Fodor's 90
The South

Fodor's Travel Publications, Inc.
New York and London

Fodor's The South

Editors: Candice Gianetti, Jacqueline Russell
Contributors: Carmen Anthony, Susan Bleecker, John Cantrell, Edgar and Patricia Cheatham, Janet Clark, John English, Wayne Greenhaw, Ellen Knox, Tom Martin, Honey Naylor, Denise Nolty, Francis X. Rocca, William Schemmel, Eileen Robinson Smith, Carol L. Timblin
Art Director: Fabrizio La Rocca
Map Editor: Suzanne Brown
Cartographer: David Lindroth
Illustrator: Karl Tanner
Cover Photograph: Hans Blohm/Masterfile

Design: Vignelli Associates

Special Sales

Contents

Foreword *vi*

Highlights '90 *viii*

Fodor's Choice *xii*

Introduction *xxii*

1 Essential Information *1*

Before You Go *2*

Visitor Information *2*
Tour Groups *2*
Package Deals for Independent Travelers *3*
Tips for British Travelers *3*
When to Go *4*
Festivals and Seasonal Events *6*
What to Pack *12*
Cash Machines *13*
Traveling with Film *13*
Car Rentals *14*
Traveling with Children *14*
Hints for Disabled Travelers *16*
Hints for Older Travelers *16*
Further Reading *17*

2 Alabama *19*

Birmingham *20*
Montgomery *36*
Mobile and the Gulf Coast *50*
Elsewhere in the State *63*

3 Georgia *68*

Atlanta *69*
Savannah *96*
The Golden Isles and Okefenokee Swamp *117*

4 Louisiana *127*

New Orleans *128*
South Louisiana *159*
Baton Rouge and Plantation Country *172*

5 Mississippi *182*

The Gulf Coast *185*
The Natchez Trace *194*

Holly Springs and Oxford *213*
The Delta *219*

6 North Carolina *228*

Charlotte *229*
Raleigh *246*
Winston-Salem *255*
Outer Banks and Historic Albemarle *259*
Asheville *266*
North Carolina High Country *271*

7 South Carolina *278*

Charleston *282*
Myrtle Beach and the Grand Strand *305*
Hilton Head and Beyond *315*

8 Tennessee *327*

Memphis *328*
Nashville *348*
East Tennessee *367*

9 Virginia *384*

Shenandoah Valley and the Highlands *385*
Charlottesville Area *399*
Northern Virginia *405*
Richmond *417*
Tidewater and the Eastern Shore *427*

Index *442*

Maps

The South *xviii–xix*
World Time Zones *xx–xxi*
Alabama *21*
Birmingham *24*
Birmingham Dining and Lodging *31*
Downtown Montgomery *39*
Montgomery Dining and Lodging *45*
Mobile and the Gulf Coast *53*
Elsewhere in the State *64*
Georgia *70–71*
Atlanta *76–77*
Atlanta Dining and Lodging *86*
Savannah Historical District *100*
Savannah Historical District Dining and Lodging *111*
The Golden Isles *118*
Louisiana *130–131*
French Quarter and Central Business District *134–135*
New Orleans Dining and Lodging *148–149*
South Louisiana *161*
Baton Rouge and Plantation Country *174*

Mississippi *184*
The Natchez Trace *197*
The Mississippi Delta *221*
North Carolina *230*
Charlotte *234*
Charlotte Dining and Lodging *240*
Outer Banks *261*
South Carolina *280–281*
Charleston *286*
Charleston Dining and Lodging *297*
Tennessee *329*
Memphis *332*
Memphis Dining and Lodging *341*
Nashville *351*
Nashville Dining and Lodging *360*
East Tennessee *369*
Virginia *386*
Shenandoah Valley and the Highlands *389*
Northern Virginia *408*
Richmond *420*
Richmond Dining and Lodging *425*
Tidewater and the Eastern Shore *430*

Foreword

This is an exciting time for Fodor's, as we continue our ambitious program to rewrite, reformat, and redesign all 140 of our guides. Here are just a few of the new features:

★ Brand-new computer-generated maps locating all the top attractions, hotels, restaurants, and shops

★ A unique system of numbers and legends to help readers move effortlessly between text and maps

★ A new star rating system for hotels and restaurants

★ Restaurant reviews by major food critics around the world

★ Stamped, self-addressed postcards, bound into every guide, to give readers an opportunity to help evaluate hotels and restaurants

★ Complete page redesign for instant retrieval of information

★ FODOR'S CHOICE—Our favorite museums, beaches, cafes, romantic hideaways, festivals, and more

★ HIGHLIGHTS—An insider's look at the most important developments in tourism during the past year

★ TIME OUT—The best and most convenient lunch stops along the shopping and exploring routes

★ A mini-journal for travelers to keep track of their own itineraries and addresses

We wish to thank Cheryl Hargrove at Travel South for her assistance in the preparation of this guidebook.

While every care has been taken to assure the accuracy of the information in this guide, the passage of time will always bring change, and consequently, the publisher cannot accept responsibility for errors that may occur.

All prices and opening times quoted here are based on information available to us at press time. Hours and admission fees may change, however, and the prudent traveler will avoid inconvenience by calling ahead.

Fodor's wants to hear about your travel experiences, both pleasant and unpleasant. When a hotel or restaurant fails to live up to its billing, let us know and we will investigate the complaint and revise our entries where the facts warrant it.

Send your letters to the editors of Fodor's Travel Publications, 201 E. 50th Street, New York, NY 10022.

Highlights '90 and Fodor's Choice

Highlights '90

Alabama

On the coast of **Mobile Bay,** Stouffer's has opened a new hotel with a 28-story river view; it houses Julia's Restaurant, which features sparkling chandeliers and mirrored columns. In the same area, the Grand Hotel, dating back to 1847, has been recently refurbished by Marriott. On its landscaped 550 acres, guests can enjoy tennis, deep-sea fishing, sailing, horseback riding, and golf at the recently completed Lakewood Golf Club.

The Alabama Space and Rocket Center in **Huntsville,** home of NASA's full-scale space shuttle orbiter and NASA's skylab engineering module, has become a major scientific and research center. A highlight for visitors is the new spacedome, where a 70-foot movie screen and high-quality sound system simulate the sensation of blasting off in space vehicles. You can experience weightlessness in one of the exhibits or participate in a week-long astronaut training course offered by the Space Academy and Camp, a popular new addition to the center.

Dotham has restored its Opera House, which can seat 640 for stage or speaking events. Built in 1915 as a civic auditorium, it is listed on the National Register of Historic Places.

Georgia

Eight to ten million visitors a year are expected to visit the newly opened Underground Atlanta, a $142-million entertainment and shopping complex in the heart of Five Points in downtown **Atlanta.** Comprised of three levels, one of which is underground, the complex features nearly 100 specialty retailers, 20 food court vendors, and 22 restaurants and nightclubs. There are two large public plazas, 1,250 parking spaces in two garages, and a variety of special attractions. The six-block, twelve-acre complex will cater to the convention trade.

The Atlanta International Museum of Art and Design will be opening its doors in Peach Tree Center, downtown Atlanta.

Louisiana

On January 1, 1989, Louisiana became the first state in the USA to create a sales-tax refund system for foreign tourists. The law provides for state and local sales tax exemptions on tangible personal property bought by foreign travelers. Cash refunds or checks will be given to tourists when they leave the state for their home countries.

The New Orleans Hilton Riverside & Towers has finally opened, complete with The River Center Tennis & Racquetball Club and Pete Fountain's Club. The New Orleans Airport Hilton and Conference Center opened near Kenner Airport in January 1989 with a business center, airport shuttle, tennis courts, and a heated outdoor pool.

Air travelers interested in flying from New Orleans to Baton Rouge or Shreveport should note that Emerald has taken some of the routes once covered by Royal Airlines, which is no longer in business. For those traveling by car, the Crescent City Connection, formerly called the Greater New Orleans Bridge, opened its second span in September of 1988. The $500-million project was undertaken to connect the east and west banks of the Mississippi River in New Orleans.

A four-alarm fire in 1988 damaged the roof and top floor of the Cabildo in New Orleans. Repairs are under way and the museum is scheduled to reopen in late 1990. The Old State Capitol has been restored.

In the summer of 1990, an 18-acre, $5.2-million theme park called Vermillionville will open in **Beaver Park,** three miles south of Interstate 10. Flat-bottomed boat rides on the bayou and food, music, and dance indigenous to South Louisiana will be featured. There will be a collection of Acadian and Creole houses, where artisans will make baskets, boats, and other native crafts, as well as a 100-seat family-style restaurant modeled after an overseer's house. The Armand Broussard House, a West Indies–style house dating back to 1790, will be moved here from New Orleans. Scheduled for completion by the summer of 1990 is a 250-seat performance center resembling a 19th century cotton gin, where there will be plays, dances, and folkloric presentations of Cajun and Zydeco music.

Mississippi

At **Gulfport Harbor** you can hop aboard the 900-passenger *Pride of Mississippi* to cruise away from Mississippi waters and Mississippi law for a day of gambling in the ship's casino. The cruise lasts from 5 to 8 hours. Once a month, the ship goes to Mexico, but reservations must be made in advance.

North Carolina

New on the **Raleigh-Durham** hotel scene are Embassy Suites Hotel, Fairfield Inn, Hampton Inn, Hospitality Inn–Stony Brook, Quality Suites Hotel, Red Roof Inn, and Sundown Inn–North. The Fearrington House in **Chapel Hill** is a new bed-and-breakfast inn.

Kitty Hawk Aerotours, which leaves from the First Flight Airstrip, has expanded its operation to include charter flights to Norfolk through a subsidiary called Outerbanks Airways.

Spirit Square, the arts center in **Charlotte,** is under renovation and is expected to reopen in 1990. The Public Library, which includes a mural of a Romare Bearden painting, reopened on North Tryon Street in mid-1989 and the Afro-American Cultural Center, a black arts center with galleries, a theater, and bookstore, is housed in a restored building that formerly served as the Little Rock AME Zion Church.

New to Charlotte in the past year are The Dunhill Hotel, Compri, Embassy Suites, and Days Inn Hotel.

April 1, 1989, saw the opening of the Richard Petty Museum in the stock-car racer's home town of **Level Cross.** The museum, open to the public Monday through Saturday, displays race cars, trophies, awards, and personal mementos.

At press time, despite a direct hit from **Hurricane Hugo,** everything in Charlotte was open for business as usual—albeit minus several of the city's huge old trees that were uprooted by the force of the storm.

South Carolina

In late September 1989, **Hurricane Hugo** cut a vicious swath through South Carolina, hitting the greater Charleston area and some of the barrier islands dead-center. Property damage was greatest along the shore and in residential and rural areas close to the coast, where clean-up and rebuilding efforts are expected to last for some time.

Charleston's historic district was spared serious damage, and within a month of the storm the city had returned pretty much to normal, with power fully restored and some 90% of all area businesses reopened. Outside Charleston, **Magnolia Plantation and Gardens** lost some trees but reopened only a few weeks after the storm. Heavily damaged **Cypress Gardens** lost two buildings and is closed until an unspecified date in 1990.

Hugo virtually by-passed **Hilton Head Island** and **Beaufort County,** though the **Isle of Palms** was devastated, and **Wild Dunes Resort** there is not expected to reopen for some time. **Kiawah Island** and **Seabrook Island** resorts were damaged but reopened by the end of 1989. Along the **Grand Strand,** which includes **Myrtle Beach,** damaged beaches are being renourished and hotels are reopening every day, though some of the seasonal properties closed following Hugo, using the fall to make repairs and prepare for their scheduled spring reopenings. All but one of the area's 63 golf courses are open. In hard-hit **Georgetown County** south of Myrtle Beach, much cleanup remains to be done along the inlets. The **Litchfield Inn** is still closed, but Georgetown it-self is intact and accommodations there are open.

The South Carolina State Museum in **Columbia** is a 50,000-square-foot facility in the process of expanding. Housed in a building that served as the first electric textile mill in 1894, the museum displays, among other exhibits, a replica of the first locomotive built in America for both passengers and freight service. The Charles H. Townes Center celebrates the achievement of the South Carolina Nobel laureate who pioneered the laser. Other achievements of South Carolina residents can be found in the History Hall, which chronicles 14,000 years of the state's history, and the Palmetto Gallery, which exhibits works of South Carolina artists. The art gallery features a variety of changing exhibits.

The Koger Center for Performing Arts, one of the South's finest new performing arts complexes, opened its doors in January, 1989. Connected with the University of South Carolina in Columbia, the center, which cost $15 million to complete, contains 2,256 seats on three levels. Programs in 1990 will include performances by the London Philharmonic, the Warsaw Ballet, the New York City Opera, the Moscow Philharmonic, Taj Mahal, and the Boston Chambers Players.

Tennessee

American Airlines has increased service to **Nashville** and provides nonstop or direct service between Nashville and a score of other cities on its route system.

Visitors to The Hermitage, outside of Nashville, will find The Andrew Jackson Center, a 28,000-square-foot museum, visitor, and education center that opened in 1989. It contains many Jackson artifacts never before exhibited as well as a 16-minute film, "Old Hickory," that is shown in its auditorium.

Nashville is also the site of the Stouffer Nashville hotel, a new high rise that has gone up next to the Nashville Convention Center. The hotel is also connected to the new Church Street Center Mall.

Virginia

Visitors to **Colonial Williamsburg** will discover a new indoor museum complex, which will be fully open in 1990. At press time, plans stood to change Festival Park's name to Jamestown Settlement. The park is open daily year-round except Christmas and New Year's.

The Golden Sands motel in **Virginia Beach** has been replaced by the Idlewhyle Motel, which caters to families and is situated right on the beach.

Fodor's Choice

No two people will agree on what makes a perfect vacation, but it's fun and helpful to know what others think. We hope you'll have a chance to experience some of Fodor's Choices yourself while visiting the American South. For detailed information about each entry, refer to the appropriate chapters within this guidebook.

Alabama

Special Moments A drive through the elegant Birmingham suburb of Mountain Brook

Standing at the pulpit where Dr. Martin Luther King, Jr., first preached, at the Dexter Avenue Memorial Baptist Church, Montgomery

Festivals Azalea Trail Festival, Mobile

Alabama Shakespeare Festival, Montgomery

Dining Sahara Restaurant, Montgomery *(Expensive)*

Vintage Year, Montgomery *(Expensive)*

Highlands: A Bar and Grill, Birmingham *(Expensive)*

The Pillars, Mobile *(Expensive)*

Lodging Governor's House Hotel, Montgomery *(Expensive–Very Expensive)*

Sheraton Riverfront Station, Montgomery *(Expensive)*

Wynfrey Hotel, Birmingham *(Expensive)*

Quality Inn, Gulf Shores *(Moderate–Very Expensive)*

Pickwick Hotel, Birmingham *(Moderate)*

The Malaga Inn, Mobile *(Inexpensive)*

Museums Alabama Sports Hall of Fame, Birmingham

Oakleigh, Mobile

Georgia

Special Moments Cold beers and camaraderie at Manuel's Tavern, Atlanta

The view from the lounge atop the Westin Peachtree Plaza Hotel, Atlanta

Sights, scents, and sounds of the DeKalb Farmer's Market, Atlanta

The choir singing at Ebenezer Baptist Church, Atlanta

Intellectual schmoozing at the Oxford Bookstore's Cup and Chaucer, Atlanta

St. Patrick's Day in Savannah

Scenic Drives	Buckhead residential area during Dogwood Festival, Atlanta
Festivals	Peachtree Road Race on July 4th, Atlanta
	Piedmont Arts Festival in Piedmont Park, Atlanta
Dining	The Dining Room at the Ritz-Carlton, Atlanta *(Very Expensive)*
	LaGrotta Ristorante Italiano, Atlanta *(Expensive)*
	Elizabeth on 37th, Savannah *(Inexpensive–Expensive)*
	Buckhead Diner, Atlanta *(Inexpensive)*
	Mrs. Wilke's Boarding House, Savannah *(Inexpensive)*
Lodging	The Cloister, Sea Island *(Very Expensive)*
	Ritz-Carlton Downtown, Atlanta *(Very Expensive)*
	Eliza Thompson House, Savannah *(Expensive)*
	Jesse Mount House, Savannah *(Expensive)*
Museums	High Museum of Art, Atlanta
Nightlife	The hip rock scene at Club Rio, Atlanta
	Dancing at Johnny's Hideaway, Atlanta
	Blues and beers at Blues Harbor, Atlanta
	Early breakfast at the Majestic, Atlanta

Louisiana

Special Moments	Pirates Alley in the early morning mists, New Orleans
	The view of the French Quarter from a riverboat, New Orleans
	Waking up in the Madewood plantation house, Napoleonville
	Midday jazz at the Gazebo, New Orleans
	Strolling through Longue Vue House and Gardens, New Orleans
	Browsing for posters and postcards on Royal Street, New Orleans
	The Zulu parade on Mardi Gras day, New Orleans
Festivals	Mardi Gras in Lafayette
	Crawfish Festival, Breaux Bridge
	Festival International de Louisiane, Lafayette
Scenic Drives	Creole Nature Trail (LA 27), Sulpher to Lake Charles
Dining	Brennan's, New Orleans *(Very Expensive)*

Commander's Palace, New Orleans, *(Very Expensive)*

Arnaud's, New Orleans *(Expensive)*

Cafe Margaux, Lake Charles *(Moderate)*

Chef Hans, Monroe *(Inexpensive)*

Lodging   Maison de Ville, New Orleans *(Expensive)*

Olivier House, New Orleans *(Expensive)*

Remington Suites, Shreveport *(Expensive)*

The Windsor Court, New Orleans *(Expensive)*

Hotel Acadiana, Lafayette *(Moderate)*

Museums   Gallier House, New Orleans

Pitot House, New Orleans

Hermann-Grima House, New Orleans

Nightlife   Dancing at Mulate's, Breaux Bridge

Cajun night at the Maple Leaf Bar, New Orleans

Sipping a Pimm's cup on the patio of the Napoleon House, New Orleans

---

Mississippi

Special Moments   Looking out at the Mississippi River from Vicksburg

A drink and the spectacular view at the Delta Point Restaurant, Vicksburg

Feeling William Faulkner's presence in his study at Rowan Oak, Oxford

Standing under the live oaks in the grove at Jefferson Davis's home, Beauvoir, near Gulfport

A visit to Elvis's birthplace in Tupelo

Festivals   Tobacco Spit in Billy John Crumpton's pasture, outside Raleigh

The Neshoba County Fair, off the Natchez Trace

Delta Blues Festival, Greenville

Scenic Drives   The Natchez Trace (especially between Jackson and Natchez)

Lodging   Millsaps-Buie House, Jackson *(Expensive–Very Expensive)*

Oliver-Britt House, Oxford *(Moderate)*

Dining   Nick's, Jackson *(Very Expensive)*

Walker's Drive-In, Jackson *(Expensive)*

The Sweet Olive, Boyle *(Inexpensive)*

Museums   Walter Anderson's Home, Ocean Springs

Mary Buie Museum, Oxford

**Off the
Beaten Track** Ethel Wright Mohamed's Stitchery Museum,
Belzoni

North Carolina

Special Moments Standing under the Gothic arches of Duke Chapel

Shooting the rapids on the Nantahala

Recalling the life of Carl Sandburg at Flat Rock

Observing 19th-century living at Old Salem

Festivals Brevard Music Festival

North Carolina Shakespeare Festival, High Point

Mountain Dance and Folk Festival, Asheville

Dining Jonathan's Uptown, Charlotte *(Very Expensive)*

The Marketplace, Asheville *(Expensive–Very Expensive)*

The Angus Barn, Raleigh *(Expensive)*

Claire's, Blowing Rock *(Expensive)*

The Jarrett House, Dillsboro *(Moderate)*

Justine's, Wilmington *(Moderate)*

Lodging Green Park Inn, Blowing Rock *(Expensive–Very
Expensive)*

The Greenwich, Greensboro *(Expensive)*

Grove Park Inn and Country Club, Asheville *(Expensive)*

Oakwood Inn, Raleigh *(Expensive)*

Brookstown Inn, Winston-Salem *(Moderate–Expensive)*

The Morehead, Charlotte *(Moderate–Expensive)*

South Carolina

Special Moments Riding a mule-drawn farm wagon at the Plantation
Stableyards in Middleton Place

Collecting shells and sand dollars on the beach at Kiawah
Island

Boat tour among spring blooms reflecting in the black
waters at Cypress Gardens

Relaxing in a rocking chair overlooking luxury yachts in
the Harbour Town marina, Sea Pines on Hilton Head

Festivals Charleston Historic Foundation's Festival of Houses

Spoleto Festival USA and Piccolo Spoleto, Charleston

Dining Henry's, Charleston *(Expensive)*

The Rusty Anchor, Charleston *(Expensive)*

The Shaftesbury Room, Charleston *(Expensive)*

Lodging   Mills House Hotel, Charleston *(Very Expensive)*

Omni Hotel, Charleston *(Very Expensive)*

Planters Inn, Charleston *(Very Expensive)*

Myrtle Beach Hilton and Golf Club, Myrtle Beach *(Very Expensive)*

Hotel Inter-Continental Hilton Head, Hilton Head Island *(Very Expensive)*

Museums   Charleston Museum, Charleston

Gibbes Art Gallery, Charleston

Patriots Point Naval and Maritime Museum, north of Charleston

Brookgreen Gardens, Murrells Inlet

The Rice Museum, Georgetown

Tennessee

Special Moments   Ducks on parade in the Peabody Hotel lobby, Memphis

Roy Acuff balancing his fiddle bow on his nose at the Grand Ole Opry, Nashville

Viewing the Great Smokies from Lookout Tower at Clingmans Dome, East Tennessee

Rhododendron Gardens in spring atop Roan Mountain, East Tennessee

Blues spilling into the afternoon from the porch of the Handy Home, Memphis

Festivals   International Barbecue Cooking Contest, Memphis

National Storytelling Festival, Jonesborough

Dining   Chez Philippe, Memphis *(Very Expensive)*

Chef Sigy's, Nashville *(Expensive)*

Burning Bush, Gatlinburg *(Moderate–Expensive)*

Miss Mary Bobo's Boarding House, Lynchburg *(Inexpensive)*

Lodging   Buckhorn Inn, Gatlinburg *(Very Expensive)*

Opryland Hotel, Nashville *(Very Expensive)*

The Peabody, Memphis *(Very Expensive)*

Radisson Union Station Hotel, Nashville *(Very Expensive)*

Hyatt Regency Knoxville *(Moderate–Expensive)*

Museums   Mississippi River Museum, Mud Island, Memphis

Tennessee State Museum, Jackson

Country Music Hall of Fame and Museum, Nashville

Museum of Appalachia, Norris

Netherland Inn, Kingsport

Christus Gardens, Gatlinburg

American Museum of Science and Energy, Oak Ridge

Off the Beaten Track Agricenter International, Memphis

Lichterman Nature Center, Memphis

Joe L. Evins Appalachian Center for Crafts, Smithville

Virginia

Special Moments Changing of the guard at the Tomb of the Unknown Soldier, Arlington Cemetery

Running of the ponies at Chincoteague Island

Festivals The spring and fall Foxfield Races, Charlottesville

Virginia Highlands Festival, Abingdon

Dining The Waterwheel Restaurant, Warm Springs *(Expensive)*

Eastern Standard, Charlottesville *(Expensive)*

Lodging Hotel Roanoke *(Expensive)*

Mayhurst, Orange *(Expensive)*

Museums Lee Memorial Chapel and Museum, Lexington

The Museum of American Frontier Culture, Staunton

Nightlife Whitey's, Arlington

The Mine Shaft, Charlottesville

Off the Beaten Track Association for Research and Enlightenment, Virginia Beach

Phillip Morris Plant, Richmond

Great Drives Blue Ridge Parkway

Skyline Drive

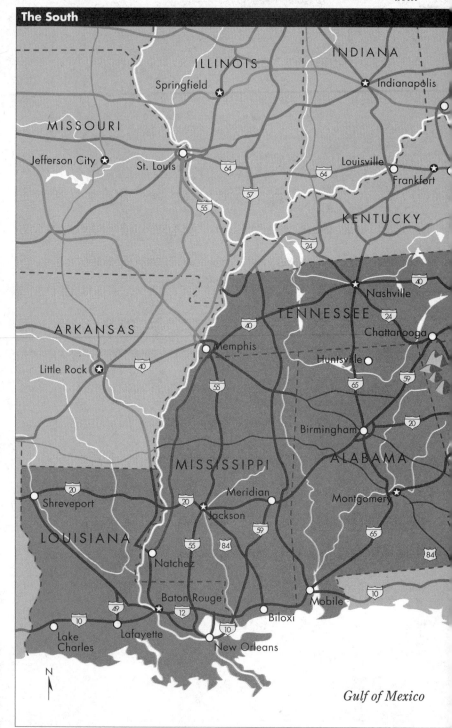

The South

Gulf of Mexico

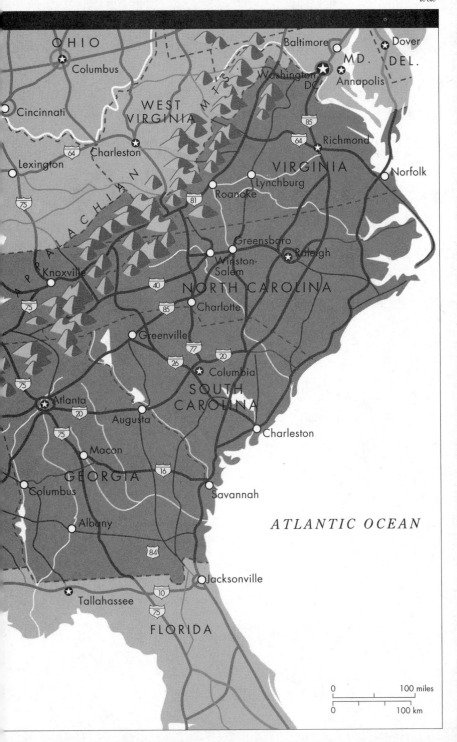

World Time Zones

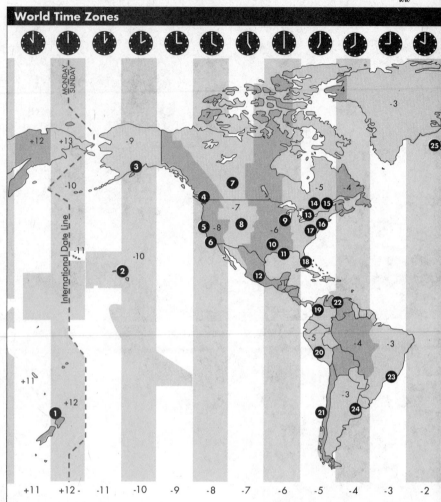

Numbers below vertical bands relate each zone to Greenwich Mean Time (0 hrs.).
Local times may differ, as indicated by lightface numbers on the map.

Algiers, **29**
Anchorage, **3**
Athens, **41**
Auckland, **1**
Baghdad, **46**
Bangkok, **50**
Beijing, **54**

Berlin, **34**
Bogotá, **19**
Budapest, **37**
Buenos Aires, **24**
Caracas, **22**
Chicago, **9**
Copenhagen, **33**
Dallas, **10**

Delhi, **48**
Denver, **8**
Djakarta, **53**
Dublin, **26**
Edmonton, **7**
Hong Kong, **56**
Honolulu, **2**

Istanbul, **40**
Jerusalem, **42**
Johannesburg, **44**
Lima, **20**
Lisbon, **28**
London (Greenwich), **27**
Los Angeles, **6**
Madrid, **38**
Manila, **57**

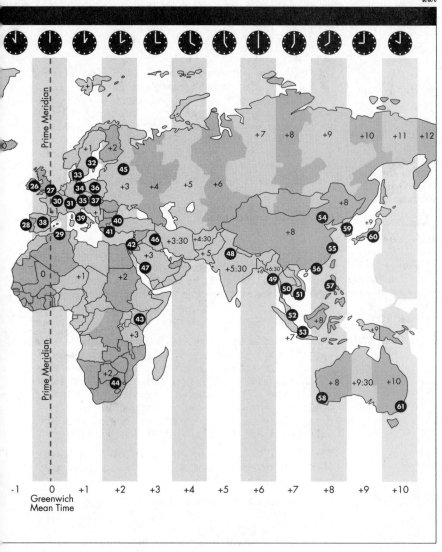

Mecca, **47**	Ottawa, **14**	San Francisco, **5**	Toronto, **13**
Mexico City, **12**	Paris, **30**	Santiago, **21**	Vancouver, **4**
Miami, **18**	Perth, **58**	Seoul, **59**	Vienna, **35**
Montreal, **15**	Reykjavík, **25**	Shanghai, **55**	Warsaw, **36**
Moscow, **45**	Rio de Janeiro, **23**	Singapore, **52**	Washington, DC, **17**
Nairobi, **43**	Rome, **39**	Stockholm, **32**	Yangon, **49**
New Orleans, **11**	Saigon, **51**	Sydney, **61**	Zürich, **31**
New York City, **16**		Tokyo, **60**	

Introduction

by Honey Naylor

Real-live Southerner Honey Naylor is a freelance writer whose features have appeared in Travel & Leisure, New Orleans Magazine, USA Today, *and other national publications. She is also the author of* Fodor's Pocket New Orleans *and a contributor to* Fodor's New Orleans 1989.

If you hear a Southern farmhand threaten to cut off one of his arms and eat it, don't scream and call for help. That's just his way of saying that he is hungry—or, as he is also likely to put it, "so hungry my stomach thinks my throat's been cut." A Southern man is not just tired or ill-used. He feels "like I've been rode hard and put up wet" (the reference being to letting a hard-ridden horse unlather before stabling it). A Southern woman in the midst of a tizzy is "running around setting my hair on fire." And if things don't work out right, she may "have to go to bed with a cold rag on my head"; in an extreme case, she may "go completely to pieces."

A proclivity to exaggerate is at the very core of every Southerner's soul, and he will take any opportunity to exercise it—for all Southerners simply *love* to talk. A Southerner setting out to make a transaction, whether it's buying a Coke or a condo, is viscerally aware that in the South the first order of business is almost never business. It's "visiting"—passing the time of day.

Out of these two tendencies—to talk and to talk big—has sprung the age-old Southern tradition of spinning colorfully embroidered stories, which in turn has spawned some great American storytellers. The original version of Thomas Wolfe's novel *Of Time and the River* was about the length of 12 average novels, or twice the length of *War and Peace*. Simply unable to stem the flow of words, he stopped writing only after his editor told him that the novel was finished.

Thomas Wolfe was a Southerner, a native of Asheville, North Carolina, which means that he was born with a bad case of logorrhea.

Other notable Southern storytellers are Mississippi's two Pulitzer Prize winners, Tennessee Williams and Eudora Welty, and its Nobel Prize winner, William Faulkner. All three wrote of eccentric, complex, and occasionally bizarre characters caught up in Byzantine plots, as did Savannah-born Flannery O'Connor, author of *Wise Blood*.

Faulkner wrote his first novel in an apartment overlooking Pirates Alley in New Orleans—a city that gave the world Truman Capote and Lillian Hellman, and which Tennessee Williams called "my spiritual home." A Pulitzer was awarded posthumously to New Orleanian John Kennedy Toole, who wrote the wildly funny *A Confederacy of Dunces*. Frances Parkinson Keyes bought a historic home in the French Quarter of New Orleans, where she wrote *Dinner at Antoine's* and *Steamboat Gothic*. The brilliant Walker Percy, a native of Birmingham, won the National Book Award for his first novel, *The Moviegoer*, and continues to turn out literary gems from his home in Covington, Louisiana.

In Flat Rock, North Carolina, the home of Pulitzer Prize–winning poet and biographer Carl Sandburg is a National Historic Site. Tom Wolfe, author of *The Right Stuff*, was born in Richmond, and Pat Conroy, who wrote *Prince of Tides*, lives in Atlanta. Margaret Mitchell, also of Atlanta, wrote only one book in her life, but that book was *Gone With the Wind*—the biggest-selling novel of all time.

For other Southerners, the words soar off the page and into the air. The Southland gave birth to the blues, to jazz, and to songwriters and singers of every stripe. The King—Elvis—grew up in Tupelo, Mississippi, and launched his astonishing career in a Memphis recording studio. Each year millions of Presley fans make the pilgrimage to Graceland, his showy home and final resting place in Memphis. Florence, Alabama, gave us W. C. Handy, who first played his "St. Louis Blues" in a Memphis saloon, and Savannah produced Johnny Mercer, a songwriter of considerable notes. The versatile Wynton Marsalis, the late Louis Armstrong, and the lively Pete Fountain are among the scores of great jazzmen from New Orleans, where jazz itself was born. Leontyne Price of Laurel, Mississippi, sang the role of Bess on Broadway in *Porgy and Bess* before giving voice to opera on a grand scale.

Speaking of which, opera lovers the world over flock to the annual Spoleto Festival USA in Charleston and to Wolf Trap Farm in Virginia, both of which also feature theater, ballet, and jazz. In the spring, musicians from as far away as Australia and Finland turn up for the Jazz and Heritage Festival in New Orleans, a city that is not exactly jazzless the rest of the year. Out in the bayous of South Louisiana, contagious Cajun music has virtually the whole world two-stepping; and up in the Blue Ridge Mountains of Virginia and North Carolina, the hills sing with bluegrass music. Tennessee has produced more country-music songwriters, singers, and musicians than you can shake a mike at, and Nashville, the "Country Music Capital of the World," is the foot-stomping ground of the Grand Ole Opry.

"Dixie," incidentally, penned in 1859 by Yankee Dan Emmett, was a marching song originally played by bands of both the North and the South as they paraded into the Recent Unpleasantness—a period of time known to everyone but Southerners as the Civil War.

The Civil War, with a few exceptions, notably Gettysburg, was fought on Southern soil. South Carolina, inflamed by the rhetoric of firebrand John C. Calhoun, was the first state to secede, causing a Union loyalist to snap, "South Carolina is too small for a republic and too big for a lunatic asylum." But the first shots rang out over Charleston Harbor, and the bloody war began. Virtually every Southern city, country crossroad, and sleepy creek was touched by the war, and even now the memories linger on, preserved for all time in yet more colorful stories, passed along from generation to generation in the rooms of antebellum mansions throughout the South.

Today, south of the Mason-Dixon Line (surveyed in the 1700s by British astronomers Charles Mason and Jeremiah Dixon to settle a territorial dispute between Pennsylvania and Maryland), there are almost as many Civil War commemorative plaques as there are black-eyed peas. A slew of the South's most famous sights were once the scenes of hideous battles. Glitzy, modern Atlanta literally grew up out of the ashes Sherman left behind, and Virginia's luxuriant Shenandoah Valley was savaged by Phil Sheridan. Lookout Mountain, Tennessee, with its stunning view, was a vantage point that both sides fought for pretty keenly, and down in Mississippi, Vicksburg held Grant off for 47 days and nights before surrendering. New Orleans fell not long after Farragut shouted, "Damn the torpedoes, full speed ahead!"

The region is also fertile territory for aficionados of earlier American history. Notwithstanding the fame of that piece of rock up in Massachusetts, the first permanent English settlement in the New World was established in Jamestown, Virginia. Pocahontas had saved John Smith's life, married John Rolfe, gone to England to be presented to the king and queen, and died, all before the Pilgrims turned up. Fort Moultrie, South Carolina, is the site of the fledgling nation's first decisive victory over the British during the Revolutionary War, and in Yorktown, Virginia, Cornwallis surrendered to General George Washington after the "victory that made a Nation."

Natchitoches, Louisiana, was the first permanent settlement in the territory comprising the Louisiana Purchase, and the town has a small but beautifully restored historic district. (Holding title to the "oldest" or "first in this country" is dear to the hearts of tradition-cherishing Southerners, and visitors may find themselves deluged with the latter adjectives.) New Orleans's French Quarter, famed for Bourbon Street jazz haunts and exquisite Creole cuisine, is the original colony founded by French Creoles, and there are important historic districts in Savannah, Charleston, and Mobile. At Colonial Williamsburg, capital of Virginia from 1699 to 1779, a whole village has been created with costumed bakers, blacksmiths, and craftsmen demonstrating various aspects of early Colonial life in authentic surroundings. Adjacent to the Colonial village is the serene green campus of the College of William and Mary, whose illustrious graduates include Thomas Jefferson and James Madison.

But the South is much more than time-honored historic sites. It is a vast sports arena for snow-skiers and water-skiers, scuba divers and horseback riders, spelunkers and hunters, shrimpers and saltwater anglers, hikers, bikers, tennis buffs, golfers, and beachcombers.

Lush carpets of white sand roll down the Atlantic Coast and sweep along the Gulf of Mexico. Seekers of sun and fun head for such resorts as Virginia Beach, Virginia; Sea Island, Georgia; and, in the Carolinas, Cape Hatteras, Hilton Head Island, and Myrtle Beach. Alabama barely sticks its big toe in the Gulf, but Mobile Bay's swank resorts and colorful artists' colonies are among the state's most popular attractions. Twenty-six miles of sun-kissed beaches stretch along the Mississippi coast, dotted with resorts like Pascagoula, Pass Christian, and Biloxi.

If beaches bore you, there are plenty of hills to head for. The breathtakingly beautiful Blue Ridge Mountains roll through Virginia, the Carolinas, and northern Georgia, and the Great Smokies soar over the North Carolina–Tennessee border. Playgrounds abound in "them thar hills," such as Gatlinburg, Tennessee, and Blowing Rock, North Carolina. From lookout points on Virginia's serpentine Skyline Drive there are soul-stirring views of the mountains and the Shenandoah Valley.

One last note before you go: If you expect to hear the Hollywood version of a Southern accent, you're likely to be surprised. About the only generalization that can be made is that the Southern voice is gentle and soft—except at football games and hog-calling contests. You *will* hear drawls and "y'alls." ("Y'all," incidentally, is a contraction of "you all." It's the equivalent of "you guys," something you will almost never hear a Southerner say). The Tidewater Virginia accent bears little resemblance to the sounds of south Louisiana, where the language isn't even English—it's Cajun French. And in New Orleans you'll hear an accent that is soft, slightly slurred, but decidedly Brooklynese.

The truth is, the voices of the South are as rich and varied as the land itself. In its shops, restaurants, and homes you can be sure you'll hear those melodic Southern voices say, "Y'all come back."

And that's not just whistling Dixie.

1 Essential Information

Before You Go

Visitor Information

Contact each of the following state travel bureaus for free tourist information. If you wish to speak to a travel representative, you must call the bureau directly; for a free travel information packet, call the toll-free "800" number.

Alabama State Bureau of Tourism and Travel (532 S. Perry St., Montgomery, AL 36130, tel. 205/261–4169 or 800/ALABAMA).

Georgia Department of Industry and Trade (Tourism Division, Box 1776, Atlanta, GA 30301, tel. 404/656–3590 or 800/VISIT GA).

Louisiana Department of Tourism (666 N. Foster, Box 94291, Baton Rouge, LA 70804, tel. 504/342–8100 or 800/334–8626).

Mississippi Division of Tourism (Box 22825, Jackson, MS 39205, tel. 601/359–3414 or 800/647–2290).

North Carolina Division of Travel and Tourism (430 N. Salisbury, Raleigh, NC 27611, tel. 919/733–4171 or 800/VISIT NC).

South Carolina Division of Tourism (Box 71, Columbia, SC 29202, tel. 803/734–0122).

Tennessee Department of Tourism (Box 23170, Nashville, TN 37202, tel. 615/741–2158).

Virginia Division of Tourism (Suite 500, 202 N. 9th St., Richmond, VA 23219, tel. 804/786–4484 or 800/VISIT VA).

Tour Groups

If you prefer to have someone else drive while you sit back and enjoy the ride, you might do well to consider a package tour. Although you will have to march to the beat of a tour guide's drum rather than your own, you are likely to save money on airfare, hotels, and ground transportation while covering a lot of territory. For the more experienced or adventurous traveler, there are a variety of special-interest and independent packages available. Listed below is a sample of available options. Check with your travel agent for additional resources.

When considering a tour, be sure to find out exactly what expenses are included (particularly tips, taxes, side trips, additional meals, and entertainment), ratings of all hotels on the itinerary and the facilities they offer, cancellation policies for both you and for the tour operator, and if you are traveling alone, what the single supplement is. Most tour operators request that bookings be made through a travel agent; there is no additional charge for doing so.

General-Interest Tours

Cosmos/Tourama (150 S. Los Robles Ave., Suite 860, Pasadena, CA 91101, tel. 818/449–0919 or 800/556–5454) offers three colorful Southern tours: "Heritage of the Deep South" concentrates on Louisiana, Mississippi, and Alabama. "Country Western USA" highlights Memphis and Nashville. "The Old South and the Golden Isles" winds its way from Atlanta to Charleston, with a stopover on Jekyll Island, among other spots.

Domenico Tours (751 Broadway, Bayonne, NJ 07002, tel. 800/554–TOUR) offers tours of New Orleans, New Orleans/Memphis/Nashville, and Nashville.

Maupintour (Box 807, Lawrence, KS 66044, tel. 913/843–1211 or 800/255–4266) takes a step back in time with "Historic Savannah and Charleston."

Special-Interest Tours **Adventure:** *Wilderness Southeast* (711 Sandtown Rd., Savannah, GA 31410, tel. 912/897–5108) runs rugged trips through places like the Okefenokee Swamp in Georgia and the Everglades in Florida.

Black History: Groups of 10 to 44 who are interested in exploring America's black heritage may want to check out the Virginia tours organized by **Pepper Bird Express** (Box 69081, Hampton, VA 23669, tel. 804/723–1106). They will customize a trip to your needs, or you can join in on a set three-day tour including Hampton University, Yorktown, Colonial Williamsburg, Monticello, and more.

Package Deals for Independent Travelers

American Fly AAway Vacations (tel. 817/355–1234 or 800/433–7300) offers city packages with discounts on hotels and car rental. Also check with **Delta Air Lines** (tel. 404/765–2952 or 800/241–6108) and **Eastern Airlines** (tel. 305/873–3000) for packages. **American Express** has similar city packages, with half-day sightseeing tours (tel. 800/241–1700).

Tips for British Travelers

Government Tourist Office The United States Travel and Tourism Administration (22 Sackville St., London W1X 2EA, tel. 01/439–7433) will send brochures and advise you on your trip to the American South.

Passports and Visas You will need a valid 10-year passport. You do not need a visa if you are staying for less than 90 days, have a return ticket, and are flying with a participating airline. There are some exceptions to this, so check with your travel agent or with the United States Embassy (Visa and Immigration Dept., 5 Upper Grosvenor St., London W1A 2JB, tel. 01/499–3443). No vaccinations are required.

Customs Visitors 21 or over can take in 200 cigarettes or 50 cigars or 3 pounds of tobacco; 1 U.S. quart of alcohol; duty-free gifts to a value of $100. Be careful not to try to take in meat or meat products, seeds, plants, fruits, etc. Avoid illegal drugs like the plague.

Returning to Britain, you may bring home: (1) 200 cigarettes or 100 cigarillos or 50 cigars or 250 grams of tobacco; (2) two liters of table wine with additional allowances for (a) one liter of alcohol over 22% by volume (38.8° proof, most spirits), (b) two liters of alcohol under 22% by volume, or (c) two more liters of table wine; (3) 50 grams of perfume and a quarter-liter of toilet water; and (4) other goods up to a value of £32.

Insurance We recommend that you insure yourself to cover health and motoring mishaps. **Europ Assistance** (252 High St., Croydon, Surrey CRO 1NF, tel. 01/680–1234) offers comprehensive policies. It is also wise to take out insurance to cover loss of luggage (though check that this isn't already covered in an existing homeowner's policy). Trip-cancellation insurance is another wise buy. **The Association of British Insurers** (Aldermary House, Queen St., London EC4N 1TT, tel. 01/248–4477) will give advice on all aspects of vacation insurance.

Tour Operators **Albany Travel** (190 Deansgate, Manchester M3 3WD, tel. 061/833–0202) offers a 16-day North-South Discovery tour, including Washington, Williamsburg, Charleston, and Savannah, for around £1,000. **Poundstretcher** (Hazelwick Ave., Three Bridges, Crawley RH10 1NP, tel. 0293/518022) offers a three-center holiday in Atlanta, New Orleans, and Orlando, with prices for seven nights (including airfare) beginning at £855.

Airfares If you are traveling independently, your best bets for a low-price air ticket are APEX fares. APEX round-trip fares to Birmingham start at £513, to Atlanta £399, to New Orleans £377, to Nashville £333, and to Richmond £388. Check with the major airlines: **American Airlines** (tel. 01/834–5151), **British Airways** (tel. 01/897–4000), **Continental Airlines** (tel. 0293/776464), **Delta Airlines** (tel. 0800/414767), **Pan American Airlines** (tel. 01/409–3377), and **Virgin Atlantic Airways** (tel. 0293/38222).

If you can afford to be flexible about when you travel, try the small ads in daily or Sunday newspapers for last-minute flight bargains, but check that all airport taxes are included in the price quoted.

When to Go

Spring is probably the most attractive season in this part of the United States. Cherry blossoms are followed throughout the region by azaleas, dogwood, and camellias from April into May, and apple blossoms in May.

Seasonal and special events occur throughout the year. Festivals (folk, craft, art, and music) tend to take place in the summer, as do sports events. State and local fairs are held mainly in August and September, though there are a few in early July and into October. Historical commemorations are likely to occur at any time of the year.

Climate In winter, temperatures generally average in the low 40s in inland areas, in the 60s by the shore. Summer temperatures, modified by mountains in some areas, by sea breezes in others, range from the high 70s to the mid-80s, now and then the low 90s.

The following are average daily maximum and minimum temperatures for sample Southern cities.

Birmingham, Alabama								
Jan.	56F	13C	**May**	81F	27C	**Sept.**	86F	30C
	38	3		61	16		67	19
Feb.	58F	14C	**June**	88F	31C	**Oct.**	76F	24C
	38	3		68	20		56	13
Mar.	67F	19C	**July**	90F	32C	**Nov.**	65F	18C
	47	8		70	21		45	7
Apr.	74F	23C	**Aug.**	90F	32C	**Dec.**	56F	13C
	54	12		70	21		38	3

Atlanta, Georgia	Jan.	52F 36	11C 2	May	79F 61	26C 16	Sept.	83F 65	28C 18
	Feb.	54F 38	12C 3	June	86F 67	30C 19	Oct.	72F 54	22C 12
	Mar.	63F 43	17C 6	July	88F 70	31C 21	Nov.	61F 43	16C 6
	Apr.	72F 52	22C 11	Aug.	86F 70	30C 21	Dec.	52F 38	11C 3

New Orleans, Louisiana	Jan.	63F 47	17C 8	May	83F 68	28C 20	Sept.	86F 74	30C 23
	Feb.	65F 50	18C 10	June	88F 74	31C 23	Oct.	79F 65	26C 18
	Mar.	72F 56	22C 13	July	90F 76	32C 24	Nov.	70F 56	21C 13
	Apr.	77F 61	25C 16	Aug.	90F 76	32C 24	Dec.	65F 49	18C 9

Jackson, Mississippi	Jan.	59F 38	15C 3	May	85F 63	29C 17	Sept.	88F 65	31C 18
	Feb.	63F 41	17C 5	June	92F 70	33C 21	Oct.	81F 54	27C 12
	Mar.	68F 47	20C 8	July	94F 72	34C 22	Nov.	67F 43	19C 6
	Apr.	76F 54	24C 12	Aug.	94F 70	34C 21	Dec.	61F 40	16C 4

Raleigh, North Carolina	Jan.	52F 32	11C 0	May	79F 56	26C 13	Sept.	83F 61	28C 16
	Feb.	56F 34	13C 1	June	86F 63	30C 17	Oct.	72F 49	22C 9
	Mar.	61F 38	16C 3	July	90F 68	32C 20	Nov.	61F 38	16C 3
	Apr.	72F 47	22C 8	Aug.	88F 67	31C 19	Dec.	52F 31	11C −1

Charleston, South Carolina	Jan.	58F 43	14C 6	May	81F 67	27C 19	Sept.	83F 72	28C 22
	Feb.	69F 45	15C 7	June	86F 74	30C 23	Oct.	76F 61	24C 16
	Mar.	67F 50	19C 10	July	88F 76	31C 24	Nov.	67F 52	19C 11
	Apr.	74F 58	23C 14	Aug.	88F 76	31C 24	Dec.	59F 45	15C 7

Nashville, Tennessee	Jan.	47F 31	8C −1	May	79F 58	26C 14	Sept.	83F 63	28C 17
	Feb.	50F 34	10C 1	June	86F 67	30C 19	Oct.	72F 50	22C 10
	Mar.	59F 40	15C 4	July	90F 70	32C 21	Nov.	58F 40	14C 4
	Apr.	70F 49	21C 9	Aug.	88F 68	31C 20	Dec.	49F 34	9C 1

Norfolk, Virginia	Jan.	49F 34	9C 1	**May**	76F 58	24C 14	**Sept.**	81F 65	27C 18
	Feb.	50F 34	10C 1	**June**	83F 67	28C 19	**Oct.**	70F 56	21C 13
	Mar.	58F 40	14C 4	**July**	88F 72	31C 22	**Nov.**	61F 45	16C 7
	Apr.	67F 49	19C 9	**Aug.**	85F 70	29C 21	**Dec.**	52F 36	11C 2

Current weather information on 235 cities around the world—180 of them in the United States—is only a phone call away. To obtain the **Weather Trak** telephone number for your area, call 800/247–3282. The local number plays a taped message that tells you to dial the three-digit access code for the destination you're interested in. The code is either the area code (in the United States) or the first three letters of the foreign city. For a list of all access codes, send a stamped, self-addressed envelope to Cities, Box 7000, Dallas, TX 75209. For further information, phone 214/869–3035 or 800/247–3282.

Festivals and Seasonal Events

Starting with Mardi Gras in New Orleans and ending with Christmas in Natchez, Mississippi, the Southern states hold a wide variety of festivals and special events through out the year. The following is a sample. For more complete listings of events, contact the Division of Tourism in each state.

January **Alabama:** *Senior Bowl All-Star Classic* is played in Mobile. *General Robert E. Lee's Birthday* is commemorated in Montgomery at the first White House of the Confederacy.

Georgia: A *Rattlesnake Roundup* is held in Whigham. *Savannah Marathon* and *Half Marathon* are run. *Martin Luther King, Jr., Week* is celebrated in Atlanta.

Louisiana: The *Sugar Bowl Classic* is played on New Year's Day in New Orleans. *Louisiana Fur and Wildlife Festival* is held in Cameron.

Mississippi: The *National Tractor Pull* is held in Jackson.

North Carolina: *The Charlotte Observer Marathon* and *Runner's Expo* take place in Charlotte.

South Carolina: Orangeburg invites the country's finest coon dogs to compete in the *Grand American Coon Hunt*. Charleston hosts a colorful *Oyster Festival*.

Tennessee: *Reel Foot Eagle Watch* tours take place at Reel Lake.

Virginia: *Robert E. Lee's Birthday* is celebrated at his boyhood home in Alexandria. *Stonewall Jackson's Birthday* is celebrated at his home in Lexington.

February **Alabama:** *Mardi Gras* is celebrated in Mobile and Gulf Shores. *Farm-City Week* is held annually at Selma's Convention Center. *Black History Month* events are held at Tuskegee University in Tuskegee.

Georgia: *Georgia Day Event* is held in Savannah. A two-day *Arts and Crafts Georgia Festival* is held in Kennesaw.

Louisiana: *Mardi Gras* is New Orleans's—and the South's—biggest annual parade and party. *The International Crawfish Tasting and Trade Show* is held in Lafayette.

Mississippi: Biloxi and Natchez celebrate *Mardi Gras*. In Jackson, the *Dixie National Livestock Show* runs most of the month in conjunction with the *Dixie National Rodeo* and the *Dixie National Western Festival*.

North Carolina: Asheville welcomes visitors to its annual *Winterfest Arts and Crafts Show*.

South Carolina: *Black Heritage Celebration* continues all month in North Charleston. Greenville rings with the *Festival of American Music*. The *Southern Gospel Music Festival* is held in Fort Mill.

Tennessee: Nashville hosts the *Americana Craft Sampler* show. *Heart of the Country Antiques* is at Opryland.

Virginia: *Mardi Gras* is celebrated in Norfolk. Mount Vernon commemorates *George Washington's Birthday*. A *Revolutionary War Encampment and Skirmish* is reenacted in Alexandria.

March **Alabama:** The *Sea Oats Jamboree* is held in Gulf Shores. The *Azalea Trail and Festival* is in Mobile. *Cherry Festival* is held in Montgomery. The annual *Turkey Calling Class* is held in Bessemer; the *Southeastern Turkey Calling Contest* is in Montgomery. Fairhope hosts the annual *Arts and Crafts Festival*.

Georgia: *Rattlesnake Roundup* is held in Claxton. Macon hosts its *Cherry Blossom Festival*. The *Okefenokee Spring Fling* is held in Waycross. And *St. Patrick's Day* is especially colorful in Atlanta and Dublin.

Louisiana: Ville Platte hosts the *Boggy Bayou Festival*. Iowa celebrates its *Rabbit Festival*. The *Tennessee Williams/New Orleans Literary Festival* is a three-day event in New Orleans.

Mississippi: The *Natchez Pilgrimage* begins, as do similar house tours in Port Gibson, Vicksburg, and Columbus.

North Carolina: An 18th-century military encampment and Revolutionary War battle reenactment bring history to life on the *Anniversary of the Battle of Guilford Courthouse* in Greensboro. Mooresville hosts the annual *Old Time Fiddlers' and Bluegrass Convention*. Amateur and professional golfers compete in the *K-Mart Greater Greensboro Open*.

South Carolina: *Springfest* lasts all month on Hilton Head Island. Charleston welcomes visitors to its *Festival of Houses*, its *Founder's Festival*, and *The American Seafood Challenge*.

Tennessee: Gatlinburg hosts the *Great Smoky Arts and Crafts Community Spring Show*.

Virginia: Virginia Beach holds the *Mid-Atlantic Wildfowl Festival*. Fredericksburg welcomes more than 130 artists to its annual *Fine Arts Festival*. *St. Patrick's Day* is cause for big celebrations in Norfolk. *National Wildlife Week Celebration* takes place at the Virginia Living Museum in Newport News.

April **Alabama:** *Fort Blakely Battle Festival* takes place in Spanish Fort.

Georgia: *Atlanta Dogwood Festival* is held throughout the capital. *River Days* are celebrated at River Front Park in Albany. The *Rose Festival* is in Thomasville, and the *Masters Golf Tournament* is held in Augusta.

Louisiana: The *Louisiana Crawfish Festival* takes place in St. Bernard. In New Orleans, major events include the *French Quarter Festival*, *Spring Fiesta*, and the *New Orleans Jazz and Heritage Festival*. *Festival International de Louisiane* is an extravaganza in Lafayette and the *Strawberry Festival* in Ponchatoula is a must.

Mississippi: Eleven Gulf Coast communities hold *Spring Pilgrimages* of historic homes. The *World Catfish Festival* is celebrated in Belzoni. *The Landing of d'Iberville* is reenacted in Ocean Springs.

North Carolina: Fayetteville dresses up for its *Dogwood Festival*. Wilmington hosts the *North Carolina Azalea Festival*. Late in the month, Charlotte holds its annual *Springfest* and Chadburn its annual *North Carolina Strawberry Festival*.

South Carolina: *Allendale County Spring Cooter Festival* is held in Allendale. The *World Grits Festival* is held in St. George. *Riverfest* is held in Columbia.

Tennessee: Knoxville holds a *Dogwood Arts Festival*. *The World's Biggest Fish Fry* is held in Paris. The annual *Spring Wildflower Pilgrimage* sets off from Gatlinburg.

Virginia: On Chincoteague, there's an *Easter Decoy Carver Festival*. An annual *Dogwood Festival* is held in Charlottesville. Norfolk holds the *International Azalea Festival*.

May **Alabama:** The *Alabama Jubilee Hot Air Balloon Classic* takes place in Decatur and the Montgomery Jubilee happens near the month's end.

Georgia: *Arts-on-the-River Weekend* is held in Savannah. Athens hosts the *New Jazz Festival*. Special events mark *Memorial Day* weekend on Jekyll Island and in Savannah.

Louisiana: May brings the *Rose Festival* in Shreveport, the *Louisiana Praline Festival* in Houma, and the *Breaux Bridge Crawfish Festival* in odd-numbered years.

Mississippi: *Jubilee Jam* in Jackson features music and the arts, as do the *Gum Tree Festival* in Tupelo and the *Atwood Music Festival* in Monticello.

North Carolina: *Tarheel Association of Storytellers' Festival* is held in Winston-Salem. Nags Head is the location for the annual *Hang Gliding Spectacular*.

South Carolina: *Spoleto Festival USA* in Charleston is one of the world's biggest arts festivals. Running concurrently with Spoleto is *Piccolo Spoleto*, which showcases local and regional talent. *Mayfest* takes place in Columbia.

Tennessee: *Memphis in May International Festival* is celebrated all month. *International Folkfest* is held in Murfreesboro. *Knoxville Water Sports Festival* means canoe, kayak, and rowing competitions.

Virginia: *Storytelling Festival at Busch Gardens* and the *Jamestown Landing Celebration* are held in Williamsburg. In

Front Royal, Miss Toadstool is crowned during the *Virginia Mushroom Festival*. The *Shenandoah Apple Blossom Festival* is in Winchester.

June **Alabama:** A *Seafood Festival* is held throughout the summer in Bayou la Batre. *MOWA Choctaw Indian Pow Wow* is held in McIntosh. The *Blessing of the Shrimp Fleet* is celebrated in Bayou la Batre.

Georgia: Stone Mountain Village holds an annual *Festival of the Arts*. *COA Blueberry Festival* is held in Alma.

Louisiana: June is food month, with the *Okra Festival* in Kenner, the *Jambalaya Festival* in Gonzales, the *Great French Market Tomato Festival* and *La Fete* in New Orleans, the *Louisiana Blueberry Festival* in Mansfield, the *Feliciana Peach Festival* in Clinton, and the famed *Louisiana Catfish Festival* in Des Allemands.

Mississippi: Biloxi hosts the colorful *Blessing of the Fleet, Shrimp Festival,* and *Fais Do Do. Art Mart* in Batesville is a juried art show. In Raleigh, contestants gather for the *National Tobacco Spitting Contest*. The *Bear Creek Festival* is hailed in Dennis and Natchez celebrates *Steamboat Jubilee*.

North Carolina: The *Kitty Hawk Triathlon* includes hang gliding, windsurfing, and sailing at Nags Head. Asheville hosts the annual *Highland Heritage Art and Craft Show*.

South Carolina: *Sun Fun Festival* is held in the Grand Strand. *Colonial Life Days* are reenacted in Charleston. Hampton hosts the *Hampton County Watermelon Festival*.

Tennessee: The *International Country Music Fan Fair* is held in Nashville, and the *Carnival Music Festival* is held in Memphis.

Virginia: The *June Jubilee* is held in Richmond. Norfolk's *Harborfest* enlivens that city's waterfront.

July **Alabama:** *Alabama Deep Sea Fishing Rodeo* is held in Mobile and on Dauphin Island.

Georgia: In Atlanta, there's the *Independence Festival* and the popular *Peachtree Road Race*. Major *July Fourth* celebrations are held in Savannah and Columbus.

Louisiana: Galliano hosts the *Louisiana Oyster Festival. Cajun Bastille Day* is celebrated in Baton Rouge for three days and Franklinton hosts the *Washington Parish Watermelon Festival*.

Mississippi: The *Deep Sea Fishing Rodeo* in Gulfport is one of the largest fishing contests in the South. In Philadelphia, a major event is the *Choctaw Indian Fair;* the *Watermelon Festival* is held in Mize.

North Carolina: In Asheville, clog and figure dancing are part of the *Shindig-on-the-Green*. Among the many Independence Day celebrations is Winston-Salem's *Fourth of July Torchlight Procession* at Old Salem. Mid-July in Winston-Salem is the *Andy Griffith Show Celebration/Mayberry Convention*. Kill Devil Hills hosts the *Wright Kite Festival*.

South Carolina: *July Fourth* is commemorated in several communities, including Clemson, Conway, Greenville, and Gilbert. The *South Carolina Peach Festival* is held in Gaffney. Myrtle Beach hosts *Art in the Park*.

Tennessee: The *Tennessee Peach Festival* is held in Brownsville. *Kingsport Fun Fest* is in Kingsport and Sportsfest is in Morristown.

Virginia: *Independence Day* celebrations are annual traditions around the state, including Yorktown, where America's independence was won. Richmond hosts the savory annual *World Invitational Rib Championship. Shenandoah Valley Music Festival* is held in Orkney Springs. The *Virginia Highlands Festival* is celebrated in Abingdon.

August **Alabama:** The famed *W.C. Handy Festival* goes on in Florence for a week.

Georgia: A *Beach Music Festival* is held on Jekyll Island. *Sea Island Festival* is centered in St. Simons. *Labor Day Bluegrass Festival* is held in Fort Yargo State Park, and the *Green Corn Festival* is in Calhoun.

Louisiana: Morgan City hosts the *Louisiana Shrimp and Petroleum Festival*.

Mississippi: The *Old Brook Festival* is held in Brookhaven. Greenwoods hosts *Crop Day*, celebrating the history of cotton.

North Carolina: Asheville holds the annual *Mountain Dance and Folk Festival* and, later in the month, the *Annual Summerfest Art and Craft Show*. Kill Devil Hills celebrates *National Aviation Day*. The *North Carolina Apple Festival* is held in Hendersonville.

South Carolina: *Palmetto Upstate Festival* is in Woodruff. *South Carolina Peanut Party* is held in Pelion. The *Waccamaw Riverfest* is a citywide event in Conway.

Tennessee: *Elvis International Tribute Week* is held in Memphis. The *Appalachian Fair* is held in Gray, and Shelbyville hosts the *Tennessee Walking Horse National Celebration*.

Virginia: Norfolk hosts a *Festival of Nations*. In Manassas, the *Prince William County Fair* is a large agricultural and industrial exposition.

September **Alabama:** Gulf Shores hosts the annual *Orange Beach Fishing Rodeo*.

Georgia: *Oktoberfest* begins in Helen, and the *Hot Air Balloon Festival* is held there also. Atlanta hosts the *Fine Arts and Crafts Festival* in Piedmont Park. In Old Town Sharpsburg there's the *Fall Festival*, and in Carollton, the *Autumn Leaves Arts and Crafts Festival*.

Louisiana: Truly a festival month, some of the best are Houma's *Labor Day Piroque Race Festival;* the Southwest *Zydeco Music Festival* in Plaisance; the *Frog Festival* in Rayne; *Festival Acadiens* in Lafayette, and the *Louisiana Sugar Cane Festival* in New Iberia.

Mississippi: Natchez hosts the *Indian Festival*, Indianola the *Indian Bayou Arts and Crafts Festival*, and Biloxi the *Seafood Festival*. The *Delta Blues Festival* is held in Greenville.

North Carolina: The annual *Woolly Worm Festival* takes place in Banner Elk.

South Carolina: *South Carolina Apple Festival* is held in Westminster. Hilton Head Island hosts the *American Festival of Fitness and Sport.* Chesterfield celebrates its *Fall Festival.*

Tennessee: Nashville hosts the *Tennessee State Fair. Artfest* brings visual and performing arts to Knoxville. The *Mid-South Fair* is held in Memphis.

Virginia: *International Children's Festival* is celebrated in Vienna. The *Mountain Music and Dance Convention* is held in Lexington. Virginia Beach hosts the *Virginia Neptune Festival.* The *State Fair of Virginia* is held in Richmond.

October **Alabama:** *National Shrimp Festival* is held in Gulf Shores. Spanish Fort hosts the annual *Blakeley Bluegrass Festival* and the *National Peanut Festival* takes place in Dothen.

Georgia: *Cotton Days Festival* begins in Marietta. Athens hosts the *North Georgia Folk Festival.* The annual *Fall Bluegrass Festival* is held in Blue Ridge. *National Pecan Festival* is held in Albany. Savannah celebrates its *Oktoberfest,* and *Heritage Holidays* are commemorated in Rome.

Louisiana: Shreveport hosts the week-long *Red River Revel Arts Festival.* The *Gumbo Festival* is held in Bridge City. The *Louisiana Cotton Festival* is held in Ville Platte. Shreveport hosts the *Louisiana State Fair.* New Orleans hosts the *Festa d'Italia.*

Mississippi: *Mississippi State Fair* is held in Jackson. Natchez stages the *Fall Pilgrimage.* Jackson has its *Mistletoe Market* late in the month, and Vaughn has *Hobo Day.*

North Carolina: The annual *Indian Summer Art and Craft Show* is held in Asheville. Wilmington is the scene of the spooky *Halloween Festival.*

South Carolina: *Moja Arts Festival* in Charleston celebrates African, American, and Caribbean cultures. *Halloween* festivities are especially colorful in Charleston, Greenville, and Georgetown.

Tennessee: *Dollywood National Crafts Festival* is held all month in Pigeon Forge. The *Gatlinburg Fall Craftsmen's Fair* is also month-long. Jonesborough hosts the popular *National Storytelling Festival.* Memphis and Clarkesville celebrate *Oktoberfest.*

Virginia: Charlottesville revels during the *Bacchanalian Feast/Monticello Wine Festival.* Fairfax stages the *Halloween Happening* and Portsmouth the *Olde Towne Ghost Walk.*

November **Alabama:** *Creek Indian Thanksgiving Day Homecoming* is held in Poarch, near Atmore.

Georgia: *Mistletoe Market* is held in Albany. Savannah holds its *Festival of Trees. Cane grinding parties* are thrown in Tifton and Juliette.

Louisiana: *Louisiana Pecan Festival* is held in Colfax. Shreveport's *Christmas in Roseland* begins this month and continues through December.

Mississippi: *Scottish Highland Games* are held in Biloxi as well as the *Old Biloxi Fall Festival.*

North Carolina: The annual *High Country Christmas Art and Craft Show* is held in Asheville.

South Carolina: *Christmas Connection* enlivens Myrtle Beach, as does *Dickens Christmas Show and Festival.*

Tennessee: *Mid-South Arts and Crafts Show/Sale* is held in Memphis.

Virginia: *Holidays in the City* is celebrated in Norfolk. *Virginia Thanksgiving Festival* at Berkeley Plantation in Charles City County commemorates the first official Thanksgiving in 1619.

December   **Alabama:** *Christmas on the River* is held at Demopolis.

Georgia: *Sugarplum Festival* is held at Stone Mountain Village. Atlanta hosts its *Holiday Tour of Homes* and the *Peach Bowl and Parade.* Special Christmas celebrations are held in Savannah, at Callaway Gardens, and on Jekyll Island.

Louisiana: *Creole Christmas* is celebrated in the French Quarter of New Orleans. The *Plaquemines Parish Fair and Orange Festival* is held at Fort Jackson. Natchitoches becomes the *City of Lights* with displays along the Cane River.

Mississippi: Special Christmas events are held in Jackson, Natchez, Meridian, Greenwood, Leland, Inverness, and Vicksburg. Biloxi celebrates with *Christmas on the Water.*

North Carolina: Historic homes are open to visitors during the *Candlelight Tour of Chapel Hill.* Winston-Salem re-creates a Moravian Christmas during *Old Salem Christmas.* The *Historic Oakwood Candlelight Tour* is held in Raleigh. *First Night Charlotte* is a New Year's Eve festival on the Town Square.

South Carolina: Christmas in Charleston lasts all month and the *Elgin Catfish Stomp* takes place in Elgin.

Tennessee: *Christmas in the City* is a month-long Knoxville celebration. *Smoky Mountain Christmas* is held in Gatlinburg. Nashville's *Trees of Christmas* light up all month at Cheekwood.

Virginia: *Grand Illumination* takes place in Colonial Williamsburg. The *Spirit of Christmas* enlivens Williamsburg, Jamestown, and Yorktown. *Christmas at Belle Grove* is a Middletown tradition as is the *Yule Log Lighting* in Norfolk. Norfolk also celebrates a *waterfront New Year's Eve Festival.*

What to Pack

Pack light because porters and luggage trolleys are hard to find. Luggage allowances on domestic flights vary slightly from airline to airline. Most allow three checked pieces and one carry-on. Some give you the option of two checked and two carry-on. In all cases, check-in bags cannot weigh more than 70 pounds per piece or be larger than 62 inches (length + width + height) and must fit under the seat or in the overhead luggage compartment.

Generally, the South has hot, humid weather during the summer and sunny, mild weather in the winter. For winters in the southernmost tier of states, pack a lightweight coat, slacks, and sweaters. The northern tier of Southern states can be very cold and damp in the winter. Snow is not unusual, so be prepared. For summer visits, keep the high humidity level in mind and pack cotton and natural fabrics that breathe. You'll need an umbrella for sudden summer showers, but leave the plastic raincoats behind because the humidity makes them extremely uncomfortable. Take a jacket or sweater for summer evenings, or for restaurants that have air-conditioning going full blast. Always take insect repellent during the summer because the mosquitoes come out in full force after sunset.

Cash Machines

Virtually all U.S. banks belong to a network of ATMs (automatic teller machines), which accept bank cards and spit out cash 24 hours a day in cities throughout the country. There are eight major networks in the United States, the largest of which are Cirrus, owned by MasterCard, and Plus, affiliated with Visa. Some banks belong to more than one network. These cards are not automatically issued; you have to ask for them. If your bank doesn't belong to at least one network, you should consider moving funds, for ATMs are becoming as essential as check cashing. Cards issued by Visa and MasterCard may also be used in the ATMs, but the fees are usually higher than the fees on bank cards, and there is a daily interest charge on the "loan," even if monthly bills are paid on time. Each network has a toll-free number you can call to locate machines in a given city. The Cirrus number is 800/4–CIRRUS; the Plus number is 800/THE–PLUS. Check with your bank for fees and for the amount of cash you can withdraw on any given day.

Traveling with Film

If your camera is new, shoot and develop a few rolls before leaving home. Pack some lens tissue and an extra battery for your built-in light meter. Invest about $10 in a skylight filter and screw it onto the front of your lens. It will protect the lens and also reduce haze.

Film doesn't like hot weather. If you're driving in summer, don't store film in the glove compartment or on the shelf under the rear window. Put it behind the front seat on the floor, on the side opposite the exhaust pipe.

On a plane trip, never pack unprocessed film in check-in luggage; if your bags get X-rayed, you can say goodbye to your pictures. Always carry undeveloped film with you through security and ask to have it inspected by hand. (It helps to isolate your film in a plastic bag, ready for quick inspection.) Inspectors at American airports are required by law to honor requests for hand inspection; abroad, you'll have to depend on the kindness of strangers.

The old airport scanning machines—still in use in some Third World countries—use heavy doses of radiation that can turn a family portrait into an early morning fog. The newer models—used in all U.S. airports—are safe for anything from five to 500 scans, depending on the speed of your film. The effects are cumulative; you can put the same roll of film through several scans without worry. After five scans, though, you're asking for trouble.

If your film gets fogged and you want an explanation, send it to the National Association of Photographic Manufacturers (600 Mamaroneck Ave., Harrison, NY 10528). They will try to determine what went wrong. The service is free.

Car Rentals

Outside of south Florida, New Orleans and Atlanta are the South's biggest car rental centers. **Hertz** (tel. 800/654–3131), **Avis** (tel. 800/331–1212), **National** (tel. 800/328–4567), **Budget** (tel. 800/527–0700), **Thrifty** (tel. 800/367–2277), **American International** (tel. 800/527–0202), **Sears** (tel. 800/527–0770), and **Dollar** (tel. 800/421–6868) have airport locations in New Orleans, Atlanta, Memphis, Jackson, Birmingham, Nashville, Louisville, Charleston, Columbia, and Raleigh. Mid-size cities like Fayetteville, Baton Rouge, and Augusta have at least three or four of the above companies, plus local and regional firms. Expect to pay $35–$45 daily for a subcompact in larger cities, with 75–100 free miles daily. **Alamo** (tel. 800/327–9633) offers some of the region's lowest rates, though it does not have offices in all cities. Unlimited free mileage these days seems to be the exception rather than the rule. Be careful renting a car for a multistate Southern trip: many rental companies tack instate driving restrictions onto their unlimited-mileage specials.

Local and regional companies sometimes skirt the over-25 age restriction and credit-card requirements of many large companies; sometimes they have lower rates, too. Birmingham has **Agency** (tel. 800/321–1972). Nashville has **Agency** plus **Holiday Payless** (tel. 800/237–2804). Memphis also has **Holiday Payless** and **Agency.** Jackson has **Just A Ride** (tel. 601/355–7433) and **ATR** (tel. 601/948–3391, a Mississippi-wide company). Raleigh has **Enterprise** (tel. 800/325–8007), **Able-Leith** (tel. 919/832–2921), **Triangle** (tel. 919/851–2555), and **Choice** (tel. 919/832–2121). Charleston has **Alamo, Holiday Payless, Enterprise,** and **Freedom** (tel. 803/554–9829). Columbia, SC, has **Not A Lemon Rent-A-Car** (tel. 803/782–2640).

It's always best to know a few essentials *before* you arrive at the car-rental counter. Find out what the collision damage waiver (usually an $8–$12 daily surcharge) covers and whether your corporate or personal insurance already covers damage to a rental car (if so, bring a photocopy of the benefits section along). More and more companies are now also holding renters responsible for theft and vandalism damages if they don't buy the CDW; in response, some credit-card and insurance companies are extending *their* coverage to rental cars. These include Dreyfuss Bank Gold and Silver MasterCards (tel. 800/847–9700), Chase Manhattan Bank Visa cards (tel. 800/645–7352), and Access America (tel. 800/851–2800). Find out, too, if you must pay for a full tank of gas whether you use it or not; and make sure you get a reservation number.

Traveling with Children

Publications   *Family Travel Times,* an 8- to 12-page newsletter published 10 times a year by Travel with Your Children (80 Eighth Ave., New York, NY 10011, tel. 212/206–0688). Subscription includes access to back issues and twice-weekly opportunities to call in for specific advice.

Great Vacations with Your Kids: The Complete Guide to Family Vacations in the U.S., by Dorothy Ann Jordon and Marjorie Adoff Cohen (E.P. Dutton, 2 Park Ave., New York, NY 10016; $9.95), details everything from city vacations to adventure vacations to child-care resources.

Bimonthly and monthly publications filled with events listings, resources, and advice for parents and available free at such places as libraries, supermarkets, and museums include ***Atlanta Parent*** (Box 8506, Atlanta, GA 30306, tel. 404/325–1763) and ***Youth View*** (1401 W. Paces Ferry Rd., Suite A-217, Atlanta, GA 30327, tel. 404/231–0562). For a small fee you can usually have an issue sent to you before your trip.

Hotels **Guest Quarters Suite Hotels** (tel. 800/424–2900) offer the luxury of two-room suites with kitchen facilities, plus children's menus in the restaurants. The hotels also allow children under 18 to stay free in their parents' suite. Most **Days Inn** hotels (tel. 800/325–2525) charge only a nominal fee for children under 18 and allow those 12 and under to eat free (many offer efficiency-type apartments, too).

The Hyatt Regency Ravinia (4355 Ashford-Dunwoody Rd., Atlanta, GA 30346, tel. 404/395–1234 or 800/228–9000) shows special attention and offers discounted meals to children in its Cafe Ravinia. **The Ritz-Carlton, Buckhead** (3434 Peachtree Rd., Atlanta, GA 30326, tel. 404/237–2700 or 800/241–3333) pampers children with everything from stuffed lions in their cribs to coloring-book menus in *The Cafe*. A children's program is scheduled during the summer at both **The Cloister** (Sea Island, GA 31561, tel. 912/638–3611 or 800/732–4752) and **Sea Palms Golf and Tennis** (5445 Frederica Rd., St. Simons Island, GA 31522, tel. 912/638–3351 or 800/841–6268).

In winter and summer, kids' programs are offered at **Wintergreen Resort** (Wintergreen, VA 22958, tel. 804/325–2200).

The Outer Banks of South Carolina harbors a number of resorts with elaborate children's programs and facilities: **Kiawah Island Resort** (Box 12910, Charleston, SC 29412, tel. 803/768–2121 or 800/6–KIAWAH), **Hyatt Regency Hilton Head** (Box 6167, Hilton Head Island, SC 29938, tel. 803/785–1234 or 800/228–9000), **Inter-Continental Hilton Head** (135 S. Port Royal Dr., Hilton Head Island, SC 29928, tel. 803/681–4000 or 800/327–0200), **Marriott's Hilton Head Resort** (130 Shipyard Dr., Hilton Head Island, SC 29928, tel. 803/842–2400 or 800/334–1881), and **Palmetto Dunes Resort** (Box 5606, Hilton Head Island, SC 29938, tel. 803/785–1161 or 800/845–6130).

Condo Rentals See ***The Condo Lux Vacationer's Guide to Condominium Rentals in the Southeast,*** by Jill Little (Vintage Books/Random House, New York; $9.95).

Home Exchange See ***Home Exchanging: A Complete Sourcebook for Travelers at Home or Abroad,*** by James Dearing (Globe Pequot Press, Box Q, Chester, CT 06412, tel. 800/243–0495 or 800/962–0973 in CT).

Getting There On domestic flights, children under 2 not occupying a seat travel free. Various discounts apply to children 2–12. Reserve a seat behind the bulkhead of the plane, which offers more legroom and can usually fit a bassinet (supplied by the airline). At the same time, inquire about special children's meals or snacks, offered by most airlines. (See "TWYCH's Airline Guide," in the February 1988 issue of *Family Travel Times*, for a rundown of the services offered by 46 airlines.) Ask the airline in advance if you can bring aboard your child's car seat. (For the booklet "Child/Infant Safety Seats Acceptable for Use in Aircraft," contact the Community and Consumer Liaison Division, APA-400 Federal Aviation Administration, Washington, DC 20591, tel. 202/267–3479.)

Baby-sitting Services First check with the hotel concierge about child-care arrangements. **Sitters Unlimited** has a franchise in northern Virginia (tel. 703/250–5250).

Hints for Disabled Travelers

The Information Center for Individuals with Disabilities (20 Park Plaza, Room 330, Boston, MA 02116, tel. 617/727–5540) offers useful problem-solving assistance, including lists of travel agents that specialize in tours for the disabled.

Moss Rehabilitation Hospital Travel Information Service (12th St. and Taber Rd., Philadelphia, PA 19141, tel. 215/329–5715) provides information on tourist sights, transportation, and accommodations in destinations around the world. The fee is $5 for each destination. Allow one month for delivery.

Mobility International (Box 3551, Eugene, OR 97403, tel. 503/343–1284) has information on accommodations, organized study, etc., around the world.

The Society for the Advancement of Travel for the Handicapped (26 Court St., Brooklyn, NY 11242, tel. 718/858–5483) offers access information. Annual membership costs $40, $25 for senior travelers and students. Send a stamped, self-addressed envelope.

The Itinerary (Box 1084, Bayonne, NJ 07002, tel. 201/858–3400) is a bimonthly travel magazine for the disabled.

Access to the World: A Travel Guide for the Handicapped, by Louise Weiss, is useful but out of date. Available from Facts on File (460 Park Ave. S, New York, NY 10016, tel. 212/683–2244).

Frommer's Guide for Disabled Travelers is also useful but dated.

Greyhound-Trailways (tel. 800/531–5332) will carry a disabled person and companion for the price of a single fare. **Amtrak** (tel. 800/USA–RAIL) requests 24-hour notice to provide redcap service, special seats, and a 25% discount.

Travel Industry and Disabled Exchange (TIDE, 5435 Donna Ave., Tarzana, CA 91356, tel. 818/343–6339) is an industry-based organization with a $15-per-person annual membership fee. Members receive a quarterly newsletter and information on travel agencies and tours.

Hints for Older Travelers

The **American Association of Retired Persons** (AARP, 1909 K St. NW, Washington, DC 20049, tel. 202/662–4850) has two programs for independent travelers: (1) *The Purchase Privilege Program*, which offers discounts on hotels, airfare, car rentals, and sightseeing; and (2) the *AARP Motoring Plan*, which offers emergency aid and trip-routing information for an annual fee of $29.95 per couple. AARP also arranges group tours, through two companies: **Olson-Travelworld** (5855 Green Valley Circle, Culver City, CA 90230, tel. 800/227–7737) and **RFD, Inc.** (4401 W. 110th St., Overland Park, KS 66211, tel. 800/448–7010). AARP members must be 50 or older. Annual dues are $5 per person or per couple.

When using an AARP or other identification card, ask for a reduced hotel rate at the time you make your reservation, not when you check out. At restaurants, show your card to the maître d' before you're seated, since discounts may be limited to certain set menus, days, or hours. When renting a car, remember that economy cars, priced at promotional rates, may cost less than cars that are available with your ID card.

Elderhostel (80 Boylston St., Suite 400, Boston, MA 02116, tel. 617/426–7788) is an innovative 13-year-old program for people 60 and older. Participants live in dorms on some 1,200 campuses around the world. Mornings are devoted to lectures and seminars, afternoons to sightseeing and field trips. The all-inclusive fee for two- to three-week trips, including room, board, tuition, and round-trip transportation, is $1,700–$3,200.

National Council of Senior Citizens (925 15th St. NW, Washington, DC 20005, tel. 202/347–8800) is a nonprofit advocacy group with some 4,000 local clubs across the country. Annual membership is $10 per person or $14 per couple. Members receive a monthly newspaper with travel information and an ID card for reduced-rate hotels and car rentals.

Mature Outlook (Box 1205, Glenview, IL 60025, tel. 800/336–6330), a subsidiary of Sears Roebuck & Co., is a travel club for people over 50, with hotel and motel discounts and a bimonthly newsletter. Annual membership is $7.50 per couple. Instant membership is available at participating Holiday Inns.

Travel Tips for Senior Citizens (U.S. Dept. of State Publication 8970, revised Sept. 1987) is available for $1 from the Superintendent of Documents, U.S. Government Printing Office, Washington, DC 20402.

Golden Age Passport is a free lifetime pass to all parks, monuments, and recreation areas run by the federal government. People over 62 should pick them up in person at any national park that charges admission. A driver's license or other proof of age is required.

Further Reading

For background reading on Southern writers, take along Paul Buiding's *A Separate Country: A Literary Journey through the American South.* Chet Fuller's *I Hear Them Calling My Name* is a first-person narrative of a black journalist traveling through the South.

Eugenia Price's novels *Savannah* and *The Beloved Invader* are little known outside the South but provide a keen sense of place in a historical-romance frame. Look also for *Cold Sassy Tree,* by Olive Ann Burns.

Several good epic/romance/adventure novels are *North and South,* by John Jakes; *The Glass Flame,* by Phyllis A. Whitney; Ben Ames Williams's *House Divided; So Red the Rose,* by Stark Young; *Gone With the Wind,* by Margaret Mitchell; and *Savannah Purchase,* by Jane A. Hodge.

For engaging Southern fiction at its best, take along a few of the following: *A Christmas Memory*, by Truman Capote; *To Kill a Mockingbird*, by Capote's childhood neighbor, Harper Lee; *Edisto*, by Padgett Powell, a young boy's coming-of-age story, set near Savannah and Charleston; Carson McCullers's *Member of the Wedding;* Toni Morrison's *Song of Solomon; The Color Purple*, by Alice Walker; William Faulkner's *The Sound and the Fury*, set in the mythic Mississippi county of Yoknapatawpha; and the short-story collections of Georgia's Flannery O'Connor and Mississippi's Eudora Welty.

2 Alabama

Introduction

by Wayne
Greenhaw

Wayne Greenhaw is
the editor of
Alabama
magazine. He is
also author of
several books,
prize-winning
journalist, and
lifelong
Alabamian.

Alabama is indeed—as Governor Guy Hunt, the first Republican to win that office in Alabama in 112 years, declared it—a state of surprises. Visitors are surprised at the physical beauty: from the dramatic rocky, wooded hills and vast caves of the northeast to the expansive lakes and broad rivers of the interior to the snow-white beaches of the Gulf coast. At the high-tech world of Huntsville's Space and Rocket Center, near Redstone Arsenal, the Saturn rocket was designed. The state's largest city, Birmingham, is one of the South's major medical centers, with 22 institutions, including the University of Alabama at Birmingham Medical Center, ranked among the nation's highest in quality of health care.

The traveler who ventures off the four-lane interstates will find something surprising at almost every turn—a cascading waterfall or showy stand of wildflowers, an archaeological excavation or a Colonial fort, perhaps one of Alabama's 16 covered bridges. At Florence, in the northwest corner of the state, the tiny frame cottage where Helen Keller overcame the loss of hearing and sight sits as a monument to her inspirational life. A few miles south, tucked away on a wooded hillside, is a cemetery for coon hounds, begun in 1937 by the devoted master of Troop, its first resident. A few more miles south is a sunken park (called The Dismals) where junglelike plants, some of which are found nowhere else in this hemisphere, grow in profusion. In Alabama, expect the unexpected.

Each spring, several Alabama towns hold "pilgrimages"—tours of historic homes (including many private residences not otherwise open to the public), mansions, plantations, churches, gardens, even cemeteries. Hosts and hostesses in period costume greet visitors and tell tales of life in bygone days. It's a lovely time to visit, with the gardens decked out in dogwood, azalea, magnolia, and many other blossoms. Candlelight tours add a romantic touch. For a copy of the "Alabama Pilgrimages" brochure, contact the Alabama Bureau of Tourism and Travel (*see* Essential Information).

Birmingham

Birmingham, set in a valley below the foothills of the Appalachians, first blossomed around the coal mines and the iron industry in the latter part of the 19th century. In the 1970s, after plastics became commonplace in auto manufacturing, the steel-making plants that had polluted the valley air virtually vanished. The air cleared of soot and dust, and the University of Alabama at Birmingham, with its fast-growing medical center, became the city's largest employer.

Birmingham's image as a backward civil rights territory was reinforced in 1963 when Police Commissioner Eugene "Bull" Connor turned loose snarling dogs on peaceful demonstrators and when Dr. Martin Luther King, Jr., was put in jail for his activities. However, when the turmoil finally settled, a new city began to emerge. A sign of the change was the election in 1979 of Richard Arrington, a successful black businessman, as mayor; he is currently serving his third term.

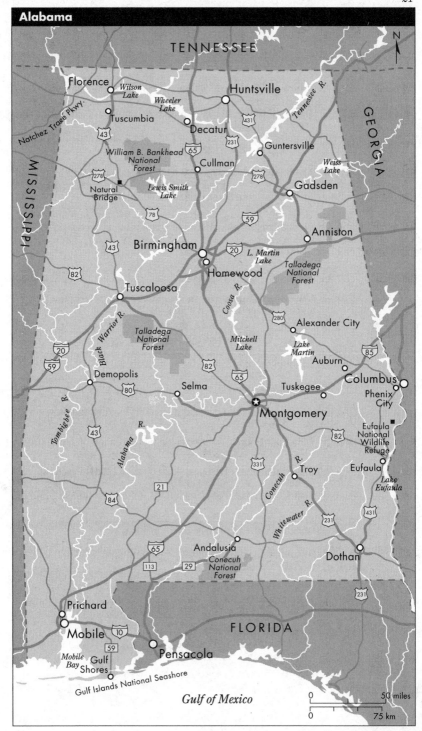

Alabama

TENNESSEE

N

Florence
Wilson Lake
Wheeler Lake
Huntsville
Natchez Trace Pkwy.
Tuscumbia
431
Decatur
Tennessee R.
GEORGIA
MISSISSIPPI
43
231
Guntersville
65
William B. Bankhead National Forest
Cullman
278
Weiss Lake
278
Natural Bridge
Lewis Smith Lake
Gadsden
78
59
Anniston
Birmingham
20
L. Martin Lake
Talladega National Forest
43
Homewood
Coosa R.
82
Tuscaloosa
Talladega National Forest
280
Alexander City
Black Warrior R.
Mitchell Lake
Lake Martin
Auburn
85
20
82
Columbus
59
Demopolis
65
Phenix City
80
Selma
Tuskegee
Tombigbee R.
Montgomery
Eufaula National Wildlife Refuge
43
Alabama R.
R.
82
331
Conecuh R.
Troy
Eufaula
21
Lake Eufaula
84
Whitewater R.
231
431
65
Andalusia
113
29
Conecuh National Forest
Dothan
231
Prichard
Mobile
10
FLORIDA
59
Pensacola
Mobile Bay
Gulf Shores
Gulf Islands National Seashore

Gulf of Mexico

50 miles

0

0

75 km

Birmingham is today a beautiful, hospitable, busy metropolis. Several 19th-century houses and commercial buildings have been restored to create a lively shopping and dining area called Five Points South. The city's last remaining antebellum mansion has been restored and functions as a museum. There's also a large, major zoo and a 67-acre Japanese and botanic garden. Looking down on it all from high atop Red Mountain—so named for the iron ore within it—is a reminder of the source of an earlier prosperity: a 55-foot-high cast-iron statue of Vulcan, god of the forge.

Arriving and Departing

By Plane
Airports and Airlines
The Birmingham Airport is less than three miles from central downtown. It is served by **American, Delta, Eastern, Braniff's Florida Express, Southwest, United,** and **USAir.**

Between the Airport and Center City
Taxis are readily available; the fare to most hotels is about $7.50. Many hotels will provide **limousine service** from the airport by prior arrangement. If traveling **by car,** follow clearly marked signs to downtown.

By Train
The **Amtrak** station is on Morris Avenue, downtown, tel. 205/324–3033.

By Bus
Greyhound/Trailways is on 19th Street North, between Fourth and Fifth avenues, tel. 800/528–0447.

By Car
I–59 goes northeast from Birmingham to Chattanooga, southwest to Tuscaloosa, and then into Mississippi. I–20 runs west to Anniston and Atlanta. I–65 goes north to Decatur and Nashville and south to Montgomery and Mobile.

Getting Around

This is a city where a car is a necessity—sites are pretty well spread out.

By Taxi
Taxis charge $2.10 for the first mile, $1.10 each additional mile. **Yellow Cab:** tel. 205/252–1131.

By Bus
Bus schedules are irregular and suited only to the more adventurous traveler. They require exact change (80¢ fare, 15¢ transfer) and run from 4 AM to 7 PM. For a schedule, call 205/328–6277.

Important Addresses and Numbers

Tourist Information
Birmingham Convention & Visitors Bureau (2027 First Ave. N, tel. 205/252–9825).

Emergencies
Dial 911 for **police** and **ambulance** in an emergency.

Doctor
The all-night emergency room closest to downtown is at **University Hospital** (1900 Fifth Ave. S, tel. 205/934–5105).

Dentist
Dental Care offers 24-hour emergency service. Call either of its two locations: in Eastwood Mall, tel. 205/956–2999, and in Homewood, tel. 205/942–6916.

24-Hour Pharmacy
Eckerd Drugs (Eastwood Mall, tel. 205/592–8149).

Guided Tours

Not much in the way of guided tours goes on in the city, except for large groups. One outfit, **Way-to-Go Carriage Co.** (tel. 205/930–9262; weekdays or by appointment), offers rides in six-passenger horse-drawn carriages through the Five Points South area. The tour lasts 15–20 minutes and costs $15 per couple; there is no narration, but the driver will be glad to answer your questions. **Alabama Limousine** (tel. 205/591–7555 or 800/633–0223) will take you around on a 2½ hour tour of the city ($12 adults; $6 children 3–11, under 3 free).

Exploring Birmingham

Numbers in the margin correspond with points of interest on the Birmingham map.

Alabama has long been noted for its excellence in sports, and at the **Alabama Sports Hall of Fame Museum,** in the Birmingham–Jefferson County Civic Center, memorabilia of some of the state's most famous heroes is on display. Among the exhibits are the houndstooth hat worn by Alabama coach Bear Bryant, the shoes in which Jesse Owens won the Olympic gold medal, uniforms once worn by Bessemer baseball great Willie Mays and Mobile outfielder Hank Aaron, and trophies won by Bart Starr and Auburn-born Heisman Trophy winner Pat Sullivan. *21st St. between Ninth and 11th Aves. N, tel. 205/323–6665. Admission: $1.50 adults, 75¢ students. Open Tues., Sun. 1–5; Wed.–Sat. 10–5; other times by appointment.*

The **Birmingham Museum of Art,** two blocks south, has one of the world's largest collections of Wedgwood, the largest collection of contemporary Chinese paintings outside the People's Republic of China, some extraordinary examples of Western American art, plus Italian Renaissance and pre-Columbian art. *2000 Eighth Ave. N, tel. 205/254–2565. Admission: $4 adults; $2 children 6–12, under 6 free. Open Tues.–Sat. 10–5 (until 9 on Thurs.), Sun. 2–6.*

At the corner of 16th Street North and Eighth Avenue North is the **16th Street Baptist Church,** site of one of the saddest and most memorable occurrences of the civil rights movement. Here, on the morning of September 15, 1963, a bomb exploded and killed four little black girls who were attending Sunday school in the basement. A plaque erected to their memory bears this legend: May Men Learn to Replace Bitterness and Violence with Love and Understanding.

From here, head south. One block past First Avenue North, running east and west between 20th and 24th streets, is **Morris Avenue,** a turn-of-the-century brick roadway lined with brick buildings of the period. Many of these buildings have been renovated and are now used as professional offices. Gaslights add to the Victorian atmosphere.

Time Out Stop in at **Maxwell's-on-Morris** (2033 Morris Ave., tel. 205/324–9821), a sort of Victorian pub, for a drink or casual dining. The specialty is hickory-smoked prime rib.

Driving east on First Avenue North, over the viaduct, you'll see signs for **Sloss Furnace.** The massive ironworks plant pro-

Arlington, **6**

Birmingham Museum of Art, **2**

Birmingham Zoo, **19**

Botanical and Japanese Gardens, **20**

Brother Bryan statue, **9**

Five Points South, **7**

Five Points Theatre, **14**

Haskins Williams House, **11**

Methodist Church, **10**

Morris Ave., **4**

Nabob Hill, **12**

Pickwick Hotel, **15**

Pickwick Place, **8**

Red Mountain Museum, **17**

Rube Burrows, **16**

16th St. Baptist Church, **3**

Sloss Furnace, **5**

Southside Baptist Church, **13**

Sports Hall of Fame Museum, **1**

Vulcan statue, **18**

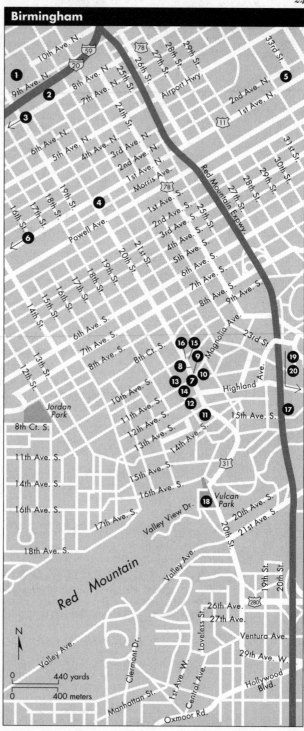

Birmingham

duced pig iron from ore dug from the hills surrounding Birmingham between 1882 and 1971. Retired blast-furnace workers who knew the heat of the flowing molten metal first-hand conduct guided tours through the plant, spicing the narrations with tales of their own experiences. *First Ave. N and 32nd St., tel. 205/324–1911. Admission free. Open Tues.–Sat. and holidays, 10–4, Sun. 12–4. Closed Thanksgiving, Christmas, and New Year's Day.*

⑥ If you head west again on First Avenue North, you'll come to **Arlington,** Birmingham's only remaining antebellum mansion. It was used as headquarters by Union General James H. Wilson in March of 1865 as he and his raiders swept south through Alabama to Selma, destroying iron furnaces along the way. In the 1950s the city purchased the classic Greek Revival structure, and 50 prominent citizens donated funds for its renovation. Today it houses Civil War memorabilia, some prime examples of 19th-century furniture, and a museum dedicated to the women of Alabama. *331 Cotton Ave. SW, tel. 205/780–5656. Admission: $2 adults; $1 children 6–18, under 6 free. Open Tues.–Sat. 10–4, Sun. 1–4; closed major holidays.*

⑦ Heading east again on First Avenue North, turn right onto 20th Street and continue for about 12 blocks to reach **Five Points South,** an outdoor museum of turn-of-the-century archi-
⑧ tecture. Start with the renovated **Pickwick Place,** a miniature open-air shopping mall between 20th Street South and Magnolia Avenue. On this site the Pickwick Ballroom once stood. Big bands played swing tunes while the belles and their beaux danced the nights away beneath the large mirrored ball that now hangs in the mall's entranceway.

Time Out At **Cosmos Pizza House** (2012 Magnolia Ave., tel. 205/930–9971), Jack makes gourmet pizza with sun-dried tomatoes, exotic cheeses, and crawfish.

⑨ Outside CAPS Restaurant and Lounge at Five Points is the kneeling stone **statue of Brother Bryan,** Birmingham's good-Samaritan minister. Across Magnolia, in front of the **Highlands**
⑩ **United Methodist Church,** is a concrete Art Deco fountain. The church, built in 1909 in the Spanish Renaissance Revival style, was designed by the same architect who was responsible for Atlanta's Fox Theatre. In the first block of 11th Avenue, in what is called the Spanish Stores for its stucco walls and tiled roofs, is **Highlands: A Bar and Grill** (*see* Dining), which has won national awards.

If you are lucky, you'll arrive on a "special weekend" (most are unannounced, with the exception of Halloween). As soon as the sun falls, the locals come out. Street bands play. Teenagers mimic denizens of London's Soho with their multihued hair and loose-fitting, wildly colored costumes. And men in drag dance in the streets. Is it any wonder local pundits have named Five Points "Bourbon Street without the sleaze"? With all the street people out, it is comforting to know that the Five Points South owners have their own security patrol, which immediately alerts the police department in case of a crime. You can walk these streets without fear.

⑪ South on 20th Street, the **Haskins Williams House** is another example of turn-of-the-century residential architecture. On the stairway is a wall of stained glass and floor-to-ceiling carved woodwork.

Time Out Behind 20th Street Antiques, through a narrow walkway, is Cobb Lane, where **The Back Alley Restaurant** (tel. 205/933–6211) has dining indoors and on an oak-shaded patio. The fare is soups, salads, sandwiches, quiche, and one or two Continental entrees each day.

Walking north on 19th Street, you'll see a ridge on your left at

⑫ 12th Avenue. Once called **Nabob Hill,** it was the site of five mansions in which the families of high-ranking Confederate officers lived. Today there's only a playground. A block beyond

⑬ (at 1016 19th St. S) stands the large, columned **Southside Baptist Church.** Built in 1911, it is a prime example of Classical Revival architecture, resembling a Roman Ionic temple.

Turning right and back toward the center of Five Points, you come to the Art Deco facade of multicolored Carrara glass that

⑭ was once the **Five Points Theatre** (1914 11th Ave. S), a popular movie house in the 1920s and '30s. Today the building houses Clyde Houston's bar and restaurant (tel. 205/251–0278).

⑮ Back on 20th Street is the **Pickwick Hotel** (1123 20th St. S; *see* Lodging), built in 1931 as the Medical Arts Building, with offices for physicians, surgeons, and pharmacists. Today it retains the original polished-marble lobby, but renovations have created roomy suites and a cozy little lounge with an etched-glass mirror showing Pickwick dancers in their finest formals.

Half a block down 20th Street, near where the walking tour of

⑯ Five Points began, is **Rube Burrows** (1005 20th St. S, tel. 205/933–5570), a watering hole and hamburger oasis named for Alabama's infamous 19th-century train robber.

After leaving the area, you can head south on U.S. 31 a short

⑰ way until you come to the **Red Mountain Museum,** showcasing rocks, fossils, and minerals of the many types found in the area. Also here is the only solar telescope in North America that is open to the public; don't miss the chance to get a look at the sun's surface. *1421 22nd St. S, tel. 205/933–4104. Donation. Open Tues.–Sat. 10–4:30, Sun. 1–4:30.*

A pleasant way to end a day would be to wend your way up Red

⑱ Mountain to visit **Vulcan.** From the enclosed observation deck at the base of the world's tallest cast-iron statue, there's a panoramic view of the city. There's also a circular stairway inside for the hardy. *Valley Ave. at U.S. 31S, tel. 205/328–6198. Admission: $1 (under 7 free). Open daily 8 AM–10:30 PM.*

The next part of the tour, a day in itself, takes you to Mountain Brook. This elegant suburb is a place for wandering along tree-shaded country roads, driving past great old and new Southern mansions. Here, too, nestled beneath a hammock of huge oaks,

⑲ is the **Birmingham Zoo.** A miniature train winds its way through the wooded acreage, or you may walk the paths at a leisurely pace. The zoo is known for the breeding of Siberian tigers, a number of which live here, along with the only self-sustaining breeding colony of golden spider monkeys in captivity. *2630 Cahaba Rd., tel. 205/879–0408. Admission: $2 adults; $1 over 64 and children 2–17, under 2 free. Open daily 9:30–5.*

20 At the nearby **Botanical and Japanese Gardens,** under a great glass dome, waterfalls cascade into pools with plants of every shade of green and flowers of every color imaginable. Outside, there is a quiet Japanese garden with small bridges over bubbling brooks and an authentic teahouse set amid Japanese ferns, mosses, and trees. For the blind, there is a touch-and-see nature trail. *2612 Lane Park Rd., tel. 205/879–1227. Admission free. Open daily sunrise to sunset.*

Birmingham for Free

Temple Sibyl. About five miles south of Vulcan on U.S. 31, atop Shades Mountain in the suburb of Vestavia Hills, is a replica of the Temple of Sibyl at Tivoli, near Rome. From this round, open-air temple, there's a grand view of the Georgian-style campus of Samford University and the whole valley below. It's a good spot for a picnic.

Vulcan Park *(see* Exploring*)*.

What to See and Do with Children

Discovery Place Children's Museum. At this hands-on museum, a child can dress up in a policeman's hat and coat, climb on a fire truck, sit in an ambulance and sound the siren, or put together the bones of a skeleton. *1320 22nd Ave. S, tel. 205/939–1176. Admission: $2 adults, $1.50 children under 16. Open Tues.–Fri. 9–3, Sat. 10–4, Sun. 1–4, Nov.–Aug.; extended hours Sat. summer.*

Red Mountain Museum *(see* Exploring*)*.

Ruffner Mountain Nature Center. Cutaway sections of the mountain ridge are labeled to explain the area's geologic history. There are also well-marked nature trails, a wildflower garden, and bird observation stations. *1214 81st St. S, tel. 205/833–8112. Admission free. Open Tues.–Sat. 9–5, Sun. 1–5. Closed Thanksgiving, December 24, Christmas, and New Year's Day.*

Off the Beaten Track

Birmingham Turf Club. To the northeast of Birmingham, just off I–459, is this 330-acre facility with room to stable more than 1,000 Thoroughbred horses in the finest style. The ultramodern clubhouse and track cost $84 million. In the middle of its first season, in 1987, the club hit financial difficulties and did not reopen in 1988. At press time, plans were to reopen in 1989. (tel. 205/838–1604 for current status).

Legion Field. If you're a fan, you know that Birmingham is known as the Football Capital of the South—perhaps even the world. Legion Field (400 Graymont Ave. W, tel. 205/251–0537; tickets, tel. 205/254–2391) is the site of the annual Alabama–Auburn Iron Bowl Classic, in which Paul "Bear" Bryant won his record-breaking game to become the winningest coach in college football. Not far from the famous stadium is **Elmwood Cemetery** (600 Martin Luther King Jr. Dr. SW), where the Alabama legend is buried.

Ollie's B-B-Q. A tradition in Birmingham, Ollie McClung's barbecue restaurant is a place where people go to meet while they eat. A strongly religious man, Ollie sells Bibles as well as bar-becue; on the walls are his favorite verses. The waitresses are very friendly, and the sauce is tangy. *515 University Blvd. off I–65, tel. 205/324–9485. Open Mon.–Sat. 9:30–8, but never on Sunday.*

Southern Living. At the offices of the most successful magazine in the South (820 Shades Creek Pkwy., tel. 205/877–6000), cooks test recipes before they are published. Free tours may be arranged.

Southern Museum of Flight. Housed here is the Alabama Avia-tion Hall of Fame, the first Delta Airlines passenger plane, and World War II bombers built at a factory in Birmingham. *4343 73rd St. N, tel. 205/833–8226. Admission: $2 adults, $1 stu-dents, preschoolers free. Open Tues.–Fri. 9:30–5, Sun. 1–5.*

Tannehill Historical State Park. Built around reconstructed ironworks and blast furnaces that produced munitions for the Confederacy, the park offers a museum, crafts demonstra-tions, a gristmill, a pioneer farm, a country store, and a train ride. The log-walled **Furnace Master Inn** serves up home cook-ing. *Bucksville exit off I–59 (about 30 mi west of Birmingham), tel. 205/477–5711. Admission: $1 adults, 50¢ children 6–12; under 6 and over 65 free. Open daily 7 AM–sunset.*

Shopping

These days, shopping is done mostly in malls and centers in the suburban areas, rather than downtown. Stores are usually open weekdays 10–6, Saturday 10–7, and closed Sunday. Sales tax is 6%. Banks are generally open weekdays 9–2.

Shopping Districts **Riverchase Galleria.** About 10 miles from downtown, at the in-tersection of I–459 and U.S. 31S (Information Center: tel. 205/ 985–3039), is one of the largest shopping malls in the South-east. Here you'll find 200 stores, including Macy's, Rich's, JC Penney, McRae's, and Parisian's department stores, plus specialty shops like Banana Republic and other purveyors of fashion high and low. At the core is a 100-foot-plus glass-domed atrium bordered by a dozen fast-food restaurants. An elegant restaurant, Winston's, is located in the adjoining Wynfrey Ho-tel (*see* Dining).

Mountain Brook Village. This small, villagelike shopping area, tucked away in the hollows of Birmingham's ritziest neighbor-hood (on Cahaba Rd.), has a number of small specialty shops, including Pappagallo. Also here is Browdy's, a New York–style deli-restaurant with imported beer (tel. 205/879–8585).

Discount Stores Off Valley Avenue at Green Springs, **Palisades** in Birmingham (tel. 205/879–3040) is a complex of 15 or 20 discount shops, in-cluding Stein Mart (with name-brand clothing).

Antiques For Depression glass, Oriental silver chests, and 19th-century memorabilia, try **20th Street Antiques** (20th St. at Cobb Ln., tel. 205/933–1472).

Day Trips from Birmingham

The sites listed below are within 150 miles of Birmingham. For information on them, *see* Elsewhere in the State.

Alabama Space and Rocket Center, Huntsville
Ave Maria Grotto, Cullman
De Soto Caverns, Childersburg
De Soto Falls, Fort Payne
Demopolis
Ivy Green, Tuscumbia
Little River Canyon, Fort Payne
Lookout Mountain Trail
Montgomery (*see* Montgomery section)
Mound State Monument, Moundville
Noccalula Falls and Park, Gadsden
Point Mallard Park, Decatur
Russell Cave National Monument, Bridgeport
Sequoyah Caverns, Valley Head
Sturdivant Hall, Selma
Tuskegee

Participant Sports

Bicycling Although the terrain is very hilly, many bikers enjoy the quiet thoroughfares around Five Points South. For rentals, try **Alabama Cycle & Equipment Co.** (tel. 205/833–1122).

Canoeing North of Birmingham at Warrior, there are several outfitters on the Black Warrior River—including **Cahaba Canoe & Kayaks Too** (tel. 205/991–5461)—that offer whitewater canoeing. South of Birmingham, beginning and intermediate canoeing can be found on the Cahaba River, especially near Montevallo. The best guidebook is John Foshee's *Canoeing in Alabama*.

Fishing The best fresh-water crappie or bass fishing is northeast of Birmingham at **Logan Martin Lake** (tel. 205/831–6860) or south at the smaller lakes in **Oak Mountain State Park** (tel. 205/663–6783) off I–65. Rentals are available at **Holiday Marine Boat Center** (tel. 205/424–0412) or **Aeromarine Inc.** (tel. 205/595–2141).

Golf Good public courses include **Charlie Boswell** (tel. 205/326–3998) and **Hawkins Park and Recreational Center** (tel. 205/836–7318).

Hiking and Jogging **Oak Mountain State Park** (tel. 205/663–6783), 15 miles south of the city in Pelham, offers trails for hiking or jogging. Joggers also favor the quiet streets in and around Five Points South.

Spectator Sports

Baseball The **Birmingham Barons** of the Southern League moved into brand-new facilities at Hoover Metropolitan Stadium (tel. 205/988–3200) in Hoover, south of Birmingham on AL 150, at the beginning of the 1988 season.

Basketball The University of Alabama at Birmingham has had a fine basketball team since it imported former UCLA coach Gene Bartow. The **Blazers** (tel. 205/934–3824) play home games at the 19,000-seat Coliseum in the Birmingham-Jefferson Civic Center (tel. 205/251–4100).

Football The annual **Iron Bowl Classic,** held at Legion Field (tel. 205/254–2391) on the Friday after Thanksgiving, matches the Auburn Tigers against the Alabama Crimson Tide. Some of Alabama's home games are also played here.

Dining

Birmingham dining moved into the big time with the opening a few years ago of Highlands: A Bar and Grill, which won praise in national magazines (including *Playboy*), sparking competition among other top Birmingham restaurants. As throughout Alabama, north of Mobile, Old South dishes prevail here: fried chicken, barbecue, roast beef, and country fried steak.

The most highly recommended restaurants in each price category are indicated by a star ★.

Category	Cost*
Expensive	$25–$35
Moderate	$15–$20
Inexpensive	under $15

per person without tax (7% in Birmingham), service, or drinks

The following credit-card abbreviations are used: AE, American Express; CB, Carte Blanche; DC, Diners Club; MC, MasterCard; V, Visa.

Downtown
Expensive
★

Highlands: A Bar and Grill. Exceptionally grand gourmet feasts are prepared here by owner-chef Frank Stitt, who worked at Chez Panisse in Berkeley and with Richard Olney in France and has received honors from *Playboy* and *Gourmet*. The room is a sophisticated peach and white, with paintings, an ornamental fireplace, brass candleholders, and fresh flowers—plus unhurried but efficient service. There's fillet of sole with a wine sauce so light it almost floats away; quail with raspberry sauce; and a tomato stuffed with chunks of lobster, crab, shrimp, and corn—all superbly done. *2011 11th Ave. S, tel. 205/ 939–1400. Dress: casual. Reservations preferred. AE, CB, DC, MC, V. Closed Sun.*

Moderate–Expensive

Bombay Cafe. The interior is very attractive, with muted colors and an Italian marble fireplace, and the food—like simple, perfectly done grilled amberjack, or snapper *en papillote* (snapper marinated in béchamel sauce and baked in parchment with oysters and crabmeat)—is superb. *2839 Seventh Ave. S, tel. 205/322–1930. Dress: casual to jacket and tie. Reservations recommended. AE, CB, DC, MC, V. Closed Sun.*

G.G. in the Park. If there's a football game in town, it's crowd time at G.G.'s for an after-game party. Prepare for lots of talking noise, and don't believe all the gossip you pick up between appetizer and main course. The sea scenes and oversize marlin that deck the walls will get you in the mood for seafood. Pick out your own Maine lobster from the tank and settle into a feast, or go for the angel-hair pasta Alfredo with lump crabmeat—it's all superior at G.G.'s. French onion soup, baked potato, garden salad, and hot rolls accompany each meal. *3625 Eighth Ave. S, tel. 205/254–3506. Dress: casual. Reservations preferred. AE, CB, DC, MC, V. Closed Sun.*

Moderate

Fish Market Restaurant. Fresh fish of all types is served here, from West Indies salad (with lump crabmeat) to seafood gumbo, grilled snapper to blackened redfish, fried scallops to

Dining
Bombay Cafe, **15**
Browdy's Fine Foods, **21**
Cabana Cafe, **22**
Christian's Classic Cuisine, **14**
Cosmo's, **11**
Dilly's Deli and Pub, **19**
Fish Market Restaurant, **9**
G.G. in the Park, **18**
Golden Rule Barbecue, **25**
Highlands: A Bar and Grill, **13**
John's, **5**
Joy Young Restaurant, **23**
Michael's Sirloin Room, **7**
Rossi's, **8**
Winston's Restaurant, **24**

Lodging
Birmingham Hilton, **10**
Days Inn, **16**
Economy Inn, **4**
Holiday Inn, **6**
Mountain Brook Inn, **20**
Pickwick Hotel, **12**
Ramada Civic Center Plaza, **2**
Ramada Inn, **17**
Tourway Inn, **1**
Tutwiler, **3**
Wynfrey Hotel, **24**

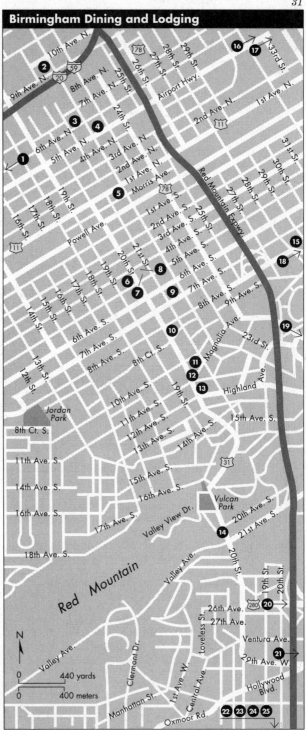

Birmingham Dining and Lodging

raw oysters. Chef George Sarris is at his best with the Greek-style fish. The decor is restaurant nautical: fish nets, lobster traps, and carved fish. *611 21st St. S, tel. 205/322–3330. Dress: casual. No reservations. AE, CB, DC, MC, V. Closed Sun.*

★ **John's.** Though rather plain in atmosphere, this restaurant has been consistently rated best in local popularity polls. After a recent expansion, the family dining establishment seats 460 and serves some 1,200 meals daily. Owner Phil Hontzas serves the freshest seafood available and constantly gets raves on the trout amandine, whole red snapper, and jumbo shrimp fried in light batter. The cole slaw, with John's famous dressing, should be ordered with any meal. And the corn sticks, an Alabama specialty, are done up proudly here. *112 21st St. N, tel. 205/322–6014. Dress: casual. Reservations for more than 5. AE, CB, DC, MC, V. Closed Sun.*

Michael's Sirloin Room. This is one of the most popular steak houses in Birmingham. It is also a sports bar, with photos of all the local sports greats from Bear Bryant to Willie Mays on the wall of fame. The talk centers on what kind of team Alabama or Auburn will have this year, and the television is always tuned to the sport of the day. The specialty is a hearty cut of prime steer butt, usually at least two inches thick, charbroiled for a smoky taste, but other dishes are served, including veal, lamb, and pork cooked Greek style: heavy on the oregano and garlic. *431 20th St. S, tel. 205/322–0419. Dress: casual. Reservations for more than 5. AE, CB, DC, MC, V. Closed Sun.*

Rossi's. It's Italian, tacky style, with plastic grapevines decorating the paintings from Napoli and piped-in music from the old country, but Rossi's always serves very good shrimp scampi, chicken cacciatore, and veal piccanti (medallions of veal in lemon butter with fettuccine) and superior veal Marsala. Go for the pasta and the Italian salad. *427 20th St. S, tel. 205/323–7111. Dress: casual. Reservations accepted Fri. and Sat. AE, CB, DC, MC, V. Closed Sun.*

Inexpensive **Cosmo's.** This is an in place with UAB students in the Five Points South neighborhood. The walls are paneled in pastel Formica, and the neon lighting makes for a colorful, lively mix. A glass wall fronting on Magnolia Street encourages people-watching. The specialty is gourmet pizza: pesto with prosciutto, sweet peppers, goat cheese, sun-dried tomatoes, and Italian sausage; or crawfish pizza in season. *2012 Magnolia Ave., tel. 205/930–9971. Dress: casual. No reservations. AE, CB, DC, MC, V. Closed Sun.*

Mountain Brook **Christian's Classic Cuisine.** This is an elegant restaurant with a
Expensive tropical look created by greenery, waterfalls, and wicker furniture. There is a fine wine selection and superior Continental-style cuisine. The catch of the day is always a winner. A specialty is lobster bisque, a lightly spiced soup made with heavy cream and sherry and chunks of fresh lobster meat. *2300 Woodcrest Pl., tel. 205/871–3222. Jacket and tie suggested. Reservations preferred. AE, CB, DC, MC, V. Closed Sun.*

Moderate **Joy Young Restaurant.** Once a Birmingham tradition down-
★ town, this Chinese restaurant, in its new location, is still one of the best in Birmingham. The windows give the place lots of light (though, unfortunately, the view is of a busy parking lot in a shopping mall), and there are modern Chinese paintings on the wall. The food is very good, especially the steamed red snapper. *547 Brookwood Blvd., tel. 205/879–7500. Dress: casu-*

al. *No reservations. AE, CB, DC, MC, V. Closed Mon. No dinner Sun.*

Inexpensive–
Moderate
★

Browdy's Fine Foods. Walk through the grocery and bakery to the rear dining room. Here, nestled behind bakery racks, is a comfortable but rather plain paneled room with red-and-white-checked tablecloths. This super deli-bakery serves some of the best baked beef short ribs in Alabama, usually with steamed cabbage. The beef brisket is served *au jus* with brown new potatoes and baby carrots. The sandwiches, from corned beef to pastrami, stand high on fresh rye (all breads are baked on the premises). Kosher deli is available. *2807 Cahaba Rd., tel. 205/879–8585. Dress: casual. No reservations. AE, MC, V.*

Cabana Cafe. In this modern atmosphere without the glitz and glitter of brass and ferns, there's a 120-item menu to choose from, including Mexican dishes. The Saturday champagne-brunch crowd crow over the eggs Benedict and seafood salad. Amberjack is coated with herb butter and grilled to a golden brown. The shrimp gumbo is good, and the Low Country Carolina chicken better. *509 Brookwood Blvd., tel. 205/870–1390. Dress: casual. No reservations. AE, MC, V. Closed Sun.*

Inexpensive

Dilly's Deli and Pub. From the looks of it, it could be located in any shopping center in any town in America, but Dilly's makes a millionare club sandwich—a triple-decker with turkey, ham, bacon, Swiss cheese, lettuce, tomato, and mayonnaise—that would be hard to beat. The hot Reuben is also especially recommended. *1624 Montclair Rd., tel. 205/956–5605. Dress: casual. No reservations. AE, MC, V. Closed Sun.*

Points Beyond
Expensive

Winston's Restaurant. This is a sophisticated hotel dining room with an English look—hunting prints and brass horns hang on dark-paneled walls. The cuisine is American gourmet, with especially good prime rib and steak. The menu usually features at least one wild game dish, like a tasty rack of venison with red-wine sauce. The lobster thermidor is steamed Maine lobster meat and sautéed shiitake mushrooms with a mustard-and-parmesan glaze, broiled and served in the shell. *Wynfrey Hotel, 1000 Riverchase Galleria, off U.S. 31, tel. 205/987–1600. Jacket and tie requested. Reservations suggested. AE, CB, DC, MC, V. Closed Sun.*

Inexpensive

Golden Rule Barbecue. This side-of-the-road joint doesn't invite leisurely dining, but it has the best barbecue in Birmingham—succulent, smoked long and evenly, and served with a mild red sauce that doesn't overpower. Booths, tables, and counter seat 70, or you can sit at picnic tables outside or take some away for a picnic of your own. *1571 Montgomery Hwy. (U.S. 31), tel. 205/823–7770. Dress: casual. No reservations. AE, MC, V. Closed Sun.*

Lodging

Many Birmingham hotels and motels offer weekend specials; inquire about special rates. In fall or winter, beware of football weekends: if the Alabama Crimson Tide or the Auburn Tigers are in town, you may find all hotels booked or at least very crowded.

The most highly recommended properties in each price category are indicated by a star ★. For a map pinpointing locations, *see* Dining.

Category	Cost*
Expensive	over $75
Moderate	$50–$75
Inexpensive	under $45

double room; add 7% for taxes

The following credit-card abbreviations are used: AE, American Express; CB, Carte Blanche; DC, Diners Club; MC, MasterCard; V, Visa.

Downtown
Expensive
Birmingham Hilton. This 14-story hotel near the University Medical Center and Five Points South was newly redecorated in 1988. The pink and green lobby, with a piano lounge, has a marble floor and Queen Anne–style furnishings. Rooms have a contemporary look, in mauve and peach tones. *808 20th St. S, 35205, tel. 205/933–9000 or 800/445–8667. 298 rooms, including 11 suites on the executive floor (3 with wet bars). Facilities: cable TV, outdoor pool, sauna, steam rooms, privileges at nearby fitness center, cocktail lounge, oyster bar. AE, CB, DC, MC, V.*

★ **Pickwick Hotel.** Part of the Five Points South area, the eight-story Pickwick was built in 1931 as an office building and converted in 1986 to a bed-and-breakfast hotel. Rooms have been decorated in an Art Deco style, with pink walls, green carpets, elegant period furnishings (including armoires) and Liberty of London bedspreads. Suites have kitchenettes, wet bars, and dining tables. High tea is served every afternoon. *1023 20th St. S, 35205, tel. 205/933–9555 or 800/255–7304. 35 rooms, 28 suites. Facilities: breakfast room, bar, sitting room with complimentary wine and cheese, meeting room. AE, CB, DC, MC, V.*

Tutwiler. A National Historic Landmark, the Tutwiler was built in 1913 as luxury apartments and converted into a hotel in 1987. The lobby is elegant, with marble floors, chandeliers, brass banisters, antiques, and lots of flowers. Rooms are furnished in antique reproductions, including armoires and high-back chairs, plus velour loveseats and king or double beds. *Park Place at 21st St. N, 35203, tel. 205/322–2100 or 800/228–0808. 96 rooms, 53 suites. Facilities: restaurant, pub, reduced rate at nearby YMCA. AE, CB, DC, MC, V.*

Moderate–Expensive
Ramada Hotel Civic Center Plaza. The lobby, decorated in soft pink and beige and filled with plants, is a restful oasis in a busy area. Rooms are traditionally furnished. Three corporate floors and a concierge floor provide such special amenities as a daily happy hour and a complimentary breakfast. *901 21st St. N, 35203, tel. 205/322–1234 or 800/272–6232. 377 rooms, 28 suites. Facilities: cable TV, outdoor pool, meeting space for 700, barbershop, 2 lounges, 2 restaurants, reduced rate at YMCA. AE, CB, DC, MC, V.*

Moderate
Holiday Inn. This 11-story hotel near the UAB campus and the Medical Center has a two-story cathedral-ceiling lobby with contemporary furniture, soft green carpeting, and green plants. Rooms are typical Holiday Inn style. *420 20th St. S, 35233, tel. 205/322–7000 or 800/465–4329. 229 rooms, 3 suites. Facilities: outdoor pool, 7 meeting rooms, restaurant, lounge. AE, CB, DC, MC. V.*

Inexpensive **Econo Lodge.** At this full-service facility near the Civic Center, all the rooms have balconies overlooking downtown. The decor in the guest rooms and public areas is contemporary. *2224 Fifth Ave. N, 35203, tel. 205/324–6688 or 800/446–6900. 127 rooms. Facilities: outdoor pool, coin laundry, restaurant, lounge. AE, CB, DC, MC, V.*

Tourway Inn. This two-story budget inn is about a mile from Legion Field and caters to business travelers and families. *1101 Sixth Ave. N, 35206, tel. 205/252–3921 or 800/633–3131. 70 rooms. Facilities: cable TV, outdoor pool, meeting room, restaurant. AE, DC, MC, V.*

Farther Out **Wynfrey Hotel.** This deluxe hotel rises 15 stories above the
Expensive Riverchase Galleria complex of 200 shops and restaurants (*see*
★ Shopping). The lobby is elegant, with Italian marble floor, Chippendale furniture, Oriental rug, enormous arrangement of fresh flowers, and brass escalator. Rooms are furnished in English and French traditional styles. The top two floors constitute the Chancellor's Club and have two bi-level suites each. *U.S. 31 S, 1000 Riverchase Galleria, 35244, tel. 205/987–1600 or 800/522–5282. 329 rooms, 19 suites. Facilities: outdoor pool, complete health club with whirlpool, concierge, cafe, Winston's restaurant (see Dining), piano lounge, "high-energy" lounge. AE, CB, DC, MC, V.*

Moderate **Mountain Brook Inn.** This eight-story glass hotel in the foothills of Red Mountain caters to the business traveler. The lobby is tastefully furnished, with marble floors, chandeliers, brass, and Oriental carpet. Eight suites are bi-level, with spiral staircases and Oriental decor; they have wet bars and refrigerators. Two suites have conference tables. *2800 U.S. 280, 35223, tel. 205/870–3100 or 800/523–7771. 162 rooms, 8 suites. Facilities: outdoor pool, privileges at nearby health club, 4 meeting rooms, ballroom (capacity: 300), restaurant, lounge. AE, CB, DC, MC, V.*

Ramada Inn. Three minutes from the airport, this 12-story hotel is a typical Ramada, except for the eye-catching winding staircase in the chandeliered lobby. *5216 Airport Hwy., 35212, tel. 205/591–7900 or 800/272–6232. 193 rooms. Facilities: outdoor pool, exercise room, 6 meeting rooms, restaurant, and lounge. AE, DC, MC, V.*

Inexpensive **Days Inn.** A typical unit of the chain, with standard blue-and-peach contemporary decor, a mile from the airport. *5101 Messer-Airport Hwy., 35212, tel. 205/592–6110 or 800/325–2525. 144 rooms (some with coffeemakers). Facilities: outdoor pool, small meeting room, restaurant, privileges at nearby fitness center. AE, DC, MC, V.*

The Arts

For an up-to-date listing of happenings in the arts, get the current issue of *Birmingham* magazine on the newsstand. For ticket information, contact the **Central Ticket Office** (1001 19th St. N, tel. 205/251–4100).

Theater The **Birmingham Jefferson Civic Center** (tel. 205/251–4500)—a four-block complex with an exhibition hall, a theater, a concert hall, and the Coliseum—hosts touring Broadway companies, major rock concerts, and exhibitions. The **Terrific New Theatre** (tel. 205/328–0868) hosts touring drama groups. **Town and**

Gown Theatre (tel. 205/934–3489), a semiprofessional community theater based on the UAB campus (but not a college theater group), puts on five musical and dramatic works from October through May. **Birmingham Children's Theater** (tel. 205/324–0470) performs for children from October through May at the Civic Center. At the 400-seat **Blue Moon Dinner Theater** (tel. 205/823–3000), touring and local performers stage musicals and comedies.

Opera The **Birmingham Opera Theater** (tel. 205/322–6737) presents four productions each season (Nov.–May).

Concerts The **Alabama Symphony Orchestra** (tel. 205/326–0100) performs at the Civic Center throughout the year, and sometimes at Sloss Furnace's covered amphitheater (tel. 205/324–1911). Rock concerts are held at the Civic Center, Sloss Furnace, and the **Oak Mountain Amphitheater** in Pelham (tel. 205/985–9797). Organ shows on a "mighty Wurlitzer" are given at the **Alabama Theatre** (tel. 205/251–0418).

Dance The **State of Alabama Ballet** (tel. 205/252–2475) performs at the Civic Center from September through March. The modern dance group **Southern Danceworks** (tel. 205/322–6483) performs October through February at the Alabama Theatre and other halls in the city, including some performances of its **Hispanic Dance Olé** division.

Festival For a month or more each spring, Birmingham celebrates the ballet, opera, painting, sculpture, literature, symphony, and other art forms of a single country at its **Festival of the Arts.** Performances and exhibits are staged at various locations throughout the city, though the Civic Center is usually the hub of activity. For more information, contact the Tourist Bureau (tel. 205/323–5461).

Nightlife

Cabaret **Broadway Joe's** (808 20th St. S, tel. 205/933–9000), off the lobby of the Hilton, always features a top singer and a jazz combo.

Discos **Cheers Lounge** (400 Beacon Pkwy. W, tel. 205/942–2031), at the Radisson Inn (formerly Regis Inn) is a friendly place with fast and loud music. **Overtures** (Riverchase Galleria, tel. 205/987–1600), at the Wynfrey Hotel, is where Yuppies meet. **The Spot** (260 Oxmoor Rd., tel. 205/942–2041), at the Ramada Inn, is frequented into the wee hours by a young crowd of fun-seekers.

Montgomery

Known as the Cradle of the Confederacy, Montgomery is a town steeped in antebellum history. While its population has grown to almost 300,000, the capital city is still reminiscent of a sleepy little town on the banks of the Alabama River. In the final year of the Civil War, Union troops, led by General John Wilson, passed through the city and burned artillery factories in Selma, but they did not destroy Montgomery. Today many of the old houses have been restored to their original splendor.

The city bears witness to another of this country's great struggles as well. Here, in 1954, after black seamstress Rosa Parks was arrested for refusing to give up her seat on a city bus to a white man, a young black minister, Martin Luther King, Jr., led a 1½-year bus boycott that spearheaded the civil rights movement. His small brick church—in the shadow of the classic-style domed capitol, at whose steps the legendary Selma-to-Montgomery march ended—stands as a monument to the birth of the movement.

While Montgomery's history has been dramatic, its present makes it the capital of stage drama in the South. With the move of the Alabama Shakespeare Festival into world-class facilities (costing $21.5 million), some of the best actors in America have been lured to the area to perform at the 750-seat festival stage and the 225-seat Octagon theater. Also in the 250-acre Wynton M. Blount Cultural Park—named for the former postmaster general of the United States, who donated the land and the festival building to the city—is the new $6.1 million Montgomery Museum of Fine Arts. Blount, an international construction contractor, plans to develop a series of British-style formal gardens on the rolling hills of the property.

Arriving and Departing

By Plane Dannelly Field is seven miles from downtown. It is served by **Eastern** commuter planes and **Delta**.

Between the Airport and Center City **Taxis** are readily available and relatively inexpensive to most downtown hotels. Many hotels provide transportation from the airport by prior arrangement. **By car,** take U.S. 80, which connects with U.S. 31, to the first major intersection. Turn right onto the South By-Pass, where some hotels are located. To travel to downtown, turn north onto I–65, follow signs to I–85, and take the first exit, Court Street.

By Train Amtrak no longer serves Montgomery.

By Bus Greyhound/Trailways (210 Court St., downtown, tel. 205/264–4518).

By Car I–65 runs north to Birmingham and south to Mobile. I–85 begins in Montgomery and runs northeast to Atlanta. U.S. 80 runs west past the airport to Selma.

Getting Around

By Taxi Taxis charge $2.05 for the first mile, $1 for each additional mile. One company is **Yellow Cab** (tel. 205/262–5225).

By Bus City buses (tel. 205/262–7321) run from 6 AM to 4:30–6 PM, depending on the route. Exact change is required (80¢ fare, 10¢ transfer).

By Trolley A quiet, comfortable, inexpensive (free) way to see downtown is by old-style trolley (tel. 205/262–7321). (Montgomery was the site of the first electric trolley.) It runs from the Crampton Bowl parking lot (two blocks behind the capitol) to the capitol, west on Dexter Avenue, through downtown, and to the parking lot in front of the old Union Station, next to the river. Get on and off at any of its stops, walk around, see the area, shop, and then get back on when it next makes its hourly rounds (8–6).

Important Addresses and Numbers

Tourist Information Montgomery Chamber of Commerce (41 Commerce St., tel. 205/834–5200). **Visitor Information Center** (220 N. Hull St., tel. 205/262–0013). **Alabama Bureau of Tourism and Travel** (532 S. Perry St., tel. 205/261–4169).

Emergencies Dial 911 for **police** or **ambulance** in an emergency.

24-Hour Pharmacy **Eckerd Drugs** (Capitol Plaza Shopping Center, South By-Pass, tel. 205/281–1312).

Guided Tours

The only guided tours available in Montgomery are restricted to groups. A cassette driving tour of the downtown area is available from the **Landmarks Foundation** (310 N. Hull St., tel. 205/263–4355). The **Visitor Information Center** (*see* Important Addresses and Numbers) has a free 15-minute video on the city that will help you organize your own tour. Also, the **Old North Hull Street Historic District** gives combined cassette/guided tours of the district (*see* A Walking Tour in Exploring).

Exploring Montgomery

Numbers in the margin correspond with points of interest on the Montgomery map.

A Walking Tour

1 Begin with the handsome **State Capitol,** at present undergoing extensive restoration at the hands of some of the best restoration architects and builders in the United States. It was built in 1851 and from 1860 served as the first capitol for the Confederate States of America. Just inside the huge double doors (with a bronze star marking the spot where Jefferson Davis stood to take the oath of office as president of the Confederacy) there is an amazing piece of interior design. The stairway curling up the sides of the circular hallway is free-standing, without visible support. The state's rich history has been caught by an artist's brush in great, colorful murals. In the large House chamber and smaller Senate chamber, gigantic brick fireplaces, long hidden by additions, have been uncovered and will be fully operational when the building is reopened (probably not until 1990). *Bainbridge St. at Dexter Ave.; call Visitor Information Center for information. Free guided tours available weekdays 8–5, weekends 9–5. Closed major holidays.*

2 Walk west on Dexter Avenue for one block. On your left, at no. 454, is the **Dexter Avenue King Memorial Baptist Church** (tel. 205/263–3970), where Dr. Martin Luther King, Jr., began his career as a minister in 1955. The church's sanctuary and the basement Sunday-school rooms are open to visitors. A mural covering one basement wall depicts people and events associated with Dr. King and the movement.

3 Walk back to the capitol and turn right onto Bainbridge. At the corner of Bainbridge and Washington is the **Alabama Department of Archives and History,** a memorial to the soldiers who lost their lives in World War I. Newly restored, it is lined with Alabama marble and contains outstanding exhibits of artifacts documenting the state's history from its Indian days. *624 Washington Ave., tel. 205/261–4361. Open weekdays 8–5, with free guided tours, weekends 9–5.*

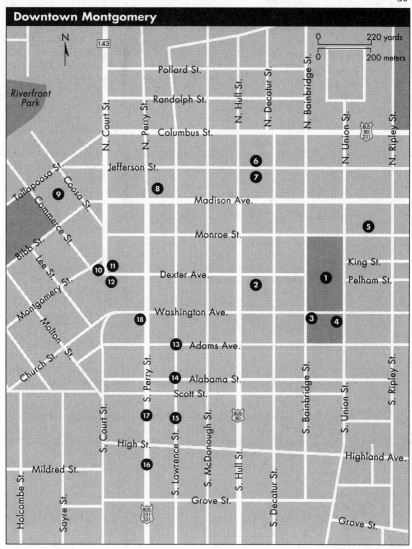

Downtown Montgomery

Arts and Humanities
State Council
Building, **11**

Confederate Post
Office, **18**

Court House
Fountain, **10**

Dept. of Archives and
History, **3**

Dexter Ave. King
Mem. Baptist
Church, **2**

Falconer House, **15**

1st White House of the
Confederacy, **4**

Governor Shorter
Mansion, **14**

House of Mayors, **16**

Lower Commerce St.
Hist. Dist., **9**

Lucas Tavern, **6**

Lurleen Burns Wallace
Museum, **5**

Ordeman-Shaw
House, **7**

St. John's, **8**

St. Peter's, **13**

State Capitol, **1**

Teague House, **17**

Winter Building, **12**

At the corner of Washington Avenue and Union Street stands
❹ the **First White House of the Confederacy,** built in 1840. The
house was occupied by Jefferson Davis and his family while
the Confederacy was being organized at the State Capitol
across the street. Today it contains many of their possessions,
plus artifacts of the Civil War period. *644 Washington Ave.,
tel. 205/261–4624. Free tours weekdays 8–5, weekends 9–5.*

Continue walking north on Union, then turn right onto Monroe
❺ Street. A half-block east is the **Lurleen Burns Wallace Memorial Museum,** housed (with the Alabama Historical Commission's
offices) in the 1850s Rice-Semple-Haardt House. With its wide
porch and angular roof, it is reminiscent of the French- and
Spanish-influenced designs often found in Louisiana; the lat-
ticed arches on the L-shaped porch were a feature of many early
Montgomery homes. The museum displays many possessions of
Alabama's first woman governor, and a free nine-minute film
tells the story of this courageous woman, who died of cancer
while in office. *725 Monroe St., tel. 205/261–3183. Admission
free. Open daily 8–5.*

The **Old North Hull Street Historic District**—about six blocks
northwest of the capitol, between Madison Avenue and Columbus Street—comprises 24 newly restored houses, barns,
stores, and other structures from 1818 to the turn of the century. Most were moved here from their original sites. Eleven of
these buildings are house museums; the remainder are rented
to private businesses.

❻ The reception center for the district is in the old **Lucas Tavern**
(310 N. Hull St., tel. 205/263–4355), built in 1818 on the Old
Federal Road traveled by early settlers to the area; in 1825, the
French general Lafayette stayed at the tavern on his way to
Montgomery. A free slide show here tells the story of the dis-
trict. A cassette walking tour is available that includes 10
❼ house museums. For the 11th—the **Ordeman-Shaw House** (230
N. Hull St.), an Italianate town house with restored outbuild-
ings and gardens—you get a human guide. *Tel. 205/263–4355.
Cassette tour: $4 adults; $1.50 children 6–18, under 6 free.
Ordeman-Shaw House: $1 adults, children free with adult.
Open Mon.–Sat. 9:30–3:30, Sun. 1:30–3:30. Closed Thanks-
giving, Christmas, and New Year's Day.*

A Driving Tour From North Hull Street, drive west on Madison Avenue for
three blocks. The imposing, high-spired church on the right is
❽ **St. John's Episcopal Church** (113 Madison Ave.). Built in 1856,
it has colorful stained-glass windows and a bronze plaque
marking the pew where Jefferson Davis worshiped.

Continue west on Madison Avenue, veer left onto Bibb Street,
then turn right onto Commerce Street. On your right, between
❾ Court Square and the Riverfront, is the **Lower Commerce
Street Historic District,** a group of renovated Victorian structures dating from the end of the last century and now used as
office buildings. This area was the trade-and-transportation
hub of the busy 19th-century town, which prospered from the
business of the Alabama River; there cotton was loaded onto
great riverboats and transported downstream and finally out
to sea, headed for the textile mills of New England.

Time Out At the end of Commerce Street is the Alabama River. On its grassy banks is a park that is a perfect spot for a picnic. The riverboat *General Richard Montgomery,* a replica of a 19th-century sternwheeler, is docked here; to book a sunset cruise, call 205/834–9862. *Fare: $5 adults, $4.50 over 65, $3 couples and children 2–12, under 2 free; $2 Tues.–Wed.*

Drive south on Commerce Street to Dexter Avenue. At the junction is **Court House Fountain,** built in 1885. Hebe, cup-bearer to the gods, looks north down Commerce Street to the river. To the left on Dexter is the extraordinary **Arts and Humanities State Council building** (1 Dexter Ave., tel. 205/261–4076), patterned after a Venetian palazzo. Works by Alabama artists are always on display in the magnificent lobby with its banistered balcony. Free tours may be arranged.

Across the avenue is another newly renovated structure, the **Winter Building** (2 Dexter Ave.), built in the 1840s as the office of the Southern Telegraph Company. It was from here that the Confederate leaders sent a telegram ordering their soldiers to fire on Fort Sumter, thereby starting the Civil War.

Drive east on Dexter Avenue, then south on Lawrence Street, to **St. Peter's Roman Catholic Church** (219 Adams Ave.), built in 1852. Its unusual Spanish-style architecture may reflect the Cuban and Mexican origins of some of the building funds. To have a look inside, enter through the rectory.

Continue south on Lawrence Street past the new Montgomery County Courthouse. At the corner of Lawrence and Alabama streets is the **Governor Shorter Mansion** (305 S. Lawrence St.) with its Greek Revival portico, home in the 19th-century to Governor John Gill Shorter. It has been renovated and now houses offices.

In the next block is the **Falconer House** (428 S. Lawrence St.), built in 1840 for Montgomery's first postmaster, John Falconer. With its bracketed eaves and low-hipped roof, this cottage is characteristic of many that once lined these historic streets.

Turn right onto High Street and drive one block. To the left on South Perry Street is the brick **House of Mayors.** Once the home of Jack Thorington and Mordecai Moses, both mayors of Montgomery during the 19th century, and Joseph Norwood, who became mayor of nearby Fort Deposit in the 1880s, this mansion now houses the Alabama State Bureau of Tourism and Travel. Inside, free information about the state is available. *532 S. Perry St., tel. 205/261–4169. Open weekdays 8–5.*

One block north is the **Teague House** (468 S. Perry St.), a fine example of late Greek Revival architecture in the South and now owned by the Alabama Business Council. Continuing north on Perry Street, you'll see the **Old Confederate Post Office** (39 S. Perry St., corner of Washington St.). One of the oldest buildings in town, it was once the law office of U.S. Congressman William Lowndes Yancey, who spoke eloquently in Congress in the mid-1800s about why the South should secede from the Union. The building served as the Confederate Post Office in 1861. Today it houses private offices.

Montgomery for Free

Concerts Each spring and fall, Blount International sponsors **concerts at Court Square** on Fridays at noon near the Court Square Fountain. During the Christmas season, the **First Baptist Church** (305 S. Perry St., tel. 205/834–6310) performs "The Living Christmas Tree," with the choir arranged in the shape of a tree and singing hymns of the season.

Lectures **Auburn University** at Montgomery (off I–85N, 8 mi east of downtown, tel. 205/271–9300) offers entertaining and informative lectures throughout the year.

What to See and Do with Children

Montgomery Zoo. Among the zoo's offerings is an open-air exhibit of exotic birds; a hands-on petting zoo with such barnyard pets as goats, donkeys, chickens, and calves; and a community of eagles that have been treated for wounds at Auburn University's veterinary clinic but can no longer fly. *329 Vandiver Blvd., tel. 205/832–2637. Admission: $1.50 adults and children over 12; 25¢ children 2–12, under 2 free; senior citizens free. Open Mon.–Sat. 9:30–4:30, Sun. 1–5.; closed Christmas and New Year's Day.*

W. A. Gayle Planetarium. Photographs and objects from the stars and outer space are exhibited. Daily shows are continuously updated. *1010 Forest Ave., in Oak Park, tel. 205/832–2625. Admission free. Open Mon.–Sat. 9–5, Sun. 1–4. Shows weekends at 2 PM, children's shows Mon. and Wed. at 10 AM, closed last 2 weeks Aug., Dec. Show admission: $1.50 adults, 75¢ 6–17, under 6 free.*

Off the Beaten Track

Hank Williams Memorial. Montgomery was the home of country-music singer and songwriter Hank Williams, and after his untimely death at age 29 on New Year's Day, 1953, he was brought here for one of the city's grandest funerals. It was held at City Hall, with the top country stars of the time delivering eulogies and singing sad songs. He was buried in the Oakwood Cemetery Annex, (1305 Upper Wetumpka Rd., tel. 205/264–4938), beneath a stone that depicts his likeness and sheet music from his most popular songs, such as "Your Cheatin' Heart."

Jasmine Hill Gardens. Here, atop a wooded hill, are 17 acres of beautiful gardens with replicas of Greek sculptures and of the ruins of the Temple of Hera. Musical performances are sometimes given at the outdoor theater. *1500 Jasmine Hill Rd., tel. 205/567–6463. Admission: $3.50 adults; $2 children 6–12, under 6 free. Open Tues.–Sun. and Mon. holidays. 9–5, May–Sept.*

Shopping

Most Montgomery stores are open Monday–Saturday 10–6 and closed Sunday. From Thanksgiving to Christmas they remain open until 9 PM. The sales tax is 8%. Banks are open Monday–Thursday 9–1, 2–4; Friday 9–2, 3–5; Saturday 9–noon.

Shopping Districts Almost all of Montgomery's shopping is done in the centers and malls surrounding the city. Here are the biggest and best:

Eastdale Mall. In addition to its anchor stores—Sears, Parisian's, McRae's, and Gayfer's—Eastdale has specialty stores, record and book stores, an Italian fast-food restaurant, three movie theaters, and a popular ice rink. *I–85N to Eastern By-Pass, take exit to Wetumpka, follow Eastern By-Pass north to Eastdale exit, tel. 205/277–7359.*

Montgomery Mall. This is an old shopping area that has recently undergone a face lift and enlargement. A glass atrium at the center, flickering gaslights, and miniature trees, plus a replica of the famous old Klein's Jewelry clock that for many years stood outside One Dexter Avenue, give the mall a plush downtown-street look. The main stores are Gayfer's, McRae's, and JC Penney. *Intersection of South By-Pass and U.S. 231S, tel. 205/284–1533.*

Zelda Place. This Deco-style shopping area is Yuppie headquarters, with many small shops like Nancy Blount (women's high fashion), The Hub (men's clothes), B. Dalton, and the New York Kitchen Shoppe. Joe's delicatessen (tel. 205/244–0440), a Montgomery tradition that recently moved to this trendy location, serves super breakfasts and whopping corned beef and pastrami sandwiches. *I–85N to Ann St. exit, south on Ann St.*

Specialty Stores
Antiques **Herron House** (422 Herron St., tel. 205/265–2063) has the city's largest stock of porcelain, glass, and silver, plus 18th- and 19th-century furniture. **Bodiford's Antique Mall** (919 Hampton St., tel. 205/265–4220) is several small stores gathered under one big roof. Depression pieces abound. **Blue Ridge Antique Junction** (Eastern By-Pass to U.S. 231N exit to Wetumpka; 7 mi from exit, on left atop Jasmine Hill, tel. 205/567–6106) are two very large buildings packed with antiques. There is also an old drugstore put together by the owners for your viewing pleasure.

Jewelry **Lauda Inc.** has very fine, expensive, distinctive jewelry. *Hillwood Office Center, 2800 Zelda Rd., tel. 205/271–4431. By private appointment only.*

Leather and Luggage For the best in leather goods and luggage as well as unique gifts, try **Brenner's Montgomery Shoe Factory and Luggage Shop**. *Two locations: 105 S. Court St., tel. 205/262–3134; Normandale Shopping Mall, tel. 205/288–6994.*

Day Trips from Montgomery

The sites listed below are within 100 miles of Montgomery. For information on them, *see* Elsewhere in the State.

Birmingham (*see* Birmingham section)
De Soto Caverns, Childersburg
Demopolis
Mound State Monument, Moundville
Pike Pioneer Museum, Troy
Shorter Mansion, Eufaula
Sturdivant Hall, Selma
Tuskegee

Participant Sports

Bicycling   **Breakaway Bicycles** (tel. 205/271–2453) rents bicycles for rides in Oak Park or in the country.

Golf   **Lagoon Park** (tel. 205/271–7000).

Miniature Golf   **Mountasia Fantasy Golf** (tel. 205/277–4653) takes golfers on a safari through and around a man-made mountain, large model elephants and other animals, and a cave.

Tennis   **Lagoon Park** (tel. 205/271–7001) and **O'Connor Tennis Center** (tel. 205/832–2608).

Spectator Sports

Dog Racing   One of the most successful greyhound dog-racing facilities in the United States is **Victoryland,** about 20 miles east of Montgomery, just off I–85N in Tuskegee (tel. 205/727–0540). There's racing and pari-mutuel betting every night but Sunday, and several matinees during the week.

Dining

The most highly recommended restaurants in each price category are indicated by a star ★ .

Category	Cost*
Expensive	Over $25
Moderate	$15–$20
Inexpensive	Under $15

per person without tax (8% in Montgomery), service, or drinks

The following credit-card abbreviations are used: AE, American Express; CB, Carte Blanche; DC, Diners Club; MC, MasterCard; V, Visa.

Downtown   **Elite Restaurant.** Pronounced "E-light," this is a downtown
Moderate   tradition going back to 1911. Always operated by the Xides
★   family and recently renovated to give the dining room a modern flair, the Elite is a favorite with legislators and downtown businessmen at lunch. The Mediterranean tenderloin, marinated in olive oil with much garlic and oregano, is a rich Greek splendor. The seafood is always fresh; in season, the sautéed pompano with a light amandine sauce is outstanding. *129 Montgomery St., tel. 205/263–2832. Dress: casual. Reservations preferred. AE, DC, MC, V. Closed Sun. No dinner Mon.*

Inexpensive   **Chris' Hot Dog Stand.** A Montgomery tradition for over 50 years, this stand is about 15 feet wide and 50 feet deep, with a counter that is always busy at lunchtime. Mr. Chris's famous sauce combines chili peppers, onions, and a variety of herbs that give his hot dogs a one-of-a-kind flavor. A booth at the rear gives a good view of knickknacks the 84-year-old owner has brought back from trips to his Greek-island homeland, as well as a plaster bust of his favorite U.S. president, Franklin Delano Roosevelt. For a special treat, try the hot dog with "kitchen chili," a heavy, hot chili of beans and onions that you

Dining

Bates House of Turkey, **23**

Capitol Oyster Bar, **13**

Catfish House, **10**

Chris' Hot Dog Stand, **6**

Christopher's, **17**

Elite Restaurant, **3**

Farmer's Market Cafeteria, **7**

Green Lantern, **21**

Jim's Barbecue, **11**

Jubilee Seafood Company, **18**

Martin's Restaurant, **19**

Red Bird Inn, **16**

Sahara Restaurant, **15**

Vintage Year, **14**

Lodging

Best Western-Montgomery Lodge, **12**

Capitol Inn, **1**

Governor's House Hotel, **20**

Hampton Inn, **25**

La Quinta Motor Inn, **24**

Madison Hotel, The, **5**

Ramada Inn East, **22**

Sheraton Riverfront Station, **2**

State House Inn, **9**

Town Plaza Motor Hotel, **8**

Whitley Hotel, **4**

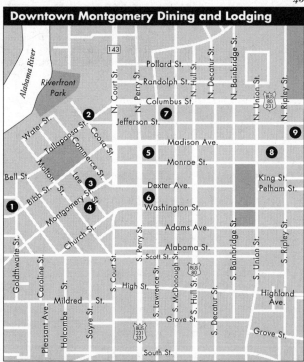

Downtown Montgomery Dining and Lodging

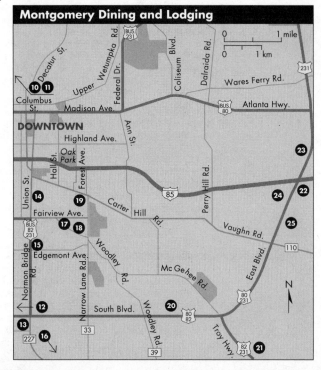

Montgomery Dining and Lodging

have to eat with a knife and fork. It's scrumptious—especially on a cold winter day. *138 Dexter Ave., tel. 205/265–6850. Dress: casual. No reservations. No credit cards. Closed Sun.*

Farmer's Market Cafeteria. Located in a downtown industrial-style metal building, the cafeteria is about as plain as a restaurant can be, except for the photos on the walls reminding diners of past heroes of the gridiron and the baseball diamond. Fried chicken, catfish, country smothered steak, and fresh vegetables are served cafeteria fashion. A hearty breakfast with smoked bacon and homemade biscuits begins many mornings for downtown businessmen. *315 N. McDonough St., tel. 205/262–9163. Dress: casual. No reservations. No credit cards. Closed Sun. Breakfast, lunch only.*

Cloverdale
Expensive
★

Sahara Restaurant. Recently renovated after a kitchen fire, the Sahara—in the suburb of Cloverdale—is Montgomery's finest restaurant. Joe and Mike Deep carry on a family tradition with their friendly service, which is also the best in town. The snapper, delivered twice weekly from the Gulf, is fried in a very light batter; the white meat flakes exactly as it should. Choice steaks are grilled over coals. And the seafood gumbo is wonderful: the okra is whole and not cooked to bits, and there's plenty of shrimp and oysters. *511 E. Edgemont Ave., tel. 205/262–1215. Jacket and tie required. Reservations preferred. AE, CB, DC, MC, V. Closed Sun.*

★ **Vintage Year.** This is a gourmet's delight. Chef Judy Martin is a prize-winner for her Cajun pecan-butter fish with *meunière* sauce, quail with raspberry sauce, and red snapper Niçoise (baked in a light sauce of tomatoes, scallions, and olives). Among the favorite appetizers are the baked artichoke bottoms with crabmeat and Monterey Jack cheese, and the crab taco with lump crabmeat sautéed in butter and served with fresh spinach, Jack cheese, and salsa. Vintage Year is an elegant restaurant with excellent service and a cozy bar that is fast becoming a neighborhood meeting place; Henry Pugh plays jazz piano Saturday evenings. *405 Cloverdale Rd., tel. 205/264–8463. Jacket and tie required. Reservations required. AE, MC, V. Closed Sun. Dinner only.*

Moderate
★

Christopher's. Near the renovated Capri Theater, an art-film house, Christopher's is one of the newest and best restaurants in Montgomery, an intimate little place with tasteful decor and a chef direct from Italy. Every dish is a delight. Littleneck clams from Boston are served with garlic, Parmesan cheese, and bread crumbs. Scampi Romano is jumbo shrimp and artichoke hearts swimming in a garlic, butter, and cream sauce. New York strip steak is sautéed in olive oil, garlic, and Italian spices and served with potatoes baked in the same sauce. *1018 E. Fairview Ave., tel. 205/269–5600. Jacket and tie requested. No reservations. AE, MC, V. Closed Sun.*

Jubilee Seafood Company. In a very pleasant, small cafe setting, Bud Skinner cooks some of the finest and freshest seafood dishes in town. His crabmeat omelet—with onion, garlic, peppers, and a generous helping of crab—is mouth-watering. Steamed Florida clams are a delicious seasonal treat. Oysters on the half-shell are shucked before your eyes. A Cajun-style dish—served only on special occasions—is "oysters in rue": oysters lightly poached and dropped into a spicy, tomato-based sauce with mucho garlic, onions, peppers, and more. *1057 Woodley Rd., Cloverdale Plaza, tel. 205/262–*

6224. Dress: casual. No reservations. AE, MC, V. Closed Sun.

Inexpensive **Martin's Restaurant.** In this plain but comfortable eatery in a small shopping center, you'll find generous helpings of home-cooked fresh vegetables, Southern fried chicken, and delicious panfried catfish fresh from Alabama ponds. The cornbread sticks literally melt in your mouth; you don't even need to put butter on them, they are so rich and crisp. *1716 Carter Hill Rd., tel. 205/265–1767. Dress: casual. No reservations. No credit cards. Closed Sun.*

Points Beyond **Catfish House.** Fried fresh Alabama-grown catfish is the spe-
Moderate cialty at this rustic, cabinlike restaurant, set in a grove of pine trees overlooking a pond. *Cobbs Ford Rd. in Millbrook, 10 mi north of Montgomery (take Exit 179 off I–65 toward Millbrook, ½ mi east), tel. 205/285–7225. Dress: casual. No reservations. AE, MC, V. Closed Sun. Dinner only.*

Green Lantern. In a rustic country setting, with jukebox music, fireplaces, and long tables, the Green Lantern is famous for its cheese biscuits, which many locals take home by the sackfuls. The waitresses bark out the menu, which is not printed. It consists of several types of steaks, all charbroiled, boiled shrimp, and fried chicken. The best is the steak, with huge baked potatoes and all the cheese biscuits you can eat. *Troy Hwy., 5 mi southeast on U.S. 231, tel. 205/288–9947. Dress: casual. Reservations preferred, especially with large parties. No credit cards. Closed Sun. Dinner only.*

Inexpensive **Bates House of Turkey.** There are only two like this in the world, so far as we know—here and 34 miles south at Greenville. In a small but well-polished down-home dining room, with photographs of the biggest turkey farm in central Alabama, Bates House of Turkey serves nothing but turkey: turkey sandwiches, turkey chili, turkey sausage, even quick-frozen smoked turkey breasts. *1060 Eastern By-Pass, 1 blk north of I–85, tel. 205/272–9701. Dress: casual. No reservations. No credit cards. Closed Sun.*

Capitol Oyster Bar. Here is a good-ol'-boy hangout that looks like an old Kentucky Fried Chicken franchise. That's because it *is* an old Kentucky Fried Chicken franchise, now a smelly oyster bar with the freshest seafood around. The grouper is fried in hand-size chunks, and the oysters are cracked from the shell while you wait. The gumbo is a bit watery for some tastes. A specialty is the generous oyster poboy: piping-hot breaded oysters served on a fresh French roll with homemade mayonnaise-and-relish sauce. On the walls are portraits of Alabama giants like Coach Bear Bryant and Governor George Wallace. *109 E. South By-Pass on service road between Court St. and Norman Bridge Rd., tel. 205/288–4217. Dress: casual. No reservations. No credit cards. Closed Sun.*

★ **Jim's Barbecue.** The best pork barbecue in the area is worth all the effort of finding it. (Drive 10 miles north on I–65, take Exit 179, turn left toward Prattville to the junction with U.S. 31, turn left, and travel south one-half mile.) Another former Kentucky Fried, Jim's is a small, unassuming place with plate-glass windows covering three walls and a counter across the fourth. Mama will take your order, which should be a barbecue-pork plate. The pork is tender, the sauce is tangy-tasty, and the hospitality is first-rate. Jim himself barbecues the top-grade shoulder at his pit some 20 miles north on U.S. 82, where he still sells 100-plus pounds of pork every time the Alabama Crimson Tide play in Tuscaloosa. *Montgomery Hwy., in Prattville, tel. 205/361–9346. Dress: casual. No reservations. No credit cards. Closed Sun. Lunch only.*

Red Bird Inn. Montgomery's crispiest fried chicken, good french fries, and fried onion rings have come out of this old house on the outskirts of town for at least 50 years. Enter through the front door, find a room down a shotgun hallway, play the jukebox, unpop your bottle, and order. There is nothing fancy here, but the down-home atmosphere is friendly, and the chicken is splendid. *Off U.S. 331 on Seibels Rd., tel. 205/288–5005. Dress: casual. No reservations. No credit cards. Closed Sun.*

Lodging

The most highly recommended properties in each price category are indicated by a star ★. For a map pinpointing locations, *see* Dining.

Category	Cost*
Very Expensive	over $60
Expensive	$45–$60
Moderate	$30–$45
Inexpensive	under $30

*double room; add 8% for taxes

The following credit-card abbreviations are used: AE, American Express; CB, Carte Blanche; DC, Diners Club; MC, MasterCard; V, Visa.

Downtown
Very Expensive

Madison Hotel. Elvis Presley slept here, but you're more likely to run into legislators and businessmen than rock stars at the Madison. The six-story atrium lobby is furnished in Oriental style and filled with lush greenery, fountains, and caged parrots and other birds that sing and talk throughout the day. The guest rooms were recently renovated and carry on the tropical/Far East theme. The Civic Center is two blocks away. *120 Madison Ave., 36104, tel. 205/264–2231. 184 rooms, 6 suites. Facilities: cable TV, outdoor pool, 2 restaurants, 2 lounges, large ballroom, 11 meeting rooms. AE, CB, DC, MC, V.*

Expensive–
Very Expensive
★

Sheraton Riverfront Station. A converted historic railway depot, this Sheraton retains many original elements, resulting in an 1890s feel in the lobby and lounge. Every guest room has a brass bed; other furnishings vary from room to room. Second-floor rooms have cathedral ceilings and original brick and beams. The Civic Center is just a block away. *200 Coosa St., 36104, tel. 205/834–4300 or 800/325–3535. 130 rooms, including 6 suites. Facilities: cable TV, outdoor pool, restaurant, coffee shop, 2 lounges, 5 meeting rooms. AE, CB, DC, MC, V.*

Moderate

Capitol Inn. One of Montgomery's oldest motels—a two-story building with iron grillwork along the length of the facade—the Capitol is well situated in the heart of downtown. Some rooms have balconies with a grand view of the Union Station–Lower Commerce Street Historic District. *205 N. Goldthwaite*

St., 36101, tel. 205/265–0541. 97 rooms. Facilities: cable TV, outdoor pool, restaurant, lounge, 3 meeting rooms. AE, CB, DC, MC, V.

State House Inn. The hotel (formerly a Holiday Inn) has been attractively redecorated with a pleasing color scheme of mauve and gray throughout the terra-cotta-tiled lobby and the large guest rooms. The location is central; the State Capitol is a block away. *924 Madison Ave., 36104, tel. 205/265–0741. 168 rooms, 2 suites. Facilities: cable TV, outdoor pool, restaurant, lounge, 9 meeting rooms. AE, CB, DC, MC, V.*

Whitley Hotel. The hotel's Early American/Victorian–style building, dating to 1929, houses classrooms for Troy State University on two of its six floors. A well-established clientele returns year after year for the hotel's quiet, old-fashioned ambience, reflected in the lobby's marble walls and columns and the bathrooms' original brass fixtures. All the small guest rooms, however, are furnished in a modern style. *231 Montgomery St., 36104, tel. 205/262–6461. 125 rooms. Facilities: dining room, coffee shop, lounges. AE, DC, MC, V.*

Inexpensive **Town Plaza Motor Hotel.** This is a basic two-story L-shaped motel, built in the early '60s. All rooms have balconies with a view of the capitol, (two blocks south), are decorated in modern style, and come with coffeemakers. *743 Madison Ave., 36104, tel. 205/269–1561. 38 rooms. Facilities: cable TV. AE, MC, V.*

Outskirts **Governor's House Hotel.** Located 15 minutes from the airport
Expensive– and within walking distance of shopping and entertainment,
Very Expensive this two-story hotel is brick with white shutters and a lighted
★ fountain out front. The lobby is decorated in Queen Anne style, guest rooms in contemporary white modular and light wood. Each room has a drip coffeemaker. *2705 E. South Blvd., 36116, tel. 205/288–2800 or 800/334–8459. 202 rooms, 3 suites, some with Jacuzzi, whirlpool, wet bar, refrigerator. Facilities: cable TV, outdoor pool (in the shape of Alabama), restaurant, lounge, putting green, privileges at nearby health club possible, 10 meeting rooms (largest seats 1,000). AE, MC, V.*

Ramada Inn East. This two-story inn is off I–85, about eight miles from downtown and 1½ miles from Lagoon Park (a sports facility with eight softball fields, 10 tennis courts, and a golf course). A complete redecoration has injected lighter, brighter colors and contemporary furnishings. There are coffeemakers in each room; suites have refrigerators, wet bars, and boardroom tables. *1355 Eastern By-Pass, 36117, tel. 205/277–2200 or 800/272–6232. 154 rooms, 2 suites. Facilities: cable TV, outdoor pool, restaurant, lounge, reduced rate at adjacent health club. AE, CB, DC, MC, V.*

Moderate– **Best Western–Montgomery Lodge.** This is a two-story hotel
Expensive three miles from the airport. The lobby bookcase is stocked for guests' use. Rooms have been redecorated in royal blue or cranberry; most have recliners, and three have king-size water beds. *977 W. South Blvd., 36105, tel. 205/288–5740 or 800/528–1234. 100 rooms, 1 suite. Facilities: cable TV, outdoor pool, Jacuzzi, coin laundry, restaurant, lounge, 2 meeting rooms. AE, CB, DC, MC, V.*

La Quinta Motor Inn. The lobby has been remodeled in muted tones, with terra-cotta-tile floor and silk flowers. Rooms are contemporary, in light earth tones. The location is near the Hampton Inn. *1280 Eastern By-Pass, 36117–2231, tel. 205/271–*

*1620 or 800/531–5900. 130 rooms, 2 suites. Facilities: cable TV,
outdoor pool. AE, CB, DC, MC, V.*

Moderate **Hampton Inn.** Off I–65, next door to the Ramada, this two-
story inn—one of the chain's best—caters to businessmen. The
lobby is homey, with lots of plants. Guest rooms are furnished
in contemporary style. *1401 Eastern By-Pass, 36117, tel. 205/
277–2400 or 800/426–7866. 103 rooms, 2 suites. Facilities: cable
TV, outdoor pool, reduced rate at nearby health club, free local
calls. AE, CB, DC, MC, V.*

The Arts

For a listing of weekly events, get a current issue of *Montgomery!* magazine, which is given away in the lobbies of most hotels
and motels.

Theater **Alabama Shakespeare Festival.** Shakespearean plays, modern
drama, and musicals are performed on two stages at the multi-
million dollar festival (tel. 205/277–2273) on the outskirts of
Montgomery. (From downtown, drive east on I–85 to the Eastern By-Pass exit, then follow signs.) Stratford-upon-Avon
drama authorities have called it the finest facility of its kind in
the world.

A superb amateur-theater group performs at the **Montgomery
Little Theatre** (tel. 205/263–4856) in fall and winter. Traveling
theater groups play at the large auditorium at the **Civic Center**
(tel. 205/241–2105). At the **Faulkner University Dinner Theater**
(tel. 205/272–5820), student musicians and singers perform after dinner. At the campus theater of **Auburn University at
Montgomery** (tel. 205/271–9632), student actors perform drama and comedy.

Concerts The **Montgomery Community Symphony Orchestra** performs at
the newly renovated Davis Theatre for the Performing Arts
(tel. 205/262–0322). Other arts-related events are held at the
1,200-plus-seat auditorium as well.

Dance The **Montgomery School of Ballet** (tel. 205/265–1653
or 205/288–7980 if no answer) performs at different locations in
the city.

Nightlife

Country At the **Diplomat Lounge** (tel. 205/288–1999), top names from
and Western Nashville perform regularly. Local country bands and singers
perform at **The Gambler** (tel. 205/288–9068), which is open
seven days a week, 24 hours a day.

Rock and Roll **Stagger Lee's** (tel. 205/269–9611) has '50s and '60s knock-down-
drag-out good music and fast dancing for the Yuppie crowd.

Hotel Lounges There's live entertainment at **Zeiggy's Lounge** (Holiday Inn
Montgomery East–I–85, tel. 205/272–0370).

Mobile and the Gulf Coast

Mobile, one of the oldest cities in Alabama, is perhaps the most
graceful. Its main thoroughfare, Government Street, is bordered with live oaks, and many antebellum buildings survive
as a bridge with a treasured past. The city is also rich in
azaleas—a feature that is highlighted each spring with the

Azalea Trail Festival. Nearby is Bellingrath Gardens, one of
the most spectacular public gardens in the country.

In Mobile, Mardi Gras was created before New Orleans ever
celebrated Fat Tuesday, and today the predominantly Catholic
city still glories in its pre-Lenten partying with parades and
merrymaking day and night during the second weekend of February.

The area of the Gulf coast around Gulf Shores, to the south of
Mobile, encompasses about 50 miles of pure white sand beach,
including a former peninsula called Pleasure Island and some
smaller islands to the west. Though hotels and condominiums
take up a good deal of the beachfront, several miles of it remain
public. Here you'll find small-town Southern beach life, with
excellent deep-sea fishing, as well as freshwater fishing in the
bays and bayous, plus water sports of all types.

Those with more time might explore the eastern shore of Mobile Bay—Spanish Fort, Daphne, and Fairhope—which has a
laid-back atmosphere of yesteryear: live oaks laced with Spanish moss; sprawling clapboard houses with wide porches
overlooking the lazy, dark water of the bay; and interesting watering holes where local artists and writers meet informally.
At Point Clear, south of Fairhope, is the Victorian-style Grand
Hotel, host for the past 50 years to the vacationing wealthy.

Getting Around

By Plane The Mobile Municipal Airport at Bates Field, about five miles
west of the city, is served by **Air New Orleans** (for flights to Gulf
Shores; Pensacola and other points in Florida; and New Orleans), plus **American, Delta, Eastern, Republic,** and **Skyways.**
Air New Orleans, **Continental, Delta, Eastern, USAir,** and
Royale have flights into the Pensacola Regional Airport, some
40 miles east of Gulf Shores in Florida.

By Car I–10 travels east from Mobile into Florida through Pensacola,
west into Mississippi. I–65 slices Alabama in half vertically,
passing through Birmingham and Montgomery and ending at
Mobile. Gulf Shores is connected with Mobile via I–10 and Rte.
59; Rtes. 180 and 182 are the main beach routes.

By Train **Amtrak** does not serve Mobile, Gulf Shores, or Pensacola.

By Bus **Greyhound/Trailways** has stations in Mobile (201 Government
St., tel. 205/432–1861) and Pensacola (505 W. Burgess Rd., tel.
904/476–4800).

Guided Tours

Gray Line Tours (tel. 205/432–2229 or 800/338–5597), in Mobile,
offers one- to 3½-hour trolley or motorcoach tours to Mobile's
historic points of interest, Bellingrath Gardens, and the USS
Alabama.

Important Addresses and Numbers

Tourist **Mobile Convention and Visitors Corp.** (1 St. Louis Center, Suite
Information 2002, Mobile 36602, tel. 205/433–5100). **Mobile Chamber of
Commerce** (451 Government St., tel. 205/433–6951). **Fort
Condé,** the official visitor center for Mobile (150 S. Royal St.,
tel. 205/438–7304). **Alabama Gulf Coast Convention and Visi-**

tors Bureau (Hwy. 59, Gulf Shores Pkwy., Drawer 457, Gulf Shores 36542, tel. 205/968–7511). **Orange Beach Chamber of Commerce** (Hwy. 182, P.O. Drawer 399, Orange Beach 36561, tel. 205/981–8000).

Emergencies Dial 911 for **police** or **ambulance** in an emergency.

Exploring Mobile and the Gulf Coast

Numbers in the margin correspond with points of interest on the Mobile and the Gulf Coast map.

Mobile The busy port city of **Mobile,** on the western bank of the Mobile
❶ River and at the top of Mobile Bay, overlaps past and present. Despite a raking-over by Hurricane Frederick in 1979, gracious old mansions, iron-grillwork balconies, and lovely gardens abound—belying the madness of the city's annual Mardi Gras (for 10 days preceding Shrove Tuesday, in February). Many businesses in town are conducted from buildings that predate the Civil War.

Fort Condé was the name the French gave the site in 1711; around it blossomed the first white settlement in what is now Alabama. For eight years it was the capital of the French colonial empire, and it remained under French control until 1763, long after the capital had moved to New Orleans. This French connection survives in the area's cuisine, which is strongly Creole-flavored and rivals New Orleans in fieriness.

Fort Condé, too, survives, thanks to a $2.2-million restoration, which preserved it when its remains were discovered—150 years after the fort was destroyed—during construction of the I–10 interchange (an I–10 tunnel now runs under the fort). A reconstructed portion houses the visitor center for the city, as well as a museum and several re-created rooms. Costumed guides interpret and enlighten. *150 S. Royal St., tel. 205/434–7304. Admission free. Open daily 9–5. Closed Christmas.*

Mobile today is noted for its tree-lined boulevards fanning out from **Bienville Square,** at the center of the city. Once upon a time, the square was a showplace, where the town's finest dressers would stroll beneath the live oaks and listen to bands playing on the ornate wrought iron, gazebo-style bandstand. On special occasions—unfortunately few and far between these days—bands play again. One such occasion is the September Celebration, when weekend musical celebrations fill the air.

The city's main thoroughfare is Government Street. From here, signs lead to **Oakleigh,** a gorgeous white antebellum mansion with twin stairways circling under ancient live oaks to meet at a small portico. The high-ceilinged half-timber house was built between 1833 and 1838 and is typical of the most expensive dwellings of its day. Fine period furniture, portraits, silver, jewelry, kitchen implements, toys, and more are displayed throughout. Tickets may be purchased next door at the **Cox-Deasy House,** another antebellum home that is not quite as old as Oakleigh (1850) and by no means as grand. It is, rather, a cottage, built for middle-class folk, and is furnished in simple 19th-century pieces. *350 Oakleigh Place, tel. 205/432–1281. Admission: $4 adults, $3 over 65, $2 college students with ID, $1 children 6–18, under 6 free. Open Mon.–Sat. 10–4, Sun. 2–4. Guided tours conducted every half-hour. Closed major holidays and Christmas week.*

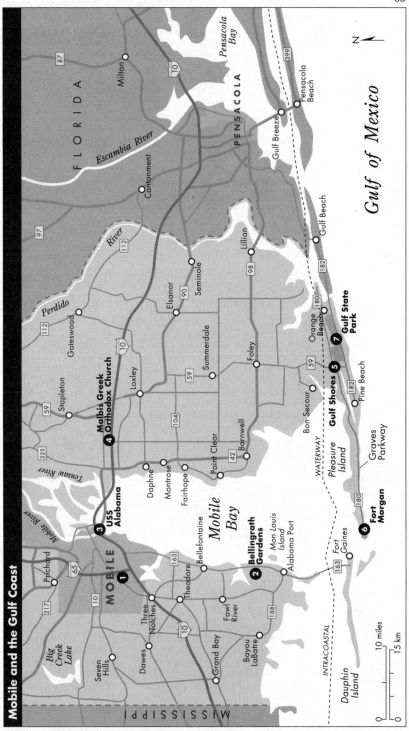

Mobile and the Gulf Coast

Less than 20 miles south of Mobile off I–10 (turn south onto Bellingrath Rd. at the town of Theodore) is **Bellingrath Gardens and Home,** site of one of the world's most magnificent azalea gardens. Here, set amid a 905-acre semitropical landscape, are some 65 spectacular acres of gardens. Showtime for its azaleas is spring, when some 250,000 plantings of 200 different species are ablaze with color. But Bellingrath is a year-round wonder. In summer, 2,500 rosebushes are in bloom; in autumn, 60,000 chrysanthemum plants; in winter, fields of poinsettias. And countless other species and varieties of flowering plants spring up along a river or stream or around a lake populated by ducks and swans.

Guides are on hand throughout the gardens to assist or explain, but a free map lets you plan your own strolls along flagstone paths and charming bridges. One special area is the Oriental-American Garden, a lovely, tranquil setting with teahouses and bridges. The gardens are a sanctuary to over 200 species of birds; especially good times to visit for those ornithologically inclined are April and October, when large numbers of migratory birds drop by.

Coca-Cola bottling pioneer Walter D. Bellingrath began the nucleus of the gardens in 1917, when he and his wife bought a large tract as a fishing camp. Their travels, however, prompted them to create, instead, a garden rivaling some they had seen in Europe, and before long they opened it to the public. Today their brick home on the property is also open to visitors and offers one of the finest collections of antiques in the Southeast. Along with furniture, Meissen porcelain figurines, Dresden china, and other objets d'art amassed by Mrs. Bellingrath is the world's largest collection of Boehm porcelain birds. *Tel. 205/973–2217. Admission: gardens, $4.40 adults, $2.20 6–11, under 6 free; combination admission with house $10. Gardens open daily 7 AM–sunset; house open daily 8–4:30 (until 6 in summer). Closed Christmas.*

Mobile is at its loveliest during the **Azalea Trail Festival** in March or April, on the Saturday following the 10K Azalea Trail Run. The trail twines for 35 well-marked miles in and around the city, showing off azaleas at their best. Throughout the preceding week, scores of special events celebrate the yearly blossoming, from concerts to art exhibits and, of course, the crowning of a queen—America's Junior Miss.

March is also the time of the **Historic Mobile Homes Tour,** when 19th-century Federal-style town houses, Creole cottages, and antebellum plantation homes—36 in all, public and private—are opened to visitors in grand style, including candlelight tours. *For information, write to Historic Mobile Homes Tours, Box 2187, Mobile 36652, or call 205/433–0259.*

To the Shore   From Mobile, there are two ways to reach Pleasure Island, a 30-mile region for romping along the Gulf of Mexico. One is to take a scenic drive south along Rte. 163, perhaps stopping off at Bellingrath Gardens, and cross over the bridge to Dauphin Island, where you catch the **Mobile Bay Ferry** (tel. 205/973–2251) for the 30-minute trip over to Fort Morgan, at the tip of Pleasure Island. This coastal route is shorter in mileage, though probably not in time. The other approach—the one our tour follows—is via U.S. 90E through the Bankhead Tunnel, then south on AL 59.

❸ On the way, stop to pay a call aboard the USS *Alabama,* anchored in Mobile Bay just east of Mobile off I–10. Public subscription saved the mighty gray battleship from being scrapped ignominiously after her heroic World War II service, which ranged from Scapa Flow to the South Pacific. A tour of the ship gives a facinating look into the life of a 2,500-member crew. Anchored next to the battleship is the submarine USS *Drum,* another active battle weapon during World War II, also open to visitors. Other exhibits in the 100-acre Battleship Park include a B-52 bomber called *Calamity Jane* and a P–51 Mustang fighter plane. *Battleship Pkwy., tel. 205/433–2703. Admission: $5 age 12 and up; $2.50 ages 6–11, under 6 free. Parking fee: $1. Open 8 AM–sunset. Closed Christmas.*

Twelve miles east of Mobile, on U.S. 90, just off I–10, is the ❹ **Malbis Greek Orthodox Church,** a replica of a beautiful Byzantine church in Athens, Greece. It was built in 1965, at a cost of more than $1 million, as a memorial to the faith of a Greek immigrant and former monk, Jason Malbis, who founded the community but died before his dream for a cathedral could be realized. The marble for the interior was imported from the same quarries that provided stone for the Parthenon, and a master painter was brought over from Greece to paint murals on the walls and the 75-foot dome of the rotunda. The stained-glass windows are stunning. *County Route 27, tel. 205/626–3050. Admission free. Tours daily 9 AM–noon, 2–5 PM.*

When you're ready for some sun and surf, take AL 59 south to the end. At AL 182, head west. A block later, turn right for a ❺ circular drive next to the **Gulf Shores** public beach area, crowded with Alabama high school and college students at spring break and everyone in summer. There's ample free parking—though the traffic is bumper-to-bumper at peak times—and the beach is as white as snow.

At the western tip of Pleasure Island, 20 miles from Gulf ❻ Shores at the end of AL 180, is **Fort Morgan,** built in the early 1800s to guard the entrance to Mobile Bay. The fort saw fiery action during the Battle of Mobile Bay in 1864: Confederate torpedoes sank the ironclad *Tecumseh,* on which Admiral David Farragut gave his famous command "Damn the torpedoes! Full speed ahead!" The original outer walls still stand; inside, a museum chronicles the fort's history and displays artifacts from Indian days through World War II, with an emphasis on the Civil War. *Mobile Point, tel. 205/540–7125. Admission: $2 adults; $1 over 61 and children 6–18, under 6 free. Open daily 9–5 PM. Closed major holidays.*

❼ Five miles east of Gulf Shores on AL 182 is **Gulf State Park,** which covers more than 6,000 acres of Pleasure Island. Along with 2½ miles of pure white beaches and glimmering dunes, the park also has two freshwater lakes with canoeing and fishing, plus biking, hiking, and jogging trails through pine forests. There is a large beach pavilion with a snack bar, restrooms, and showers, and nearby is a concrete fishing pier that juts 825 feet into the Gulf. There is also a resort inn and convention center, 468 campsites, and 21 cottages, plus tennis courts and an 18-hole golf course. *For information, write Gulf State Park, Rte. 2, Box 9, Gulf Shores 36542. Tel.: cabins and bike, canoe, and motorless flat-bottom fishing boat rentals, 205/968–7544; camping, 205/968–6353; resort inn, 205/968–7531. Open year-round.*

What to See and Do with Children

Fort Condé (*see* Mobile in Exploring).
Fort Morgan (*see* To the Shore in Exploring).
Gulf State Park (*see* To the Shore in Exploring).
Romar Miniature Golf. This 18-hole miniature golf course is set among tropical palms and waterfalls (Beach Rd. E, Gulf Shores, tel. 205/981–4418).
USS *Alabama* (*see* To the Shore in Exploring).
Waterville USA. This water park set on 17 acres has a 750,000-gallon wave pool (creates three-foot waves), seven exciting water slides, and a lazy river ride around the park. For younger children there are gentler rides in a supervised play area. There is also a 36-hole miniature golf course and a video-game arcade. *AL 59, Gulf Shores, tel. 205/948–2106. Admission: $9.95, children under 3 free. Open Memorial Day–Labor Day.*

Off the Beaten Track

Naval Aviation Museum. At the Naval Air Station in Pensacola, many planes used in both world wars and later—including a Gemini space capsule, F-18s, Corsairs, and Spitfires—are displayed on a rotating basis. And they're everywhere—outdoors, in hangars, or inside, on the floor or suspended from the ceiling. From Gulf Shores, follow the Beach Road east to Blue Angel Parkway, then to Sherman Field, where the precision-flying team the Blue Angels are based. (They practice here during the week when they are not doing shows elsewhere.) When the USS *Lexington* aircraft carrier is in port, you can go aboard between 9 and 3 on weekends. *Tel. 904/452–3604. Admission free. Open daily 9–5. Closed major holidays.*

Shopping

Mobile Most shopping in Mobile is done in malls and centers in the suburban areas. Stores are generally open Monday–Saturday 10–9, Sunday 1–6. Sales tax is 7%. Banks are generally open weekdays 9–2.

Shopping Districts. The **Bel Air Mall** (one block east of I–65 Beltline off Airport Blvd., tel. 205/478–1893) has some 175 stores under one roof, including JC Penney and Sears, plus a food court. **Springdale Mall-Plaza** (Airport Blvd. and I–65, tel. 205/471–1945), anchored by Gayfer's, McRae's, and Montgomery Ward, recently expanded and now has more than 100 stores.

Antiques At **Allen's Antiques & Collectibles** (121 Telegraph Rd., in Chickasaw, just north of Mobile, tel. 205/452–0717), the specialty is wicker. **Al Atchison Courtyard Antiques** (601 Government St., tel. 205/438–9421), one of the largest antiques dealers in the South, is packed with antique brass beds and other American and European antique furniture.

Discount Stores **Festival Center Mall** (3725 Airport Blvd., tel. 205/341–0500) has such stores as Walmart and Marshall's, as well as a 24-hour supermarket.

Gulf Shores For swimsuits, air-brushed T-shirts, souvenirs, gifts, and cam-
Beach Gear era supplies, try **Beach Bazaar** (Gulf Shores Pkwy., tel. 205/948–7233).

Gifts   The **Green Parrot** (AL 59, tel. 205/948–7078) has unusual vases
made from driftwood, round five-gallon designer aquariums
with tropical fish, and custom-made jewelry. China, crystal,
wicker teacarts, beach paintings, and other home accessories
are found at **Holiday Treasures** (Gulfview Sq., tel. 205/981–
9177). For shell jewelry, brass items, and National Shrimp Festival posters and T-shirts, try **Sunburst** (Bayou Village on AL
59, tel. 205/948–7862; **Sunburst Galleries** at Romar Beach, tel.
205/981–9655).

Participant Sports

Biking   **Gulf State Park** (tel. 205/948–7275) in Gulf Shores has biking
trails through pine forests and rents bicycles. **Island Recreation Services** (tel. 205/948–7334) in Gulf Shores rents bikes,
mopeds, and water-sports equipment (see Water Sports).

Canoeing   **Sunshine Canoe Rentals** (tel. 205/344–8664) runs canoe trips at
Escatawpa River, 15 miles west of Mobile. The river has no rapids, but makes for pleasant, leisurely travel past lots of white
sandbars.

Fishing   The freshwater and saltwater fishing in the Gulf area is excellent. **Gulf State Park** has fishing from an 825-foot pier and rents
flat-bottom boats for lake fishing. Deep-sea fishing from charter boats is very popular; in Gulf Shores, you can sign on board
the *Marina Queen* (tel. 205/981–8499) for a full- or half-day
fishing expedition, and Orange Beach has 40 boats to choose
from. For a brochure on Orange Beach's offerings, call 205/981–
8000; two choices are the 98-foot *Moreno Queen* (tel. 205/981–
8499) and the 48-foot *Island Lady* (tel. 205/981–4510). Catches
from these deep-sea expeditions include king mackerel, amberjack, tuna, white marlin, blue marlin, grouper, bonita, sailfish,
and red snapper. Nonresidents 16 or over may not fish anywhere in Alabama without a valid fishing license; for information, call 205/261–3260.

Golf   A good public 18-hole course in Mobile is the **Spring Hill College
Golf Course** (tel. 205/343–2356); the 18-hole **Azalea City Golf
Club** (tel. 205/342–4221) is rather flat and not a great challenge.
Gulf Shores Golf Club (tel. 205/968–7366) has an 18-hole, 72-par
championship course. The 18-hole course at the **Gulf State
Park Resort** (tel. 205/948–4653) is one of the most beautiful,
with moss-hung live oaks and giant magnolia trees. The newest
links in the area, **Lakeview Golf Club** (off AL 59 on Rte. 20 south
of Foley, tel. 205/943–4653), has 27 holes and six lakes and is
well sand-trapped. Only 25 minutes from Gulf Shores, on the
Beach Road East in Florida, is **Perdido Bay Resort** (tel. 904/492
–1223), the home of October's Pensacola Open.

Horseback Riding   **Horseback Beach Rides** (tel. 205/943–6674) offers guided group
rides along country trails or along the beach at Gulf Shores.

Jogging   **Gulf State Park** has trails through a forest.

Sailing   Sailboats that can be rented with captain ($24 for three
hours) include the *Cyrus King* (tel. 205/968–6775) and the
Daedalus (tel. 205/986–7018) in Gulf Shores. **Island Recreation Services** (tel. 205/948–7334), in Gulf Shores; and **Land 'N'
Sea** (tel. 205/943–3600), in Foley, rent sailboats without captain.

Tennis   **Gulf State Park** has courts.

Water Sports **Fun Marina** (tel. 205/981–8587) in Orange Beach rents Jet Skis, pontoon boats, and 16-foot bay-fishing boats. In Gulf Shores, **Island Recreation Services** (tel. 205/948–7334) rents boogie boards, body boards, surf boats, and sailboats.

Spectator Sports

Dog Racing At the **Mobile Greyhound Park** (off I–10W, about 10 mi from Mobile, tel. 205/653–5000) and at the **Pensacola Greyhound Track** (U.S. 98, about 40 mi east of Gulf Shores in Florida, tel. 904/455–8595 or 800/345–3997), there's pari-mutuel betting and a restaurant overlooking the finish line.

Dining

In Mobile and throughout the Gulf area, the specialty is fresh seafood, often prepared in Creole style, with peppery spices, crabmeat dressing, and sometimes a tomato-based sauce. Mobile, in fact, prides itself on being the only city in Alabama with a cuisine of its own, whose precedence (in time, at least) over New Orleans's it has been claiming for years. The basis of the claim is history: the founders of Mobile, French explorers Bienville and Iberville, came here first, then moved west to New Orleans.

The most highly recommended restaurants in each price category are indicated by a star ★.

Category	Cost*
Expensive	over $25
Moderate	$15–$25
Inexpensive	under $15

per person without tax (9% in Mobile), service, or drinks

The following credit-card abbreviations are used: AE, American Express; CB, Carte Blanche; DC, Diners Club; MC, MasterCard; V, Visa.

Mobile **John Word's.** Word of mouth is fast spreading the fame of this
Expensive restaurant in an ancient town house in downtown Mobile. You
★ have to search for the place—the sign is so small, it looks like a lawyer's shingle. Inside, it's quietly elegant. The scamp—a white fish caught in the Gulf—is flaky and delicious. The steaks, too, are wonderful: prime meat perfectly cooked. In the upstairs bistro, top-notch jazz performers entertain ($5 cover charge). *358 Dauphin St., tel. 205/433–7955. Jacket and tie requested. Reservations suggested. AE, CB, DC, MC, V. Closed Sun.*

La Louisiana. This antiques-filled old house on the outskirts is a delightful setting in which to dine. The seafood is fresh, prepared with a touch of French Creole. Shrimp dishes are heavy with cream sauces unless you order them lightly fried. The seafood gumbo is made the Mobile way: heavy on shrimp, oysters, and okra. *2400 Airport Blvd., tel. 205/476–8130. Jacket and tie requested. Reservations preferred. AE, MC, V. Closed Sun. Dinner only.*

★ **The Pillars.** Sitting amid fine antiques from the 18th and 19th centuries in a huge old mansion with wide porches overlooking the live oaks in the yard, it is easy to imagine oneself in another time, listening to the latest news from the battlefront at Vicksburg or Shiloh. The beautifully cooked snapper with a white-wine-and-cream sauce and the snapper with crabmeat and a pecan Creole sauce are delicious. The lamb chops are cut thick and cooked just the way you like them over a charcoal grill. *1757 Government St., tel. 205/478–6341. Dress: formal. Reservations preferred. AE, CB, DC, MC, V. Closed Sun. Dinner only.*

Moderate **The Malaga Restaurant.** This is a small, intimate restaurant in the former carriage house of The Malaga Inn (*see* Lodging). At the end of one of its two rooms, a set of French doors lets in lots of light and a view out to the pool, landscaped with banana trees and other tropical plants. The walls are a mixture of old brick and a cream-and-green floral-print wallpaper. The menu is a mix of Creole-style seafood and Continental dishes. One of the most popular choices is snapper Brennan—fresh Gulf snapper served with a sauce of crabmeat, mushrooms, wine, and other delights. Continental choices include chateaubriand and steak Diane. *359 Church St., tel. 205/433–5858. Dress: casual. Reservations preferred for dinner. AE, CB, DC, MC, V.*

Rousso's Restaurant. A local favorite, with a nautical look created by lots of fishnets and scenes of ships at sea, Rousso's is known for its crab claws, fried in a light batter and served with a catsup-horseradish sauce. *166 S. Royal St., tel. 205/433–3322. Dress: casual. Reservations accepted. AE, CB, DC, MC, V. Closed Sun.*

Inexpensive **Wintzell's Oyster House.** Opened in 1938, this is a place to see and be seen. All the local celebrities (not to mention a movie or TV star or two) eat here—especially at the raw bar. Every piece of space on the walls and ceilings is covered with Wintzell's favorite sayings and photographs of celebrities and political figures. The seafood is fresh from the Gulf, fried or broiled—perfectly complemented by good draft beer. *605 Dauphin St., tel. 205/433–1004. Dress: casual. No reservations. AE, CB, DC, MC, V. Closed Sun.*

Gulf Coast **Original Oyster House.** A rustic but very clean, plant-filled res-
Moderate taurant overlooking the bayou, this has become a Gulf Shores tradition. Oysters on the half-shell, fresh out of nearby Perdido Bay, are the specialty of the house. The Cajun-style gumbo—a concoction of crab claws, shrimp, amberjack, grouper, redfish, okra and other vegetables, and Cajun spices—has won 20 major awards. *Bayou Village Shopping Ctr., AL 59, tel. 205/948–2445. Dress: casual. No reservations. AE, DC, MC, V.*

Prudhomme's Hemingway's. Gourmet Cajun cuisine is served from the kitchen of a cousin of the famous New Orleans chef—he even looks like Chef Paul. A specialty is eggplant Pirouge: Eggplant is carved into the shape of a boat, deep-fried, filled with a sauce of shrimp, crabmeat, green onions, and mushrooms, and topped by a thin layer of cheese and three deep-fried jumbo shrimp in Cajun seasoning. The restaurant itself has a nautical look, with bamboo wallpaper and natural wood accents. *Orange Beach Marina, Rte. 2, tel. 205/981–9791. Dress: casual. No reservations. AE, DC, MC, V.*

Inexpensive **Dempsey's Restaurant.** The setting is tropical, enhanced by a 20-foot waterfall, at this lakeside dining room. Cajun seafood specialties are arranged temptingly at the all-you-can-eat dinner buffet that includes such seafood dishes as stuffed jumbo shrimp. There's also nightly blues and a small dance floor. *AL*

182, Romar Beach, tel. 205/981–6800. Dress: casual. No reservations. AE, CB, DC, MC, V.

Hazel's Family Restaurant. Former Alabama Governor Fob James, a resident of Gulf Shores, says Hazel's has "the best biscuits in the state." The plain but tasteful family-style restaurant serves a good, hearty breakfast, soup-and-salad lunches, and adequate buffet dinners featuring such seafood dishes as flounder Florentine or crab-stuffed broiled snapper. *Gulf View Square Shopping Ctr., Romar Beach, tel. 205/981–4628. Dress: casual. No reservations. No credit cards.*

Maw Maw's Cajun Cafe. At this small, fern-hung restaurant across from Gulf Shores beach, café au lait and beignets New Orleans–style are the order of the day for breakfast, Cajun cooking—such as spicy peppered snapper stuffed with crabmeat dressing—for lunch and dinner. The Big Maw Maw's Cajun Platter is barbecued shrimp, blackened fish, and fried oysters, served with french fries, a salad, and gumbo. *Econo Lodge, W. Beach Blvd., tel. 205/948–8141. Dress: casual. No reservations. AE, CB, DC, MC, V.*

Pompano's. All seats at this hotel restaurant have a view of the Gulf; one of the four high-ceilinged rooms has two glass walls. Furnishings are blond wood with green upholstery, gray tablecloths, and maroon napkins. The specialty is local seafood, served in a "coastal tradition." The Captain's Platter features Gulf jumbo shrimp, oysters, flounder, and bay scallops, all fried in a light batter. *Quality Inn Beachside, W. Beach Blvd., tel. 205/948–6874. Dress: casual. No reservations. AE, CB, DC, MC, V.*

Lodging

The most highly recommended properties in each price category are indicated by a star ★.

Category	Cost*
Very Expensive	over $95
Expensive	$70–$95
Moderate	$50–$70
Inexpensive	under $50

*double room; add 10% for taxes in Mobile, 8% on the coast

The following credit-card abbreviations are used: AE, American Express; CB, Carte Blanche; DC, Diners Club; MC, MasterCard; V, Visa.

Mobile
Expensive–
Very Expensive
★

Radisson Admiral Semmes Hotel. An old hotel that was renovated several years ago, this is a favorite with local politicians. It is also popular with partygoers, particularly during Mardi Gras, because of its excellent location directly on the parade route. Rooms are furnished in Queen Anne and Chippendale styles. *250 Government St., Box 1209, 36633, tel. 205/432–8000 or 800/228–9822. 147 rooms, 22 suites. Facilities: cable TV/free movies, outdoor pool, Jacuzzi, Oliver's Restaurant, specializing in Cajun, Creole cuisines, Admiral's Corner Lounge, privileges at Y. AE, CB, DC, MC, V.*

★ **Stouffer's Riverview Plaza.** A stylish new contemporary structure, the 28-story Riverview offers panoramic views of the

Mobile River and downtown Mobile. The lobby and guest rooms are decorated in a contemporary style. *64 S. Water St., 36602, tel. 205/438–4000 or 800/468–3571. 365 rooms, 10 suites. Facilities: outdoor pool, sauna, whirlpool, deli, lounge, Julia's Restaurant, with sparkling chandeliers, mirrored columns, sweeping views of the riverfront. AE, CB, DC, MC, V.*

Expensive– **Ramada Resort and Conference Center.** This glass-and-brick
Very Expensive hotel, with a four-story main section and a two-story wing, is known for having the most "happening" bar in town. Suites are large, and all rooms are decorated in a contemporary style. *600 S. Beltline Hwy. 36608, tel. 205/344–8030 or 800/272–6232. 230 rooms, 6 suites. Facilities: cable TV/free movies, heated indoor pool with Jacuzzi, outdoor pool, Nautilus room, putting green, lighted tennis court, restaurant, lounge, bar, 8 meeting rooms. AE, CB, DC, MC, V.*

Inexpensive– **The Malaga Inn.** A delightful, romantic getaway place, The
Moderate Malaga comprises two town houses built by a wealthy landown-
★ er in 1862. The lobby is furnished with 19th-century antiques and opens onto a tropically landscaped central courtyard with a fountain. The rooms are large, airy, and furnished with massive antiques. Ask for the front suite, with 14-foot ceilings and crimson velveteen wallpaper. *359 Church St., 36602, tel. 205/ 438–4701. 40 rooms. Facilities: cable TV, outdoor pool, restaurant (see Dining), lounge. AE, CB, DC, MC, V.*

Gulf Coast **Marriott's Grand Hotel.** Nestled amid 550 acres of beautifully
Expensive– landscaped grounds, the "Grand" has been a cherished tradi-
Very Expensive tion since 1847. Extensively refurbished by Marriott, it is one
★ of the South's premier resorts. Its two-story cypress–paneled and beamed lobby evokes an aura of traditional elegance. Spacious rooms and cottages are also traditionally furnished. *On Mobile Bay, US Scenic 98, Point Clear 36564, tel. 205/928–9201 or 800/228–9290. 308 units, including some suites, 2 rooms with refrigerators. Facilities: cable TV, movies, pool, beach, sauna and whirlpool, marina with rental boats, sailing, charter fishing, social program, complimentary Grand Fun Camp for youngsters Mon.–Sat., rental bicycles, playground, 10 tennis courts, 36 holes golf, horseback riding, 3 dining rooms, including award-winning Magnolia Room, coffee shop, lounge with entertainment. AE, DC, MC, V.*

Gulf Shores Holiday Inn. This four-story beachfront hotel has Gulf-front, poolside, and king leisure rooms in a contemporary style. *E. Beach Blvd., Box 417, Gulf Shores 36542, tel. 205/968– 6191 or 800/465–4329. 118 rooms. Facilities: cable TV/free movies, outdoor pool, poolside, 2 lighted tennis courts, restaurant, lounge, 3 meeting rooms. AE, CB, DC, MC, V.*

Perdido Beach Hilton. The eight- and nine-story towers are Mediterranean stucco and red tile. The lobby is tiled in terracotta and decorated with mosaics by Venetian artists and a brass sculpture of gulls in flight. Rooms are furnished in luxurious Mediterranean style, and all have a beach view and balcony. *AL 182E, Box 400, Orange Beach 36561, tel. 205/981– 9811 or 800/634–8001. 345 units, including 16 suites. Facilities: heated indoor/outdoor pool, whirlpool, sauna, exercise room overlooking beach, 4 lighted tennis courts, pool bar, cafe, restaurant. AE, CB, DC, MC, V.*

★ **Quality Inn.** This luxury motel is made up of two buildings, one five years old (three stories) and a new one (six stories). All the guest rooms are modern and luxurious, decorated in pastels, with private balconies; most face the Gulf; half have kitchens. In the Art Deco–style atrium lobby, with glass-brick walls, is a 70-foot swimming pool and a waterfall. Glass-walled elevators rise six stories. *921 W. Gulf Shores Blvd., Box 1013, Gulf Shores 36542, tel. 205/948–6874 or 800/228–5151. 158 rooms. Facilities: cable TV, exercise room, large hot tub, outdoor pool, pool bar, piano bar, Pompano's restaurant (see Dining), deli. AE, DC, MC, V.*

Moderate–Expensive **Lighthouse.** This complex of five two- to four-story buildings, surrounded by brightly colored exotic flowers, is set on a 580-foot private beach. The waterfront rooms have private balconies, and some units have kitchens. All have contemporary furnishings. *E. Beach Blvd., Box 233, Gulf Shores 36542, tel. 205/948–6188. 124 rooms. Facilities: cable TV/movies, 2 outdoor pools (1 heated, with large Jacuzzi). AE, CB, DC, MC, V.*

Moderate **Budget Host.** Across the street from Gulf Shores beach, this four-story hotel has some rooms (20) with kitchenettes. *201 E. Beach Blvd., Box 955, Gulf Shores 36542, tel. 205/968–6844. 52 rooms. Facilities: cable TV, restaurant, lounge with live music and dance floor. AE, CB, DC, MC, V.*

Inexpensive–Moderate **Port of Call.** At this three-story facility across the highway from Gulf Shores beach, suites have full kitchens and separate living rooms. Some units have balconies. *W. Beach Blvd., Box 978, Gulf Shores 36542, tel. 205/948–7739. 18 suites, 3 efficiencies. Facilities: cable TV, outdoor pool, coin laundry. MC, V.*

The Arts

Theater   The **Joe Jefferson Players** (tel. 205/471–1534), a well-established group of amateur actors and actresses, perform plays and musicals at various locations around Mobile throughout the year. They often perform at the Saenger Theater (tel. 205/438–5686) or the Mobile Municipal Auditorium (tel. 205/434–7381), as do **The Pixie Players** (tel. 205/344–1537), a children's theatrical group.

Nightlife

Hotel Lounges   **Adam's** (Airport Blvd.–Beltline Hwy., tel. 205/344–8030), at Mobile's Ramada Inn Airport, is popular among younger partygoers who enjoy loud, fast music. There's live entertainment in **Admiral's Corner** at the Radisson Admiral Semmes Hotel (251 Government St., tel. 205/432–8000) and live entertainment and dancing in the **Jubilation** lounge of the Holiday Inn (I–10 and U.S. 90, tel. 205/666–5600).

Honky-tonk   On the Alabama–Florida line is the **Flora-Bama Lounge** (Beach Rd., tel. 205/981–8555), with country-and-western music performed by a local band and vocalist. It's the place where Mobile native Jimmy Buffet got his start to stardom.

Swing   At **Shirley & Wayne's** (AL 182, Romar Beach, tel. 205/981–4818), Wayne Perdew and his band play swing and country Monday–Saturday nights while you dine and/or dance.

Elsewhere in the State

Numbers in the margin correspond with points of interest on the Elsewhere in the State map.

6 **Alabama Space and Rocket Center, Huntsville.** Home to the U.S. Space Camp, where youngsters learn about space exploration, the center offers a bus tour of the NASA labs and shuttle test sites, a 45-minute Omnimax film (in which the screen extends above and around you) on space exploration, hands-on exhibits in the museum, and an outdoor park filled with spacecraft. *100 mi from Birmingham via I–65N to U.S. 72E. 1 Tranquillity Base, Huntsville, tel. 205/837–3400. Admission: $12 adults, $8 over 60 and children 3–12, under 3 free; includes museum, film, NASA tour. Open daily 8–6 Memorial Day–Labor Day, 9–5 rest of year. Closed Christmas.*

7 **Ave Maria Grotto, Cullman.** Take a leisurely stroll through this hillside garden grotto to view over 125 miniature churches, buildings, and shrines, painstakingly created by a Benedictine monk over the course of 50 years from originals in the United States and Europe. Standing only a few feet in height, these tiny buildings were constructed from rare materials, such as marble and semiprecious stones, gathered from around the world. *50 mi from Birmingham via I–65N to U.S. 278E, St. Bernard's Abbey, Cullman, tel. 205/734–4110. Admission: $3 adults; $2.50 senior citizens; $1.50 children 6–12, under 6 free. Open daily 7 AM–sunset.*

8 **DeSoto Caverns, Childersburg.** The site of a 2,000-year-old Indian burial ground, these vast onyx caves were rediscovered in 1540 by Hernando DeSoto and later served as a Confederate gunpowder mining center and a Prohibition speakeasy. Curious rock formations created by stalagmites and stalactites allow the imagination free reign. During the tour, the largest cave (over 12 stories high) hosts a sound, light, and water show. *85 mi from Montgomery via U.S. 231N to Rte. 76. 60 mi from Birmingham via U.S. 280S to Rte. 76. Tel. 205/378–7252. Admission: $7 adults; $4 children 4–11, under 4 free. Open Mon.–Sat. 9–5:30, Sun. 12:30–5:30 Apr.–Sept.; Mon.–Sat. 9–5, Sun. 12:30–5 rest of year. Closed Thanksgiving and Christmas.*

13 **DeSoto Falls, Fort Payne.** This 100-foot waterfall is one of the loveliest attractions in the 5,000-acre DeSoto State Resort Park. Unsupervised swimming is allowed in the lake, and there is a supervised pool, picnic area, and campgrounds nearby. *90 mi from Birmingham via I–59N to Exit 218 (AL 35) to Co. Rd. 89. Tel. 205/845–5380 or 800/ALA–PARK. Admission free, picnicking 50¢. Open daily 7 AM–dusk.*

2 **Demopolis.** This town takes great pride in its rich Southern heritage. A five-mile self-guided-tour map provides detailed histories of the numerous antebellum homes in the area, and a cassette driving tour will take you past the 18th-century buildings in the historic downtown area. The 10,000-acre **Demopolis Lake** offers fishing, boating, swimming, picnicking, and campgrounds. *100 mi from Montgomery via U.S. 80W. 115 mi from Birmingham via I–59S to U.S. 43W. Maps, cassettes, and tape players are available, free of charge, from the Demopolis Area Chamber of Commerce, 213 N. Walnut St., tel. 205/289–0270, open weekdays 8–5, or from the Information Center at the Best*

Alabama Space and
Rocket Center, **6**

Ave Maria Grotto, **7**

DeSoto Caverns, **8**

DeSoto Falls, **13**

Demopolis, **2**

Ivy Green, **1**

Little River
Canyon, **13**

Lookout Mountain
Trail, **10**

Mound State
Monument, **3**

Noccalula Falls and
Park, **10**

Pike Pioneer
Museum, **9**

Point Mallard Park, **4**

Russell Cave Natl.
Monument, **11**

Sequoyah Caverns, **12**

Shorter Mansion, **15**

Sturdivant Hall, **5**

Tuskegee, **14**

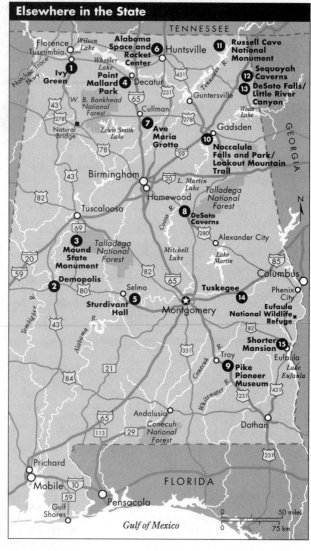

Elsewhere in the State

Western Hotel on Hwy. 80, tel. 205/289–5772, open evenings and weekends.

Two fine antebellum homes in Demopolis are open to the public. **Gaineswood,** built in 1860, has been called one of the finest Greek Revival mansions in the South. The house has been extensively restored, down to reproductions of the original French wallpapers. It is unique in that it contains the original furnishings, including carved four-posters and a flutina—a one-of-a-kind musical instrument invented by the original owner (who also designed Gaineswood itself). Interior architectural elements include elaborate columns and pilasters; friezes and medallions of wood, plaster, cast iron, and leather; veined marble mantels; and ceiling-dome skylights. **Bluff Hall** was built in 1832 as a Federal-style house and remodeled in the Greek Revival style several years later. It stands on a chalky cliff above the Tombigbee River and features a columned front portico, a huge double parlor with Corinthian columns, and Empire and Victorian furnishings donated by friends and descendants of the original owner. Also on display is a collection of period clothing. Like Gaineswood, Bluff Hall is listed on the National Historic Register. *Gaineswood: 805 Cedar St. E, tel. 205/289–4846. Admission: $3 adults, $2 students, 50¢ children under 13. Open Mon.–Sat. 9–5, Sun. 1–5. Closed holidays. Bluff Hall: N. Commissioners Ave., tel. 205/289–1666. Admission: $2 adults, 50¢ children 5–12, children under 5 free. Open Tues.–Sat. 10–5, Sun. 2–5. Closed Thanksgiving, Christmas, and New Year's Day.*

❶ Ivy Green, Tuscumbia. Visitors can tour the grounds and childhood home of Helen Keller. It was here, at the carriage house, where Annie Sullivan taught her the meaning of language. *The Miracle Worker* is performed on the grounds Friday and Saturday nights in June and July. *110 mi from Birmingham via I–65N to State Rd. 157N to U.S. 72W to Rte. 55N. 300 W. North Commons, tel. 205/383–4066. Admission: $2 adults, 50¢ children 6–11, under 6 free. Miracle Worker general admission: $3, $2 children 6–11, under 6 free. Open Mon.–Sat. 8:30–4, Sun. 1–4. Closed Labor Day, Christmas, and New Year's.*

⓭ Little River Canyon, Fort Payne. The deepest canyon east of the Rocky Mountains can be found in DeSoto State Park. Almost 600 feet at its deepest point and 16 miles wide, the canyon is surrounded by a breathtaking 22-mile scenic drive. *95 mi northeast of Birmingham via I–59 to Hwy. 176 near Fort Payne, tel. 800/ALA–PARK. Admission free, 50¢ for use of picnic area.*

⓾ Lookout Mountain Trail. Stretching north from Gadsden, Alabama, to Chattanooga, Tennessee, this trail along a mountain ridge offers 125 miles of the prettiest scenery in the state for the adventurous hiker's delight. *Gadsden is 45 mi from Birmingham via I–59N. Tel. 800/ALABAMA for information.*

❸ Mound State Monument, Moundville. The museum contains a number of prehistoric Indian artifacts discovered in the area. On the grounds are 20 earthen temple mounds, the largest of which supports a reconstructed Indian temple. Also on the grounds are a reconstructed Indian village, a nature trail leading to the Black Warrior River, picnic areas, and a campground. *100 mi from Montgomery via U.S. 82N to Hwy. 69S. 65 mi from Birmingham via I–59S to Hwy. 69S. Tel. 205/ 371–2572. Admission: $2 adults, $1 students and senior citizens, children under 6 free. Open daily 9–5. Closed Thanksgiving, Christmas, and New Year's.*

⓾ Noccalula Falls and Park Gadsden. Highlights of this 100-acre woodland park include a 90-foot waterfall, miniature golf, train rides, a small zoo, a botanic garden, and a 1776 pioneer homestead—four log cabins were moved here from the backwoods of Tennessee. There are also campgrounds and picnic areas. *50 mi from Birmingham via I–59N to Exit 188. 1400 Noccalula Rd., Gadsden, tel. 205/543–7412. Admission to pioneer homestead and botanic garden: $1.50 adults, $1 over 60, children under 12; train ride 75¢, 50¢ over 65 and under 12. Open daily 9–dark.*

❾ Pike Pioneer Museum, Troy. This museum has captured the essence of 18th- and 19th-century Pike County in its 10,000 museum pieces, ranging from pioneer farm tools to turn-of-the-century household goods. These artifacts are displayed in 10 buildings that are themselves museum pieces, including a log house, a jail, a general store, and even an outhouse, all moved here from other parts of the state. *48 mi from Montgomery via U.S. 231S. Address: 248 U.S. 231N, Troy, tel. 205/566–3597. Admission: $2 adults, 50¢ students, children under 6 free. Open Mon.–Sat. 10–5, Sun. 1–5.*

❹ Point Mallard Park, Decatur. Facilities at this 749-acre park include a swimming pool, a wave pool, and a water slide (summer only); plus an ice rink (mid-Nov.–mid-Mar.), campgrounds, an 18-hole championship golf course, miniature golf, a duck pond, and a four-mile hiking and biking trail. *130 mi from Birmingham via I–65N to Exit 334 to Rte. 67N. Eighth St., tel. 205/350–3000. Individual fees. Open Mon., Wed., Fri.–Sun. 10–6; Tues., Thurs. 10–9. Closed Labor Day.*

⓫ Russell Cave National Monument, Bridgeport. This archaeological site was occupied by the American Indian's prehistoric ancestors for 8,000 years before the arrival of European settlers. Visitors today can tour the cave shelter—the entrance to over seven miles of cavernous passages–and view museum exhibits of prehistoric artifacts and an Indian burial ground. There are also tool and cooking demonstrations, a slide program, a nature trail, an Indian garden, a hiking trail, and picnic grounds. *130 mi from Birmingham via I–59N to Hwy. 117N to U.S. 72N to Co. Rd. 75. Tel. 205/495–2672. Admission free. Open daily 8–5. Closed Christmas.*

⓬ Sequoyah Caverns, Valley Head. A half-mile guided tour through the caverns in Sand Mountain brings visitors past rock formations mirrored in lakes. In the 1930s, dances were held in the largest room, now called the Ballroom. Outside, there's a picnic area, a campground, a small zoo, a swimming pool, a playground, and hiking trails. *110 mi from Birmingham via I–59N to U.S. 11N. Sequoyah Rd., tel. 205/635–6423. Admission: $5 adults; $4.50 senior citizens; $3.50 children 6–12, under 3 free. Open daily 8:30–6 Memorial Day–Labor Day; 8:30–5 Labor Day–Nov. and Mar.–Memorial Day; weekends only 8:30–5 Dec.–Feb.*

⓯ Shorter Mansion, Eufaula. This house museum, built in 1884, is a fine example of Neoclassical Revival architecture. It should be noted for its dedication to both Eufaula's and Barbour County's history, particularly as shown in the Governor's Parlor, a room containing portraits and memorabilia from the terms in office of the six Alabama governors who hailed from Barbour County. *90 mi from Montgomery via U.S. 82S. 340 N. Eufaula Ave., tel. 205/687–3793. Admission: $3 adults, 50¢ children under 12. Open Mon.–Sat. 10–4, Sun. 1–4. Closed national holidays.*

❺ Sturdivant Hall, Selma. Built in 1853 by architect Thomas Helm Lee, Robert E. Lee's cousin, this antebellum house museum is an excellent example of Greek Revival architecture. Now restored to its original grandeur, the house boasts beautiful grillwork and lovely gardens. Furnishings include a few original pieces and period antiques. Each year in late March, a Historic Selma Pilgrimage takes visitors through Sturdivant

Hall and other antebellum and Victorian homes (for information, call 800/ALABAMA). *50 mi from Montgomery via U.S. 80W. 80 mi from Birmingham via I–65S to Rte. 31S to U.S. 80W. 713 Mabry St., tel. 205/872–5626. Admission: $3 adults, $1.50 children 6–18, under 6 free. Open Tues.–Sat. 9–4, Sun. 2–4. Closed Mon. and major holidays.*

⑭ Tuskegee. The **Tuskegee National Forest** (tel. 205/727–2652), spread over 1,000 acres, includes an 8½-mile hiking trail, a firing range, and a botanic garden, as well as a replica of the childhood home of Booker T. Washington. His actual home, **The Oaks,** is part of the **George Washington Carver Museum** on the Tuskegee University campus. This museum includes Carver's original laboratory, his artwork, and a historical study of the **Tuskegee Institute.** *120 mi from Birmingham via I–65S to I–85E to U.S. 29S. 30 mi from Montgomery via I–85E to U.S. 29S. Tuskegee Institute National Historic Site, tel. 205/727–3200. Admission free. Open weekdays 8–noon, 1–4:30. Closed major holidays.*

3 Georgia

Atlanta

by John English
and William
Schemmel

A transplanted
Georgian since
1970, John English
teaches journalism
at the university in
Athens, Georgia.
Native son Bill
Schemmel is a
freelance writer
based in Atlanta.

"Her patron saint is Scarlett O'Hara," writer James Street once said of Atlanta, "and the town is just like her—shrewd, proud and full of gumption—her Confederate slip showing under a Yankee mink coat."

It's true that the Yankee influence has long given Atlanta its vitality, while its Southern traditions have made it one of America's most livable cities.

But make no mistake: Atlanta is located in the heart of the South. The state of Georgia continues to celebrate Confederate Memorial Day as a holiday every April. *The Atlanta Constitution's* Sunday section of regional news is still called "Dixie Living." And one of the top tourist attractions in this metropolis is the Cyclorama, a diorama depicting the famous Battle of Atlanta, which leveled the city during what locals call the "War Between the States."

Despite the mystique of *Gone With the Wind*, which Margaret Mitchell cranked out in a still-remaining apartment house at 10th and Peachtree streets, Atlanta has never really been part of the moonlight and magnolias myth common in many antebellum cities of the Old South.

Atlanta's chief asset has always been the accessibility of its location. From its earliest days, it was an important freight center, and it is still a major distribution center for trains, trucks, and planes. The city has long been called the "Crossroads of the South" because three interstates (I–85, I–75, and I–20) converge near downtown and because Atlanta's Hartsfield Airport has become the hub of the entire Southeast. There is an old local saying that goes, "It makes little difference whether you wind up in heaven or hell; in either case, you still have to pass through Atlanta."

In short order, Atlanta boasted other important assets. It became a banking center, and Peachtree Street is often tagged the "Wall Street of the South." In recent years, the city moved into the global arena with the opening of foreign banks and consulates and trade offices. Direct flights to Europe, South America, and Asia have stimulated new international business.

No mention of Atlanta would be complete without talking about its reputation as a "city too busy to hate." For the past three decades, Atlanta has been linked to the civil rights movement. It was Ralph McGill, the crusading editor of the *Constitution*, who guided the city through the civil rights struggle with unfaltering pragmatism. He insisted that folks simply do what needed to be done because it was right. In the 1960s, Atlanta quietly integrated its school system. The fact that peaceful desegregation and a soaring economy seemed to go hand in glove was not lost on anyone. Yet McGill was still a controversial figure during this critical period. It was often said that 50% of the local citizenry could not eat breakfast before reading Ralph McGill's daily column and that the other half couldn't eat after reading his column!

Among the accomplishments of Atlanta's black community was the Nobel Peace Prize that Martin Luther King, Jr., won in 1964. In 1972, Andrew Young was reelected the first black congressman from the South since Reconstruction. After serving

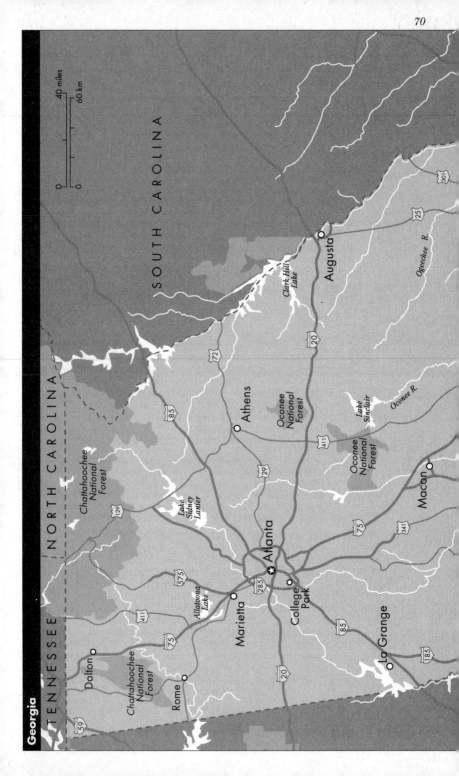

Georgia

TENNESSEE

NORTH CAROLINA

SOUTH CAROLINA

Dalton

Chattahoochee
National
Forest

Rome

59

411

75

575

Chattahoochee
National
Forest

129

Lake Sidney Lanier

Allatoona
Lake

Marietta

285

Atlanta

College
Park

85

La Grange

185

20

75

341

Macon

85

29

411

Oconee
National
Forest

Athens

72

85

Oconee
National
Forest

Lake
Sinclair

Oconee R.

20

Clark Hill
Lake

Augusta

25

301

Ogeechee R.

40 miles
60 km

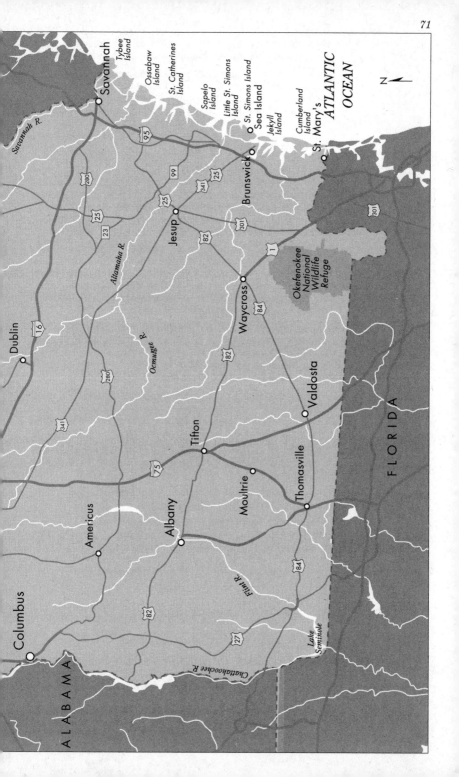

as Ambassador to the United Nations during President Jimmy Carter's administration, Young was elected mayor of Atlanta.

In recent years, Atlanta has been ranked among the best places in the country to live. Some would attribute these high ratings to the area's pleasant year-round climate; but others insist that Atlanta just has the right mix of people who have worked together to build a pleasant community.

Arriving and Departing

By Plane Hartsfield International Airport, off I–85 and I–285, 13 miles south of downtown, is one of the world's busiest jet complexes. Airlines servicing it include **Aeromexico, Air Jamaica, American, Bahamasair, British Airways, Cayman Islands Airways, Continental, Delta, Eastern, Japan Airlines, KLM, Lufthansa, Northwest, Sabena, Swissair, TWA, United,** and **USAir.**

Between the Airport and Center City **Atlanta Airport shuttle vans** (tel. 404/766–5312) operate every half hour between 6 AM and 11:30 PM. The trip ($7 one way) takes about 20 minutes and stops at major hotels. Vans also go to Emory University and Lenox Square ($10 one way). **Northside Airport Express buses** (tel. 404/455–1600) operate from 6 AM to midnight between the airport ($9.75–$15 one way).

If your luggage is light, you can also take **MARTA**'s (Metropolitan Atlanta Rapid Transit Authority, tel. 404/848–4711) high-speed trains between the airport and downtown and other locations. Trains operate 5:30 AM–1:30 AM. The trip downtown takes about 13 minutes and the fare is 85¢.

Taxi fare between the airport and downtown hotels is fixed at $13.50 for one person; $7 each for two people; $5 each for three people. Taxis aren't one of Atlanta's strong suits, so be certain your driver is familiar with your destination.

By Train **Amtrak**'s *Crescent* (tel. 800/USA–RAIL) operates daily to New Orleans, Washington DC, and New York from Atlanta's Brookwood Station (1688 Peachtree St.).

By Bus Hop a bus to Atlanta via **Greyhound/Trailways Bus Lines** (81 International Blvd., tel. 404/522–6300).

By Car Atlanta is the hub of four interstate highways: I–85, running northeast to southwest from the South Carolina to the Alabama border; I–75, north–south from Tennessee to Florida; I–20, east–west from South Carolina to Alabama; and I–285, the Perimeter Highway, circling the metropolitan area for 65 miles.

Getting Around

By Bus The **Metropolitan Atlanta Rapid Transit Authority (MARTA,** tel. 404/848–4711) operates a modern, efficient bus system. The fare is 85¢, and exact change is required.

By Subway MARTA's clean, luxurious rapid-rail subway trains link downtown with most major landmarks. The rail system's two lines connect at the **Five Points Station** downtown, where information on public transportation is available at the **Ride Store** (weekdays 7 AM–7 PM). Trains run 5 AM–1:30 AM, and parking (85¢ all day) can be found around most suburban stations. The fare is 85¢ one way, and exact change is required. Transfers, valid on buses or trains, are free.

By Taxi Taxis start at $1 and go up 20¢ for each 1/5 of a mile or 40 seconds of waiting time. Each additional person costs 50¢. When traveling in the Downtown, Convention Zone a flat rate of $3 for one person or $2 per person will be charged for any destination within the zone.

Guided Tours

Orientation Tours **Alpha-Omega Tours** (tel. 404/584–7712) is a small, local company offering customized tours of the city's historic landmarks and places of interest. Tours are in a 47-passenger motor coach. Guides are personable and knowledgeable.

Burton's Tours (tel. 404/525–3415), owned by the city's most famous soul-food chef, covers black historical landmarks like the Martin Luther King, Jr., National Historic District and the Atlanta University Center area. Tours are in motor coaches, with guides full of anecdotes about the city's past and present.

Special-Interest Tours **Atlanta Carriage Co.** (tel. 404/584–9960) gives 30-minute horse-drawn carriage tours through downtown Atlanta ($25 a couple). The congested streets may lack the romantic charm of Savannah and Charleston, but with a little moonlight, a little champagne, who knows?

Walking Tours **The Atlanta Preservation Center** (401 Flatiron Bldg., tel. 404/522–4345) offers a half-dozen walking tours of historic areas and other places of interest from April through October ($3 per person). The tour of the Fox Theatre, with backstage looks at the city's elaborate 1920s picture palace, is especially recommended.

Important Addresses and Numbers

Tourist Information To plan your trip write to the Department of Tourism (233 Peachtree St. NE, Suite 2000, Atlanta 30303). When you are in Atlanta, the Convention and Visitors Bureau has three visitor information centers stocked with maps and brochures: **Peachtree Center Mall** (233 Peachtree St. NE, tel. 404/521–6633), **Hartsfield International Airport** (Airport Welcome Center, tel. 404/767–3231), and **Lenox Square Mall** (3393 Peachtree Rd. NE, tel. 404/266–1398).

Emergencies Dial 911 for assistance. For hospital emergencies both **Grady Memorial Hospital** (80 Butler St., tel. 404/589–4307) and **Georgia Baptist Medical Center** (300 Boulevard NE tel. 404/653–4000) have 24-hour emergency room service.

Pharmacy **Treasury Drug** (1061 Ponce de Leon Ave. NE, tel. 404/876–0381).

Exploring Atlanta

Orientation Atlanta's beltway is most often called "the Perimeter," but it's also known as "The Big O around the Big A," or simply I–285. The interstate's completion in 1969 reaffirmed the city's relentless development to the north. In fact, so many office parks, shopping centers, and multifamily housing developments have cropped up along the northern arc of I–285, that the name of one typical project, "Perimeter Center," may no longer just be an oxymoron. In the southern arc is the massive Atlanta Hartsfield International Airport.

Most of metro Atlanta is located within Fulton and DeKalb counties, but the southern part of the city is in Clayton County. Cobb and Gwinnett counties are in the burgeoning northern sector.

Some visitors are confused by Atlanta's lack of a strict grid system of streets or by its confluence of streets into five-point intersections. One generous explanation is that Atlanta's streets were originally cow paths and Indian trails, which were paved, renamed, and given lights; others blame topography and the meandering Chattahoochee River.

Atlanta is a city shaped like a cursive capital *I*. At the bottom is the downtown area, and at the top is the Lenox Square-Phipps Plaza area. Along the shank of the *I* runs the city's main thoroughfare, the famed Peachtree Street. Actually, Peachtree Street runs only about three miles north from downtown, then changes its name, without notice, to Peachtree Road. Past the Lenox Square area, the grand avenue becomes Peachtree Industrial Boulevard, a name that befits its environment. (Newcomers to the city should be forewarned that there are some three dozen arteries with "Peachtree" in their names, so one must be wary of pretenders.)

Seven distinct sections of the city are plotted along Atlanta's "big I": downtown, midtown, Ansley Park, Brookwood Hills, Peachtree Hills, Garden Hills, Buckhead, and Peachtree Park, which includes the Lenox area.

Numbers in the margin correspond with points of interest on the Downtown Atlanta and Atlanta Vicinity maps.

Downtown   The ideal way to get acquainted with Atlanta is to begin with its past. Atlanta is not a historic city like Savannah or Boston, yet its history can be traced to the mid-19th century. A good way to start is with a saunter through **Oakland Cemetery.** Buried here are many of Georgia's notable politicians and businessmen. There is also a Jewish section and a section for Confederate soldiers. Margaret Mitchell, author of *Gone With the Wind* and a favorite daughter of the city, and golfer Bobby Jones are interred here. *248 Oakland Ave., tel. 404/577–8163. Free tours on weekends. Open daily sunrise–sunset.*

Continue to the Martin Luther King, Jr., National Historic District on Auburn Avenue, a couple of blocks north on Boulevard. Dr. King's white marble tomb with its eternal flame is located next to the **Ebenezer Baptist Church** (407 Auburn Ave.). For three genera-tions the King family preached here. During the civil rights struggle in the 1960s, and after Dr. King was awarded the Nobel Peace Prize in 1964, Ebenezer Baptist was recognized as the spiritual center of the movement. After King's assassination in 1968, his widow, Coretta Scott King, established the adjoining **Center for Nonviolent Social Change.** It contains a museum with King memorabilia, a library and a souvenir gift shop, and frequently sponsors educational programs for the community. *449 Auburn Ave., tel. 404/ 524–1956. Admission free. Open weekdays 9–5:30, weekends 10–5:30.*

A few doors up the street is **Dr. King's birthplace** (501 Auburn Ave.). The home, a Victorian structure in the Queen Anne style, is managed by the National Park Service and is open to the public daily.

⑤ **Auburn Avenue** is the heart of the black community's business district. The landmark **Atlanta Life Insurance Company,** founded by Alonzo Herndon, was located in modest quarters at 148 Auburn Avenue until the new modern complex was opened in 1980 at no. 100.

⑥ At 145 Auburn Avenue is the **Atlanta Daily World** building, home of one the nation's oldest black newspapers. The church with the "Jesus Saves" sign on its steeple is the Big Bethel African Methodist Episcopal Church. Nearby is the **Royal Peacock Night Club,** a hot spot for black entertainers.

For a history of Auburn Avenue, stop in at the **African American Panoramic Experience** to see the permanent exhibit, as well as their other collections and displays. *135 Auburn Ave., tel. 404/521–2654. Admission: $2 adults, $1 children. Open Mon.–Tues., Thurs.–Fri. 10–5; Wed. 10–6; Sat. 10–4; Sun. noon–4.*

⑦ If you're interested in a free, guided walking tour of the so-called Sweet Auburn neighborhood, you can arrange one at the **National Park Service Rangers Station** (440 Auburn Ave., tel. 404/331–3919) located across from the King Center.

⑧ Closer to town, on Edgewood Avenue, is the **Municipal Market,** a thriving produce market where you can buy every part of the pig but the oink. At 125 Edgewood Avenue is the site of the first bottling plant for the Coca-Cola Company; today the site is oc- **⑨** cupied by the **Baptist Student Center** for the adjoining campus of **Georgia State University.** Mosey through the urban GSU **⑩** campus toward the gold dome of the **Georgia State Capitol building** (206 Washington St.). If you read the state historical markers on the grounds, you'll realize that Atlanta has been virtually rebuilt since General Sherman's urban renewal program more than a century ago. The dome of the capitol is covered with gold leaf, originally mined from Dahlonega, in north Georgia. In addition to housing politicos, it also contains a Georgia history museum, which is open to the public. *Georgia State Capitol, tel. 404/656–2844. Free guided tours of the legislative chambers and museums are given weekdays at 10 and 11 AM and 1 and 2 PM.*

⑪ Behind the capitol is the **Fulton County Stadium,** where the Atlanta Braves and Falcons play. Across the street from the **⑫** capitol is Atlanta's **City Hall** (68 Mitchell St.). When this 14-story neo-Gothic structure with its lavish marble interior was first built in 1926, wags dubbed it "The Painted Lady of Mitchell Street."

⑬ Up Central Avenue to Upper Alabama Street is an entrance to the city's newest attraction, **Underground Atlanta** (tel. 404/522–1793). This reincarnated six-block entertainment-shopping district, opened in June 1989, now accommodates some 100 specialty retail shops, 20 food-court vendors and 22 restaurants and nightclubs on two levels. The entertainment area, Kenny's Alley, hopes to be a sophisticated version of New Orleans's Bourbon Street, with bars and night spots offering comedy acts, a variety of music (Dixieland, country, pop, folk, jazz) and dancing. Don't miss the ship decor at Dante's Down the Hatch on Lower Alabama Street.

The center of the $142-million joint venture between the city and The Rouse Co. will be the Peachtree Fountains Plaza, with

Downtown Atlanta

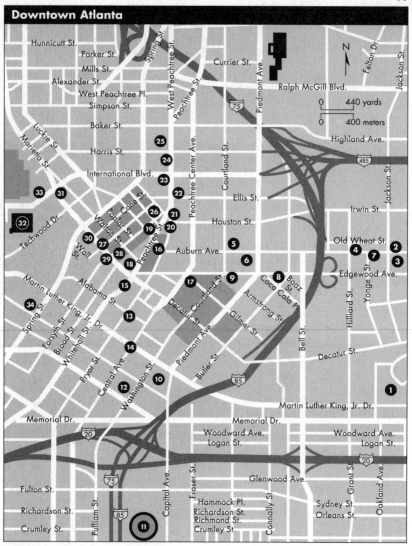

Atlanta Daily World, **6**
Atlanta-Fulton County Public Library, **26**
Atlanta Historical Society, **46**
Atlanta Life Insurance Company, **5**
Atlanta Newspapers Inc., **30**

Bank South Building, **27**
Baptist Student Center, **9**
Buckhead, **43**
Candler Building, **20**
Capital City Club, **25**
"Castle", The, **37**
Center for Nonviolent Social Change, **3**

Citizens and Southern National Bank, **28**
City Hall, **12**
CNN Center, **31**
Dr. King's birthplace, **4**
Ebenezer Baptist Church, **2**

Federal Reserve Bank, **30**
Five Points MARTA, **15**
Flatiron Building, **19**
Fox Theater, **35**
Fulton County Stadium, **11**
Georgia Governor's Mansion, **45**

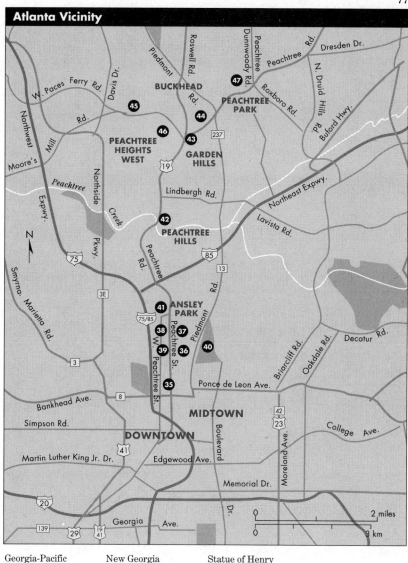

Atlanta Vicinity

Georgia-Pacific Building, **21**

Georgia State Capitol, **10**

Heath Gallery, **44**

High Museum of Art, **39**

Hurt building, **17**

IBM Tower, **36**

Municipal Market, **8**

National Park Service Rangers Station, **7**

New Georgia Railroad, **14**

Oakland Cemetery, **1**

Omni, **32**

Peachtree Battle Shopping Center, **42**

Peachtree Center, **24**

Phipps Plaza, **47**

Piedmont Park, **40**

Rhodes Hall, **41**

Richard B. Russell Federal building, **34**

Ritz-Carlton, **22**

Statue of Henry Grady, **29**

Underground Atlanta, **13**

Westin-Peachtree Plaza Hotel, **23**

William Oliver building, **18**

Woodruff Arts Center, **38**

Woodruff Park, **16**

World Congress Center, **33**

its distinctive 138-foot light tower. Across the street is an information center and on-site security unit. Two parking garages are on Martin Luther King, Jr. Drive. The new Underground is almost three times larger than the first renovation, which opened in 1969 and closed in 1980.

Two other special attractions will become part of Underground during 1990. A pavilion, called **The World of Coca-Cola** will display historical memorabilia from corporate archives and have interactive exhibits at a four-story, $10-million facility located across the Depot Plaza on Central Avenue. **Atlanta Heritage Row,** on Upper Alabama Street within Underground Atlanta, will feature a multimedia presentation in a 100-seat theatre. Six historical vignettes will tell the story of the city's past and present spirit.

⑭ At the Central Avenue entrance to the Underground Atlanta complex is the **New Georgia Railroad** (1 Martin Luther King, Jr., Dr., tel. 404/656–0769). The vintage locomotive and antique passenger coaches make an 18-mile loop around the city three Saturdays a month. One Saturday each month they travel to **Stone Mountain Park and Village,** a suburb that's grown up around the largest granite outcropping in the world, with a monumental Civil War sculpture carved on its side (*see* What to See and Do with Children, below). *Trips at 10 and 2. Loop fare is $10; Stone Mtn. $12.50. Both trips $5 children 3–12. Loop trips are nonstop and take about an hour.*

⑮ The **Five Points MARTA** station (Corner of Peachtree and Wall Sts., downtown) is the city's major crossroads, the one tied to the economic lifeblood of the city, with its surrounding bank towers and offices of high-powered law firms. This is pinstripes and power-lunch territory.

On the corner of Peachtree and Alabama streets, outside the station, notice the old-fashioned gas street light, with its historical marker proclaiming it as the **Eternal Flame of the Confederacy.**

⑯ At **Woodruff Park** (Corner of Peachtree St. and Park Pl.), named after the city's great philanthropist, Robert W. Woodruff, the late Coca-Cola magnate, you can see a virtual cross section of Atlanta life. During lunchtime on weekdays, the park is filled with executives and secretaries, street preachers, politicians, Georgia State University students, and an array of other characters. If you want to join in, pick up lunch at one of the franchises or Chinese eateries around the park and find an empty bench. For people-watching, the scene rarely gets better than this.

Not much of old Atlanta still exists downtown, although a few turn-of-the-century buildings remain. These elaborately decorated structures stand in sharp contrast to the severe ⑰ modernism of the skyscrapers of recent decades. **The Hurt Building** (45 Edgewood Ave.) features intricate architectural ⑱ details, grillwork, and an elaborate marble staircase. **The William Oliver Building** (32 Peachtree St.) is an Art Deco gem. Walk through its lobby and admire the ceiling mural, brass ⑲ grills, and elevator doors. **The Flatiron Building** (at the Peachtree and Broad Sts. triangle) dates from 1897 and is the city's oldest high rise. Perhaps the most prestigious address in the ⑳ legal profession is the **Candler Building** (127 Peachtree St.), which is notable for its decorative details, including marble friezes. Its elegant lobby reeks of Old Atlanta Money, Power, and Influence.

㉑ The towering **Georgia–Pacific Building** (133 Peachtree St.) occupies hallowed ground, the precise site of the old Loew's Grand Theatre, where *Gone With the Wind* premiered back in 1939. One of the architectural oddities about this red marble high rise is that from certain angles the building appears to be two-dimensional or flat against the sky. There's a small branch of the **High Museum of Art** *inside the building. Tel. 404/577–6940. Admission free. Open weekdays 11–5.*

㉒ On the adjacent corner is the downtown **Ritz-Carlton Hotel** (181 Peachtree St.), a stylish place for a cocktail or afternoon high tea.

Next to **Macy's** department store (180 Peachtree St.), is the
㉓ **Westin–Peachtree Plaza Hotel** (210 Peachtree St.), at 73 stories the world's tallest hotel. Designed by Atlanta architect John Portman, the round tower with its trademark exterior elevator features a postmodern interior and a revolving bar/restaurant offering the best panoramic view of the city and the surrounding countryside.

㉔ In the next block, on both sides of the street, is **Peachtree Center**, a city within the city, also designed by John Portman. This complex of buildings, with its connecting skywalks, includes the massive **Merchandise Mart**; the twin office towers of Peachtree Center, with an underground arcade and plaza; **the Apparel Mart;** and the **Hyatt Regency Hotel.** The Hyatt, with its bunkerlike exterior, low entrance, and soaring atrium, earned its place in history by being the first of its type back in 1967.

Within Peachtree Center, the **Atlanta International Museum of Art and Design** shows crafts from around the globe. *245 Peachtree Center Ave., tel. 404/876–3600. Admission free. Open Mon.–Sat. 11–6.*

㉕ The **Capital City Club** (7 Harris St.), is another haunt of the city's power brokers. Its modest size makes it a holdout in the neighborhood, which attests to its clout.

㉖ Back down at the Georgia-Pacific intersection, pause at **Margaret Mitchell Park,** with its cascading waterfall and stately columned sculpture. Across the street, heading south, is the **Atlanta-Fulton County Public Library** (126 Carnegie Way), which houses a large collection of *Gone With the Wind* memorabilia.

Head down Forsyth Street five blocks, to Marietta Street. Notice the renovated **Healy Building** (57 Forsyth St.), an early skyscraper in Commercial style with Tudor decoration.
㉗ Through the lobby is a pretty rotunda. The **Bank South Building** (55 Marietta St.) was briefly Atlanta's tallest building, from 1955 until 1964, when it was superseded by the National
㉘ Bank of Georgia Building. Around the corner is the **Citizens and Southern National Bank** (35 Broad St.), embellished with an exquisite marble floor and bronze banking tables.

㉙ At the corner of Marietta and Forsyth streets is a bronze **statue of Henry Grady,** the post–Civil War editor of *The Atlanta Constitution* and early champion of the so-called "New South." Farther down Marietta Street are the offices of the **Atlanta**
㉚ **Newspapers Inc.** Next door is the **Federal Reserve Bank** (104

Marietta St.). Tours of its monetary museum can be arranged (tel. 404/521–8500).

Two blocks away, at the corner of Marietta Street and
③ Techwood Drive, is the **CNN Center** (1 CNN Center, 100 International Blvd.), the home of media mogul Ted Turner's Cable News Network. If you want to gawk at the high-tech world of "tee-vee" land and get a behind-the-scenes look at newscasters in action, take a 45-minute tour. The tour begins with a ride up the world's longest escalator to an eighth floor exhibit on Turner's global broadcasting empire. The film version of *Gone With the Wind*, which Turner now owns, plays continuously at the **CNN Cinemas** (tel. 404/577–6928). *Tel. 404/827–2400. Tours: $4 adults, $2 senior citizens and children 5–12. Open weekdays 10–5, weekends 10–4.*

③ Behind the CNN Center is the **Omni** (100 Techwood Dr.), where the Atlanta Hawks play and other special events such as
③ rock concerts are staged. The **World Congress Center** (285 International Blvd.), where Jimmy Carter held his rally the night he was elected president, and where the Democratic National Convention was held during the summer of 1988, is also nearby.
③ A short distance away is the **Richard B. Russell Federal Building** (Spring St. between Mitchell and Martin Luther King, Jr. Dr.), where former President Carter has an office. Its lobby has a tile mosaic that is worth seeing.

Midtown A couple of miles north, up Peachtree Street, is midtown. The
③ **Fox Theatre** (660 Peachtree St., tel. 404/881–1977) is a classic movie palace, built in the 1920s in Moorish-Egyption style.

Time Out If you want authentic Southern home-style cooking, don't miss **Mary Mac's Tea Room** (tel. 404/875–4337), just a few blocks from the Fox. Owner Margaret Lupo serves tasty plate lunches with cornbread. *224 Ponce de Leon Ave., tel. 404/875–4337. No credit cards accepted. Inexpensive.*

Peachtree Street at 10th Street used to be the heart of the hippie scene in Atlanta during the early 1970s. New construction has leveled vast areas of this district, but its residential blocks still include large 1920s bungalows and mansions converted into multiunit apartments. Gentrification has brought the Yuppie crowd into the area, so trendy and ethnic eateries and bars have followed.

Down 14th Street is Atlanta's newest, tallest, and most elegant
③ skyscraper, the **IBM Tower** (1201 W. Peachtree St.). This postmodern high rise, which is visible from many parts of the city, was designed with a Gothic motif by Philip Johnson.

On 15th Street, across from the Woodruff Arts Center, is an
③ imposing old stone home known as **The Castle** (87 15th St.), which preservationists are struggling to hold on to.

③ The **Woodruff Arts Center** (1280 Peachtree St.) is home to the renowned **Atlanta Symphony** and the **Alliance Theatre,** which has more subscribers than does any other regional theater in the country. The Alliance has two venues: a main stage, where mainstream works are produced for general audiences, and a studio downstairs, which does offbeat productions for a more broad-minded public.

39 Next door is the white-enamel **High Museum of Art,** a high-tech showplace whose permanent collection is strong on the decorative arts and African folk arts. *1280 Peachtree St., tel. 404/892–4444. Admission: $2 adults, $1 students and senior citizens; free on Thurs. Special exhibits often have an additional charge. Open Tues. 10–5, Wed. 10–9, Thurs.–Sat. 10–5, Sun. noon–5.*

40 A few blocks off Peachtree Street is **Piedmont Park,** the outdoor recreation center of the city. Here you'll find tennis courts, a swimming pool, and paths for biking, hiking, and jogging.

The Botanical Garden, located on 30 acres inside the park, has five acres of formal gardens, a 15-acre hardwood forest with walking trails, a serene Japanese garden and a new conservatory, which features unusual, flamboyant and threatened flora from both tropical and desert climates. Don't overlook the whimsical dragon topiary at the entrance. *Tel. 404/876–5858. Admission: $4.50 adults, $2.25 children and senior citizens, free on Thurs. afternoons. Open Tues.–Sat. 9–6, Sun. noon–6.*

41 North on Peachtree Street is **Rhodes Hall,** headquarters of the **Georgia Trust for Historic Preservation.** A permanent exhibit focuses on Atlanta architecture of earlier eras. *1516 Peachtree St., tel. 404/881–9980. Admission $2.50. Open weekdays 11–4.*

In the Brookwood Hills area, across I–85, Peachtree Street becomes **Peachtree Road,** and turns into a strip of popular dining places. You'll also note that flowering peach trees once again thrive along various stretches of the road.

42 The **Peachtree Battle Shopping Center,** on your right, has Atlanta's largest bookstore, **Oxford Books** (2345 Peachtree Rd., tel. 404/262–3333).

Buckhead Past Peachtree Hills and Garden Hills is **Buckhead,** the heart of
43 affluent and trendy Atlanta. Many of Atlanta's finest restaurants and most popular watering spots are in this area. The
44 city's major art galleries are here, too. Start at **Heath Gallery** (416 E. Paces Ferry Rd.) and pick up a guidebook for the location of other galleries.

45 A short drive out West Paces Ferry Road will bring you to the **Georgia Governor's Mansion.** Built some 20 years ago, in Greek Revival style, the house features Federal-period antiques in its public rooms. *391 W. Paces Ferry Rd., tel. 404/261–1776. Open for free guided tours Tues.–Thurs. 10–11:30 AM.*

46 In the same area is the **Atlanta Historical Society.** Of interest on the 26-acre site are the **Swan House,** an Italianate villa filled with European furnishings and art; the **Tullie Smith Plantation,** an 1830s farm house; and **McElreath Hall,** an exhibition space for artifacts from Atlanta's history. *3101 Andrews Dr., tel. 404/261–1837. All inclusive admission: $4.50 adults, $4 senior citizens, and $2 children. Open Mon.–Sat. 9–5:30, Sun. noon–5.*

If you want to gaze at the lovely lawns, gardens, and mansions of Atlanta's well-to-do, drive around in this area, especially along Tuxedo, Blackland, and Habersham roads. Follow the green-and-white "Scenic Drive" signs past an impressive array of Greek Revival, Spanish, Italianate, English Tudor, and French château showplaces.

At the intersection of Peachtree Street and Lenox Road is **Phipps Plaza,** which includes such fashionable shops as Lord & Taylor, Saks Fifth Avenue, Abercrombie & Fitch, Gucci, and Tiffany. On the other corner is the **Ritz-Carlton Buckhead,** which features Atlanta's only five-star restaurant, **The Dining Room** (*see* Dining). If you intend to splurge, this is the place.

Atlanta for Free

Alonzo F. Herndon Home. Founder of the Atlanta Life Insurance Co., the nation's second-largest black-owned insurance company, Alonzo Herndon built this 15-room mansion in 1910. A museum contains furnishings, artwork, photographs, memorabilia. *587 University Pl., tel. 404/581–9813. Open Tues.–Sat. 10–4.*

Concerts. On summer Sunday evenings, the **Atlanta Symphony Orchestra** performs free concerts for thousands of patrons who spread blankets and picnic suppers on the former golf course at Piedmont Park (Piedmont Ave. between 10th and 14th Sts.).

Emory University Museum of Art and Archeology. The pristine interior of this Beaux Arts building on the Emory campus was designed by architect Michael Graves. Exhibits range from an Egyptian mummy to contemporary art. *Emory University, Kilgo Cir., tel. 404/727–7522. Open Tues.–Sat. 10–4:30, Sun. noon–5.*

Telephone Museum. The advances of the telephone over the last century are chronicled in 10 exhibit areas. *Southern Bell Center, Plaza Level, 675 W. Peachtree St. NE, tel. 404/529–7334. Open weekdays 11–1.*

Georgia Governor's Mansion (*see* Exploring).

What to See and Do with Children

The "Weekend" tabloid section of Saturday's *Atlanta Journal–Constitution* has a listing called "Kids," which highlights special happenings around the city for young people.

Fernbank Science Center. The large planetarium here is the only one in the nation owned by a public school system. The museum exhibits focus on geology. A forest behind the center is a treasure itself. *Admission: $2 adults, $1 children. 156 Heaton Park Dr. NE, tel. 404/378–4311. Open Tues.–Fri. 8:30–10, Mon. 8:30–5, Sat. 10–5, and Sun. 1–5.*

Center for Puppetry Arts Museum. The large display of puppets from all over the world is designed to teach visitors about the craft. *1404 Spring St., tel. 404/873–3391. Admission: $2. Open Mon.–Sat. 9–4.*

SciTrek. A new science and technology museum has some 100 hands-on exhibits in four halls—Simple Machines; Light, Color, and Perception; Electricity and Magnetism; and Kidspace, for 2–7 year-olds. *395 Piedmont Ave. NE, tel. 404/522–5500. Admission: $5 adults, $3 children, under 3 free. Open Tues.–Sun. 10–5.*

Six Flags Over Georgia is Atlanta's major theme park, with over 100 rides, musical revues, performing tropical birds and dolphins; and concerts by top-name artists. *I–20W at Six Flags Dr., tel. 404/948–9290. Admission: (all-inclusive one-day* *pass) $18.20 adults, $11.20 children 42" tall and seniors 55 and older; $3 parking fee. Opens 10 AM daily in summer and weekends year round; closing times vary. Take MARTA's West Line to Hightower Station and connect with the Six Flags bus (No. 201).*

Stone Mountain Park is the largest granite outcropping on earth. The Confederate Memorial on the north face of the 825-foot-high, five-mile-around monolith is the world's largest sculpture. A 3,200-acre park includes a skylift to the mountaintop, a steam locomotive train ride around the base, an antebellum plantation, an ice skating rink, golf course, swimming beach, campground, paddlewheel steamboat, and Civil War museum. *U.S. 78, Stone Mountain Freeway, tel. 404/498-5600. Admission: $4 per car, additional fees for attractions. Open daily 6 AM–midnight.*

Zoo Atlanta has made a spectacular recovery from a rash of bad publicity (poor management and treatment of animals) a few years ago. An ongoing $35-million renovation program has already resulted in a new Birds of Prey Amphitheater, Flamingo Lagoon, and African Rain Forest. *Grant Park, 800 Cherokee Ave., tel. 404/622-7627. Admission: $3 adults, $2 children 4–11. Open weekdays 10–5, weekends 10–6.*

Off the Beaten Track

Deacon Burton's Grill. The holy grail of Atlanta soul food, this is the place to savor the authentic flavors of glorious Southern fried chicken, chitlins, fried fish, barbecue, turnip greens, cornbread, and cobblers. The chef and maitre d' is "Deacon" Lyndell Burton, an ageless wizard of the iron frying pan. *1029 Edgewood Ave. (across from Inman Park MARTA Station), tel. 404/525-3415. As the sign over the register says, The Credit Manager Is Out, Please Pay Cash. Inexpensive.*

Carter Presidential Center. The museum and archives focus on Jimmy Carter's political career. But it sponsors other activities as well—projects on world food issues, children, foreign affairs conferences. Its Japanese garden is also a serene spot to unwind. *One Copenhill Ave. NE, tel. 404/331-3942. Admission: $2.50 adults, $1.50 senior citizens, children under 16 free. Open Mon.–Sat. 9–4:45, Sun. noon–4:45. Cafeteria open 11–4.*

Shopping

Atlanta's department stores, specialty shops, and flea markets are magnets for shoppers from across the Southeast. Most stores are open Monday–Saturday 10 AM–9:30 PM, and Sunday noon–6 PM. Many downtown stores close on Sunday. Sales tax is 6% in the city of Atlanta and Fulton County and varies in suburban counties.

Shopping Districts The downtown shopping area is anchored on the south by **Rich's Department Store** (45 Broad St., tel. 404/586-4636) and on the north by **Macy's** (180 Peachtree St., tel. 404/221-7221). Both carry top-name apparel and merchandise, but the fashion-conscious prefer Macy's. Smaller stores include **Brooks Brothers** (134 Peachtree St., tel. 404/577-4040) and **Muse's** (52 Peachtree St., tel. 404/522-5400), the latter a long-established local favorite for conservative men's and women's clothing.

At the intersection of Peachtree and Lenox roads, eight miles north of downtown, is Atlanta's high-fashion shopping district. **Lenox Square Mall** has branches of **Neiman Marcus, Macy's, Rich's,** and 300 other specialty stores and restaurants. **Phipps Plaza** houses branches of **Saks Fifth Avenue, Lord & Taylor, Gucci,** and **Tiffany.**

Specialty Shops There's a large cluster of antiques shops and flea markets
Antiques around the intersection of Peachtree and Broad streets in north suburban Chamblee (not to be confused with the Peachtree/ Broad streets junction in downtown Atlanta). The many stores include **Broad Street Antique Mall** (3550 Broad St., tel. 404/ 458–6316) and **Whipporwill Co.** (3519 Broad St., tel. 404/455– 8357).

If "junking" is your pleasure, you'll reach nirvana in the area around the intersection of Moreland and Euclid avenues, which is loaded with vintage clothing stores, used record and book shops, and some stores that defy description.

Books Atlanta's largest selection of books and newspapers is at **Oxford Book Store** (Peachtree Battle Shopping Center, 2345 Peachtree Rd., tel. 404/262–3332) and **McGuire's Bookshop** (1055 Ponce de Leon Ave., tel. 404/875–7323). Books are not the only inducement to visit the Oxford Bookstore; along the store's narrow balcony is a coffee shop wonderfully named **The Cup and Chaucer.**

Food **DeKalb Farmers Market** (3000 E. Ponce de Leon Ave., Decatur, tel. 404/377–6400) has 106,000 square feet of exotic fruits, cheeses, seafood, sausages, breads, and delicacies from around the world. Closed Monday.

Participant Sports

Bicycling **Piedmont Park** (Piedmont Ave. between 10th and 14th Sts.) is closed to traffic and popular for biking. **Skate Escape** (across from the park at 1086 Piedmont Ave., tel. 404/892–1292) has rental bikes and skates. The **Southern Bicycle League** (tel. 404/ 294–1594) has regularly scheduled tours.

Golf The best public courses are **Stone Mountain Park** (U.S. 78, 16 mi east of downtown, tel. 404/498–5600), **Chastain Park** (216 W. Wieuca Rd., tel. 404/255–0723), and **Sugar Creek** (2706 Bouldercrest Rd., tel. 404/241–7671). Carts and rental clubs are available at all three.

Health Clubs Health clubs open to the public include **Midtown Gym** (1107 Peachtree St., tel. 404/892–0287) and branches of the **YMCA** (tel. 404/588–9622). Hotels with health clubs open to guests include the **Westin Peachtree Plaza** and the **Atlanta Marriott Marquis** (*see* Lodging).

Jogging Joggers quickly learn that this is a very hilly city, shaded by many trees. **Piedmont Park** is a traffic-free place perfect for running. Contact the **Atlanta Track Club** (3097 Shadowlawn Ave., tel. 404/231–9064) for other running zones.

Swimming **Piedmont Park** (tel. 404/892–0117) has the city's largest public pool. **White Water Park** (250 North Cobb Pkwy. (U.S. 41), Marietta, tel. 404/424–9283) has a huge wave pool, several water slides, picnic areas, lockers, and showers.

Tennis **Bitsy Grant Tennis Center** (2125 Northside Dr., tel. 404/351–2774) is the area's best public facility. **Piedmont Park** (tel. 404/872–1507) has clay courts only (no locker facilities).

Spectator Sports

Much of Atlanta's reputation as a big-league city must be credited to Hank Aaron, who not only broke Babe Ruth's long-standing home run record but did it in Atlanta playing for the Braves. The National League's **Atlanta Braves** play home games at Atlanta–Fulton County Stadium (521 Capitol Ave., tel. 404/577–9100). The National Basketball Association's **Atlanta Hawks** play home games at the Omni Coliseum (100 Techwood Dr., tel. 404/681–3605). The National Football League's **Atlanta Falcons** play home games at Atlanta–Fulton County Stadium (521 Capitol Ave., tel. 404/261–5400).

Dining

by Christine Lauterbach

Atlanta offers a full range of eating options worthy of its new image as a dynamic international city. From a million–dollar diner to a humble meat–and–three, one can find almost anything in the capital of the New South: prestigious kitchens run by Michelin chefs, fashionable bistros in reclaimed neighborhoods, a multitude of ethnic restaurants, and more fried chicken outlets than anywhere else in the country. But despite the best efforts of the convention and hospitality industry, the Old South is conspicuously absent.

The dining public is value oriented and prices are still low in Atlanta. A full plate means a lot to the average consumer and it is the rare restaurant that does not meet this expectation. The local taste for things sweet and fried cannot be discounted. Try to catch the flavor of the South at breakfast and lunch in modest establishments and to reserve your evenings for more ambitious culinary exploration.

The most highly recommended restaurants in each price category are indicated by a star ★.

Category	Cost*
Very Expensive	over $45
Expensive	$35–$45
Moderate	$25–$35
Inexpensive	under $15

*per person without tax (6%), service, or drinks

Downtown
Very expensive
★

City Grill. This posh but breezy new restaurant has made the most of its grand location in the recently renovated historic Hurt building. The bustle of success greets you at the door while bucolic murals and stunning high ceilings help create a feeling of glamour. The menu is traditional American: steaks, chops, and grilled fish. There are a few weaknesses, but you can't go wrong with the splendid lamb chops, the fresh salmon or any of the delicious vegetable specialties such as cauliflower soufflé. Club-style service is by a well-trained staff. *55 Hurt Plaza, tel. 404/524–2489. Valet parking. Jacket recommended.*

Dining
City Grill, **8**
Dailey's, **9**
Delectables, **5**
Mick's, **11**
Nikolai's Roof, **13**
Savannah Fish
Company, **4**
The Abbey, **14**
Thelma's, **2**

Lodging
Atlanta Hilton &
Towers, **13**
Atlanta Marriott
Marquis, **10**
Barclay, **3**
Colony Square, **12**
Hyatt Regency, **6**
Omni, **1**
Ritz-Carlton, **7**
Westin Peachtree
Plaza, **4**

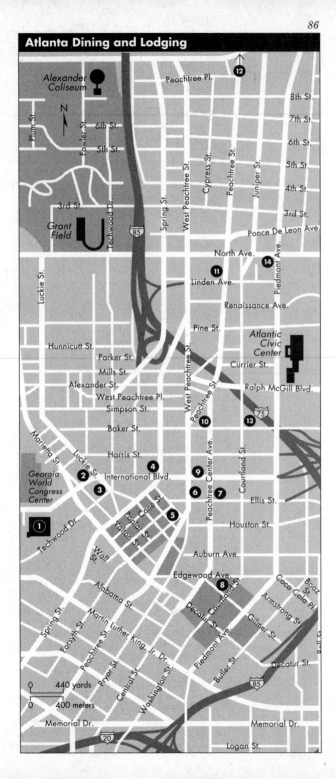

Atlanta Dining and Lodging

Reservations required, weeks ahead for weekend dining. AE, CB, DC, MC, V. No lunch weekends.

Nikolai's Roof. Once Atlanta's best restaurant, it has been living on its reputation ever since. Rounds of flavored vodka, cossacks rattling off a verbal menu, and complicated dishes under silver cloches make for an impressive show in this Russian-inspired restaurant. Piroshki and borscht (both excellent) are followed by fancy Continental preparations, especially game. The menu changes monthly but you'll find reliable dessert soufflés. *Top of the Atlanta Hilton, 255 Courtland St. tel. 404/659-2000. Jacket and tie requested. Reservations must be made 2 to 3 weeks in advance for a weeknight, 2 to 3 months on weekends. AE, CB, DC, MC, V. Dinner only (two formal seatings 6:30 and 9:30).*

Expensive **Savannah Fish Company.** Have a drink in the revolving lounge at the top of the hotel, but come down to the ground floor for a smashingly good and simple meal of fresh fish, grilled or sautéed without ado. Entrees are served with a bamboo steamer of fresh vegetables. Ignore overpriced appetizers and enjoy the house's saffron and fennel flavored fish stew. Pass up generic cakes for the simple Savannah fried puffs sprinkled with sugar and served with three sauces. There's a hint of Asian simplicity in the pared-down decor. *Westin Peachtree Plaza, Peachtree St. at International Blvd., tel. 404/589-7456. Jacket optional. Reservations accepted for lunch only. AE, CB, DC, MC, V.*

Moderate **Dailey's.** There's always something going on at the bar and in the two dining rooms of this enormous converted warehouse. Downstairs is casual fun. Upstairs there's spectacular decor (merry-go-round horses, enormous shop lamps, both in perfect scale with the imposing space) and more serious dining: veal with Pommery mustard, amberjack au poivre, crisp duck, generous salad, and fried rolls). The menu is recited, the service flashy. Revved-up versions of pastry classics are paraded before the adoring eyes of the crowd on an astounding dessert bar. *17 International Blvd., tel. 404/681-3303. Dress: casual. No reservations; expect a wait. AE, CB, DC, MC, V. No lunch weekends.*

Inexpensive **Delectables.** One of downtown's best kept secrets, don't let the
★ location (inside the Central Public Library) or the format (cafeteria) deter you. This is a very sophisticated little operation serving ravishing salads, wholesome soups, yummy cookies, and freshly baked cakes. Sandwiches are fair. You can enjoy your meal immersed in jazz music and sunshine, on the patio. *Public Library, corner of Margaret Mitchell Sq. and Carnegie Way (enter through Carnegie Way), tel. 404/681-2909. Dress: casual. No reservations. No credit cards. Lunch and coffee break only. Weekdays only.*

Harold's Barbecue. It's a short distance from downtown, but worth the ride. Legislators, political groupies, and small fry from the Capitol sit side by side, wolfing down delicious chopped pork sandwiches, huge platters of freshly sliced meat, and overflowing bowls of Brunswick stew. Don't miss the crackling bread. The knotty pine, tacky art, and management haven't changed in 25 years. *171 McDonough Blvd. near the Federal Penitentiary, tel. 404/627-9268. Dress: casual. No reservations. No credit cards. Closed Sun.*

Thelma's. Honest-to-goodness soul food is served in a squat cinder block building with a cafeteria counter and cramped dining room. Go early at lunchtime to beat the crowds lining up for baked chicken, okra cakes, twice-cooked potatoes, and some of the best flavored greens around town at this cheerful family-run eatery. *190 Luckie St., tel. 404/688–5855. Dress: casual. No reservations. No credit cards. Breakfast and lunch only. Closed weekends.*

The Varsity. Part of Atlanta's collective past, people from all walks of life are likely to run into this enormous, sprawling diner to get one of the famous chili dogs, a glorified hamburger, or a gigantic order of fresh and delicious—but greasy—onion rings. Line up behind the locals and pay close attention to the lingo: "One naked dog, walking and a bag o' rags," will get you a plain hot dog and some french fries. Connoisseurs drink orange frosties. Folks in a hurry get curb service. *61 North Ave., tel. 404/881–1706. Dress: casual. No reservations. No credit cards. Open late.*

Midtown   **The Abbey.** Dining in a church, attended by mock–friars, and
Very Expensive   listening to a harpist plucking away above the altar could be the ultimate in tourist tacky, but it isn't, somehow. The church is a pleasant old building, the chef is young and ambitious, and the wine list is exceptional down to its many selections by the glass or half-bottle. Warm goat cheese salad, poached oysters with pepper confetti, and grilled grouper with zucchini pasta show that high volume and fine food are not mutually exclusive. Ponderous service, however, can drag the meal beyond reason. *163 Ponce de Leon Ave., tel. 404/876–8831. Jacket and tie recommended. Reservations recommended. AE, CB, DC, MC, V. Dinner only.*

Moderate–Expensive   **Chefs' Café.** Living in a symbiotic relationship with the bud-
   ★   get lounge in which it is located, this casual San Francisco-style bistro has taught Atlanta to enjoy fashionable food without high-pressure trappings. The menu changes with the seasons but grilled fish, fresh pasta, and creative garnishes can always be found. Grilled eggplant, warm Georgia goat cheese, crab cakes, and roasted lamb sandwich with cilantro mayonnaise are among the specialties. Lunch and Sunday brunch rank high for value. There's an excellent small wine list. *2115 Piedmont Rd. in La Quinta Inn, tel. 404/872–2284. Jacket optional. Reservations recommended. AE, MC, V. Closed Mon. lunch.*

   ★   **Indigo.** Sizzling and trendy, the creative coastal cuisine proves it can be taken seriously. The owner is a former fashion editor with a great eye for catchy details. Lime and cilantro flavor many of the dishes. Conch fritters, lamb turnovers, grilled oysters with chipotle peppers and tequila, and fish and fresh herbs in a twist of parchment are particularly recommended. Don't miss the refreshing Key lime pie or the sautéed bananas with run and lime. There's brown paper on the tables and gliders on the sidewalk. It's always crowded, but waiting for a table can become part of the fun. *1897 N. Highland Ave., tel. 404/876–0676. Dress: casual. No reservations. AE, MC, V. Dinner only. Closed Sun.*

   ★   **Partners.** Next door to Indigo, it is also owned by Alix Kenagy. Upbeat and noisy, the creative decor is an appropriate backdrop for an excellent light menu that includes freshly made ravioli with a different stuffing and sauce every day, Cajun mixed grill, Vietnamese chicken cakes, and nostalgic, old-fashioned desserts. An appealing small wine list is full of good values. *1399 N. Highland Ave., tel. 404/875–0202. Dress: casu-*

al. No reservations; expect a wait. AE, MC, V. Dinner only. Closed Sun.

Sierra Grill. Quite trendy, with sparse, witty Southwestern decor, the creative cuisine here involves much grilling and smoking. In-depth knowledge of chili peppers gives many of the dishes a zippy, joyous flavor. Smoked chicken quesadillas, stuffed trout in corn husks, and grilled vegetables are representative of the best options. *1529 Piedmont Rd., tel. 404/873–5630. Dress: informal. No reservations. AE, MC, V. Closed Sun., closed Sat. lunch.*

Inexpensive **Mick's.** Casual and hip, with a well-researched and implemented menu, this restaurant serves the kind of food America never stopped loving: yummy burgers, great chicken sandwiches, big cream pies. The menu also includes fresh pasta, grilled vegetable plates, and soda fountain specials. Great people-watching opportunities abound in a pertly renovated old drugstore. *557 Peachtree St., tel. 404/875–6425 (two other locations: 3393 Peachtree St., tel. 404/262–6425; 4505 Ashford-Dunwoody Rd., tel. 404/394–6425). Dress: casual. No reservations. AE, CB, DC, MC, V. Open late.*

Buckhead **Bone's.** In this brash, New York-style steakhouse, the rich and
Very Expensive powerful rub egos and compare lifestyles over steaks, chops, lobster, and potatoes baked in a crust of salt. Most patrons wear jackets, but if your idea of fun is spending big bucks in a sport shirt, they won't turn you down. *3130 Piedmont Rd., tel. 404/874–0904. Jacket and tie suggested. Reservations recommended. AE, CB, DC, MC, V. No lunch weekends.*

★ **The Dining Room, in The Ritz-Carlton Buckhead.** This is the best restaurant in town and among the country's ten greatest. Under Chef Guenter Seeger, haute cuisine is not flashy or ostentatious. Strictly limiting himself to the freshest regional products, Seeger doesn't like calling attention to the culinary process. The menu, handwritten every day, is likely to involve local sun-dried sweet potatoes (in ravioli), Vidalia onions (with lobster and lobster coral sauce), or persimmons (a mousse with muscadine sorbet and Georgia golden raspberries). Quivering creamy textures (especially fresh duck liver or any kind of seafood) are the result of the chef's own cooking magic. Don't ask for your food to be well-done. Surrender to this imperious genius and the exquisite, discreet service. *3434 Peachtree Rd., tel. 404/237–2700. Jacket and tie requested. Reservations required, several days ahead for weekend dining. AE, CB, DC, MC, V. Dinner only. Closed Sun.*

Hedgerose Heights Inn. Chef Heinz Schwab has equal amounts of talent and common sense. Born in Switzerland, trained in prestigious resort hotels, he now runs a beautiful restaurant in the classic European sense. Pirozki with an impeccable Béarnaise; minced veal in cream with roesti potatoes; and venison, buffalo, duck, and goose liver pâté rolled in minced truffles are some of the dishes he perfected when he headed the kitchen at Nikolai's Roof. His dessert soufflés are among the most luscious in town. Salt can be a problem in some of specialties. The service may be intimidating and the tables are very close together in the pretty, soft dining room. *490 E. Paces Ferry Rd., tel. 404/233–7673. Jacket required. Reservations required (two seatings). AE, CB, DC, MC, V. Dinner only. Closed Sun. and Mon.*

★ **103 West.** An ornate facade and porte cochère add to the proud image of Atlanta's poshest, most palatial restaurant. Antique tapestries, watered silks, and glorious details fill the dining rooms. The kitchen matches this lavish classicism. Here's the place to gorge on crab cakes with beurre blanc, sweet basil and red pepper rouille; or fresh veal sweetbreads with madeira sauce and fresh grapes on a bed of wilted spinach. Glamour dishes include smoked mountain trout with lump crab meat, venison with wild mushrooms and mustard fruit, and an amazing "Grand Dessert" sampler. *103 W. Paces Ferry Rd., tel. 404/ 233–5993. Jacket and tie required. Reservations required. AE, CB, DC, MC, V. Dinner only. Closed Sun.*

The Coach & Six. This has been one of Atlanta's most famous and most idiosyncratic restaurants for nearly three decades. No place can make you feel more like an outsider, yet no place provides a better opportunity to see the Atlanta that was, and still is, a mercantile boom-town. Marvelous New York-style rolls, raw vegetables, olives, cheese toast, and spinach pie are presented before the meal even begins. The menu focuses on steaks, roasts, chops, and fresh fish. There's also an impressive pastry cart. The service aims for formality but is sometimes uncaring. *1776 Peachtree Rd., tel. 404/872–6666. Jacket and tie required. Reservations required, well in advance for weekends. AE, CB, DC, MC, V. No weekend lunch.*

★ **La Grotta.** Despite its odd location in the basement of an apartment building, this is one of the best-managed dining rooms in town. Magnetic, dynamic Sergio Favalli is a superb host and the waiters are on their toes. The kitchen experiments cautiously with new concepts and trendy ingredients, but old Northern Italian favorites remain at the core of the menu. Don't miss the cold grilled wild mushrooms, the baby quails over polenta, or the special tiramisu dessert. Veal and fresh pasta are outstanding. There's an excellent wine list. *2637 Peachtree Rd., tel. 404/231–1368. Jacket and tie required. Reservations required well in advance. AE, CB, DC, MC, V. Dinner only. Closed Sun. and Mon.*

Expensive **Pano's and Paul's.** An Atlanta classic, it's now in its 10th year of stylish pampering. Pano Karatassos and Paul Albrecht hit gold, thanks to their single-minded devotion to their customers' whims and needs, including dietary restriction. Lovely lights and rich fabrics fill the dining rooms designed by Penny Goldwasser. Many new ideas percolate through the kitchen; state-of-the-art dishes are introduced as specials and eventually included in the menu. Look for roasted Georgia quails with foie gras and trumpet mushrooms, smoked salmon crêpes with truffle horseradish sauce, and a combination of Maine lobster and capon breast with a mousseline of potato and celery. *1232 W. Paces Ferry Rd., tel. 404/261–3662. Jacket required. Reservations required (days, sometimes weeks ahead for a prime slot). AE, CB, DC, MC, V. Dinner only. Closed Mon.*

Moderate–Expensive **Buckhead Diner.** This million-dollar fantasy by the owners of
★ *Pano's and Paul's* is one of the hottest restaurants in town, a shimmering faux-diner wrapped in luscious hues of neon. Inlaid wood, Italian leather, hand-cut marble and mellow lights establish a langorous ambience reminiscent of the Orient Express. The cuisine is anything but diner: neo-Asian shrimp wonton, buffalo milk mozzarella melted in fresh tomato coulis, veal meatloaf, and homemade banana walnut ice cream are some of the treats prepared by gifted young Gerry Klaskala. Interesting wines are available by the glass. *3073 Piedmont*

Rd., tel. 404/262-3336. Dress: informal. No reservations; expect a long wait. AE, CB, DC, MC, V. Closed Sun.

Inexpensive **OK Café.** You'll go "back to the future" in this witty take-off on small town cafés. There's a great cast of cheeky waitresses, whimsical art, and very comfortable booths. Particularly good breakfasts (fried French toast, stout omelets) are served, but blue-plate-specials are not always reliable. The desserts are excellent. *3345 Lenox Rd., tel. 404/261-2888; also 1248 W. Paces Ferry Rd., tel. 404/233-2888. Dress: casual. No reservations. AE, MC, V. Open late.*

Wyolene's. Impudent and saucy, this amusing roadhouse winks an eye at the '50s. Free jukebox, big patio with dishevelled palm tree, and bags of white bread on the tables are part of its charm. Wyo's comfort food is the real thing, with no props: meatloaf, chicken-fried steak, macaroni and cheese, home-cooked vegetables, soft-serve ice cream. *2890 Peachtree Rd., tel. 404/365-0360. Dress: casual. No reservations. AE, DC, MC, V.*

Outside the **Aunt Fanny's Cabin.** This is a place where the real and the fake
Perimeter interlock. There are some overdone folksy touches, but the old
Moderate building and its many additions are always packed with people having a good time. Whole Greyhound busloads come to drink mint juleps (that taste like a blend of chemicals). They also eat fried chicken (not better or worse than many) and country ham (its usual leathery, salty self). *2155 Campbell Rd. in Smyrna, tel. 404/436-5218. Dress: informal. Reservations for 12 or more. AE, CB, DC, MC, V. Dinner only.*

Lodging

One of America's three most popular convention destinations, Atlanta offers a broad range of lodgings. More than 12,000 rooms are in the compact downtown area, close to the Georgia World Congress Center, Atlanta Civic Center, Atlanta Merchandise Mart and Apparel Mart, and Omni Coliseum. Other clusters are in the affluent Buckhead corporate and retail area, and around Hartsfield International Airport.

Category	Cost*
Very Expensive	over $100
Expensive	$75–$100
Moderate	$50–$75
Inexpensive	under $50

*double room; add 11% for taxes

The following credit-card abbreviations are used: AE, American Express; CB, Carte Blanche; DC, Diners Club; MC, MasterCard; V, Visa.

Downtown and **Atlanta Hilton & Towers.** The Hilton provides for the needs of
Midtown the business traveler. The top three Tower floors are comprised
Very Expensive of suites in Early American, contemporary, French Provincial and Oriental styles; the remaining floors were recently renovated along contemporary, modular lines. Nikolai's Roof, a Russian restaurant, and Trader Vic's are excellent and popular. *255 Courtland St., 30043, tel. 404/659-2000 or 800/*

HILTONS. 1,250 rooms and suites. Facilities: jogging track, 4 tennis courts, pool, health club, lounges, 4 restaurants including Trader Vic's, a rooftop nightclub. AE, CB, DC, MC, V.

Atlanta Marriott Marquis. Immense and coolly contemporary, the Marquis seems to go on forever as you stand under the lobby's huge fabric sculpture that appears to be floating down from the sky-lit roof 50 stories above. Each guest room opens onto this atrium. *265 Peachtree Center Ave., 30303, tel. 404/521 –0000 or 800/228–9290. 1,674 rooms and suites. Facilities: 5 restaurants, 4 bars and lounges, health club, indoor/outdoor pool. AE, CB, DC, MC, V.*

Colony Square Hotel. Theatricality and opulence are epitomized by the dimly lit lobby with overhanging balconies, piano music, and fresh flowers. The hotel is one block from MARTA's Art Center station, across from the Woodruff Arts Center and the High Museum of Art, and it anchors the Colony Square office/residential/retail complex. *Peachtree and 14th Sts. (1 block from MARTA's Art Center rail station), 30361, tel. 404/ 892–6000 or 800/422–7895. 434 rooms, 32 suites. Facilities: lobby lounge, 2 restaurants, access (for a fee) to the Colony Club health club, racquetball courts, outdoor pool. AE, CB, DC, MC, V.*

Hyatt Regency Atlanta. The Hyatt's 23-story atrium/lobby (built in 1965) launched the chain's "atrium look." The rooms were recently renovated in honor of the hotel's 20th anniversary. Most guests are conventioneers. *264 Peachtree St. (connected to MARTA's Peachtree Center Station), 30303, tel. 404/577–1234. 1,279 rooms and 56 suites. Facilities: 4 restaurants, outdoor pool, health club, sauna. 2 ballrooms. AE, CB, DC, MC, V.*

Omni Hotel at CNN Center. The hotel is adjacent to the CNN Center, home of Ted Turner's Cable News Network. The lobby combines Old World and modern accents, with marble floors, Oriental rugs, exotic floral and plant arrangements, and contemporary furnishings. *100 CNN Center, near MARTA's Omni station stop, 30335, tel. 404/659–0000. 470 rooms. Facilities: 2 restaurants, lounge, access to the Downtown Athletic Club. AE, CB, DC, MC, V.*

Ritz-Carlton Atlanta. The mood here is set by traditional afternoon tea served in the intimate, sunken lobby beneath an 18th-century chandelier. Guest rooms are luxuriously decorated with marble writing tables, sofas, four-poster beds, and marble bathrooms. *181 Peachtree St., 30303, tel. 404/659–0400 or 800/241–3333. 454 rooms. Facilities: 2 restaurants, bar with live jazz, access (for a nominal fee) to the adjacent Phoenix Athletic Club. AE, CB, DC, MC, V.*

The Westin Peachtree Plaza. Every photograph of Atlanta's skyline taken in the last 10 years features this cylindrical glass tower, the tallest hotel in North America. The five-story atrium lobby is classic John Portman—the Atlanta-based architect who set a modern hotel style for the world. The hotel was recently renovated top to bottom to the tune of $35 million. For the best views, ask for floor 45 or higher. *210 Peachtree St. at International Blvd., 30303, tel. 404/659–1400 or 800/228–3000. 1,074 rooms. Facilities: 3 restaurants, 3 bars, a rooftop indoor/ outdoor pool, health club, sauna, shopping gallery, kosher kitchen. AE, CB, DC, MC, V.*

Inexpensive **Barclay Hotel.** This is a quiet, older downtown hotel patronized by budget travelers. The hotel's Wild Wild West Nightclub and

Soda Club is geared toward teenagers under the drinking age. *Directly behind the Peachtree Center at 89 Luckie St. NW, 30303, tel. 404/524–7991. 73 rooms. Facilities: rooftop swimming pool and sun deck, restaurant. AE, CB, DC, MC, V.*

Buckhead
Very Expensive

French Quarter Suites. A baby grand plays daily in the atrium lobby. All one-bedroom suites are decorated with contemporary furnishings and have Jacuzzis. Some have refrigerators. *2780 Whitley Rd., 30339, tel. 404/980–1900 or 800/843–5858. 155 suites. Facilities: Café Orleans, bar, lounge with live entertainment, outdoor pool, and exercise and sauna rooms. AE, CB, DC, MC, V.*

The Ritz-Carlton, Buckhead. Not to be confused with the Ritz-Carlton in Atlanta, its classy downtown cousin, this suburban hotel caters more to social events and shopping lovers. *3434 Peachtree Rd., 30326, tel. 404/237–2700 or 800/241–3333. 553 rooms. Facilities: The Café, with live music and dance floor; The Dining Room, The Bar, with evening entertainment, indoor swimming pool and deck, health center. AE, CB, DC, MC, V.*

Westin Lenox. This elegant 25-story hotel opened in Lenox Square in December 1988. It is sumptuous, but in a subdued style emphasizing intimacy and comfort. Irregularly shaped rooms have spacious baths with separate shower stall and tub. Homey traditional decor and tasteful reproduction antique furniture add to its informal tone. *3300 Lenox Rd., 30326, tel. 404/262–3344. 371 rooms, including 3 club floors and suites. Facilities: indoor pool, health club, 2 lounges, Swan Room restaurant, ballroom and meeting rooms. AE, CB, DC, MC, V.*

Moderate

Beverly Hills Inn. This three-story inn has hardwood floors and English antiques. Most rooms and suites have kitchen facilities and dinettes. Downstairs is the library/parlor and the garden room, where complimentary breakfasts are served. *65 Sheridan Dr., 30305, tel. 404/233–8520. 18 rooms, 4 suites. AE, MC, V.*

The Arts

Culture here now means more than church suppers, stock-car racing, and country music. The Atlanta Symphony Orchestra plays the great halls of Europe and New York, the Atlanta Ballet is rated one of the top companies in the country, and the Alliance Theatre sells more season tickets than any other regional theater in the country.

For the most complete schedule of cultural events, check the "Weekend" tabloid section of Saturday's *Atlanta Journal-Constitution.* Also check *Creative Loafing,* a lively community weekly distributed at restaurants, bars, and stores throughout the metro area.

SEATS, Inc. (tel. 404/577–2626) handles tickets for the Fox Theatre, Atlanta Civic Center, and other large houses. However, most companies sell tickets through their own box offices.

Theater

Consistently one of the city's best, the **Alliance Theatre** performs everything from Shakespeare to the latest Broadway and off-Broadway shows in the Woodruff Arts Center *(see Exploring).*

Academy Theatre. The city's oldest theater troupe moved into a new theater complex in 1987. The mainstage theater seats 450;

new plays are showcased in the 200-seat First Stage and 75-seat Lab Theatre. Also using the Academy complex is **Jomandi Productions,** the city's major African-American company. *173 14th St. NW, tel. 404/892–0880.*

Horizon Theatre Co. This experimental company produces new works by contemporary playwrights as well as mime shows. *1038 Austin Ave. in Little Five Points, tel. 404/584–7450.*

Touring Braodway musicals, pop music, and dance concerts are presented in **The Atlanta Civic Center** (395 Piedmont Ave., tel. 404/523–6275) and the **Fox Theatre** (660 Peachtree St., tel. 404/881–1977. See Exploring).

Concerts Modeled after the Viennese choir, the **Atlanta Boy's Choir** (tel. 404/378–0064) performs frequently at Atlanta locations and makes national and international tours.

The long-established **Atlanta Chamber Players** (tel. 404/872–3360) perform classical works at various Atlanta locations.

The city's **Atlanta Symphony Orchestra** (tel. 404/892–2414) performs its fall–spring subscription series in the 1,800-seat Symphony Hall at Woodruff Arts Center. During the summer, the orchestra accompanies big-name artists in Chastain Park and plays free Sunday evening concerts in Piedmont Park.

Opera **The Atlanta Opera Association** (tel. 404/872–1706), made up of local singers and musicians, is augmented by internationally known artists.

Dance **The Atlanta Ballet Company** (tel. 404/873–5811), founded in 1929, has received international recognition for its high-quality productions of classical and contemporary works. Performances are at the Fox Theatre and Atlanta Civic Center.

Nightlife

"We entertain at home," Atlantans proudly sniffed some 20 years ago. Today, the pursuit of entertainment—from midtown to Buckhead—is known as the "Peachtree Shuffle." Throughout the city you will find a vibrant nightlife, with everything from piano bars to high-energy dance clubs. Locals seem to take pride in the fact that Atlanta has always had more saloons than churches . . . and, in the south, that's saying something.

Most bars and clubs are open seven nights, until 2–4 AM. Those featuring live entertainment usually have a cover charge. For a listing of entertainment, consult both the "Weekend" section of Saturday's *Atlanta Journal-Constitution* and *Creative Loafing.*

Blues New Orleans–style blues send jam-packed crowds into a frenzy at **Blind Willie's** (818 N. Highland Ave., tel. 404/456–4433), a storefront club in trendy Virginia/Highland. Chicago-style blues and zydeco are on the musical menu at the popular **Blue's Harbor** (Underground Atlanta, tel. 404/261–6717).

Jazz **The Bar** at the Ritz-Carlton Buckhead *(see* Lodging) has dark wood paneling, a small museum's worth of original art, a real fire crackling in the hearth throughout the winter, fashionably dressed patrons sipping drinks while a jazz combo plays. Atlanta doesn't get any more uptown than this.

Dante's Down the Hatch (3380 Peachtree Rd., tel. 404/266–1600) is one of the city's best-known showplaces, where The Paul Mitchell Trio conjures silky-smooth sounds in the "hold" of a make-believe sailing ship. Fondues and a large wine selection add to the experience.

Highland Brewing Co. (816 N. Highland Ave., tel 404/876–7115) presents jazz Thursday through Sunday starting at 9 in a snug Art-Deco style cellar cafe.

Rock   **The Cotton Club** (1021 Peachtree St., tel. 404/874–2523) is a loud, usually packed, midtown club that features both local and national performers in a variety of musical styles.

Club Rio (195 Luckie St., tel. 404/525–7467), a late-night downtown club, is the "in" place to be seen dancing to hot new music. The action begins about midnight and roars until 6.

Little Five Points Pub (1174 Euclid Ave., tel. 404/577–7767) is a scruffy club that often showcases top talent in folk, rock, and progressive music.

Bars and Lounges   **Atkins Park Bar & Grill** (794 N. Highland Ave., tel. 404/876–7249), one of Atlanta's oldest neighborhood bars, is packed nightly with a mostly young crowd. It's a fun place to meet-and-mingle in a nonmeat-market atmosphere.

Confetti (3909 Roswell Rd., tel. 404/237–4238) is the consummate singles bar, which attracts a young crowd perpetually on the make. Good drinks and loud music around a congenial bar and postage-stamp-size dance floor.

Sexy, well-dressed single professionals mingle, dine, and dance in **élan** (4505 Ashford-Dunwoody Rd., tel. 404/393–1333), a glossy suburban club that has held its magnetism for nearly 10 years.

The antithesis of hip-and-trendy, 30-year-old **Manuel's Tavern** (602 N. Highland Ave., tel. 404/525–3447)—ancient by Atlanta standards—is a neighborhood saloon in the truest sense. A blend of families, politicians, writers, students, professionals, and blue-collar workers enjoy good drinks, bar food (chili dogs, french fries, strip steaks), and conversations. A lively summertime Shakespeare festival is staged in an adjoining room.

Nonalcoholic   **Joyful Noise** (2669 Church St., tel. 404/768–5100), a Christian supper club on Atlanta's south side, has a buffet supper and live entertainment performed by gospel and other religious musical groups.

Savannah

by Honey Naylor

Savannah. The very sound of the word conjures up misty images of mint juleps, live oaks dripping with Spanish moss, handsome mansions, and a somewhat decadent city moving at a lazy Southern pace. Why, you can hardly say "Savannah" without drawling.

Well, brace yourself. The mint juleps are there all right, along with the moss and the mansions and the easygoing pace, but this Southern belle rings with surprises.

Take, for example, St. Patrick's Day: Why on earth does Savannah, of all places, have a St. Patrick's Day celebration second only to New York's? The greening of Savannah began more than 164 years ago and nobody seems to know why, although everybody in town talks a blue (green) streak about St. Patrick's Day. Everything turns green on March 17, including the faces of startled visitors when green scrambled eggs and green grits are put before them. One year, some well-oiled revelers even tried to dye the Savannah River green.

Savannah's beginning was February 12, 1733, when English General James Edward Oglethorpe and 120 colonists arrived at Yamacraw Bluff on the Savannah River to found the 13th and last colony in the New World. As the port city grew, Englishmen, Scottish Highlanders, French Huguenots, Germans, Austrian Salzburgers, Sephardic Jews from Spain and Portugal, Moravians, Italians, Swiss, Welsh, and Irishmen all arrived to create what could be called a rich gumbo.

In 1793, Eli Whitney of Connecticut, who was tutoring on a plantation near Savannah, invented a mechanized means of "ginning" seeds from cotton bolls. Cotton soon became king, and Savannah, already a busy seaport, flourished under its reign. Waterfront warehouses were filled with "white gold," and factors, or brokers, trading in the Savannah Cotton Exchange set world prices. The white gold brought in solid gold, and fine mansions were built in the prospering city.

It was a Yankee who ushered in Savannah's Golden Age, and it was Yankees who shattered it. In 1864, Savannahians, having seen what Sherman did to the rest of Georgia, surrendered their city to the Union general rather than see it torched. In December of that year, Sherman sent a now-famous telegram to Lincoln. It read, "I beg to present to you as a Christmas gift, the City of Savannah with 150 heavy guns and plenty of ammunition and also about 25,000 bales of cotton."

Following Reconstruction and the collapse of the cotton market, Savannah itself virtually collapsed. The city languished for more than 50 years. Elegant mansions were either razed or allowed to decay, and cobwebs replaced cotton in the decaying riverfront warehouses.

But in 1955, Savannah's spirits rose again. News that the exquisite Isaiah Davenport home (324 E. State St.) was to be destroyed prompted seven outraged ladies to raise enough money to buy the house. They saved it the very day before the wrecking ball was to swing.

Thus was born the Historic Savannah Foundation, the organization responsible for the restoration of downtown Savannah.

More than 1,000 structures have been restored in the 2.5-square-mile Historic District, the nation's largest urban Historic Landmark district, and many of them are open to the public during the annual tour of homes (Mar. 24–28).

When visiting the city, you'll hear a lot about the "Savannah colors." As old buildings were scraped down in preparation for restoration, Savannah showed its true colors—rich mauves, blues, grays, and golds appearing beneath old layers of paint. Those colors are in full view now, making Savannah one of the nation's most colorful cities.

Arriving and Departing

By Plane Savannah International Airport, eight miles west of downtown, is served by **American, Continental, Delta, Eastern, United,** and **USAir.** There is no international passenger service.

Between the Airport **Vans** operated by **McCalls Coastal Express** (tel. 912/966–5364)
and Center City leave the airport daily between 7 AM and 10 PM destined for downtown locations. The trip takes 20–30 minutes, and the one-way fare is $8.

Taxi fare from the airport to downtown hotels is $15 for one person, $3 for each additional person.

By car, drive south on Dean Forest Drive to I–16, then east on I–16 into downtown Savannah.

By Train Amtrak (800/USA–RAIL) has regular service along the Eastern Seaboard, with daily stops in Savannah. The Amtrak station (2611 Seaboard Coastline Dr., tel. 912/234–2611) is four miles southwest of downtown. Cab fare into the city is about $4.

By Bus The **Greyhound/Trailways** station (tel. 912/233–7723) is downtown at 610 W. Oglethorpe Avenue. You can travel nonstop between Atlanta and Savannah on minivans operated by **Peachtree Express** (tel. 912/355–0459; in GA 800/627–3900).

By Car I–95 slices north–south along the Eastern Seaboard, intersecting 10 miles west of town with east–west I–16, which dead-ends in downtown Savannah. U.S. 17, the Coastal Highway, also runs north–south through town. U.S. 80, which connects the Atlantic to the Pacific, is another east–west route through Savannah.

Getting Around

Despite its size, the downtown Historic District should be explored on foot. Its grid shape makes getting around a breeze, and you'll find any number of places to stop and rest.

By Bus Buses require 75¢ in exact change, and 5¢ extra for a transfer. **Chatham Area Transit (CAT)** (tel. 912/233–5767) operates buses in Savannah and Chatham County Monday–Saturday from 6 AM to 11:30 PM, Sunday 6 AM to 6:30 PM.

By Taxi Taxis start at 60¢ and cost $1.20 for each mile. **Adam Cab Co.** (tel. 912/927–7466) is a reliable, 24-hour taxi service.

Important Addresses and Numbers

Tourist For trip planning information, write to the **Savannah Area Con-**
Information **vention and Visitors Bureau** (222 W. Oglethorpe Ave.,

Savannah 31499, tel. 800/444–CHARM). The **Savannah Visitors Center** (301 W. Broad St., tel. 912/944–0455) has free maps
and brochures, lots of friendly advice, and an audiovisual overview of the city. The center is also the starting point for a
number of guided tours. *Open Mon.–Fri. 8:30–5, weekends
and holidays 9–5.*

Emergencies Dial 911 for **police** and **ambulance** in an emergency.

Hospitals Area hospitals with 24-hour emergency rooms are **Candler
General Hospital** (5353 Reynolds St., tel. 912/356–6037) and
Memorial Medical Center (4700 Waters Ave., tel. 912/356–
8390).

Pharmacies **Revco Discount Drug Center** (Medical Arts Shopping Center,
4800 Waters Ave., tel. 912/355–7111) and **Pharmor** (7400
Abercorn St., tel. 912/352–8127).

Guided Tours

Orientation Tours The **Historic Savannah Foundation Tours** (tel. 912/234–TOUR)
are conducted by members of the nonprofit organization that
began, and continues, restoration of the city's fine old buildings. Guides are both knowledgeable and enthusiastic, and
you'll ride in sleek, 20-passenger, climate-controlled vans.
Tours of the Historic District and of the Victorian District each
take about two hours. **Colonial Historic Tours** (tel. 912/233–
0083) will take you on a two-hour tool around town on minibuses
or on an "Old Time Trolley."

**Special-Interest
Tours** **Helen Bryant's Shoppers Walk** (tel. 912/355–7731) is a three-
hour browse for hidden treasures with a native Savannahian.
The **Garden Club of Savannah** (tel. 912/238–0248) takes you into
private gardens tucked behind old-brick walls and wrought-
iron gates. The **Negro Heritage Trail** (tel. 912/234–8000), tracing the city's 250-year black history, is a van tour with a
knowledgeable guide who will tell you about the Gullah culture
of the Georgia and Carolina sea islands. Tours commence at the
Black Heritage Museum in the King-Tisdell Cottage (514 E.
Huntingdon St.).

Cap'n Sam's Cruises (tel. 912/234–7248) churn along the Savannah River in small, colorful paddlewheelers. Cap'n Sam Stevens
has been a fixture on the riverfront for more than 50 years. He
and his guides offer a wealth of information and trivia about Savannah's historic ties to its river. There are two-hour narrated
harbor tours, twilight cocktail cruises, and moonlight dinner
cruises, with daily departures from the dock on Riverfront
Plaza/River Street behind City Hall.

Carriage Tours of Savannah (tel. 912/236–6756) show you the
Historic District by day or by night at a 19th-century clip-clop
pace, with coachmen spinning tales and telling ghost stories
along the way. A romantic evening champagne tour in a private
carriage will set you back $50–$60, plus $16 per bottle of bub-
bly. Regular tours are a more modest $9.50 adults, $4.50
children 11 and under. Daily departures are from City Market
and Madison Square; evening departures are behind the Hyatt
Regency Hotel.

Low-Country Tours The **Historic Savannah Foundation Tours** (tel. 912/234–TOUR),
Colonial Historic Tours (912/233–0083), and **Gray Line** (tel. 912/
236–9604) all make four-hour excursions to the fishing village of

Thunderbolt; the Isle of Hope, with stately mansions lining Bluff Drive; the much-photographed Bonaventure Cemetery on the banks of the Wilmington River, with 200-year-old oaks draping Spanish moss over the graves of many notable Savannahians; and Wormsloe Plantation, with its mile-long avenue of arching oaks.

Walking Tours The **Historic Savannah Foundation** (tel. 912/234–TOUR) offers two strolls through the Historic District, one of which includes breakfast at Mrs. Wilkes's Boarding House. Both of the personalized strolls focus on the city's architecture and gardens.

Cycle Carriage Company (346 Whitaker St., tel. 912/234–8277) is in a class by itself. Its canopied contraptions look a bit like old-time Tin Lizzies but are actually bicycles built for four. The four-wheel critters have baskets up front, where small children get a free ride, and two seats to the rear, where the big folks do the steering—and the pedaling. Regular bicycles are also available.

Exploring Savannah

Numbers in the margin correspond with points of interest on the Savannah Historical District map.

General Oglethorpe himself designed the original town of Savannah and laid it out in a perfect grid. The Historic District is neatly hemmed in by the Savannah River, Gaston Street, and East and West Broad streets. Streets are arrow-straight, public squares of varying sizes are tucked into the grid at precise intervals, and each block is sliced in half by an alley. Bull Street, anchored on the north by City Hall and the south by Forsyth Park, charges down the center of the grid and lunges around the five public squares that stand in its way. (Maneuvering a car around Savannah's squares is a minor art form.)

The Historic
District
❶
There are two excellent reasons for making your first stop the **Savannah Visitors Center** *(see* Tourist Information in Important Addresses and Numbers), the most obvious being the maps and brochures you'll need for exploring. The other reason is the structure that houses the Center. The big red-brick building with its high ceilings and sweeping arches was the old Central of Georgia railway station, completed in 1860.

The Visitors Center lies just north of the **site of the Siege of Savannah.** During the American Revolution, the Redcoats seized Savannah in 1778, and the Colonial forces made several attempts to retake it. In 1779, the Colonials, led by Polish Count Casimir Pulaski, laid siege to the city. They were beaten back, and Pulaski was killed while leading a cavalry charge against the British.

❷
On the battle site, adjacent to the Visitors Center in a restored shed of the railway station, the **Great Savannah Exposition** offers an excellent introduction to the city. Two theaters present special-effects depictions of Oglethorpe's landing and of the siege. There are various exhibits, ranging from old locomotives to a tribute to Savannah's own world-famous songwriter Johnny Mercer, as well as two restored dining cars that aren't going anywhere, but you can climb aboard for a bite to eat. *303 W. Broad St., tel. 912/238–1779. Admission: $3.75 adults; $2.50 children 4–12, under 4 free. Open daily 9–5.*

Andrew Low House, **18**

Cathedral of St. John, **16**

Chippewa Square, **14**

Colonial Park Service Cemetery, **15**

Emmet Park, **8**

Factors Walk, **5**

Forsyth Park, **24**

Great Savannah Exposition, **2**

Green-Meldrim House, **20**

Isaiah Davenport House, **9**

Johnson Square, **4**

Juliette Gordon Low House, **13**

Lafayette Square, **17**

Madison Square, **19**

Massie Center, **23**

Owens-Thomas House, **10**

River Street, **6**

Scarbrough House, **3**

Ships of the Sea Museum, **7**

Telfair Mansion and Museum, **12**

Temple Mickve Israel, **21**

Visitor's Center, **1**

Wesley Monumental Church, **22**

Wright Square, **11**

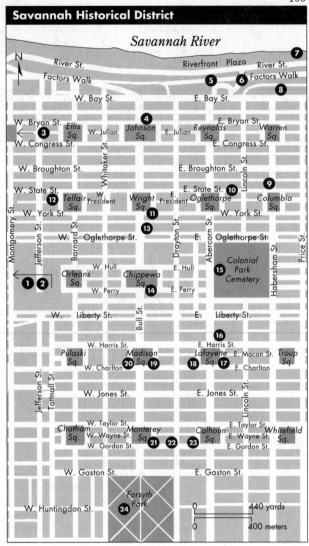

Savannah Historical District

Turn left on Broad Street and walk two blocks to the **Scarbrough House** headquarters for the Historic Savannah Foundation. The exuberant Regency mansion was built during the 1819 cotton boom for Savannah merchant prince William Scarbrough and designed by English architect William Jay. A Doric portico is capped by one of Jay's characteristic half-moon windows. Four massive Greek Doric columns form a peristyle in the atrium entrance hall. Three stories overhead is an arched, sky-blue ceiling with sunshine filtering through a skylight. Exhibits of works by local artists are displayed throughout the house. *41 W. Broad St., tel. 912/233-7787. Admission: $1.50 adults, 75¢ children. Open Mon.–Sat. 10–4.*

Continue east across Franklin Square and stroll through City Market, with its sidewalk cafes, jazz joints, and shops. Now ❹ head east on St. Julian Street to **Johnson Square.** Laid out in 1733 and named for South Carolina Governor Robert Johnson, this was the earliest of Oglethorpe's original 24 squares. The square was once a popular gathering place, where Savannahians came to welcome President Monroe in 1819, to greet the Marquis de Lafayette in 1825, and to cheer for Georgia's secession in 1861. It was here that Lafayette laid the cornerstone for the monument that marks the grave of his friend and Revolutionary War hero, Major-General Nathaniel Greene. (It was on Greene's plantation after the war that Eli Whitney invented the cotton gin.)

Time Out Food carts are parked in Johnson Square; you can pick up an ice cream cone, a hot dog, or a cold drink and relax on one of the park benches.

That building to the north with the glittering gilt dome at the foot of Bull Street is **City Hall,** dating from 1905. (The dome was regilded in 1987.) The lower stories of City Hall face the spot from which the SS *Savannah* set sail in 1819, the first steamship to cross any ocean. Just to the west of City Hall, on Yamacraw Bluff, is a marble bench, appropriately called **Oglethorpe's Bench,** that marks the site of the general's field tent.

❺ Cobblestone ramps lead from Bay Street down to **Factors Walk** ❻ and, below it, to **River Street.** Cars can enter Factors Walk via the ramps, and so can pedestrians. (These are serious cobblestones, and you will suffer if you wear anything but the most comfortable shoes you own.) There is also a network of iron walkways connecting Bay Street with the multistoried buildings that rise up from the river level, and iron stairways plunge (word used advisedly) from Bay Street down to Factors Walk.

Foreign vessels still call at the Port of Savannah, the largest port between Baltimore and New Orleans. Paper and other products have replaced the cotton exports, and in 1977 a multi-million-dollar riverfront revitalization transformed the decayed warehouses into a nine-block marketplace with everything from sleek boutiques to musty taverns.

Learning about the port and the river is a breeze aboard one of **Cap'n Sam's Cruises,** so you may want to break up your walking tour at this point to board one of his paddlewheelers *(see* Guided Tours).

There are benches all along **Riverfront Plaza** where you can watch the parade of freighters and pug-nosed tugs, and the tugboat-shape sandboxes where youngsters can play. Each weekday, Dixieland music can be heard from the cabin of the **River Street Rambler,** a brightly-painted freight train that rumbles down River Street to the port. River Street is the main venue for many of the city's celebrations, including the First Saturday festivals when flea marketeers, artists, and craftsmen display their wares and musicians entertain the crowds.

Even landlubbers can appreciate the fine craftsmanship of the ❼ ship models in the **Ships of the Sea Museum.** The four floors of the museum contain models of steamships, nuclear subs, China clippers with their sails unfurled, Columbus's ships, a showcase filled with ships-in-bottles, and a collection of fine Royal Doulton porcelain seafarers. *503 E. River St. and 504 E. Bay St., tel. 912/232–1511. Admission: $2 adults, 75¢ children 7–12. Open daily 10–5. Closed major holidays.*

If you entered the museum at the River Street entrance and worked your way up all four floors, you'll be topside again on **8** Bay Street. The tree-shaded park along Bay Street is **Emmet Park,** named for Robert Emmet, a late 18th-century Irish patriot and orator. Walk west along Bay Street and turn left onto Abercorn Street. In **Reynolds Square** you'll see the statue of John Wesley, who preached in Savannah and wrote the first English hymnal here in 1736. The monument to the founder of the Methodist Church is shaded by greenery and surrounded by park benches. On the square is the **Olde Pink House** (23 Abercorn St.). Built in 1771, it is one of the oldest buildings in town. The porticoed pink stucco Georgian mansion has been a private home, a bank, and headquarters for a Yankee general during the war. It is now a restaurant (*see* Dining).

From Reynolds Square walk south on Abercorn Street, turn left onto Broughton Street, and two blocks down turn right onto **9** Habersham Street. This will bring you to the **Isaiah Davenport House.** Semicircular stairs with wrought-iron trim lead to the recessed doorway of the red-brick Georgian mansion that master builder Isaiah Davenport built for himself in 1815. Three dormer windows poke through the sloping roof of the stately house, and inside there are polished hardwood floors, fine woodwork and plasterwork, and a soaring elliptical staircase. The furnishings are Hepplewhite, Chippendale, and Sheraton, and in the attic there is a collection of antique dolls and a dollhouse with tiny 19th-century furnishings. *324 E. State St., tel. 912/236–8097. Admission: $2.50 adults, $1.25 children. Open Mon.–Sat. 10–4:30, Sun. 1:30–4:30.*

10 Walk west on State Street two blocks to the **Owens-Thomas House.** This was William Jay's first Regency mansion in Savannah, built in 1817, and it is the city's finest example of that architectural style. The thoroughly English house was built largely with local materials, including tabby—a mixture of oyster shells, sand, and water that resembles concrete. The entry portico is of Doric design with curving stairs leading to a recessed door topped by a fanlight. Of particular note are the curving walls of the house, Greek-inspired ornamental molding, Jay's half-moon arches, stained-glass panels, and Duncan Phyfe furniture. You'll see hoopskirt chairs (whose short arms accommodated the circular skirts of many Southern belles), canopied beds, a pianoforte, and displays of ornate silver. From a wrought-iron balcony, in 1825, the Marquis de Lafayette bade a two-hour au revoir to the crowd below. *124 Abercorn St., tel. 912/233–9743. Admission: $3 adults; $2 students; $1 children 6–12, under 6 free.*

11 Stroll through **Oglethorpe Square,** across State Street, and continue two blocks west to **Wright Square.** The square was named for James Wright, Georgia's last Colonial governor. Centerpiece of the square is an elaborate monument erected in honor of William Washington Gordon, founder of the Central of Georgia Railroad. A slab of granite from Stone Mountain marks the grave of Tomo-Chi-Chi, the Yamacraw chief who befriended General Oglethorpe and the colonists.

Continue west on State Street, strolling, if you like, through
⑫ **Telfair Square** to reach the **Telfair Mansion and Art Museum.**
The South's oldest public art museum is housed in yet another
of Jay's Regency creations, this one designed in 1819. Within
its marbled halls there are American, French, and German Impressionist paintings; a large collection of works by Kahlil
Gibran; plaster casts of the Elgin Marbles, the Venus de Milo,
and the Laocoön, among other classical sculptures; and a room
that contains some of the Telfair family furnishings, including a
Duncan Phyfe sideboard and Savannah-made silver. The mansion is also notable for Jay's distinctive moldings, cornices, and
mantlepieces. *121 Barnard St., tel. 912/232-1177. Admission:
$2.50 adults, $1 students, 50¢ children 6–12; free on Sun. Open
Tues.–Sat. 10–5, Sun. 2–5.*

At the next corner, turn left onto Oglethorpe Avenue and cross
⑬ Bull Street to reach the **Juliette Gordon Low House.** This majestic Regency mansion is attributed to William Jay (and why
not?) and in 1965 was designated Savannah's first National
Historic Landmark. "Daisy" Low, founder of the Girl Scouts,
was born here, and the house is now owned and operated by the
Girl Scouts of America. Mrs. Low was also an artist, and her
paintings and other artworks are on display in the house, along
with original family furnishings of the 19th century. *142 Bull
St., tel. 912/233-4501. Admission: $2.25 adults, $1.25 children, discounts for Girl Scouts. Open Mon.–Sat. 10–4, Sun.
12:30–4:30. Closed every Wed., and Sun. in Dec. and Jan.*

⑭ **Chippewa Square** is a straight shot south on Bull Street. There
you can see the imposing bronze statue of the general himself,
James Edward Oglethorpe.

From Chippewa Square, go east on McDonough Street to reach
⑮ the **Colonial Park Cemetery.** Savannahians were buried here
from 1750 to 1853. Shaded pathways lace through the park, and
you may want to stroll through and read some of the old inscrip-
tions. There are several historical plaques in the cemetery, one
of which marks the grave of Button Gwinnett, a signer of the
Declaration of Independence.

⑯ The **Cathedral of St. John the Baptist** soars like a hymn over the
corner of Abercorn and Harris streets, two blocks south of the
cemetery. The French Gothic cathedral, with the pointed
arches and free-flowing traceries characteristic of the style, is
the seat of the Diocese of Savannah. It is the oldest Roman
Catholic church in Georgia, having been founded in the early
1700s. Fire destroyed the early structures, and the present cathedral dates from the late 19th century. Most of the
cathedral's impressive stained-glass windows were made by
Austrian glassmakers and imported around the turn of the century. The high altar is of Italian marble, and the Stations of the
Cross were imported from Munich.

⑰ Across from the cathedral is **Lafayette Square,** named for the
Marquis de Lafayette. The graceful three-tier fountain in the
square was donated by the Georgia chapter of the Colonial
Dames of America.

⑱ Across the square is the **Andrew Low House.** The house was
built for Andrew Low in 1849, and later belonged to his son William, who married Juliette Gordon. After her husband's death,
"Daisy" Low founded the Girl Scouts in this house on March 12,

1912. Robert E. Lee and William Thackeray were both entertained in this mansion. In addition to its historical significance, the house boasts some of the finest ornamental ironwork in Savannah. Members and friends of the Colonial Dames have donated fine 19th-century antiques and stunning silver to the house. *329 Abercorn St. Admission: $2 adults, $1 students, 75¢ children and Girl Scouts. Open daily 10:30–4:30. Closed Christmas, Thanksgiving, and New Years.*

⑲ Two blocks to the west is **Madison Square,** laid out in 1839 and named for James Madison. The statue depicts Sergeant William Jasper hoisting a flag and is a tribute to his bravery during the Siege of Savannah. Though mortally wounded, he rescued the colors of his regiment in the assault on the British lines.

⑳ On the west side of the square is the **Green-Meldrim House,** designed by New York architect John Norris and built about 1850 for cotton merchant Charles Green. The house was bought in 1892 by Judge Peter Meldrim, hence the hyphenated name. Meldrim's heirs sold the house to St. John's Episcopal Church, for which it is now the parish house. It was here that General Sherman established residence after taking the city in 1864. Here the general lived in a splendid Gothic Revival mansion, complete with crenelated roof and oriel windows. The gallery that sweeps around three sides of the house is awash with filigreed ironwork. The mantles are Carrara marble, the woodwork is carved black walnut, and the doorknobs and hinges are silver-plated. There is a magnificent skylight above a gracefully curved staircase. The house is furnished with 16th- and 17th-century antiques. *On Madison Sq. Admission: $2.50. Open Tues., Thurs., Fri., and Sat. 10–4. Closed during special church functions.*

Time Out Students from the Savannah College of Art and Design buy art supplies and books at **Design Works Bookstore.** There is also a soda fountain and tables in this old Victorian drugstore, where you can get short orders, burgers, and deli sandwiches. *Corner of Bull and Charlton Sts., tel. 912/238-2481. Open Mon.– Thurs. 8–8, Fri. and Sat. 9–4.*

The fifth and last of Bull Street's squares is **Monterey Square,** which commemorates the victory of General Zachary Taylor's forces in Monterey, Mexico, in 1846. The square's monument honors General Casimir Pulaski, the Polish nobleman and Revolutionary War hero who lost his life during the Siege of Savannah.

㉑ On the east side of the square stands **Temple Mickve Israel,** which was consecrated in 1878. Five months after the founding of Savannah, a group of Spanish and German Jews arrived, bringing with them the prized "Sephar Torah" that is in the present temple. The splendid Gothic Revival synagogue contains a collection of documents and letters pertaining to early Jewish life in Savannah and Georgia. *20 E. Gordon St. Admission free. Open weekdays 10–noon.*

㉒ A block east of the temple is a Gothic Revival church memorializing the founders of Methodism. The **Wesley Monumental Church,** patterned after Queen's Kirk in Amsterdam, celebrated a century of service in 1968. The church is noted for its magnificent stained-glass windows. In the Wesley Window there are busts of John and Charles Wesley.

㉓ At the **Massie Heritage Interpretation Center,** in addition to a scale model of the city, maps and plans, and architectural displays, is a "Heritage Classroom" that offers schoolchildren hands-on instruction about early Colonial life. *207 E. Gordon St., tel. 912/651-7380. Admission free, but a donation of $1.50 is appreciated. Open weekdays 9-4:30, weekends by appointment.*

㉔ The southern anchor of Bull Street is **Forsyth Park,** with 20 luxuriant acres. The glorious white fountain, dating from 1858, was restored in 1988. In addition to its Confederate and Spanish-American War memorials, the park contains the Fragrant Garden for the Blind, a project of Savannah garden clubs. There are also tennis courts and a tree-shaded jogging path. The park is often the scene of outdoor plays and picnic concerts.

The Victorian District
The **King-Tisdell Cottage,** perched behind a picket fence, is a museum dedicated to the preservation of black history and culture. The Negro Heritage Trail (*see* Special-Interest Tours) begins here, in this little Victorian house. Broad steps lead to a porch that's loaded with gewgaws, and dormer windows pop up through a steep roof. The interior is furnished to resemble a late 19th-century black coastal home. *514 E. Huntingdon St., tel. 912/234-8000. Admission: $1.50 adults, 50¢ children. Open weekdays noon-4.*

Other houses of interest in the Victorian district are at **118 E. Waldburg Street** and **111 W. Gwinnett Street.** A stroll along **Bolton Street** will be especially rewarding for fans of fanciful architecture. Of particular note is the entire 200 block, 114 W. Bolton Street, 109 W. Bolton Street, and 321 E. Bolton Street.

Day-tripping to Tybee Island

Tybee Island, which lies 18 miles east of Savannah right on the Atlantic Ocean, offers all manner of water and beach activities. The drive to Tybee takes about a half hour, and there are two historic forts to visit on the way.

To reach Tybee Island, drive east on Victory Drive (U.S. 80) all the way to the Atlantic. (The highway sometimes goes under the alias of Tybee Road.)

Fort Pulaski is 15 miles east of downtown Savannah. You'll see the entrance on your left just before Tybee Road reaches Tybee Island. A must for Civil War buffs, the fort was built on Cockspur Island between 1829 and 1847, and named for General Casimir Pulaski. Robert E. Lee's first assignment after graduating from West Point was as an engineer here. During the Civil War the fort fell on April 12, 1862, after a mere 30 hours of bombardment by newfangled rifled cannons. It was the first time such cannons had been used in warfare—and the last time a masonry fort was thought to be impregnable. The restored fortification, operated by the National Park Service, is complete with moats, drawbridges, massive ramparts, and towering walls. There is an interpretive center that offers historical demonstrations, self-guided trails, and ample picnic areas. *U.S. 80, tel. 912/786-5787. Admission: $2 adults, $1.50 students, senior citizens, and military. Open daily 8:30-5:15 in winter; 8:30-6:45 in summer. Closed Christmas and New Year's.*

Three miles farther along U.S. 80 is **Tybee Island.** "Tybee" is an Indian word meaning salt. The Yamacraw Indians came to the island to hunt and fish, and legend has it that pirates buried their treasure here.

The island is about five miles long and two miles wide, with a plethora of seafood restaurants, chain motels, condos, and shops. The entire expanse of white sand is divided into a number of public beaches, where visitors go shelling and crabbing, play on waterslides, charter fishing boats, swim, or just build sand castles.

The **Tybee Museum and Lighthouse** are at the very tip of the island. In the museum you'll see Indian artifacts, pirate pistols, powder flasks, old prints tracing the history of Savannah, even some sheet music of Johnny Mercer songs. The Civil War Room has old maps and newspaper articles pertaining to Sherman's occupation of the city. On the second floor there are model antique cars and ship models, and a collection of antique dolls. The lighthouse across the road is Georgia's oldest and tallest, dating from 1773, with an observation deck 145 feet above the sea. Bright red steps—178 of them—lead to the deck and the awesome Tybee Light. The view of the ocean will take away whatever breath you have left after the climb. *Meddin Dr. and the jumping off place, tel. 912/786-4077. Admission to both lighthouse and museum: $1 adults, 50¢ children 6-12. Museum open daily in summer 10-6; in winter weekdays 1-5, weekends 10-5. Lighthouse open daily in summer 1-5; in winter Thurs.-Mon. 1-5.*

Time Out   **Spanky's Pizza Galley & Saloon,** overlooking the beach, has seafood platters, burgers, chicken dishes, and salads. *404 Butler Dr., tel. 912/786-5520. AE, MC, V. Open daily 11 AM-midnight.*

Heading west back to Savannah, take the Islands Expressway, which becomes the President Street Extension. About 3½ miles outside the city you'll see a sign for **Fort Jackson,** located on Salter's Island. The Colonial fort was purchased in 1808 by the federal government, and is the oldest standing fort in Georgia. It was garrisoned in 1812, and was the Confederate headquarters of the river batteries. The brick fort is surrounded by a tidal moat, and there are 13 exhibit areas. Battle reenactments, blacksmithing demonstrations, and programs of 19th-century music are among the fort's schedule of activities. The Trooping of the Colors and military tattoo take place at regular intervals during summer. *1 Ft. Jackson Rd., tel. 912/232-3945. Admission: $1.75 adults, $1.25 students, senior citizens, and military. Open Mar.-Nov., Tues.-Sun. 9-5; Dec.-Feb., weekends 9-5.*

Savannah for Free

Beach at Tybee Island (*see* Exploring).

There are many **celebrations** in Savannah, and most of them take place on River Street. Arts and crafts displays, music, and entertainment are always part of special events such as the February Georgia Day Festival, Oktoberfest, the Great American 4th of July, the Seafood-Fest, and First Saturday festivals every month. About 40,000 greenish folk flock to Riverfront

Plaza after the St. Patrick's Day parade. Contact the Savannah Visitors Center (*see* Important Addresses and Numbers).

Free Concerts are given during summer months in Johnson Square (*see* Arts).

Oatland Island Education Center. Located only 15 minutes from downtown Savannah, this 175-acre maritime forest is not only a natural habitat for coastal wildlife (including timber wolves and panthers), it also offers environmental education for visitors. The center also houses the coastal offices of the Georgia Conservancy. *711 Sandtown Rd., tel 912/897–3733. Open weekdays 8:30–5; Second Saturday events Oct.–May.*

Savannah Young People's Theater (*see* What to See and Do with Children).

Skidaway Island Marine Science Complex. On the grounds of the former Modena Plantation, the complex features a 12-panel, 12,000-gallon aquarium with marine and plant life of the Continental Shelf. Other exhibits highlight archaeological discoveries and undersea life of the Georgia coast. *McWhorter Dr., Skidaway Island, tel. 912/356–2496. Open weekdays 9–4, weekends noon–5.*

Telfair Mansion and Museum charges no admission on Sundays (*see* Exploring).

Watch the parade of ships on the Savannah River.

What to See and Do with Children

Community Children's Theater (tel. 912/233–9321, ext. 132) performs puppet shows, marionette shows, and live plays especially for children; performances are given at various locations.

Explore Savannah, Inc. (418 E. State St., tel. 912/354–4560 or 912/233–5238) designs individualized activity packages and tours for children ages 4–16. Professional guides conduct full- or half-day tours, and ticket prices, which start at $10, include transportation, meals, and snacks.

Fort Pulaski and Jackson (*see* Exploring).

Juliette Gordon Low Girl Scout National Center (*see* Exploring).

Oatland Island Education Center (*see* Savannah for Free).

Exhibits at the **Savannah Science Museum** include live and mounted reptiles and amphibians, a "walk-in" human heart and mouth, a solar energy unit, Indian artifacts, plans, and planetarium shows. *4405 Paulsen St., tel. 912/355–6705. Admission: $1 adults, 50¢ children. Open Tues.–Sat. 10–5, Sun. 2–5; planetarium shows weekends at 3 PM.*

Tybee Island Museum and Lighthouse (*see* Exploring).

Off the Beaten Track

If your tastebuds are fixin' for real down-home barbecue, head for **Wall's.** There's a counter where you place your order and a couple of orange plastic booths. Entertainment is provided by a small black-and-white TV set. You reach in the refrigerator case to get your canned beverage, and your food comes served in Styrofoam cartons. A sign taped up over the counter reads, "When I work, I works hard. When I sit, I sits loose—when I think, I falls asleep." Plain? Not really. There is richness in them thar barbecued spare ribs, barbecued sandwiches, and deviled crabs (the three items make up the entire menu. A large carton of ribs costs $7. *515 E. York Ln., between Ogle-*

*thorpe Ave. and York St., tel. 912/232-9754. Dress: bibs. No
credit cards. Open Thurs. 11-10, Fri. and Sat. 11-11.*

Shopping

Regional wares to look for are handcrafted items from the Low
Country—handmade quilts and baskets; wreaths made from
Chinese tallow trees and Spanish moss; preserves, jams, and
jellies. The favorite Savannah snack, and a popular gift item, is
the benne wafer. It's about the size of a quarter and comes in a
variety of flavors.

Shopping Districts **Riverfront Plaza/River Street** is nine blocks of shops housed in
the renovated waterfront warehouses, where you can find
everything from popcorn to pottery. **City Market,** located on
West St. Julian Street between Ellis and Franklin squares, has
sidewalk cafes, jazz haunts, shops, and art galleries. If you're
in need of anything from aspirin to anklets, head for **Broughton
Street** and wander through its many variety and specialty
stores.

Savannah's major suburban shopping mall is **Oglethorpe Mall**
(7804 Abercorn St. Ext.). The enclosed center has four department stores (Sears, Penney's, Belk, and Maas Bros./Jordan
Marsh) and over 100 specialty shops, fast-food, and full-service
restaurants.

Specialty Shops **Arthur Smith** (1 W. Jones St., tel. 912/236-9701) houses four
Antiques floors of 18th- and 19th-century furniture. At **Nostalgia Station**
(307 Stiles Ave., tel. 912/236-8176) you can get some of Savannah's architecture to go—beveled and stained glass, brackets,
ornamental accent pieces. They'll crate and deliver it for you,
too. The best in bronzes, silver, crystal, and antique jewelry
can be found at **Coachlight Antiques** (423-B Bull St., tel. 912/
234-4081).

Artwork **Exhibit A** (342 Bull St., tel. 912/238-2480), the gallery of the
Savannah College of Art and Design, has hand-painted cards,
handmade jewelry, and paintings by regional artists. **Gallery
209** (209 E. River St., tel. 912/236-4583) is a co-op gallery with
paintings, watercolors, and sculptures by local artists.

Benne Wafers You can buy boxed bennes in most gift shops, but **The Cooky
Shanty** (2233 Norwood Ave., tel. 912/355-1716) is where
they originated. You can buy them and watch them being made
here.

Books The nine rooms of **E. Shaver's** (326 Bull St., tel. 912/234-7257)
bookstore, are stocked with books on architecture and regional
history, as well as used and rare books. **The Book Lady** (17 W.
York St., tel. 912/233-3628) specializes in used, rare, and out-
of-print books; it also provides a search service.

Country Crafts **Callaway Gardens Country Store** (301 E. River St., tel. 912/236-
4055) carries lots of gift-packaged preserves and jellies,
sauces, bacon and hams, cookbooks, and gifts. At **Charlotte's
Corner** (1 W. Liberty St., tel. 912/233-8061) there are handmade quilts and baskets made from quilts, regional cookbooks,
aprons, and Savannah-made potpourris. **Mulberry Tree** (17
W. Charlton St., tel. 912/236-4656) is another crafty shop for
handmade quilts and baskets, antique dolls, jams, jellies, preserves, and wreaths.

Participant Sports

Bicycling	Pedaling is a breeze on these flatlands. The **Historic Savannah Foundations** (tel. 912/233–3597) provides rental bikes at the DeSoto Hilton Hotel (Bull and Liberty Sts.) and the Hyatt Regency Hotel (2 W. Bay St.).
Bird-watching, Crabbing, Shelling	**Palmetto Coast Charters** takes small groups to the barrier islands (Box 536, Tybee Island 31328, tel. 912/786–5403). **Coastal Island Cruises** takes in Tybee, Little Tybee, Cockspur, and Wilmington islands (525 Quarterman Dr., on Wilmington Island, behind Palmer's Seafood Restaurant at Turner's Creek, tel. 912/897–1604).
Boating	Boats can be rented at **Bellaire Woods Campground,** 2½ miles west of I–95 on GA 204 (15 mi from downtown Savannah, tel. 912/748–4000) and at **Water Way RV Park** on the Ogeechee River (U.S. 17, tel. 912/756–2296). Pedal boats can be rented for pedaling around **Lake Mayer** (Lake Mayer Park, Sallie Mood Dr. and Montgomery Crossroads Dr., tel. 912/352–1660). There are public boat ramps at **Bell's Landing** on the Forest River (Apache Rd. off Abercorn St.); **Islands Expressway** on the Wilmington River (Islands Expressway adjacent to Frank W. Spencer Park); and **Savannah Marina** on the Wilmington River in the town of Thunderbolt.
Golf	There's a 27-hole course at **Bacon Park** (Skidaway Rd., tel. 912/354–2625), and a 9-hole course at **Mary Calder Park** (Bay St. Ext., tel. 912/238–7100).
Health Clubs	The following private clubs are open to guests for a fee:

Savannah Downtown Athletic Club (7 E. Congress St., tel. 912/236–4874). Nautilus and free-weight equipment, whirlpool, sauna, aerobics, and karate classes.

Racquet Plus (4 Oglethorpe Professional Bldg., tel. 912/355–3070). Racquetball courts, Nautilus equipment, whirlpool, and sauna.

YMCA Family Center (6400 Habersham St., tel. 912/354–6223). Gymnasium, exercise classes, pool, and tennis—for men and women.

Jewish Educational Alliance (5111 Abercorn St., tel. 912/355–8111). Racquetball courts, gymnasium, weight room, sauna, steam, whirlpool, and aerobic dance classes.

Jogging	Flat-as-a-pancake **Forsyth Park** is a favorite jogging path, with plenty of shade trees and benches. The beach at **Tybee Island** is another great favorite of joggers. Suburbanites favor the jogging trails in **Lake Mayer Park** (Montgomery Crossroads Rd. at Sallie Mood Dr.) and **Daffin Park** (1500 E. Victory Dr.).
Tennis	There are 14 lighted courts in **Bacon Park** (Skidaway Rd., tel. 912/354–5925); four lighted courts in **Forsyth Park** (Drayton and Gaston Sts., tel. 912/352–1660); and eight lighted courts in **Lake Mayer Park** (Montgomery Crossroads Rd. and Sallie Mood Dr., tel. 912/352–9915).

Dining

Situated on a river, 18 miles inland from the Atlantic Ocean, Savannah naturally has excellent seafood restaurants. Barbecue is also a local favorite, and there are a number of Continental restaurants as well. The Historic District is loaded with eateries, especially along River Street. Savannahians also like to drive out to eat in Thunderbolt and on Skidaway, Tybee, and Wilmington Islands.

The most highly recommended restaurants in each price category are indicated by a star ★.

Category	Cost*
Very Expensive	over $30
Expensive	$25–$30
Moderate	$15–$25
Inexpensive	under $15

per person without tax, service, or drinks

The following credit-card abbreviations are used: AE, American Express; CB, Carte Blanche; DC, Diners Club; MC, MasterCard; V, Visa.

American
Very Expensive

Olde Pink House. The brick Georgian mansion, built for James Habersham in 1771, is one of Savannah's oldest structures. The cozily elegant tavern has original Georgia pine floors and crystal chandeliers, and antique furniture that was shipped from England. Cocktails are served below in the romantic Planters Tavern, where black leather chairs are pulled up around an open fireplace in the wintertime. Veal Thomas Jefferson is a sautéed cutlet topped with fresh crabmeat and béarnaise sauce, and garnished with asparagus and shrimp. "Mr. and Mrs. Habersham's Dinner," purportedly the favorite dinner of the original occupants, begins with a shrimp appetizer and moves on to black-turtle bean soup, salad, "an intermission of sorbet," chateaubriand carved tableside, and a dessert. *23 Abercorn St., tel. 912/232–4286. Jacket and tie required for dinner. Reservations suggested for dinner. AE, DC, MC, V.*

Expensive
★

45 South. This was a popular southside eatery that moved in 1988 to the sprawling Pirates' House complex. 45 South is a small, stylish restaurant with contemporary decor in lush mauve and green Savannah colors. There is a changing menu that might include lunch entrees of grilled marinated swordfish steak served with a bean, asparagus, and radicchio salad; or medallions of pork tenderloin with grilled onions, peppers, and rosemary. Dinner entrees include peppered breast of duck with acorn squash and fresh spinach; and trout with a ragout of zucchini and basil. *20 E. Broad St., tel. 912/354–0444. Jacket and tie required. Reservations accepted. MC, V.*

Inexpensive
★

Crystal Beer Parlor. A comfortable family tavern famed for hamburgers, thick-cut french fries, onion rings, and frosted mugs of draft beer. The menu also offers fried oyster sandwiches, gumbo, and shrimp salad. *301 W. Jones St. at Jefferson St., tel. 912/232–1153. Dress: informal. No reservations. No credit cards.*

★ **Mrs. Wilkes Boarding House.** There's no sign out front, but you won't have any trouble finding this famed establishment. At breakfast time and noon (no dinner is served) there are long lines of folks waiting to get in for a culinary orgy. Charles Kuralt and David Brinkley are among the celebrities who have

Dining
Crystal Beer Parlor, **1**
45 South, **18**
LaToque, **20**
Mrs. Wilkes Boarding
House, **5**
Olde Pink House, **15**
Pirates' House, **19**
River House, **4**
Shrimp Factory, **12**

Lodging
Ballastone Inn, **10**
Days Inn, **3**
DeSoto Hilton, **11**
Eliza Thompson
House, **9**
Foley House, **8**
Forsyth Park Inn, **6**
The Gastonian, **16**
Hyatt, **7**
Jesse Mount House, **2**
The Mulberry, **17**
Olde Harbour Inn, **13**
River Street Inn, **14**

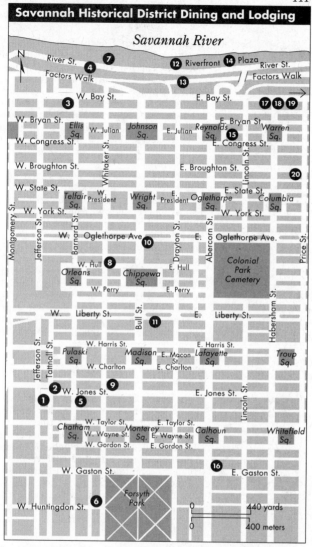

Savannah Historical District Dining and Lodging

feasted on the fine Southern food, served at big family-style tables. For breakfast there are eggs, sausage, piping hot biscuits, and grits. At lunch, bowl after bowl is passed around the table. Fried or roast chicken, collard greens, okra, mashed potatoes, cornbread, biscuits—the dishes just keep coming. *107 W. Jones St., tel. 912/232–5997. Dress: informal. No reservations. No credit cards.*

Continental
Moderate–Expensive
★

LaToque. Swiss-born owner/chef Christian Bigler prepares fish, shellfish, veal, duckling, and pork in traditional European style, with rich brandy, wine, and cream sauces. The dining room has an understated elegance, with starched white tablecloths and dark red decor. *420 E. Broughton St., tel. 912/*

238–0138. Jacket and tie required. Reservations accepted. AE, MC, V. Closed Sun.

Seafood
Expensive
★

Elizabeth on 37th. Elizabeth and Michael Terry's restaurant is in an elegant turn-of-the-century mansion, with hardwood floors and spacious rooms. Elizabeth is the chef, called by *Town & Country* magazine, "One of America's great new women chefs." Among her specialties is flounder Elizabeth, a filet broiled in a crab, cream, and sherry sauce. While the emphasis is on sea creatures served in delicate sauces, there are other excellent offerings, including steak au poivre, quail, lamb, and chicken dishes. *105 E. 37th St., tel. 912/236–5547. Jacket and tie required. Reservations suggested for dinner. AE, MC, V. Closed Sun.*

Pirates' House. You'll probably start hearing about the Pirates' House about 10 minutes after you hit town. There are all sorts of legends about it involving shanghaied sailors and ghosts. It's a sprawling complex with nautical and piratical trappings, and 23 rooms with names like The Jolly Roger and The Black Hole; children love the place. The menu is almost as big as the building, with heavy emphasis on sea critters. For starters there are oysters, escargots, and soft-shell crabs. The large portions of gumbo and seafood bisque come in iron kettles. Flounder Belle Franklin is crabmeat, shrimp, and filet of flounder baked in butter with herbs and wines and a glaze of cheeses and toasted almonds. You can pick out your live Maine lobster from a big saltwater tank. There are 40 listings on the dessert menu; try the warm chocolate-chip pie topped with whipped cream. The large bar upstairs has a ceiling all a-twinkle with ersatz stars. *20 E. Broad St., tel. 912/233–5757. Dress: informal. Reservations accepted. AE, CB, DC, MC, V. Sun. jazz brunch.*

Moderate–Expensive

River House. This stylish restaurant sits over the spot where the SS *Savannah* set sail for her maiden voyage across the ocean in 1819. For starters try the snails wrapped in puff pastry, baked and served with beurre blanc sauce; or oysters on the half shell. There are a number of mesquite-grilled entrees, including swordfish topped with raspberry butter sauce and grouper Florentine, served with creamed spinach and a fresh dill and lemon butter sauce. Entrees are served with hush puppies, and fish dishes come with freshly made angel-hair pasta. *125 W. River St., tel. 912/234–1900. Dress: informal for lunch; jacket and tie required for dinner. Reservations accepted. AE, DC, MC, V.*

Inexpensive–Moderate
★

Seashell House. It may not look like much from the outside, but the steamed seafood inside is regarded by many to be the best in the city. It specializes in crab, shrimp and oysters, as well as a Low Country Boil that includes shrimp, sausage, corn, and whatever else comes to mind that day. It also features a seafood platter second to none. Be prepared to roll up your sleeves and dig in. *3111 Skidaway Rd., tel. 912/352–8116. Dress: casual. No reservations. AE, MC, V.*

Shrimp Factory. Like all riverfront restaurants, this was once an old warehouse. Now it's a light and airy place with exposed brick, wood paneling, beamed ceilings, and huge windows that let you watch the parade of ships on the water. A house specialty is pine bark stew—five native seafoods simmered with potatoes, onions, and herbs, and served with blueberry muffins. The extensive lunch and dinner menus have few offerings that don't come from the sea. Blackened dolphin filet is smothered with herbs and julienned sweet red peppers in butter sauce. Baked deviled crabs are served with chicken baked rice. Fish entrees are accompanied by angel-hair pasta, and there is a delicious whipped cheese spread for the warm French bread. *313 E. River St., tel. 912/236–4229. Dress: informal. Reservations accepted. AE, DC, MC, V.*

Lodging

While Savannah has plenty of chain hotels and motels, ranging from the simple to the sublime, the city's most distinctive lodgings are the historic inns. There are more than two dozen historic inns, guest houses, and bed-and-breakfasts in the Historic District.

If "historic inn" brings to your mind images of roughing it in picturesque but shabby genteel mansions with slightly antiquated plumbing, you're in for a surprise. Most of the inns are in mansions, most of them with high ceilings, spacious rooms, and ornate carved millwork. Most have canopied, four-poster, or Victorian brass beds and 19th-century antiques. Most of them *also* have enormous marble baths with whirlpools, hot tubs, or Jacuzzis (if not all of the above), and many of them have a film library for the in-room VCRs. Virtually all have turndown service with a chocolate or praline and, in some, a discreet brandy is placed on your nightstand. In most cases, Continental breakfast and afternoon aperitifs are included in the rate.

The most highly recommended properties in each price category are indicated by a star ★.

Category	Cost*
Very Expensive	over $100
Expensive	$75–$100
Moderate	$50–$75
Inexpensive	under $50

*double room; add taxes or service

The following credit-card abbreviations are used: AE, American Express; CB, Carte Blanche; DC, Diners Club; MC, MasterCard; V, Visa.

Inns and Guest Houses
Very Expensive
★

Ballastone Inn. This sumptuous inn is located within a mansion, dating from 1835, that was once, so it is said, a bordello. The Ballastone is notable for the wildly dramatic designs of its Scalamandre wallpaper and fabrics, which show off the Savannah colors to full advantage. Each of the 19 rooms has a different theme, with distinctive colors, ambience, and 18th-or 19th-century antiques. In Scarborough Fair, a vivid red and yellow room, the fabric pattern was adapted from a Victorian china serving platter in the Davenport House. That exquisite third-floor room has two queen-size Victorian brass beds, a Queen Anne lowboy and writing desk, and a Victorian slipper chair. On the garden level (there are three stories in addition to the garden level), rooms are small and cozy, with exposed brick walls, beamed ceilings, and in some cases windows at eye level with the lush courtyard. One such room is the Sorghum Cane, trimmed in the bronze color of sugar cane molasses; it has two queen-size brass beds, wicker furniture, and wall fabric patterned after the etched glass window of a restored local house. Afternoon tea or wine served daily; bedtime turn-downs with chocolate and brandy. *14 E. Oglethorpe Ave., 31401, tel. 912/236–1484. 19 rooms with bath. Facilities: concierge, courtyard, Jacuzzis, in-room VCR, film library. AE, MC, V.*

Foley House. In the parlor of this four-story 1896 house, carved gargoyles flank the original fireplace and there is a graceful brass-and-crystal chandelier. On the newel post in the hall there is an elaborate lamp that worked as an extra in *Gone With the Wind.* There are four rooms in the carriage house and 16 spacious rooms (four with Jacuzzis) in the main house, all with canopied or four-poster beds, polished hardwood floors covered with Oriental rugs, and 19th-century antiques. There is a splendid tapestry in the Essex Room (an especially romantic room with a balcony on Chippewa Square), a king-size bed and day bed, and an extra large bath with whirlpool. When you call to reserve, ask about the special package deals. *14 W. Hull St., 31401, tel. 912/232–6622, in GA 800/822–4658, outside GA 800/647–3708. 20 rooms with bath. Facilities: concierge, courtyard with hot tub, VCRs, film library. AE, MC, V.*

★ **The Gastonian.** Hugh and Roberta Lineberger's inn will probably, to put it modestly, knock your socks off. The mansion was built in 1868, and each of its 13 sumptuous suites is distinguished with vivid Scalamandre colors. The Caracalla Suite is named for the marble bath with an eight-foot whirlpool tub. The huge bedroom has a king-size canopy bed, working fireplace, and a lounge with a mirrored wet bar. The French Room, resembling a 19th-century French boudoir, is done in blues and whites, with Oriental rugs and flocked wallpaper. All rooms have working fireplaces and antiques from the Georgian and Regency periods. In the morning, a full breakfast is served in the formal dining room—pancakes, eggs, waffles, country ham, grits, fresh fruit, biscuits, and juice—or you can opt for a Continental breakfast in your room. Each guest receives a fruit basket and split of wine upon arrival. *220 E. Gaston St., 31401, tel. 912/232–2869. 13 suites with bath. Facilities: concierge, VCRs, film library, whirlpools, courtyard, and sun deck with hot tub. AE, MC, V.*

Expensive–
Very Expensive
Olde Harbour Inn. The building dates from 1892, when it was built on the riverfront as a warehouse and processing plant, but the old inn is actually a thoroughly modern facility that housed condos until 1987. Each suite has a fully equipped kitchen, including dishwasher and detergent. All suites overlook the river, and have wall-to-wall carpeting, exposed brick walls painted white, and a canopied or four-poster bed. There are studio suites; regular suites with living room, bedroom, kitchen, and bath; and loft suites. (The latter are lofty indeed, with 25-foot ceilings, balconies overlooking the water, huge skylights, and ample room to sleep six.) Each evening a dish of sherbet is brought to your room and placed in the freezer, and each morning croissants, blueberry muffins, juice, and coffee are served in a cozy breakfast room. *508 E. Factors Walk, 31401, tel. 912/234–4100 or 800/553–6533. 24 suites with bath.*

Facilities: concierge, room service, fully equipped kitchen, cable TV with remote control, VCR, film library, honor bar, valet laundry, and parking. AE, MC, V.

Expensive **Eliza Thompson House.** This 25-room guest house, located on
★ one of the Historic District's prettiest tree-lined streets, was originally built in 1847 for "Miss Eliza." There are king- and queen-size four-poster and canopied beds; some rooms with wall-to-wall carpeting, others with Oriental rugs covering the Georgia pine floors. The choice rooms overlook the large brick courtyard, which is a popular place for wedding receptions. In nice weather the complimentary breakfast is served at tables placed around a tiered fountain. *5 W. Jones St., 31401, tel. 912/ 236–3620 or 800/845–7638. 25 rooms with bath. Facilities: concierge. AE, MC, V.*

★ **Forsyth Park Inn.** As the name suggests, this Victorian mansion sits across the street from Forsyth Park. In the foyer is a grand piano, and afternoon wines and cheeses are taken to the accompaniment of Mercer and Gershwin music. Rooms are outfitted with 19th-century furnishings, including king- and queen-size four-poster beds, and have working fireplaces, large marble baths (some with whirlpools). The carriage house, just off the courtyard, has a suite with bath, complete kitchen, and a screened porch. *109 W. Hall St., 31401, tel. 912/ 233–6800. 9 rooms with private bath; 1 private guest cottage. AE, V, MC.*

Bed-and-Breakfast **Jesse Mount House.** The Georgian home of Lois and Howard
Expensive Crawford (the house is named for the original owner in 1854)
★ has two full floors for guests, one on the garden level and the other on the second floor. The three-bedroom suite on the upper level has a sunny sitting room with white-iron furniture, shower-bath, refrigerator and coffeemaker, wineglasses, and dishes; two of the bedrooms have fireplaces with gas logs. Breakfast (freshly squeezed orange juice, croissants, blueberry muffins, coffee) can be taken either in your own quarters or with the Crawfords in the formal dining room. *209 W. Jones St., 31401, tel. 912/236–1774. 2 3-bedroom suites with bath. Facilities: cable TV, private phones. No credit cards.*

R.S.V.P. Savannah (417 E. Charlton St., 31401, tel. 912/232– RSVP) is a bed-and-breakfast service that can reserve accommodations for you in Savannah, Tybee, and the surrounding area.

Hotels and Motels **DeSoto Hilton.** Three massive chandeliers glisten over the jar-
Expensive– dinieres, fresh flowers, and discreetly placed conversation
Very Expensive areas of the spacious lobby. The chandeliers are from the his-
★ toric DeSoto Hotel that stood on this site long ago. Guest rooms are on the cushy side, in Savannah peach and green, with wall-to-wall carpeting, traditional furniture, and king, queen, or two double beds. (Best view is from the corner kings, which have the added attraction of coffeemakers, refrigerators, and such). Suites have kitchens and custom-made contemporary furnishings in the bedroom, sitting room, and dining area. *15 E. Liberty St., 31401, tel. 912/232–9000 or 800/445–8667. 254 rooms; 9 suites with bath. Facilities: concierge, free parking, restaurant and lounge, outdoor pool with sundeck, golf and tennis privileges at area clubs. AE, CB, DC, MC.*

Hyatt. When this riverfront hotel was built in 1981, preservationists opposed a seven-story structure in the historic district. Its modern design has a towering atrium and a pleasant central lounge, as well as glass elevators. Its rooms have mauve furnishings and balconies overlooking the atrium, the Savannah River, or Bay St. MD's Lounge is the ideal spot to have a drink and watch the river traffic drift by. *2 W. Bay St., tel. 912/238–1234 or 800/228–9000. 346 rooms. Facilities: 2 restaurants, 2 lounges, indoor pool, gift shop, AE, CB, DC, MC, V.*

★ **The Mulberry.** There are so many objets d'art in the public rooms that the management has obligingly provided a walking tour brochure. There are, to mention but a few, 18th-century oil paintings, an English grandfather clock dating from 1803, Chinese vases from the Ching Dynasty, an ornate Empire game table—and to think this was once a Coca-Cola bottling plant. The restaurant is a sophisticated affair with crystal chandeliers and mauve velvet Regency furniture. There is a spacious courtyard covered with a mosquito net, which keeps it about 10 degrees cooler in the summer. The guest rooms are in a traditional motif; suites have queen-size beds, wet bars, amenity packages, and river views. *601 E. Bay St., 31401, tel. 912/238–1200 or 800/554–5544 (in GA 800/282–9198). 100 rooms, 25 suites with bath. Facilities: concierge, bar, restaurant, outdoor pool, rooftop deck with Jacuzzi, accommodations for nonsmokers and the handicapped. AE, DC, MC, V.*

River Street Inn. This elegant Legacy Hotel offers panoramic views of the Savannah River. Rooms are furnished with antiques and reproductions from the era of King Cotton. Amenities include turn-down service. The interior is so lavish, it's difficult to believe it was only recently a vacant warehouse dating back to 1830. One floor includes charming shops, another a New Orleans-style restaurant and blues club. *115 E. River St., tel. 912/234–6400. 44 rooms. Facilities: restaurant, lounge, shops. AE, DC, MC, V.*

Moderate **Days Inn.** This downtown hotel is located in the Historic District near the City Market, only a block off River Street. Its compact rooms have modular furnishings and most amenities, including HBO/ESPN on the tube and valet service. Interior corridors and an adjacent parking garage minimize its motel qualities. *201 W. Bay St., tel. 912/236–4440 or 800/325–2525. 235 rooms. Facilities: restaurant, pool, gift shop. AE, DC, MC, V.*

Nightlife

Savannah's nightlife is a reflection of the city's laid-back, easygoing personality. Some clubs feature live reggae, hard rock, and other contemporary music, but most stay with traditional blues, jazz, and piano bar vocalists. After-dark merrymakers usually head for watering holes on Riverfront Plaza or the southside.

Jazz Clubs **Savannah Blues** (117 E. River St., tel. 912/234–6400, ext. 107) offers a variety of live music, including blues, on Tuesdays, Fridays and Saturdays in the brick basement of a cotton warehouse.

Bars and **Congress Street Station** (121 W. Congress St., tel. 912/236–
Nightclubs 7309) is a small dark club that formerly was called Nightflight. It's still the city's liveliest music hall, featuring a variety of name performers in rock, blues, jazz, reggae, folk, country and

comedy. The age of the crowd on the tiny dance floor depends on who's on the bandstand.

Kevin Barry's Irish Pub (117 W. River St., tel. 912/233–9626), a cozy pub with a friendly bar and traditional Irish music, is *the* place to be on St. Patrick's Day. The rest of the year there's a mixed bag of tourists and locals, young and old. **Hollywood's** (9 W. Bay St., tel. 912/233–8347), across from the Hyatt Regency, is a very active singles bar, where young locals and out-of-towners mix it up to taped Top-40 music.

The Golden Isles and Okefenokee Swamp

The Golden Isles are a string of lush, subtropical barrier islands meandering lazily down Georgia's Atlantic coast from Savannah to the Florida border. Three of the islands—Jekyll Island, Sea Island, and St. Simons Island—are connected to the mainland by bridges in the vicinity of Brunswick; these are the only ones accessible by automobile. The Cumberland Island National Seashore is accessible by ferry from St. Mary's. Little St. Simons Island, a privately owned retreat with a guest lodge, is reached by a private launch from St. Simons.

The islands have a long history of human habitation; Indian relics have been found on them that date back to about 2500 BC. According to legend, the various Indian nations agreed that no wars would be fought there and that tribal members would visit only in a spirit of friendship.

Each Golden Isle has a distinctive personality, shaped by its history and ecology. About 50 miles inland is the Okefenokee Swamp National Wildlife Refuge, which has a character all its own.

Cumberland Island National Seashore

Numbers in the margin correspond with points of interest on the Golden Isles map.

The largest, most southerly, and most primitive of Georgia's coastal islands is **Cumberland,** a 16-by-3-mile sanctuary of marshes, dunes, beaches, forests, lakes and ponds, estuaries and inlets. Waterways are home to gators, otters, snowy egrets, great blue herons, ibis, wood storks, and more than 300 other bird species. In the forests are armadillo, wild horses, deer, raccoons, and an assortment of reptiles.

After the ancient Guale Indians came 16th-century Spanish missionaries, 18th-century English soldiers, and 19th-century planters. During the 1880s, Thomas Carnegie of Pittsburgh built several lavish homes here, but the island remained largely as nature created it. In the early 1970s, the federal government established the Cumberland Island National Seashore and opened this natural treasure to the public.

Getting Around   The only public access to the island is by *The Cumberland Queen,* a reservations-only, 150-passenger ferry based near the National Park Service Information Center at the docks at St. Mary's on the mainland. From mid-May through Labor Day, the *Queen* departs from St. Mary's daily at 9 and 11:45 AM

Golden Isles

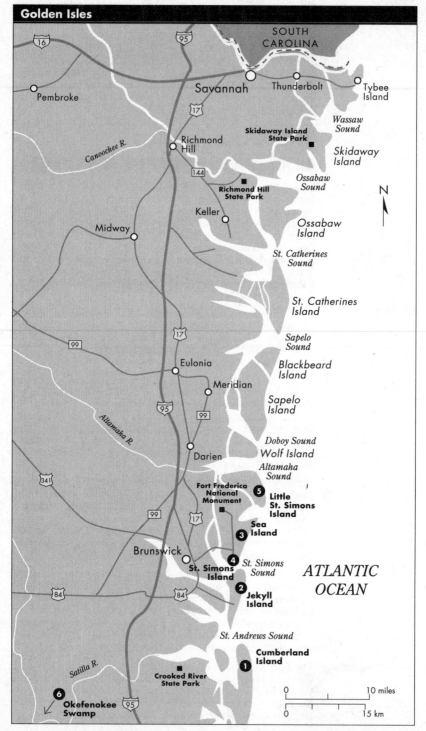

South Carolina

Pembroke

16
95

Savannah
Thunderbolt
Tybee Island

17

Wassaw Sound

Skidaway Island State Park

Richmond Hill

144

Skidaway Island

Ossabaw Sound

Richmond Hill State Park

Keller

Canoochee R.

Midway

Ossabaw Island

St. Catherines Sound

St. Catherines Island

N

99

17

Sapelo Sound

Eulonia

Blackbeard Island

Meridian

95

99

Sapelo Island

Altamaha R.

341

Darien

Doboy Sound
Wolf Island

Altamaha Sound

Fort Frederica National Monument

5 Little St. Simons Island

99

17

3 Sea Island

Brunswick

4 St. Simons Sound

St. Simons Island

ATLANTIC OCEAN

84

84

2 Jekyll Island

St. Andrews Sound

1 Cumberland Island

Satilla R.

Crooked River State Park

6 Okefenokee Swamp

95

| 0 | | 10 miles |
| 0 | | 15 km |

and departs from Cumberland at 10:15 AM and 4:45 PM. The trip takes 45 minutes. For the remainder of the year there is no ferry on Tuesday and Wednesday.

Important Addresses and Numbers To make ferry reservations or obtain further information, contact the **National Park Service** (Cumberland Island National Seashore, Box 806, St. Mary's 31558, tel. 912/882–4335). Ferry bookings are very heavy during summer, but cancellations and no-shows often make last-minute space available.

Exploring From the Park Service docks at the island's southern end, you can follow wooded nature trails, swim and sun on 18 miles of undeveloped beaches, go fishing and bird-watching, and view the ruins of Carnegie's great estate, **Dungeness.** You can also join history and nature walks led by Park Service rangers. There is no transportation on the island, so the length of your explorations will be determined by your own interests and energy. Bear in mind that summers are hot and humid, and that you must bring your own food, soft drinks, sunscreen, and a reliable insect repellant. *Nothing can be purchased on the island.*

Lodging Camping Novice campers usually prefer **Sea Camp,** a five-minute walk from the *Cumberland Queen* dock, with rest rooms and showers adjacent to campsites. The beach is just beyond the dunes. Experienced campers will want to hike 3–10 miles to several areas where cold-water spigots are the only amenities. Contact the National Park Service (*see* Important Addresses and Numbers).

Hotels **Greyfield Inn.** The island's only hotel lodgings are in a turn-of-the-century Carnegie family home. Greyfield's public areas are filled with family mementoes, furnishings, and portraits (you may feel as though you've stepped into one of Agatha Christie's mysterious Cornwall manors). Prices include all meals, sales tax, mandatory gratuity, and pickup and drop off by the inn's ferry at Fernandina Beach, Florida. *Drawer B, Fernandina Beach, FL 32034, tel. 904/261–6408. 9 rooms. MC, V. Very Expensive (over $100).*

Riverview Hotel. Rooms are spartan but air-conditioned in this hotel opposite the Park Service docks in St. Mary's. Seagle's Restaurant serves inexpensive breakfast, lunch, dinner, and cocktails. *105 Osborne St., St. Mary's 31558, tel. 912/882–3242. 18 rooms. Facilities: restaurant, lounge. AE, DC, MC, V. Moderate ($50–$75).*

Jekyll Island

For 56 winters, between 1886 and 1942, America's rich and famous faithfully came south to **Jekyll Island.** Through the Gilded Age, the Great War, the Roaring '20s, and the Great Depression, Vanderbilts and Rockefellers, Morgans and Astors, Macys, Pulitzers, and Goodyears shuttered their Fifth Avenue castles and retreated to the serenity of their wild Georgia island. There they built elegant "cottages," played golf and tennis, and socialized. Early in World War II, the millionaires departed for the last time. In 1947, the state of Georgia purchased the entire island for the bargain price of $650,000.

Getting Around *By Plane*	Glynco Jetport, six miles north of Brunswick, is served by **Atlantic Southeast Airlines** (tel. 404/765–2000) flights from Atlanta.
By Car	From Brunswick by car, take the Jekyll Island Causeway ($1 per car).
Important Addresses and Numbers	**The Jekyll Island Convention and Visitors Bureau** (901 Jekyll Island Causeway, Jekyll Island 31520, tel. 912/635–3636), at the end of the causeway, is open daily 9–5.
Guided Tours	Tours of the **Jekyll Island Club Historic District** originate at the Museum Orientation Center on Stable Road. Ninety-minute tours are given in open-air trolleys. Sites include several restored homes and buildings in the 240-acre historic district: Indian Mound; William Rockefeller's shingled cottage; and Faith Chapel, illuminated by stained-glass windows signed by Louis Comfort Tiffany. Audiovisual orientations are presented a half-hour before each tour departs. *Exit 35, tel. 912/635–2236. Admission: $6 adults, $4 children 6–18. Tours operate daily Labor Day–Memorial Day 10 AM, noon, 2 PM; Memorial Day–Labor Day, tours at 10 AM, noon, 2 and 4 PM.*
Exploring	Jekyll Island is still a vast playground, but no longer restricted to the rich and famous. For recreation, there is golf (63 holes), tennis, fishing, biking, and jogging. There is also a new water park, picnic grounds, and tours of the historic homes.
	One side of the island is flanked by nearly 10 miles of hard-packed Atlantic beaches; the other, by the Intracoastal Waterway and picturesque salt marshes. Deer and wild turkeys inhabit interior forests of pine, magnolia, and moss-veiled live oaks. Egrets, pelicans, herons, and sandpipers skim the gentle surf.
	Jekyll's clean, mostly uncommercialized beaches are free and open to the public year-round. Bathhouses with rest rooms, changing areas, and showers are open at regular intervals along the beach. Beachwear, suntan lotion, rafts, snacks, and drinks are available at the **Jekyll Shopping Center,** facing the beach at Beachview Drive.
Participant Sports *Golf*	Jekyll's 63 holes of golf include three 18-hole courses (tel. 912/635–2368) with a main clubhouse on Capt. Wylly Rd. and a 9-hole course (tel. 912/635–2170) on Beachview Dr.
Tennis	Nine courts include J.P. Morgan's indoor court (tel. 912/635–2860).
Water Park	**Summer Waves,** an 11-acre water park, opened in June 1988 with an 18,000-square-foot wave pool; two 330-foot water slides; a children's activity pool; and a 1,000-foot river for tubing and rafting. *210 Riverview Dr., tel. 912/635–2074. Admission: $7.95 adults, $5.95 children 4–8. Open daily 10–6.*
Dining	**The Grand Dining Room.** In the Jekyll Island Club Hotel the dining room sparkles with silver and crystal. What sets the meals apart from the ordinary are the sauces that flavor the dishes of fresh seafood, beef, veal, and chicken. *371 Riverview Dr., tel. 912/635–2600, ext. 1002. Jacket required for dinner. Reservations recommended. AE, CB, DC, MC, V. Expensive ($30–$40).*
	Saint Andrews Landing. This locally popular restaurant specializes in seafood. Recommended is the pecan shrimp and the

Friday night seafood buffet (seasonal). The candle-lit dining room has sweeping ocean views. The Hunt Club Lounge upstairs has live entertainment Tuesday–Saturday, and drinks are served poolside at the Barefoot Bar. *975 N. Beachview Dr., tel. 912/635–2531. Dress: informal. Reservations for large parties. AE, CB, DC, MC, V. Moderate–Expensive ($20–$40).*

Lodging **Jekyll Island Club Hotel.** Built in 1887, the four-story clubhouse, with wraparound verandas, towers, and turrets, once served as dining area, social center, and guest accommodations for some of the wealthiest families in the United States. In 1985, a group of Georgia businessmen spent $17 million restoring it to a splendor that would astonish even the Astors and Vanderbilts. The guest rooms and suites are custom-decorated with mahogany beds, armoires, and plush sofas and chairs. All have flowery views of the Intracoastal Waterway. All suites have Jacuzzis. The adjacent Sans Souci Apartments, former "bachelor quarters" built in 1886 by J.P. Morgan and William Rockefeller, have been converted into guest rooms. The hotel is operated as a Radisson Hotels resort. *371 Riverview Dr., Jekyll Island 31520, tel. 800/822–1886 or 800/843–5355 in GA. 60 rooms. Facilities: restaurant, outdoor pool, free shuttle to nearby beaches, tennis courts. AE, CB, DC, MC, V. Very Expensive (over $100).*

Holiday Inn Beach Resort. Nestled amid natural dunes and oaks in a secluded oceanfront setting, this hotel has a private beach, but its rooms with balconies still don't have an ocean view. Its recreational activities include outdoor pool and playground, tennis courts and 63 holes of golf. *200 S. Beachview Dr., Jekyll Island 31520, tel. 912/635–3311 or 800-HOLIDAY. 205 rooms. Facilities: restaurant, lounge with live entertainment, satellite cinema, some in-room saunas and whirlpools, bike rentals. AE, CB, DC, MC, V. Expensive ($75-$100).*

Jekyll Inn. The largest facility on the island, once a Hilton Inn, changed its affiliation to Best Western in 1989. Located on a landscaped 15-acre site, these oceanfront units, including some villas with kitchenettes, also underwent a $2.5 million renovation. Rooms were redecorated with new lighting and carpeting and saunas and Jacuzzis in some bathrooms. Island decor was added to the second-floor Ocean View lounge. *975 Beachview Dr., Jekyll Island 31520, tel. 912/635–2531 or 800/528–1234. 264 rooms. Facilities: restaurant, large pool, playground. AE, CB, DC, MC, V. Moderate-Very Expensive ($75-over $100).*

Sea Island

❸ **Sea Island** has been the domain of the **Cloister Hotel** since 1928. Attached to St. Simons Island by a bridge over a narrow waterway, and a good many steps up the social ladder, the resort lives up to its celebrity status. Guests lodge in spacious, comfortably appointed rooms and suites in the Spanish Mediterranean main hotel and in beachside cottages and villas.

For recreation, there's a choice of golf, tennis, swimming in pools or at the beach, skeet shooting, horseback riding, sailing, biking, lawn games, surf and deep-sea fishing. After dinner, a big-band orchestra plays for dancing in the lounge.

Like a person of some years, the Cloister has its eccentricities. Guest rooms were only recently equipped with TVs. Credit cards are not honored, but personal checks are accepted. Gentlemen must cover their arms in the dining rooms, even at breakfast. And for the most part, nouvelle cuisine, new American cuisine, and other culinary trends trends of the '80s have yet to breach the hotel's traditional menus.

There is no admission gate, and nonguests are free to admire the beautifully planted grounds and to drive past the mansions lining Sea Island Drive. Space permitting, they may also play at the Sea Island Golf Course and on the tennis courts and dine in the main dining room. *The Cloister, Sea Island 31561, tel. 912/638–3611, reservations 800/SEA–ISLAND. 264 rooms, 450 cottages, 44 condos. Full American Plan. No credit cards, but personal checks are accepted. Very Expensive (over $100).*

St. Simons Island

As large as Manhattan, with over 10,000 year-round residents, St. Simons is the Golden Isles' most complete and commercial resort destination. Fortunately, the accelerated development of condos, shopping districts, and other amenities in recent years has failed to spoil the natural beauty of the island's regal live oaks, beaches, and wavering salt marshes. Visits are highlighted by swimming and sunning on hard-packed beaches, biking, hiking, fishing, horseback riding, touring historic sites, and feasting on fresh local seafood at a growing number of restaurants. All of Georgia's beaches are in the public domain.

Getting Around Glynco Jetport, six miles north of Brunswick, is served by
By Plane **Atlantic Southeast Airlines** (tel. 404/765–2000) flights from Atlanta.

By Car Reach St. Simons by crossing the Torras Causeway from Brunswick. The island's accommodations and sights are widespread, so you'll need a car.

Important **St. Simons Island Chamber of Commerce** (Neptune Park, St.
Addresses and Simons Island 31522, tel. 912/638–9014) can provide helpful in-
Numbers formation about the area.

Exploring Many sights and activities are in **the village** area along Mallery Street at the south end of the island. Shops sell groceries, beachwear, and gifts. There are also several restaurants, pubs, and a popular public pier.

Also on the island's southern end is **Neptune Park,** which includes picnic tables, miniature golf, and beach access. In the summer, a freshwater swimming pool, with showers and rest rooms, is open in the **Neptune Park Casino** (tel. 912/638–2393), in addition to a roller-skating rink, bowling lanes, and snack bars. Also in the park is **St. Simons Lighthouse,** a beacon since 1872. The **Museum of Coastal History** in the lightkeeper's cottage has permanent and changing exhibits of coastal history. *Tel. 912/638–4666. Admission (including the lighthouse): $1.50 adults, $1 children 6–12. Open Tues.–Sat. 1–4, Sun. 1:30–4.*

Ft. Frederica National Monument, at the north end of the island, includes the tabby ruins of a fort built by English troops in the mid-1730s as a bulwark against a Spanish invasion from Florida. Around the fort are the foundations of homes and shops built by soldiers and civilians. Start your tour at the **National Park Service Visitors Center,** which has a film and displays. *Tel. 912/638–3639. Admission: $1 adults, 50¢ children. Open daily 9–5.*

On your way to Frederica, pause at **Christ Episcopal Church** on Frederica Road. Consecrated in 1886 following an earlier structure's desecration by Union troops, the white frame Gothic structure is surrounded by live oaks, dogwoods, and azaleas. The interior is highlighted by beautiful stained-glass windows. Donations welcome.

Dining   **Alfonza's Olde Plantation Supper Club.** Seafood, superb steaks, and plantation fried chicken are served in a gracious and relaxed environment. The club also has a cocktail lounge. *Harrington Ln., tel. 912/638–9883. Dress: informal. Reservations recommended. MC, V. Moderate ($20–$30).*

Blanche's Courtyard. Located in the village, this lively restaurant/nightclub is gussied up in "Bayou Victorian" dress, with lots of antiques and nostalgic memorabilia. True to its bayou decor, the menu features Cajun-style seafood as well as your basic steak and chicken. A ragtime band plays for dancers on the weekends. *440 Kings Way, tel. 912/638–3030. Dress: informal. Reservations accepted. AE, DC, MC, V. Moderate ($20–$30).*

Emmeline & Hessie. A large dining room and bar offer patrons a spectacular view of the marina and marshes. Specialties are seafood, steak, and lobster. There's also a bakery, a deli, and a seafood market on the premises. There's usually a line here, but it's well worth the wait to watch the sun set over the marshes as you dine. During the summer months, live bands play on the outdoor terrace. *Golden Isles Marina, tel. 912/638–9084. Dress: informal. No reservations. AE, MC, V. Inexpensive–Moderate ($15–$30).*

The Crab Trap. One of the island's most popular spots, the Crab Trap offers a variety of fried and broiled fresh seafood, oysters on the half shell, clam chowder, heaps of batter fries, and hush puppies. The atmosphere is rustic-casual—there's a hole in the middle of every table to deposit corn cobs and shrimp shells. *1209 Ocean Blvd., tel. 912/638–3552. Dress: informal. No reservations. MC, V. Inexpensive (under $20).*

Spanky's. This trendy restaurant and bar in the Golden Isles Marina is popular for hamburgers, pizza, salads, sandwiches, seafood, beer, and cocktails. The panoramic view is also a drawing point. *225 Marina Dr., tel. 912/638–0918. Dress: informal. No reservations. AE, MC, V. Inexpensive (under $20).*

Lodging   **The King and Prince Hotel and Villas.** This hotel facing the beach stepped into the deluxe resort category with a recently completed, multimillion-dollar modernization and expansion. Guest rooms are spacious, and villas offer from two to three bedrooms. *Box 798, 201 Arnold Rd., St. Simons Island 31522, tel. 912/638–3631. 124 rooms, 44 villas. Facilities: restaurant, indoor/outdoor pool, tennis, golf, bike rentals. AE, CB, DC, MC, V. Very Expensive (over $100).*

Sea Palms Golf and Tennis Resort. A contemporary resort complex with fully furnished, ultramodern villas nestled on an 800-acre site. *5445 Frederica Rd., St. Simons Island 31522, tel. 912/638–3351. 263 rooms. Facilities: restaurant, 2 pools, health club, 27-hole golf course, tennis, waterskiing, children's recreation programs. AE, CB, DC, MC, V. Very Expensive (over $100).*

Queen's Court. This family-oriented complex in the village has clean, modest rooms, some with kitchenettes. The grounds are beautiful. *437 Kings Way, St. Simons Island 31522, tel. 912/638 –8459. 23 rooms. Facilities: color cable TV, shower baths, pool. MC, V. Inexpensive (under $50).*

Little St. Simons Island

Six miles long, two to three miles wide, skirted by Atlantic beaches and salt marshes teeming with birds and wildlife, **Little St. Simons** is custom-made for Robinson Crusoe–style getaways. The island has been owned by one family since the early 1900s, and the only development is a rustic but comfortable guest compound. The island's forests and marshes are inhabited by deer, armadillos, horses, raccoons, gators, otters, and over 200 species of birds.

Guests are free to walk the six miles of undisturbed beaches, swim in the mild surf, fish from the dock, and seine for shrimp and crabs in the marshes. There are also horses to ride, nature walks with experts, and other island explorations that can be made by boat or in the back of a pickup truck.

Lodging and Dining **River Lodge and Cedar House.** Up to 24 guests can be accommodated in the lodge and house. Each has four bedrooms with twin or king-size beds, private baths, sitting rooms, and screened porches. Older hunting lodges have some private and some shared baths. None of the rooms are air-conditioned, but ceiling fans make sleeping comfortable. The rates include all meals and dinner wines (cocktails available at additional cost). Meals, often featuring fresh fish, pecan pie, and home-baked breads, are served family-style in the lodge dining room. *Box 1078, Little St. Simons Island 31522, tel. 912/638–7472. Facilities: stables, pool, beach, transportation from St. Simons Island, transportation on the island, fishing boats, interpretive guides. Minimum two-night reservations. MC, V. Very Expensive (over $100).*

Okefenokee Swamp National Wildlife Refuge

Covering more than 700 square miles of southeast Georgia, spilling over into northeast Florida, the mysterious rivers and lakes of the **Okefenokee Swamp** bristle with seen and unseen life. Scientists agree that Okefenokee is not duplicated anywhere else on Earth. The swamp is actually a vast peat bog, remarkable in geologic origin and history. Once part of the ocean floor, it now rises more than 100 feet above sea level.

As you travel by canoe or speedboat among the water-lily islands and the great stands of live oaks and cypress, be on the lookout for otters, egrets, muskrats, herons, cranes, and gators cruising the dark channels like iron-clad subs. The Okefenokee Swamp Park, eight miles south of Waycross, is a major visitor gateway to the refuge. The Swamp Park is a nonprofit development operating under a long-term lease. There are two other gateways to the swamp: an eastern entrance in the Suwanee Canal Recreation Area, near Folkston; and a western entrance at Stephen C. Foster State Park, outside the town of Fargo.

Seminole Indians, in their migrations south toward Florida's Everglades, once took refuge in the Great Okefenokee. Noting the many floating islands, they provided its name—"Land of the Trembling Earth."

Exploring **Okefenokee Swamp Park.** South of Waycross, via U.S. 1, the park offers orientation programs, exhibits, observation areas, wilderness walkways, an outdoor museum of pioneer life, and boat tours into the swamp that reveal its ecological uniqueness. A boardwalk and 90-foot tower are excellent places to glimpse cruising gators and a variety of birds. Gate admission includes a guided boat tour and all exhibits and shows. You may also arrange for lengthier explorations with a guide and a boat. *Waycross 31501, tel. 912/283–0583. Admission: $6 adults, $4 children 6–11. Open daily spring and summer, 9–6:30; fall and winter, 9–5:30.*

Suwanee Canal Recreation Area. This area, eight miles south of Folkston, via GA 121/23, is administered by the U.S. Fish and Wildlife Service. Stop first at the Visitor Information Center, which has an orientation film and exhibits on the Okefenokee's flora and fauna. A boardwalk takes you over the water to a 40-foot observation tower. At the concession building you may purchase snacks and sign up for guided boat tours into an 11-mile waterway, which resulted from efforts to drain the swamp a century ago. Hikers, bicyclists, and private motor vehicles are welcome on the Swamp Island Drive; several interpretive walking trails may be taken along the way. Picnicking is allowed. *Park Supt., Box 336, Folkston 31537, tel. 912/496–7156. Admission to the park is free. 1-hr tours: $4.25 adults, $2 children 5–11; 2-hr tours: $8.50 adults, $4 children 5–11. Refuge open Mar.–Sept., 10, 7 AM–7:30 PM; Sept. 11–Feb., 8–6. Closed major holidays.*

Stephen C. Foster State Park. Eighteen miles from Fargo, via GA 11, is an 80-acre island park entirely within the Okefenokee Swamp National Wildlife Refuge. The park encompasses a large cypress and black gum forest, a majestic backdrop for one of the thickest growths of vegetation in the southeastern United States. The lush terrain and the mirrorlike black waters of the swamp provide at least a part-time home for more than 225 species of birds, 41 species of mammals, 54 species of reptiles, 32 species of amphibians, and 37 species of fish. Park naturalists leading boat tours will spill out a wealth of swamp lore as riders observe gators, many bird species, and native trees and plants. You may also take a self-guided excursion in rental canoes and fishing boats. Camping is also available here (*see* Lodging). *Fargo 31631, tel. 912/637–5274. Admission free. Open Mar.–Sept. 14, 6:30 AM–8:30 PM; Sept. 15–Feb., 7 AM–7 PM.*

Lodging **Laura S. Walker State Park.** Near Okefenokee Swamp Park,
Camping but not in the swamp, are campsites ($8 a night) with electrical and water hookups. Be sure to pick up food and supplies on the way to the park. *Park Supt., Waycross 31501, tel. 912/283–*

4424. Facilities: playground, fishing docks, pool, picnic areas. Inexpensive (under $20).

Stephen C. Foster State Park. The park has furnished two-bedroom cottages ($45 a night Sun.–Thurs.; $55 weekends) and campsites with water, electricity, rest rooms, and showers ($8 a night). Because of roaming wildlife and poachers, the park's gates close between sunset and sunrise. If you're staying overnight, stop for groceries in Fargo beforehand. *Park Supt., Fargo 31631, tel. 912/637-5274. Inexpensive–Moderate ($8–$75).*

4 Louisiana

by Honey Naylor Louisiana is a state clearly divided. Locals refer to *North* Louisiana and *South* Louisiana, and even in conversation you can detect a capitalized distinction. *North* Louisiana is Southern and *South* Louisiana is not, except for those parishes (counties) north of Baton Rouge, which have a more Southern flavor than the rest of South Louisiana.

Louisiana's Mason-Dixon line is Alexandria, in the state's midsection. In sharp contrast to the rolling hills of North Louisiana, the terrain south of Alexandria is flat and marshy. There, amid canebrakes, rice paddies, and marshlands, Cajun fiddles tune up for fais-do-dos (dances); tables are laden with jambalaya, gumbo, and crawfish; and pirogues—small flat-bottom boats—are poled through bayous. One of the state's so-briquets is "Sportsman's Paradise," and this indeed is fishing, camping, and hunting territory, with the Gulf of Mexico sneaking into the coastal marshes.

Not a month goes by in Louisiana without a festival of some sort, and at press time plans were being made for a major statewide, year-long bash called Open House 1990.

New Orleans

The jewel in the South Louisiana crown is New Orleans, home of the splashiest festival in all of North America—Mardi Gras. When Rhett Butler took Scarlett O'Hara to New Orleans on their honeymoon, the city was scarred by war, carpetbaggers were looting the town, and decent folk feared for their lives. But gone with the wind the city wasn't. Captain Butler and his bride were entertained at a continuous round of lavish parties, suppers, and plays.

In the 1980s, New Orleans, like most cities, has its problems with crime and a depressed economy. But its reputation as a good-time town is intact. Despite its problems, New Orleans is forever finding something to celebrate. As well as world-famous Mardi Gras, new festivals crop up at the drop of a Panama hat. New Orleans party animals even celebrated a new addition to the Audubon Zoo.

The city's most famous party place is the French Quarter. Also called the Vieux Carré (Old Square), the Quarter is the original colony, founded in 1718 by French Creoles. As you explore its famous restaurants, antiques shops, and jazz haunts, try to imagine a handful of determined early 18th-century settlers living in crude palmetto huts, battling swamps, floods, hurricanes, and yellow fever. Two cataclysmic fires in the late 18th century virtually leveled the town. The Old Ursuline Convent on Chartres Street is the only remaining original French Colonial structure. Survival was a struggle for the Creoles, and the sobriquet "The City That Care Forgot" stems from a determination not only to live life but to celebrate it, come what may.

Necessity may be the mother of invention, but it was the Father of Waters that forced Crescent City denizens to devise a new vocabulary for dealing with directions. The Mississippi River moves in mysterious waves, looping around the city and wreaking havoc with ordinary directions. New Orleanians, ever resourceful, refer instead to lakeside (toward Lake Pont-

chartrain), riverside (toward the Mississippi), upriver (also
called uptown), and downriver (downtown).

Arriving and Departing

By Plane **New Orleans International Airport** (Moisant Field), located 15
miles west of New Orleans in Kenner, is served by American,
Continental, Delta, Eastern, Midway, Northwest, Royale,
Southwest, TWA, United, and USAir. Foreign carriers serving
the city include Aviateca, Lacsa, Sahsa, and Taca.

Between the Airport **Buses** operated by Louisiana Transit (tel. 504/737–9611) run
and Center City (every 22 minutes between the airport and Elk Place in the
Central Business District (CBD). Hours of operation are 6 AM
to 6:20 PM; the last bus leaves the airport at 5:40 PM. The $1.10
trip downtown takes about an hour.

Limousines of Rhodes Transportation (tel. 504/469–4555) leave
the airport every 5–10 minutes, 24 hours a day, for the 20- to
30-minute trip into town. The limos, which are really small
vans, drop passengers off at their hotels, so arrival time at your
destination will depend upon the number of stops the van
makes en route. Per-person fare is $7.

Taxi fare is $18 for up to three passengers, and $6 for each additional person. If you share a cab with three or four people in the
taxi line, the driver may agree to charge each of you the $7 limo
rate.

Driving from Kenner into New Orleans is via Airline Highway
(U.S. 61) or I–10. Hertz, Avis, Budget, and other major car-
rental agencies have outlets at the airport.

By Train **Amtrak** (800/USA–RAIL) trains pull into the CBD's Union
senger Terminal (1001 Loyola Ave., tel. 504/528–1610).

By Bus **Greyhound/Trailways** buses arrive and depart from Union Passenger Terminal (1001 Loyola Ave., tel. 504/525–9371 or 800/
237–8211).

By Car I–10 runs from Florida through New Orleans and on to California. I–55 is the north–south route, connecting with I–10 to the
west of New Orleans; I–59 heads for the northeast. U.S. 61 and
0 also run through New Orleans.

Getting Around

The French Quarter, laid out in a perfect grid pattern, covers
about a square mile and is best explored on foot. Should your
feet fail you, look for the Vieux Carré shuttle that loops around
the Quarter.

Several of the CBD sights are clustered together near the river
and can also be seen on a walking tour.

By Bus Buses require 60¢ exact change (except for the CBD shuttle,
which is 30¢). Transfers are 5¢ extra. The CBD shuttle bus
operates weekdays from 6:30 AM to 6 PM, and the Vieux
Carré shuttle operates weekdays from 5 AM to 7:23 PM. The
Regional Transit Authority (RTA) puts out a color-coded
RideGuide, available free at the tourist welcome centers
(*see* Tourist Information), and has a 24-hour information
service (tel. 504/569–2700; for the hearing impaired, 504/569–
2838).

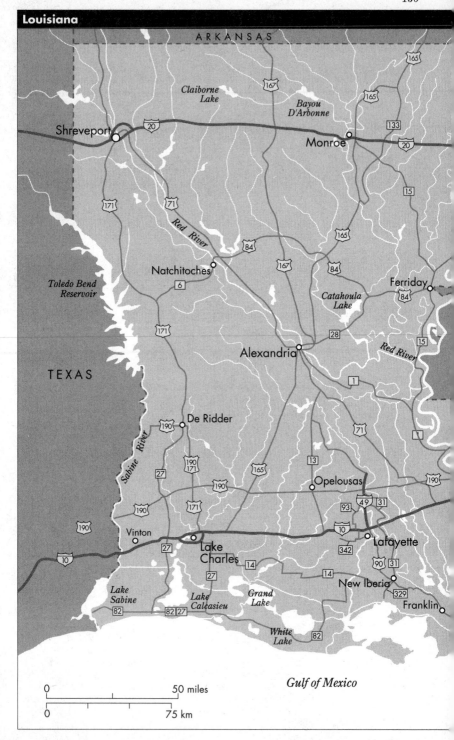

Louisiana

ARKANSAS

Shreveport

Claiborne
Lake

Bayou
D'Arbonne

Monroe

165

165

133

20

171

71

Red River

84

167

84

Ferriday

Natchitoches

6

Catahoula
Lake

84

15

Toledo Bend
Reservoir

171

28

Red River

15

Alexandria

1

TEXAS

De Ridder

190

71

1

Sabine River

27

190
171

13

190

165

Opelousas

190

190

171

93 49 31

Vinton

27

10

342

Lafayette

10

Lake
Charles

14

90 31

Lake
Sabine

27

Lake
Calcasieu

Grand
Lake

14

New Iberia

329

Franklin

82

82 27

White
Lake

82

Gulf of Mexico

0   50 miles

0   75 km

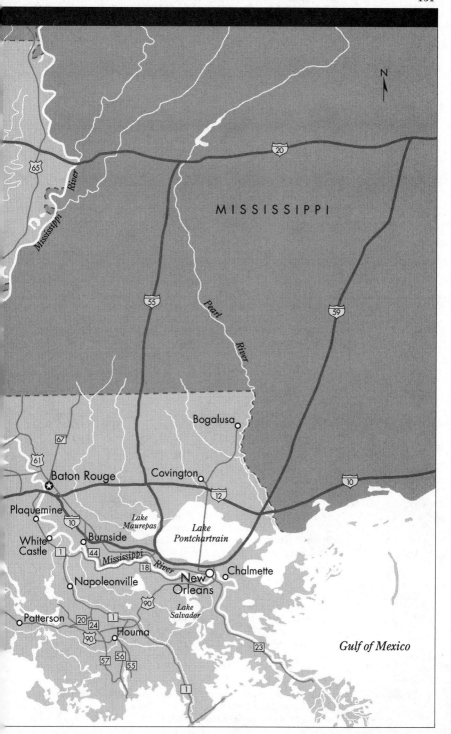

By Streetcar The St. Charles Streetcar, New Orleans's moving Historic Landmark, clangs up St. Charles Avenue through the Garden District, past the Audubon Zoo and other Uptown sights. The streetcar can be boarded in the CBD at Canal and Carondelet Streets (60¢ exact change). A round-trip sightseeing jaunt covers just over 13 miles and takes about 90 minutes. The streetcar operates daily, every five minutes between 7:30 AM and 6 PM, every 15–20 minutes between 6 PM and midnight, and hourly between midnight and 7 AM.

The Riverfront Streetcar rolls along the river between Esplanade Avenue and the Robin Street Wharf. It makes ten stops, five above and five below Canal St. Fare is 60¢ (exact change), and it operates weekdays from 6 AM–midnight; weekends 8 AM–midnight.

By Taxi Taxi fares start at $1.10, adding 20¢ for each fifth of a mile or 40 seconds of waiting time.

By Ferry A free ferry crosses the Mississippi from the Canal Street Wharf to Algiers, leaving the pier every 25 minutes.

Important Addresses and Numbers

Tourist Information To plan your trip, write to **The Greater New Orleans Tourist and Convention Commission** (1520 Sugar Bowl Dr., New Orleans, LA 70112). The Tourist Commission staffs a desk near the customs desk at New Orleans International Airport, but its main outlet is the **New Orleans Welcome Center.** *529 St. Ann St. in French Quarter, tel. 504/566–5031. Open daily Mar.–Nov. 10–6, Dec.–Feb. 9–5. Closed Thanksgiving, Christmas, Mardi Gras, and New Year's Day.*

Emergencies Dial 911 for **police** or **ambulance** in an emergency.

Doctor The following hospital emergency rooms are open all night: **Tulane Medical Center** (1415 Tulane Ave., tel. 504/588–5711), in the CBD near the French Quarter; **Touro Infirmary** (1401 Foucher St., tel. 504/897–8250), near the Garden District.

24-Hour Pharmacy **Eckerd's** (3400 Canal St., tel. 504/488–6661).

Guided Tours

Orientation Tours If you prefer a "known" in an unknown city, go in an air-conditioned, 45-passenger **Gray Line** bus (tel. 504/587–0861) for a two-hour tour of New Orleans's major sights. **Tours by Isabelle** (tel. 504/367–3963) uses air-conditioned, 14-passenger vans for a more personalized and multilingual three-hour tool around town. Both companies provide hotel pickup, and reservations can be made through your hotel.

Special-Interest Tours **Let's Go Antiquing** (tel. 504/899–3027) takes you under the wing of a knowledgeable guide to the city's antiques shops. **Specialty Tours** (tel. 504/861–2921) tailors tours to your taste, covering everything from architecture to voodoo. Statistics for the **Superdome** (tel. 504/587–3810) are staggering and you can learn all about the huge facility during daily tours. On the flatboats of **Honey Island Swamp Tours** (tel. 504/641–1769), steered by a professional wetland ecologist, you can tour one of the country's best-preserved river swamps. **Tours by Isabelle** (tel. 504/367–3963) takes you to the bayous for a visit with a Cajun alligator hunter. **Acadian-Creole Tours** (tel. 504/524–1700 or

504/524–1800) travels to a famous old sugar plantation. **Preservation Resource Center** (tel. 504/581–7032) occasionally conducts two-hour architectural tours of the CBD.

Exploring New Orleans

Numbers in the margin correspond with points of interest on the French Quarter and Central Business District map.

Tucked in between Canal Street, Esplanade Avenue, Rampart Street, and the Mississippi River, the Vieux Carré is a carefully preserved historic district. But the Quarter is also home to some 7,000 residents, some of the most famous of the French Creole restaurants, and many a jazz club. An eclectic crowd, which includes some of the world's best jazz musicians, ambles in and out of small two- and three-story frame, old-brick, and pastel-painted stucco buildings. Baskets of splashy subtropical plants dangle from the eaves of buildings with filigreed galleries, dollops of gingerbread, and dormer windows. Built flush with the *banquettes* (sidewalks), the houses, most of which date from the early to mid-19th century, front secluded courtyards awash with greenery and brilliant blossoms.

In the early 19th century, the American Sector was just upriver of the French Quarter. For that reason, street names change as you cross Canal Street from the French Quarter: Bourbon Street to Carondelet Street, Royal Street to St. Charles Avenue, and so on.

Nerve center of the nation's second-largest port and main parade route during Mardi Gras, the CBD cuts a wide swath between Uptown and Downtown, with Canal Street the official dividing line. Bordered by Canal Street, the river, Howard Avenue, and Loyola Avenue, the CBD has the city's newest high-tech convention hotels, along with ritzy new shopping malls, age-old department stores, foreign agencies, fast-food chains, monuments, and the monumental Superdome.

Nestled in between St. Charles Avenue, Louisiana Avenue, Jackson Avenue, and Magazine Street, the Garden District is aptly named. The Americans who built their estates upriver surrounded their homes with lavish lawns, forgoing the Creoles' preference for secluded courtyards. Many of the elegant Garden District homes were built during New Orleans's Golden Age, from 1830 until the Civil War. Magazine Street is heaven on earth for shoppers. Joggers, golfers, tennis buffs, and horseback riders head for Audubon Park, and animal lovers can get close to many different species at the Audubon Zoo.

The French Quarter Make your first stop the **New Orleans Welcome Center** (529 St. Ann St.), for free maps, brochures, and friendly advice.

❶ ❷ The **Welcome Center** is in the heart of **Jackson Square,** near a large equestrian statue of General Andrew Jackson, for whom the square is named. Jackson Square was known as Place d'Armes to the Creoles; it was renamed in the mid-19th century for the man who defeated the British in the Battle of New Orleans. Place d'Armes was the center of all Colonial life, home to parading militia, religious ceremonies, social gatherings, food vendors, entertainers, and pirates. The square remains a social hub today. Pirate attire is not uncommon in the colorful crowd that flocks to the square. The only thing missing is the militia.

The French Quarter and Central Business District

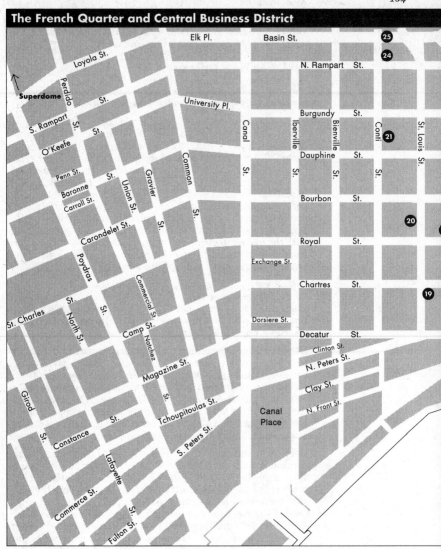

Beauregard-Keyes House, **8**

Café du Monde, **5**

Cornstalk Fence, **11**

First Skyscraper, **15**

Gallier House, **9**

Hermann-Grima House, **20**

Historic New Orleans Collection, **17**

Jackson Square, **2**

LaBranche House, **14**

Lafitte's Blacksmith Shop, **10**

Louis Armstrong Park, **22**

Louisiana State Museum, **4**

Madame John's Legacy, **13**

Musée Conti, **21**

Napoleon House, **19**

Old Ursuline Convent, **7**

Old U.S. Mint, **6**

Our Lady of Guadalupe, **24**

Preservation Hall, **16**

Pharmacy Museum, **18**

St. Louis Cathedral, **3**

St. Louis Cemetery No. 1, **25**

Theatre for the Performing Arts, **23**

Voodoo Museum, **12**

Welcome Center, **1**

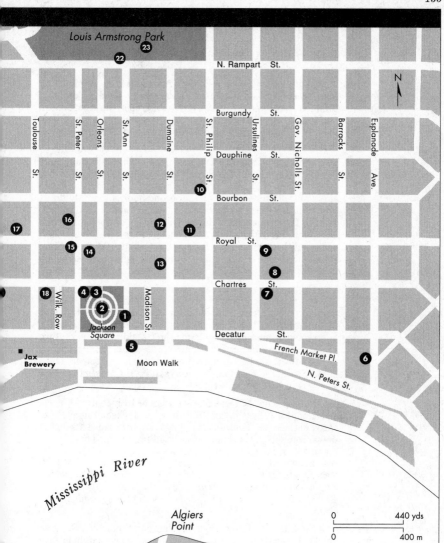

Louis Armstrong Park

N. Rampart   St.

Burgundy   St.

Dauphine   St.

Bourbon   St.

Royal   St.

Chartres   St.

Decatur   St.

French Market Pl.

N. Peters St.

Toulouse   St.

St. Peter   St.

Orleans   St.

St. Ann   St.

Dumaine   St.

St. Philip   St.

Ursulines   St.

Gov. Nicholls St.

Barracks   St.

Esplanade   Ave.

Wilk. Row

Madison St.

Jackson Square

Jax Brewery

Moon Walk

Mississippi   River

Algiers Point

0   440 yds

0   400 m

❸ St. Louis Cathedral, soaring above the earthly activity taking place right in its front yard, is a quiet reminder of the spiritual life of New Orleans citizens. The present church dates from 1794, and it was restored in 1849. Tours are conducted daily except during services.

Alongside the church are **Pirate's Alley** and **Père Antoine's Alley.** Those cracked-flagstone passageways seem redolent of infamous plots and pirate intrigue—but, alas, the streets were laid long after Jean Lafitte and his Baratarian band had vanished. William Faulkner wrote his first novel, *A Soldier's Pay,* while living at **624 Pirate's Alley.**

❹ The church is flanked by two buildings of the **Louisiana State Museum.** As you face the church, the **Cabildo** is on the left, the **Presbytere** on the right. Transfer papers for the Louisiana Purchase of 1803 were signed on the second floor of the Cabildo. It now holds historic documents, works of art, and artifacts pertinent to the region, including a death mask of Napoleon, who was a hero for many a New Orleanian. A four-alarm fire in 1988 damaged the roof and top floor of the Cabildo. At press time, repairs were under way and the museum is scheduled to reopen in 1990.

The Presbytere was built as a home for priests of the church, but was never used for this purpose. Like the Cabildo, it is also a museum, with changing exhibits. The odd-shaped structure in the arcade of the Presbytere is a Confederate submarine. Hours and admission charges for the Cabildo and Presbytere are the same. *Jackson Sq., tel. 504/568–6968. Admission: $3 adults; $2 students, children 3–17, and senior citizens. Open Wed.–Sun. 10–5. Closed Thanksgiving, Christmas, New Year's Day, and Mardi Gras.*

You can see what life was like for upscale 19th-century Creole apartment dwellers in the **1850 House** in Jackson Square. Located in the lower Pontalba Buildings (lower because it's on the downriver side of the square), the building contains period furnishings, antique dolls, and evidence of cushy Creole living. It, too, is part of the Louisiana State Museum complex. *525 St. Ann St., Jackson Sq., tel. 504/568–6968. Admission: $3 adults, $2 students and senior citizens. Open Wed.–Sun. 10–5. Closed Christmas, Thanksgiving, New Year's Day, and Mardi Gras.*

The **Pontalba Buildings** that line Jackson Square on St. Ann and St. Peter streets are among the oldest apartment houses in the country. Built between 1849 and 1851, they were constructed under the supervision of the baroness Micaela Pontalba, who occasionally lent a helping hand to the laborers.

The promenade of **Washington Artillery Park,** across Decatur Street, affords a splendid perspective of the square on one side and Old Man River rolling along on the other. On the **Moon Walk** promenade, across the tracks from the park, you can sit on a bench or stroll down the steps to the water's edge.

Washington Artillery Park is anchored on the upriver side by the **Jackson Brewery and Millhouse,** and downriver by the **French Market.** Jax Beer used to be brewed in the brewery, and the market is on the site of a late 17th-century Indian trading post. Both are now filled with boutiques and restaurants. Toward Canal Street on Decatur Street is the Jackson Brewery

Corporation's latest addition, **The Marketplace,** on Decatur Street, home of yet more restaurants and retail outlets.

By 1991 the **Aquarium of the Americas and Riverfront Park** are set to be completed. Ground has already been broken and things are coming along swimmingly for the aquarium and park, which will cover 16 acres behind the Bienville Street Wharf.

⑤ **Café du Monde** in the French Market, a 24-hour haven for café au lait and *beignets* (square, puffy, holeless doughnuts sprinkled with powdered sugar), is a traditional last stop after a night out on the town, and a New Orleans institution.

Make a right and continue down Decatur Street to Esplanade Avenue. *This area on the fringe of the Quarter should be avoided at night,* but you'll be safe during the day when you visit the Jazz and Mardi Gras Exhibits in the **Old U.S. Mint.** This
⑥ was the first branch of the U.S. Mint, and it turned out money hand over fist from 1838 until Something (the Civil War) stopped it in 1861. It's now a part of the Louisiana State Museum. **A Streetcar Named Desire,** one of the cars from the old Desire line, is in mint condition and on display behind the building. *400 Esplanade Ave., tel. 504/568-6968. Admission: $3 adults; $2 students and senior citizens, children under 12 free. Open Wed.–Fri. 10–5. Closed Mardi Gras, Thanksgiving, Christmas, and New Year's Day.*

Speaking of streetcars, the upriver trip is now a breeze since the Riverfront Streetcar began rolling. The streetcar rumbles right along the river from Esplanade Avenue all the way up to the Robin Street Wharf, where the *Mississippi Queen* and the *Delta Queen* dock.

After viewing the mint, make a left; after one block, turn left
⑦ again at Chartres Street and walk three blocks to **The Old Ursuline Convent** (1114 Chartres St.). Erected in 1749 by order of Louis XV, it is the only building remaining from the original colony. The Sisters of Ursula, who arrived in New Orleans in 1727, occupied the building from 1749 to 1824. It is now an archival and research center for the archdiocese and not open to the public.

The Greek Revival raised cottage across the street is the
⑧ **Beauregard-Keyes House.** General P.G.T. Beauregard, the man who ordered the first shot at Fort Sumter, lived in the house after the Civil War. In the mid-1940s the house was bought by novelist Frances Parkinson Keyes (author of *Dinner at Antoine's*), whose office was in the slave quarters. Costumed docents will tell you all about the dwelling and its dwellers. *1113 Chartres St., tel. 504/523-7257. Admission: $3 adults, $2 senior citizens and students, $1 children under 12. Open Mon.–Sat. 10–3. Closed Christmas, Thanksgiving, and Mardi Gras.*

At the corner turn right onto Ursulines Street and walk one
⑨ block to Royal Street, where you'll find the **Gallier House.** Built about 1857 by famed architect James Gallier, Jr., this is one of the best-researched house museums in the city. The Galliers were Irish, but this is a fine example of how well-heeled Creoles lived. *1118-32 Royal St., tel. 504/523-6722. Admission: $3.75 adults, $3 senior citizens, AAA members, and students, children under 12, $2.25; $9 families. Tours Mon.–Sat. 10:30–3:45. Closed Thanksgiving, Christmas, and Mardi Gras.*

Back on Ursulines Street, turn right and walk one block to Bourbon Street, turn left, and go one more block. The tattered cottage is **Lafitte's Blacksmith Shop** (941 Bourbon St.). The house dates back to 1772, and it is typical of houses built by the earliest settlers. According to a cherished legend, the cottage was once a front for freebooter Jean Lafitte's smuggling and slave trade. Today it's a neighborhood bar, and for a long time it has been a favorite haunt of artists and writers, the well-known and the never-known (*see* Nightlife).

Go down St. Philip Street one block and turn right for a look at the **Cornstalk Fence** (915 Royal St.). Morning glories and ears of corn are intricately intertwined in the cast-iron fence.

At the corner of Royal Street turn right onto Dumaine Street. The **Voodoo Museum** is an "only in New Orleans" phenomenon and either spooky or campy (or both), depending upon what spirits move you. Remembrances of voodoo queen Marie Laveau are prominently displayed, along with altars, artifacts, and everything you need for a voodoo to-do. *724 Dumaine St., tel. 504/523–7685. Admission: $3 adults, $2 students and senior citizens; $1 children 6–12. Open Sun.–Thurs. 10–7, Fri. and Sat. 10–10.*

As you leave the museum, turn right and walk one block on Dumaine Street. **Madame John's Legacy** (632 Dumaine St.) is so named for a character in the short story "'Tite Poulette,'" by 19th-century New Orleans writer George Washington Cable. The West Indies–style house was built in 1788 on the site of the birthplace of Renato Beluche, a Lafitte lieutenant who helped Andrew Jackson in the Battle of New Orleans. Part of the Louisiana State Museum (tel. 504/568–6968), the house is open sporadically, depending upon the state's financial situation.

Go back to Royal Street, turn left and walk two blocks past the quiet, green **Cathedral Garden,** which is at the rear of St. Louis Cathedral. One block more will bring you to St. Peter Street and the most-photographed building in the city. The **LaBranche House** (740 Royal St.), dating from about 1840, wraps around the corner of Royal Street and runs halfway down St. Peter Street. Its filigreed double galleries are cast iron with an oak-leaf-and-acorn motif.

Directly across the street is the **First Skyscraper** (640 St. Peter St.). Built between 1795 and 1811, it was a three-story high rise; rumor has it that the fourth floor was added later so that it might retain its towering title. Behind weathered walls is **Preservation Hall** (726 St. Peter St.), home of the world's best traditional and Dixieland jazz (*see* Nightlife).

Continue on Royal Street one block to the **Historic New Orleans Collection.** The **Merieult House** was one of the few buildings to survive the fire of 1794, and it now contains an extensive collection of documents and research materials pertaining to the city. Exhibits in the **Williams Gallery** on the ground floor can be seen for free, and for a nominal fee you can take a guided tour and hear the legends of the historic house. *533 Royal St., tel. 504/523–4662. Admission: $2. Open Tues.–Sat. 10–4:30. Closed Christmas, Thanksgiving, Mardi Gras, and New Year's Day.*

Turn left and then right onto Toulouse Street, walk toward the
18 river, and turn right on to Chartres Street. The **New Orleans Pharmacy Museum** is a musty old place where Louis Dufilho had his pharmacy in 1823. It's full of ancient and mysterious medicinal items, and there is an Italian marble fountain used by 19th-century soda jerks. *514 Chartres St., tel. 504/ 524–9077. Admission: $1. Open Tues.–Sun. 10–5. Closed Mon.*

19 At the corner of Chartres and St. Louis streets is the **Napoleon House** (500 Chartres St.), a long-time favorite haunt of artists and writers. The bar fairly oozes atmosphere from every splinter, with peeling sepia walls, Napoleonic memorabilia, and taped classical music to back up your libation. It is entirely possible—and this is a proven fact—to laze away an entire afternoon sitting by an open door and watch rain splatter down on the pavement (*see* Dining).

If you can wrench yourself away, turn right at the corner and walk along St. Louis Street past Antoine's Restaurant and go
20 one more block to the **Hermann-Grima House.** Guides will steer you through the American-style town house, built in 1831, and on winter Thursdays you can get a taste of Creole during cooking demonstrations. *820 St. Louis St., tel. 504/525–5661. Admission: $3 adults, $2.50 AAA members, $2 senior citizens and students, children under 8 free. Open Mon.–Sat. 10–4. Closed Thanksgiving, Christmas, and Mardi Gras.*

Turn left as you leave the house, left again on Dauphine Street,
21 and then right on Conti Street to reach the **Musée Conti Wax Museum.** The museum waxes lifelike on Louisiana legends, among them Andrew Jackson, Jean Lafitte, Marie Laveau, and former governor Edwin Edwards. *917 Conti St., tel. 504/525–2605. Admission: $4 adults, $3.50 senior citizens and AAA members, $3 students, $2.50 children 6–12. Open daily 10–5:30. Closed Christmas and Mardi Gras.*

Time Out Nearby **Arnaud's Grill** has mosaic-tile floors, ceiling fans, and a player piano as the backdrop for its mixed drinks. *813 Bienville St., tel. 504/523–5433. AE, CB, DC, MC, V.*

We'll now take a look at some of the attractions on unattractive, run-down Rampart Street, but we'll do so with a warning: The section of the street between St. Peter and Canal streets is relatively safe during daylight hours, but *should be avoided at night. Avoid the section between St. Peter Street and Esplanade Avenue day* and *night.*

22 At St. Ann Street, a large arch hovers over the entrance to **Louis Armstrong Park,** which is named for native son Louis
23 "Satchmo" Armstrong. Inside the park are the **Municipal Auditorium** and the **Theatre for the Performing Arts.** The auditorium is on the site of Congo Square, scene of 18th- and 19th-century slave gatherings. Congo Square is believed to have been the birthplace of jazz, with the voodoo Afro-Caribbean rhythms of the slaves' songs and chants influencing the new music. Large crowds attend the opera and ballet at the theater, and many a Carnival ball is still held at the auditorium. *Do not venture into the park alone, even in the daytime.*

24 **Our Lady of Guadalupe Catholic Church** (411 N. Rampart St.) was dedicated in 1827, when it was known as the Mortuary Chapel. It was originally used only for funerals, usually for victims of yellow fever and cholera. A midnight Jazz Mass, which combines the city's religious and musical traditions, is celebrated every Saturday in the chapel. This church is home to one of the city's legends, St. Expedite. The story is that a statue was delivered to the church in a crate marked simply "Expedite." It was expeditiously mounted, and it can be seen to the right as you enter the church.

25 Just behind the church on Basin Street is **St. Louis Cemetery No. 1,** between St. Louis and Conti streets. This is New Orleans's oldest City of the Dead, so called because the stark white above-ground tombs resemble tiny houses. The cemetery dates from 1789, and well-worn paths lead through a maze of tombs and mausoleums, many with the same ornate grilles and ironwork as the houses where live folks live. Many a well-known early New Orleanian is buried here, and voodoo doings mark the tomb believed to be that of Marie Laveau. (Some say she is buried in St. Louis Cemetery No. 2.) *Warning: The cemetery is adjacent to a crime-ridden housing project, and you should not visit it alone. Go on a tour, such as the one conducted by the Park Rangers (see* Guided Tours).

Audubon Park and Zoo Rolled out across St. Charles Avenue from Tulane and Loyola universities is **Audubon Park and Zoo.** You can board the **St. Charles Streetcar** at Poydras Street and St. Charles Avenue to tool off Uptown. The Friends of the Zoo operate a free shuttle that boards in front of Tulane every 15 to 20 minutes for a ride to the zoo, which lies on the 58 acres of the park nearest the river. It is entirely possible to while away an entire day exploring Audubon Zoo. A wooden walkway strings through the zoo, and a miniature train rings around a part of it. More than 1,500 animals roam free in natural habitats, such as the **Australian exhibit,** where kangaroos hop-nob with wallabies, and the **Louisiana Swamp exhibit,** where alligators bask on the bayou. A special treat is the feeding of the sea lions, which is occupied by a great deal of flapping about and barking. The **Wisner Children's Village** has a petting zoo and elephant and camel rides. *Tel. 504/861–2537. Admission: $5.50 adults, $2.75 senior citizens and children 2–12. Open weekdays 9:30–5; weekends (winter) 9:30–5, during daylight savings time 9:30–6. Closed Thanksgiving, Christmas, and Mardi Gras.*

The 400-acre Audubon Park, with live oaks and lush tropical plants, was once part of the plantation of Etienne de Bore and his son-in-law Pierre Foucher. In 1795, de Bore figured out how to granulate sugar for commercial purposes, thereby revolutionizing the sugar industry.

In addition to the 18-hole golf course, there is a two-mile jogging track with 18 exercise stations along the way, a **stable** that offers guided trail rides, and 10 tennis courts. The park is also eminently suitable for lolling about under a tree and doing nothing. Note, however, that you should stay *out* of the park after dark.

Around Town City Park Avenue, Bayou St. John, Robert E. Lee Boulevard, and Orleans Avenue embrace the 1,500 luxuriant acres of **City Park,** which can be reached via the Esplanade or the City Park bus. You can spend a great deal of time simply admiring the lagoons and majestic live oaks, whose gnarled branches bow and scrape to Mother Earth, but there is plenty to keep you busy if you are not an idler. There are four 18-hole golf courses, a double-deck driving range, 39 lighted courts in the Wisner Tennis Center, Botanical Gardens, baseball diamonds, and stables. At the casino on Dreyfous Avenue you can rent **bikes, boats,** and **canoes**—or just have a bite to eat—and at the amusement park, you can ride the turn-of-the-century carousel and miniature train. **Storyland** offers puppet shows, talking storybooks, storybook exhibits, and storytelling—hence its name. Unfortunately, it is no fairy tale that City Park is *not safe at night.*

The **New Orleans Museum of Art** (NOMA), located in the park, displays from its collections Italian paintings from the 13th to 18th centuries, 20th-century European and American paintings and sculptures, Chinese jades, and the Imperial Treasures by Peter Carl Fabergé. *Lelong Ave., City Park, tel. 504/488–2631. Open Tues.–Sun. 10–5. Admission: $3 adults, $1.50 senior citizens and children 3–17; admission free on Thurs. Closed Thanksgiving, Christmas, Mardi Gras.*

To reach the **Pitot House** from NOMA, walk along Lelong Avenue, cross over the Bayou St. John Bridge, and make a right turn on Moss Street. Continue following Moss Street as it winds alongside the bayou, and look for the house on your left. The West Indies–style house was built in the late 18th century and bought in 1810 by New Orleans mayor James Pitot. It is furnished with Louisiana and other American 19th-century antiques. *1440 Moss St., tel. 504/482–0312. Admission: $3 adults, $1 children under 12. Open Wed.–Sat. 10–3. Closed Thanksgiving, Christmas, New Year's Day, Mardi Gras.*

Longue Vue House & Gardens sits right on the border between Orleans and Jefferson parishes, about a $5 cab ride from the Quarter. To describe this mansion, the word "opulent" immediately comes to mind. The house is furnished with elegant antiques and sits on eight acres of landscaped gardens. Yes, opulent is the word. *7 Bamboo Rd., tel. 504/488–5488. Admission: $5 adults, $3 students and children. Open Tues.–Fri. 10–4:30, weekends 1–5. Closed Mon., Thanksgiving, Christmas, New Year's, Mardi Gras, July 4th.*

New Orleans for Free

A free **ferry** runs from the foot of Canal Street across the Mississippi to Algiers Point. A round-trip excursion takes about 25 minutes.

New Orleans Museum of Art. Admission to the museum is free on Thursdays (*see* Around Town in Exploring).

New Orleans **street musicians** perform regularly in Jackson Square and on Bourbon, Royal, and Chartres streets. There are free **concerts** on weekends in Dutch Alley in the French Market. You can also lean against a lamppost on Bourbon Street and listen to the music that pours out of jazz clubs.

Free **tours** of the French Quarter, St. Louis Cemetery No. 1, and the Garden District (although you must hand over 60¢ for the streetcar fare for the last) are given by park rangers. Reservations are necessary for the cemetery and Garden District tours. *Walks begin at the Folklife & Visitor Center, 916–18 N. Peters St., in the French Market, tel. 504/589–2636.*

What to See and Do with Children

Audubon Zoo (*see* The Garden District and Uptown in Exploring).
City Park (*see* Around Town in Exploring).
Jackson Square (*see* The French Quarter in Exploring).
Le Petit Théâtre du Vieux Carré (616 St. Peter St., tel. 504/522–2081). The Children's Corner often puts on plays for the little ones.
Musée Conti Wax Museum (*see* the French Quarter section in Exploring).
Ripley's Believe It or Not Museum. Exhibits of oddities from Robert Ripley's collections. *501 Bourbon St., tel. 504/529–5131. Admission: $5 adults; $2.75 children 6–12, under 6 free. Open daily 10 AM–midnight.*
Riverboat Rides. Steamboat and ferry rides on the Mississippi hold a particular fascination for children. Aside from the view of the city and the water lapping at the sides of the boats, kids love to watch the big sternwheel turning. The mighty *Natchez* (tel. 504/586–8777), with its off-key steam calliope blasting out tunes, and the *Cotton Blossom* (tel. 504/586–8777), with its hour-long trip upriver to the Audubon Zoo, are great fun.
St. Charles Streetcar (*see* Getting Around).
Roman Candy Man. Look for the old-fashioned horse-drawn cart of the candy man just outside the zoo.
Parades and Festivals (*see* Festivals and Seasonal Events in Before You Go).

Off the Beaten Track

Ever get nostalgic for the old-fashioned drugstore, which is not to be confused with today's discount chains? Well, there's a tiny one in New Orleans. At **Schweickhardt Drugs,** you can shop for sundries on one side and have a sundae at the soda fountain on the other. A big sign in the window proclaims the fame of its Nectar Soda, which is indeed quite well-known to locals. (It's $1.65 at the counter, $1.91 to go.) Sandwiches and plate lunches are also served at the lunch counter. The drugstore is easily reached, because it's right on the streetcar line. *1438 S. Carrollton Ave., tel. 504/866–1833. Open daily 8–6:30.*

Shopping

Pralines, chicory coffee, Mardi Gras masks, nostalgia clothing, and jazz records are usually hot tickets for tourists (as well as for locals). The packaging of New Orleans food to go is a growing trend.

Shopping Districts New Orleans shops string along the Mississippi all the way from the French Quarter to Riverbend (at the Uptown bend in the river) and beyond. **The French Quarter** is the place to search for antiques shops, art galleries, designer boutiques, bookstores, and all sorts of shops in all sorts of edifices. Among **Canal Place's** (333 Canal St.) lofty tenants you'll find Saks Fifth Avenue, Laura Ashley, Gucci, Charles Jourdan, and Benetton. **Riverwalk** (1 Poydras St.) is a long, tunnel-like marketplace brightened by over 200 splashy shops, restaurants, food courts, and huge windows overlooking the Mississippi. The tony **New Orleans Centre,** between The Hyatt Regency Hotel and the

Superdome on Poydras St., boasts more than 100 occupants, including Macy's and Lord & Taylor. Along six miles of **Magazine Street** are Victorian houses and small cottages filled with antiques and collectibles. Stop at the **New Orleans Welcome Center** for a copy of the shopper's guide published by the Magazine Street Merchants Association. Turn-of-the-century Creole cottages cradle everything from toy shops to designer boutiques and delis in the **Riverbend** (Maple St. and Carrollton Ave.). At **Uptown Square** (200 Broadway), boutiques and restaurants surround—guess what?—a square. Macy's, D. H. Holmes, and Mervyn's are among the 155 shops in Metairie's glittering three-level **Esplanade Mall** (1401 W. Esplanade Ave.).

Department Stores Woolworth's (737 Canal St., tel. 504/522–6426) has budget shopping to a New Orleans beat.

Specialty Stores **As You Like It** (3025 Magazine St., tel. 504/897–6915) carries
Antiques obsolete patterns in silver and silverplate. **Mid-America Shop** (3128 Magazine St., tel. 504/895–4226) offers the best in crystal and Depression glass. **M. S. Rau** (630 Royal St., tel 504/523–5660) has a fine selection of American and Victorian cut glass.

Flea Market Jazz is within earshot and "junque" at your fingertips, at the **French Market Flea Market** on weekends from 7 to 7.

Food to Go **Bayou To Go** (New Orleans International Airport, Concourse C, tel 504/468–8040) has a full line of Louisiana food products, including fresh, frozen, and cooked seafood packed to check or carry on the plane.

Jazz Records Chances are you'll find the hard-to-find vintage stuff at **Record Ron's** (1129 Decatur St. and 407 Decatur St., tel. 504/524–9444).

Masks **Hidden Images** (523 Dumaine St., tel. 504/524–8730), has a whole store full of handmade leather, feather, and frilly Mardi Gras masks. For exotic handmade masks to decorate your face or your wall, try **Rumors** (513 Royal St., tel. 504/525–0292).

Pralines For the best pralines in town; try **Old Town Praline Shop** (627 Royal St., tel. 504/525–1413).

Participant Sports

Biking For scenic cycling around City Park rent a bike at the **City Park Casino** (Dreyfous Ave., City Park, tel. 504/482–4888). In the French Quarter, Bourbon and Royal streets are closed to all but pedalers and pedestrians. Rentals are available at **Bicycle Michael's** (618 Frenchmen St., tel. 504/945–9505).

Golf There are four 18-hole golf courses in City Park, plus a double-decker driving range. You can rent clubs, handcarts, and electric carts at the **Main Clubhouse** (1040 Filmore Dr., tel. 504/283–3458). To rent clubs and tee off on Audubon Park's luscious links, check into **Audubon Park's Clubhouse** (473 Walnut St., tel. 504/865–8260). The **Joe Bartholomew Municipal Golf Course** (6514 Congress Dr., tel. 504/288–0928) has an 18-hole course in Pontchartrain Park.

Tennis There are 39 courts in the **City Park Wisner Tennis Center** (Victory Rd. in City Park, tel. 504/482–2230). **Audubon Park** (tel. 504/895–1042) has 10 courts near Tchoupitoulas Street. **Pontchartrain Park Tennis Center** (5104 Hayne Blvd., tel. 504/283–

9734) lets you lob on 10 courts, and there are 11 courts at the Hilton's **River Center Tennis & Racquetball Club** (2 Poydras St., tel. 504/587–7242).

Spectator Sports

Baseball The **Tulane Green Wave** plays home games at the school's St. Charles Avenue campus (tel. 504/861–3661). The **University of New Orleans Privateers** take on foes at the Lakefront (tel. 504/286–7240).

Basketball The **Sugar Bowl Basketball Classic** is played in the Superdome the week preceding the annual football classic.

Football The **New Orleans Saints** play NFL games in the Superdome (tel. 504/522–2600). Home games of **Tulane University** are also played in the Dome (tel. 504/861–3661). The annual **Sugar Bowl Football Classic** (tel. 504/525–8573) is played in the Dome on New Year's Day, and in late November the **Bayou Classic** (tel. 504/587–3663) pits Southern University against Grambling University.

Dining

by Lisa LeBlanc-Berry

The "Urbane Gourmet" food critic for Gambit *newspaper, Lisa LeBlanc-Berry gives weekly restaurant reviews on New Orleans's radio station WWIW. She is currently the editor of* Where Magazine *in New Orleans.*

New Orleans usually means excellent dining. The Big Easy is recognized almost as much for hot and spicy culinary delights as it is for hot and steamy jazz. Louisiana styles of cooking are becoming increasingly popular worldwide—but what is a fad elsewhere is a tradition here.

As a general rule, expect to tip from 15% to 20%. Most establishments do not automatically add a service charge.

Apart from K-Paul's and Galatoire's, where people stand in line to be served on a first-come basis, you are strongly advised to make reservations and to book well in advance for weekends, particularly during holiday periods or conventions.

Most of the more pricey restaurants adhere to a moderate dress code—jackets for men, and in some places, a tie. New Orleans is a conservative city; dining out is an honored ritual, and people are expected to dress the part. A man in faded jeans and sports coat may not be turned away, but he may not feel terribly comfortable either. Credit cards are accepted in most, but not all, dining establishments; it's wise to check in advance.

Lunch hours are 11:30 AM to 2:30 PM. Dinner is almost always served from 6 to 10 PM, although some restaurants will close an hour earlier or later depending on volume of business and season.

The following terms will appear frequently throughout this section:

andouille (an-*dooey*)—Cajun sausage made with pork blade meat, onion, smoked flavorings, and garlic.
boudin (boo-*dan*)—hot, spicy pork with onions, rice, and herbs stuffed in sausage casing.
bananas Foster—a dessert of bananas sautéed with butter, brown sugar, and cinnamon, flambéed in white rum and banana liqueur, and served on ice cream.
barbecue shrimp—large shrimp baked in the shell, covered with butter, rosemary, herbs, and spices. They are not barbecued at all.

court bouillon (coo–bee–*yon*)—a thick, hearty soup made with a roux, vegetables, and fish, and served over rice.

crawfish (pronounced as spelled)—also known as "mud-bugs," because they live in the mud of freshwater streams. They resemble miniature lobsters and are served in a great variety of ways.

etouffee (ay-to-*fay*)—crawfish etouffee is made with a butter and flour roux of celery and onion, then cooked for a short period of time and served over rice. Shrimp etouffee is heartier, made with an oil and flour roux or tomato paste, celery, onion, bell pepper, tomatoes, and chicken stock, cooked for approximately an hour and served over rice.

filé (fee-*lay*)—ground sassafras, used to season gumbo and many other Creole specialties.

grillades (gree-*yads*)—bite-size pieces of veal rounds or beef chuck, braised in red wine, beef stock, garlic, herbs, and seasoning, served for brunch with grits and with rice for dinner.

gumbo—a hearty soup prepared in a variety of combinations (okra gumbo, shrimp gumbo, chicken gumbo, to name a few).

jambalaya (jum-bo-*lie*-yah)—a spicy rice dish cooked with stock and chopped seasoning, and made with any number of ingredients including sausage, shrimp, ham, and chicken.

muffuletta—a large, round loaf of bread filled with cheese, ham, and salami smothered in a heavy, garlicky olive salad.

remoulade—a cold dressing that accompanies shrimp (sometimes crabmeat) over shredded lettuce, made of mayonnaise and Creole mustard, oil and vinegar, horseradish, paprika, celery, and green onion.

praline (praw-*leen*)—candy patty most commonly made from sugar, water or butter, and pecans. There are many different flavors and kinds.

New Orleans is renowned for *Creole* cuisine. A Creole, by definition, is a person of French or Spanish ancestry born in the New World. However, Creole is also a word of elastic implications, and in culinary terms, Creole refers to a distinctive cuisine indigenous to New Orleans that has its roots in European dishes enhanced by the liberal usage of local seasonings such as *filé*. The French influence is also strong, but the essence of Creole is in sauces, herbs, and the prominent use of seafood.

In recent years the term *Nouvelle Creole* has been popularized by local restaurateurs. Instead of gumbo or jambalaya, a nouvelle menu might include hickory-grilled items, seafood served with pasta, or smoked meats and fish. There has also been a strong Italian influence in Creole cuisine in the last decade, creating yet another marriage of styles.

The initial restaurant listings here are divided into five Creole categories: *Classic Creole*, those restaurants devoted to traditional Louisiana cuisine with minimal French overtones; *French Creole*, indicating a more expansive Continental accent; *Italian Creole*, Creole with an Italian flair; *Soul Creole*, black cuisine of Creole origin; and *Creole-Inspired*, meaning the newer breed of cooking styles that incorporate Nouvelle Creole dishes, new American cooking, and classic Creole. Please note that the above categories often overlap; it is not unusual to find a blend of varying Creole cuisines on any given menu.

Cajun cuisine was brought from Nova Scotia to the bayou country of Louisiana by the Acadians over 250 years ago. Cajun cooks generally use less expensive ingredients than their Creole counterparts, and they are heavy-handed on the herbs and spices.

Cajun cuisine is rarely served in its purest form in New Orleans; rather it is often blended with Creole to create what's known as "New Orleans–style" cooking. There is a difference, though, between the two: Creole is distinguished by its rich and heavy sauces; Cajun, by its tendency to be spicy and hot.

The most highly recommended restaurants in each price category are indicated by a star ★.

Category	Cost*
Very Expensive	over $35
Expensive	$25–$35
Moderate	$15–$25
Inexpensive	under $15

*per person without tax (9% in New Orleans), service, or drinks

The following credit-card abbreviations are used: AE, American Express; CB, Carte Blanche; DC, Diners Club; MC, MasterCard; V, Visa.

Louisiana Cuisine

Cajun-Inspired **K-Paul's Louisiana Kitchen.** National celebrity chef Paul Prudhomme made blackened redfish so famous that a fishing ban was levied and restaurateurs can no longer acquire the fish. K-Paul's now serves blackened yellowfin tuna. Strangers often must share tables, and the "no reservations" policy makes for long lines outside. But K-Paul's is a shrine to the popular concept of New Orleans Cajun cooking. *416 Chartres St., French Quarter, tel. 504/942–7500. Dress: informal. No reservations. AE. Closed Sat. and Sun. Expensive.*

Olde N'Awlins Cookery. Inspired by K-Paul's, but with more atmosphere, this restaurant is adorned with quaint photographs and slowly spinning ceiling fans. Alligator sausage is among the appetizers, and, predictably, there are a couple of blackened dishes on the menu. *629 Conti St., French Quarter, tel. 504/529–3663. Dress: informal. No reservations. No credit cards. Moderate.*

Classic Creole **Arnaud's.** Beveled glass, ceiling fans, and tile floors cast an
★ aura of traditional Southern dining. The lively Sunday jazz brunch is a classic New Orleans experience. Pompano *en croûte*, veal Wohl, and filet Charlemond topped with two sauces are savory entree selections, and there is little on the menu there that isn't excellent. *813 Bienville St., French Quarter, tel. 504/523–5433. Jackets required. Reservations required. AE, MC, V. Expensive.*

★ **Galatoire's.** Operated by the fourth generation, Galatoire's is a tradition in New Orleans. Creole specialties, moderately priced by New Orleans standards, are served in a large, brightly lit room with mirrors on all sides. Lunch is served all afternoon, and you can avoid the long lines by arriving after 1:30 PM. An extensive menu offers every imaginable Creole dish. Seafood is the most diverse category, but there is also a fine lineup of steaks, sweetbreads, and chicken dishes. *209 Bourbon St., French Quarter, tel. 504/525–2021. Jacket and tie required after 5 and all day Sun. No reservations. No credit cards. Closed Mon. Moderate.*

Tujague's. In the city's second-oldest eatery, one of the dining rooms is decorated with memorabilia relating to Madame Begue, the late and legendary restaurateur who had an establishment housed on the same spot many long years ago. The six-course dinner menu always includes shrimp remoulade, soup, boiled beef brisket, a choice of three entrees, vegetables, and bread pudding. *823 Decatur St., French Quarter, tel. 504/525–8676. Dress: informal. Reservations advised for dinner. AE, MC, V. Moderate.*

French Creole **Antoine's.** Established in 1840, Antoine's is the oldest restau-
★ rant in the United States under continuous family ownership. The enormous restaurant is popular with locals, and waiters tend to cater to their regular customers. You can best appreciate this fine old restaurant if you are accompanied by a regular. The menu is in French, but the waiter will give you a rundown of the various specialties. Oysters Rockefeller originated here, as did pompano *en papillote* and puffed-up soufflé potatoes. *Tournedos marchand de vin* is a legend in its own wine. Be sure and tour the restaurant after dinner. Among other things, you'll see the 25,000-bottle wine cellar, the Rex Room, filled with tributes to kings of Carnival, and the Germanic Red Room, filled with tributes to Antoine's. *713 St. Louis St., French Quarter, tel. 504/581–4422. Jackets required for dinner. Reservations advised on weekends. AE, DC, MC, V. Very Expensive.*

★ **Brennan's.** Opened in 1946, Brennan's is one of the city's premier dining establishments. Breakfast at Brennan's is a tradition unto itself. The extensive menu includes rich, creamy eggs Benedict, Sardou, and Houssarde. The traditional breakfast dessert is bananas Foster, flamed with liqueur in a tableside ritual. The oysters tournedos Chanteclair, three prime cuts each with a different sauce, represents one of the restaurant's strong suits: excellent French sauces with a Creole stamp. Brennan's also serves brunch on weekends. *417 Royal St., French Quarter, tel. 504/525–9711. Reservations advised. AE, DC, MC, V. Very Expensive.*

★ **Commander's Palace.** Housed in a renovated Victorian mansion, this elegant restaurant offers the best sampling of old Creole cooking prepared with a combination of American and French styles. Entree selections include veal chop Tchoupitoulas, trout with roasted pecans, and tournedos. Commander's serves a one-of-a-kind bread pudding soufflé. Jazz brunch Saturday and Sunday, a festive affair with balloons and lots of Creole egg dishes, is best enjoyed in the Garden Room overlooking the patio. *1403 Washington Ave., Garden District, tel. 504/899–8221. Jackets required. Reservations required. AE, DC, MC, V. Very Expensive.*

Seb's. This new restaurant overlooking the Mississippi River has a strong emphasis on fish—right down to the decor. You can sample a variety of dishes in taster portions here, which is the concept of the menu. The cold taster is shrimp remoulade Royal, crabmeat Decatur, and seafood seviche. *Jackson Brewery Millhouse, 5th floor, 600 Decatur St., French Quarter, tel. 504/522–1696. Dress: informal. Reservations advised weekends. AE, MC, V. Closed Sat. for lunch. Very Expensive.*

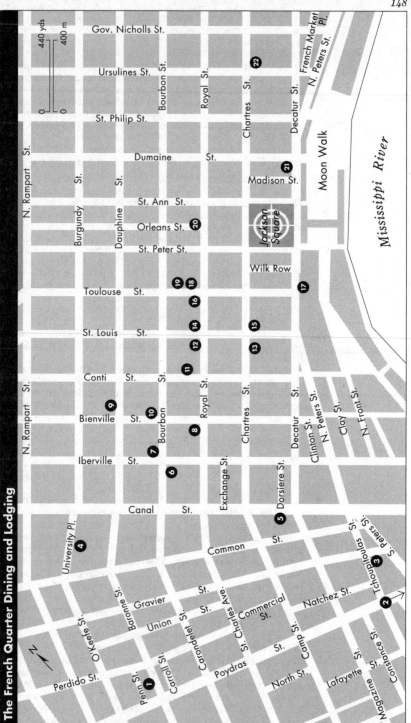

The French Quarter Dining and Lodging

Mississippi River

Moon Walk

Jackson Square

Gov. Nicholls St.

Ursulines St.

St. Philip St.

Dumaine St.

Madison St.

St. Ann St.

Orleans St.

St. Peter St.

Wilk Row

Toulouse St.

St. Louis St.

Conti St.

Bienville St.

Iberville St.

Canal St.

Common St.

Gravier St.

Union St.

Poydras St.

Perdido St.

N. Rampart St.

Burgundy St.

Dauphine St.

Bourbon St.

Royal St.

Chartres St.

Decatur St.

French Market Pl.

N. Peters St.

Exchange St.

Dorsiere St.

Clinton St.

N. Peters St.

Clay St.

N. Front St.

University Pl.

O'Keefe St.

Baronne St.

Carroll St.

Carondelet St.

St. Charles Ave.

Commercial St.

Camp St.

North St.

Magazine St.

Constance St.

Lafayette St.

Natchez St.

Tchoupitoulas St.

S. Peters St.

Penn St.

440 yds
400 m

149

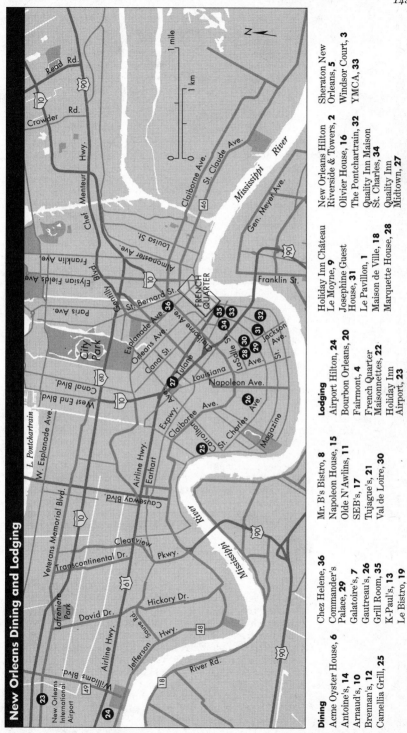

New Orleans Dining and Lodging

Dining
Acme Oyster House, **6**
Antoine's, **14**
Arnaud's, **10**
Brennan's, **12**
Camellia Grill, **25**

Chez Helene, **36**
Commander's Palace, **29**
Galatoire's, **7**
Gautreau's, **26**
Grill Room, **35**
K-Paul's, **13**
Le Bistro, **19**

Mr. B's Bistro, **8**
Napoleon House, **15**
Olde N'Awlins, **11**
SEB's, **17**
Tujague's, **21**
Val de Loire, **30**

Lodging
Airport Hilton, **24**
Bourbon Orleans, **20**
Fairmont, **4**
French Quarter Maisonnettes, **22**
Holiday Inn Airport, **23**

Holiday Inn Château Le Moyne, **9**
Josephine Guest House, **31**
Le Pavillon, **1**
Maison de Ville, **18**
Marquette House, **28**

Sheraton New Orleans, **5**
Olivier House, **2**
Windsor Court, **3**
The Pontchartrain, **32**
Quality Inn Maison St. Charles, **34**
Quality Inn Midtown, **27**
YMCA, **33**

★ **Gautreau's.** This is one of the most popular restaurants in the Uptown area: a small cafe converted from an old pharmacy. The food is straightforward but imaginative, while being comfortably Creole. Lunches are very light and include many good soups and salads with the entrees. The dinner menu consists entirely of specials; perhaps the best of those regularly appearing are the various manifestations of filet mignon, but the fish and veal are also consistent winners. *1728 Soniat St., Uptown, tel. 504/899–7397. Dress: informal. Reservations advised. MC, V. Closed for lunch; closed for dinner Sun. Moderate.*

Creole-Inspired **Mr. B's Bistro.** You can tell you're near this classy bistro by the
★ aroma of fish and steaks roasting on hickory and pecan logs. The shrimp Chippewa and hickory-grilled fish are highly recommended, and the gumbo ya-ya is first-rate. The wine list is solid, with some very good wines by the glass available at the bar. The lively jazz brunch offers New Orleans classic egg dishes, and then some. *201 Royal St., French Quarter, tel. 504/ 523–2078. Dress: informal. Reservations advised. AE, MC, V. Sun. brunch. Moderate.*

Soul Creole **Chez Helene.** Stuffed bell peppers, fried chicken, Creole gumbo, and smothered okra are just some of the fine recipes of Helene Howard, whose nephew, Austin Leslie, opened the second Chez Helene (316 Chartres St. in the de la Poste Hotel, French Quarter, tel. 525–6130). The popular television series *Frank's Place* is based on Leslie and his soulful establishment. The soul and Cajun specialties are marked by spiciness and fresh herbs—no bottled, dried, or dehydrated condiments. The Creole jambalaya and crawfish étouffée are among the city's simplest and best; the fresh corn bread is a joy. *1540 N. Robertson St., Mid-City, tel. 504/947–1206. Dress: informal. Reservations accepted. AE, MC, V. Moderate. Open weekends until 1 AM.*

International **Grill Room.** Among locals, this is one of the most highly cele-
Cuisines brated of the newer hotel dining rooms. The opulence begins
Continental with a Lalique crystal table at the entrance and continues with
★ an array of original art. Chef John Carey calls the cuisine New American, although there are strong Continental overtones. Especially recommended are the steamed halibut on Swiss mâche with Beluga caviar, and the saddle of red deer with red currant sauce. There is a grill here (as the name suggests) over which much good fish is prepared. The wine cellar was assembled with the rich collections of two local claret fans; it is not only mind-boggling but fairly priced, too. *Windsor Court Hotel, 300 Gravier St., Central Business District, tel. 504/523– 6000. Dress: informal. Reservations advised. AE, MC, V. Very Expensive.*

★ **Le Bistro.** A small, elegant restaurant with the flavor of a fin-de-siècle Parisian bistro. The cuisine is a blend of Mediterranean and Provençal styles. The eggplant caviar appetizer is roasted, chilled, seasoned with garlic, olive oil, and basil, and served in ramekins. The spinach salad, sautéed oysters, and the grilled shrimp are recommended, as are the daily pasta dishes. The filet mignon with boursin cheese and sweetbreads in a butter caper sauce is delicious. A miniature courtyard behind the restaurant is a fitting spot to enjoy desserts and coffee at your leisure. *733 Toulouse St., French Quarter, tel. 504/528– 9206. Dress: informal. Reservations advised. AE, MC, V. Closed Sun. for lunch. Moderate.*

Val de Loire New Orleans. The restaurant resembles some of the finer bistros in Paris. Windows overlook Washington Avenue, and pastries are displayed at the bar, a tempting sight. The new chef-owner Steven Lopez serves mostly French cuisine, but with a healthy offering of Creole dishes. Try the chef's selection of the day—a gourmet tray of several appetizers, which makes a full meal if accompanied by a salad. Oyster mushroom pie is an especially recommended appetizer. Good entree choices include smoked fish du jour, grilled items, and baby veal with mushrooms, brandy and cream. Try the bananas Foster for dessert, or the white chocolate mousse. *2727 Prytania St., Uptown, tel. 504/891–1973. Dress: informal. Reservations advised for dinner. AE, MC, V. Closed lunch; closed Sun.*

Back to Basics
Seafood
★

Acme Oyster House. The granddaddy of local oyster bars, the Acme has a big old marble counter at which you stand and eat dozen after dozen of oysters, opened before your eyes by old pros. Next to that is another bar where you get your beer, the preferred drink with cold oysters. You order your sandwiches from the cooking station, where you can see them frying the oysters. The wait can be aggravating if it's a crowded day, but it's worth it. A recent addition is a very limited salad bar. You can eat oysters on the half shell at a table, but this isn't the style of the natives. *724 Iberville St., French Quarter, tel. 504/522–5973. Dress: informal. No reservations. AE, MC, V. Closes Sun. at 7 PM. Inexpensive.*

Grills and Coffee Shops
★

Camellia Grill. This is the class act among lunch counters, with linen napkins and a maître d'. The omelets are the best in town. Especially good is the ham, cheese, and onion—huge and fluffy. Good red beans and rice on Monday. Great hamburgers, pecan pie, cheesecake, and banana-cream pie. The chocolate freezes are also popular. Dining here is entertaining, mainly due to the somewhat theatrical waiters. Expect long lines on weekends for breakfast. *626 S. Carrollton Ave., Uptown, tel. 504/866–9573. Dress: informal. No reservations. Inexpensive.*

★ **Napoleon House.** The tables in the front room of this ancient bar open on to the street, and there's a charming courtyard in the back. The very limited menu offers several po' boys, appetizers, a salad bar for lunch weekdays, and a few desserts. But people come here for the muffuletta, one of the best in town. The popular drink is still the Pimm's cup, cool and light with a slice of cucumber. The classical music and mellow ambience make this an alluring spot for repose. Very popular with locals. *500 Chartres St., French Quarter, tel. 504/524–9752. Dress: informal. AE, MC, V. Closes Sun. at 6 PM. Inexpensive.*

Lodging

Visitors to New Orleans have a wide variety of accommodations to choose from: posh high-rise hotels, antiques-filled antebellum homes, Creole cottages, or old slave quarters.

When planning a stay in New Orleans, try to reserve well in advance, especially during Mardi Gras or other seasonal events. Frequently, hotels offer special packages at reduced rates, but never during Mardi Gras, when almost every accommodation raises its rates higher than listed here. Many chain or associated hotels and motels offer the additional convenience of advance reservations at affiliated hostelries of your choosing along your route.

The most highly recommended properties in each price category are indicated by a star ★.

Category	Cost*
Very Expensive	over $120
Expensive	$90–$120
Moderate	$50–$90
Inexpensive	under $50

* *double room; add 11% tax*

The following credit-card abbreviations are used: AE, American Express; CB, Carte Blanche; DC, Diners Club; MC, MasterCard; V, Visa.

Hotels
Central Business District

Staying in the Central Business District will appeal to visitors who prefer accommodations in luxurious high-rise hotels. All the hotels listed here are within walking distance of the French Quarter, but shuttles, taxis, buses, and the streetcar are available if your feet hurt.

★ **Fairmont Hotel.** The Fairmont is one of the oldest grand hotels in America. The red and gold Victorian splendor of the massive lobby evokes a more elegant and gracious era. The hotel is composed of three separate buildings. The Baronne and University sections have spacious rooms. Rooms in the Shell section, however, are small and require a hike as there is no elevator service in this building. Decorating varies from room to room and is a continuous project. Special touches in every room include four down pillows, electric shoe-buffers, and bathroom scales. Impressive murals depicting life in the South enliven the walls of the famed Sazerac Bar; the herbs used in the restaurants are grown on the roof and delivered to the kitchens within 20 minutes of being cut. The Sazerac Restaurant has had a face-lift that removed the old world ambience and replaced it with a contemporary look. The Blue Room, the oldest supper club in the country, featuring dining, dancing, and big-name entertainment six nights a week, is also a must. *University Pl., 70140, tel. 504/529–7111 or 800/527–4727. 685 rooms, 50 suites. Facilities: 4 restaurants with bars, heated outdoor pool, 2 lighted tennis courts, beauty salon, gift shop, newsstand, florist, jewelry store, public stenographer, valet parking. AE, CB, DC, MC, V. Very Expensive.*

★ **Le Pavillon Hotel.** Magnificent chandeliers grace the European-style lobby of this historic hotel (built in 1905). Another pièce de résistance is the marble railing in Le Cafée Trianon, originally from the Grand Hotel in Paris. High-ceiling rooms boast hand-carved furnishings; try to get one of the 36 rooms with a bay window. *833 Poydras St., 70140, tel. 504/581–3111 or 800/535–9095. 220 rooms, 8 suites. Facilities: 2 restaurants, lounge, rooftop pool and sun deck, 2 nonsmoking floors, valet laundry, parking. AE, CB, DC, MC, V. Moderate.*

★ **Windsor Court Hotel.** Exquisite, gracious, elegant, eminently civilized—these words frequently are used to describe Windsor Court, but all fail to capture its wonderful quality. From Le Salon's scrumptious high tea, served each afternoon in the lobby, to the unbelievably large guest rooms, this is one of *the* places to stay in New Orleans. Plush carpeting, canopy and four-poster beds, stocked wet bars, marble vanities, oversize mirrors, dressing areas—all contribute to the elegance and luxury of the Windsor Court. Located across from the Rivergate and four blocks from the French Quarter. *300 Gravier St., 70140, tel. 504/523–6000 or 800/262–2662. 58 rooms, 266 suites. Facilities: 2 restaurants, lounge, entertainment, Olympic-size outdoor pool, health club, Jacuzzi, steambath, sauna, gift shop, shoe shine, valet laundry, parking. AE, DC, MC, V. Very Expensive.*

French Quarter   Since most people who visit New Orleans stay in the Quarter, the 96-square-block area abounds with every type of guest accommodation. The selections that follow are all quality establishments chosen to provide variety in location, atmosphere, and price. Reservations are usually a must.

★   **Bourbon Orleans.** Entering the lobby of this historic hotel is like being received in a grand French drawing room: a wall of French doors overlooks Orleans Street, conversation areas are tastefully arranged, and cocktails are served at an intimate bar. A grand piano and a magnificent spiral staircase that leads to the Orleans Ballroom on the third floor complete the picture. The 1815 ballroom, now restored to its original beauty, was the site of innumerable masquerade and quadroon balls. The large guest rooms have Queen Anne furnishings, and most of the king-size beds have canopies. Bathrooms are fitted with telephones and mini-TVs. Even-numbered rooms face a beautiful courtyard, but you can still hear the Bourbon Street noise. The suites are bilevel and have two entrances. *717 Orleans St., 70116, tel. 504/523–2222 or 800/521–5338. 164 rooms, 47 suites. Facilities: restaurant, lounge, entertainment, outdoor pool, secretarial service, valet service, parking. AE, CB, DC, MC, V. Very Expensive.*

★   **Hotel Maison de Ville.** This small, romantic hotel lies in seclusion amid the hustle and bustle of the French Quarter. Tapestry-covered chairs, a fire burning in the sitting room, and antiques-furnished rooms all contribute to a 19th-century atmosphere. Some rooms are in former slave quarters in the courtyard; others are on the upper floors of the main house. Fully stocked minibars and robes are provided for all guests. The complimentary Continental breakfast is served with a rose on a silver tray. Other meals can be enjoyed at a small adjacent restaurant called Le Bistro, where the garlic soup is a must. Visitors who seek a special hideaway will love the hotel's cottages—located off the street in a private, enclosed area, each with a kitchen and individual patio—two blocks from the hotel. *727 Toulouse St., 70130, tel. 504/561–5858 or 800/634–1600. 14 rooms, 2 suites, 7 cottages. Facilities: restaurant, outdoor pool at cottage location, valet service, parking. No children under 12. AE, CB, MC, V. Expensive–Very Expensive.*

★   **Olivier House Hotel.** Located half a block off Bourbon Street, this small hotel has 40 rooms in two 1836 town houses. The enormous hand-carved mirror gracing the entrance hall and the chandeliers are from the house's original furnishings. Room design and decor varies. Some rooms have lofts, many have complete kitchens; baths in suites feature raised tub areas; gas-burning fireplaces are found throughout. Most are a comfortable mixture of antique and traditional decor; some have a tropical atmosphere with wicker furnishings and sunny colors. Both children and pets are welcome. *828 Toulouse St., 70112, tel. 504/525–8456. 40 rooms. Facilities: pool, quiet, plant-shaded courtyard; elevator. AE, CB, DC, MC, V. Moderate–Very Expensive.*

Garden District/ Uptown Visitors to New Orleans who prefer accommodations away from Downtown will find the historic Garden District and Uptown area ideal. All are located on or close to fashionable, mansion-lined St. Charles Avenue, where the St. Charles Avenue streetcar runs (24 hours), making the CBD and French Quarter a mere 15–20 minutes away.

★ **The Pontchartrain Hotel.** Maintaining the grand tradition is the hallmark of this quiet, elegant European-style hotel that has reigned on St. Charles Avenue for more than 60 years. From the canopied entrance, through the marble foyer, to the white-gloved elevator operator, the hotel's commitment to quality, service, and taste comes through clearly. Each room or suite is different in design or decor. The one common denominator is that all are lavish. The internationally known Caribbean Room restaurant provides memorable dining. *2031 St. Charles Ave., 70140, tel. 504/524–0581 or 800/952–8092. 50 rooms, 25 suites. Facilities: 2 restaurants, piano bar, 24-hr concierge, limousine, valet service, parking. AE, CB, DC, MC, V. Very Expensive.*

Guest Houses French Quarter **French Quarter Maisonnettes.** The Maisonnettes, located in the residential part of the Vieux Carré, are for those who want to ★ open a wrought-iron gate, walk through a flagstone carriageway, and find themselves in the private courtyard of a past century. All of the maisonnettes (some with two and three rooms) open directly on to the courtyard. Homey furnishings, private baths, and TVs are included; private phones are not available. Mrs. Underwood, the chatelaine, offers a special brochure to guests that gives inside information on what to see and do in the area. She will organize individualized tours upon request. Children over 12 and well-trained pets are welcomed. *1130 Chartres St., 70116, tel. 504/524–9918. 1 room, 7 suites. No credit cards. Closed July. Inexpensive.*

Garden District **The Josephine Guest House.** This Italianate-style mansion, ★ built in 1870, has been perfectly restored to provide visitors with the pleasures of the graceful lifestyle of an old New Orleans home. French antiques fill the rooms, and Oriental rugs cover gleaming hardwood floors. Four rooms and a parlor are in the main house; there are two smaller but spacious rooms in the garçonnier (quarters where the original owners' sons stayed). The bathrooms are impressive in both size and decor. A complimentary Creole breakfast of fresh-squeezed orange juice, café au lait, and homemade biscuits can be brought to your room (Wedgwood china on a silver tray) or served on the secluded patio. Phones can be installed in rooms upon request. *1450 Josephine St., 70130, 1 blk from St. Charles Ave., tel. 504/524–6361. 6 rooms. AE, CB, DC, MC, V. Moderate.*

National Hotel and Motel Chains In addition to the many excellent independent hotels and motels throughout the area, there are also many that belong to national or regional chains. A major advantage of the chains is the ease of making reservations either en route or in advance. If you are a guest at a member hotel or motel one night, the management will be delighted to secure a booking at one of their affiliated hotels at no cost to you. Chains usually have toll-free lines to assist you.

New Orleans Hilton Riverside & Towers. It's located on the banks of the Mississippi, with Riverwalk sprawled out around it and the New Orleans Convention Center just down the street. Pete Fountain's Club is here, as well as a swirl of other bars, restaurants, and lounges. The River Center Tennis & Racquetball Club is a handy spot for working off all the calories you'll consume at Winston's, Kabby's, and Cafe Bromeliad. VIPs check into the Tower suites, where a concierge looks after things, but the best views of the river are in the appropriately named Riverside section. *Poydras St. at the Mississippi River, 70130, tel. 504/561–0500 or 800–HILTONS. 1602 rooms, 86 suites. Facilities: 5 restaurants, 6 lounges, 2 outdoor pools, tennis and racquetball club, business center. AE, CB, DC, MC, V. Moderate–Very Expensive.*

★ **Sheraton New Orleans.** On Canal Street, across from the French Quarter. Lobby is large and user-friendly. A tropical atmosphere permeates the Gazebo Lounge, which features jazz nightly. Café Promenade encircles the second level. There's a $79 rate here that's not always available, but ask! Executive rooms on the top floors come with many special amenities. Expect top-quality service. *500 Canal St., 70130, tel. 504/525–2500 or 800/325–3535. 1,200 rooms, 84 suites. Facilities: restaurant, lounge, entertainment, outdoor swimming pool with restaurant, gift shop, video checkout, nonsmoking rooms, valet service, and parking. AE, CB, DC, MC, V. Moderate–Very Expensive.*

Quality Inn—Midtown. Too far to walk but only a short drive from the French Quarter. *3900 Tulane Ave., 70119, tel. 504/486–5541 or 800/228–5151. 102 rooms. Facilities: restaurant, lounge, entertainment, outdoor pool, whirlpool, nonsmoking rooms, airport shuttle, free parking. AE, CB, DC, MC, V. Moderate.*

French Quarter **Holiday Inn Chateau Le Moyne.** Old World atmosphere and de-
★ cor; 8 suites located in slave quarters off a tropical courtyard. *301 Dauphine St., 70112, tel. 504/581–1303 or 800/HOLIDAY. 160 rooms, 11 suites. Facilities: restaurant, lounge, outdoor heated pool, valet parking. AE, CB, DC, MC, V. Moderate–Expensive.*

Garden District **Quality Inn Maison St. Charles.** Lovely property in five historic
★ buildings along St. Charles Avenue. Home of Patout's fine restaurant. *1319 St. Charles Ave., 70130, tel. 504/522–0187 or 800/228–5151. 121 rooms, 11 suites. Facilities: lounge, outdoor pool, heated whirlpool, nonsmoking rooms, valet parking. AE, CB, DC, MC, V. Moderate.*

Kenner/Airport **New Orleans Airport Hilton & Conference Center.** This brand-new facility (opened in January 1989) is directly opposite the New Orleans International Airport. *901 Airline Hwy., Kenner 70062, tel. 504/469–5000 or 800/HILTON. 315 rooms. Facilities: restaurant, lounge, heated outdoor pool, tennis court, fitness center, business center, valet service, airport shuttle. AE, CB, DC, MC, V. Moderate–Expensive.*

Holiday Inn–Airport Holidome. Many of the rooms here face the dome-covered pool area. *I–10 and Williams Blvd., Kenner 70062, tel. 504/467–5611 or 800/HOLIDAY. 301 rooms, 1 suite. Facilities: restaurant, lounge, indoor pool, exercise room, sauna, Jacuzzi, airport shuttle, free parking. AE, CB, DC, MC, V. Moderate.*

Bed-and-Breakfasts Bed-and-breakfast means overnight lodging and breakfast in a private residence. Begin by writing or calling a reservation service and discussing price range, type of residence, location, and length of stay. The service in turn will provide you with descriptions of several choices of B&Bs that meet your criteria. From these choices you'll make a decision and send a 20% deposit. You'll receive the address and other pertinent details before you arrive.

Bed & Breakfast, Inc.—Reservations Service. This service offers a variety of accommodations in all areas of New Orleans. Some homes are 19th-century, others are contemporary. Guest cottages, rooms, and suites are also available. Prices range from $40 to $110. *Write or call Hazel Boyce, 1360 Moss St., Box 52257, New Orleans 70152, tel. 504/525–4640 or 800/228–9711–Dial Tone–184. No credit cards. Inexpensive–Expensive.*

New Orleans Bed & Breakfast. Among 300 properties citywide are private homes, apartments, and condos. Prices range from $35 to $150. *Contact Sarah-Margaret Brown, Box 8163, New Orleans 70182, tel. 504/822–5046 or 504/822–5038. AE, MC, V. Inexpensive–Very Expensive.*

Hostels **International Center YMCA.** Accommodations are for both men and women. Rooms in Pratt Building are newer and have TVs. Hint for Mardi Gras: 20 of these rooms face St. Charles Avenue or Lee Circle and provide excellent parade views. There are bathrooms and showers on each floor. *936 St. Charles Ave., 70130, tel. 504/568–9622. 150 rooms, no private baths. Facilities: restaurant, gym, weight room, track, indoor pool, parking. MC, V. Inexpensive.*

Marquette House, New Orleans International Hostel. This is the fourth-largest youth hostel in the country, run by Steve and Alma Cross. It is located in a 100-year-old lower Garden District home, one block from St. Charles Avenue and the streetcar. There are bunk beds in dorms, and private rooms with double beds also available. *2253 Carondelet St., 70130, tel. 504/523–3014. 80 beds, 5 private rooms, no private baths. Facilities: 2 lounge areas with TV (1 nonsmoking), 2 equipped community kitchens, dining room, coin-operated laundry, lockers, garden patio with picnic tables. AE, MC, V. Inexpensive.*

The Arts

Comprehensive listings of events can be found in the weekly newspaper *Gambit*, which is distributed free at newsstands, supermarkets, and bookstores. The Friday edition of the daily *Times-Picayune* carries a "Lagniappe" tabloid that lists weekend events. The monthly *New Orleans Magazine* also has a Calendar section. Credit-card purchases of tickets for events at the Saenger Performing Arts Center, the Orpheum Theater, and UNO Lakefront Arena can be made through TicketMaster (tel. 504/888–8181).

Theater The avant-garde, the off-beat, and the satirical are among theatrical offerings at **Contemporary Arts Center** (900 Camp St., tel. 504/523–1216). At **Le Petit Théâtre du Vieux Carré** (616 St. Peter St., tel. 504/522–2081), classics, contemporary drama, children's theater, and musicals are presented. Touring Broadway shows, dance companies, and top-name talent appear at the **Saenger Performing Arts Center** (143 N. Rampart St., tel. 504/524–2490).

Concerts Free jazz concerts are held on weekends in **Dutch Alley**. Pick up a schedule at the information kiosk (French Market at St. Philip St., tel. 504/522–2621). The New Orleans Symphony performs at the **Orpheum Theatre** (129 University Pl., tel. 504/525–0500), which also presents jazz and pop concerts.

Nightlife

Jazz was born in New Orleans, and the music refuses to be confined to nighttime. Weekend jazz brunches are enormously popular and are featured all over town. But a stroll down Bourbon Street will give you a taste of the city's eclectic rhythms. You'll hear Cajun, gutbucket, R&B, rock, ragtime, New Wave, and you name it, and you'll hear it almost around the clock. During the annual Jazz and Heritage Festival, held from the last weekend in April through the first weekend in May, musicians pour in from all over the world to mix it up with local talent, and the music never misses a beat.

New Orleans is a 24-hour town, meaning that there are no legal closing times and it ain't over till it's over. Closing times, especially on Bourbon Street, depend on how business is. Your best bet is to call and ask before tooling out to bar-hop at 2 AM. It is also a superb idea to call and ask about current credit-card policy, cover, and minimum.

Gambit, the free weekly newspaper, has a complete listing of who's doing what where. Things can change between press and performance times, so if there's an artist you're especially eager to hear, it's wise to call and confirm before turning up.

Jazz Aboard the *Creole Queen* (Poydras St. Wharf, tel. 504/524–0814 or 504/529–4567) you'll cruise on the river with Andrew Hall's Society Jazz Band and there's a buffet to boot. If you've an ounce of romance racing through your veins, do it.

Weekdays you can lunch to the tune of ragtime piano at the **Gazebo** (1018 Decatur St., tel. 504/522–0862), and on weekends Chris Clifton's Dixieland band takes the stand. The open-air cafe is a great local favorite on weekend afternoons, when it almost lifts off the ground and soars with the sounds.

Pete Fountain (2 Poydras St., tel. 504/523–4374) is a New Orleans legend with his clarinet and his band that plays in a plush 500-seat room on the third floor of the Hilton Hotel. This is Pete's home base, and the man's on the stand Tuesday, Wednesday, Friday, and Saturday when he's in town. But he makes frequent appearances around the country, so it's wise to call first.

Speaking of legends, the old-time jazz greats lay out the best traditional jazz in the world in a musty, funky hall that's short on comfort, long on talent. **Preservation Hall** (726 St. Peter St., day tel. 504/522–2238, night tel. 504/523–8939) is *the* place for traditional jazz, and it costs you a mere $2 at the door. You may have to stand in line to get in, but it will help if you get there around 7:30.

Dixieland is the name of the tune at the **Seaport Cafe & Bar** (424 Bourbon St., tel. 504/568–0981). You can dine on seafood and Cajun dishes while sitting on a balcony and watching the movable feast down on "the Street."

There's yet more Dixieland Friday and Saturday nights at **Fritzel's** (733 Bourbon St., tel. 561–0432) Clarinet player Chris Burke and his New Orleans Band come on around 10 PM and jazz things up till . . .

Rambling, rustic, and raucous **Snug Harbor** (626 Frenchmen St., tel. 504/949–0696) is where greybeards and undergrads get a big bang out of the likes of the Dirty Dozen, Charmaine Neville, the David Torkanowsky Trio, and Maria Muldaur.

The 350-seat **Storyville Jazz Hall** (1104 Decatur St., tel. 504/525–8199) has a dance floor where you can eat and listen to the beat. Traditional jazz stomps off around 8, with R&B and rock coming up on the late show. Top-name talent is sometimes booked, at which time there's a cover.

R&B, Cajun, Rock, New Wave Industrial-strength rock rolls out of the sound system at the **Hard Rock Cafe** (418 N. Peters, tel. 504/529–5617). Hard Rock Hurricanes are dispensed at a guitar shaped bar, and the place is filled with rock 'n' roll memorabilia. Hamburgers, salads, and steaks are served.

The college crowd raises the rafters at **Jimmy's** (8200 Willow St., tel. 504/861–8200). The music, by national as well as local groups, is rock, New Wave, reggae, R&B . . . whatever.

Benny's Bar (938 Valence, tel. 504/895–9405) is a laid-back lair for blues and reggae. There's never a cover here.

An institution, **Tipitina's** (501 Napoleon Ave., tel. 504/891–TIPS) is sort of a microcosm of the Jazz Fest, featuring progressive jazz, reggae, R&B, rock, New Wave, and blues. Its name comes from a song by Professor Longhair, who was posthumously awarded a Grammy for Best Traditional Blues Recording, and the place is dedicated to his memory. Funky, mellow, loaded with laid-back locals. $3–$10 cover.

Another popular hangout, with a mixed bag of locals and a mixed bag of music—pop, hard rock, R&B, jazz—is **Tyler's** (5234 Magazine St., tel. 504/891–4989). James Rivers and The James Rivers Movement is one of the main attractions, and oysters sell for 15¢ each. Happy hour Tuesday to Saturday from 4 to 7.

Bars One of the world's best-known bars and home of the Hurricane (a sweetly potent concoction of rum and fruit juices) is **Pat O'Brien's** (718 St. Peter St., tel. 504/525–4823). There are three bars, including a lively piano bar and a large courtyard bar, and mobs of collegians and tourists line up to get in. Very lively, very loud, very late.

Dancing **Forty-one Forty-one** (4141 St. Charles Ave., tel. 504/891–9873) is a stylish bastion for disco dancing and mingling singles.

Two-stepping to a Cajun band is billed as the "spécialité de la maison," but the **Maple Leaf Bar** (8316 Oak St., tel. 504/866–LEAF) moves with rock, R&B, reggae, and gospel as well. (Cajun nights *are* special.) There's a $2–$5 cover, depending on what's up.

If you're into heavy-duty dancing to Top-40s discs, check out **Club Galleria West** (The Galleria, 1 Galleria Blvd., Metairie, tel. 504/836–5055). The glitzy disco draws a loyal crowd of young locals.

Supper Club For more than 50 years the **Blue Room** (Fairmont Hotel, tel. 504/529–4744) was the place for big-band, big-name entertainment. You may remember the coast-to-coast radio broadcasts, "brought to you live from the Blue Room of the Roosevelt Hotel." The Roosevelt has been the Fairmont since 1965, and the Blue Room has recently undergone a change. The big names are still booked, and dinner is still served; however, in an effort to attract more young people, the club has slashed the cover charge to $7 weeknights, $9 weekends.

South Louisiana

Just as the state has two distinct regions, so, too, does South Louisiana. We'll make two separate tours of South Louisiana, beginning with Acadiana. Also called French Louisiana, the region is the cradle of the Cajun craze that's swept the nation. Our second tour will cover Baton Rouge, the state capital, and continue to plantation country—the only Southern section of South Louisiana.

Cajuns are descendants of 17th-century French settlers who established a colony they called l'Acadie in the present-day Canadian provinces of Nova Scotia and New Brunswick. The Acadians—"Cajun" is a corruption of "Acadian"—were expelled by the British in the mid-18th century. Their exile was described by Henry Wadsworth Longfellow in his epic poem *Evangeline*. They eventually found a home in South Louisiana, and there they have been since 1762, imbuing the region, the state, and the nation with their unique cuisine and culture. The flavor of the region is summed up in the Cajun phrase *"Laissez les bons temps rouler!"* Let the good times roll.

Cajun Country is made for meandering. We're going to take some scenic routes and state highways, and we encourage you to take to the country roads along the way to further explore the backroads and byways of bayou country.

Getting Around

By Car   The fastest route from New Orleans through Cajun Country to Lafayette and Lake Charles is via I–10, which cuts coast-to-coast across the southern United States. However, if you've time, do take the leisurely scenic drives for exploring.

Great Drives: LA 56 to LA 57 is a circular drive out of Houma, along which you can see shrimp and oyster boats docked along the bayous from May to December. Another circular drive is the Creole Nature Trail (LA 27) out of Lake Charles. LA 82 (Hug-the-Coast Highway) runs through the coastal marshes along the Gulf of Mexico.

By Train   **Amtrak** (tel. 800/USA–RAIL) serves Franklin, Schriever (12 miles from Houma), Lafayette, New Iberia, and Thibodaux (the station is five miles from town).

By Bus   **Greyhound/Trailways** (tel. 800/237–8211) has frequent daily departures to Franklin, Houma, Lafayette, Lake Charles, Morgan City, New Iberia, Opelousas, and Thibodaux.

Guided Tours

Acadiana to Go (tel. 318/981–3918) gives guided tours of Acadiana, as well as the rest of Louisiana. **Allons à Lafayette** (tel. 318/269–9607) offers customized tours, with bilingual guides and itinerary planning for Lafayette and Cajun Country. **Annie Miller's Terrebonne Swamp & Marsh Tours** (tel. 504/879–3934) is especially popular with the kids. The lady who gets along great with gators does daily tours March 1–November 1 out of Houma into the swamps. **Atchafalaya Basin Backwater Adventure** (tel. 504/575–2371) gives two-hour tours of the swamps surrounding Gibson and four-hour forays into the Great Chacahoula Swamp. **Hammond's Flying Service** (tel. 504/876–0584) has air tours, which soar out of Houma over the swamps, marshlands, and the Gulf of Mexico. **McGee's Landing** (tel. 318/228–2384) conducts pontoon-boat tours from the levee in Henderson into the 800,000-acre Atchafalaya Basin.

Important Addresses and Numbers

Tourist Information The **Iberia Parish Tourist Commission,** 2690 Centre St., New Iberia, tel. 318/365–1540. Open daily 9–5. The **Lafayette Convention and Visitors Commission,** 16th Street and Evangeline Thruway, tel. 318/232–3808. Open weekdays 8:30–5, weekends 9–5. The **Southwest Louisiana Convention & Tourist Bureau,** 1211 N. Lakeshore Drive, Lake Charles, tel. 318/436–9588. Open weekdays 8–5. From May 1 to Sept. 4, also open weekends 10:30–3:30.

Emergencies Dial 911 for assistance, or try the emergency room at **Hamilton Medical Center** (2810 Ambassador Caffery Pkwy, Lafayette, tel. 318/981–2949); in Lake Charles, **St. Patrick's Hospital** (524 S. Ryan St., tel. 318/436–2511).

24-Hour Pharmacy **Eckerd's,** (3601 Johnston St., Lafayette, tel. 318/984–5220). In Lake Charles, when pharmacies are closed at night contact **St. Patrick's Hospital** (*see* Emergencies).

Exploring South Louisiana

Numbers in the margin correspond with points of interest on the South Louisiana map.

U.S. 90 drops down into Houma in the marshlands south of New Orleans, an area that abounds with campgrounds and charter boats for fresh- and saltwater fishing. Our route will take us through Morgan City, where the first Tarzan film was made; Franklin, an official Main Street USA town; and the state's only Indian reservation. We'll follow the rambling Bayou Teche (pronounced "tesh") into St. Martinville in Evangeline Country, and next we'll head for Lafayette, which proudly calls itself, with some justification, the capital of French Louisiana. The scenic route to Lake Charles is LA 14, which is fishing, camping, and bird-watching territory. Looping back toward Baton Rouge, we'll go through the area famed for the *Courir du Mardi Gras*, or Mardi Gras Run, during which masked and costumed horseback riders make a mad dash throughout the countryside. Last stop on this trip is Baton Rouge on the Mississippi River, where we'll begin our second tour.

❶ **Houma,** in Terrebonne Parish, dates from 1795 and is located in the heart of the old Hache Spanish Land Grant. The town is named for the Houmas Indians (incidentally, the stressed first syllable of Houma sounds like "home"). Terrebonne Parish is a major center for shrimp and oyster fisheries, and the blessing

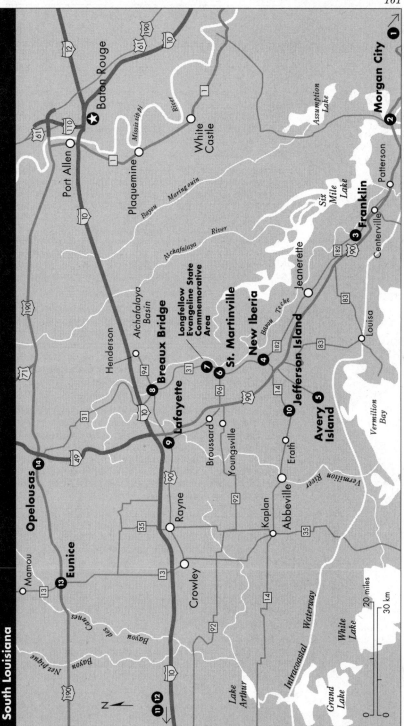

of the shrimp fleets in Chauvin and Dulac is a colorful April event.

The 21-room **Southdown Plantation** was built in 1859 as a one-story Greek Revival house, but the addition in 1893 of the second floor transformed it into a castlelike Queen Anne mansion. The house contains a display of 135 Boehm and Doughty porcelain birds. U.S. Senator Allen Ellender called Houma home, and the house contains a re-creation of his Washington office. *LA 311 at St. Charles St., Houma, tel. 504/851–0154. Admission: $5 adults, $2 senior citizens, $1 students. Open daily 10–4. Closed Thanksgiving, Christmas, New Year's Day, and Easter.*

② Traveling northwesterly now on U.S. 90, we'll come to **Morgan City**, smack on the Atchafalaya River. This city struck it rich when the first producing offshore oil well was completed on November 14, 1947, and the Kerr-McGee Rig No. 16 ushered in the "black gold rush." If you're an aficionado of vintage films, head for the **Turn-of-the-Century House,** where you can see the original 1917 *Tarzan of the Apes* movie, which was filmed in Morgan City. *715 Second St., tel. 504/385–6159. Admission: $2 adults, $1 children. Open weekdays 9–5, weekends 1–5. Closed Thanksgiving, Christmas, New Year's Day, Mardi Gras, and Easter.*

③ The little town of **Franklin** lies 30 miles northwest of Morgan City on U.S. 90. However, we recommend that you get there via LA 182, which you pick up just outside of Patterson. This is Bayou Teche country, and the state highways follow the writhing bayou along some stretches. (Teche is an Indian word meaning snake. According to an ancient Indian legend, the death throes of a giant snake carved the bayou.)

If you're of a nostalgic bent, Franklin's Main Street may bring tears of joy to your eyes. The official Main Street USA status was bestowed on it by the National Trust for Historic Preservation. The street rolls out beneath an arcade of live oaks, and old-fashioned street lamps with No Hitching signs line the boulevard. Franklin is nestled along a bend in the bayou, and there is a splendid view of it from **Parc sur le Teche.** (To reach the park as you drive north through town, turn right on Willow Street by the courthouse square.)

The **Chitimacha Indian Reservation,** three miles northeast of Franklin, is the state's only Indian reservation. For centuries the Chitimacha flourished along the shores of Bayou Atchafalaya. The tribe's main settlement was in Charenton, site of the present reservation. The tribe was famed for its weaving, and Chitimacha baskets, as well as other small craft items, can be found in the reservation's craft shop. *LA 326, Charenton, tel. 318/923–4830. Admission free. Open weekdays 8–4:30. Closed weekends, Christmas, Thanksgiving, New Year's, and Labor Day.*

④ **New Iberia**—the "Queen City of the Teche"—is the next stop along LA 182. New Iberia was founded in 1779 by Spanish settlers, who named the town after the Iberian Peninsula. The town is a blend of Spanish, French, and Acadian cultures.

Set in two lush acres on the bank of the bayou, in the shadows of moss-draped oaks, **Shadows-on-the-Teche** is one of the South's best-known plantation homes. Built in 1834 for sugar planter

David Weeks, this fine old home is the epitome of what went with the wind. *117 E. Main St., New Iberia, tel. 318/369-6446. Admission: $4 adults; $2 children 6-11, children under 11 free. Open daily 9-4:30. Closed Christmas, Thanksgiving, and New Year's Day.*

Down the street a piece from the Shadows, **Mintmere Plantation** is a Greek Revival raised cottage built circa 1857. Many skirmishes took place in this area during the Civil War, and a Union general occupied this house. Also on the grounds is the **Armand Broussard House,** a West Indies–style house dating from about 1790. Present plans call for it to be moved to the new Vermilionville site in Lafayette. Mintmere is open to bed-and-breakfasters. *1400 E. Main St., New Iberia, tel. 318/364-6210. Admission: $3.50 adults, $3 senior citizens and AAA members, $2.50 students. Open daily 10-4 Oct.–Apr., 10-4:30 May–Sept. Closed Christmas, Thanksgiving, New Year's, and Easter.*

City Park is a 45-acre area across the Teche from Main Street, with tennis courts, playgrounds, baseball and softball fields, a fishing pond, boat ramps, and picnic shelters with barbecue facilities. *Admission free. Open weekdays 8 AM–9 PM, Sat. 1-9, Sun. 1-5. Closed Christmas, New Year's Day, Easter, and Thanksgiving.*

Make a short detour, nine miles south of New Iberia, to see **⑤ Avery Island.** The factory on the "island" (it's actually a salt dome) is the birthplace of Tabasco sauce, and descendants of Edmund McIlhenny continue making the hot sauce he invented in the mid-1800s. Other attractions are the 200-acre Jungle Garden, lush with tropical plants, and Bird City, a sanctuary with flurries of snow-white egrets. *LA 329, tel. 318/369-6243. Admission to the gardens and sanctuary: $4 adults; $3 children 6-12, under 6 free. Admission to the Tabasco factory is free. Open daily 9-5.*

LA 31 hugs, as best it can, the Teche from New Iberia north to **⑥ St. Martinville** in the heart of Evangeline Country. This little town is awash with legends. Longfellow's poem was based on the true story of Emmeline Labiche and Louis Arceneaux, two young lovers who were separated for years during the Acadian exile. St. Martinville was a major point of debarkation for Arcadian refugees in the mid-18th century. Louis arrived in the town first and waited many long years hoping to find Emmeline. He eventually despaired of ever seeing her again and became engaged to another woman. Emmeline finally did reach St. Martinville, and, the story is told, Louis saw her by chance as she stepped ashore. Pale with shock, he told her that he was betrothed to another, turned on his heel, and disappeared. Their last, unhappy meeting place was beneath the **Evangeline Oak** (Port St. and Bayou Teche). The *Romance of Evangeline* was filmed in St. Martinville in 1929. Dolores Del Rio starred as Evangeline, and posed for the bronze statue that the cast and crew donated to the town.

You can see the statue in the cemetery behind the church of **St. Martin de Tours** (123 S. Main St.), near the grave of Emmeline Labiche. St. Martin de Tours, Mother Church of the Acadians, is one of the oldest Catholic churches in the country. Inside there is a replica of the Lourdes Grotto and a baptismal font said to have been a gift from Louis XVI. In the late 18th century, St. Martinville was known as Petit Paris because it was a major refuge for royalists who escaped during the French Revolution. "Little Paris" was the scene of many regal balls, soirees, and operas.

❼ Just north of the city limits, on LA 31 and the banks of the Teche, the **Longfellow-Evangeline State Commemorative Area** is a 157-acre park shaded by majestic, moss-draped live oaks. The park contains picnic tables and pavilions, a boat launch, and early Acadian structures. *Tel. 318/394–3754. Admission to the grounds: $2 per vehicle. Open daily 9–7 Apr. 1– Sept. 30, 9–5 rest of year.*

❽ Continue northward on LA 31 for a look at the little town of **Breaux Bridge.** Breaux Bridge is home to world-famous **Mulate's** (*see* Dining) and calls itself the Crawfish Capital of the World. The **Crawfish Festival,** held in May of even-numbered years, draws upwards of 100,000 people.

❾ About 15 minutes from Breaux Bridge on LA 94 is **Lafayette,** a major center of Cajun lore and life. Stop in at the **Lafayette Convention and Visitors Bureau** (16th St. and Evangeline Thruway) and load up your tote bag with maps and brochures.

The **Acadian Village,** nestled in 10 wooded acres, is a re-creation of an early 19th-century bayou settlement. There is a general store, a blacksmith shop, a chapel, and houses representing different styles of Acadian architecture. *H. Mouton Rd., south of LA 342, tel. 318/981–2364. Admission: $4 adults, $3 senior citizens, $1.50 children 6–14. Open daily 10–5. Closed Thanksgiving, Christmas Eve, Christmas Day, New Year's, and Mardi Gras.*

Time Out | **Dwyer's Cafe** serves Cajun plate lunches, burgers, and sandwiches. *323 Jefferson St., tel. 318/235–9364. Open weekdays 4 AM–4 PM, Sat. 4 AM–2 PM. No credit cards. Inexpensive.*

The Louisiana Live Oak Society was founded in Lafayette more than 50 years ago. A charter member of that silent but leafy set dominates the 900 block of St. John Street. The **St. John Oak** is 400 years old and has a matronly waistline of about 19 feet. It is on the grounds of the **Cathedral of St. John the Evangelist** (914 St. John St.), a Romanesque church with Byzantine touches.

The **Lafayette Natural History Museum** is a busy place, with workshops, movies, concerts, light shows, and a planetarium. It's also the venue for the annual September Louisiana Native Crafts Festival. *637 Girard Park Dr., Lafayette, tel. 318/268–5544. Admission free. Open Mon., Wed., Thurs., and Fri. 9–5, Tues. 9–9, weekends 1–5.*

The museum's sister facility is **The Acadiana Park Nature Station,** a three-story cypress pole structure with an interpretive center and discovery boxes to help children get acquainted with the wildflowers, birds, and other things they'll see along a 3½-mile trail. *E. Alexandre St., Lafayette, tel. 318/235–6181. Admission free. Open weekdays 9–5, weekends 11–3.*

The *Vermilion Queen* lazes out on Bayou Vermilion for sightseeing, dinner, and moonlight cruises. *1604 Pinhook Rd., Lafayette, tel. 318/235–1776. Admission: noon cruises, $7 adults, $4 children 4–12; dinner cruises, $19.50 adults, $11.50 children; moonlight cruise $8 (adults only).*

In the summer of 1990, an 18-acre, $5.2 million theme park called **Vermilionville** will open within Beaver Park, three miles south of Interstate 10. For more information, contact the Lafayette Parish Bayou Vermilion District, Box 4736, Lafayette 70502, tel. 318/233–6220.

We'll hitch up with U.S. 90 now and go 15 miles south to the junction with LA 675, where a right turn will take us to **Live Oak Gardens.** American actor Joseph Jefferson, who toured the country in the 19th century portraying Rip Van Winkle, bought several thousand acres of land in South Louisiana and built his winter home on what came to be called **Jefferson Island.** In 1980, the salt dome on which the "island" rested collapsed, causing severe damage to the property. The area, now called Live Oak Gardens, has been completely restored to its former grandeur, with formal and informal gardens and groves of live oaks. Jefferson's house is a three-story, comfortably opulent, Southern Gothic home with Moorish touches. *284 Rip Van Winkle Rd., off LA 14, tel. 318/367–3485. Admission: $5 adults, $3.50 senior citizens, $2.50 children 5–16. Open daily 9–5 during daylight savings time, 9–4 during winter. Closed Christmas and New Year's.*

At this point, we'll strike out on LA 14 and head for **Lake Charles,** the state's third seaport. The city dates from the 1760s, when the first French settlers arrived. The first home was built by Charles Sallier on the shell beach by the lake, and the town was originally called Charlie's Lake. The city is blessed with more than 50 miles of rivers, lakes, canals, and bayous, making it a paradise for sailing, fishing, canoeing, shrimping, and crabbing.

North Beach (admission $1 per vehicle) is a white-sand beach on the north shore of the lake, where you can loll in the sun, swim, or rent a sailboat. Twelve miles north of the city on LA 378, **Sam Houston Jones State Park** is a 1,068-acre area that beckons sports and nature enthusiasts.

The **Imperial Calcasieu Museum,** on the site of Charles Sallier's home, has an extensive collection pertaining to Lake Charles and Imperial Calcasieu Parish. The museum includes an old-fashioned pharmacy, an Audubon collection, a Gay Nineties barbershop, and a modern fine-arts gallery. *204 W. Sallier St., Lake Charles, tel. 318/439–3797. Admission free. Open Tues.–Fri. 10–5, weekends 1–5. Closed Mon., Thanksgiving, Christmas, New Year's Day, Easter, and Mardi Gras.*

The **Creole Nature Trail** is a 105-mile loop beginning on LA 27 in **Sulphur,** dipping down along the Gulf of Mexico on LA 82, and winding up back in Lake Charles. Beautiful in the spring, this drive takes you to the **Sabine Wildlife Refuge** (admission free) where a paved 1½ mile trail takes you right into the wilds. There is an audio-visual center and a tower at the end of the trail, which gives you an excellent view of the wilderness. (Take along some insect repellent!)

You can make a detour off the Creole Nature Trail and continue east on LA 82 (Hug-the-Coast Highway), which whips along the windswept coastal marshes through **Grand Chenier** to the **Rockefeller Wildlife Refuge,** an 84,000-acre tract where thousands of ducks, geese, 'gators, wading birds, otters, and others while away the winter months.

We'll leave Lake Charles on I–10E, and exit on U.S. 165 headed north. An 18-mile drive will put us at the intersection of U.S. 190, where we'll head east again.

⑬ This route will take us through the tiny town of **Eunice,** home of the **Cajun Radio Show** (*see* Nightlife) and of the **Eunice Museum.** The museum is in a former railroad depot and contains displays on Cajun culture, including Cajun music and Cajun Mardi Gras. *220 S. C.C. Duson Dr., Eunice, tel. 318/457–1208. Admission free. Open Tues.–Sat. 8–noon and 1–5.*

The area surrounding Eunice is the major stomping grounds for the annual Courir du Mardi Gras, which takes place the Sunday before Fat Tuesday (Mardi Gras day). *Le Capitaine* leads a band of masked and costumed horseback riders on a mad dash through the countryside, stopping at farmhouses along the way to shout, *"Voulez-vous recevoir cette bande de Mardi Gras?"* (Do you wish to receive the Mardi Gras?) The answer is always Yes, and the group enlarges and continues, gathering food for the street festivals that wind things up.

⑭ Farther east on U.S. 190 is **Opelousas,** the third-oldest town in the state. Poste de Opelousas was founded in 1720 by the French as a trading post. The town is named for the Appalousa Indians, who lived in the area centuries before the French and Spanish arrived. For a brief period during the Civil War, Opelousas served as the state capital.

As you approach the town from the east on U.S. 190, look for the **Acadiana Tourist Center** (tel. 318/948–6263), where you can get plenty of information and also arrange for tours of some of the town's historic homes.

Adjacent to the tourist center is the **Jim Bowie Museum.** This was Bowie's boyhood home, and the museum has memorabilia pertaining to his life and times, including the famous Bowie knife. *U.S. 190E, tel. 318/948–6263. Admission free. Open daily 8–4.*

A 15-minute drive south of Opelousas on I–49, exiting on LA 93, will put you on Main Street in **Grand Coteau.** Grand Coteau is a religious and educational center, and the entire peaceful little village is on the National Register of Historic Places. Of particular note here is the **Church of St. Charles Borromeo,** a simple wooden structure with an ornate high-baroque interior. There are 36 works of art in the church, most of which were done by Erasmus Humbrecht, whose works can also be seen in St. Louis Cathedral in New Orleans. The church's unusual bell tower is one of the area's most-photographed sights. The church can be toured (for a $1 donation per person), but you must call (tel. 318/662–5279) to make arrangements in advance.

Time Out	**The Kitchen Shop,** in a quaint cypress cottage, sells gourmet cookware and Louisiana crafts. There's also a tiny sun-filled room and a patio where you can relax over desserts, tea, and gourmet coffee. *Main St., Grand Coteau, tel. 318/662–3500. MC, V. Open Mon.–Sat. 9– 5. Inexpensive.*

Cretien Point Plantation, not far away, is noted not only for its grandeur but also for the role it played in *Gone With the Wind.* In the 1930s, a photographer infatuated with the house took pictures of it and sent them to Hollywood. As a result, its staircase was the model for the one in Scarlett O'Hara's Tara. *About 4 mi from Sunset on the Bristol/Bosco Rd., tel. 318/662–5876 or 318/233–7050. Admission: $5 adults, $2.50 children under 12, under 4 free. Open daily 10–5. Closed Thanksgiving, Christmas, and New Year's Day.*

You can continue on to Baton Rouge via either U.S. 190 or I–10, as Grand Coteau is cradled in between the two thoroughfares. We'll begin our next tour in Baton Rouge and continue into plantation country.

What to See and Do with Children

Acadian Village, Lafayette (*see* Exploring).
Annie Miller's Terrebonne Swamp & Marsh Tours (*see* Guided Tours).
Atchafalaya Basin Backwater Adventure (*see* Guided Tours).
Avery Island (*see* Exploring).
Cajun Queen boat tours on Bayou Teche. *La Place d'Evangeline, Port St. and Bayou Teche, St. Martinville, tel. 318/394–4010. Admission: $5 adults, $2.50 children.*
Chitimacha Indian Reservation, Charenton (*see* Exploring).
City Park, New Iberia (*see* Exploring).
Creole Nature Trail, Lake Charles (*see* Exploring).
Hammond's Flying Service, Air Tours, Houma (*see* Exploring).
Heaven on Earth Amusement Park, with air-inflated rides, water wobble, roller racers, skill games, toddle town (geared for children 1–14). *3512 Kirkman St., Lake Charles, tel. 318/478–7529. Admission free for adults accompanied by children; $4.25 children 8–14, $3.25 children 1–7. Open Tues.–Thurs. 3–6, Fri. 9–8, Sat. 10–8, Sun. 2–6.*
Jim Bowie Museum, Opelousas (*see* Exploring).
Lafayette Natural History Museum & Nature Station (*see* Exploring).
Live Oak Gardens (*see* Exploring).
McGee's Landing, Atchafalaya Basin Tours (*see* Guided Tours).
North Beach, Lake Charles (*see* Exploring).
Turn-of-the-Century House (Tarzan film), Morgan City (*see* Exploring).

Off the Beaten Track

People all over the world have a hankering for Cajun chank-a-chanking (dancing). In order to play Cajun music, musicians need those special triangles, accordions, and fiddles. A number of places in Cajun Country make not only music but musical instruments as well. Among them is the **Savoy Music Center Accordion Factory** in Eunice. The front half of the building is a music store, and behind it, Cajun accordions are made from scratch. Proprietor Marc Savoy says his factory turns out about five accordions a month and fills orders all the way from Alaska to New Zealand. On Saturday mornings, accordions and other instruments tune up and take off during the weekly jam sessions held in the shop. There's beer to drink, two-stepping to do, and musicians from all over the area dropping over to sit in on the informal sessions. *U.S. 190, 3 mi east of Eunice, tel. 318/457–9563. Admission free. Open Tues.–Fri. 9–5, Sat. 9–noon.*

Participant Sports

Louisiana is not called Sportsman's Paradise for nothing. Hunting and fishing are a way of life in this state. There are approximately 1.7 million acres of publicly owned or managed lands open to hunting. For information on permits, limits, and seasons, contact the **Louisiana Department of Wildlife & Fisheries,** Box 15570, Baton Rouge 70895, tel. 504/342–5868.

Biking These flatlands and lush parks make for easy riding. Bikes can be rented at **Pack & Paddle** (601 E. Pinhook Rd., Lafayette, tel. 318/232–5854, and W. College Dr., Lake Charles, tel. 318/478–9298).

Canoeing Paddling is almost a breeze on the easy-going Whisky Chitto Creek. Canoes can be rented at **Pack & Paddle** (117 W. College Dr., Lake Charles, tel. 318/478–9298).

Fishing Trips to fish, sightsee, bird-watch, or hunt can be arranged at **Cajun Fishing Tours** (1925 E. Main St., New Iberia, tel. 318/364–7141). **Sportsman's Paradise** (tel. 504/594–2414) is a charter fishing facility 20 miles south of Houma, with six boats available year-round. **Salt, Inc. Charter Fishing Service** (tel. 504/594–6626 or 504/594–7581), LA 56 south of Houma at Coco Marina, offers fishing trips in the bays and barrier islands of lower Terrebonne Parish, as well as into the Gulf of Mexico.

Golf You can tee off at **Pine Shadows Golf Center** (750 Goodman Rd., Lake Charles, tel. 318/433–8681), **City Park Golf Course** (Mudd Ave. and Eighth St., Lafayette, tel. 318/261–8385), and **Vieux Chene Golf Course** (Youngsville Hwy., Broussard, tel. 318/837–1159).

Hiking/Nature Trails The Old Stagecoach Road in **Sam Houston Jones State Park** is a favorite for hikers who want to explore the park and the various tributaries of the Calcasieu River. The **Louisiana State Arboretum** (Ville Platte, tel. 318/363–2503) is a 600-acre facility with four miles of nature trails.

Horseback Riding There are trail rides, pony rides, and even hayrides at **Broken Arrow Stables** (Segura Rd. off LA 3013, New Iberia, tel. 318/369–PONY).

Dining and Lodging

Dining Graced as the state is with waterways, Louisiana tables are laden with seafood in every imaginable and innovative variety. In South Louisiana, sea creatures are prepared with a Cajun flair, which usually means hot and spicy.

Category	Cost*
Very Expensive	over $35
Expensive	$25–$35
Moderate	$15–$20
Inexpensive	under $15

per person without tax (7½%), service, or drinks

Lodging Sleeping accommodations run from homey bed-and-breakfasts to chain motels to luxury hotels to elegant antebellum mansions open for overnighters.

Category	Cost*
Very Expensive	over $120
Expensive	$90–$120
Moderate	$50–$90
Inexpensive	under $50

double room; add 6% for taxes

The following credit-card abbreviations are used: AE, American Express; CB, Carte Blanche; DC, Diners Club; MC, MasterCard; V, Visa.

Breaux Bridge **Mulate's.** A roadhouse with flashing yellow lights outside and
Dining plastic checkered cloths inside, Mulate's is an eatery, a dance
★ hall, an age-old family gathering spot, and a celebrity, having been featured on "The Today Show" and "Good Morning, America," among other airings. A dressed-down crowd digs into the likes of stuffed crabs and the Super Seafood Platters. *325 Mills Ave., tel. in LA 800/634–9880 or in USA 800/42–CAJUN. Dress: informal. Reservations not required. AE, MC, V. Open Sun.–Thurs. 7 AM–10:30 PM, Fri. and Sat. 7 AM–11 PM. Closed Christmas Day. Inexpensive.*

Carencro **Prudhomme's Cajun Cafe.** In a suburb of Lafayette, celebrity
Dining chef Paul Prudhomme's sister Enola—a major contributor to *The Prudhomme Family Cookbook*—has her country kitchen in a cypress cottage. Her specialties are blackened redfish, eggplant pirogue, and panfried rabbit in cream sauce—plus homemade jalapeño-and-cheese bread. *4676 N.E. Evangeline Thruway, tel. 318/896–7964. Dress: informal. Reservations not required. MC, V. Closed Mon. Inexpensive.*

Lafayette **Cafe Vermilionville.** A 19th-century inn with crisp white na-
Dining pery, old-brick fireplaces, and a casual elegance. Among the specialties are Redfish Anna, with lump crabmeat, artichoke hearts, and béarnaise sauce, and fried soft-shell crab with crawfish fettuccine. *1304 W. Pinhook Rd., tel. 318/237–0100. Dress: informal. Reservations advised. AE, MC, V. Closed Christmas and New Year's Day. Inexpensive.*

Prejean's. Housed in a cypress cottage, this local favorite has a cozy oyster bar, red-checkered cloths, and live music nightly. Specialties include Prejean's Platter (seafood gumbo, fried shrimp, oysters, catfish, and seafood-stuffed bell peppers) and Crawfish Dinner, with étouffée, bisqued, and fried mudbugs. *3480 U.S. 167N, next to Evangeline Downs, tel. 318/896–3247. Dress: informal. Reservations not required. AE, CB, DC, MC, V. Closed Christmas and Thanksgiving. Inexpensive.*

Lodging **Holiday Inn Central–Holidome.** Seventeen acres containing virtually everything you'd ever need for a long and yuppie life. *Box 91807, 70509, tel. 318/233–6815 or 800/HOLIDAY. 250 rooms. Facilities: airport shuttle, cable TV, cocktail lounge, restaurant, heated indoor pool with whirlpool, sauna, outdoor pool, 2 lighted tennis courts, 24-hr jogging track, game rooms, playgrounds, picnic areas, baby-sitting service. AE, CB, DC, MC, V. Moderate.*

Hotel Acadiana. Cushy lobby lit by a huge brass chandelier, concierge floor, and standard rooms with thick carpeting, marble-top dressers, and wet bars. Even-numbered rooms face the pool. Built in 1980 across the road from the *Vermilion*

Queen riverboat landing. *1801 W. Pinhook Rd., 70508, tel. 318/233–8120, in LA 800/874–4664 or in USA 800/826–8386. 304 rooms. Facilities: cable TV with ESPN, cocktail lounge, restaurant, free parking, facilities for handicapped, 2 outdoor pools. AE, DC, MC, V. Inexpensive.*

Lake Charles
Dining

Cafe Margaux. Candlelight, soft pinks, white linens, French waiters, and a 9,000-bottle mahogany wine cellar. Specialties include rack of lamb *en croute* and fillet of flounder with lump crabmeat and brown meunière sauce. *765 Bayou Pines East, tel. 318/433–2902. Jacket and tie required. Reservations recommended. AE, MC, V. Closed Sun., Christmas, July 4th, Thanksgiving, New Year's. Moderate.*

Chez Oca. Across the street from Cafe Margaux is this glassed-in restaurant with white napery, candlelight, exposed beams, and old brick. Two of the more popular items on an extensive menu are filet mignon with green peppercorns and fillet of red snapper with crabmeat and crawfish sauce. *615 Bayou Pines E, tel. 318/439–8364. Jacket and tie required. Reservations recommended. AE, DC, MC, V. Closed Sun., Christmas Eve, Christmas Day, Thanksgiving, Good Friday, and Memorial Day. Moderate.*

Lodging

Hilton Inn, Lake Charles. Built in 1982 between the lake and the interstate, the Hilton has traditional furnishings in rooms done in soothing earth tones. The four-story structure offers 10 rooms for nonsmokers and five for the handicapped. Rooms on the lakeside are infinitely preferable to those on the interstate side. *505 N. Lakeshore Dr., 70601, tel. 318/433–7121 or 800/367–1814. 269 rooms. Facilities: free airport shuttle, cable TV, coffee shop, restaurant, concierge, currency exchange, free parking, gift shop, laundry, room service, safety deposit box, outdoor swimming pool. AE, DC, MC, V. Moderate.*

Chateau Charles Hotel and Conference Center. A New Orleans-style structure with wrought-iron trim and beamed ceilings, the hotel is located on 25 wooded acres, three minutes from downtown. There are four two-bedroom suites with wet bars, six nonsmokers' rooms, and easy access for the handicapped in the all-ground-level hotel. The facility was built in 1955 and completely renovated in 1983. *Box 1381, 70602, tel. 318/882–6130, in LA 800/227–3138 or in USA 800/227–2605. 260 rooms. Facilities: free airport shuttle, free shuttle to local health clubs, cable TV, restaurant, cocktail lounge, laundry, and room service. AE, CB, DC, MC, V. Inexpensive.*

Downtowner Motor Inn. Smack on the lake, adjacent to the Hilton but about 10 years its senior, the Downtowner boasts a boat dock, splashy garden, large sun deck, and contemporary rooms in green and rust. Ask for a room overlooking the lake. *507 N. Lakeshore Dr., 70601, tel. 318/433–0541 or 800/238–6161. 134 rooms. Facilities: free airport shuttle, cable TV with free Showtime, cocktail lounge, 24-hr restaurant, room service. AE, CB, DC, MC, V. Inexpensive.*

Lodging

Mintmere Plantation. A Greek Revival raised cottage built on the banks of Bayou Teche in 1857 and occupied by a Union general during the Civil War. Yankees nowadays find somewhat easier access to the house, which is furnished with antebellum Louisiana antiques. *1400 Main St., 70560, tel. 318/364–6210. 2 1-bedroom suites and 1 2-bedroom suite, all with private bath. No credit cards. Closed Thanksgiving, Christmas, New Year's Day, and Easter. Expensive.*

Opelousas
Dining

The Palace Café. A down-home coffee shop on the town square, operated by the same family for more than 60 years. Locals flock here for the cafe's famous homemade pies and baklava. Among the eclectic specialties are baked eggplant stuffed with Alaskan king crabmeat dressing, and Greek salad with feta cheese, black and green olives, and anchovies. There are also steaks, fried chicken, sandwiches, burgers and seafood. *167 W. Landry St., tel. 318/942–2142. Dress: informal. Reservations not required. MC, V. Closed Easter, July 4th, Thanksgiving, Christmas Eve, Christmas Day, and New Year's Day. Inexpensive.*

St. Martinville
Dining

La Place d'Evangeline. In the historic red-brick Castillo Hotel, on the banks of the Bayou Teche beneath the branches of the Evangeline Oak, dine in high-ceiling rooms where 18th-century royalists once held lavish balls and operas. An extensive menu includes steak Evangeline, stuffed with lump crabmeat; redfish Gabriel, topped with seafood sauce; and alligator meat. Do not pass up the homemade bread. Proprietors Peggy and Gerald Hulin are renovating the upstairs part of the old hotel, and five rooms are now open for overnight guests. *Port St. at Bayou Teche, tel. 318/394–4010. Dress: informal. Reservations not necessary. AE, MC, V. Closed Christmas. Moderate.*

The Arts

Concerts

Major concert attractions are booked into the **Cajundome** in Lafayette (444 Cajundome Blvd., tel. 318/265–2100) and the **Lake Charles Civic Center** (900 Lakeshore Dr., tel. 318/ 491–1256).

Theater

The Lake Charles Little Theater (813 Enterprise Blvd., Lake Charles, tel. 318/433–7988) puts on a variety of plays and musicals. **The Theatre 'Cadien** (200 S. State St., Abbeville, tel. 318/893–2936) performs plays in French in conjunction with the Abbey Players. **Lafayette Community Theatre** (529 Jefferson St., tel. 318/235–1532) offers contemporary plays with a Cajun flair.

Nightlife

Louisiana is alive with all kinds of music, but while we're in Cajun Country our focus will be on the music of the Cajuns. And we'll introduce you to chank-a-chanking at a fais do-do. Translation? The little iron triangles in most Cajun bands make a rhythmic "chank-a-chank" sound, and most folks call dancing to the rhythm chank-a-chanking. As for fais do-do (pronounced "fay doh-doh"), that's the dance, or party, where you go to chank-a-chank. Fais do-dos crop up all over Cajun Country, sometimes in the town square, sometimes at somebody's house. There are also restaurants, dance halls, and lounges that regularly feature live Cajun music. The *Times of Acadiana* is a free newspaper that comes out every Wednesday and is available in hotels, restaurants, and shops. Check the "On the Town" section to see what's doing in the area.

The following restaurants and lounges regularly feature music for two-stepping, waltzing, and chank-a-chanking. ("Regularly" does not necessarily mean every night.) Sunday afternoon (*all* afternoon) is often devoted to dancing. Be sure and call to find out what the schedule is.

Mulate's (*see* Beaux Bridge Dining).

Prejean's (*see* Lafayette Dining).

Randol's (2320 Kaliste Saloom Rd., Lafayette, tel. 318/981–7080). Hot dancing in a greenhouse setting.

La Poussière (1212 Grand Pointe Rd., Breaux Bridge, tel. 318/332–1721). One of the oldest dance halls around.

Belizaire's (2307 N. Parkerson Ave., Crowley, tel. 318/788–2501). Take a look at the Cajun Music Hall of Fame before you take to the floor.

Slim's Y-Ki-Ki (LA 167, Washington Rd., Opelousas., tel. 318/942–9980). *Louisiana Life* magazine rated this black Cajun club the best Cajun dancing place in the state.

Fred's Lounge (420 Sixth St., Mamou, tel. 318/468–5411). Saturday morning radio broadcasts (complete with music, of course), have been aired from Fred Tate's place for more than 40 years. It starts at 8 AM and goes on till 1 PM.

Cajun Music Show. A live radio show, mostly in French, that's been described as a combination of the "Grand Ole Opry", the "Louisiana Hayride," and the "Prairie Home Companion." *Eunice, tel. 318/457–3329. Admission: $1. Saturday nights from 6 to 8 in the Liberty Theatre, Park Ave. at Second St.*

Baton Rouge and Plantation Country

Our meandering amble through South Louisiana brings us now to Baton Rouge, the state capital. Legend has it that in 1699 French explorers observed that a red stick planted in the ground on a high bluff overlooking the Mississippi served as a boundary between two Indian tribes. Sieur d'Iberville, leader of the expedition, noted *le baton rouge*—the red stick—in his journal, and *voila!* Baton Rouge.

This is the city from which Huey P. Long ruled the state and also the site of his assassination. Even today, more than half a century after Long's death, legends abound of the colorful, cunning, and controversial governor and U.S. senator.

The parishes to the north of Baton Rouge are quiet and bucolic, with gently rolling hills, high bluffs, and historic districts. John James Audubon lived in West Feliciana Parish in 1821, tutoring local children and painting 80 of his famous bird studies. In both terrain and traits, this region is more akin to North Louisiana than to South Louisiana—which is to say, the area is very Southern.

As you are by now aware, Louisiana is graced with many stately mansions. But the area designated Plantation Country begins with a reservoir of fine old homes north of Baton Rouge that cascades all the way down the Great River Road to New Orleans.

Getting Around

By Plane Baton Rouge Metropolitan Airport (tel. 504/355–0333), 12 miles north of downtown, is served by **American, Continental, Delta, and Northwest.**

By Car I–10 and U.S. 190 run east–west through Baton Rouge. I–12 heads east, connecting with north–south I–55 and I–59. U.S.

61 leads from New Orleans to Baton Rouge and northward through Mississippi.

Great Drives: LA 1 travels along False River, which is a blue "oxbow lake" created ages ago when the mischievous, muddy Mississippi changed its course. Water lazily nudges the shore along the route, which wanders past gracious homes and small lake houses.

By Bus **Greyhound-Trailways** (tel. 504/343–4891 or 800/237–8211) has frequent daily service to Baton Rouge and surrounding towns.

Guided Tours

Lagniappe Tours (tel. 504/387–2464) has daily van tours of Baton Rouge, Cajun Country, and plantations.
Louisiana Heritage Tours (tel. 504/293–8189) takes small groups on plantation tours.
Feliciana Travel & Tours (tel. 504/635–3582 or 504/381–9512 from Baton Rouge) gives tours in a 15-passenger minibus with pickups in the Baton Rouge area.

Important Addresses and Numbers

Tourist Information
The **Louisiana Visitor Information Center** will supply you with maps and brochures to just about anywhere. *Louisiana State Capitol, State Capitol Dr., Baton Rouge, tel. 504/342–7317. Tourist information can be obtained by calling 800/33–GUMBO (outside LA) or 504/342–8119 (in LA). Open daily 9–4:30. Closed Thanksgiving, Christmas, New Year's Day, Mardi Gras.*

West Feliciana Historical Society Information Center is another useful stop for advice and information. *364 Ferdinand St., St. Francisville, tel. 504/635–6330. Open Mon.–Sat. 9–4, Sun. 1–4.*

Emergencies
Dial 911 for assistance. Hospital emergency rooms are open 24 hours a day. **Baton Rouge General Medical Center** (3600 Florida Blvd., tel. 504/387–7000); **Our Lady of the Lake Medical Center** (5000 Hennessy Blvd., tel. 504/765–6565).

Pharmacy
Eckerd's (3651 Perkins Rd., tel. 504/344–9459; 14455 Greenville Springs Rd., tel. 504/261–6541).

Exploring Baton Rouge and Plantation Country

Numbers in the margin correspond with points of interest on the Baton Rouge and Plantation Country map.

After touring the state capital, we'll take LA 67 to see the historic districts and plantations in the parishes north of Baton Rouge. An overnight stay in one of the plantation bed-and-breakfasts is recommended. From St. Francisville, we'll take the free ferry at the tip of town and start south on LA 1 to see the antebellum gems that decorate the Great River Road between Baton Rouge and New Orleans.

❶ Start your tour of **Baton Rouge** at the Visitors Information Center in the lobby of the **State Capitol Building.** Armed with maps and brochures, you can take a tour of the first floor, which includes the spot where Huey Long was shot. This building is America's tallest state capitol, standing 34 stories tall. There is

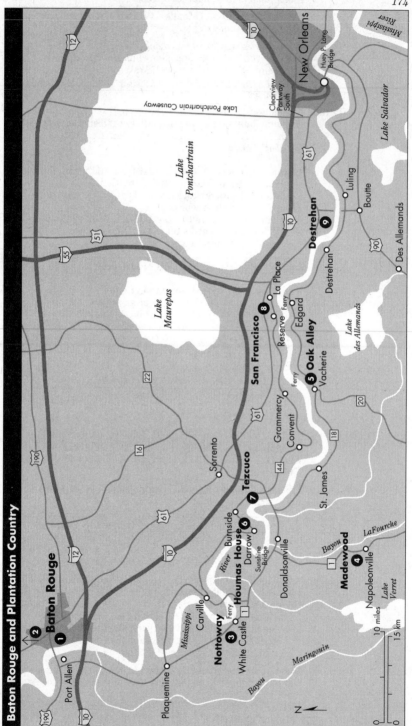

Baton Rouge and Plantation Country

an observation deck on the 27th floor that affords a spectacular view of the Mississippi River and the city. *State Capitol Dr., tel. 504/342–7317. Admission free. Open daily 8–4:30; last tour at 4 PM. Closed Thanksgiving, Christmas, New Year's, and Mardi Gras.*

A museum in the **Pentagon Barracks** has exhibits that acquaint visitors with the Capitol complex. The barracks were originally built in 1819 to quarter U.S. Army personnel, and when Louisiana State University moved from Pineville to Baton Rouge in 1869, it was located in these buildings. *900 North Blvd. (Riverside Mall on the State Capitol grounds), tel. 504/387–2464. Admission free. Open Tues.–Sat. 10–4, Sun. 1–4. Closed Christmas, Thanksgiving, New Year's Day, Easter, and Mardi Gras.*

Only one battle of the American Revolution was fought outside the 13 original colonies, and it was fought on these capitol grounds. At press time, one of the historic buildings, the **Old Arsenal Museum,** a heavy-duty structure dating from about 1835, was being restored. It's scheduled to reopen in 1990.

Although the restored **Old State Capitol** contains no exhibits, the building itself is worth seeing. When it was completed in 1849 it was to some a masterpiece, to others a monstrosity. In any case, the Gothic Revival castlelike structure stands on a bluff; its name is on the list of National Historic Landmarks. *150 North Blvd., tel. 504/342–8211. Admission free. Open Tues.–Sat. 9:30–4.*

Across the street from the Old State Capitol is the **Louisiana Arts & Science Center Riverside Museum,** housed in an old railroad station. There is a fine arts museum with changing exhibits, an Egyptian tomb exhibit, restored trains from the 1890s to the 1950s, and a Discovery Depot with a children's art gallery and workshop. *100 S. River Rd., tel. 504/344–9463. Admission: $1.50 adults; 75¢ students, senior citizens, and children 6–12; children under 6 free. Museum does not charge admission on Sat. 10–noon. Open Tues.–Fri. 10–3, Sat. 10–4, Sun. 2–4. Closed Thanksgiving, Christmas, New Year's, and Mardi Gras.*

The *Samuel Clemens Riverboat* gives one-hour narrated tours of Baton Rouge harbor and evening supper cruises. *Departures from Florida Blvd. at the River, tel. 504/381–9606. Admission: $5 adults, $3 children under 12. 1-hr. tours 10 AM, noon, and 2 PM; Apr.–Aug. daily Sept.–Nov. and March, Wed.–Sun.; call for schedule Dec.–Feb. Closed Thanksgiving and Christmas.*

The **Louisiana Arts & Science Center** is in the restored Old Governor's Mansion, which was built in 1930 during Huey Long's administration. Rooms in the antiques-filled house are dedicated to the memories of Louisiana governors. *502 North Blvd., tel. 504/344–9463. Admission: $1.50 adults; 75¢ students, senior citizens, and children 6–12. Open Sat. 10–4, Sun. 1–4. Closed Thanksgiving, Christmas, New Year's, and Mardi Gras.*

Time Out   At the **Blackforest** you can get German food, deli sandwiches, plate lunches, and imported beer. *321 North Blvd., tel. 504/334–0059. No credit cards. Inexpensive.*

The **Louisiana Governor's Mansion** was built in 1963 and is designed along the lines of a Greek Revival plantation. *1001 Capital Access Rd., tel. 504/342–5855. Admission free. Open weekdays 9–11 and 2–4. Reservations are required.*

About a mile-and-a-half from the center of town, **Magnolia Mound Plantation** is an early 19th-century raised cottage furnished with American Federal antiques and Louisiana artifacts. On Tuesday, Thursday, and Saturday from October through April cooking demonstrations are conducted in the outbuildings. *2161 Nicholson Dr., tel. 504/343–4955. Admission: $3.50 adults, $2.50 senior citizens, $1.50 students, 75¢ children. Open Tues.–Sat. 10–4, Sun. 1–4. Closed Thanksgiving, Christmas, New Year's Day, Easter, and Mardi Gras.*

Continuing south on Nicholson Drive you'll come to **Louisiana State University.** LSU was founded in Pineville in 1860 as the Louisiana State Seminary of Learning and Military Academy. Its president was William Tecumseh Sherman, who resigned when war broke out and four years later made his famous march through Georgia. The 200-acre campus has several museums of interest, as well as Indian Mounds that are of particular interest to archaeologists and archaeology buffs.

Baton Rouge's other major institution of higher learning is **Southern University,** about five miles north of town on U.S. 61. Founded in 1880, Southern U. is the nation's largest predominantly black university.

Fourteen miles north of Baton Rouge on U.S. 61, you'll come to the **Port Hudson State Commemorative Area.** The 650-acre park is the site of a fiercely fought Civil War battle, and the longest siege in American military history. There are high viewing towers, gun trenches, and, on a more peaceful note, seven miles of hiking trails. *756 W. Plains-Port Hudson Rd. (U.S. 61), tel. 504/654–3775. Admission free. Open daily April 1–Sept. 30 9–7, Oct. 1–Mar. 31 9–5. Closed Thanksgiving, Christmas, and New Year's.*

❷ St. Francisville has been described as a town two miles long and two yards wide. Much of the long, skinny town is listed on the National Register of Historic Places. Allow plenty of time for your visit to **Rosedown Plantation and Gardens.** This house and its surroundings bring on a bad attack of hyperbole. Suffice it to say that the opulent house dates from 1835, is beautifully restored, and nestles in 28 acres of exquisite formal gardens. *LA 10, just off U.S. 61, tel. 504/635–3332. Admission: $5 to the house and gardens, $3 for the gardens only. Open daily 9–5 Mar.–Oct., 10–4 Nov.–Feb. Closed Christmas Eve and Christmas Day.*

A few miles south of St. Francisville, off U.S. 61, you'll find the 100-acre **Audubon State Commemorative Area,** where Audubon did a major portion of his "Birds of America" studies. The 3-story Oakley Plantation House on the grounds is where Audubon tutored the young Eliza Pirrie. *LA 956, tel. 504/635–3739. Admission to the park and plantation: $2 per vehicle of 4 people. Grounds open daily 9–7 Apr. 1–Sept. 30, 9–5 daily Oct. 1–Mar. 31. Oakley open daily 9–5. Closed Christmas, Thanksgiving, and New Year's.*

The Myrtles bills itself as America's Most Haunted House and hosts Mystery Weekends, Halloween Tours, and such. The Myrtles is best noted for its 110-foot gallery with Wedgwood blue cast-iron grillwork. The house was built around 1796, and has elegant formal parlors with rich molding and faux marbre paneling. *5 mi north of St. Francisville on U.S. 61, tel. 504/635 –6277. Admission: $4.50 adults, $2.50 children. Open daily 9–5. Closed Christmas.*

Drive aboard the free ferry just outside St. Francisville for a breezy ride across the Mississippi. Pick up LA 1 in New Roads and head south. You'll be driving right alongside **False River,** which was an abandoned riverbed that became a lake. In contrast to the muddy Mississippi, the waters of False River are dark blue. This is an excellent fishing area, and you'll see long piers and fishing boats tied up all along the route.

③ Sixteen miles south of Baton Rouge is **Nottoway,** the South's largest plantation home, built in 1859 by famed architect Henry Howard. The Greek Revival/Italianate mansion has 64 rooms filled with antiques and is especially noted for its white ballroom, which has original crystal chandeliers and hand-carved Corinthian columns. Several of the rooms are open for overnighters. Before you leave the lush grounds of Nottoway, walk across the road and go up on the levee for a splendid view of Old Man River. *LA 1, 2 mi north of White Castle, tel. 504/ 545–2730. Admission: $8 adults, $2 children under 12. Open daily 9–5. Closed Christmas Day.*

④ Henry Howard was also the architect for **Madewood,** a magnificent 21-room Greek Revival mansion with double galleries and white columns. *A Woman Called Moses,* starring Cicely Tyson, was filmed in the house. This, too, is an elegant antebellum bed and breakfast. *LA 308, 15 mi south of Donaldsonville, tel. 504/ 524–1988. Admission: $4 adults, $3 students, $2 children under 12; 10% discount for senior citizens. Open daily 10–5. Closed Christmas and Thanksgiving.*

⑤ **Oak Alley** is also a movie star, having served as the setting for the Don Johnson-Cybil Shepherd TV remake of *The Long Hot Summer.* The house dates from 1839, and the 28 gnarled and arching live oaks trees that give the house its name were planted in the early 1700s. There is a splendid view of those trees from the upper gallery. *LA 18, 6 mi upriver of the Gramercy-Vacherie ferry, tel. 504/523–4351. Admission: $5 adults, $2.50 students, $1.50 children 6–12. Open daily 9–5. Closed Christmas, Thanksgiving, and New Year's.*

On the East Bank of the River, docents in antebellum garb
⑥ guide you through **Houmas House,** a Greek Revival masterpiece famed for its three-story spiral staircase. *Hush Hush, Sweet Charlotte,* with Bette Davis and Olivia de Haviland, was filmed here, as was the pilot for the TV series "Longstreet." *LA 942, ½ mi off LA 44 near Burnside, tel. 504/522–2262. Admission: $5 adults, $3 students, $2 children 6–12. Open daily Feb.–Oct. 10–5, Nov.–Jan. 10–4. Closed Christmas Day.*

⑦ Built in 1835, **Tezcuco** is a graceful raised cottage with delicate wrought-iron galleries, ornate friezes, and ceiling medallions. *LA 44, about 7 mi above Sunshine Bridge, tel. 504/562–3929. Admission: $5 adults, $2.50 children 4–12, $3.50 students and senior citizens. Open daily 10–5. Closed Thanksgiving, Christmas, and New Year's Day.*

8 **San Francisco,** completed in 1856, is an elaborate "Steamboat Gothic" house noted for its ornate millwork and ceiling frescoes. *LA 44 near Reserve, tel. 504/535-2341. Admission: $5 adults, $3.50 students, $2.25 children 6-11. Open daily 10-4. Closed Thanksgiving, Christmas, New Year's Day, Mardi Gras, and Easter.*

9 **Destrehan Plantation** is the oldest plantation left intact in the lower Mississippi Valley. The simple West Indies–style house, dating from 1787, is typical of the homes built by the earliest planters in the region. *9999 River Rd., tel. 504/764-9315. Admission: $4.25 adults, $3.25 students and senior citizens, $2.25 children 6-11. Open daily 10-4. Closed Thanksgiving, Christmas, New Year's Day, Mardi Gras, and Easter.*

Destrehan is about an hour's drive from New Orleans, and U.S. 61 will take you right into the city from which you departed.

What to See and Do with Children

Samuel Clemens Riverboat (*see* Exploring).
LSU Museum of Geoscience (*see* Exploring).
Planetarium (*see* Exploring).
Louisiana Arts & Science Riverside Museum (*see* Exploring).

Off the Beaten Track

LA 942 is a peaceful back road that drifts off U.S. 61 just north of Baton Rouge and winds through woodlands and past green pastures with grazing horses and lazing cattle. At the intersection of LA 3004, there is a tiny community called **Plains.** A marker notes that during the Civil War the Battle of Plains took place here.

Plains's small-town features include the **Volunteer Fire Department** building; the **Plains Super Market,** and next to it the **Plains Presbyterian Church.**

Participant Sports

Golf   Baton Rouge boasts three 18-hole championship golf courses that are open to the public: **Greenwood Park** (Lavey Ln., Baker, tel. 504/775-9166); **Howell Park** (5511 Winbourne Ave., Baton Rouge, tel. 504/357-9292); and **Webb Park** (1351 Country Club Dr., Baton Rouge, tel. 504/383-4919).

Hiking   There are seven miles of hiking trails in the **Port Hudson State Commemorative Area** (756 W. Plains-Port Hudson Rd. [Hwy 61], tel. 504/654-3775).

Swimming   A couple of good pooling around places are **Howell Park** (5509 Winbourne Ave., tel. 504/357-5374) and **Thunderbird Beach** (7400 Thunderbird Beach Ln., Denham Springs, tel. 504/664-2990).

Tennis   You can lob and volley at **City Park** (1440 City Park Ave., Baton Rouge, tel. 504/344-4501 or 923-2792); **Highland Road Park** (Highland and Amiss Rd., Baton Rouge, tel. 504/766-0247); and **Independence Park** (549 Lobdell Ave., Baton Rouge, tel. 504/923-1792).

Dining and Lodging

Dining   Cajun is *the* way to go here. Dine and dance at the new Mulate's in Baton Rouge, or try the po'boys at The Cabin in Burnside.

Category	Cost*
Very Expensive	over $35
Expensive	$25–$35
Moderate	$15–$20
Inexpensive	under $15

*per person without tax (7% in Baton Rouge), service, or drinks

Lodging   Staying on the plantation is your best bet for lodging in South Louisiana, but if you are stuck in the city or budget conscious, you'll have no problem finding suitable accommodations.

Category	Cost*
Very Expensive	over $120
Expensive	$90–$120
Moderate	$50–$90
Inexpensive	under $50

*double room; add 9% for taxes

The following credit-card abbreviations are used: AE, American Express; CB, Carte Blanche; DC, Diners Club; MC, MasterCard; V, Visa.

The most highly recommended establishments in each price category are indicated by a star ★.

Baton Rouge
Dining

Chalet Brandt. Swiss-born Charles Brandt has created an Alpine house that lacks only the Alps. The elegant dining rooms gleam with brass and china collectibles from around the globe, and many of the edibles are also imported. Brandt's motto is "Continental cuisine with Louisianians in mind." There is a changing menu that might include fresh poached Norwegian salmon with mousseline sauce; veal tournedos topped with foie gras, truffles, and madeira sauce; or speckled trout with crawfish Cardinale sauce. *7655 Old Hammond Hwy. tel. 504/927–6040. Jacket and tie required. Reservations suggested. AE, MC, V. Expensive.*

★ **Mulate's.** Dennis Quaid was among the celebrities on hand for the festive 1988 opening of Mulate's Baton Rouge branch. A rustic place with cypress beams, red-checkered cloths, and artwork by Cajun artist George Rodrigue, Mulate's offers shrimp and oyster en brochette, a Super Seafood Platter, and live Cajun music every night. *8322 Bluebonnet Road, tel. 504/767–4797 or 800/634–9880. Dress: informal. Reservations not required. MC, V. Inexpensive.*

Mike Anderson's. Former LSU football player Mike Anderson believes in serving up enormous portions and almost single-handedly supports the folks who manufacture doggie bags. His rustic, barnlike restaurant features the freshest of Louisiana seafood, with specialties like trout Norman (fried trout filet with crabmeat au gratin). Don't pass up the fried onion rings. Lowly cole slaw is elevated here to heavenly realms. *1031 W. Lee Dr., tel. 504/766–7823. Dress: informal. Reservations not required. AE, MC, V. Closed Thanksgiving, Christmas, New Year's, Easter. Inexpensive.*

Lodging **Baton Rouge Hilton.** This Hilton bills itself as a city resort hotel and boasts that it's the only capital city hotel with 24-hour room service. Centrally located at I–10 and College Drive, the tall, skinny white high rise offers a nonsmoking floor and half a floor with facilities for the handicapped. Traditional furnishings throughout, in hues of plum and blue. *5500 Hilton Ave., 70808, tel. 504/924–5000, 800/621–5116, or in LA 800/221–2584. 305 rooms. Facilities: free airport shuttle, cable TV, cocktail lounge, coffee shop, restaurant, concierge, free parking, gift shop, laundry, room service, lighted tennis courts, sauna, health club, jogging track. AE, CB, DC, MC, V. Moderate.*

Embassy Suites Hotel. Located in central Baton Rouge, this 1985 all-suites hotel was designed in a southwestern motif. Each two-room suite, with complexions of peaches and greens, has a galley kitchen with microwave, and custom-made mahogany furniture. *4914 Constitution Ave., 70808, tel. 504/924–6566 or 800/EMBASSY. 224 suites. Facilities: free airport shuttle, cable TV, cocktail lounge, coffee shop, restaurant, free parking, gift shop, handicapped facilities, laundry, room service, indoor pool, sauna, and steam room. AE, CB, DC, MC, V. Moderate.*

★ **Residence Inn.** One- and two-bedroom suites with dens, dining rooms, wood-burning fireplaces, and kitchens equipped with everything right down to popcorn poppers. The two-bedroom suites come with Jacuzzis. Traditional furnishings in the centrally located hotel, which opened in 1984. *5522 Corporate Blvd., 70808, tel. 504/927–5630 or 800/331–3131. 80 suites. Facilities: cable TV, concierge, free parking, handicapped facilities, laundry service, spa/health club, outdoor pool. AE, DC, MC, V. Moderate.*

Days Inn. If all else fails, this is a convenient and clean place to lay your weary head. *10245 Airline Hwy., 70816, tel. 504/293–9680 or 800/325–2525. 222 rooms. Facilities: cable TV, free parking, laundry service, outdoor pool. AE, DC, MC, V. Inexpensive.*

Burnside **The Cabin.** Rustic 150-year-old slave cabin-cum-restaurant
Dining with yellowed newspapers covering the walls and ancient tools
★ dangling here and there. Crawfish stew and crawfish étouffée are featured, but there are po'boys, steaks, and burgers, too. *Junction of LA 44 and 22, tel. 504/473–3007. Dress: informal. Reservations not required. AE, MC, V. Closed Christmas, Thanksgiving, New Year's. Moderate.*

Napoleonville **Madewood.** Expect gracious Southern hospitality in this
Lodging antiques-filled Greek Revival mansion, which is both elegant and cozy. The $150 price for a room in the main house includes not only breakfast but wine and cheeses in the parlor, followed by a candlelit gourmet dinner in the stately dining room. There are also suites in restored outbuildings on the plantation grounds ($85, plus $20 if you'd like the gourmet dinner). *New Orleans Office: 420 Julia St., New Orleans, 70130, tel. 504/524–1988. Napoleonville Office: Rte. 2, Box 478, Napoleonville, 70390, tel. 504/369–7151. All rooms with pri-*

vate bath. AE, V. Closed Christmas and Thanksgiving. Expensive.

White Castle **Nottoway.** A massive Italianate mansion with 64 rooms filled
Lodging with antique treasures, this is reputed to be one of the most
stunning B&Bs in the nation. Thirteen of its elegant rooms are
let to overnight guests, who are welcomed with complimentary
sherry upon arrival. Your first breakfast of croissants, juice,
and coffee is served in your room; second breakfast is a full feast
in Randolph Hall. *2 mi north of White Castle on LA 1, White
Castle 70788, tel. 504/545–2730. All rooms have private baths.
AE, DC, MC, V. Closed Christmas Day. Expensive–Very Expensive.*

The Arts

Theater Top name stars like Alabama and Neil Diamond are booked into
the **Centroplex Theatre for the Performing Arts.** (tel. 504/389–
3030).
The **Baton Rouge Little Theatre** (7155 Florida Blvd., tel. 504/
924–6496) has been presenting musicals, comedies, and dramas
for more than 40 years.

Concerts Guest soloists perform frequently with the **Baton Rouge Symphony Orchestra** (Centroplex Theatre for the Performing Arts,
tel. 504/387–6166). LSU's annual **Festival of Contemporary Music** (tel. 504/388–5118), which takes place in February, is more
than 40 years old.

Nightlife

Baton Rouge The new **Mulate's** (8322 Bluebonnet Rd., tel. 504/767–4794) in
Cajun Clubs Baton Rouge is a chip off the famed old Breaux Bridge block.
Cajun dance lessons every Wednesday night at **Ric Seeley's
Club Dance** (11224 Boardwalk, tel. 504/273–3090).

Country/Western The **Texas Club** (456 N. Donmoor Ave., tel. 504/926–0867) is the
hot spot for top-name country artists. A down-home crowd
drops in to shoot pool and dance at the **Gold Dust Lounge** (8146
Greenwell Springs Rd., tel. 504/924–9189).

Bars and An LSU crowd congregates at the **Bayou** (124 W. Chimes St.,
Nightclubs tel. 504/346–1765), where there is occasional live music Saturday night. The **Bengal** (2286 Highland Rd., tel. 504/387–5571)
draws a young disco crowd to its dance floor, game room, and
patio. Live bands and DJs alternate at **Sports Illustrated Bar**
(1176 Bob Pettit Blvd., tel. 504/766–6794). The young and not
so young dance in a tropical setting at **TD's** (Baton Rouge Hilton Hotel, tel. 504/924–5000).

5 Mississippi

by Janet Clark

Janet Clark writes for various Mississippi publications from her home north of Jackson.

Mississippians are fascinated with each other and spend a lot of time telling what they know. Once I corrected a friend who was recounting an event with no regard for the facts. "Hush!" she said. "This is a *story*." Stories are important here, so hush and listen.

If you mind your manners, Mississippi folks will get interested in you, too. As soon as you hit Iuka or Olive Branch you're sure to be asked, "Where y'all from?" even if there's just one of "y'all" at the moment. This is how Mississippi's famous hospitality begins. We see you, like some fabulous creature, with your story spread bright behind you like a tail. And spend some time considering whether you've got Mississippi relatives. The next questions are "What's your name? Any kin to those Henleys over in Tutwiler?"

You'll want to try out some Mississippi storytellers before you come. You'll feel exalted reading William Faulkner's Nobel Prize address, and you'll laugh at the characters in Eudora Welty's short stories—and get a lesson on Southern accents at the same time. B.B. King, Mose Allison, Son Thomas, John Lee Hooker, and Muddy Waters will give you the authentic Mississippi blues. Jimmie Rodgers will tell you all you need to know about country music. And then, of course, there's Elvis.

Prepare for weather. Mississippi is strong on weather. You can swelter from May to October and then suddenly freeze, just for a few days at Fair time in October. Winter is damp and colder than you'd expect, but Christmas Day is usually good for riding new bikes. On any day record highs and lows can vary by 60 degrees. February is generally interrupted by "blackberry winter" and everyone rushes to plant marigolds, which die in the short March cold snap. Once or twice it has snowed for a day in April. In spring and fall, though, you're generally talking *wonderful*, with temperatures in the 60s and 70s and azaleas bursting out everywhere.

Check on festivals, those down-home celebrations when Mississippians are most themselves. The Mississippi Department of Tourism (Box 849, Jackson 39205, tel. 601/359–3414) can give you a monthly blow by blow, which includes such wonders as the National Tobacco Spit held each June in Billy John Crumpton's pasture (five miles outside Raleigh) and the Delta Blues Festival each September in Greenville. There's the Catfish Festival in Belzoni in April, the Watermelon Festival in Mize in July, the unique Neshoba County Fair—the world's largest houseparty—in August, the Gumbo Festival of the Universe at Necaise Crossing (Bay St. Louis) in October, and the Sweet Potato Festival in Vardaman in November.

Start your tour of Mississippi by crossing interstate highways off your map. You won't discover the real Mississippi by sticking to them. The best roads in Mississippi have wonderful names like "the Natchez Trace," "Old Taylor Road," "The Great River Road," or no names at all.

Wherever you go in Mississippi, and whenever, remember the traveler in 1915 who wrote from a tiny, isolated hamlet near the coast: "Am stranded in this typical Mississippi town with a broken auto. Am having a good time."

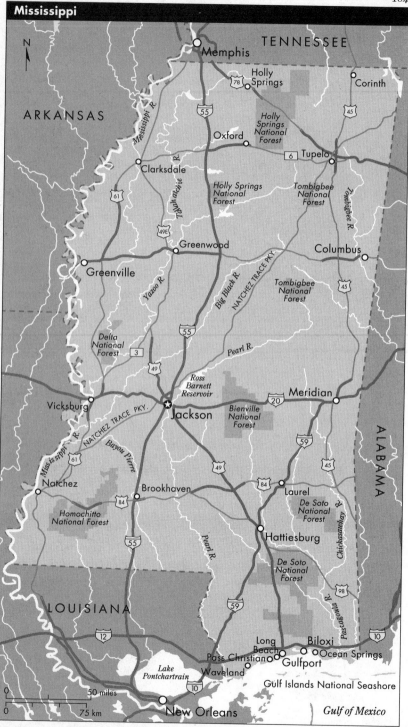

Mississippi

The Gulf Coast

The Mississippi Gulf Coast runs along U.S. 90 from Alabama to Louisiana. The traveler seeking a boisterous good time will find it in the restaurants, bars, hotels, motels, and souvenir shops that jostle for space along U.S. 90's busy four lanes.

Don't let the clamor of this neon strip hide the coast's quieter treasures: the ancient land, sculpted by wind and water, continually changing; serene beachfront houses set on green and shady lawns; the teeming wildlife of the Mississippi Sound and its adjacent bayous and marshes; the unspoiled natural beauty of the seven barrier islands that separate the Gulf of Mexico from the Mississippi Sound.

On a clear day, if you have good eyesight or a good imagination, you can see these islands. Their names (from east to west) are Petit Bois (anglicized as "Petty Boy"), Horn, East and West Ship, and Cat. Two others, Round and Deer, lie within the Mississippi Sound. The islands are constantly shifting as the tides and prevailing winds work on their fragile sands. In 1969 Hurricane Camille's furious onslaught cut Ship Island in two.

During the 1700s France, England, and Spain ruled the area, according to their fortunes in international wars. Street names, family names, and traditions still reflect this colorful heritage. In the late 19th and early 20th centuries, the coast became a fashionable vacation spot for wealthy New Orleanians and Delta planters eager to escape yellow fever epidemics. Elegant hotels, imposing beachfront mansions, and smaller summer homes sprang up. Edgewater Plaza shopping mall now stands on the site of the queen of the early hotels, the Edgewater Gulf, which in its heyday had its own stop on the L & N Railroad. Today the homes that have endured the vagaries of time and hurricanes stand along the beach—brave and beautiful survivors.

The coast's people today are known as easygoing and tolerant, artistic and hardy. Though individualistic, they are linked by a reliance on the sea and its bounty, and by a love of the water and its Gulf shores.

Take your cue from the natives and ignore any urge to swim in the sound. It's too murky (at best). Instead, admire the stately live oaks and accept the salutes of crabs. Go floundering and spear your supper. Above all, slow down. On the Mississippi Coast only the traffic on U.S. 90 moves quickly.

Getting Around

By Car   You can drive across the entire coast in 1½ hours on I–10 and U.S. 90, reaching New Orleans in just over an hour from Gulfport. Jackson is three hours straight up U.S. 49, north from Gulfport.

By Plane   Fly into Gulfport-Biloxi Regional Airport (Airport Road, off Washington Ave., Gulfport) and you can be on the beach in 15 minutes. **Northwest** flies to Memphis, **Continental** to New Orleans, and **Eastern Metro Express** to Atlanta.

By Bus   **Gulf Area Transit** (DeBuys Rd., Gulfport, tel. 601/896–8080) provides a coastwide public transportation system.

Greyhound/Trailways connects the coast with Jackson, New Orleans, and Mobile. (Biloxi: 502 W. Railroad Ave., tel. 601/374–4200; Gulfport: 11205 25th Ave., tel. 601/863–1022; Bay St. Louis: 512 Ulman Ave., tel. 601/467–4272.)

Important Addresses and Numbers

Tourist Information   Get a free *Attractions and Accommodations* guide to the Gulf Coast area at the **Mississippi Gulf Coast Convention and Visitors Bureau** *Box 6128, Gulfport, 39506, tel. 896–6699 or 800/237–9493. Open weekdays 8–5; Memorial Day–Labor Day, open weekdays 8 AM–10 PM, Sat. noon–10 PM.*

Emergencies   For assistance dial 911, call the **Mississippi Highway Patrol** (601/864–1314), or go to the emergency room at **Biloxi Regional Medical Center** (300 Reynoir, Biloxi, tel. 601/432–1571).

Guided Tours

Celebrity Limousine and Tours Service (111 South Shore Dr., Biloxi, tel. 601/388–1384) charters bus tours of the coastal area and New Orleans.

Coasting, Inc. (Box 7408, Gulfport, tel. 601/864–2044) custom-plans tours and entertainment for groups.

Exploring the Gulf Coast

Ocean Springs   To begin at the beginning, at least as far as Mississippi is concerned, start in **Ocean Springs**. Here, in 1699, the French commander Pierre LeMoyne Sieur D'Iberville established Fort Maurepas to shore up France's claim to the central part of North America. This first colony was temporary, but is fondly remembered by Ocean Springs in its annual spring festival celebrating D'Iberville's landing.

Ocean Springs is famous as the home of Walter Anderson (1903–1965), an artist of genius and grand eccentricity who enjoyed an ecstatic communion with nature, which he revealed in thousands of drawings and watercolors, most of them kept secret until his death. You can discover his work at the Anderson family compound, which includes **Shearwater Pottery and Showroom** and **Anderson's Cottage,** gloriously decorated with murals. The Pottery and Showroom feature the art of Walter Anderson, some of it for sale at prices for serious collectors. *102 Shearwater Dr., tel. 601/875–7320. Admission free. Cottage open Thurs. 1–4, or by appointment. Showroom open weekdays 9–5:30, Sun. 1–5:30.*

Magnificent oaks shade the sleepy town center, a pleasant area of small shops to explore on foot. The interior of the **Community Center** was painted with intricate murals by Walter Anderson for a fee of $1; they are appraised at $1 million. *514 Washington Ave., tel. 601/875–1193. Admission free. Get key from Chamber of Commerce (1100 Washington Ave). Open weekdays 10–4, Sat. 2–4, or by appointment.*

A brochure from the **Ocean Springs Chamber of Commerce** (tel. 601/875–4424) will guide you on a driving tour of the D'Iberville Trail, shaded by moss-draped trees and bordered by summer houses.

Gulf Islands National Seashore—which includes Ship, Horn, and Petit Bois Islands—has its headquarters on Ocean Springs's Davis Bayou. In the summer you can explore the marshes by boat with a U.S. Park Ranger as your guide. When heat and humidity allow, picnic here and explore the nature trails. *4000 Hanley Rd. on Davis Bayou off U.S. 90, tel. 601/ 875-9057. Ranger boat tours begin at 6:30 PM Thurs.–Sun.; rangers start taking reservations at 6 PM (limit of 20 people).*

Biloxi From Ocean Springs, cross the Biloxi–Ocean Springs bridge to **Biloxi,** practicing the correct pronunciation, "Bi-LUX-i," as you go. Biloxi is the oldest continuous settlement on the Gulf Coast and the second largest city in Mississippi. When Pierre LeMoyne Sieur D'Iberville met the Indians who called themselves Biloxi, or "first people," he gave their name to the area and to the bay. The French constructed Fort Louis here; it served as the capital of the Louisiana Territory from 1720 to 1722, when the capital was moved to New Orleans.

At the foot of the Biloxi–Ocean Springs Bridge, on the south, is **Gulf Marine State Park,** jutting over the water on wooden decks. Through its telescopes you can glimpse **Deer Island** 12 miles away or watch gulls and pelicans, sailboats and sailboards. This is a great spot for fishing, 24 hours a day. Bait and tackle are sold here and fishing poles may be rented daily 9–5. *Just south of U.S. 90 at the west end of the Biloxi–Ocean Springs Bridge. Open daily.*

Adjacent to Gulf Marine State Park is the **Marine Education Center,** featuring live exhibits of Gulf Coast animals and a spectacular 40,000-gallon aquarium. *1650 E. Beach Blvd., Biloxi, tel. 601/374-5550. Admission: $2 adults, $1 children and senior citizens. Open Mon.–Sat. 9–4.*

Across U.S. 90 is **Point Cadet Plaza,** a waterfront complex now under development, which has a marina and a seafood industry museum. In the 1880s Point Cadet was home to European emmigrants who flocked to Biloxi to work in the seafood canneries.

Biloxi's **Small Craft Harbor,** off U.S. 90 on the sound, captures the atmosphere of a lazy fishing village. Catch the **Sailfish Shrimp Tour** boat here to experience 80 minutes as a shrimper. Cast your nets upon the waters and let the crew identify your catch, however bizarre, for you. *1500 E. Beach Blvd., tel. 601/ 374-5718. Admission: $6 adults, $5 children. Runs begin at 10 AM daily; call for schedule.*

Biloxi's landmark 65-foot **lighthouse** on U.S. 90 was erected in 1848. During the Civil War, Federal forces, operating from Ship Island, blockaded the Mississippi Sound and cut Biloxi off from much-needed supplies. When the Yankees demanded that Biloxi submit or starve, the reply was that the Union would have to "blockade the mullet" first. Ever since, mullet has been known as "Biloxi bacon" and honored with its own festival each October. (You may want to try it if you've eaten your fill of delicate redfish, fresh crabmeat, plump Gulf oysters, and tender shrimp.) The city defended itself with what appeared to be a formidable cannon array near the lighthouse but what was actually only two cannons and many logs painted black! *U.S. 90. Admission: $1 adults, 50 cents children under 12. Open Wed.– Sun. 10–6:30. Closed Oct.–April.*

The lighthouse is the starting point for the **Biloxi Tour Train,** which bumps you past historic mansions and shrimp trawlers, new banks and old restaurants. *U.S. 90 at Porter Ave. Six tours daily, Mar. 1–Labor Day. Admission: $1.50 adults, $1 children.*

Time Out Mary Mahoney's **Old French House Restaurant** is in a renovated 1737 mansion with several elegant dining rooms and enclosed patios. Locals swear by it, perhaps more for the comfort of its old brick and age-darkened wood and for the memory of Mary herself (who always went from table to table, chatting with customers) than for the food. Come for drinks in the Old Slave Quarter Lounge (11 AM–11 PM) and for Le Café's beignets, coffee, gumbo, and po'boys served 24 hours a day (there's take-out, too). *138 Rue Magnolia, tel. 601/374–0163. Reservations recommended for lunch and dinner in the elegant main dining rooms. AE, DC, MC, V. Very Expensive.*

Four miles from Gulfport is **Beauvoir,** the antebellum beachfront mansion that was the last home of Jefferson Davis. Here the president of the Confederacy wrote his memoirs and his book *The Rise and Fall of the Confederate Government.* This National Historic Landmark is maintained much as it was when Davis lived here. The serene, raised cottage-style house, with its sweeping front stairs, is flanked by pavilions and set on a broad lawn shaded by ancient live oaks. A Confederate cemetery on the grounds includes the Tomb of the Unknown Soldier of the Confederacy. *On U.S. 90 between Biloxi and Gulfport, tel. 601/388–1313. Admission: $4 adults, $2 children, $3 senior citizens. Open daily 9–5. Closed Christmas Day.*

Gulfport **Gulfport** merges seamlessly with Biloxi along U.S. 90. If you have time for only one activity on the coast, make it a getaway to **Ship Island** on the passenger ferry from the Gulfport Harbor. At **Ship Island** a U.S. Park Ranger will guide you through Fort Massachusetts, built in 1859 and used by Federal troops to blockade the sound during the Civil War. The rangers will treat you to tales of the island's colorful past, including the story of the *filles aux casquettes*—young women sent by the French government as brides for the lonely early colonists. Each girl *(fille)* carried a small hope chest *(casquette).* If you bring your own casquette filled with a picnic lunch, you can skip the snack bar and head straight for the surf on the island's southern shore. Spend the day sunning, swimming in the clear green water, and beachcombing for treasures washed up by the surf. You'll feel a world away (just remember to return on the last boat). *Ticket office at Gulfport Harbor in the Joseph T. Jones Memorial Park, just east of the intersection of U.S. 49 and U.S. 90, tel. 601/864–1014. Cost (round-trip): $11 adults, $5 children 3–10. 1–3 trips daily, Mar.–Oct.*

At Gulfport Harbor you can hop aboard the 900-passenger **Pride of Mississippi** and cruise away from Mississippi waters— and Mississippi law—for a day of gambling in the ship's casino. Dance to live music, enjoy continuous live entertainment and Las Vegas-style stage shows, and feast on all-you-can-eat buffets (tickets include two meals). *Cruises daily, 2 on Sat. from the Port of Gulfport, U.S. Hwy. 90 at U.S. Hwy. 49, tel. 800/237–0077 or 601/867–2715. Cost varies depending on time and season: $36.95-$69.95, children under 12 half price on Sun. when planned activities will entertain 8–12 year-olds.*

West of Gulfport the landscape grows increasingly broad, wild, and lovely. The highway runs between stately homes on the north and shimmering water on the south from Long Beach through Pass Christian and from Bay St. Louis to Waveland.

Pass Christian (Chris-chi-ANN) suffered the full fury of Hurricane Camille on August 17, 1969, but not even Camille could erase its history. Here sailboat racing began in the South, and here the second yacht club in the country was formed (it still exists today). Louisiana landowner Zachary Taylor was at the yacht club when he was persuaded to run for the presidency. In 1913, President Woodrow Wilson and his family spent a Christmas vacation here, but his Dixie White House, the Herndon Home, was destroyed by Camille.

Waveland boasts the best beach in Mississippi, located on E. Beach Boulevard, two miles south of U.S. 90. Take a beach walk or drive through Buccanneer State Park's mossy live oaks to enjoy the splendid, unimpeded view of sparkling waters.

What to See and Do with Children

Boating *(see* Participant Sports below).
The Doll House accommodates a collection of contemporary and antique dolls and stuffed animals. *3201 Bienville Blvd., on U.S. 90, Ocean Springs, tel. 601/872–3971. Cost: donation for YMCA Pet Shelter. Open 1–6. Closed Mon.*
Fishing *(see* Participant Sports below).
Funtime USA will entertain children for hours, with its water slides, playground, bumper boats and cars, and over 100 arcade games. *1300 Beach Blvd., Gulfport, tel. 601/896–7315. Open daily, 9AM–midnight.*
Marine Education Center *(see* Exploring).
Marine Life offers continuous shows with performing dolphins, sea lions, and macaws. *Joseph T. Jones Memorial Park, just east of the intersection of U.S. 49 and U.S. 90., tel. 601/896–3981. Admission: $7.95 adults, $5.25 children 3–11, children under 3 free. Open daily 9–6. Closed Thanksgiving and Christmas.*

Shopping

Gifts   At **Ballard's Pewter** (1110 Government St., Ocean Springs, tel. 601/875–7550) you can find necklaces and earrings made from sand dollars and crabs, or have the pewtersmith fashion a "bespoke" (custom-made) piece.

Outfit yourself at **Realizations** (1000 Washington St., Ocean Springs, tel. 601/875–0503) in T-shirts, skirts, blouses, and dresses silk-screened with Walter Anderson's swirling block print designs. Books, reproductions, and posters of the artist's work are also available.

Beaches

Twenty-six miles of man-made beach extend from Biloxi to Pass Christian. Toward the west the beaches become less commercialized and crowded; **Waveland**'s is the best of all. Tan, sail, jetski, or beachcomb, but *don't* swim; it's shallow and not clean.

Participant Sports

Boating	Sailboats, sailboards, jet skis, and catamarans may be rented from the many vendors who station themselves along the beach. You can also rent 14-foot motorboats at **End of the Wharf** (1020 E. Beach Blvd., Biloxi), just behind Fisherman's Wharf Restaurant.
Camping	Take U.S. 90 to Waveland, turn south on Nicholson, and follow the signs to **Buccaneer State Park** (tel. 601/467–3822), which conceals 129 campsites in a grove of live oaks streaming with moss. An Olympic-size wave pool may lure you from the nature trail and picnic sites. No cabins, but toilet and shower facilities.
Fishing and Crabbing	For **floundering** you'll need nighttime, a light, and a gig. Head for the sound, roll up your jeans, and spear your supper! A chicken neck and a string will put you in the **crabbing** business at any public pier. If you want to be lazy, substitute a crab trap for the string.
	Charter boats for half-day and full-day **deep-sea fishing** can be found at marinas and harbors all along the Gulf Coast. Prices range upward from $30 per person, averaging $55; group rates are usually available. The Mississippi Gulf Coast Convention and Visitors Bureau (tel. 601/388–8000) can assist you.
Golf	The coast's climate allows for year-round golfing, and many golf packages are offered by hotels and motels. The Mississippi Coast Coliseum sponsors **indoor golf clinics**, day and night, February–April. Contact the Mississippi Gulf Coast Convention and Visitors Bureau (tel. 601/388–8000) for details. Diamondhead's **Pine** and **Cardinal courses** (7600 Country Club Circle, Bay St. Louis, tel. 601/255–2525) offer 36 holes that can challenge all but the pros. Wooded, gently rolling, and well-kept, they are ringed by the large, elegant houses and condominiums of Diamondhead resort community.
	Hickory Hill Country Club and Golf Course (900 Hickory Hill Dr., Gautier, tel. 601/497–5575, ext. 204) offers visitors fairways lined with whispering pines, tall oaks, magnolias, and dogwoods. Flowers surround the teeing areas.
	Pine Island Golf Course (Gulf Park Estates 2 ¼ mi east of Ocean Springs, 3 mi south of U.S. 90, tel. 601/875–1674) was designed by Pete Dye, who created the tournament players course in Jacksonville. This course spans three islands, and its abundant wildlife, beautiful setting, and club house can console you for any bogeys.
	Windance Country Club (94 Champion Circle, Gulfport, tel. 601/832–4871) has a public golf course ranked among the top 100 in the United States by *Golf Digest*.

Dining and Lodging

Dining	Fresh Gulf seafood, particularly redfish, flounder, and speckled trout dishes, stars in coast restaurants. Soft-shell crab is a coast specialty, and crab claws are a traditional appetizer. Coast natives are fond of quaffing Barq's root beer with their seafood.

Category	Cost*
Very Expensive	over $20
Expensive	$15–$20
Moderate	$10–$15
Inexpensive	$5–$10

per person without tax (8%), service, or drinks

Lodging Recent economic conditions have battered the Gulf Coast like a hurricane, but good lodgings can still be found.

Category	Cost*
Very Expensive	over $70
Expensive	$50–$70
Moderate	$30–$50
Inexpensive	$20–$30

double room; add 9% for taxes

The following credit-card abbreviations are used: AE, American Express; CB, Carte Blanche; DC, Diners Club; MC, MasterCard; V, Visa.

Bay St. Louis **Diamondhead Inn.** This standard-issue motel attracts golfers
Lodging who play the nearby Diamondhead Pine and Cardinal courses (see Participant Sports). The wooden walks and balconies are nicked by cleats; some walls are scarred, presumably by golfers' rages or rowdies. Each room has a balcony and kitchenette (actually just a fridge for beer). *4300 Aloha Circle, Bay St. Louis 39520, tel. 601/255–1421 or outside MS 800/647–9550. 72 rooms. Facilities: yacht club, marina, tennis courts, 36-hole golf course, stable, and a nearby 3,500-ft lighted airstrip. AE, MC, V. Expensive.*

Biloxi **Fisherman's Wharf.** A neighboring shrimp factory perfumes
Dining the parking lot here, but race inside to fresher air and views of oyster shuckers at work on the pier. Crabmeat salad for lunch; broiled catch-of-the-day for dinner; and always, the only dessert, the mysterious Fisherman's Wharf pie. *1020 E. Beach Blvd., tel. 601/436–4513. Dress: informal. Reservations recommended. AE, MC, V. Expensive.*

White Pillars. This lovely mansion just off the beach combines intimate dining rooms with an airy enclosed dining patio. Linen-covered tables are set with sparkling silverware, with elegant results. Nevertheless, when ordering, think *simple*. Go for the broiled catch-of-the-day and avoid the overrated but highly touted eggplant Josephine. Save your calories for the popular dessert bar; sample three for the price of one. *100 Rodenburg Ave., tel. 601/432–8741. Jacket and tie required. Reservations recommended. AE, MC, V. Expensive.*

Baricev's. The restaurant's large, plain dining room is enhanced by display cases of shrimp, fish, and oysters heaped on ice, and by sweeping views of the ocean where the creatures so recently cavorted. Fried soft-shell crab, a specialty, is succulent inside a thick, flaky crust. If you scorn "fry," other specialties are snapper Baricev, rolled in seasoned cracker crumbs and broiled in olive oil; and oysters Baricev, a casserole of plump oysters, green onions, garlic, cheese, and olive oil. Baricev's is Yugoslavian, but the hearty gumbo bespeaks a proper French *roux*. *633 Central Beach Blvd., tel. 601/436–3526. Dress: informal. No reservations. AE, MC, V. Moderate.*

The Marina. Unwind with a cocktail on the Marina's patio, overlooking the scalloped slips of the Broadwater Marina. Then move inside to enjoy beach views (with lighthouse) from the comfortable, if nondescript, bar and dining room. The heaping seafood platter combines the menu's specialties: stuffed crab; fried shrimp, oysters, and scallops; and trout. The thick steaks sizzle with juice, if you dare to eat beef on the Gulf. *U.S. 90 at the Broadwater Beach Marina, tel. 601/ 388–2211. Dress: informal. No reservations. AE, MC, V. Moderate.*

McElroy's Harbor House Seafood Restaurant. Biloxi natives and real shrimpers eat hearty breakfasts, lunches, and dinners here in functional surroundings. Notable are the po'boys, oysters on the half shell, broiled stuffed flounder, and stuffed crabs. You can also try "Biloxi bacon." *Biloxi Small Craft Harbor, tel. 601/436–5000. Dress: informal. AE. DC, MC, V. Inexpensive.*

Lodging **Biloxi Hilton.** A high-rise hotel flanked by motel-like wings, the Hilton gains distinction from tropical plantings. Rooms can be tired and musty. *3580 W. Beach Blvd., Biloxi 39531, tel. 601/ 388–7000. 450 rooms. Facilities: lounge with entertainment, 6 lighted tennis courts, championship golf course, swimming pool, 2 playgrounds, game room. AE, MC, V. Expensive–Very Expensive.*

Royal d'Iberville Hotel-Days Inn. This Day's Inn has gone upscale since a recent decoration that left the spacious rooms bright with chintz. Furniture is hotel-functional; the large public areas are comfortably contemporary. *3250 W. Beach Blvd. Biloxi 39531, tel. 601/388–6610; 800/647–3955; in MS, 800/222–3906. 264 rooms. Facilities: beachfront lounge, entertainment, 2 swimming pools, restaurants, children's playground, tennis, golf, meeting facilities, suites, babysitting. AE, DC, MC, V. Expensive–Very Expensive.*

Beachwater Inn. Set among live oaks that contrast with its contemporary lines, this family-owned motel attracts repeat customers. Its owners are experts on coast attractions and events. The rooms are fresh and neat, though not elegant. *2872 W. Beach Blvd., Biloxi 39531, tel. 601/432–1984. 31 rooms, some with cooking nooks and porches; beach views. Facilities: tree deck, babysitting, swimming pool, golf packages, deep-sea fishing, and activity director. No restaurant. AE, MC, V. Rates depend on season. Moderate.*

Gulfport **Vrazel's.** In 1969, Hurricane Camille blew away the restaurant
Dining that had long stood here; the brick building that replaced it gets its charm from soft lighting and dining nooks with large windows facing the beach. Added attractions include the red snapper, Gulf trout, flounder, and shrimp prepared every which way: étouffée, au gratin à la Cajun, amandine, à la Vrazel, blackened, Pontchartrain, meuniere. Snapper Lenwood is a specialty, teaming broiled snapper with crabmeat and crawfish in a Cajun-style sauce. For the best of land and sea, try veal Aaron (crabmeat, mushrooms, and lemon sauce combined with tender veal medallions). *3206 W. Beach Blvd. (U.S. 90), tel. 601/863–2220. Jacket and tie required. Dinner reservations recommended. AE, MC, V. Moderate.*

Guided Tours

Special-Interest Tours In Jackson, **Mississippi Tours, Incorporated** (Box 16623, Jackson 39236, tel. 601/362–8525), offers a "Mansions Along the Mississippi" tour designed for groups of up to 30 as well as for couples. Group tours are conducted in motor coaches, and couples travel by car. Both spend two nights each in mansions and historic inns in Vicksburg and Natchez. (The tour may also include New Orleans's French Quarter.) The company has also just instituted a four-night antiques and architectural tour of these cities.

Vicksburg Historic Tours (1104 Monroe St., Vicksburg 39180, tel. 601/638–8888) gives morning bus tours daily, which cover the Vicksburg National Military Park, the USS *Cairo*, and antebellum homes throughout the city. Afternoon tours, offered Monday through Saturday, drive through the city visiting antebellum homes.

In Natchez, **Pilgrimage Tours, Inc.** (Box 347 Natchez 39121, tel. 601/446–6631 or 800/647–6742) takes groups of 20 or more to tour 13 antebellum homes year-round (during Pilgrimage, between 24 and 30 homes are open). Tours are conducted mornings and afternoons, and bus tickets can be bought at six of the area's hotels. Tour tickets can be bought only at the office on the corner of Canal and State streets.

Important Addresses and Numbers

Tourist Information **Corinth/Alcorn Area Chamber of Commerce.** *810 Tate St., Corinth 38834, tel. 601/287–5269. Open weekdays 8–5. Closed for lunch.* **Jackson Convention and Visitors Bureau.** *Box 1450, Jackson 39205, tel. 601/960–1891. Open weekdays 8:30–5.* **Jackson Visitor Information Center.** *Located at the entrance to the Mississippi Agriculture and Forestry Museum, 1150 Lakeland Dr. east of I–55, tel. 601/9600–1800. Open weekdays 8:30–5.* **Natchez Trace Parkway Visitor Center.** *Rte. 1, NT-143, Tupelo 38801; on the Natchez Trace Pkwy., milepost 266, tel. 601/845–1572. Open daily 8–5. Closed Christmas Day.* **Natchez-Adams County Chamber of Commerce.** *300 N. Commerce, Natchez 39120, tel. 601/445–4611. Open weekdays 8:30–5.* **Natchez Pilgrimage.** This is the only place to purchase tickets for Pilgrimage; all Pilgrimage tours originate here. *Canal St. at State St., Box 347, Natchez 39120, tel. 601/446–6631 or 800/647–6742 (out-of-state). AE, MC, V. Open daily 8:30–5:30.* **Tupelo Convention and Visitors Bureau.** *712 E. President St., Box 1485, Tupelo 38801, tel. 601/841–6521. Open weekdays 8–5.*

Emergencies In Tupelo, Jackson, and Natchez, dial 911 for **police** or **ambulance** in an emergency. For help on the Natchez Trace, dial 0 and ask for the nearest Park Ranger.

Seek medical help at **North Mississippi Regional Medical Center** (830 S. Gloster St., Tupelo, tel. 601/841–3000), **Mississippi Baptist Medical Center** (1225 N. State St., Jackson, tel. 601/968–1776), and **Jefferson Davis Hospital** (Sgt. Prentiss Dr., Natchez, tel. 601/442–2871).

24-Hour Pharmacy **Jim Bain's Pharmacy** (519 N. Gloster St., Tupelo, tel. 601/844–4530) has a 24-hour answering service. In Jacksonville, **Eckerd's** (DeVille Plaza, I–55N, E. Frontage Rd., tel. 601/

956–5143). In Natchez, **Lessley's Pharmacy** (115 Jefferson Davis Blvd., tel. 601/446–6331 or after 6 PM 601/442–4272).

Exploring the Natchez Trace

Numbers in the margin correspond with points of interest on the Natchez Trace map.

The Mississippi segment of the Natchez Trace begins near Tupelo, in the northeast corner of the state. It wanders through a hilly landscape of dense forests and sparkling streams.

❶ Named for J.P. Coleman, Mississippi's governor from 1955 to 1959, **J.P. Coleman State Park** vies with Tishomingo State Park for the title of most spectacular Mississippi state park. There are wooded campsites for tents and RVs, and 10 secluded cabins, some of them old and rustic (no air-conditioning); others from the 1970s with fireplaces and central air and heat. Rooms at the balconied lodge overlook the shale beaches of serene Pickwick Lake. Visitors explore nature trails, rent canoes and boats, fish, swim, waterski, drink beer, or play canasta under the oaks and virgin pines. *Rte. 5, Box 503, Iuka 38852 (13 mi north of Iuka off U.S. 25), tel. 601/423–6515.*

❷ **Tishomingo State Park** lies in the Appalachian foothills, making its terrain unique in Mississippi. If you're feeling peppy, a 13-mile nature trail winds through a canyon along steep hills by waterfalls, granite outcrops, and a swinging bridge; otherwise, take the winding roads through forests so leafy they can hide the brightest day in shadow. Eight-mile canoe trips and float trips are offered from mid-March to October. Around Haynes Lake are primitive campsites, hookups, and five rustic cabins to rent. Bring your own provisions. *Rte. 1, Box 310, Dennis 38838 (15 mi south of Iuka, and 3 mi north of Dennis off U.S. 25), tel. 601/438–6914.*

❸ **Corinth** is a town of special interest for Civil War enthusiasts. The Battles of Shiloh and Corinth are commemorated with markers and displays throughout the area. Corinth was settled just seven years before the war and assumed military importance because of its two railroad lines.

In April 1862, after the bloody battle of Shiloh, near Shiloh Church in Tennessee, 21 miles to the north, the Confederates turned Corinth into a vast medical center. In May 1862, the Confederates, under General P.G.T. Beauregard, were forced to withdraw further; their retreat involved the most ingenious hoax of the war: To fool the Federal forces, campfires were lighted, dummy cannoneers were placed at fake cannons, empty trains were cheered as if they brought reinforcements, and buglers moved along the deserted works, playing taps. Union forces occupied the town and, in October 1862, a Confederate attempt to recapture the town.

To visit all of Corinth's Civil War sites, follow the street markers, using the self-guided tour brochure available free at the **Northeast Mississippi Museum.** *Fourth St., at Washington St., tel. 601/287–2231. Admission: $1.50 adults, 50¢ children. Open daily 1–4. Closed Thurs. and the month of Jan.*

❹ Between Corinth and Tupelo is **Jacinto,** a ghost town with a restored Federal-style courthouse (1854) surrounded by pre-1870 buildings that are slowly being restored.

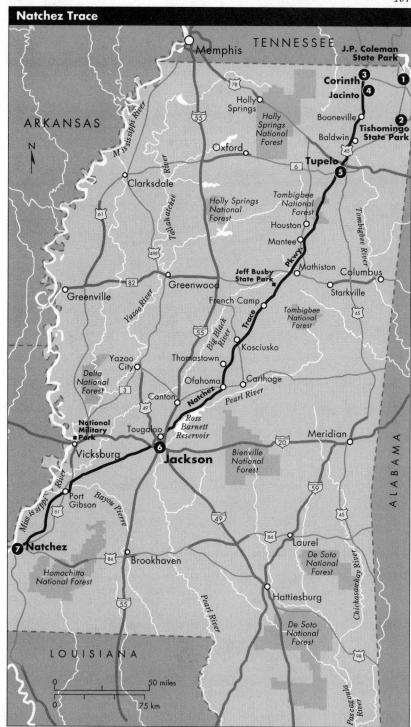

Natchez Trace

Jacinto also has nature trails that lead to mineral springs, and a swinging bridge. A new recreational park provides hookups for eight campers, a playground, and a picnic area with grills. *On MS 356, 9 mi east of U.S. 45 between Corinth and Tupelo, tel. 601/287–4296. Admission free. Open Tues.–Sun. 1–5, other times by appointment.*

The **Natchez Trace Parkway Visitor Center** *(see* Tourist Information) is located five miles north of Tupelo on the Trace. The Visitor Center offers exhibits, a 12-minute film, a hands-on area for children, and the *Official Map and Guide*, which opens to a four-foot length to give detailed, mile-by-mile information from Nashville to Natchez.

Tupelo
❺
The largest city in north Mississippi, **Tupelo** (named after the tupelo gum tree), was founded in 1859 and is a city of accomplishment. Progressive leaders have successfully lured business and industry to an area that only 30 years ago was predominantly agricultural. The arts flourish here, and the medical center is the largest in the state. The scenic hill country provides beautiful places to camp, swim, fish, jog, and bike.

Why do so many tourists flock here? Because this is a city of destiny: the birthplace of Elvis Presley, the one-and-only king of rock and roll. The **Tupelo Convention and Visitor's Center** is a good place to start your tour *(see* Tourist Information). From here, head to **Elvis Presley's birthplace,** a tiny, two-room "shotgun" house built by his father, Vernon Presley, for $180. Elvis Aaron Presley was born here on January 8, 1935. The home has been restored and furnished much as it was when the Presleys lived in it. The house is now surrounded by **Elvis Presley Park,** land purchased with proceeds from Elvis's 1956 concert at the Mississippi-Alabama Fair. The park includes a swimming pool, tennis courts, playground, and a gift shop (for Elvis souvenirs) in the Youth Center. The **Elvis Presley Memorial Chapel,** suggested by the singer in 1971 as a place for his fans to meditate, was dedicated in 1979, two years after Presley's death. *Off Old Hwy. 78, at 306 Elvis Presley Dr., tel. 601/841–1245. Admission: $1 adults, 50¢ children. Open Mon.–Sat. 9–5:30, Sun. 1–5.*

Five miles north of the Presley birthplace is **Elvis Presley Lake and Campground** where you can swim, ski, sun, and fish—and think about Elvis. *Off Canal St. extended, tel. 601/841–1304. Primitive and full-service campsites. Separate fees for swimming, camping, fishing, and boat launching.*

The **Tupelo Museum** displays further Presley memorabilia along with other exhibits, including a turn-of-the-century Western Union office, a working sorghum mill, a train depot and caboose, and an old-time country store. *Located in James J. Ballard Park, off MS 6W, tel. 601/841–6438. Admission: $1 adults; 50¢ children 3–11, under 3 free. Group tours by appointment. Open Tues.–Fri. 10–4, weekends 1–5.*

Once you've satisfied your Elvis mania, turn your thoughts to the Civil War Battle of Tupelo. In 1864, Union General A. J. Smith marched 14,000 troops against Nathan Bedford Forrest's forces near Tupelo. Smith's goal was to end the constant Southern harrassment of supply lines to Sherman's army besieging Atlanta. The battle, on July 14, 1864, was the last major battle in Mississippi and one of the bloodiest. A **National**

Battlefield site on West Main Street (MS 6), inside the city limits, commemorates the battle with monuments and displays.

From Tupelo, the trip to Jackson takes three hours if you don't stop. It can easily take an entire day, however, if you stop to read the brown wooden markers, explore nature trails, and admire the neat fields, trees, and wildflower meadows.

Bynum Mounds (milepost 232.4) are ceremonial hills that were constructed between 100 BC and AD 200 by prehistoric people. Exhibits describe their daily existence.

Jeff Busby State Park (milepost 193.9) was named for the Mississippi congressman who introduced legislation creating the Natchez Trace Parkway. The park includes an overlook at one of the state's highest points (603 feet) and a 20-minute nature trail that identifies native plants and describes their use by pioneers. Campers may wish to spend the night. For more information contact the State Parks (Box 20305, Jackson 39209).

The **Little Mountain Service Station** is located at the campground entrance. This privately owned station is the only place to fuel up right on the parkway.

At **French Camp** (milepost 180.7), where Frenchman Louis LeFleur established a stand (or inn) in 1812, you can watch sorghum molasses being made on Saturdays in late September and October.

At **Beaver Creek** (milepost 145.1) a short (5- to 10-minute), self-guided nature trail explains beavers' habits.

Cypress Swamp (milepost 122.0), a pleasure today, was once a treacherous, mosquito-infested morass for early travelers. A 20-minute self-guided nature walk takes you through the gloom of a tupelo/bald cypress swamp.

The **Ridgeland Crafts Center** displays and sells high quality crafts in a dogtrot log cabin. Members of the Craftsman's Guild of Mississippi have created Choctaw Indian baskets of seamless doubleweave, splint baskets of Mississippi white oak, wooden plates and utensils, handwoven and handscreened clothing, pottery, pewter jewelry, and sturdy, whimsical wooden toys. The Center sponsors free demonstrations (usually on weekends) of basketweaving, Indian dances and games, bread baking in an outdoor stone oven, and glassblowing. *Natchez Trace at Ridgeland (milepost 102.4) tel. 601/856–7456. Restrooms, picnic tables, water fountain. Admission free. Open daily 9–5.*

The parkway is incomplete from milepost 101.5 to 87.0. I–55, I–20, and I–220 are connecting routes. To reach Jackson, follow I–55 south from the Trace.

Jackson
6
At its spangled edges, **Jackson** has little to distinguish it, but the state capital becomes increasingly original toward its shady heart. The downtown area has many small museums and most of the city's notable architecture.

The city is named for Andrew Jackson, who was popular with Mississippians long before he became president. As Major General Jackson, he helped negotiate the Treaty of Doak's Stand by which the Choctaw Indians ceded large chunks of Mississippi to the United States, on October 18, 1820. The City of

Jackson is the county seat of Hinds County, named for another negotiator, Major General Thomas Hinds, an enterprising and daring hero of the Battle of New Orleans in the War of 1812.

The **Jackson Visitor Information Center** is a small log cabin with anachronistic plate glass windows and a good stock of brochures. *At the Mississippi Agriculture and Forestry Museum, 1150 Lakeland Dr., east of I–55, tel. 601/960–1800. Open weekdays 8:30–5.*

The **Agriculture and Forestry Museum** looks like an old farm marooned in the midst of expanding suburbs, but the city was actually here first. The 10 farm buildings were brought here to stand exactly as they once did in Jefferson Davis County, Mississippi. They are still surrounded by a working farm with fields of corn and cotton, and pastures for sheep, goats, and horses. A crossroads town, similar to small Mississippi towns in the 1920s, has also been assembled. Work goes on in a blacksmith's shop and a cotton gin, meetings are held in the old Masonic Lodge, and the 1897 Epiphany Episcopal church building can be rented for weddings. The General Store sells soft drinks, snacks, and souvenirs. A complete tour of the museum will take about 90 minutes. *1150 Lakeland Dr., Tour Coordinator, Box 1609, Jackson 39215, tel. 601/354–6113. Admission: $3 adults; $1 children 6–18, under 6 free. Group tours available. Open Tues.–Sat. 9–5, Sun. 1–5. Summer hours: Tues.–Sat. 10–7, Sun. 1–5.*

The **Old Capitol Building** sits serenely on Capitol Green, with the **War Memorial Building** (1940) to the north and the **Mississippi Archives Building** (1971) to the south. Begun in 1833 and completed in 1840, the Old Capitol, with its simple columns and elegant proportions, is an excellent example of Greek Revival architecture. The building was restored in 1959–61 for use as the **State Historical Museum.** Capitol Green is a leafy reminder of the checkerboard pattern of alternating squares of buildings and parks recommended by President Thomas Jefferson and proposed for Jackson by Peter A. Vandorn. Vandorn submitted a map and plan for the new city in April 1822. The Vandorn map and other exhibits depicting Mississippi's history are on display in the museum. *100 North State St., tel. 601/354–6222. Admission free. Guided tours available. Open weekdays 8–5, Sat. 9:30–4:30, Sun. 12:30–4:30.*

The **Spengler's Corner Building** (101 N. State St.) is one of Jackson's oldest commercial structures. In 1840 Joseph Spengler opened a tavern here that was popular with legislators, but when the New Capitol was built, the inn closed. Many other businesses occupied the building, which was restored as a law office in 1976. Adjoining it to the north are attractive late-19th- and early 20th-century buildings, with the stucco and bay windows making them primarily Victorian-Italianate in style.

The **Harding Building** (500 E. Capitol St.) occupies the corner that was once the site of Mississippi's first statehouse, which was used from 1822 until the completion of the Old Capitol in 1840. The Harding Building, a Victorian Italianate design, was renovated for offices in the early 1980s.

The old **Central Fire Station** (201 N. President St.) is a three-story brick structure completed in 1905; it served as Central Station No. 1 until 1975. The Jackson Chamber of Commerce restored it in 1978.

City Hall (203 S. President St.) is a white Greek Revival building that has served continuously as Jackson's center of government since its opening in 1847. A Masonic Hall originally occupied the third floor. During the Civil War, City Hall was used as a hospital. Look into the tiny City Council chamber with its black and white floors and heavy red velvet curtains. On the west side of the building is the formal Josh Halbert Garden, with a statue of Andrew Jackson designed in 1968.

In the **Mississippi Arts Center** you will find the **Mississippi Museum of Art** and the **Impressions Gallery.** The museum has changing exhibits and a permanent collection of regional paintings. In the high-tech, hands-on Impressions Gallery, you can create music by walking through beams of light, wave your arms to send colors rippling from your shadow, and more—all in the name of education and art. *201 E. Pascagoula St., tel. 601/960–1515. Admission: $2 adults, $1 children. The Impressions Gallery is free. Museum open Tues.–Fri 10–5, weekends noon–4. Closed Mon.*

Davis Planetarium is the largest planetarium in the Southeast and one of the world's best-equipped, but its shows vary wildly in quality. Seek local guidance or reviews in the *Clarion-Ledger* newspaper. *201 E. Pascagoula St., tel. 601/960–1550. Admission: $3 adults, $2 children 12 and under, $2 senior citizens. Closed Mon.*

The **U.S. Federal Courthouse** (245 E. Capitol St.) is a good example in concrete and sandstone of the streamlined Art Deco style that was popular between the world wars, a time when many Jackson buildings were constructed. This building was completed in 1934 and served as Jackson's post office and as a federal court building until 1988, when a new post office was built. The motifs of eagles, stars, and geometric designs on the exterior are repeated throughout the interior and on the free-standing aluminum light fixtures around the building.

St. Andrew's Episcopal Cathedral (305 E. Capitol St.) offers free musical programs at noon each Wednesday (except in the summer), followed by sandwiches at a nominal fee. The original building is an important example of Gothic Revival architecture enhanced by fine stained glass windows.

The Lamar Life Building, adjacent to St. Andrew's, was designed to complement the cathedral. Although it has lost the alligators that once flanked its doors, it still exhibits other Gothic designs and a crenellated clock tower. The president of Lamar Life during the building's construction (1924–25) was C.W. Welty, father of Eudora Welty, Pulitzer Prize–winning author and lifelong Jackson resident.

The **Mississippi Governor's Mansion** has been continuously in use as the official home of the state's first family since its completion in 1841. At that time, Jackson was a tiny city and this grand Greek Revival dwelling was an optimistic statement. General Sherman presumably lived here during his occupation of Jackson in 1863. An addition in the rear serves the governor's family. The original building was carefully restored in the 1970s and furnished with museum-quality antiques that the state could never have afforded in the 1800s. Invest 30 minutes in the lively tours, strong on legend as well as fact. *300 E. Capitol St., tel. 601/350–3175. Admission free. Tours Tues.–Fri. 9:30–11:30.*

Smith Park is the only public square that remains from the 1822 checkerboard plan of the city. It is the center of the Smith Park Historic District. The park was a grazing area for animals until 1884, when James Smith of Glasgow, Scotland, a former Jacksonian, donated $100 to fence and beautify it, and the park was named for him. It is the setting for a famous short story, "The Winds," by Eudora Welty. The park hosts frequent concerts, festivals, picnics, and art exhibits. A popular "Fridays in Smith Park" program offers noontime entertainment in April and October.

The **Cathedral of St. Peter the Apostle** (203 N. West St.), built 1897–1900, is the third building of the congregation, which organized in 1846. Their first building was burned by Federal troops in 1863, as were many others in the city. Their second church, now in the very center of the downtown area, at the site of the present rectory (123 N. West St.), was criticized for its remoteness from town.

Across Yazoo Street from Smith Park is a Greek Revival building with graceful columns. Constructed of slave-made brick in 1843–44, this simple, elegant structure housed the First Baptist Church until 1893, then a Methodist church, followed by the Central Church of Christ. After several years as an apartment house, it became an office building in 1959, and it now belongs once more to the Methodists.

The **Galloway House** (304 N. Congress St.) is a two-story house built in the Victorian "Second Empire" style. Completed in 1889, this house was built for Methodist Bishop Charles Galloway, a distinguished churchman of international reknown. In 1983 it was renovated for use as a law office.

The **New Capitol** sits in Beaux Arts splendor at the junction of Mississippi and North Congress streets, its dome surmounted by a gold-plated copper eagle with a 15-foot wingspan. Completed in 1903 at a cost of $1 million, the Capitol enjoyed a $19-million renovation from 1979 to 1983. It was designed by the German architect Theodore C. Link, who was strongly influenced by the national capitol in Washington, DC. Elaborate architectural details inside the building include a Tiffany window. Ride up in the ornate brass-and-wood elevator if the grand staircase outside daunts you. *High St., tel. 601/359–3114. Admission free. Open weekdays 8–5, Sat. 10–4, Sun. 1–4. Guided tours: weekdays 9, 10, 11, 1:30, 2:30, 3:30.*

Eudora Welty Library (300 N. State St.), the largest public library in Mississippi, is named in honor of the city's famed short-story writer and novelist *(The Ponder Heart, Losing Battles, The Optimist's Daughter)*. The library opened in 1986; it has a 42-foot-long circulation desk, handcrafted of African rosewood and curly maple by local craftsman Fletcher Cox. *300 N. State St., tel. 601/968–5811. Open Mon.–Thurs. 10–9, Fri. and Sat. 10–6, and (Sept.–May) Sun. 1–5.*

A few Victorian homes stand on North State Street between College Street and Fortification Street, the survivors of the many large houses that lined this street in its heyday as Jackson's best address. The **Morris House** (505 N. State St.) is a Classic Revival house built about 1900. The **Virden-Patton House** (512 N. State St.), built about 1849, was undamaged in the Civil War, suggesting that Union officers may have used it as headquarters. The **Millsaps-Buie House** (628 N. State St.), built in 1888, has been restored as a bed-and-breakfast inn *(see* Lodging). It was built by Major Reuben Webster Millsaps, the founder of Millsaps College in Jackson. Two doors north is the **Garner Green House** (1910), with an imposing portico of Corinthian columns. This house was moved across the street from its original location and restored in 1988 to become an office building. **Greenbrook Flowers** (c. 1895–97; 705 N. State St.) occupies the former St. Andrew's Episcopal rectory; it has been greatly altered.

Time Out | **Kitchen Delights** offers takeout food as appealing as its tomato-red building. The fresh herbs in the front garden show up in plate lunches like tarragon chicken breast over rice and salads like fresh tomato and mozzarella with basil. Other specialties are crawfish and crabmeat quiche (in season), fresh-baked breads, and raisin-walnut cookies. *709 Poplar Blvd., tel. 601/ 353–FOOD. Cash only. Open weekdays 9–5:30. Inexpensive (unless you stock up on fresh cheeses and pâtés).*

The **Manship House** was built about 1857 by Charles H. Manship, the Jackson mayor who surrendered the city to General William Tecumseh Sherman on July 16, 1863. The museum is a careful restoration of a small Gothic Revival–style home with examples of wood graining painted by Manship himself. *420 E. Fortification St. (enter parking area from Congress St.), tel. 601/961–4724. Admission free. Tours: Tues.–Fri. 9–4, weekends 1–4. Closed Mon.*

C.W. Welty and his wife Chestina built the house at **741 North Congress Street** in 1907. Their daughter Eudora was born here in 1909 in the master bedroom on the second floor. Welty used images of this house and neighborhood in many of her literary works, including *The Golden Apples.* It has been restored for use as a law office.

Jackson's oldest house, **The Oaks,** was built by James Hervey Boyd, mayor of Jackson between 1853 and 1858. *823 N. Jefferson St., tel. 601/353–9339. Admission: $1.50. Open Tues.–Sat. 10–4, Sun. 2–4. Closed Mon.*

Jackson is a city of neat, tree-shaded neighborhoods, excellent for walking, jogging, or "Sunday driving," especially the **Belhaven area** bounded by Riverside Drive, I–55, Fortification Street, and North State Street. **Carlisle, Poplar, Peachtree,** and **Fairview streets** are distinguished by fine homes.

Rocky Springs (milepost 54.8) was a stop for post riders during the early 1800s, and General Grant's army camped here on its march to Jackson and Vicksburg during the Civil War. You can camp here, too. It's a first-come, first-served race, especially on weekends, but at least you needn't worry about Confederate sharpshooters. Overhung by ancient trees, the stream ripples and sings like mountain waters. Trails meander through the woods and up a steep hill to a tiny old cemetery and **Rocky Springs Methodist Church** (1837), where services are still held on Sundays.

At milepost 41.5 is a portion of the **Old Trace,** a short section of the original Indian Trace of loess soil (easily eroded and compacted earth). You can park and walk along it for a short way.

Port Gibson is the earliest town to grow up along the Trace that is still in existence. On Church Street is the much-photographed **First Presbyterian Church** (1859), its spire topped by a 12-foot hand pointing heavenward. The church chandeliers came from the old steamboat *Robert E. Lee.* Also on Church Street are the double-galleried **Disharoon House** (no building date is known); Port Gibson's largest antebellum house; **Englesing House** (1817), distinguished by its sturdy end chimneys and formal garden; **Gage House** (1830), with double doors, surrounded by heavy molding, and a handsome detached kitchen; and **St. Joseph's Catholic Church** (1850), Gothic in style, with pointed arches and buttresses.

Unless you're a brave and lucky navigator, you'll need a map from the **Port Gibson Chamber of Commerce** to negotiate the winding roads that plunge through dense forests to historic sites around the city.

Grand Gulf Military Monument commemorates the once-thriving town of Grand Gulf that was left in ruins by Federal gunboats during the Civil War. On a steep hill, the old town site has become a museum with an 1863 cannon, a collection of carriages, an 1820s dogtrot cabin, an old Catholic church, and a Spanish house from the 1790s. *North of Port Gibson off U.S. 61. Rte. 2, Box 389, Port Gibson 39150. Admission: $1 adults, 50¢ children. Open Mon.–Sat. 8–noon, 1–5; Sun. 1–6.*

Time Out Handmade bonnets swing in the breeze on the porch of **The Old Country Store,** which has been in business at Lorman since 1890. Its longleaf-pine flooring is jammed with display cases, most installed when the store was built, and you can buy souvenirs, soft drinks, and snacks, including mellow hoop cheese sliced with an antique cutter. *U.S. 61, south of Lorman, tel. 601/437–3661. MC, V.*

Northwest of Lorman, on MS 552, are 23 vine-clad columns that are the romantic ruins of **Windsor,** a huge Greek Revival mansion that was built in 1861 and burned down in 1890. **Rodney** is a ghost town that was celebrated by Eudora Welty in "At the Landing."

Just off the Trace near milepost 20 is **Springfield,** a plantation home built in Jefferson County in 1791. Tradition says Andrew Jackson married Rachel Donelson Robards here soon after the house was completed. *Rte. 1, Box 201, Fayette 39069, west of Natchez Trace on MS 553, tel. 601/786–3802. Admission: $4 adults, $2 children under 12. Open spring and summer daily 10–8, fall 10–6, winter 10:30–5:30.*

Emerald Mound (milepost 10.3) is the second largest Indian mound in the country, covering almost eight acres. It was built around 1300 for religious ceremonies practiced by ancestors of the Natchez Indians. It's a good place to picnic, view a sunset, fly a kite, and let your children run loose.

The Parkway abruptly ends, putting you on U.S. 61 as you near Natchez. Here is the little town of **Washington,** with the buildings of **Historic Jefferson College** meticulously restored. Washington was the capital of the Mississippi Territory from 1802 to 1817, and Jefferson College was chartered in 1802 as the territory's first educational institution. Here Aaron Burr, who served as Thomas Jefferson's vice president, was arraigned for treason, under an oak tree, which still stands. Burr was lionized by Natchez society while he awaited trial. *U.S. 61 at Natchez, tel. 601/442–2901. Admission free. Buildings open Mon.–Sat. 9–5, Sun. 1–5.*

Natchez **Natchez** is named for the mound-building, sun-worshiping
❼ Natchez Indians who lived here, undisturbed, in small villages before the French built Fort Rosalie in 1716. Later the city came under British rule (1763–1779), and the district known today as **Natchez-under-the-Hill** grew up at the Mississippi River landing beneath the bluff. The Spanish took control in 1795; they left their mark on the city by establishing straight streets—which intersect at right angles, atop the bluff—and green parkland that overlooks the river. The United States claimed Natchez by treaty in 1795. The city gave its name to the Natchez Trace and prospered as travelers heading for Nashville passed through with money in their pockets and a willingness to spend it on a rowdy good time.

The real glory days came between 1819 and 1860, when cotton plantations and the bustling river port poured riches into Natchez. Wealthy planters built stylish town houses and ringed the city with opulent plantation homes. Because the city had little military significance, it survived the Civil War almost untouched, but its economy was wrecked. The city entered a decline that actually saved its architectural treasures. No one could afford to tear houses down or even to remodel them. In 1932, the women of Natchez originated the idea of a pilgrimage, which would raise money for preservation. The Natchez Pilgrimage is now held twice a year, three weeks in October and four weeks in March and April. Many houses are open only during Pilgrimage weeks, when crowds flock to see them, but others are open year-round.

Begin your sightseeing at one of the tourist information centers (*see* Important Addresses and Numbers). The Chamber of Commerce offers a free self-guided walking tour. At the **Pilgrimage Tour Headquarters** (Canal and State Sts., tel. 601/446–6631 or 800/647–6742) you can purchase *Natchez: Walking Guide to the Old Town* ($4.95) and *The Great Houses of Natchez*, a coffee-table tome with color photographs and a reliable text; too heavy to carry on a walking tour but a good souvenir if its price ($35) isn't too heavy as well.

Rosalie (1823) established the ideal form of the "Southern mansion" with its white columns, hipped roof, and red bricks. Furnishings purchased for the house in 1858 include a famous Belter parlor set. *100 Orleans St., tel. 601/445–4555. Admission: $4 adults, $2 children over 10. Open daily 9–5.*

Magnolia Hall (c. 1858) was shelled by the Union gunboat *Essex* during the Civil War. The shell reportedly exploded in a soup tureen, scalding several diners. The Greek Revival mansion has scored stucco walls and fluted columns topped with curving Ionic capitals. Note the plaster magnolia blossoms on the parlor ceiling. *215 S. Pearl St., tel. 601/442–7259. Admission: $4 adults, $2 children. Overnight lodgings. Daily tours 9–5.*

Dunleith (1856) stands like a Greek temple on a knoll surrounded by 40 acres of green pastures and wooded bayous (with the culture shock of a Wal-Mart department store across the way). The Greek Revival mansion is completely encircled by 26 columns, each two stories high. It has extensive gardens and restored outbuildings. It was also used as a backdrop for scenes in the film *Huckleberry Finn* (the 1970 version) and *Showboat* (the 1950s version). *84 Homochitto St., tel. 601/446–8500. Bed-and-breakfast inn, tel. 601/446–6631 or 800/647–6742. Admission: $4 adults, $2 children. Open Mon.–Sat. 9–5:30, Sun. 12:30–5:30.*

Longwood (1860–61) is the largest octagonal house in the United States. When the Civil War broke out, Northern workers fled to their homes, preventing the immensely wealthy Dr. Haller Nutt from completing the mansion. Hoping to finish the house at the war's end, Nutt moved his family into the basement, but he died in 1864. Still unfinished, Longwood is now a museum for the Pilgrimage Garden Club. *140 Lower Woodville Rd., tel. 601/442–5193. Admission: $4 adults, $2 children. Open daily 9–5.*

During Pilgrimage you can tour only those homes that are open on a given day. To the list above try to add **Mount Repose** (Pine Ridge Rd.), **Hawthorne** (Lower Woodville Rd.), **Fair Oaks** (U.S. 61S), **The Parsonage** (305 S. Broadway), and **Elmscourt** (John R. Junkin Dr.).

What to See and Do with Children

Jackson **Atari Adventure.** Large video arcade. *N. Park Mall, 1200 E. County Line Rd., tel. 601/956–7315. Open Mon.–Sat. 10–9:30, Sun. 1–6.*
Chuck E. Cheese's Pizza Time Theatre. Arcade and entertainment for the under-12 set. *5465 I–55N, tel. 601/956–5252. Open Mon.–Thurs. 11–9:30, Fri. and Sat. 11–11, Sun. noon–9:30.*
Impressions Gallery (*see* Exploring).
Mississippi Agriculture and Forestry Museum (*see* Exploring).
The New Capitol is awe-inspiring enough in its decorations (4,500 bare light bulbs, and plenty of gilt) to interest even young children (*see* Exploring).
Zoological Park. Family recreational spot features animals in natural settings, including many endangered species. *2918 W. Capitol St., tel. 601/960–1575 or 601/960–1576. Admission: $2 adults, $1 children. Open summer 9–6, winter 9–5.*

Natchez **Carriage rides** are a fun way to see downtown Natchez. Tours begin at Natchez Pilgrimage Tour Headquarters (Canal St. at State St.) or the Eola Hotel (110 N. Pearl St.). A tour lasts about 30 minutes and costs $7 per person.
Grand Village of the Natchez Indians. The archaeological park and museum depicts the culture of the Natchez Indians, which reached its zenith in the 1500s. *400 Jefferson Davis Blvd., tel. 601/445–6502. Admission free. Open Mon.–Sat. 9–5, Sun. 1:30–5.*
Longwood. An air of mystery surrounds this uncompleted octagonal house, making it the only Natchez mansion guaranteed to interest children (*see* Exploring).

Port Gibson **Grand Gulf Military Monument.** Children love the steep trail, the observation tower, the old waterwheel, and the blood-stained uniforms (*see* Exploring).

Tupelo **Elvis Presley Birthplace.** One tourist said to her grandchild, "I'm not paying 50¢ for you to see furniture that wasn't even his." You, however, may want to (*see* Exploring).

Elvis Presley Park (*see* Exploring).
Elvis Presley Lake and Campground (*see* Exploring).

Off the Beaten Track

Waverley Mansion (1852), near Columbus, is one of the finest plantation homes in Mississippi and a National Historic Landmark, inspiring not only as architecture but as the labor of love of its present owners, Donna and Robert Allen Snow. The Snows and their children have restored the once-abandoned house to splendor over a 25-year period, proceeding room by room and doing most of the work themselves. Waverley's twin spiral staircases have 718 hand-turned spindles. *6 mi from Columbus, off MS 50, Rte. 2, Box 234, West Point 39773, tel. 601/494-1399. Cost: $4. Open year-round, dawn–dusk.*

Go off to war—the Civil War—in an authentic uniform crafted by the **Jarnagin Company.** Union and Confederate "soldiers" from Vicksburg to Virginia are outfitted by John and Carolyn Jarnagin for re-creations of the war's great battles, as well as for educational programs presented by museums and for Army ceremonial duties. The standard Federal coat, which looks like a dark blue blazer, is cut from special wool and costs $49.50. Union or Confederate trousers, also 100% wool, cost $50, and five canteen models run from $18.50 to $29.50. *5 min east of Corinth on the Oakland–Central Rd., Rte. 3, Box 217, Corinth 38834, tel. 601/287-4977. Open weekdays 7 AM–3:30 PM. MC, V.*

Shopping–Jackson

Antiques **Antiques Et Cetera** (Highland Village Shopping Center, I-55N at E. Northside Dr., tel. 601/981-3666) fills its large store with English furnishings and new and antique decorative accessories. **Bobbie King's** (Woodland Hills Shopping Center, Old Canton Rd. at Duling Ave., tel. 601/362-9803) specializes in heirloom textiles and exhibits them in lavish displays with one-of-a-kind accessories to wear or with which to decorate your home. **Cottage Antiques** (4074 N. State St., tel. 601/362-6510; closed Sat.) carries fine American antiques, accessories, and textiles. **C.W. Fewel III & Co., Antiquarians** (840 N. State St., tel. 601/355-5375) specializes in fine 18th- and 19th-century furnishings and accessories.

Books Books by Mississippi authors and about Mississippi are available from knowledgeable booksellers at **Lemuria** (202 Banner Hall, tel. 601/366-7619). **Choctaw Books** (406 Manship St., tel. 601/352-7281) stocks first editions of Southern writers' works. **The Bookworm** (Highland Village, tel. 601/362-4018) is also recommended.

Gifts The members of the Craftsman's Guild of Mississippi have raised crafts from their "arts and crafts" status to "craft *as* art." Their work is sold in the Jackson area (*see* Exploring) at **Ridgeland Crafts Center,** the **Old Capitol Museum** shop, the **Mississippi Arts Center** shop, and the **Mississippi Crafts Gallery** (111 Bldg., 111 E. Capitol St., tel. 601/354-0856).

The Everyday Gourmet stocks state products, including pecan pie, bread, and biscuit mixes; muscadine jelly; jams and chutneys; cookbooks; fine ceramic tableware, and a complete stock

of kitchenware and gourmet foods (2905 Old Canton Rd., tel.
601/362–0723).

Participant Sports

Golf   In Jackson: **Lefleur's Bluff State Park,** 18 holes (Highland Dr.,
tel. 601/960–1436).

Jogging   In Jackson: Jog on paths that curve under tall pines and stretch
down to a sunny meadow in **Parham Bridges Park** (5055 Old
Canton Rd.).

In Natchez: An asphalt road runs about one-and-a-half miles
through **Duncan Park** (Duncan St. at Auburn Ave.).

Tennis   In Jackson: **Tennis Center South** (2827 Oak Forest Dr., off Mc-
Dowell Rd., tel. 601/960–1712) and **Parham Bridges Park** (5055
Old Canton Rd., tel. 601/956–1105).

In Natchez: There are courts in **Duncan Park** (Duncan St. at
Auburn Ave.).

Dining and Lodging

Dining   In Tupelo, Jackson, and Natchez you can find everything from
caviar to chitlins. Fine food often comes in casual surroundings. Jackson boasts several elegant restaurants, and Natchez
offers plantation breakfasts in antebellum opulence. Tupelo offers a wide variety, but specializes in down-home cooking. If
you're eating on the run, Jackson's County Line Road east of
I–55 and the East Frontage Roads along I–55N are jammed
with fast food joints. Blue plate dinners of fresh Mississippi
vegetables are a widely available alternative.

Category	Cost*
Very Expensive	over $20
Expensive	$15–$20
Moderate	$10–$15
Inexpensive	under $10

per person without tax (8%), service, or drinks

Lodging   National hotel and motel chains are found in Jackson and Tupelo. The choice is greater in Jackson. In Natchez, travelers will
find plantation homes that open their doors in bed-and-
breakfast courtesy.

Category	Cost*
Very Expensive	over $70
Expensive	$50–$70
Moderate	$30–$50
Inexpensive	under $30

double room; add 7% for taxes

The following credit-card abbreviations are used: AE, American Express; CB, Carte Blanche; DC, Diners Club; MC,
MasterCard; V, Visa.

Jackson   **Nick's.** This large restaurant plays white tablecloths, mirrors,
Dining   and pale oak walls against the dark green of a thick rug to create an elegant background for nouvelle versions of regional
dishes. Lunch specialties are grilled catfish and Biloxi snapper.
Dinner specialties include eggplant stuffed with deviled crab,
grilled salmon with cognac and paprika, and blackfish. *1501
Lakeland Dr., tel. 601/981–8017. Jacket and tie required. Reservations accepted, except on Fri. and Sat. nights. AE, MC, V.
Very Expensive.*

The Silver Platter. The specialties of this tiny brick house are
rib-eye steaks and milk-fed veal. *219 N. President St., tel. 601/
969–3413. Jacket and tie required. Reservations recommended. AE, DC, MC, V. Closed Sun. Expensive.*

Walker's Drive-In. The Art Deco building looks like a diner inside, but the food is the work of a talented chef. Specialties are
soft-shell crab, blackfish, and fettuccine. Lunch is for the blue-
plate special crowd (chicken pot pie on Thursday is $3.95, with
vegetables and Miss Hazel's bread pudding). BYOB at night.
*3016 N. State St., tel. 601/981–8069. Dress: informal. No reser-
vations. MC, V. Closed Sun. Expensive.*

Hal and Mel's Restaurant and Oyster Bar. This vast warehouse
has been converted with the help of neon, 1930s antiques and
memorabilia, and terrific entertainment. A mixed crowd of artistic, business, and collegiate types comes to this trendy spot
for such specialties as grilled fresh fish, grilled chicken, and
oyster po'boys. *200 Commerce St., tel. 601/948–0888. Dress:
informal. Reservations recommended for dinner. MC, V.
Closed Sun. Moderate.*

The Mayflower. A perfect 1930s period piece with black and
white tile floors, straight-back booths, and formica-topped coffee counter, this cafe specializes in Greek salads, fresh fish
sautéed in lemon butter, and people-watching till all hours. *123
W. Capitol St., tel. 601/355–4122. Dress: informal, elegant, or
odd. No reservations. No credit cards. Moderate.*

Gridley's. Mexican tile tables and floors enhance small, sunny
dining areas. Eat pancakes as big as a plate ($1 each) for break-
fast, and spicy barbecued pork and ribs anytime else. *1428 Old
Square Rd., tel. 601/362–8600. Dress: informal. No reservations. AE, MC, V. Inexpensive.*

Lodging   **Millsaps-Buie House.** This Queen Anne–style home, with its
corner turret and tall-columned porch, was built in 1888 for
Jackson financier and philanthropist Major Reuben Webster
Millsaps, founder of Millsaps College in Jackson; it is listed
on the National Register of Historic Places. Restored as a B&B
in 1987, its guest rooms are individually decorated with antiques. An attentive staff serves morning coffee and pastries
in your room or in the Victorian dining room. *628 N. State
St., 39202, tel. 601/352–0221. 11 rooms, each with telephone
and private bath. AE, DC, MC, V. Expensive–Very Expensive.*

Holiday Inn Downtown. Convention hotel with cheerful guest
rooms (those on the east side overlook the Cathedral of St. Peter the Apostle and Smith Park) and a convenient downtown
location. *200 E. Amite St., 39201, tel. 601/969–5100 or 800/
HOLIDAY. 358 rooms. Facilities: restaurant, pool, lounge.
AE, DC, MC, V. Expensive.*

Ramada Renaissance Hotel. This new high-rise convention motel is sleekly contemporary. *1001 County Line Rd., 39211, tel.
601/957–2800 or 800/272–6232. 300 rooms. Facilities: airport*

*courtesy van, restaurant with live entertainment, jazz in the
lobby bar, gift shop, barber shop. AE, DC, MC, V. Expensive.*
Radisson Walthall Hotel. The cornerstone and huge brass mail-
box near the elevators are almost all that remain of the original
Walthall Hotel. The dismal motel that occupied the site next
was transformed into the new Radisson. The marble floors,
gleaming brass, a panelled library/writing room, and cozy bar
almost fool you into thinking this is a restoration. *25 E. Capitol
St., 39201, tel. 601/948–6161 or 800/228–9822. AE, DC, MC, V.
211 rooms. Facilities: heated pool, Jacuzzi, transportation to
airport, copy machines, 24-hr notary public. Moderate–
Expensive.*

Natchez   **Confederate Room.** The restaurant serves soup and salad
Dining   lunches (curried chicken, crab, and shrimp salads) and
Natchez's best food at night (grilled smoked pork chop, broiled
snapper, and steak). *211 N. Pearl St., tel. 601/445–9014. Dress:
informal. Reservations recommended at night. MC, V. Closed
Sun. Expensive.*
Cock of the Walk. The famous original of a regional franchise,
this shanty overlooking the Mississippi River specializes in
fried catfish fillets, fried dill pickles, hush puppies, mustard
greens, and coleslaw. Waiters in red long john shirts serve
cornbread to the constant strum of banjos. *15 Silver St.,
Natchez-Under-the-Hill, tel. 601/446–8920. Dress: informal.
Reservations not required. AE, MC, V. Moderate.*
Natchez Landing. The porch tables provide a view of the Mississippi River, which is at its very best when both the *Delta Queen*
and *Mississippi Queen* steamboats dock. Specialties are barbe-
cue (pork ribs, chicken, beef) and fried and grilled catfish. *11
Silver St., Natchez-Under-the-Hill, tel. 601/442–6639. Dress:
informal. Reservations not required. AE, MC, V. Closed Sun.
Moderate.*
Ramada Hilltop Motel Restaurant. Don't be discouraged by this
motel setting; the spacious dining room has a beautiful view.
Try the noon buffet or the oyster soup and prime rib on
Wednesday night. *130 John R. Junkin Dr., tel. 601/446–6311.
Jacket and tie required. Reservations recommended at night.
AE, MC, V. Moderate.*
Scrooge's. This old storefront once housed the studio of Nor-
man of Natchez (a well-known local photographer) and the
Tango Tearoom, where locals learned to dance for a quarter.
The restaurant has a pub atmosphere downstairs and a more
subdued intimate ambience upstairs. The menu includes red
beans and rice, and mesquite-grilled chicken or shrimp with
angel-hair pasta. *315 Main St., tel. 601/446–9922. Dress: informal. Reservations not required. AE, MC, V. Moderate.*
Annex Tea Room. The tea room is airy, and bright with Natchez
chitchat and gossip. Specialties are chicken salad, gumbo,
sandwiches on homemade bread, and homebaked cakes and
pies. *209 Franklin St., tel. 601/446–6544. Dress: informal.
Reservations for groups only. MC, V. Closed Sun. Inexpensive.*
The Fare. The red, white, and blue color scheme of this Victorian Cafe creates a carnival air. The menu includes homemade
soups, sandwiches, beignets (French doughnuts), and café au
lait. *109 N. Pearl St., tel. 601/442–5299. Dress: informal. No
reservations. MC, V. Inexpensive.*
The Parlor. This parlor is a comfortable mishmash of
unmatching tables and chairs, racks of magazines, jazz posters,

and an enclosed patio with picnic tables and umbrellas. Mexican food is a specialty (the fajitas are fresh); so is grilled catfish with vegetables and seafood pasta. *116 S. Canal St., tel. 601/ 446–8511. Dress: informal. Reservations recommended. AE, MC, V. Closed Sun. Inexpensive.*

Lodging This list includes the area's most popular bed-and-breakfast inns. **Natchez Pilgrimage Tours** (Canal St. at State St., Box 347, Natchez 39120, tel. 800/647–6742) can answer questions and handle reservations. Contact **Creative Travel** (Canal St. Depot, Natchez 39120, tel. 601/442–3762) about stays in private homes, which are less expensive than the mansions.

The Burn. This elegant 1832 mansion offers a seated plantation breakfast, private tour of the home, and swimming pool. *712 N. Union St., 39120, tel. 601/445–8566 or 601/442–1344. 6 bedrooms, all with private baths. AE, MC, V. Very Expensive.*

Monmouth. This plantation mansion (c. 1818) was owned by Mississippi governor John A. Quitman from 1826 to his death in 1858. Guest rooms are decorated with tester beds and antiques. The grounds are tastefully landscaped, with a New Orleans–style courtyard, a pond, and a gazebo. Plantation breakfast; tour of home. *36 Melrose, 39120, tel. 800/828–4531. 4 bedrooms, 1 suite in main house; 5 bedrooms in servants' quarters; 4 in garden cottages. No children under 14. AE, MC, V. Expensive –Very Expensive.*

Dunleith. Stately, colonnaded Dunleith is the most popular bed-and-breakfast inn in Natchez. The inn reserves a wing for overnight guests and serves them breakfast in their rooms or across the herb garden in the former poultry house. A Southern breakfast and a tour of the house are included. *84 Homochitto St., 39120, tel. 601/446–6631. 12 guest rooms with private bath. AE, MC, V. Moderate–Very Expensive.*

Eola Hotel. This beautifully restored 1920s hotel has a tiny formal lobby and small guest rooms with antique reproduction furniture. Request rooms in the Eola guest house across the street if you want more space, some antiques, and a balcony. Its restaurant was once a liability but is now under new management. *110 N. Pearl St., 39120, tel. 601/445–6000 or 800/821–3721. 122 rooms. AE, DC, MC, V. Moderate.*

Ramada Hilltop. The typical motel decor is forgotten if your room overlooks the Mississippi River. *130 John R. Junkin Dr., 39120, tel. 601/446–6311 or 800/272–6232. AE, DC, MC, V. Moderate.*

Tupelo **Jefferson Place.** This austere 19th-century house is lively in-
Dining side, with red-checked tablecloths and bric-a-brac. The place is popular with the college crowd; short orders and steaks are the specialties. *823 Jefferson St., tel. 601/844–8696. Dress: informal. Reservations not required. AE, MC, V. Closed Sun. Expensive.*

Papa Vanelli's Pizzaria. Family pictures and scenes of Greece decorate the walls of this comfortably nondescript restaurant where tables wear traditional red-and-white checkered tablecloths. Specialties (all homemade) include pizza with 10 toppings, lasagna, moussaka, manicotti, Greek salad. Vanelli's own bakery produces breads, strudels, and pastries. *712 S. Gloster, tel. 601/844–4410. Dress: informal. Reservations not required. AE, MC, V. Inexpensive.*

Rita's Gum Tree Cafe. Down a brick-paved alley is an 1800s commercial building, originally a feed store, that now feeds 64 people in two rooms with ceiling fans. Homecooked, blue plate specials include chicken salad with fresh fruit, and fried pork chops with creamed potatoes. Don't miss the fried cornbread. *206 N. Spring St., tel. 601/842–2952. Dress: informal. Reservations not required. No credit cards. Closed weekends. Inexpensive.*

Lodging **Executive Inn.** Guest rooms in this large, contemporary hotel are plain and functional, yet new and clean. *1011 N. Gloster, 38801, tel. 601/841–2222. 119 rooms. Facilities: indoor pool, whirlpool, sauna, cable TV. AE, DC, MC, V. Moderate–Expensive.*

Ramada Inn. This modern three-story hotel caters to business travelers and conventions as well as families. Dancing nightly (except Sunday) in Bogart's Lounge. Breakfast and lunch buffets are served. *854 N. Gloster, 38801, tel. 601/844–4111 or 800/272–6232. 230 rooms, 10 executive suites. Facilities: large outdoor pool, sauna, whirlpool, coin laundry, valet service, in-room movies, barber and beauty shops. AE, DC, MC, V. Moderate.*

Best Western Trace Inn. This old, rustic inn on 15 acres near the Natchez Trace offers neat rooms and friendly service. *3400 W. Main St., 38801, tel. 601/842–5555. 165 rooms. Facilities: in-room movies, playground, pool, restaurant, entertainment and dancing nightly (except Sun.), courtesy car. AE, MC, V. Moderate–Inexpensive.*

Nightlife

Jackson **Hal & Mel's** is the city's most popular night spot (*see* Dining). There's live entertainment at **The Dock** (Main Harbor Marina at Ross Barnett Reservoir, tel. 601/856–7765) Thursday–Sunday, when some 2,000 people pass through. The restaurant, which sits on a pier, generally attracts a young crowd, but draws an older one on Sundays. The mood is set by the people who step off their boats to dine, drink, and listen to the rock and roll and rhythm and blues.

George Street Grocery (416 George St., tel. 601/969–9483) is crammed with little tables, bric-a-brac, antiques, and Mississippi legislators from the nearby new Capitol. Top-name bands perform Thursday–Saturday.

Poet's (1855 Lakeland Dr., tel. 601/982–9711) presents food, drink, and a jazz trio in an old-fashioned atmosphere, created by antiques, old signs, pressed tin ceiling, and wooden floors.

Shucker's (1216½ N. State St., tel. 601/353–7536) is a tiny room with neon lights, pool table, and outdoor deck. Blues and classic rock are performed by local bands on Friday and Saturday; drinks, po'boys, and oysters are served.

Natchez **The River City Cafe and Lounge,** at the Briars, is a rustic pavilion on the highest point of the Mississippi River between St. Louis and New Orleans. The lounge is ideal for drinks at sunset.

Pearl Street Cellar (211 N. Pearl St., tel. 601/446–5022) is popular with the young set, but draws a mixed crowd when its bar hosts a jazz combo.

Under-the-Hill Saloon (33 Silver St., tel. 601/446–8023) features live entertainment on weekends in one of the few original buildings left in Natchez-Under-the-Hill.

Holly Springs and Oxford

Holly Springs and Oxford, just east of I–55 in north Mississippi, are sophisticated versions of the Mississippi small town; both are courthouse towns incorporated in 1837. They offer visitors historic architecture, arts and crafts, literary associations, a warm welcome, and those unhurried pleasures of Southern life that remain constant from generation to generation—entertaining conversation, good food, and nostalgic walks at twilight.

Getting Around

By Car A 90-minute drive from Memphis, Holly Springs is located in north Mississippi near the Tennessee state line on U.S. 78 and MS 4, MS 7, and MS 311. Oxford is 29 miles south of Holly Springs on MS 7. Oxford is also accessible from I–55; it is 23 miles east of Batesville on MS 6.

By Bus **Greyhound/Trailways** has stations at Holly Springs (490 Craft St., tel. 601/252–1353) and Oxford (925 Van Buren, tel. 601/234–1424).

Guided Tours

Guided tours of the University of Mississippi campus are available upon request from the admissions office (tel. 601/232–7226).

Important Addresses and Numbers

Tourist Information **Holly Springs Chamber of Commerce** is located at Randall and College streets, tel. 601/252–2943. Open Monday–Wednesday and Friday 9–4. Closed Thursday afternoon and weekends.
Oxford's Information Center is in a cottage on the square next to City Hall, tel. 601/236–1610. Open Monday–Saturday 8–5. Closed for lunch noon–1, and Sunday.
Oxford-Lafayette County Chamber of Commerce is at 440 N. Lamar Avenue in Oxford, tel. 601/234–4651. Open weekdays 9–4.
Contact the **Public Relations Department of the University of Mississippi** (tel. 601/232–7236) for information about university plays, lectures, sporting events, and special events.

Emergencies In Holly Springs, dial 0 for assistance. In Oxford, dial 911. Medical help is available at **Oxford-Lafayette Medical Center** (U.S. 75, 1 mi south of the Oxford Square on S. Lamar Ave., tel. 601/234–6721).

24-Hour Pharmacy **Chaney's Eastgate Pharmacy** (Eastgate Shopping Center, University Ave. E, tel. 601/234–7221, after hours 601/234–0058).

Exploring Holly Springs and Oxford

Holly Springs **Holly Springs** arose from a crossroads of old Indian trails originally called Spring Hollow. Here Chickasaw Indians and travelers stopped to rest and bathe in the medicinal waters of springs in glades of holly trees. After the Chickasaw Cession in 1832, settlers poured into the area from the Carolinas, Virginia, and Georgia. Holly Springs became an educational, business, and cultural center as the newly arrived planters gained great wealth. Cotton barons built palatial mansions and handsome commercial buildings. Today Holly Springs has more than 300 structures listed on the National Register of Historic Places.

Holly Springs survived at least 50 raids during the Civil War. In December 1862, the Confederate army under General Earl Van Dorn destroyed $1 million worth of Union supplies intended for General Grant's use in his march against Vicksburg. Bent on reprisals against the city, Grant ordered General Benjamin Harrison Grierson to burn it in 1864. A clever Holly Springs matron, Maria Mason, invited the general into her home to chat. They discovered that they shared a love of music and that they had studied piano under the same teacher; so instead of destroying Holly Springs, Grierson enjoyed its hospitality at a series of afternoon gatherings and piano concerts. Many of Holly Springs's historic homes are open only during Pilgrimage (the last weekend in April), but the following landmarks are open daily.

Montrose (1858) was built by Albert Brooks as a wedding present for his daughter. Now leased by the Holly Springs Garden Club, this mansion has an elegant spiral staircase as well as elaborate cornices and plaster ceiling medallions. *307 E. Salem Ave., tel. 601/252–2943. Admission: $3 adults, children under 12 free. Open by appointment only.*

Rust College (N. Memphis St.), founded in 1868, contains **Oak View** (c. 1860), one of the oldest buildings in the state associated with black education. Metropolitan Opera star Leontyne Price, a native of Laurel, Mississippi, graduated from Rust.

The Yellow Fever House (104 E. Gholson Ave.), built in 1836, was Holly Springs's first brick building. It was used as a hospital during the 1878 yellow fever epidemic.

Hillcrest Cemetery (380 S. Maury St.) contains graves of 13 Confederate generals. Many of the iron fences surrounding the graves were made locally before the Civil War.

The Kate Freeman Clark Art Gallery is dedicated solely to the work of Holly Springs resident Kate Freeman Clark, who was trained in New York City during the 1890s. Clark completed more than 1,000 works on canvas and paper, including landscapes and portraits. She returned to Holly Springs in the 1920s and never painted again. Many of her friends did not know of her talent until her paintings were discovered after her death. In her will she left funds to establish a museum. *292 E. College Ave., tel. 601/252–2511. Admission free. Open by appointment (contact Holly Springs Chamber of Commerce; see Important Addresses and Numbers).*

Even the briefest visit to Holly Springs should include a look at the exteriors of several homes that are not usually open to the public. **Oakleigh**, on Salem Avenue across the street from Montrose, is a mansion with fine details: acanthus leaves on the graceful, grooved columns, a cornice emphasized by recessed dentil moldings and projecting pendants, and the pediment with a semicircular window. The interior is equally grand. Also on Salem Avenue are **Cedarhurst** and **Airliewood**, brick houses constructed in the Gothic style popularized in the 1850s by Andrew Jackson Downing. General Grant used Airliewood as his headquarters and General Ord used Cedarhurst as his during their occupation of Holly Springs.

Oxford   Oxford and Lafayette County were immortalized as "Jefferson" and "Yoknapatawpha County" in the novels of Oxford native William Faulkner, but even if you're not a Faulkner fan, this is a great place to experience small town living. You won't be bored; the characters who fascinated Faulkner still live here, and the University of Mississippi keeps things lively.

Faulkner received the Nobel Prize for Literature in 1950, and his readers will enjoy exploring the town that inspired *The Hamlet, The Town,* and *The Mansion.* "I discovered that my own little postage stamp of native soil was worth writing about, and that I would never live long enough to exhaust it," said Faulkner. "I created a cosmos of my own."

Many people who knew the eccentric Mr. Bill still live in Oxford and are willing to share stories about him. You may encounter them around **Courthouse Square.** The Square is a National Historic Landmark, and at its center is the white sandstone **Lafayette** (pronounced "Luh-FAY-it") **County Courthouse,** named for the French Revolutionary War hero the Marquis de Lafayette. The courthouse was rebuilt in 1873 after Union troops burned it; on its south side is the obligatory monument to Confederate soldiers. The courtroom on the second floor is original.

Time Out   At **Square Books** the knowledgeable staff can guide you to Southern fiction or gourmet food in their upstairs cafe. The specialties, lemon chicken and fresh strawberry shortcake (in season), can be enjoyed on the balcony overlooking the square. Keep an eye out for well-known writers who stroll over from the university—particularly Willie Morris (*Good Ole Boy, North Toward Home*) and Barry Hannah (*Ray, Geronimo Rex*). *South side of Courthouse Square, tel. 601/236-2262. Open Mon.-Sat. 9-9, Sun. 1-5. V, MC.*

University Avenue from Courthouse Square to the University of Mississippi is one of the state's most beautiful sights when the trees flame orange and gold in the fall, or when the dogwoods blossom in the spring.

The **University Museum** displays the brightly colored primitive paintings of local artist Theora Hamblett. Hamblett gained international fame for her works depicting dreams and visions, children's games, Mississippi landscapes, and scenes from her childhood. *University Ave. at 5th St., tel. 601/232-7073. Admission free. Open Tues.-Sat. 10-4, Sun. 1-4.*

Just beyond the museum is **The University of Mississippi,** the state's beloved "Ole Miss," which opened in 1848 with 80 students. **The Grove,** the tree-shaded heart of the campus, is almost as important a meeting place as Courthouse Square. (It was supposedly here that Faulkner, just fired from his job as postmaster for writing novels on the job, said, "Never again will I be at the beck and call of every son-of-bitch who's got two cents to buy a stamp.")

Across the Grove, antebellum **Barnard Observatory** houses **The Center for the Study of Southern Culture,** with exhibits on Southern music, folklore, and literature, and the world's largest blues archive (40,000 records). The center's annual Faulkner seminar attracts Faulkner scholars from around the world (*see* The Arts). The center's new *Encyclopedia of Southern Culture* is for sale here. *Barnard Observatory, University of Mississippi, tel. 601/343–5993. Admission free. Open weekdays 8:15–4:45.*

The **Mississippi Room** in the John Davis Williams Library contains both a permanent exhibit on Faulkner, including his Nobel Prize medal, and first editions of other Mississippi authors. *University Ave., at 5th St. Admission free. Open weekdays 8:30–5, Sat. 10–4.*

Rowan Oak was the home of William Faulkner from 1930 until his death in 1962. Although this is one of Mississippi's most famous attractions, there are no signs to direct you to the home, nor is there a marker at the site. The house and its surrounding 31 acres are as serene and private as they were when Faulkner lived and wrote there.

Built around 1844 by Colonel Robert Sheegog, the two-story, white-frame house with square columns represents the so-called planter style of architecture common to many Mississippi antebellum homes. After the Civil War it fell into disrepair and, in 1930, was purchased by Faulkner and his bride of one year, Estelle Oldham Franklin. The house was both a sanctuary and a financial burden to the author; it is now a National Historic Landmark owned by the University of Mississippi.

Faulkner made improvements and additions to the house, including a porch on the east side that he surrounded with a brick wall to shield him from curious strangers. After winning the Nobel Prize, he added the study where his bed, typewriter, desk, and other personal items, such as his sunglasses, a Colgate shave stick refill, an ink bottle, and a can of dog repellent, still evoke his presence.

Faulkner wrote an outline for his novel *The Fable* on the walls of the study, which is reputed to be the most photographed room in the state. The days of the week are neatly printed over the head and length of the bed, and to the right of the door leading into the room is the notation, "Tomorrow." *Old Taylor Rd., tel. 601/234–3284. Admission free. Open Mon.–Wed. 10–noon and 2–4, Sat. 10–noon, Sun. 2–4.*

Faulkner's funeral was held at Rowan Oak, and he was buried in the family plot in **St. Peter's Cemetery** at Jefferson and North 16th streets, beside his relatives. Also buried here is Caroline Barr, "Mammy Callie," Faulkner's childhood nurse. The tomb of the author's brother, Dean Faulkner, who was killed in an airplane crash, bears the same epitaph as the one Faulkner had given to John Sartoris in the novel *Pylon*.

Off the Beaten Track

William Faulkner was married in little **College Hill Presbyterian Church** (8 mi northwest of Oxford on College Hill Rd.) on June 20, 1929. The slave gallery doors and original pews are intact, although it's believed that Sherman stabled horses here during his occupation of College Hill in 1862. Behind the church is one of north Mississippi's oldest cemeteries.

From Oxford take MS 7S, to MS 328 to reach Taylor. Downtown **Taylor** is just three stores, but they house artists' studios and the old Taylor Grocery, which has a restaurant in the back (tel. 601/236–1716; no credit cards; closed Mon.). Here you can eat crisp fried catfish and mounds of hush puppies. In sculptor **William Beckwith's studio** you can see his statue of Temple Drake, the character who waited for the train in Taylor in Faulkner's novel *Sanctuary*. Small as it is, Taylor is achieving cult status; it's proper to brag about coming here!

What to See and Do with Children

Chewalla Lake and Recreation Area *(see* Participant Sports).

Oxford **Avent Park** *(see* Participant Sports).

Holly Springs **Square Books** has a large collection of children's books *(see* Exploring).
The Union, the University of Mississippi's student center, has pool rooms, a video arcade, and a book store. *Open weekdays 8 AM–10 PM, Sat. 4 PM–midnight, Sun. 4 PM–9 PM.*

Participant Sports

Holly Springs's Chewalla Lake and Recreation Area are part of Holly Springs National Forest and have nature trails, picnic areas, swimming, boating, camping, and fishing (license required). *From Holly Springs take MS 4 to Higdon Rd. Turn east; go 7 mi to entrance. Information: National Forests, Mississippi, 100 W. Capitol St., Suite 1141, Jackson 39269, tel. 601/960–4391.*
Oxford's Avent Park (Park Rd., the continuation of Bramlett Rd. after Jackson Ave.) offers tennis courts, a playground, picnic areas, and a jogging trail.

Dining and Lodging

Dining You don't have to travel far in these small towns to find one-of-a-kind dining experiences. Food, not decor, is usually the focus.

Category	Cost*
Very Expensive	over $20
Expensive	$15–$20
Moderate	$10–$15
Inexpensive	under $10

*per person without tax (8%), service, or drinks

Lodging When staying overnight in Oxford try the Oliver-Britt House, especially if you'd like to hear town gossip from your innkeeper. For more conventional lodgings, try the Alumni House on the University of Mississippi campus or, more conventional yet, the Holiday Inn.

Category	Cost*
Very Expensive	over $70
Expensive	$50–$70

Moderate	$30–$50
Inexpensive	$20–$30

*double room; add 8% for taxes

The following credit-card abbreviations are used: AE, American Express; CB, Carte Blanche; DC, Diners Club; MC, MasterCard; V, Visa.

Holly Springs **Phillips Grocery.** The building was constructed in 1882 as a sa-
Dining loon for railroad workers. Today it's decorated with antiques and crafts, and serves big, old-fashioned hamburgers. *541-A Van Dorn across from the old depot, tel. 601/252–4671. Dress: informal. No reservations. Open weekdays 9–5, Sat. 9–6. Inexpensive.*

Oxford **Villa Elena.** Gold-painted walls, gold plates, and sparkling mir-
Dining rors create a Mediterranean ambience for Northern Italian and Continental cuisine. Specialties from the extensive menu include veal piccata, filet mignon with béarnaise sauce, and broiled red snapper. *1726 University Ave., tel. 601/236–4413. Jacket and tie required. Reservations recommended. AE, MC, V. Closed Sun. Moderate.*

Smitty's. Homestyle cooking features red-eye gravy and grits, biscuits with blackberry preserves, fried catfish, chicken and dumplings, cornbread, and black-eyed peas. The menu says, If'n You Need Anything That Ain't on Here, Holler at the Cook. *On the Square, tel. 601/234–9111. Dress: informal. No credit cards. Inexpensive.*

Starnes Catfish Place. This rustic wooden cabin serves fried catfish with the traditional trimmings—crisp hush puppies, and creamy coleslaw. BYOB. *Hurricane Landing Rd. off MS 7N, tel. 601/234–7251. Dress: informal. No reservations. Closed Mon., Tues. MC, V. Inexpensive.*

Lodging **Alumni House.** Rooms are plain and clean; the only real plus is their location on the Ole Miss campus. *The University of Mississippi, 38677, tel. 601/234–2331. MC, V. Inexpensive–Moderate.*

Holiday Inn. These functional rooms have no surprises. The restaurant, however, can do a surprisingly good breakfast, though you'll probably choose Smitty's for the biscuits *(see* Dining). *400 N. Lamar, 38655, tel. 601/234–3031. 100 rooms. Facilities: pool, lounge, travel agency, HBO. AE, DC, MC, V. Moderate.*

Oliver-Britt House. There are five pleasant rooms, each with its own bath and color TV, in a restored home built about 1900 and run in a helter-skelter fashion as a B&B. The location, midway between the university and Courthouse Square, is convenient. Lunch and Sunday brunch are served. *512 Van Buren Ave., 38655, tel. 601/234–8043. AE, MC, V. Moderate.*

The Arts

Faulkner and Yoknapatawpha Conference. This week-long event includes lectures by Faulkner scholars and field trips in "Yoknapatawpha County." For information, write to the Center for the Study of Southern Culture, University, Oxford 38677.

Nightlife

Oxford Current entertainers at **The Gin** (E. Harrison St. and S. 14th St., tel. 601/234–0024) follow in the footsteps of Mose Allison and Taj Mahal, who once played here.

The Hoka, (304 S. 14th St., tel. 601/234–3057), a warehouse turned movie theater-restaurant, has been called the "only Bohemian cafe in Mississippi" by author Barry Hannah. Hard wooden booths, jukebox, unbelievable clutter. BYOB to enjoy arty movies and short-order food, especially the cheesecake.

In an old livery stable once owned by Murry Faulkner (William's father), **Syd and Harry's** (1118 Van Buren Ave., tel. 601/236–3194) restaurant/bar has plenty of exposed brick, wooden floors, and a spare Mississippi charm. Music is rock and roll and the blues.

The Delta

"The Delta begins in the lobby of the Peabody Hotel in Memphis and ends on Catfish Row in Vicksburg," said journalist David Kohn of Greenville. In between is a vast agricultural plain created by the Mississippi River and an intimate set of personal relationships.

The Delta inspires passion in its people; outsiders may greet all that flatness with a yawn. The best way to understand the area is to be born in it, in towns like Egypt or Midnight or Alligator. If it's too late for that, try to find some Delta relatives who'll invite you to the famous Delta parties. Hunting and fishing in the Delta's swamps and streams can also give you an entree.

If life should give you only one day in the Delta, use it to cruise down U.S. 61 and the Great River Road (MS 1) from Memphis to Vicksburg. Time it right for lunch in Clarksdale, Merigold, or Boyle, and dinner at Doe's in Greenville. Then on a Saturday night you'll be able to pick up public radio's "Highway 61" with host Bill Ferris, creator and director of the Center for Southern Folk Culture. He'll be playing the blues about the time you glimpse the first kudzu near Vicksburg.

Getting Around

By Car U.S. 61 runs from Memphis through the Delta to Vicksburg, Natchez, and Baton Rouge, LA. The Great River Road (MS 1) parallels U.S. 61 and the river through part of this route.

By Plane Greenville is served by **Northwest Airlink** (tel. 601/335–5362).

By Bus **Greyhound/Trailways** stops in Belzoni (West Side Grocery, 711 Francis St., tel. 601/247–2150), Clarksdale (1604 State St., tel. 601/627–7893), Cleveland (U.S. 61N, tel. 601/843–5113), Greenville (1849 U.S. 82E, tel. 601/335–2633), and Vicksburg (1511 Walnut St., tel. 601/638–8389).

Guided Tours

Vicksburg **Vicksburg Historic Tours, Inc.** Tours of Vicksburg National Military Park and historic homes. *1104 Monroe St., tel. 601/638–8888. Admission: $10–$15 adults, $6–$7 children.*

Important Addresses and Numbers

Tourist Information
Clarksdale-Coahoma County Chamber of Commerce, Sunflower Ave., Box 160, Clarksdale 38614, tel. 601/627–7337. Open weekdays 8:30–5.
Cleveland-Bolivar County Chamber of Commerce. Third St., Box 490, Cleveland 38732, tel. 601/843–2712. Open weekdays 8:30–5 (closed noon–1).
Greenville Chamber of Commerce. Box 933, Greenville 38701, tel. 601/378–3141. Open weekdays 9–5.
Mississippi Welcome Center. 4210 Warrenton Rd., Vicksburg 39180, tel. 601/638–4269. Open Monday–Saturday 8–5, Sunday 1–5.
Vicksburg-Warren County Tourist Commission Information Center. Clay St. and Old U.S. 27, Box 110, Vicksburg 39180, tel. 601/636–9421. Open daily 8–5.
Washington County Welcome Center. U.S. 82 at Reed Rd., Box 6022, Greenville 38701, tel. 601/332–2378. Open weekdays 8–5, Sun. 1–5.

Emergencies
In Greenville and Vicksburg, dial 911. Seek emergency medical help at **Delta Medical Center** (1400 E. Union Ave., Greenville, tel. 601/334–2000) and at **Mercy Regional Medical Center** (100 McAuley Dr., Vicksburg, tel. 601/631–2131).

Exploring the Delta

Numbers in the margin correspond with points of interest on the Mississippi Delta map.

Head down U.S. 61 from Memphis through the Mississippi Delta. Fifty miles south you'll enter **Coahoma County** (from the Choctaw word "Co-i-humma," meaning "red panther"). At **Rich,** swing west on U.S. 49 for a spectacular view of
❶ the Mississippi River from the **Mississippi-Arkansas Bridge.** Continue south on MS 1 to skirt serene **Moon Lake** and **Friars Point.** The levee parallels MS 1 for most of the southbound trip; park and climb up for a look at the "Father of Waters."

❷ At **Rena Lara,** turn west to **Sunflower Landing** on Desoto Lake. Near here, in May 1541, Hernando DeSoto "discovered" the Mississippi River. Return to Rena Lara, backtrack to **Sherard,**
❸ and head east on MS 322 to **Clarksdale.**

As a child, author Tennessee Williams spent time here, visiting his grandfather, the rector of St. George's Episcopal Church. (In Williams's *Cat on a Hot Tin Roof,* Brick was running high hurdles at nearby Friars Point when he broke his leg.)

The Delta Blues Museum is a testament to the important role played by Clarksdale and Coahoma County in the history of the blues. The museum features exhibits and programs highlighting the history of the blues, tracing its influence on rock, jazz, and pop music through videotapes, slides, records, and books. *Housed in the Carnegie Public Library, Clarksdale, tel. 601/624–4461. Admission free. Open weekdays 9–5.*

❹ Continue to **Merigold** on U.S. 61. Here you can taste muscadine wine made at the state's first winery since Prohibition. The **Winery Rushing** uses grapes from the vineyard just across the

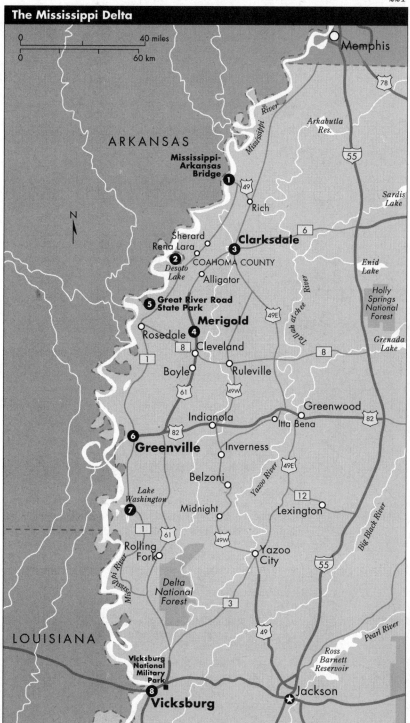

The Mississippi Delta

bayou. A gristmill grinds cornmeal, which is for sale in the Winery's gift shop. You can also eat here in the tearoom, the Top of the Cellar, but you may want to wait because the Sweet Olive at Boyle is not far away *(see* Dining and Lodging). *Old Drew Rd., Box F, Merigold 38759, tel. 601/748–2731. Admission free. Open Tues.–Sat. 10–5.*

The **McCartys of Merigold** are famous throughout the state for their pale stoneware. Their shop features their pottery and handcrafted jewelry; in the spring and summer you may get a peek at their gardens. *Corner of Goff and St. Mary Sts., tel. 601/748–2293. Open Tues.–Sat. 9:30–5. Closed Sun., Mon., and month of Jan.*

From Merigold continue through Cleveland to Boyle if you're planning to lunch at the Sweet Olive, or turn west on MS 8 to pastoral **Rosedale** for sweeping views of the Mississippi River.
⑤ The Great River Road State Park (the world's longest park) has a 75-foot-high overlook tower. *Located off MS 1 in Rosedale, Box 292, Rosedale, 38769, tel. 601/759–6762. Open daily 8–5.*

⑥ From Rosedale, follow MS 1 into **Greenville,** the county seat of Washington County. The city is named for Revolutionary War hero General Nathaniel Greene, a close friend of George Washington, for whom the county is named. The city's history has been dominated by the Mississippi River. The river created the rich soil in which cotton flourished, and Greenville was—and is—the port used by the massive Delta plantations to ship their bales to market. During the Civil War battle for Vicksburg, Union troops burned Greenville to the ground. The citizens rebuilt the town only to suffer a yellow fever epidemic in 1877. Then, in 1890, the city suffered disastrous flooding; levees finally solved the problem after the great flood of 1927. At the turn of the century Greenville developed into a major river port.

Greenville probably has produced more writers than any other city of its size in the country. These include William Alexander Percy *(Lanterns on the Levee)*, his nephew Walker Percy *(The Last Southern Gentleman, The Moviegoer)*, Ellen Douglas *(A Family's Affair, The Magic Carpet)*, Hodding Carter (Pulitzer Prize–winning, crusading journalist), Shelby Foote *(The Civil War, Love in a Dry Season)*, and Hodding Carter III (television news commentator and journalist). The best reason to visit Greenville, however, is to eat at **Doe's** *(see* Dining).

Continue south on MS 1, 17 miles to Lake Washington to tour
⑦ Mount Holly (1856), one of the best Mississippi examples of a Victorian-Italianate house. *Box 140, Chatham 38731, tel. 601/827–2652. Admission: $4 adults, $2 children 12 and under. Tours Tues.–Sun. 1–5. Closed Mon. Bed-and-breakfast lodgings by reservation.*

At MS 436, go west two miles to photograph the vine-covered ruins of **St. John's Episcopal Church.** Only its walls and bell tower remain; its windows were removed during the Civil War so that the leading could be melted to make bullets.

At MS 14, go east to Rolling Fork, then south on U.S. 61
⑧ through fields and wildlife areas to **Vicksburg.**

Vicksburg Near the site of present-day Vicksburg, the Spanish established Fort Nogales in 1790. Vicksburg itself began as a mission founded by the Reverend Newitt Vick in 1814. He chose a spot high on the bluffs above a bend in the Mississippi River, a location that would have important consequences for the young city and for the nation not 50 years later.

During the War Between the States, the Confederacy and the Union vied for control of this strategic location. U.S. Grant's men doggedly slogged through canals and bayous in five futile attempts to capture the city, which was called the Gibraltar of the Confederacy because of its almost impregnable defenses. Then, in a series of raids and battles, Grant laid waste the area between Vicksburg and Jackson to the east and Port Gibson to the south. Grant's attacks on Vicksburg were repulsed once again; he then laid siege to the city for 47 days. On July 4, 1863, the city surrendered, giving the Union control of the river and sounding the death knell for the Confederacy.

The suffering at Vicksburg was profound. The land was devastated; today's green and serene countryside was a region of blasted trees and blackened hills. Vicksburg's **National Military Park** marks the spot where the town was under siege. Battle positions are marked, and monuments line the 16-mile drive through the park. The Visitor Center offers orientation programs and exhibits. A guided tour is a good investment, should time and money ($15 for two hours) permit. The self-guided driving tour is well marked, however, and a cassette tape may be rented for $4.50. *Entrance and Visitor Center located on Clay St. (U.S. 80), 1 mi from I-20, Exit 4B, tel. 601/ 636–0583. 18-min film shown on the hour and half-hour. Admission: $3 per car load. Open daily 8–5; summer 8–6. Closed Christmas Day.*

The Union gunboat, the **USS** *Cairo,* was the first ironclad ever sunk by an electrically-detonated mine. It has been raised from the Yazoo River and restored. A small museum adjacent to it displays Civil War artifacts recovered from the *Cairo. 3201 Clay St., Vicksburg Military Park, tel. 601/636–2199. Admission free. Open daily 9–5, summer 9–6.*

The Vanishing Glory is a multimedia, 15-projector show portraying the sights and sounds of Vicksburg under siege. *Waterfront Theatre, 500 Grove St., tel. 601/634–1863. Admission: $3.50 adults, $2 students. Open daily 10–8.*

Vicksburg's historic homes may have cannonballs imbedded in their walls, but they have been beautifully restored. Worth a visit are **Cedar Grove** (2200 Oak St.), **Balfour House** (Crawford and Cherry Sts.), and the **Martha Vick House** (1300 Grove St.).

A riverboat ride on *The Spirit of Vicksburg* will show you the Confederate gun emplacements, the remains of the steamboat *Sprague,* and activity in the port. *Foot of Clay St., tel. 601/634– 6059. Admission: $5.50 adults, $2.50 children under 12. 1½-, 2- and 3-hr cruises offered daily. Sightseeing, dinner, and dance cruises.*

In 1894 Coca-Cola was first bottled at the **Biedenharn Candy Company,** which is now a Coke museum. *1107 Washington St., tel. 601/638–6514. Admission: $1.75 adults, $1.25 children under 12. Open Mon.–Sat. 9–5, Sun. 1:30–4:30.*

What to See and Do with Children

National Military Park (*see* Exploring).
Biedenharn Candy Company (see Exploring).
The USS *Cairo* and the *Cairo* Museum *(see* Exploring).
Spirit of Vicksburg **riverboat** *(see* Exploring).
Toys and Soldiers Museum. Thousands of toy soldiers, a minia-
ture circus, antique trains, and old toys are on display. *1100
Cherry St., tel. 601/638–1986. Admission: $2 adults, $1.50
grades 1–12, free for preschoolers. Open Mon.–Sat. 9–4:30,
Sun. 1:30–4:30.*

Off the Beaten Track

The **Ethel Wright Mohamed Stitchery Museum** in Belzoni contains pictures embroidered by Mrs. Mohamed, who took up
needlework in her 60s to record her life in the Delta with her
storekeeper husband and eight children. (In some of the works,
she and husband Hassan fly around on the "bluebird of happi-
ness." Some of Mrs. Mohamed's work is in the Smithsonian's
permanent collection. The gallery is in the Mohamed family
home, and the pictures cover every wall. Mrs. Mohamed herself
may be your guide, laughing and adding memories to the
stitchery. "I never pull out a stitch," she says. "Sometimes I
make an ugly face, but I just say, 'You were born that way and
that's the way you'll stay." *The Share Cropper* ($16.50) is a
cookbook with colorful reproductions of Mrs. Mohamed's works
and an entertaining text. *307 Central St., Belzoni 39038, tel.
601/247–1433. Admission free. Open by appointment.*

In Indianola, the **Crown Restaurant** in the **Antique Mall** serves
lunch in a setting reminiscent of an English pub. You can buy
your plate, chair, or table, or the antique English furnishings
and accessories that fill the large restaurant/shop. If you come
here on U.S. 82 from Greenville, you'll pass through prime
antiqueing territory. *MS 448, Indianola. Antique Mall open
Tues.–Sat. 9–5. The Crown Restaurant, tel. 601/887–2522.*

Shopping

Antiques **The Antique Mall,** Indianola *(see* Exploring).

Gifts Climb up into the **Attic Gallery** (1406 Washington St., Vicksburg, tel. 601/638–3987) to see paintings by Vicksburg artists,
pottery, handmade baskets, and local crafts.

Participant Sports

Jogging The hilly roads in the **Vicksburg National Military Park** (I–20,
Exit 4-B, Clay St.) are a challenging course for joggers.

Tennis **Carrie Stern Courts** (Eureka St., Greenville), **Ward Park** (MS
1S, Greenville), and **Clear Creek** (I–20, Bovina exit 7, Vicksburg).

Dining and Lodging

Dining Whether they need to celebrate the cotton crop or bemoan it,
Delta folks love to get together and will drive for hours to party
or eat out. Good food and drink are required; fancy surroundings aren't.

Category	Cost*
Very Expensive	over $20
Expensive	$15–$20
Moderate	$10–$15
Inexpensive	under $10

*per person without tax (7%), service, or drinks

Lodging	Category	Cost*
	Very Expensive	over $70
	Expensive	$50–$70
	Moderate	$30–$50
	Inexpensive	under $30

*double room; add 7% for taxes

The following credit-card abbreviations are used: AE, American Express; CB, Carte Blanche; DC, Diners Club; MC, MasterCard; V, Visa.

Boyle
Dining

Sweet Olive. Lunch and dinner are served in the living and dining rooms of this restored Victorian home. Lunch varies with the chef's whim—chicken in a sour-cream sauce with fruit salad, perhaps, or for dessert, praline cheesecake or ice cream pie. *328 N. Bayou Ave., off U.S. 61 at Boyle, tel. 601/846–1100. Dress: informal. Reservations recommended. Open Tues.– Sat. 11:30 AM–2 AM. Closed Sun. and Mon. No credit cards. Inexpensive.*

Clarksdale
Dining

Chamoun's. The Delta has a large Lebanese community, so Lebanese food is authentic regional fare. Chamoun's is an old Lebanese grocery store, but the real action is at the picnic tables, where visitors try such specialties as kibbie (seasoned lean ground steak with cracked wheat); spinach and meat pies; and cabbage rolls. Daily plate lunch specials include chicken and dumplings, and red beans and sausage over rice. *303 McGuire St. (old Friar's Point Rd.), tel. 601/627–9035. Dress: informal. Reservations recommended for groups. Inexpensive.*

Greenville
Dining

Doe's. This is a tumbledown building, visually as uninspiring as any restaurant you'll find—Formica-top tables, mismatched chairs, mismatched cutlery, mismatched plates—and you're practically eating in the kitchen. But when you see that huge steak hanging off your plate, you'll know why this place is famous. Hot tamales (a popular take-out item) and the house salad dressing (olive oil, lemon juice, garlic) are specialties. *502 Nelson St., tel. 601/334–3315. Dress: informal. Reservations recommended. MC, V. Moderate–Expensive.*

Merigold
Dining

Top of the Cellar. In an old house next door to the Winery Rushing is the Rushing family's restaurant, redone in an Old World style with stucco, half-timbers, and geraniums in window boxes. You'll eat on tables and chairs handmade by a local artisan and dine on plates created by the McCartys of Merigold (see Exploring). The two plate lunches might include seafood quiche or cream of mushroom soup made with Delta oyster mushrooms. A complimentary glass of wine is served. Desserts might include muscadine cobbler or strawberry trifle. *On Old Drew Rd., tel. 601/748–2731. Dress: informal. Reservations required (28-person capacity). 2 seatings for lunch: 11:30 and 1. No credit cards. Inexpensive.*

Vicksburg Dining

Delta Point. This large, elegant restaurant sits high on the bluff, and its picture windows provide excellent views of the Mississippi River. Service is impeccable, the menu varied and ambitious, and the food sometimes erratic. China, crystal, and flowers contribute to the gracious mood. Specialties are beef tenderloin stuffed with marinated Bing cherries; shrimp and fettuccine; and cherries jubilee and bananas Foster. *4155 Washington St., tel. 601/636–5317. Jacket and tie required. Reservations recommended. Sun. brunch. AE, DC, MC, V. Expensive.*

Maxwell's. This candlelit place looks neither tacky nor chic; however, its food is consistently well prepared. It serves a homestyle noon buffet (baked ham and raisin sauce; chicken livers with mushrooms) and goes fancy at night with such specialties as oysters Rockefeller, stuffed mushrooms, fresh redfish with shrimp sauce, and prime rib. Live entertainment. *4207 Clay St., tel. 601/636–1344 or 601/636–9656. Dress: informal. Reservations recommended. Closed Sun. AE, MC, V. Expensive.*

Pemberton Cafeteria. This cafeteria has the recipe for family dining: red vinyl chairs and booths, Southern-style cooking, quick and easy service on trays from the buffet. The after-church crowd flocks here on Sunday. Specialties are fried shrimp, roast beef, shrimp Creole, squash casserole, strawberry shortcake, and Mississippi mud cake. *Pemberton Mall, I–20 at U.S. 71S, tel. 601/636–1700. Dress: informal. AE, MC, V. Inexpensive.*

Lodging

Anchuca. Guests stay in the slave quarters or a turn-of-the-century cottage of this antebellum mansion. Rooms are decorated in period antiques and fabrics. A plantation breakfast and house tour are included. *1010 1st East St., 39180, tel. 601/636–4931 or 800/262–4822. 9 rooms, each with private bath. Facilities: pool, hot tub. AE, MC, V. Very Expensive.*

Duff Green Mansion. This 1856 mansion was used as a hospital during the Civil War. Each guest room is individually decorated with antiques, including half-tester beds. A large, Southern-style breakfast and a tour of the home are included. *1114 1st East St., 39180, tel. 601/638–6662. 5 rooms, 1 suite, all with private baths. Facilities: pool, courtyard, gazebo. AE, MC, V. Very Expensive.*

Cedar Grove. This bed-and-breakfast inn offers mint juleps and Southern breakfasts. Guest rooms are elegantly furnished with antiques. *2200 Oak St., 39180, tel. 601/636–1605 or 800/862–1300. 17 rooms, all with private baths. Facilities: pool, gardens. MC, V. Expensive–Very Expensive.*

Holiday Inn. A large Holiday Inn that looks like, well, a large Holiday Inn, adjacent to Vicksburg National Military Park. *U.S. 80E/I–20, Frontage Rd., tel. 601/636–4551 or 800/HOLIDAY. 325 rooms. Facilities: indoor and outdoor pool, playground, jogging course, tennis courts, game room, gift shop, cocktail lounge, whirlpool. AE, MC, V. Moderate.*

Comfort Inn. Functional, clean rooms in a new motel. *I–20 Frontage Road S., 39180, tel. 601/634–8607 or 800/228–5150.*

50 rooms. Facilities: swimming pool, exercise room, whirlpool, sauna. AE, DC, MC, V. Inexpensive–Moderate.

Nightlife

Maxwell's in Vicksburg *(see* Dining) offers live entertainment in its lounge. **Miller's Still,** in the Velchoff Corner Restaurant (1101 Washington St., Vicksburg, tel. 601/638–8661), opens at 11 AM Mon.–Sat. and at 4 PM Sun., with live entertainment Thurs.–Sat.

6 North Carolina

by Carol Timblin

The author won first place in the Lowell Thomas Travel Journalism Competition and the Discover America Award in 1988, was a contributor to Rand McNally's Guide to Shenandoah National Park, Great Smoky Mountains National Park, *and* Blue Ridge Parkway *(1984), and is the coauthor of* Insiders' Guide to Charlotte.

Bluish purple mountains covered with mist. Clear streams and large expanses of freshwater lakes. Growing cities surrounded by industrial plants and patches of red clay. Pine barrens and golf courses scattered in the Sandhills that were once the beaches of the Atlantic. Great flat fields of soybeans, corn, and tobacco in the east. Fleets of boats and ships anchored at marinas on the Intracoastal Waterway. Tall dunes, sprinkled with sea oats, and long stretches of sandy beaches. A string of lighthouses along a chain of barrier islands, over a hundred miles long.

This is North Carolina. Though its profile is currently changing to high-tech, with a concentration of activities at the Research Triangle Park near Raleigh and the University Research Park at Charlotte, there are no huge megalopolises, and the largest city, Charlotte, has a population of only 390,000. What goes on in the small towns and medium-size cities still sets the tone for much of the state—with great emphasis on civic and church functions, festivals and celebrations, friendliness and hospitality.

In Colonial days, North Carolina produced mostly tar, pitch, and turpentine. During the Civil War, Confederate Army General Robert E. Lee gave the state its nickname—the Tar Heel State. He borrowed the tar heel image from compatriot Jefferson Davis, who alleged he would coat the heels of his soldiers with tar to help them stand their ground.

Geography has dramatically carved out three distinct regions in North Carolina. The Appalachian Mountains give way to the rolling hills of the Piedmont Plateau, which in turn evolve into the Coastal Plain—a stretch of more than 500 miles from the Tennessee border to the Atlantic Ocean. Each region has its own unique place in the state's rich history, spanning four centuries. Charlotte and the capital city of Raleigh lead the state in growth and development, with Greensboro, Winston-Salem, and High Point (the Triad) following. Wilmington is a bustling port city, in marked contrast to the tranquil villages along the Outer Banks. Golf is the recreational focus of the Sandhills, while snow skiing has taken hold in The High Country (Boone, Blowing Rock, Banner Elk). Asheville has maintained its status as a resort city for over 100 years and continues to grow in popularity as a travel destination.

North Carolina has courted visitors since the first English settlers arrived here in 1584. During the Depression of the 1930s, state officials began to realize anew the importance of tourism and put up a hospitality sign. Since then, a good highway system and excellent airport facilities have been developed. Eight welcome centers now serve visitors throughout the state. Tourism is growing here, and industry officials predict it will overtake tobacco and textiles by the year 2000. The welcome mat is out in North Carolina, so make the most of it while exploring and enjoying the treasures of the Tar Heel State.

Charlotte

Charlotte, once a sleepy Southern crossroads, is growing up to be one of the nation's most sophisticated cities—with luxury hotels, world-class restaurants, sporting events, and varied cultural activities. Even stock car racing at the Charlotte Motor Speedway has become trendy with the opening of an adja-

North Carolina

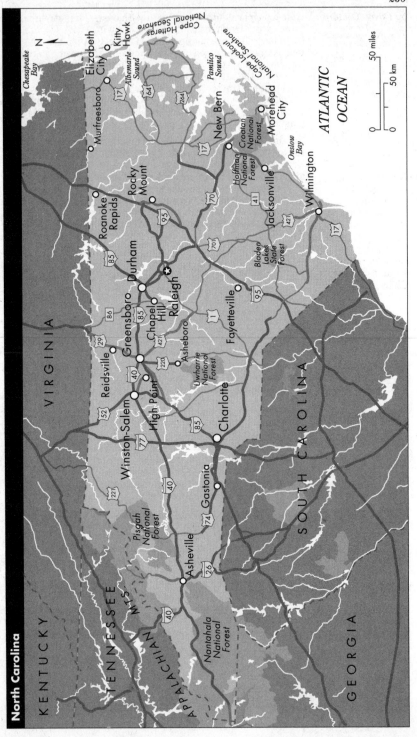

cent $20 million office building and an exclusive Speedway Club overlooking the track. Charlotte is the banking capital of the Southeast and home to national and international corporations that have played a vital role in shaping the city's history. Charlotte-Douglas International Airport is one of the fastest-growing in the country.

Though Charlotte dates to Revolutionary times (it is named for King George III's wife, Queen Charlotte), its Uptown is sparkling new with an ever-changing skyline. In recent years, urban revival has brought people back to the city to enjoy entertainment and cultural events. Cityfair, a complex of shops and restaurants, has recently added new vitality to the city, and further plans call for a new performing arts center to be built at The Square (Trade and Tryons Sts.). The new National Basketball Association team—the Charlotte Hornets—has led the league in attendance during its first season in the new 23,000-seat Coliseum. Hornet mania has gripped the city, with fans wearing teal and purple team colors and sporting various likenesses of Hugo the hornet on their cars.

In spite of all the new glitz and glamour, Charlotte has not outgrown its down-home flavor, and people still love the traditional pleasures of spreading a picnic in Freedom Park as they listen to the Charlotte Pops, politicking and munching barbecue at Mallard Creek Church, or watching the fireworks at Memorial Stadium on the Fourth of July.

Arriving and Departing

By Plane
Airports and Airlines

Charlotte-Douglas International Airport (tel. 704/359–4000), located on the west side of the city off I–85, serves the metropolitan area. Carriers include **American, Delta, Eastern, Pan American, TWA, United,** and **USAir. Henson Aviation** and **USAir Express** provide service to nearby cities and towns.

Between the Airport and Center City

By Bus. You can take a bus into the city during peak business hours (6–9 AM and 3–6 PM). The fare is 70¢ per person. **By Taxi.** To get to the central city, take a taxi or limousine. Taxis cost around $11 per person ($2 each additional person); limousines are approximately $4 per person.

By Car. Follow the road leading from the airport to the Billy Graham Parkway and then go north. Take I–85 north to the Brookshire Freeway (NC 16E) exit. Follow that route to the Tryon Street exit, which leads to the Uptown area.

By Train

Amtrak (1914 N. Tryon St., tel. 704/376–4416 or 800/872–7245) offers daily service to Washington, DC, to Atlanta, GA, and points beyond. Both trains depart in the wee hours of the morning.

By Bus

Greyhound/Trailways (601 W. Trade St., tel. 704/527–9393) serves the Charlotte area.

By Car

Charlotte is a transportation hub of the Southeast. I–85 and I–77, north–south routes, run through the city, and I–40, an east–west route, is 40 miles to the north. U.S. 74, a major east–west route, also serves the city. I–277 and Charlotte 4 are inner–city loops. An outer beltway is planned, but at this time NC 51 is something of a perimeter route around part of the city, connecting Pineville, Matthews, and Mint Hill. Harris Boulevard connects I–77 to the University City area.

Getting Around

By Bus **Charlotte Transit** (tel. 704/336–3366) provides public transportation throughout the city. The Transit Mall has bus shelters on Trade and Tryon streets in Uptown. Fares are 70¢ for local rides and $1 for express service; senior citizens with ID cards pay 25¢ between 9 and 3, after 6, and on weekends. Free bus service is available between Mint and Kings Drive on Trade and between Stonewall and 11th on Tryon weekdays 9–3.

By Taxi Visitors may choose from a half dozen different taxi companies. **Yellow Cab** (tel. 704/332–6161) has a shiny fleet of cars, and **Crown Cab** (tel. 704/334–6666), distinguished by its white cars with a crown on top, gets high marks. Passengers pay a set flat rate.

Important Addresses and Numbers

Tourist Information The **Visitor Information Center** is operated by the Charlotte Convention and Visitors Bureau (229 N. Church St., tel. 704/ 371–8700. Open weekdays 8:30–5. Parking is limited). The **N.C. Welcome Center** (on I–77 north at the North Carolina–South Carolina line, tel. 704/588–2660. Open daily 8–5 except Christmas, New Year's Day, and a half day on Thanksgiving) provides information on Charlotte and the entire state. The **Charlotte-Douglas International Airport** has unmanned information kiosks (open at all times).

Emergencies Dial 911 for **police** and **ambulance** in an emergency. Hospital emergency rooms are open 24 hours a day. **Care Connection,** operated by Presbyterian Hospital, will give physician referrals and make appointments (tel. 704/371–4111, open weekdays 8:30–4:30). **Healthfinder,** run by Mercy Hospital, is a similar operation (tel. 704/379–6100, open weekdays 8:30–5). Another option is the Mecklenburg County Medical Society, which also gives physician referrals (tel. 704/376–3688, open weekdays 9–noon).

Pharmacy **Eckerd Drugs** (Park Road Shopping Center, tel. 704/523–3031; and 3740 Independence Blvd., tel. 704/536–1010).

Guided Tours

Five balloon companies give aerial tours, which end with champagne: **Air Fair Balloons** (tel. 704/522–0965), **Balloons Over Charlotte** (tel. 704/541–7058), **Big Oh Balloons** (tel. 704/563–0818), **Fantasy Flights** (tel. 704/552–0469), and **Windborne Adventures** (tel. 704/376–8955).

Exploring Charlotte

Numbers in the margin correspond with points of interest on the Charlotte map.

Uptown Charlotte is ideal for walking, but some form of transportation is needed for visiting surrounding sites. Buses are adequate for getting around within the city limits; otherwise, you will need a car. Discovery Place provides free parking for its visitors; the Convention Center and Cityfair offer parking at a reasonable rate. The original city was laid out into four wards from The Square, at Trade and Tryon streets. The Visitor Information Center, on Church Street, can provide information on a self-guided walking tour of Fourth Ward and a historic tour of Uptown, as well as maps and brochures covering other areas.

Uptown Charlotte Walking Tour A walking tour of Charlotte may take a half hour or a full day, depending on whether you're interested in shopping, architecture, or history. Take time to stroll down **Tryon Street** and enjoy the ambience of this revitalized area. Take note of the outdoor sculptures and the creative architecture of some of the newer buildings, particularly the **First Union Tower,** currently Charlotte's signature building. During the warm months there will probably be some lunchtime entertainment going on at various plazas. Be sure to wander through the **Overstreet Mall,** a labyrinthian maze of shops and restaurants between the major office buildings.

1 Begin your tour at **Discovery Place,** across the street from the **Visitor Information Center** on Church Street. You'll want to make the hands-on **Science Museum** a priority, so plan to set aside at least two hours for this experience. The museum is for children of all ages. Enjoy the aquariums, the rain forest, and science theater, and check the schedule for special exhibits. The museum has begun an $18-million renovation, which will include an Omnimax theatre to be completed in early 1991. *301 N. Tryon St., tel. 704/372–6261. Admission: $4 adults, $3 senior citizens, $2 children 3–5. Vistascope films $1. Open daily except Thanksgiving and Christmas, weekdays 9–5 (9–6 during June, July, and Aug.), Sat. 9–6, and Sun. 1–6.*

2 **Fourth Ward,** Charlotte's new "old" city, which lies just west of Discovery Place, offers a refreshing change from the newly developed parts of town. A self-guided tour, available from the Visitor Information Center, points to 18 historic sites in the area, including the **Old North Carolina Medical College Building** (229 N. Church St.), where the center itself is located. Be sure to stop by **Old Settlers Cemetery,** just a few paces from the center. Some of the stones date to the 1700s, including the grave of Thomas Polk, a founding father. **First Presbyterian Church,** which takes up a city block and faces W. Trade Street, reflects the prosperity of the early settlers and their descendants. By the turn of the last century, they had built this Gothic Revival complex with stained glass to replace a much simpler meeting house. **Fourth Ward Park** is an oasis in the middle of the city. It is filled with thousands of people during the annual SpringFest. You can't miss the flamingo pink **Overcarsh House** (1879), perched above the park. It is one of two bed-and-breakfast houses in Fourth Ward. **Alexander Michael's** (401 W. Ninth St.), is a favorite eatery. **Poplar Street Books** is housed in the Victorian Young-Morrison House (226 W. Tenth St.). U.S. President Taft spent the night in the **Liddell-McNinch House** (51 N. Church St.) when he visited Charlotte in 1909.

Spirit Square (110 E. Seventh St.), Charlotte's arts center, is under renovation and is expected to reopen in 1990. The Public Library, which includes a mural of a Romare Bearden painting, reopened on North Tryon Street in mid–1989. Open weekdays 9–9, Sat. 9–6, and Sun. 2–6. Cityfair is a shopping-restaurant cluster on College Street.

Charlotte

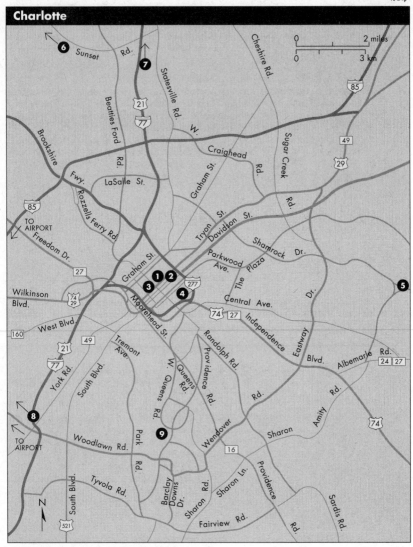

The Afro-American
Cultural Center, **4**

Discovery Place, **1**

The Energy
Explorium, **7**

Fourth Ward, **2**

Hezekiah Alexander
Homesite, **5**

The James K. Polk
Memorial, **8**

Latta Plantation
Park, **6**

The Overstreet Mall, **3**

Wing Haven Gardens
and Bird Sanctuary, **9**

❸ The **Overstreet Mall** is a good place to wind up a walking tour. You'll find some expensive specialty shops and several informal restaurants here.

Other Charlotte Area Attractions Driving Tour Other attractions are spread out across the city, so you may want to concentrate on one or two. You can reach the Afro-American Cultural Center, Hezekiah Alexander Homesite, Mint Museum, and Charlotte Nature Museum by city bus; for visits elsewhere, a car is needed.

From Uptown Charlotte, follow Seventh Street east until you **❹** get to N. Myers Street. The **Afro-American Cultural Center,** a black arts center, including galleries, a theater, and bookstore, is housed in the restored building that formerly served as the Little Rock AME Zion Church. *Open Tues.–Sat. 10–6, Sun. 1–6.*

From Seventh Street, take Central Avenue east to Eastway Drive. Turn left on Eastway and follow it for several blocks un- **❺** til you turn right on Shamrock Drive, where the **Hezekiah Alexander Homesite and History Museum** is preserved as a memorial to one of the Mecklenburg County's earliest settlers. The stone house, built in 1774, is the oldest dwelling in the county. Here, Alexander and his wife Mary reared 10 children and farmed the land. Costumed docents give guided tours of the homesite, including the reconstructed spring house and log kitchen. Special seasonal events, held during the spring, summer, and at Christmastime, commemorate the early days. *3500 Shamrock Dr., tel. 704/568–1774. Admission: $1 adults, 50¢ children 6–16. Open Tues.–Fri. 10–5, weekends 2–5. Closed holidays.*

❻ Latta Plantation Park, located northwest of town (off I–77, near Huntersville), centers around a Catawba River plantation house, built by merchant James Latta in the early 1800s. Costumed guides give tours of the house, which is on the National Register of Historic Places. In addition to the house, visitors enjoy the farm animals, an equestrian center, Audubon center, and the Carolina Raptor Center, where injured wildlife is cared for. *5225 Sample Rd., Huntersville, tel. 704/875–1391. Admission: $1 adults, 50¢ for students in grades K–12. Park open daily 7 AM to dark. House tours are offered Wed.–Sun. at 2, 3, and 4 PM.*

❼ Continue on I–77N to **The Energy Explorium,** operated by Duke Power Company on Lake Norman. Hands-on exhibits allow you to experience the excitement of creating nuclear power and other kinds of energy. A wildflower garden and picnic area offer diversion of a different kind. *McGuire Nuclear Plant, off I–77 and NC 73, Cornelius, tel. 704/875–5600. Admission free. Open Mon.–Sat. 9–5, Sun. noon–5 (June–Aug., Sun. noon–6). Closed major holidays.*

What to See and Do with Children

Carowinds, an 83-acre theme amusement park, straddles the North Carolina–South Carolina line. Young children love the Kids Karnival and teenagers seek thrills on the White Water Falls water coaster. For grown-ups, there are serene rides and Broadway-style shows. The Paladium offers musical concerts with star entertainers. *Carowinds Blvd., tel. 704/588–2600.*

Open daily 10–8; closed Fri. June–Aug.; closed weekends Mar.–Apr., Sept.–early Oct. Call 800/822–4428 for ticket prices.

The Nature Museum, a sister to Discovery Place, is a delight to young children. It features some live animals and exhibits, plus a small planetarium. *1658 Sterling Rd., tel. 704/332–4140. Admission: $1. Open weekdays 9–5, Sat. 9–6, Sun. 1–5. Closed Thanksgiving and Christmas.*

Freedom Park, across the footbridge from the Nature Museum, offers acres of space and a shimmering lake where you can feed the ducks. Children love climbing on the train engine, fire trucks, and airplanes, as well as using the playground equipment. *2435 Cumberland Ave., tel. 704/336–2663. Admission free.*

8 The **James K. Polk Memorial,** now a state historic site, marks the humble 1795 birthplace of the 11th president. Guided tours of the log cabins are available, and the buildings are decorated with fresh pine boughs and candles at Christmastime. Exhibits in the center depict early life in Mecklenburg County. *U.S. 521, Pineville, tel. 704/889–7145. Admission free. Open Apr.–Oct., Mon.–Sat. 9–5, Sun. 1–5; Nov.–Mar., Tues.–Sat. 10–4 and Sun. 1–4.*

Reed Gold Mine, east of Charlotte in Cabarrus County, is where America's first gold rush began following Conrad Reed's discovery of a 17-pound nugget in 1799. Visitors may explore the underground mine shaft and gold holes, pan for gold during the summer months, learn about the history of gold mining, or enjoy a picnic. *Off NC 27 between Midland and Stanfield, tel. 704/786–8337. Gold panning is $3 (group rate $1 per person), but admission is free. Open Mon.–Sat. 9–5, Sun. 1–5 Apr.–Oct.; Tues.–Sat. 10–4, Sun. 1–4 Nov.–Mar.*

The recently renovated **Schiele Museum of Natural History and Planetarium** in Gastonia offers some outstanding exhibits, including one on the natural history of the state and another on land mammals of North America. Visitors also enjoy the living history demonstrations at the pioneer site, as well as the nature trail. *Garrison Blvd., Gastonia, tel. 704/866–6902. Admission free. Open Tues.–Fri. 9–5, weekends 2–5. Closed on Thanksgiving Day and Christmas week.*

The **Spencer Shops–N.C. Transportation Museum,** north of Salisbury, was once Southern Railway's largest repair facility between Washington, DC, and Atlanta, GA. A restored train takes passengers on a short ride over the 57-acre complex, with a stop at the round house. The museum, a state historic site, traces the development of transportation in North Carolina from Indian times to the present. There are some unique train memorabilia in the gift shop. *Off I–85 at Spencer, tel. 704/ 636–2889. Admission free. Train rides $1–$3. Open Mon.– Sat. 9–5, Sun. 1–5 Apr.–Oct. Tues.–Sat. 10–4, Sun. 1–4, Nov.–Mar.*

Off the Beaten Track

9 A visit to **Wing Haven Gardens and Bird Sanctuary** will take you into Myers Park, one of Charlotte's loveliest neighborhoods. The three-acre garden, developed by the Clarkson family, is home to more than 135 species of birds. *248 Ridgewood Rd., tel.*

704/331–0664. Admission free. Open Sun. 2–5, Tues.–Wed. 3–5 or by appointment.

Davidson is a delightful college town several miles north of Charlotte, via I–77. Throughout the year, Davidson College, a small Presbyterian liberal arts college with a national reputation for excellence, offers a number of cultural activities—including plays, concerts, art exhibits, and lectures. The shopping district has received a face lift in recent years. Stop in at the M & M Soda Shop to find out what really goes on in this quaint village. *For more information, contact the Town of Davidson, tel. 704/892–7591.*

Shopping

Charlotte is the largest retail center in the Carolinas. Uptown Charlotte, as well as suburban malls, cater to shoppers' needs. Villages and towns in outlying areas offer some regional specialties. Uptown shops are open 10–5:30 daily except Sunday. Malls are open Monday–Saturday 10–9 and Sunday 1–6. Sales tax is 5%.

Shopping Districts **Uptown Charlotte** is fun and exciting, especially with the addition of *Cityfair*, a 120,000-square-foot retail and entertainment center.

Midtown Square, located in the old Charlottetown Mall (the city's first indoor mall), has maintained a fresh look since it was renovated a few years ago. Here you can find savings at such outlets as the Dress Barn and Burlington Coat Factory.

Park Road Shopping Center is one of the city's first modern shopping developments. It features an old-fashioned Woolworth's store, J.C. Penney's, Bush Stationers, and other shops. *Villa Square*, in Myers Park, houses a number of upscale trendy shops in what was once a private estate built to look like an Italian villa. *SouthPark*, located in the most affluent section of the city, caters to upscale customers. *Belk*, *Ivey's*, *Thalheimers*, *Montaldo's*, and *Sears* are here. *Specialty Shops on the Park*, across from Southpark, is another cluster of expensive shops. *Eastland Mall*, on the east side of town, features an ice skating rink, plus Ivey's, Belk, J.C. Penney's, Sears, and other retail stores. *Windsor Square* is a large complex of outlet stores.

Department Stores *Belk, Ivey's, Montaldo's, Thalheimers*, and *Upton's* all offer quality merchandise.

Specialty Stores The towns of Waxhaw, Pineville, and Matthews are the best
Antiques places to find antiques. Each has a number of shops, and Waxhaw sponsors an annual antiques fair each February. If you want to combine shopping with lunch, Matthews offers a choice of restaurants. Shops are usually open Monday through Saturday in Pineville and Matthews. In Waxhaw, some shops are open on Sunday but closed on Monday. You can also find a good selection of antiques at the Metroliner Expo, which is the first and third weekends of the month.

Books There are some excellent bookshops in Charlotte. Sure-bets are the **Intimate** at Eastland and South Park, the **Little Professor Book Shop** in the Park Road Shopping Center and **Matthews Festival, Poplar Street Books** in Fourth Ward, and **Brandywine Books** on Selwyn Avenue.

Crafts The best buys are in the **Metroliner Expo**. The **Carolina Christmas Craft Show** in October, the **Southern Christmas Show** in November, the **Southern Spring Show** in February, and the **Carolina Spring Craft Show** in late March offer shoppers the opportunity to see a variety of crafts in one setting.

Participant Sports

Bicycling There is a 10-mile designated route between Southpark and Uptown Charlotte. North Carolina has designated tours stretching from the coast to the mountains. Route maps are available from the NC Department of Transportation (Box 25201, Raleigh 27611).

Camping Near Charlotte, try McDowell Park and Nature Reserve, Carowinds and Duke Power State Park. In neighboring South Carolina, try Heritage USA or Kings Mountain State Park.

Canoeing Inlets on Lake Norman and Lake Wylie are ideal for canoeing, as are some spots of the Catawba River. The Pee Dee River east of Charlotte and the New River offer other options.

Fishing Enthusiasts enjoy fishing in Charlotte's neighboring lakes and streams, as well as farther away on the coast and in mountain streams. A state license is required and may be purchased at local bait and tackle shops. For details, contact the Division of Boating and Inland Fishing (tel. 919/733–3633).

Golf Charlotte has several good public golf courses, among them Crystal Springs, Renaissance, and Pebble Creek. The Visitor Information Center (tel. 704/371–8700) can provide a complete list. The renowned Pinehurst-Southern Pines golf area is only a two-hour drive from Charlotte.

Hiking Crowder's Mountain and Kings Mountain near Gastonia and the Uwharrie Mountains east of Charlotte offer plenty of varied terrain and challenge for hikers.

Jogging Jogging trails and tracks can be found in most city and county parks and at many local schools. Contact the Mecklenburg County Parks and Recreation Department (tel. 704/336–3854). or Charlotte Parks and Recreation (tel. 704/336–2884).

Physical Fitness The Charlotte YWCAs and YMCAs will permit guests who have a Y membership in another location to use their facilities for a $5 fee. Many hotels in town also offer fitness centers.

Tennis Courts are available in several city parks, including Freedom, Hornet's Nest, Park Road, and Veterans. A growing number of hotels and motels provide courts as well. For details on city-county courts call the Charlotte Parks and Recreation Department (tel. 704/336–2884).

Spectator Sports

Baseball The Charlotte Knights play April–August at Knight Stadium, I–77 and Gold Hill Road (tel. 704/332–3746).

Basketball The Charlotte Hornets have taken the city by storm. Some tickets are available through the ticket office (tel. 704/357–4738) or Rigby's restaurants (tel. 704/525–5752).

Racing NASCAR races, such as the Coca-Cola 600 and the Oakwood Homes 500, draw huge crowds at the Charlotte Motor Speedway near Concord (tel. 704/455–2121).

Dining

by Peg Robarchek The choice of good places to eat in Charlotte is extremely varied, including many restaurants specializing in international cuisine. Local specialties include barbecued pork and chicken, fresh seafood, fried chicken, and country ham. Hush puppies, made from cornmeal batter and fried in deep fat, almost always accompany fish and barbecue here. Grits is another Southern specialty widely served in North Carolina, usually with breakfast. There is also a wide selection of places that feature steaks and roast prime ribs of beef.

The most highly recommended restaurants in each price category are indicated by a star ★.

Category	Cost*
Very Expensive	over $20
Expensive	$15–$20
Moderate	$10–$15
Inexpensive	under $10

per person without tax (5% in Charlotte), service, or drinks

The following credit-card abbreviations are used: AE, American Express; CB, Carte Blanche; DC, Diners Club; MC, MasterCard; V, Visa.

American **Jonathan's Uptown.** Next door to Spirit Square performing arts
Very Expensive center, Jonathan's is an easy walk from most Uptown hotels.
★ And it is as noted for the lively entertainment in its Jazz Cellar as it is for its food, which changes weekly to highlight the distinctive cuisines of different regions of the U.S. Dinner specialties include sautéed venison loin, grilled or blackened mahi mahi, a variety of steaks, and roast duck with regional sauces and stuffings. Fresh food is flown in every day from Chesapeake Bay, Bayou Lafourche, and elsewhere. Coolly dark and elegantly appointed, Jonathan's has a comfortable bar as well as a roomy dining area. *330 N. Tryon St., tel. 704/332–3663. Jacket and tie suggested. Reservations recommended for lunch and dinner. AE, DC, MC, V. Very Expensive.*

Moderate– **Longhorn Restaurant and Saloon.** Longneck beers, buckets of
Expensive roasted peanuts, and Margaritas that live up to the Texas tradi-
★ tion of being the biggest and the strongest will help you make it through the wait, which stretches to an hour on weekends at this popular watering hole. The atmosphere is loose but not raucous. The menu concentrates on steaks, including a filet mignon as thick and tender as any you'll ever order. *700 E. Morehead St., tel. 704/332–2300. Dress: informal. Reservations not accepted. AE, MC, V.*

Inexpensive– **Catherine's on Providence.** Elegant food is seldom served under
Moderate the same roof with low prices, but Catherine's has cornered the
★ market on this unlikely pairing. Vegetables get an image boost

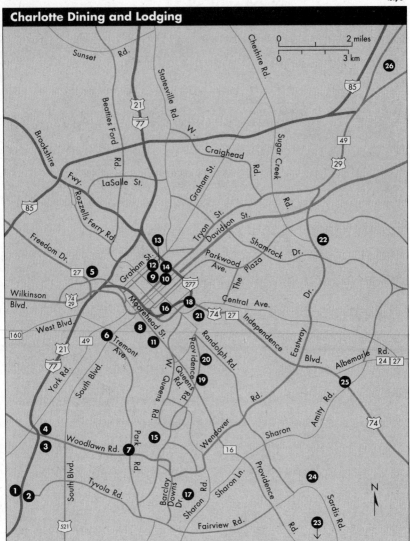

Charlotte Dining and Lodging

Dining

Alexander Michael's, **12**

Anntony's Caribbean Cafe, **21**

Bavarian Haus, **7**

Cafe Society, **15**

Catherine's on Providence, **19**

Dickadee's Front Porch, **25**

Hog Heaven, **22**

Jonathan's Uptown, **14**

La Paz, **20**

Lizzie's, **3**

Longhorn, **8**

The Open Kitchen, **5**

Pewter Rose Bistro, **6**

Lodging

Adam's Mark, **16**

The Dunhill, **13**

511 Queens Road, **18**

Hilton at University Place, **26**

Holiday Inn at Woodlawn, **4**

The Homeplace, **24**

Inn on Providence, **23**

Marriott City Center, **10**

Marriott Executive Park, **1**

The Morehead, **11**

The Park Hotel, **17**

Radisson Plaza Hotel, **9**

The Royce, **2**

at Catherine's, where the menu changes daily. Smothered cabbage, marinated cucumbers, and Greek tomato salad are good examples of the way ordinary produce is transformed into gourmet food. Tender rib roast and roast pork loin with mustard sauce are menu regulars. Breakfast also ventures away from the usual, with homemade corned beef hash, ovenbrowned potatoes, and Catherine's own blend of granola topped with fresh fruit. Soft candlelight and warm woods create a cozy feeling, but the noise level is a bit high for intimacy. *829 Providence Rd., tel. 704/372-8199. Dress: informal. Reservations not accepted. AE, MC, V.*

Caribbean **Anntony's Caribbean Cafe.** This recently expanded diner is al-
Inexpensive most hidden at the far end of a nondescript shopping center on the fringes of the Elizabeth neighborhood. But crowds quickly discovered its low, low prices and extraordinary food. Tender, tangy Caribbean barbecued chicken and Trinidad spareribs are weekday specialties, with the added weekend bonus of four-alarm curry sauce with either beef, chicken, lamb, or beef. Come early: Anntony's is notorious for selling out. *Pecan Point Shopping Center, 2001 E. 7th St., tel. 704/342-0749. Dress: casual. Reservations not accepted. No credit cards.*

Continental **Cafe Society.** This elegant restaurant in a neighborhood half-
Very Expensive way between Uptown and SouthPark is small, quiet, and softly
★ lit. The unobtrusive, strictly professional service is almost as pleasurable as the superbly prepared food. Fine wines by the glass and elegant appetizers—smoked salmon or baked brie— prepare you for a leisurely meal. Pasta for the sophisticated palate and tender veal prepared a half-dozen surprisingly different ways put this establishment at the top of the list for fine dining in Charlotte. *2839 Selwyn Ave., tel. 704/332-1166. Jacket and tie suggested. Reservations recommended on weekends. AE, MC, V.*

Lizzie's. The biggest draw at Lizzie's is the entertainment. The piano bar is packed most nights with people who love to dance to the '30s and '40s standards sung by owner Liz King and other talented vocalists. Sunday evening jam sessions often draw some of the best musicians in town. While food here is average, the prices are not. Highlights are steak tartar, black bean soup, veal Oscar, coconut shrimp, roast duckling flambéed with Grand Marnier, and fresh rainbow trout stuffed with crabmeat. The menu suggests a wine to go with each entree, and also offers to fill any special request if you give the kitchen 48 hours notice. Reservations for dinner in a booth near the dance floor are sometimes your best bet for hearing the show. *4809 S. Tryon St., tel. 704/527-3064. Jacket and tie suggested. Reservations recommended. AE, MC, V.*

Expensive **Alexander Michael's.** This is one of the city's most popular restaurants and watering holes. The biggest attraction is the location, in the heart of restored Fourth Ward, a few blocks from uptown. You'll want to roam the historic neighborhood to walk off your crabmeat quesadillas, shrimp primavera, or chicken in Sauvignon and garlic cream sauce. Alexander Michael's also has a wide selection of unusual beers and fine wines. *401 W. 9th St., tel. 704/332-6789. Dress: informal. Reservations not accepted. AE, MC, V.*

★ **Dikadee's Front Porch.** Owner Nick Colias named his restaurant from childhood memories of his grandmother's front porch. Although nowadays you'll find no front porch on which to enjoy your meal, you will enjoy the homey atmosphere. Desserts are a specialty, including Nick's famous white chocolate Basket of Sin and Sex in a Pan. The Louisiana filet mignon, prepared Creole-style, is one of the best variations on a filet you'll find. All the food is lightly prepared, with the emphasis on delicate seasonings. Intimate dining areas and candlelit tables make this a perfect romantic getaway. *4329 E. Independence Blvd., tel. 704/537-3873. Dress: informal. Reservations accepted Mon.–Thurs. AE, DC, MC, V. Closed Sun.*

French **Pewter Rose Bistro.** Housed in the second-floor loft of a reno-
Moderate vated textile mill in historic Dilworth, just a five-minute drive from Uptown, the Pewter Rose Bistro is a favorite hangout for Charlotte's young professionals. Subtly offbeat in decor, the Pewter Rose specializes in fresh seasonal foods. Highlights of the menu are marinated grilled tuna steaks with a butter seasoned with ground horseradish root; fettuccine with cognac dill cream sauce and optional smoked salmon and caviar; and a decadent chocolate cranberry torte. The bar is pleasant and roomy, filled with comfy sofas and chairs to make the wait enjoyable. *1820 South Blvd., tel. 704/332-8149. Dress: informal. Reservations not accepted. AE, MC, V. Closed Sun., Mon.*

German **Bavarian Haus.** If your schedule is tight, make another choice.
Moderate But if you have time and if a cold, dark beer, sauerkraut that bites back, and—on weekends—conversation to accordion accompaniment have appeal, search out Bavarian Haus. A five-minute drive from the SouthPark area, it offers authentic *wiener schnitzel*, *schweinebraten*, and plump potato dumplings, along with bratwurst and fresh apple strudel. *Park Road Shopping Center, 4151-A Park Rd., tel. 704/523-2406. Dress: informal. Reservations recommended. AE, DC, MC, V.*

Italian **The Open Kitchen.** The overabundance of kitsch—everything
Moderate from college pennants to Chianti bottles strung across an archway—is part of the fun at The Open Kitchen, which has been packing in Charlotteans since 1952. The food is standard Italian fare: spaghetti with practically any kind of sauce you want, lasagna, chicken or shrimp cacciatore, fettuccine alfredo that's a bit too heavy on the sauce, and pizza. But the noisy, boisterous atmosphere and the quickly delivered food give the feeling that you've been dropped into the middle of an Italian family dinner. *1318 W. Morehead St., tel. 704/375-7449. Dress: casual. Reservations accepted. AE.*

Mexican **La Paz.** The food is worth the wait at La Paz. Crowd into the
Moderate tiny upstairs bar, grab a Dos Equis or a Margarita and a basket
★ of chips and hot sauce and be prepared to wait—easily an hour during peak dinner hours. Outstanding Mexican cuisine rewards your patience—*chiles rellenos*, king crab and gulf shrimp *burritos* and *fajitas*. The setting is intimate, if a bit crowded. Located near Uptown, off Providence Road (an extension of East Third Street from Uptown). *523 Fenton Pl., tel. 704/372-4169. Dress: informal. Reservations not accepted. AE, DC, MC, V.*

Southern **Hog Heaven.** North Carolinians are as serious about their bar-
Inexpensive becue as they are about basketball. So don't ask where to go for the best barbecue, just head for Hog Heaven, a tiny restaurant

decorated in Early Auto Racing—complete with checkered flags and laminated photos of racetrack legends. In addition to barbecued chicken or ribs, the beef or pork sandwiches here are generous and filled with the undeniable flavor of long, slow, hickory-smoked cooking. Sandwiches are made with barbecued slaw, so unless you're ready for the full North Carolina experience, ask for your slaw on the side. Homemade pies for dessert. *1600 Purser Dr., tel. 704/535-0154. Dress: casual. Reservations not accepted. No credit cards.*

Lodging

At the rate Charlotte keeps adding hotel rooms, visitors should have no trouble locating rooms: approximately 15,000 are available. You can choose from economy motels, convention hotels, or bed-and-breakfast houses. Most of the major chains are represented, including Hilton, Marriott, Sheraton, and Royce, as are less expensive options—EconoLodge, Comfort Inn, Days Inn, La Quinta, Motel 6, Hampton, Sterling Inn, and Red Roof Inn. Mid-priced motel chains include Holiday Inn, Howard Johnson, Ramada Inn, and Quality Inn. Some hotels offer great weekend packages. New to Charlotte in the past year are The Dunhill Hotel, Compri, Embassy Suites, Days Hotel, and other hotels. A 3% accommodations tax and 5% sales tax are added to every room charge. The Charlotte Convention and Visitors Bureau publishes a comprehensive accommodations brochure on the area (tel. 704/371-8700).

Category	Cost*
Very Expensive	over $100
Expensive	$60–$100
Moderate	$30–$60
Inexpensive	under $30

*double room; add 8% for taxes

The following credit-card abbreviations are used: AE, American Express; CB, Carte Blanche; DC, Diners Club; MC, MasterCard; V, Visa.

Hotels
Moderate–
Very Expensive

511 Queens Road. This all-suite hotel is in the heart of Myers Park, the city's classiest neighborhood. The suites—which have living rooms, dining rooms, kitchens, and bedrooms—are ideal for families. Guests receive complimentary breakfast. *511 Queens Rd., 28207, tel. 704/336-6700. AE, DC, MC, V.*

Expensive

The Dunhill. This upscale small hotel in the heart of Uptown caters to those in search of service and special amenities. Guests are picked up in a Rolls Royce at the airport. High tea, evening cocktails, and a full breakfast are complimentary. Thistles Restaurant serves three meals a day. *237 N. Tryon St., 28202, tel. 704/332-4141 or 800/252-4666. 60 rooms, small meeting rooms, terry robes, guest privileges at YMCA. AE, MC, V, DC.*

Marriott City Center. This high-rise hotel sits in the middle of The Square in Uptown Charlotte. An atrium links the hotel with shops and offices. The lobby is dazzling but not imposing. Guests have the choice of dining in the elegant Chardonnay's or the more casual atmosphere of Sweetbay, which serves great hamburgers. Nightlife is centered in Chatfield's and the Lobby Bar, featuring piano music and complimentary hors d'oeuvres. *100 W. Trade St., 28202, tel. 704/333–9000. 431 rooms and suites. Facilities: indoor pool, whirlpool, sauna, health club, meeting rooms, airport shuttle. AE, CB, DC, MC, V.*

The Park Hotel. The ultimate in class, the Park offers both elegance and intimacy. The decor is 18th century, accented with original artwork commissioned by the hotel. Guests enjoy Morrocrofts Restaurant and Bar and Beau's Lounge. Special amenities include telephones with two incoming lines, and complimentary newspapers. *2200 Rexford Rd., 28211, tel. 704/364–8220. 196 rooms and suites. Facilities: swimming pool, health club, airport limousine service. AE, CB, DC, MC, V.*

Radisson Plaza Hotel. The Radisson set the stage for the redevelopment of Uptown Charlotte a few years ago and has remained a pacesetter. The 15-story hotel is a first-class property offering convenience and contemporary elegance. It is connected to major buildings and department stores by the Overstreet Mall. Guests may choose the casualness of Cafe Promenade or the sophistication of Reflections for dining. There's even a comedy club in the bar. If you join the Radisson Hospitality Club, you get a complimentary breakfast, happy hour drinks, unlimited local calls, and reduced car rental. All guests enjoy complimentary newspapers and free parking. *2 NCNB Plaza, 28280, tel. 704/377–0400. 381 rooms and suites. Facilities: outdoor pool, meeting rooms, airport transportation. AE, CB, DC, MC, V.*

Royce Hotel. This is one of Charlotte's most glitzy hotels. The lobby is all marble and glass. Dining is offered in The Veranda and entertainment in a trendy nightclub called Chelsea's. *5624 Westpark Dr. at I–77, 28217, tel. 704/527–8000. 184 rooms and suites. Facilities: outdoor pool, health club, complimentary airport transportation. AE, DC, MC, V.*

Moderate–Expensive **Adam's Mark.** This is one of the best places in town to have a meeting. The public rooms in this high-rise hotel are large and attractively decorated in rust tones. Rooms on the west side, overlooking McDowell Park, afford great views of the Charlotte skyline. There's a one-mile fitness trail in the park nearby. Guests enjoy dining in the Marker restaurant and relaxing in the adjoining lounge. Appleby's offers more casual meals. The high-energy disco atmosphere of Players Lounge attracts a large following. *555 S. McDowell St., 28204, tel. 704/372–4100. 588 rooms and suites. Facilities: indoor and outdoor pools, Nautilus-equipped health club, whirlpool, sauna, racquetball courts, meeting rooms, airport transportation. AE, CB, DC, MC, V.*

Charlotte Marriott Executive Park. This high-rise property commands a large presence in the I–77 cluster of hotels and motels. The public rooms are attractively decorated in rust colors, and the flooring is made of sand-colored tiles. Guests have a choice of gourmet dining at Ashley's or the more casual atmosphere of The Market. Cahoots is one of Charlotte's hot spots. The hotel also has a raw bar and the only wine bar in the city. *I–77 and Tyvola Rd., 28217, tel. 704/527–9650. 300 rooms and suites. Facilities: indoor and outdoor pools, tennis courts, exercise room, outdoor fitness center, concierge, game room, meeting rooms, airport shuttle. AE, CB, DC, MC, V.*

Hilton at University Place. The hotel dominates the European-style shopping and entertainment village near the University of North Carolina at Charlotte. Movies, restaurants, shops, a bank, and even a hospital are just a few steps from the hotel door. The interior of this high-rise features a three-story atrium. Dining is offered in Justin's, overlooking the adjacent lake. There is a happy hour buffet at the Lakeside Lounge. The 11th and 12th floors offer a number of special amenities, including concierge services, complimentary breakfast, evening hors d'oeuvres, and cocktails. *U.S. 29 and Harris Blvd., 28213, tel. 704/547–7444. 250 rooms and suites. Facilities: fitness center, outdoor lap pool, meeting rooms, airport transportation. AE, CB, DC, MC, V.*

Sheraton Airport Plaza. The atrium lobby is decorated with contemporary furnishings. Golf privileges are available at a nearby club. Amenities include newspapers, fresh fruit, and complimentary cocktail hour on Tuesday and Wednesday. *3315 I–85 at Billy Graham Parkway, 28208, tel. 704/392–1200. 226 rooms and suites. Facilities: indoor/outdoor pool, sauna, whirlpool, exercise room, meeting rooms, airport shuttle, car rental office. AE, CB, DC, MC, V.*

Woodlawn Holiday Inn is the largest of six properties in this chain in the Charlotte area. The contemporary lobby has a marble floor, and the Atrium restaurant resembles a large indoor garden with fountains. Guests have privileges at the American Fitness and Athletic Club on South Blvd. *Woodlawn and I–77, 28213, tel. 704/525–8350. 432 rooms and suites. Facilities: outdoor pool, hydra-spa, health club, meeting rooms, airport transportation, airline ticket office. AE, CB, DC, MC, V.*

Inns
Moderate–Expensive

The Morehead Inn. The historic inn is an attractive alternative to hotel living without sacrificing city convenience. The former private residence is located in the Dilworth neighborhood. Public rooms are spacious and inviting and can be used for corporate meetings. Guests have the option of 12 distinct rooms, each with a private bath. A Continental breakfast is included. *1122 E. Morehead St., 28204, tel. 376–3357. 12 rooms. AE, CB, DC, MC.*

Bed-and-Breakfast
Moderate–Expensive

The Inn on Providence. Another attractive bed and breakfast option for overnight stays. Darlene and Dan MacNeill offer five luxurious bedrooms, each with private bath, plus a home-cooked breakfast. Guests enjoy the spacious grounds and swimming pool in this quiet southeast Charlotte neighborhood. *6700 Providence Rd., 28226, tel. 704/366–6700. 5 rooms. MC, V.*

Moderate

The Homeplace. This spotless turn-of-the-century Victorian gem is now a bed-and-breakfast inn filled with antiques and memorabilia from yesteryear. The inn offers four guest rooms, each with a private bath, and breakfast prepared by owners Peggy and Frank Darien. The Homeplace is located in a country/suburban neighborhood. *5901 Sardis Rd., 28226, tel. 704/365–1936. 4 rooms. AE, MC.*

Nightlife

Nightlife—if by that you mean good music, dancing, comedy, or drinking—has become more sophisticated in recent years with the coming of the larger hotel chains, though the honky-tonk bars are still prevalent.

Cahoots (5700 Westpark Dr. at I–77, tel. 704/527–9650). The walls of the Marriott vibrate from the loud music coming from this hotel bar, a popular spot for young singles.

Comedy Zone (2 NCNB Plaza, tel. 704/377–0400). Get your laughs for the evening at this spiffy club in the Radisson Plaza Hotel.

Grady's Goodtimes (5546 Albemarle Rd., tel. 704/537–4663). There's no live music at this eastside pub-restaurant, but the hospitality will compensate for it. The bartender will know your name after a drink or two.

Jazz Cellar at Jonathan's (330 N. Tryon St., tel. 704/332–3663). This is the place to hear jazz in Charlotte. Maria Howell and the 7th Street Band play here regularly, as well as regional and national groups.

Raleigh
Including Durham and Chapel Hill

North Carolina's capital city appears to be another Atlanta about to happen—from the hustle-bustle on the Beltline to the business deals being made at the 42nd Street Oyster Bar to the new glitzy convention hotels. American Airlines, which operates a major hub at the Raleigh-Durham Airport, offers service to Paris, Cancun, Bermuda, and Puerto Rico.

There's a vibrance in this overgrown college town and capital city that's unique in the state. The Duke, NC State, and UNC (Carolina) basketball teams have all become Atlantic Coast Conference (ACC) champions in recent seasons. Scientific breakthroughs are commonplace at Research Triangle Park, as is important medical research at local universities. People, however, still get as excited over barbecue as they do about politics. The City of Oaks, so called because of its profusion of oak trees, is small town and big town, Old South and New South, down-home and urbane, all in one.

Arriving and Departing

By Plane
Airports and Airlines
Raleigh is served by the Raleigh–Durham Airport (RDU, tel. 919/840–2123), located between the two cities near the Research Triangle Park, off I–40. **American, Delta, Eastern, Pan Am, TWA, United,** and **USAir** together offer over 250 daily flights. **American Eagle, USAir Express,** and **Wheeler** provide regional commuter service.

Between the Airport and Center City
Since airport bus service is not available, the best way to get downtown is by taxi or limousine. Taxis cost $15–$20; limousine service is about half that price.

By Car. From the airport, take I–40 east to Exit 285. Then follow Wade Avenue east and turn right on Downtown Boulevard, which leads into the heart of the city. The drive takes about twenty minutes.

By Train
Amtrak (320 W. Cabarrus St., tel. 919/833–7594 or 800/872–7245) connects Raleigh with Washington, DC and New York to

the north and with Florida to the south. There are two daily trains, one northbound and one southbound.

By Bus **Carolina Trailways** and **Greyhound/Trailways** (321 W. Jones St., tel. 919/828–2567).

By Car I–40 connects Raleigh to Durham, and Chapel Hill with U.S. 401, forming something of a perimeter route around the city. U.S. 70 is also a major artery connecting to I–85 west of the city and to the coast and I–95 on the east side. U.S. 1, which runs north and south, also links to I–85 going northeast. U.S. 64 runs east and west through Raleigh.

Getting Around

By Bus **Capital Area Transit** (919/833–5701) is Raleigh's public transport system. Fares are 75¢ for adults, 30¢ for senior citizens, and 60¢ for adults between 9 AM and 3:30 PM. Children under 4 ride free.

By Taxi Approximately 16 taxi companies serve the Raleigh area. Fares are calculated by the mile.

Important Addresses and Numbers

Tourist Information The **Raleigh Visitor Information Center** is operated by the Greater Raleigh Chamber of Commerce, *800 S. Salisbury St., tel. 919/833–3005. Open weekdays 8:30–5. Free parking.*

The Raleigh Convention and Visitors Bureau offers information on the area. *225 Hillsborough St., Suite 400, tel. 919/834–5900 in Raleigh; 800/552–8666; in NC, 800/868–6666.*

Capital Area Visitor Center offers information about tours through state government buildings. *301 N. Blount St., tel. 919/733–3456. Open weekdays 8–5, Sat. 9–5, Sun. 1–5.*

Emergencies Dial 911 for **police** or **ambulance** in an emergency.

Doctor Hospital emergency rooms are open 24 hours a day. For minor emergencies, the city has 10 urgent-care centers. If you are in need of a local doctor, call the **Wake County Medical Society** (tel. 919/821–2227) for a referral.

Pharmacy **Eckerd Drugs** (3427 Hillsborough Rd., Durham, tel. 919/383–5591).

Guided Tours

Capital Area Visitor Center provides free tours of the executive mansion, state capitol, legislative building, and other government buildings. *Tel. 919/733–3456. Open weekdays 8–5, Sat. 9–5, Sun. 1–5.*

Tours and Functions (tel. 919/782–8145) offers customized tours for groups in Raleigh and the surrounding area.

Exploring Raleigh

Raleigh is spread out, so a car is almost a necessity unless you limit your sightseeing to downtown. Downtown Raleigh offers plenty of parking, including public lots at the corner of Edenton and Wilmington streets and in the 400 block of N. Salisbury

Street (50¢ cents per hour or $4 per day). There's also a big parking garage at the Raleigh Civic and Convention Center, but be prepared to pay hefty fees. Watch for one-way streets when driving. With the city growing so rapidly and confusion over roads mounting, getting around Raleigh without a map is often difficult. The streets in the downtown area, however, are laid out in an orderly grid fashion with the State Capitol as the hub (a good landmark).

Most of the attractions in the downtown Raleigh walking tour are state government buildings and are free to the public. You'll need several hours just to hit the high spots, even more time if you tend to get hooked on museums.

State Capitol After stopping in at the **Capital Area Visitor Center** to pick up
Walking Tour maps and brochures, begin your tour at the **State Capitol,** which occupies the block facing Fayetteville Street Mall in the center of downtown between Wilmington and Salisbury streets. Finished in 1840 and restored during the 1976 Bicentennial, it exudes a special warmth not found in the more contemporary 1960s State Legislative Building. The old building that once housed all the functions of state government could tell many tales if its walls could talk. *Capitol Sq., tel. 919/733–4994. Open Mon.–Sat. 9–5, Sun. 1–5. Closed certain holidays.*

The **State Legislative Building,** on the corner of Halifax and Jones streets, sits one block north of the capitol. When the legislature is in session, the building hums with lawmakers and lobbyists. *Legislative Building, Jones St., tel. 919/733–7928. Open Mon.–Sat. 9–5, Sun. 1–5.*

A half block away is the **North Carolina Museum of Natural Sciences,** a favorite hang-out for children, who love its resident snakes and animal exhibits. The gift shop offers some unusual souvenirs. *1 W. Edenton St., tel. 919/733–7450. Open Tues.– Sat. 9–5, Sun. 1–5.*

Now step back in time at the **North Carolina Museum of History.** Here you'll see exhibits on period costumes, guns, and on many other subjects that chronicle the state's 400-year history. The gift shop is worth a look. *109 E. Jones St., tel. 919/733– 3894. Open Mon.–Sat. 9–5, Sun. 1–6.*

The **Executive Mansion** (200 N. Blount St., tel. 919/733–3456), a brick turn-of-the-century Queen Anne cottage-style structure with gingerbread trim, is home to the governor. Tour hours vary; check with the Capital Area Visitor Center. A stroll through the nearby **Oakwood Historic District** will introduce you to more fine examples of Victorian architecture.

Time Out The **Side Street Cafe** has some of the best sandwiches, soups, and salads in town. *225 N. Bloodworth St., tel. 919/828–4927.*

The **City Market** (Martin St. and Moore Sq.) is coming alive again, after extensive renovations, as new shops and restaurants take up residence. *Open daily 10 AM–late evening.*

Fayetteville Street Mall extends from the State Capitol to the Raleigh Civic and Convention Center. Open to pedestrians only, it offers a chance to get in touch with the city at an easy pace. In the middle of the mall is a bronze statue of Sir Walter Raleigh, who started the first colony in North Carolina and for whom the city is named.

What to See and Do with Children

Pullen Park (500 Ashe Ave., near NCSU, tel. 919/755–6468) attracts large crowds during the summer to its 1911 Dentzel carousel and train ride. You can swim here, too, and enjoy an arts and crafts center and the Theater in the Park.

At the **North Carolina Museum of Life and Science** (433 Murray Ave., off I–85 in Durham, tel. 919/477–0431) visitors encounter life-size models of dinosaurs on the nature trail and get to ride a train through the 40-acre wildlife sanctuary. New at the hands-on museum is an animal habitat featuring native North Carolina animals. The aerospace exhibit is also outstanding.

Off the Beaten Track

Patterson's Mill Country Store. Step back into yesteryear when you visit the store at Leigh Farm just outside Chapel Hill. Browse through the pharmacy or see what a doctor's office was like a century ago. Shop for wooden toys, quilts, antiques, whirligigs—all part of a fine collection of mercantile Americana. *Exit 173 to Chapel Hill off I–40. Farrington Rd., tel. 919/ 493–8149. Open Mon.–Sat. 10–5:30, Sun. 2–5:30. Closed Easter and Christmas Day.*

Historic Hillsborough. Wander through the streets of this colonial town (Exit 164 from I–85, west of Durham). Give yourself time to read the historical markers, visit the Orange County Historical Museum, or dine at the Colonial Inn, which dates to 1759. *Museum is open Tues.–Sun., 1:30–4:30.*

Shopping

Shopping Districts Because so many stores have moved to the suburbs, downtown shopping isn't what it used to be, and the stores that remain now close by 5 or 6 in the evening. The best of the surburban malls:

Cameron Village Shopping Center (Oberlin Rd. and Clark Ave.), Raleigh's oldest shopping center and one of the first in the Southeast, is anchored by JC Penney and Thalhimers.

Crabtree Valley Mall (Glenwood Ave.; U.S. 70) is the city's largest enclosed mall, with over a million square feet of retail space. Stores include Belk, Sears, Thalhimers, Miller and Rhodes.

North Hills Fashion Mall (Six Forks Rd. and Beltline) offers the latest in high fashion. Stores include Montaldo's, Tyler House, and Ivey's.

Brightleaf Square (905 W. Main St., Durham) is an upscale shopping-entertainment complex housed in old tobacco warehouses in the heart of downtown. Shoppers enjoy relaxing at the Duke of York restaurant and pub.

Specialty Stores
Books **DJ's College Textbooks** (2416 Hillsborough St., tel. 919/832–4125) is the place to buy not only used college texts but out-of-town papers and unusual magazines.

Flea Markets **Fairgrounds Flea Market.** You can find anything and everything here—from fine antiques to "early attic" furniture. *Hillsborough St. and Blue Ridge Rd., tel. 919/832–0361. Open weekends 9–5.*

Another option is the **Flea Market Mall.** *1924 North Blvd., tel. 919/839–0038. Open weekends 9–6.*

Food **Farmer's Market.** You can't go wrong on fresh produce at this Raleigh institution, which reflects the agrarian nature of the surrounding area. There's even a restaurant on site. *1491 Hodges St., tel. 919/733–7417 (market) or 919/833–7973 (restaurant). Open 24 hrs, June–September; 5 AM–6 PM, Mon.–Sat., Oct.–May.*

Participant Sports

Bicycling The city has designated 20 miles of greenways for biking, and maps are available at City Hall (tel. 919/890–3125).

Camping Try the North Carolina State Fairgrounds, William B. Umstead State Park, Clemmons State Park near Clayton, or Jordan Lake between Apex and Pittsboro. Other options are Lake Gaston and Kerr Lake near the Virginia line. *For details, call the Raleigh Convention and Visitors Bureau, tel. 919/834–5900, or the North Carolina Division of Travel and Tourism, tel. 919/733–4171.*

Canoeing Lake Wheeler and Shelley Lake are the best places for canoeing. The Eno River State Park near Durham is another option. The Haw River is popular as well, but can be treacherous after a heavy rain.

Fishing Fishing licenses may be purchased at local bait-and-tackle shops. Call the North Carolina Division of Boating and Inland Fishing (tel. 919/733–3633) for more information.

Golf The Raleigh area has more than 12 golf courses open to the public, including **Wildwood Green Golf Club** and **Wake Forest Country Club.** A complete list of courses is available from the Raleigh Convention and Visitors Bureau (tel. 919/834–5900). Pinehurst–Southern Pines, the Golf Capital of the World, offering more than 35 courses, is only a short drive away.

Hiking Jordan Lake, Lake Wheeler, William B. Umstead State Park, and Duke Forest in Durham offer thousands of acres for hiking. For trail information, call the North Carolina Division of Travel and Tourism, (tel. 919/733–4171).

Jogging Runners enjoy Shelley Lake, the track at NCSU, and the Capitol Area Greenway system, which is partially completed.

Physical Fitness The YMCA (1601 Hillsborough St., tel. 919/832–6601) will permit visitors to use their facilities for $3–$10, provided they have a YMCA membership elsewhere. The Y also accepts guests staying at certain local hotels. Hotels with fitness centers are noted in the accommodations listings.

River Rafting The Haw River is the closest place for shooting the rapids.

Skiing *(See* the North Carolina High Country and Asheville—Land of the Sky sections.)

Tennis More than 80 courts in city parks are available for use. Millbrook Exchange Park, (1905 Spring Forest Rd.) holds city tournaments. Call *Raleigh Parks and Recreation (tel. 919/876–2616) for information. Courts are also available at some hotels.*

Spectator Sports

Basketball The Raleigh area is basketball heaven with teams such as UNC–Chapel Hill, Duke, NC State, and NC Central University to cheer to victory. For information on Raleigh's favorite team—NCSU—contact the university ticket office (tel. 919/737–2106).

Dining

Dining is approaching a new sophistication in the Raleigh area, with many upscale restaurants opening around the city in addition to those found in hotels. You can also find informal places where barbecue, Brunswick stew, fried chicken, and lots of country vegetables are served in great quantities for very low prices.

Category	Cost*
Very Expensive	over $25
Expensive	$15–$25
Moderate	$8–$15
Inexpensive	under $8

per person without tax (5%), service, or drinks

The following credit-card abbreviations are used: AE, American Express; CB, Carte Blanche; DC, Diners Club; MC, MasterCard; V, Visa.

Expensive **The Angus Barn, Ltd.** This Raleigh tradition is housed in a huge rustic barn. Gingham- and denim-clad waiters and waitresses add authenticity to the farmlike scene. The astonishing wine and beer list covers 35 pages of the menu. The restaurant serves the best steaks, baby back ribs, and prime rib for miles around. Desserts are heavenly. Take-home products are sold in the Country Store. *U.S. 70W at Airport Rd., tel. 919/781–2444. Dress: informal. Reservations recommended. Sat.—first come, first served. AE, DC, MC, V.*

42nd St. Oyster Bar. This much talked-about restaurant is the place to see and be seen in Raleigh. Politicians, businessmen, and laborers sit side by side downing succulent oysters and other seafood dishes. *West and Jones Sts., tel. 919/831–2811. Dress: casual. Reservations limited. AE, DC, MC, V.*

Moderate **Est Est Est Trattoria.** The best place in town for authentic northern Italian pasta. *19 W. Hargett St., tel. 919/832–8899. Dress: informal. Reservations not required. MC, V.*

Neptune's Galley. In business for many years, this restaurant is known for its fresh seafood. Neptune's is also open for breakfast. *5111 Western Blvd., tel. 919/851–4993. Dress: casual. Reservations not required. Closed Sun. AE, CB, DC, MC, V.*

Bullock's Bar-B-Cue (Durham). If you want to experience local cuisine, try the Brunswick stew, barbecue, southern fried chicken, and hush puppies at this casual eatery that offers eat-in or carry-out service. *3330 Wortham St., tel. 919/383–3211. First-come, first-served (come early). No credit cards. Closed Sun.*

Inexpensive **Fat Daddy's Market & Grill.** A trendy establishment known for its hamburgers. *7112 Sandy Forks Rd., tel. 919/847–3738; 6201 Glenwood Ave., tel. 919/787–3773. Dress: casual. Reservations not required. AE, MC, V.*

Irregardless Cafe. This eatery is a delight to vegetarians and weight-conscious eaters. *901 W. Morgan St., tel. 919/833–8898. Dress: casual. Reservations not required. Sat. dinner only. Sun. brunch. MC, V.*

Joe's Place "Featuring Joe's Mom's Food." If you've got a farm-sized hunger, come here for a heaping plate of home-grown country food. *301 W. Martin St., tel. 919/832–5260. Dress: casual. Reservations not required. Closed Sat. and Sun.*

Lodging

Raleigh offers lodgings in all price ranges—from convention hotels to bed-and-breakfast houses to economy chains. Major hotel chains represented here are Holiday Inn, Hilton, Radisson, Marriott, and Sheraton. Inexpensive lodging is offered by Comfort Inn, Econo Lodge, Crickett Inn, and Days Inn. New on the hotel scene are Embassy Suites Hotel, Fairfield Inn, Hampton Inn, Hospitality Inn–Stony Brook, Quality Suites Hotel, Red Roof Inn, Sundown Inn–North, and others. Most lodgings also offer suites. Since Raleigh is a business town, many hotels and motels advertise special weekend rates.

Category	Cost*
Very Expensive	over $100
Expensive	$60–$100
Moderate	$30–$60
Inexpensive	under $30

double room; add 8% for taxes

Expensive **Holiday Inn State Capitol.** Built in the chain's familiar circular tower design, the hotel is easy to pick out in downtown Raleigh and affords the only panoramic view of the city. Sunday brunches, Friday buffets, and complimentary hors d'oeuvres on weekday afternoons in the Top of the Tower Restaurant and Lounge attract large crowds. The 20-story hotel has a contemporary look. It is ideally situated for people who have to conduct business downtown. Guests enjoy privileges at the nearby YMCA. *320 Hillsborough St., 27603, tel. 919/832–0501. 203 rooms and suites. Facilities: outdoor pool, exercise room, free parking, complimentary shuttle to airport and local sites, newspaper and complimentary Continental breakfast in lobby. AE, DC, V.*

The **North Raleigh Hilton Convention Center.** This is a favorite capital city spot for corporate meetings. The Tower Suites offer a complimentary Continental breakfast, free hors d'oeuvres, concierge, newspapers, and light secretarial service. Guests enjoy dining in Lofton's restaurant and listening to the piano afterwards in the lobby bar. Bowties is one of the city's hottest nightspots. *3415 Wake Forest Rd., 27609, tel. 919/872–2323. 341 rooms and suites. Facilities: indoor pool and spa, complimentary airport shuttle, meeting rooms. AE, DC, MC, V.*

The Oakwood Inn. Located in Historic Oakwood, one of the city's oldest downtown neighborhoods, this is an alternative to hotel/motel living. Built in 1871 and now on the National Register of Historic Places, the inn is furnished with Victorian period pieces. The proprietress serves a sumptous breakfast and gladly assists with dinner reservations and evening entertainment plans. *411 N. Bloodworth St., 27604, tel. 919/832–9712. 6 rooms with bath. AE, MC, V.*

Quality Inn Mission Valley is located on the site of an old Catholic mission near the NC State University campus. Over the years the motel has become a favorite gathering spot for parents and friends attending graduations and ball games. Maybe that's why each room has a card table! The lobby is as inviting as a Southern front porch. Joel Lane's Restaurant attracts a large crowd to its Sunday Brunch. *2110 Avent Ferry Rd., 27605, tel. 919/828–3173. 367 rooms and suites; efficiency apartments by the day, week, or month. Facilities: indoor pool, sauna, exercise room, meeting rooms, mini-conference center in Magnolia Cottage, complimentary airport shuttle. AE, CB, DC, MC, V.*

Radisson Plaza Raleigh. This is an architecturally exciting hotel in the heart of downtown, with brick walls and arches, cascading fountains, and an expansive atrium. The hotel is connected to the civic center via a plaza. The hotel offers the Provence Restaurant, Cafe Promenade, and the Goodies-To-Go deli. *420 Fayetteville St. Mall, 27601, tel. 919/834–9900. 362 rooms and suites. Facilities: indoor pool, whirlpool, free parking, meeting rooms, airport shuttle. AE, CB, DC, MC, V.*

Raleigh Marriott Crabtree Valley. This is one of the city's most luxurious hotels. Fresh floral arrangements adorn the elegantly decorated public rooms. Guests enjoy the intimacy of the Scotch Bonnets restaurant, the family atmosphere of Allie's, and Champions Sports Bar. The concierge floor offers complimentary Continental breakfast and hors d'oeuvres. *4500 Marriott Dr. (U.S. 70W near Crabtree Valley Mall) 27612, tel. 919/781–7000. 375 rooms and suites. Facilities: indoor/outdoor pool, whirlpool, exercise room, game room, golf and racquetball nearby, complimentary airport shuttle. AE, CB, DC, MC, V.*

The Residence Inn by Marriott. This all-suite, apartmentlike property in North Raleigh is ideal if you want to stay for a while or are traveling with your family. Each suite features a sitting area with a wood-burning fireplace and a fully equipped kitchen. The inn will even do all the cleaning and deliver your groceries and wood free of charge. Guests enjoy getting acquainted around the fireplace in the hotel's sunken lobby. *1000 Navaho Dr., 27609, tel. 919/878–6100. 144 suites. Facilities: outdoor pool, Jacuzzi, sport court, guest privileges at nearby racquet club, complimentary newspaper and breakfast buffet. AE, CB, DC, MC, V.*

The Velvet Cloak Inn. Sister to The Breakers in West Palm Beach, this hotel is in a class of its own. Curtis, the doorman who dresses to the nines in a tux and top hat, has been greeting guests here for years. Local brides have wedding receptions around the enclosed pool, and politicians frequent the bar. The Charter Room, an elegant restaurant, often features a harpist. Afternoon tea and cookies are served in the lobby. Rooms in the brick structure, decorated with delicate wrought iron, are frequently refurbished. *1505 Hillsborough St., 27605, tel. 919/828–0333. 172 rooms and suites. Facilities: enclosed pool and tropical garden, complimentary coffee and newspaper in the lobby,* *guest privileges at the YMCA next door, airport shuttle, meeting rooms. AE, DC, MC, V.*

Fearrington House (Chapel Hill). This bed-and-breakfast inn is a member of Relais & Chateaux. It features a restaurant that serves regional food prepared in a classic manner. *8 mi south of Chapel Hill on US 15–501, (postal address: Fearrington Village Center, Pittsboro 27312), tel. 919/542–2121 or 800/334–5475. 14 rooms. MC, V.*

Moderate   **The Arrowhead Inn.** This bed-and-breakfast inn, located a few miles outside Durham, offers alternative lodging in a homelike setting. The innkeepers have refurbished several rooms in this 1774 inn and are in the process of redoing others. Guests are served a hearty breakfast. *106 Mason Rd., Durham, 27712, tel. 919/477–8430. 6 rooms, some with private baths. Closed Christmas week. AE, MC, V.*

Best Western Crabtree. The Crabtree. An upscale version of this usually ho-hum motel chain. It is tastefully decorated in soft colors. Executive and Jacuzzi suites feature wet bars, king-size beds, and private balconies. Rates include Continental breakfast. The six-story motel is near restaurants and shopping. *6209 Glenwood Ave. (U.S. 70), 27612, tel. 919/782–1112. 142 rooms and suites. Facilities: outdoor pool, health spa, meeting rooms. AE, DC, MC, V.*

Brownestone Hotel. This high-rise property adjacent to Pullen Park and North Carolina State University is a favorite haunt of state government leaders. Guests who stay on the executive level receive complimentary wine and breakfast. *1707 Hillsborough St., 27605, tel. 919/828–0811. 210 rooms and suites. Facilities: outdoor pool, privileges at adjacent YMCA, jogging trails in Pullen Park, restaurant. AE, CB, DC, MC, V.*

Plaza Hotel. A full complimentary breakfast is served to guests on weekdays. The concierge level also offers hors d'oeuvres and the use of a computer. This high rise is decorated in bold colors —purple, aqua, burgundy—a refreshing change from standard hotel beige. *2101 Century Dr. (U.S. 70 at Beltline), 27612, tel. 919/782–8600. 176 rooms and suites. Facilities: indoor pool, sauna, complimentary airport shuttle. AE, CB, DC, MC, V.*

Ramada Inn Crabtree. This hotel gets the award for being the friendliest motel in town. It's also where football and basketball teams like to stay when they're here for a game, as evidenced by the helmet collection and other sports memorabilia in the Brass Bell Lounge. The Colonnade Restaurant is known for its Sunday buffets. Rooms have been refurbished recently, and the grounds are spacious and attractively landscaped. *3920 Arrow Dr. (U.S. 70 and Beltline), 27612, tel. 919/782–7525. 177 rooms and suites. Facilities: outdoor pool, jogging trail, meeting rooms, airport shuttle. AE, DC, MC, V.*

Nightlife

Much of the nightlife is centered in the larger hotels, such as the Hilton or the Marriott. **Cat's Cradle** (320 W. Franklin St., Chapel Hill, tel. 919/967–9053) is the place for rock 'n' roll, reggae, and New Wave sounds. **Charlie Goodnight's Comedy Club** (861 W. Morgan St., tel. 919/833–8356) combines dinner with a night of laughs. Mexican dishes are featured in the restaurant downstairs, steak and seafood upstairs.

Winston-Salem

The manufacture of cigarettes, textiles, furniture, and other products has built a solid economic base in the Winston-Salem area. There's also a healthy respect for the arts here. The North Carolina School of the Arts commands international attention. The Crosby golf tournament, formerly played at Pebble Beach, California, attracts the rich and famous. Old Salem, an 18th-century Moravian town within the city of Winston-Salem, has been drawing tourists since the late 1940s.

Arriving and Departing

By Plane Six major airlines serve the Piedmont Triad International Airport: **American, Delta, Eastern, Continental, United,** and **USAir.**

By Bus Contact **Greyhound/Trailways** (tel. 919/725–5692).

By Train One daily northbound and one southbound **Amtrak** train serve Greensboro (tel. 919/855–3382), about 25 miles away.

Important Addresses and Numbers

Tourist Information **Winston-Salem Convention and Visitors Bureau** (Box 1408, Winston-Salem 27102, tel. 919/725–2361 or 800/331–7018).

Emergencies Dial 911 for **police** and **ambulance** in an emergency.

Guided Tours

Contact **Piedmont Guides** (Box 10254, Greensboro 27404, tel. 919/282–8687) for group tours to Triad attractions.

Exploring Winston-Salem

Old Salem is just a few blocks from downtown Winston-Salem and only a stone's throw from I–40 (take the Old Salem/Salem College exit). The 1700s live again in this village of 60 original brick and wooden structures. The aromas of freshly baked bread, sugar cakes, and ginger snaps mix with those of beeswax candles and newly dyed flax. Tradesmen work in their shops making pewterware, cooking utensils, and other items, while the womenfolk embroider and weave cloth. The Moravians, a Protestant sect, fled to Georgia to find religious freedom. From there they went to Bethlehem, Pennsylvania, but finally found the peace they sought in the Piedmont region of North Carolina. In 1753, they built Bethabara, located on Bethabara Road., off University Parkway, and then in 1766 they built Salem. Tour tickets will get you into several restored buildings at Old Salem, but you may wander through the streets free of charge. *600 S. Main St., tel. 919/721–7300. Admission: $12 adults, $6 children ages 6–14; families $25; check into combination ticket to MESDA. Open Mon.–Sat. 9:30–4:30, Sun. 1:30–4:30.*

Time Out **Winkler Bakery** will satisfy your craving for hot, freshly baked Moravian sugar cake. The bakery is included on tours and is also open to the public. *S. Main St., tel. 919/721–7302. Open Mon.–Sat. 9:30–4:30.*

Another way to step back into time is to enter the **Museum of Early Southern Decorative Arts (MESDA)**. Twenty rooms are decorated with period furnishings. *924 S. Main St., tel. 919/721–7360. Admission: full tour $6 adults, $3 children, ages 6–14; sampler tour $4 adults, $2 children ages 6–14. Open Mon.–Sat. 10:30–5, Sun. 1:30–4:30.*

Stroh Brewery, approximately 5 miles south of downtown via U.S. 52, rolls out 5.5 million barrels of beer a year as the second-largest brewery in the country. A single machine can fill and seal up to 1,500 12-ounce cans of beer per minute. You can see it made and enjoy a complimentary drink. *Schlitz Ave., U.S. 52S at S. Main St., tel. 919/788–6710. Admission free. Open weekdays 11–4:30.*

Historic **Bethabara Park** is another vision from the 1700s. You can explore the foundations of the town, as well as the three remaining historic structures. Kids love the reconstructed Indian fort. *2147 Bethabara Rd., tel. 919/924–8191. Admission free. Open weekdays 9:30–4:30, weekends 1:30–4:30. Guided tours Apr.–Dec. 15 or by appointment.*

Reynolda House is the lavish 60-room home of the late R. J. Reynolds, the tobacco king, that today houses an outstanding collection of American art. While you're on the estate, take time also to see the gardens and the stables, dairy barn, and other outbuildings now serving as a shopping complex. The house will close for renovations in September and reopen in late 1991. *Reynolda Rd., tel. 919/725–5325. Admission: $5 adults, $3 children and senior citizens. Open Tues.–Sat. 9:30–4:30, Sun. 1:30–4:30. Closed Mon.*

SECCA (the Southeastern Center for Contemporary Art) is near Reynolda House. This unique museum is the place to see the latest in Southern painting, sculpture, and printmaking. The Tudor-style facility, the former home of the late James G. Hanes, a textile industrialist, is as interesting as the exhibits. *750 Marguerite Dr., tel. 919/725–1904. Admission free. Open Tues.–Sat. 10–5, Sun. 2–5.*

Tanglewood Park (Hwy. 158, Clemmons, tel. 919/766–0591), a 10-minute drive west from the city via I–40, is the former home of the late William and Kate Reynolds and today serves as a public park. Visitors enjoy horseback riding, golf, tennis, boating, miniature golf, swimming, and an array of other activities, including PGA golf events and polo games. Overnight accommodations range from camping to rooms in the manor house.

What to See and Do with Children

Nature Science Center of Winston Salem. Look at the stars, handle live starfish in the tidal pool, pet the lambs and goats. *Museum Dr., Winston-Salem, tel. 919/767–6730. Admission: $3 adults, children $2. Open Mon.–Sat. 10–5, Sun. 1–5.*

Shopping

Crafts The *New York Times* called the **Piedmont Craftsmen's Shop and Gallery** a "showcase for Southern crafts." *411 N. Cherry St., 919/725–8243. Open weekdays 10–6, Sat. 10–5, Sun. 1–5.*

Outlets This is a textile center, so there are many clothing outlets clustered along the interstates. **Marketplace Mall** (2101 Peters Creek Pkwy., tel. 919/722–7779) is one option. The 100 stores in **Burlington Manufacturers Outlet Center** (tel. 919/227–2872) and **Waccamaw Pottery and the Burlington Outlet Mall** (tel. 919/229–0418) make the area off I–85 near Burlington truly the outlet capital of the South. *Most stores are open Mon.–Sat. 10–9, Sun. 1–6.*

Spectator Sports

Polo On Sunday afternoons (Apr.–June and Sept.–Nov.) polo players entertain the crowds at Tanglewood Park. Contact the Forsyth County Park Authority, Inc. (Box 1040, Clemmons 27012, tel. 919/766–0591).

Dining

Traditional dining in these parts is Southern—fried chicken, ham, vegetables, biscuits, fruit cobblers, and the like. Chopped or sliced pork barbecue is also a big item. With the area becoming so sophisticated, though, there's a growing number of gourmet restaurants.

Category	Cost*
Very Expensive	over $25
Expensive	$15–$25
Moderate	$8–$15
Inexpensive	under $8

per person without tax (4.5%), service, or drinks

The following credit-card abbreviations are used: AE, American Express; CB, Carte Blanche; DC, Diners Club; MC, MasterCard; V, Visa.

Expensive **La Chadiere.** Elegantly prepared French country dishes of pheasant, rabbit, veal, and other delicacies are served here in a country French atmosphere. Soft white walls, original paintings, and fresh flowers set off this restaurant in Reynolda Village. *120 Reynolda Rd., tel. 919/748–0269. Reservations strongly recommended. Closed Mon. AE, DC, MC, V.*

Moderate– **Old Salem Tavern Dining Room.** Eat Moravian food in a
Expensive Moravian setting served by waiters in Moravian costumes, all in the heart of Old Salem. Standard menu items are chicken pie, ragout of beef, and rack of lamb. From April through October you can dine outside under the arbor. *736 S. Main St., tel. 919/748–8585. Sun. brunch. Closed Thanksgiving, Christmas Eve, and Christmas Day. AE, MC, V.*

Moderate **Leon's Cafe.** This casual eatery near Old Salem serves some of the best gourmet food in town—fresh seafood, chicken breasts with raspberry sauce, lamb, and other specialties. *825 S. Marshall, tel. 919/725–9593. Reservations not accepted. No lunch. Closed Sun.–Tues., New Year's Day, Thanksgiving, Christmas, and the last two weeks in August. MC, V.*

Zevely House. Dine on chicken or game bird in a restored 19th-century house or in the adjoining garden. A children's menu is available. *Tel. 919/725–6666. Reservations advised. Closed for lunch on Mon. and Sat., New Year's Day and Christmas Day. AE, MC, V.*

Stars at Stevens Center. Have preview cocktails and dinner, then enjoy a play or concert, and come back for coffee and dessert afterwards—all in a restored Art Deco performing arts center in the heart of downtown Winston-Salem. *401 W. 4th St., tel. 919/761–0476. Reservations advised. No lunch. Closed New Year's Day, Thanksgiving, Christmas Eve, and Christmas Day. AE, CB, MC, V.*

Lodging

Category	Cost*
Very Expensive	over $100
Expensive	$60–$100
Moderate	$30–$60
Inexpensive	under $30

**double room; add 7.5% for taxes*

The following credit-card abbreviations are used: AE, American Express; CB, Carte Blanche; DC, Diners Club; MC, MasterCard; V, Visa.

Very Expensive **Hyatt Winston-Salem.** This downtown property features an atrium and garden terrace. Redecorated in pastel colors, its large guest rooms have a soft contemporary look. *300 W. 5th St., 27101, tel. 919/725–1234 or 800/228–9000. 288 rooms. Facilities: indoor pool, Jacuzzi, exercise room; garage parking and airport transportation extra. AE, CB, DC, MC, V.*

Stouffer Winston Plaza. This hotel is centrally located, off I–40. The hotel has almost 10,000 square feet of meeting space that can be augmented by facilities at the Convention Center across the street. *425 N. Cherry St., 27101, tel. 919/725–3500. 318 rooms. Facilities: 2 restaurants, bar, indoor/outdoor pool, steam room, sauna, game room, and gift shop. AE, DC, MC, V.*

Moderate–Expensive **Brookstown Inn.** Sleep under a comfy handmade quilt in front of the fireplace or enjoy wine and cheese in the spacious lobby of this unusual bed-and-breakfast hotel, built in 1837 as one of the first textile mills in the South. Breakfast is included. *200 Brookstown Ave., 27102, tel. 919/725–1120. 52 rooms. Facilities: some rooms with whirlpools, airport transportation. AE, MC, V.*

Moderate **Ramada Hotel.** This hotel caters to convention and business clientele, with a spacious lobby decorated in beige and green. *420 High St., 27103, tel. 919/723–7911 or 800/2–RAMADA. 173 rooms. Facilities: John Casper's Lounge featuring comedy shows Fri. and Sat., restaurant, 7 meeting rooms, ballroom, outdoor pool, and van service to the airport. AE, DC, MC, V.*

Outer Banks and Historic Albemarle

North Carolina's Outer Banks are made up of a series of barrier islands stretching from the Virginia state line southward to Cedar Island. Throughout history they have posed a threat to ships, and hence the area became known as the Graveyard of the Atlantic. A network of lighthouses and lifesaving stations was built to make the Outer Banks safer for navigators. English settlers attempted to colonize the region more than 400 years ago, but the first colony disappeared mysteriously, without a trace. Their plight is retold in an annual outdoor drama, "The Lost Colony." The islands offered seclusion and privacy to pirates who hid out in the coves and inlets. The notorious pirate Blackbeard lived and died here. For many years the Outer Banks remained isolated, home only to a few families who made their living by fishing. Today the islands, linked by bridges and ferries, are popular among summer tourists. Much of the area is included in the Cape Hatteras National Seashore. The largest towns on the islands are Manteo and Nags Head.

On the inland side of the Outer Banks is the Historic Albemarle Region, a remote area of small villages and towns surrounding Albemarle Sound. Edenton served as the Colonial capital for a while, and today many of its early structures are preserved for posterity.

Getting Around

By Plane　The closest commercial airports are the Raleigh-Durham Airport and Norfolk International, both of which are served by major carriers, including **American, Continental, Delta, Eastern, Pan Am,** and **USAir.**

By Train　**Amtrak** service (tel. 800/872–7245) is available to Norfolk, VA, about 75 miles to the north.

By Car　U.S. 158 links Manteo with Norfolk and other places north. U.S. 64 and 264 are western routes. NC 12 goes south toward Ocracoke Island and north toward Corolla. Toll ferries connect Ocracoke to Cedar Island and Swan Quarter. There is a free ferry across Hatteras Inlet.

By Taxi　**Roy's Taxi Service** (tel. 919/441–6459 or nights 473–2726) serves the Outer Banks.

By Boat　Seagoing visitors travel the Intracoastal Waterway through the Outer Banks and Historic Albemarle region. Boats may dock at Elizabeth City Manteo (the Salty Dawg Marina), and other ports.

Guided Tours

Historic Albemarle Tour, Inc., (Box 759, Edenton 27932, tel. 919/482–7325), offers guided tours of Edenton and publishes a brochure on a self-guided tour of the Albemarle Region.

Kitty Hawk Aerotours (tel. 919/441–4460) leave from the First Flight Airstrip for Kitty Hawk, Corolla, Cape Hatteras, Ocracoke, Portsmouth Island, and other areas along the Outer Banks. *Mar.–Labor Day.*

Ocracoke Trolley Tours (of Ocracoke Island) depart from Trolley Stop One. NC 12, Ocracoke. Tel. 919/928–4041. *June–Labor Day, Mon.–Sat.*

Important Addresses and Numbers

Tourist Information **Dare County Tourist Bureau,** (Box 399, Manteo, tel. 919/473–2138). Historic Albemarle Tour, Inc. (Box 759, Edenton 27932, tel. 919/482–7325). Outer Banks Chamber of Commerce (Box 1757, Kill Devil Hills 27948, tel. 919/441–8144).

Emergencies Dial 911 if you are north of Oregon Inlet and Roanoke Island; 919/986–2144 for Hattaras Island; 919/928–4631 for Ocracoke. The Outer Banks Medical Center at Nags Head is open 24 hours a day, tel. 919/441–7111.

Coast Guard Tel. 919/995–5881.

Exploring the Outer Banks

Numbers in the margin correspond with points of interest on the Outer Banks map.

You can begin your tour of the Outer Banks from either the southern end of the barrier islands at Cedar Island or the northern end at Nags Head. Unless you're camping, overnight stays will probably be in Ocracoke or in the Nags Head-Manteo area, where motels and hotels are concentrated. (There's also a motel at Cedar Island on the mainland where you catch the ferry to Ocracoke.) You can drive the 70-mile stretch of barrier islands in a day, but be sure to allow plenty of time during the summer season in case you have to wait for the next ferry to the mainland. A complete schedule is included on the state map. For reservations, call 919/225–3551 for departures from Cedar Island, 919/928–3841 from Ocracoke, or 919/926–1111 from Swan Quarter. Be wary of getting stranded on the islands during major storms and hurricanes when the roads and bridges become clogged with traffic.

① **Kill Devil Hills,** on U.S. 158 Bypass, midway between Kitty Hawk and Nags Head, is such an unimpressive location, it's hard to believe its historical significance as the site of man's first flight. The **Wright Brothers National Memorial,** a granite monument that resembles the tail of an airplane, stands as a tribute to Wilbur and Orville Wright, two bicycle mechanics from Ohio who took to the air on December 17, 1903. You can see a replica of *The Flyer* and stand on the exact spot where it made four take-offs and landings, the longest being a distance of 852 feet. Exhibits and an informative talk by a National Park Service ranger make the thrilling event come to life again. The Wrights' accomplishment was no easy task in this remote area of the world in those days. Without roads or bridges, they had to bring in the airplane unassembled. They also had to bring in all their food and supplies and build a camp (the Wrights at first used tents and later built a wooden storage shed, as well as living quarters). Wilbur and Orville made four trips to the site, beginning in 1900, each time conducting experiments to determine how to achieve their goal. The annual Wilbur Wright Fly-In, held at the Dare County Regional Airport every spring, attracts vintage aircraft from all over the country. Contact the *Superintendent, National Park Service, U.S. Department of*

The Outer Banks

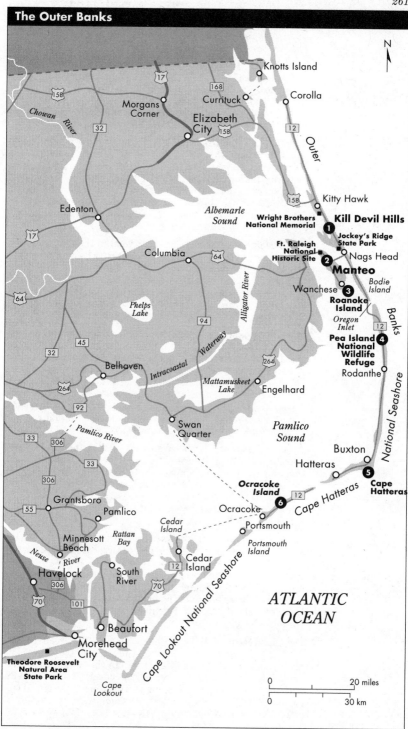

N

Knotts Island
Corolla
Currituck
Morgans Corner
Elizabeth City
Chowan River
Outer
[17]
[158]
[168]
[32]
[12]

Edenton
Albemarle Sound
Kitty Hawk
Wright Brothers National Memorial
Kill Devil Hills ❶
Jockey's Ridge State Park
[158]

Columbia
Ft. Raleigh National Historic Site
Nags Head
Manteo ❷
[64]
Wanchese
Roanoke Island ❸
Bodie Island

[64]
Phelps Lake
Alligator River
Oregon Inlet
[94]
[12]
Banks
Pea Island National Wildlife Refuge ❹

[32]
[45]
Intracoastal Waterway
[264]
Rodanthe
National Seashore

Belhaven
[92]
Mattamuskeet Lake
Engelhard
Pamlico Sound

Pamlico River
Swan Quarter
Buxton
Hatteras
Cape Hatteras ❺

[33]
[306]
Grantsboro
Pamlico
Ocracoke Island ❻
Ocracoke
[12]
Cape Hatteras
[55]
[33]
[306]
Cedar Island
Portsmouth
Portsmouth Island
Rattan Bay
Minnesott Beach
Neuse River
[12] Cedar Island
Havelock
South River
[70]
[306]
[70]
[101]
Cape Lookout National Seashore

ATLANTIC OCEAN

Beaufort
Morehead City
Theodore Roosevelt Natural Area State Park
Cape Lookout

| 0 | | 20 miles |
| 0 | 30 km | |

*the Interior, Rte. 1, Box 675, Manteo 27954, tel. 919/441–7430.
Admission $3 per car, $1 per person, Golden Passport holders
and those under 16 and over 65 free. Open daily 9–5 with extended hours in the summertime.*

A few miles south of Kill Devil Hills, via U.S. 158 Bypass, is
Jockey's Ridge State Park, the tallest sand dune in the East and
a popular spot for hang gliding and kite flying. You can join in
the activities and have a picnic here. *Rte. 158 Bypass, Milepost
12, tel. 919/441–7132. Admission free. Open daily sunrise to
sunset.*

❷ Take U.S. 64-264 from U.S. 158 Bypass to reach **Manteo** and
❸ **Roanoke Island,** the site of several attractions, including the
Elizabethan Gardens, "The Lost Colony" Waterside Amphitheatre, and Fort Raleigh. The lush gardens were established
as a memorial to the first English colonists. *U.S. 64, Manteo,
tel.919/473–3234. Admission: $2 adults, children under 12
free when accompanied by an adult. Open Mar.–Nov., daily
9–5; Dec.–Jan., weekdays 9–5.*

Fort Raleigh is a reconstruction of what is thought to be the
original fort of the first Carolinian colonists. Be sure to see the
orientation film and then take a guided tour of the fort. A nature trail leads to an outlook over Roanoke Sound. On special
occasions, musicians play 16th-century music in the visitor center. *Tel. 919/473–2111. Admission free. Open Sept.–May 9–5;
June–Aug., Mon.–Sat. 9–8; and Sun. 9–6.*

"The Lost Colony" outdoor drama reenacts the story of the first
colonists who settled here in 1584 and then disappeared during
the time that some of their party returned to England for supplies. The drama celebrated its own 50th anniversary in 1987.
*Tel. 919/473–3414. Admission: $10 adults, $4 children under
12. Reservations suggested. Performances are given from mid-
June until late Aug., Mon.–Sat. at 8:30 PM. Backstage tours
are offered afternoons, mid-June–Aug. (see the play first).
Admission: $3 adults, $1.50 children under 12.*

A short distance from Waterside Amphitheatre is the
Elizabeth II State Historic Site, a 16th-century sailing vessel
that was recreated to commemorate the 400th anniversary of
the landing of the first colonists on Roanoke Island. *Downtown
Manteo, tel. 919/473–1144. Admission: $3 adults, $2 senior citizens, $1.50 children.Open Nov.–Mar., Tues.–Sun. 10–4;
Apr.– Oct. 10–6.*

Resume your journey southward on the Outer Banks via NC 12,
a road that will take you all the way to Ocracoke Island. On the
way you will pass over **Oregon Inlet Bridge,** which arches for
three miles over the treacherous channel of water between the
ocean and Pamlico Sound. Since the bridge was built, fishing
conditions have declined. The bridge connects Bodie Island to
Hatteras Island, most of which belongs to the Cape Hatteras
National Seashore.

❹ **Pea Island National Wildlife Refuge,** on NC 12 between Oregon
Inlet and Rodanthe, is made up of more than 5,000 acres of
marsh that serves as wildlife refuge. In this vicinity was the
Pea Island Life Saving Station, whose courageous crew, led by
Richard Etheridge, made daring rescues during the late 1800s
and early 1900s. *Pea Island Refuge Headquarters, tel. 919/987–
2394. Open Apr.–Nov. weekdays 8–4.*

⑤ Cape Hatteras Lighthouse, about 30 miles south of Rodanthe, sits as a beacon to ships offshore. Threatened by erosion from the sea, the 208-foot lighthouse has been rescued numerous times by sandbagging and other methods, and its fate is still under debate. Offshore lie the remains of the *Monitor*, a Confederate ironclad ship that sank in 1862. The visitor center offers information on the national seashore. *Hatteras Island Visitor Center, tel. 919/995–4474. Open Sept.–May 9–5, June–Aug. 9–6.*

At Hatteras, board the free ferry to Ocracoke Island. Boats leave every 40 minutes, and the journey takes about half an hour.

⑥ Ocracoke Island was cut off from the world for so long that native residents still speak in quasi-Elizabethan accents; today, however, the island is a refuge for tourists. There is a village of shops, motels, and restaurants around the harbor where the infamous pirate Blackbeard met his death in 1718. The Ocracoke Lighthouse is a photographer's dream. *For information, contact the Ocracoke Visitor Center on Cedar Island, tel. 919/928–4531.*

Beaches

More than 70 miles of unspoiled beaches stretch from Nags Head to Ocracoke Island. Preserved as Cape Hatteras National Seashore, this coastal area is ideal for swimming, surfing, windsurfing, diving, boating, and any number of water activities. If you want to swim, stay in areas where there are lifeguard stations—Coquina Beach, Salvo, Cape Hatteras, Frisco, and Ocracoke. Nags Head (so named because Bankers would tie lanterns around the heads of their horses to lure merchant ships), is the most commercial beach area, with lifeguards stationed near motels and hotels. You can explore the *Laura Barnes* shipwreck site at Coquina Beach, considered the best swimming hole on the Outer Banks. Facilities here include picnic shelters, restrooms, showers, and bath houses. Divers and surfers enjoy practicing their antics around Cape Hatteras.

Participant Sports

Camping Camping is permitted in designated areas all along the Cape Hatteras National Seashore. All campgrounds in the park have cold showers, drinking water, tables, grills, and restrooms (except Ocracoke, which has pit toilets). Sanitary stations for recreational vehicles are located at Oregon Inlet, Cape Point at Cape Hatteras, and Ocracoke. Oregon Inlet, Cape Point, and Ocracoke are open from mid-April through mid-October; Salvo and Frisco, mid-June to late August. Be sure to take along extra-long tent stakes for sand, and don't forget the insect repellent. During the summer it's wise to make reservations through Ticketron offices, either in person or by writing the Ticketron headquarters at Box 2715, San Francisco, CA 94126. In addition to campsites in the National Seashore, there are many private campgrounds scattered along the Outer Banks. For information contact the North Carolina Travel and Tourism Division. tel. 919/733–4171 or 800/847–4862; ask for the *NC Camping and Outdoor Directory*.

Fishing This area is a paradise for fisherman who enjoy surf casting or deep sea fishing. You can board a charter boat or head your own craft out of Oregon Inlet. (Call 919/441–6301 for information on chartered trips.) North Carolina fishing licenses are available from local bait-and-tackle shops and marinas or from the N.C. Division of Boating and Inland Fishing (tel. 919/733–3633).

Hang Gliding Only a few miles from where Wilbur and Orville Wright first took flight, you can try your hand at hang gliding. There's probably not a safer place to attempt this aerial feat than from the giant sand dune at Jockey's Ridge State Park. Lessons are given by the **Kitty Hawk Kites,** purported to be the world's largest hang gliding school. Their shop is located on U.S. 158 at Milepost 13, tel. 919/441–4124.

Scuba Diving With over 600 known shipwrecks off the coast of the Outer Banks, diving opportunities are virtually unlimited. The *Monitor* is off-limits, however. Three dive shops along the Banks can help you organize an adventure: **Atlantic Divers** (tel. 919/441–1111), **Hatteras Divers** (tel. 919/986–2557), and **Nags Head Pro Dive Shop** (tel. 919/441–7594).

Surfing and Windsurfing The Outer Banks offer ideal conditions for these sports. Contact **Kitty Hawk Sports** (U.S. 158 at Milepost 13, tel. 919/441–4124).

Dining

Plan to get your fill of seafood during your visit to the Outer Banks; it's in abundant supply here, and a number of restaurants prepare it quite well. A complete list of restaurants is included in the *Outer Banks Vacation Guide*, published by the Dare County Tourist Bureau and the Outer Banks Chamber of Commerce.

Category	Cost*
Very Expensive	over $25
Expensive	$15–$25
Moderate	$8–$15
Inexpensive	under $8

per person without tax (5%), service, or drinks

The following credit-card abbreviations are used: AE, American Express; CB, Carte Blanche; DC, Diners Club; MC, Mastercard; V, Visa.

Kill Devil Hills
Moderate–Expensive

Evan's Crabhouse. This casual restaurant is known for its crab soups, hot and spicy steamed crabs, crab cakes, crab cocktails, crab salads, and crabs in the shell. Meals are served on oilcloth covered tables. Take-out service available. *U.S. 158 Bypass at Milepost 10, tel. 919/441–5994. Lunch only Dec.–Mar. Reservations not required. MC, V.*

Manteo
Expensive

The Elizabethan Inn. Enjoy "Pastime with Goode Companie," a show with an authentic 16th-century Elizabethan feast at this inn. *US 64, tel. 919/473–2101. Reservations required. Wed.–Fri., mid-June–late Aug. AE, CB, DC, MC, V.*

Moderate **The Weeping Radish.** This Bavarian-style restaurant is named for the radishes sprinkled with salt and served with Hoplen beer, brewed right on the premises. Waiters dressed in Bavarian costumes serve German dishes while German music plays in the background. Tours of the brewery are given upon request. *US 64, tel. 919/473–1157. Reservations required for parties of six.*

Nags Head **Owens' Restaurant.** Housed in an old Nags Head–style clap-
Expensive board cottage, Owens' has been in the same family for over 40 years. Seafood is featured here—particularly the coconut shrimp and lobster bisque. Nightly entertainment is offered in the brass and glass Station Keeper's Lounge. *U.S. 158, Milepost 17, tel. 919/441–7309. Reservations accepted for large parties only. No lunch. Closed Dec.–Mar. AE, CB, DC, MC, V.*

A Restaurant by George. Located in the onion-domed Galleon Esplanade shopping center, the restaurant is as well-known for its exotic, tropical atmosphere as for its food. Diners may choose among several intimate rooms and then mix with the lounge crowd afterward. The Continental menu features steak, seafood, and fancy desserts. *US 158 at Milepost 11, tel. 919/441–4821. Reservations advised. AE, CB, MC, V.*

Moderate **Kelly's Outer Banks Restaurant & Tavern.** This is a favorite gathering place on the Outer Banks. The menu is varied, with selections of seafood (including steamed or raw shellfish), beef, and chicken, but the restaurant is famous for its pasta and homemade desserts and breads. *U.S. 158 Bypass, Milepost 10½, tel. 919/441–4116. Reservations not required. No lunch. AE, MC, V.*

Lodging

The majority of motels and hotels are clustered in the Nags Head–Manteo area, but a small number of rooms are available in the Cape Hatteras area. There are 60 cottages for rent on Ocracoke Island, plus a dozen or so motels and tourist homes. Condos and beach cottages may be rented by the week or month through area realty companies. Consult the *Outer Banks Vacation Guide* for a complete listing of accommodations. The Outer Banks Chamber of Commerce (tel. 919/441–8144) can steer you in the direction of rental agencies.

Category	Cost*
Very Expensive	over $100
Expensive	$60–$100
Moderate	$30–$60
Inexpensive	under $30

*double room; add 7.5% for taxes

The following credit card abbreviations are used AE, American Express; CB, Carte Blanche; DC, Diners Club; MC, MasterCard; V, Visa.

Duck **Sanderling Inn and Restaurant.** If you enjoy being pampered,
Very Expensive come to this inn, located in a remote beach area north of Duck. Guests are treated to lounging robes, fruit and wine, and com-

plimentary hors d'oeuvres. For recreation you can play tennis, go swimming, or take a nature walk through the Pine Island Sanctuary and then curl up with a good book from the inn's library—or enjoy a videotape. Though it was built in 1985 and has all the contemporary conveniences, the inn has the stately, mellow look of old Nags Head. The restaurant serves three meals a day, and reservations are required for dinner. Entrees include crab cakes, roast Carolina duckling with black cherry sauce, and fricassee of shrimp. *Rte. 1200, Box 319Y, 27949, tel. 919/261–4111. 60 rooms and efficiencies. Facilities: pool, tennis, Jacuzzi, hot tub, health club, bicycles, meeting rooms. AE, MC, V.*

Kill Devil Hills
Moderate–Expensive
Ramada Inn. Rooms in this convention-style hotel have ocean views and come with refrigerators and microwave ovens. Peppercorns Restaurant, overlooking the ocean, serves breakfast and dinner, and lunch is available on the sun deck next to the pool. *US 158, Milepost 9½, Box 2716, 27948, tel. 919/441–2151. 173 rooms. Facilities: pool, Jacuzzi, meeting rooms. AE, CB, MC, V.*

Ocracoke
Moderate–Expensive
The Berkeley Center Country Inn. Once a corporate retreat, this rustic property, which resembles a life-saving station, is now a bed-and-breakfast inn. Located next to the state ferry dock, it is within easy walking distance of everything in the village. The owners, Col. and Mrs. Wesley Egan, serve a scrumptious breakfast of fresh breads, preserves, and coffee. *NC 12, Box 220, 27960, tel. 919/928–5911. Open mid-Mar.–mid-Dec. Personal and traveler's checks only, no credit cards accepted.*

Moderate
The Island Inn and Dining Room. The inn has been in operation since 1940, though it was built as a private lodge back in 1901. Guests have a choice of new or traditional rooms, including the Crow's Nest on the third floor. The dining room is known for its oyster omelet, crab cakes, and hush puppies. Reservations are advised, particularly for dinner. *NC 12, Box 9, 27960, tel. 919/928–4351 (inn) or 919/928–7821 (dining room). Open Mar.–Nov. 35 rooms. Facilities: outdoor pool. MC, V.*

Asheville

In recent years this mountain city has been rated, among cities of its size, as American's number one place to live. It has scenic beauty, low levels of pollution, a good airport and road system, a moderate four-season climate, a variety of hotels and restaurants, and plenty of cultural opportunities. It is a city where banjo pickers are as revered as violinists, where mountain folks mix with city slickers, and where everyone finds a common ground in a love for the city.

Getting Around

By Plane The Asheville Airport is served by three major air carriers: **American**–American Eagle, **Delta**–ASA, and **USAir**.

By Car I–40 runs east and west through the city. I–26 runs from Charleston to Asheville. I–240 forms a perimeter around the city. U.S. 23-19A is a major north and west route.

By Bus **Greyhound / Trailways** (tel. 704/253–5353).

Guided Tours

Three companies provide group tours: **Travel Professionals, Inc.** (tel. 704/298–3438), **Western Carolina Tours** (tel. 704/254–4603), and **Young Tour Service** (tel. 800/622–5444 in NC or 800/528–9007 in the Southeast).

Important Addresses and Numbers

Tourist Information The **Visitor Information Center** (151 Haywood St., tel. 704/258–6100) and the **Asheville Convention and Visitors Bureau** (Box 1011, 151 Haywood St., Asheville 28802, tel. 800/548–1300 in NC or 800/257–1300 outside NC).

Emergencies Dial 704/252–1110. (A 911 emergency number is being installed, but is not yet available.)

Exploring Asheville

Downtown Asheville is noted for its eclectic architecture. The **Battery Park Hotel,** built in 1924, is neo-Georgian; the **Flatiron Building** (1924) is neoclassical; the **Church of St. Lawrence** (1912) is Spanish Baroque; **Old Pack Library** (1925) is in Italian Renaissance–style; the **S & W Cafeteria** (1919) is Art Deco. A brochure entitled "Asheville Heritage Tour," details six different historic districts in the city. A guided walking tour is given every Sunday at 2 PM from June through mid-October. For details, contact the Preservation Society of Asheville and Buncombe County (Box 2806, Asheville 28802, tel. 704/254–2343).

The **Thomas Wolfe Memorial** (48 Spruce St.), built in 1880 in the Queen Anne style, is one of the oldest houses in downtown Asheville. Wolfe's mother ran a boarding house here for years, and he used it as the setting for his novel *Look Homeward, Angel.* Family pictures, clothing, and original furnishings fill the house, now a state historic site. Guided tours are available. *Tel. 704/253–8304. Admission: $1 adults, students 50¢. Open Apr.–Oct. Mon.–Sat. 9–5, Sun. 1–5; Nov.–Mar. Tues.–Sat. 9–4, Sun 1–4.*

From downtown, follow I–40 east to Exit 50 (U.S. 25). The entrance to the architecturally famous **Biltmore Estate** faces Biltmore Village, about three blocks from the interstate. Built as the private home of George Vanderbilt, the 250-room French Renaissance château is today a museum. Richard Morris Hunt designed the castle, and Frederick Law Olmsted landscaped the 125,000-acre estate. It took 1,000 men five years to complete the gargantuan project. On view are the priceless antiques and art treasures collected by the Vanderbilts, and 17 acres of gardens. *Tel. 704/255–1776. Admission: $17.50 adults, $13.50 students ages 12–17. Open daily 9–5. Evening candlelight tours during the Christmas holidays.*

Take U.S. 19-23 Bypass north, off I–240, from Asheville to Weaverville, a distance of about 18 miles. The **Zebulon B. Vance Birthplace** is located on Reems Creek Road (Route 1103). This state historic site, which includes a two-story log cabin and several outbuildings, is where Vance—North Carolina's governor during the Civil War—grew up. Crafts and chores typical of his period are often demonstrated. Picnic facilities are available.

Tel. 704/645–6706. Admission free. Open Apr.–Oct., Mon.–Sat. 9–5, Sun. 1–5; Nov.–Mar., Tues.–Sat. 9–4, Sun. 1–4.

Time Out Enjoy fresh mountain trout or chicken with pineapple raisin sauce in the turn-of-the-century **Weaverville Milling Company,** near the Vance Homestead. Waitresses dress in gingham. The craft shop on the premises sells locally made quilts and quilted pillows. *Tel. 704/645–4700. Reservations suggested. Open Mon., Tues., Thurs., Fri., 5–9, weekends 5–9:30. Closed Wed., Jan.–Mar., Mon. and Tues. MC, V. Moderate.*

Flat Rock About 20 miles south of Asheville, Flat Rock can be reached via I–26. This vacation-retirement community, long popular with Charlestonians, is home to the Flat Rock Playhouse and to the estate of poet and Lincoln biographer Carl Sandburg. **Connemara** is the home where the great Pulitzer Prize winner spent the last years of his life with his wife Lilian. The house is at same time warm and austere. Guided tours are given by the National Park Service, which manages the property. "The World of Carl Sandburg" and "Rootabaga Stories" are presented here by the Vagabond Players during the summer. *Tel. 704/693–4178. Admission free. Open daily 9–5.*

What to See and Do with Children

Sliding Rock. Slide for 150 wet and wild feet on a natural water slide located north of Brevard, off Highway 276, in Pisgah National Forest. Wear old jeans and tennis shoes and bring a towel. *Tel. 704/877–3265. Open 10–6 late May–Labor Day.*

Off the Beaten Track

Riverside Cemetery (Birch St., off Montford Ave. north of I–240 in Asheville) is the final resting place of Thomas Wolfe, O. Henry (William Sydney Porter), Zebulon Vance, and early founders and settlers of Asheville. *Open daylight hours.*

Shopping

Crafts **The Folk Art Center** (Milepost 382 on the Blue Ridge Parkway) is the best place to find authentic quality mountain crafts. *Tel. 701/298–7928. Open mid–June–early Sept. daily 9–8; 9–5 remainder of year.*

Qualla Arts and Crafts (U.S. 441 and Drama Rd., in Cherokee) features authentic Cherokee Indian crafts, as well as items from other American tribes. *Tel. 704/497–3103. Open daily 9–5.*

Biltmore Village, built by George Vanderbilt outside the entrance to his magnificent estate, houses more than 20 antique, craft, clothing, and gift shops. Be sure to check out **New Morning Gallery,** which features quality art and crafts.

Biltmore Homespun Shop, located on the grounds of the Grove Park Inn and established by Mrs. George Vanderbilt, features woven goods made on the premises. *Macon St., tel. 704/253–7651. Open Apr.–Oct., Mon.–Sat. 9–5:30; Nov.–Mar., Mon.–Sat. 9–4:30.*

Participant Sports

Camping For information on state parks, national forests, and designated sites along the Blue Ridge Parkway and in the Great Smoky Mountains National Park, request the free *NC Camping and Outdoors Directory* from the NC Travel & Tourism Division (tel. 919/733–4171 in NC or 800/847–4862 outside NC).

Canoeing/White Water Rafting The Nolichucky, French Broad, Nantahala, Ocoee, and Green Rivers offer Class I-IV rapids. About 10 outfitters serve the Asheville area, including **Cherokee River Trips** (Box 516, Cherokee, 28719, tel. 704/488–3373) and **Nantahala Outdoor Center** (U.S. 19W, Box 41, Bryson City, 28713, tel. 704/488–2175).

Gem Mining Franklin has at least a dozen mines where you can get up to your elbows in common mud in search of precious rubies, sapphires, garnets, and other stones. There are many gem shops in the area where you can have your "finds" appraised. *Location maps are available from the Franklin Chamber of Commerce (180 Porter St., Franklin 28734, tel. 704/524–3161). Admission: $4–$5 for adults, $1–$2 for children. Most mines are open mid-May–Oct. 8 to 5 or dusk.*

Golf Some 15 challenging courses are within a 60-minute drive of Asheville. Public courses are located in Asheville, Black Mountain, Brevard, Hendersonville, Lake Lure, Old Fort, and Waynesville. *Contact the Asheville Convention & Visitors Bureau (Box 1010, Asheville, 28802, tel. 800/548–1300 in NC or 800/548–1300 in Eastern USA) for a listing.*

Hiking There are hundreds of trails along the Blue Ridge Parkway and in the Great Smoky Mountains National Park. The Appalachian Trail runs along the crest of North Carolina's highest mountains. *For trail maps, contact the Superintendent (Blue Ridge Parkway, BB & T Bank Bldg., 1 Pack Sq., Asheville 28801, tel. 704/259–0779), or the Superintendent Great Smoky Mountains National Park, Gatlinburg, TN (37738, tel. 615/436–9564).*

Skiing Ski resorts in the Asheville area include **Cataloochee** (Rte. 1, Box 500, Maggie Valley 28751, tel. 704/926–0285), **Fairfield-Sapphire Valley** (Rte. 70, Box 80, Sapphire Valley 28774, tel. 704/743–3441), and **Wolf Laurel** (Rte. 3, Mars Hill, 28754, tel. 704/689–4111).

Dining

As you might expect in a resort city, dining choices are many: upscale gourmet restaurants, middle-of-the-road country fare, and fast-food establishments.

Category	Cost*
Very Expensive	over $25
Expensive	$15–$25
Moderate	$8–$15
Inexpensive	under $8

*per person without tax (4.5%), service, or drinks

The following credit-card abbreviations are used: AE, American Express; CB, Carte Blanche; DC, Diners Club; MC, MasterCard; V, Visa.

Very Expensive **The Market Place.** Nouvelle cuisine is served in a relaxed atmosphere, part chintz, part bamboo. Vegetables and herbs are regionally grown, and bread, pasta, and pastries are made on the premises. The menu changes about every 10 days. The Grille downstairs, where everything is prepared over a fire, offers a more casual atmosphere and somewhat lower prices. *10 N. Market St., tel. 704/252–4162. Reservations must be confirmed by 4 PM. No lunch. Closed Sun. and major holidays. AE, MC, V.*

Moderate **Steven's Restaurant.** International cuisine is offered in an elegant Victorian setting. The restaurant is known for its rack of lamb, freshly baked breads and desserts, and extensive wine list. *157 Charlotte St., tel. 704/253–5348. Dress: informal. Reservations recommended. Sun. brunch. AE, MC, V.*

Inexpensive– **Black Forest Restaurant.** Enjoy traditional German dishes in a
Moderate Bavarian setting. Specialties include sauerbraten, knockwurst, schnitzel, and Kassler rippchen. The restaurant celebrates Oktoberfest in the fall. *U.S. 25, tel. 704/684–8160. Reservations suggested. AE, MC. V. Closed Mon. and Christmas Day.*

Inexpensive **Bill Stanley's Barbecue and Bluegrass.** Overalls and crinoline skirts are the order at this local establishment known for its clogging, bluegrass music, barbecue, and rustic atmosphere. The locals who hang out here make everyone, including tourists and convention delegates, feel welcome. *20 Spruce St., tel. 704/ 253–4871. Reservations advised on weekends. Cover is $3 on weekends and $2 on weekdays. Closed Sun. and Mon. AE, DC, MC. Inexpensive.*

J & S Cafeteria. People come by the busloads to enjoy this above-average cafeteria. After you clean your plate, you can look for more bargains in the outlet stores that occupy the same shopping center. *800 Fairview Rd., in River Ridge Market Pl., tel. 704/298–0507. Closed Christmas Day.*

Lodging

Lodging options range from posh resorts to mountain cabins, country inns, and economy chain motels. There's a bed for virtually every pocketbook.

Category	Cost*
Very Expensive	over $100
Expensive	$60–$100
Moderate	$30–$60
Inexpensive	under $30

* *double room; add 7.5% for taxes*

The following credit card abbreviations are used: AE, American Express; CB, Carte Blanche; DC, Diners Club; MC, MasterCard; V, Visa.

Hotels and Motels **Great Smokies Hilton.** Play golf or tennis, go swimming, or just
Expensive enjoy the mountain views at this complete hotel resort. Rooms
are spacious and recently renovated; the Thomas Wolfe Room is
a favorite. *1 Hilton Dr. (U.S. 19/23) near Westgate Shopping
Center, tel. 704/254-3211. 280 rooms. Facilities: restaurant,
coffee shop and lounge, 2 pools, sauna, golf, tennis, complimentary airport shuttle. AE, CB, MC, V.*

Grove Park Inn and Country Club. This is Asheville's premier
resort, and it's just as beautiful and exciting as it was the day it
opened in 1913. The guest list has included Henry Ford, Thomas Edison, Harvey Firestone, and Warren G. Harding. Novelist
F. Scott Fitzgerald stayed here while his wife Zelda was in a
nearby sanitorium. His room was no. 441. In the past five years
the hotel has been completely renovated. The two new wings
are in keeping with the original design. Facilities include four
restaurants. *290 Macon Ave., tel. 800/438-5800. 510 rooms and
suites. Facilities: meeting rooms, pool, sauna, whirlpool, putting green, fitness center, golf, tennis, racquetball, parking
garage, airport shuttle, children's program, social program.
AE, CB, MC, V.*

Inns and B&Bs **Cedar Crest Inn.** This beautiful cottage was constructed by
Moderate–Expensive Biltmore craftsmen as a private residence around the turn of
the century. Jack and Barbara McEwan have lovingly restored
it as a bed-and-breakfast inn and filled it with Victorian antiques. Guests are treated to afternoon tea, evening coffee
or chocolate, and a breakfast of fruits, pastries, and coffee.
*674 Biltmore Ave., 28803, tel. 704/252-1389. 11 rooms. AE,
MC, V.*

Moderate **Flynt Street Inns.** These B&Bs are located in Asheville's
Montford Park. Rick and Lynne Vogel, and Rick's mother,
Marion, treat guests to a full breakfast. *100 & 116 Flint St.,
28801, tel. 704/253-6723. 8 rooms. AE, MC, V.*

North Carolina High Country

Majestic peaks, meadows, and valleys characterize the North
Carolina High Country (Alleghany, Ashe, Avery, Mitchell, and
Watauga counties) in the Blue Ridge Mountains. Once remote,
the area has boomed in the past 25 years following the introduction of snowmaking equipment. Now North Carolina is both the
Southern ski capital and a summertime playground for hiking,
bicycling, camping, fishing, and canoeing. Luxury resorts now
dot the valleys and mountaintops. The building of a 10-story
concrete condo monolith on Sugar Mountain in Banner Elk
caused a public outcry and resulted in the passage of a mountain ridge protection law to restrict this type of construction.
On the other hand, the Linn Cove Viaduct on Grandfather
Mountain, a bridge that circumvents the peaks and valleys
without disturbing them, has received rave reviews from virtually everyone, including environmentalists. The bridge, which
opened in 1987, is the final link in the Blue Ridge Parkway. Visitors to the hills take advantage of the many crafts shops, music
festivals, theater, and special events such as the Grandfather
Mountain Scottish Games. The passing of each season is a spe-

cial visual event in the High Country, with autumn's colors being the most spectacular of all.

Getting Around

By Plane **USAir Express** (tel. 800/251–5720) serves the Hickory Airport, about 40 miles from the High Country.

By Car The closest interstate is I–40, which is intersected by U.S. 321 at Hickory, NC 181 at Morganton, and U.S. 221 at Marion, leading to the High Country. U.S. 421 is a major east-west artery. The Blue Ridge Parkway, a slowly winding road, goes from Shenandoah National Park in Virginia to Great Smoky Mountains National Park in North Carolina and Tennessee, and passes over the crests of mountains in the High Country.

By Bus Service from Charlotte to Boone is provided by **Greyhound/ Trailways** (tel. 704/262–0501), with arrivals and departures from the Appalcart Bus Station on Winklers Creek Road, off U.S. 321 in Boone.

Important Addresses and Numbers

Tourist Information **North Carolina High Country Host** (701 Blowing Rock Rd., Boone 28607, tel. 800/222–7515 in NC or 800/438–7500 in the eastern U.S.).

Emergencies Dial 911 for emergency assistance or go to the emergency room at **Watauga County Hospital** in Boone (tel. 704/262–4100), **Cannon Memorial Hospital** in Banner Elk (tel. 704/898–5111), or the **Blowing Rock Hospital** in Blowing Rock (tel. 704/295–3136).

Exploring North Carolina High Country

Blowing Rock, a tourist mecca since the 1880s, has retained the flavor of a quiet mountain village. Only a few hundred people are permanent residents, but the population swells each summer. The town is named for a large outcropping of rock, which has become the state's oldest tourist attraction. The town of Blowing Rock boasts some of the best restaurants in the High Country and offers a variety of accommodations.

The Blowing Rock (off U.S. 321, on the southern outskirts of town), looms 3,000 feet over the Johns River Gorge. If you throw your hat over the sheer precipice, it may come back to you, should the wind gods be playful. The story goes that a Cherokee brave and a Chickasaw maiden fell in love. Torn between returning to his tribe or staying with her, he jumped from the cliff. Her prayer to the Great Spirit resulted in his safe return to her. During the Depression of the '30s, a local family by the name of Robbins who owned the big rock decided to make it a tourist attraction and charge admission to see it. The formula worked. The family also owns the Tweetsie Railroad theme park. Today's visitors to the Blowing Rock enjoy views from an observation tower and a garden landscaped with mountain laurel, rhododendron, and other native plants. *Tel. 704/295– 7111. Admission: $3 adults, $1 children 6–11. Open daily Apr.–May 9–6, June–Oct. 8–8.*

From downtown Blowing Rock, follow U.S. 221 one mile south to the **Blue Ridge Parkway**—a scenic asphalt ribbon that stretches over mountain crests from northern Virginia to Tennessee and North Carolina. Here are quiet vistas, dramatic mountain ranges, and remnants of pioneer life. Mileposts help tourists find the sites. Consider a stop at the **Moses H. Cone Park** (Mileposts 297.7–295) to see the manor house where the textile magnate lived.

If you want to go hiking, canoe on a mountain lake, fish for trout in a rushing stream, or pitch a tent, head for the 4,000 acres of forest in **Julian Price Park** (Mileposts 295.1–298). Keep driving south and you'll come to Grandfather Mountain, Linville Falls, Asheville, and Cherokee; head north from the park and you'll soon be at Doughton Park, the Peaks of Otter, and Roanoke. The Blue Ridge Parkway is open year-round, but it often closes during heavy snows. Maps and information are available at visitor centers along the highway. *For more information, contact the Superintendent (Blue Ridge Pkwy., BB & T Bldg., 1 Pack Sq., Asheville 28801, tel. 704/259–0779).*

From Blowing Rock, head north toward Boone, via U.S. 321, until you come to **Tweetsie Railroad,** a theme park popular with young children. In its heyday, Tweetsie provided passenger service between Johnson City, Tennessee, and Boone, but the tracks were washed away in a flood in the '40s and never rebuilt. In 1956, the train was placed on a three-mile track and opened as an attraction. The park also features a petting zoo, rides, gold panning, a saloon show, and concessions. *Tel. 704/264–9061. Admission: $10 adults, $8 children ages 4–12. Open late May–Labor Day daily 9–6; Sept.–Oct. weekdays 9–5 and weekends 9–6.*

Boone, named for frontiersman Daniel Boone, is a city of several thousand residents at the convergence of three major highways—U.S. 321, U.S. 421, and NC 105. **"Horn in the West,"** a project of the Southern Highlands Historical Association, is an outdoor drama that traces the story of Boone's life. *The amphitheater is located off U.S. 321, tel. 704/264–2120. Admission: $8 adults, $4 children under 13. Curtain time is 8:30 nightly except Mon. mid-June through mid-Aug.*

To reach **Ashe County (Jefferson-West Jefferson),** travel five miles east on U.S. 421 to the Blue Ridge Parkway, and follow the parkway north for about 15 miles to Milepost 258.6 near Glendale Springs. The scene quickly changes from commercial strips to mountain vistas and rural landscapes dotted with manicured farms and quiet villages.

The **Blue Ridge Mountain Frescoes** at Glendale Springs and Beaver Creek were painted by North Carolina artist Ben Long. Long found the abandoned churches and painted four big-as-life frescoes, applying rich earthy pigments to wet plaster. "The Last Supper" (measuring 17 × 19.5 feet) is in the Glendale Springs Holy Trinity Church. The others are in St. Mary's Episcopal Church at Beaver Creek, including "Mary, Great with Child," which won the Leonardo da Vinci International Award. *Tel. 919/982–3076. Admission free. Open 24 hours a day. Guide service available 9:30–4:30.*

You can go in another direction from Boone by following NC 105 south (about 14 miles) to NC 184, which leads to **Banner Elk.** This college and ski resort town is surrounded by the lofty peaks of Grandfather, Hanging Rock, Beech, and Sugar. Banner Elk is home to Elk River Club, fast becoming one of the most prestigious residential developments on the East Coast.

Linville, eight miles from Banner Elk at the intersection of U.S. 221 and NC 105, sits at the base of Grandfather Mountain. This resort town, distinguished by its chestnut bark homes and lodges, has not changed much since it was built in the 1880s.

Grandfather Mountain is long known for its mile-high **Swinging Bridge,** stretching between two prominent peaks. Two big events draw record crowds to the mountain. The annual Singing on the Mountain is an opportunity to hear old-time gospel music and preaching in late June. Scottish clans from all over North America gather for athletic events and Highland dancing in July. At other times of the year the mountain is a great place for hiking and picnicking. *Blue Ridge Parkway and US 221, Linville 28646, tel. 704/733–2013. Admission to the Swinging Bridge: $6 adults, $3 children ages 4–12. Hiking permits are $3 per day and may be obtained at the gate or at the Scotchman on NC 105. Open Apr.–mid-Nov., 8 until dusk; mid-Nov.–Mar., 9–4, weather permitting.*

Follow U.S. 221 south for about 10 miles to **Linville Caverns,** the only caverns in the Carolinas. The caverns go 2,000 feet underground and have a year-round temperature of 51 degrees. *Tel. 704/756–4171. Admission: $3 adults, $1.50 children 5–11. Open Apr.–Oct., daily 9–6; Nov.–Mar., weekends 9–5.*

What to See and Do with Children

Emerald Village. Grab a bucket of dirt and get muddy while looking for gems at this old mine that was established by the Bon Ami Company years ago. Then go to the Mining Museum on the site and try to identify your treasures. *Located on Rtes. 1002 and 1100, off U.S. 19E, near Spruce Pine, tel. 704/765–6463. Admission: $3 adults, $2 students and senior citizens. Open May–Oct., 9–5.*

Off the Beaten Track

You'll find everything from ribbons and calico to brogans and overalls in the **Mast Store,** an authentic general store that has been the center of the Valle Crucis community for over 100 years. *NC 194 in Valle Crucis, tel. 704/963–6511. Open Mon.–Sat. 6:30–6:30, Sun. 12:30–7.*

Shopping

Crafts High-quality handmade brooms, quilts, pottery, jewelry, and other items made by members of the Southern Highland Handicraft Guild can be found at the **Parkway Craft Center,** which operates out of the Moses H. Cone mansion. *Moses H. Cone Park, tel. 704/295–7938. Open daily 9–5:30.*

Handwoven Goods The **Goodwin Weavers** create bedspreads, tablecloths, and afghans on Civil War–era looms and then sell them in their shop. *Off U.S. 321 Bypass, Blowing Rock, tel. 704/295–3577. Open Mon.–Sat. 9–5, Sun. 1–5.*

Wicker and Wood Factory-made household items produced in the Boone area are sold at the **American Wicker and Wood Factory Outlet and Gift**

Shop. *NC 105 S., Boone, tel. 704/264–8136. Open Mon.–Sat. 10–6, Sun. 1–6.*

Participant Sports

Canoeing | The wild and scenic New River (Class I and II) provides hours of excitement, as do the Watauga River (Class I and II), Wilson Creek, and Toe River (Class II and III). Outfitters include **Edge of the World Outfitters** (Banner Elk, tel. 704/898–9550) and **Wahoo's Wild Whitewater Rafting** (Boone, tel. 704/262–5774).

Golf | The High Country has 18 golf courses, including **Boone Golf Club** (tel. 704/264–8760), **Hanging Rock Golf Course** at Seven Devils/Foscoe (tel. 704/963–6565), and **Mountain Glen Golf Club** at Newland (tel. 704/733–5804). A list of golf courses is available from NC High County Host, 701 Blowing Rock Rd. (U.S. 321), Boone 28607, tel. 800/438–7500 or 800/222–7515 in NC.

Hiking | Trails abound in wilderness areas of national forests and near the Blue Ridge Parkway. The Boone Fork Trail in Julian Price Park, near Blowing Rock, is an easy hike for most people; Shanty Springs, on Grandfather Mountain, is more difficult. The Appalachian Trail follows the not-too-distant North Carolina–Tennessee border. Trail maps are available at the entrance gate of Grandfather Mountain (tel. 704/733–4337) at the Scotchman at NC 105; or from the Superintendent (Blue Ridge Pkwy., 700 BB & T Bldg., 1 Pack Sq., Asheville 28801, tel. 704/259–0779).

Rock Climbing | One of the most challenging climbs in the country is the Linville Gorge, off NC 181. Permits are available from the District Forest Ranger's Office in Marion (tel. 704/652–2144) or from the Linville Falls Texaco Station on U.S. 221. **Appalachian Mountain Sports** in Boone (tel. 704/264–3170) provides instruction and guided trips.

Skiing | The High Country offers six alpine ski areas, plus many cross-country opportunities. For ski conditions, call 800/438–7500 in the eastern U.S. or 800/222–7515 in North Carolina. Downhill skiing is available at **Appalachian Ski Mountain** (Box 106, Blowing Rock 28605, tel. 704/295–7828), **Ski Beech** (Box 1118, Beech Mountain 28604, tel. 704/387–2011), **Ski Hawksnest** (Rte. 1, Box 256, Banner Elk 28604, tel. 704/963–6561), **Hound Ears Club** (Box 188, Blowing Rock 28605, tel. 704/963–4321), **Sugar Mountain** (Box 369, Banner Elk 28604, tel. 704/898–4521), and **Ski Mill Ridge** (U.S. 105 at Foscoe, tel. 704/963–4500). Cross-country skiing is offered at **Moses Cone Park** and at **Linville Falls** on the Blue Ridge Parkway (tel. 704/295–7591), and **Roan Mountain** (tel. 615/772–3303) or **Appalachian Mountain Sports** (tel. 704/264–3170).

Dining and Lodging

Dining | In the past 25 years the High Country has seen a tremendous increase in restaurants, from upscale gourmet restaurants to fast-food establishments. Many now serve alcoholic beverages in various ways (restrictions of previous years have been lifted). Boone has beer/wine and brown bagging (carrying your own in a paper bag); Blowing Rock and Beech Mountain, beer/

wine and liquor by the drink; Banner Elk, wine and brown bagging.

Category	Cost*
Very Expensive	over $25
Expensive	$15–$25
Moderate	$8–$15
Inexpensive	under $8

per person without tax (4.5%), service, or drinks

Lodging Overnight lodging in the High Country ranges from mom-and-pop motels to luxurious mountaintop condos and chalets. Contact North Carolina High Country Host (tel. 800/438–7500 in eastern U.S. or 800/222–7515 in NC) for complete information.

Category	Cost*
Very Expensive	over $100
Expensive	$60–$100
Moderate	$30–$60
Inexpensive	under $30

double room; add 7.5% for taxes

The following credit-card abbreviations are used: AE, American Express; CB, Carte Blanche; DC, Diners Club; MC, MasterCard; V, Visa.

Blowing Rock
Dining and Lodging

Green Park Inn. This 100-year-plus Victorian charmer on the eastern continental divide offers spacious, luxurious rooms, wide porches with rocking chairs, and large public rooms decorated in bright colors and wicker. Old photographs and mementoes highlight the illustrious history of the grand hotel. The bilevel restaurant has won high ratings and is often the setting for dinner theater productions and murder mystery weekends. *U.S. 321, Box 7, 28605, tel. 704/295–3141. Open May–Dec. 88 rooms. Facilities: pool, golf, tennis, meeting rooms. MC, V. Expensive–Very Expensive.*
Hound Ears Club. This Alpine inn, overlooking Grandfather Mountain and a lush golf course, offers comfortable, well-kept rooms dressed in Waverly print fabrics. *Off NC 105, 8 mi from Boone; Box 188, 28605, tel. 704/963–4321. Open Apr.–Feb. 27 rooms. Facilities: restaurant, pool, golf, tennis. MC, V. Very Expensive (price includes meals).*
Ragged Garden Inn. Rooms in this intimate inn are decorated in a Colonial style. Continental breakfasts and northern Italian dishes are prepared by owner/chef Joe Villani. Breakfast is served only to inn guests, but the dining room is open to the public. *Sunset Dr., Box 1927, 28605, tel. 704/295–9703. Dinner reservations suggested. Open Apr.–Jan. AE, MC, V. Expensive.*
Sunshine Inn. Guests love the warmth and charm of this restored country inn, which has a family-style restaurant open to the public. *Sunset Dr., Box 528, 28605, tel. 704/295–3487. Open May–Nov. 5 rooms. MC, V. Inexpensive.*

Boone
Dining
Claire's. Formerly in Blowing Rock, this Colonial-style restaurant has moved to Boone. The menu features veal, marinated beef tenderloin, grilled breast of chicken, shrimp creole, fresh mountain trout, and other dishes. *101 N. King St., tel. 704/264–6152. Dress: casual. Dinner reservations suggested. Open for lunch and dinner Apr. 15–Feb., Fri. and Sat. dinner only Mar.–Apr. 15. MC, V, Moderate–Expensive.*

Witch's Hollow Restaurant This 9,000-square-foot log cabin, decorated in Colonial-style furnishings, serves Continental cuisine. Specialties are veal and mountain trout. *NC 105, 8 mi south of Boone, tel. 704/963–4365. Reservations suggested. Casual dinner attire. No lunch. Closed Sun. and Dec.–Apr. AE, MC, V. Moderate.*

Lodging
Broyhill Inn. Though primarily a conference center, this contemporary hotel on the ASU campus is attractive to individual travelers who enjoy a university atmosphere. The dining room offers a great view of the mountains. *96 Bodenheimer Dr., 28607, tel. 800/222–8636 or 800/438–6022. 83 rooms. Facilities: meeting rooms, restaurant. AE, MC, V. Moderate.*

Banner Elk
Dining
Stonewalls. This contemporary rustic restaurant enjoys one of the best views of Beech Mountain. Fare includes steak, prime rib, fresh seafood, chicken, and homemade desserts. *Hwy. 184, tel. 704/898–5550. Reservations required for groups of 7 or more. Casual dinner attire. AE, MC, V. No lunch. Moderate.*

Lodging
Holiday Inn. Convenient to all the ski slopes, this inn is situated on an old farm in Moon Valley. Rooms are standard for this hotel chain, and attractively decorated. *NC 184, Box 1478, 28604, tel. 704/898–4571 or 800/HOLIDAY. 102 rooms. Facilities: restaurant, lounge, pool, horseshoes, soccer, badminton. AE, CB, DC, MC, V. Moderate.*

Linville
Dining and Lodging
Eseeola Lodge and Restaurant. Built in the 1880s, this lodge is the cornerstone of Linville. Rich chestnut paneling and stonework grace the interior rooms. *U.S. 221, tel. 704/733–4311. 28 rooms. Facilities: restaurant, lounge, golf, tennis, pool. Open June–Labor Day. MC, V. Very Expensive.*

7 South Carolina

Introduction

by Edgar and Patricia Cheatham

Award-winning travel writers Edgar and Patricia Cheatham are based in Charlotte, North Carolina. They are members of the Society of American Travel Writers and the American Society of Journalists and Authors.

From its Low Country shoreline, with wide sand beaches, spacious bays, and forests of palmettos and moss-strewn live oaks, South Carolina extends into an undulating interior region rich with fertile farmlands, then reaches toward the Blue Ridge Mountains, studded with scenic lakes, forests, and wilderness hideaways. What this smallest of Southern states lacks in land area it makes up in diversity.

The historic port city of Charleston, lovingly preserved, links past with present. Many of its treasured double-galleried antebellum homes were built at right angles to the streets to conserve space and catch ocean breezes. Some are now authentically furnished house museums where visitors savor gracious early-era eloquence. Culturally vibrant, the city nurtures theatre, dance, music, and visual arts, showcased each spring during the internationally acclaimed Spoleto Festival USA.

Myrtle Beach is the hub of the Grand Strand, a 55-mile stretch of wide golden-sand beaches and countless family entertainment and recreational activities (especially golf, a top attraction throughout the state). To the south, tasteful, low-key Hilton Head—a sea island tucked between the Intracoastal Waterway and the ocean and divided into several sophisticated, self-contained resorts—also offers beautiful beaches and some of the world's best golf and tennis. Nearby is the port city of Beaufort, where the most rewarding activity is wandering the lovely streets dotted with preserved 18th-century homes, live oaks, and palmettos.

Columbia, the state capital, is a lively (and of course historic) city cleaved by a rushing river. In addition to several museums, a good minor-league baseball team, and a library of Movietonews film clips, the city has one of the country's top zoos. It is also home to the newly opened State Museum and one of the South's finest new performing arts complexes, Koger Center for Performing Arts. Nearby lakes and state parks offer abundant outdoor recreation and first-rate fishing.

Thoroughbred Country, centered around the town of Aiken, is a peaceful area of rolling pastures where some of the world's top race horses are trained. It is also notable for magnificent mansions built by wealthy Northerners who vacationed here at the turn of the century.

Upcountry South Carolina, at the northwestern tip of the state, is less visited than most of the rest of the state but well repays time spent with dramatic mountain scenery, excellent hiking, and challenging white-water rafting.

Since 1670, when the British established the first permanent European settlement at Charleston, the history of the Palmetto State has been characterized by periods of great prosperity contrasted with eras of dismal depression. This vibrant past—from the pioneer, Colonial, Revolutionary, and antebellum periods through the bitter Civil War and Reconstruction years and beyond—is preserved in cherished traditions and an enduring belief in family that give resonance to the optimism and vitality of today's South Carolina.

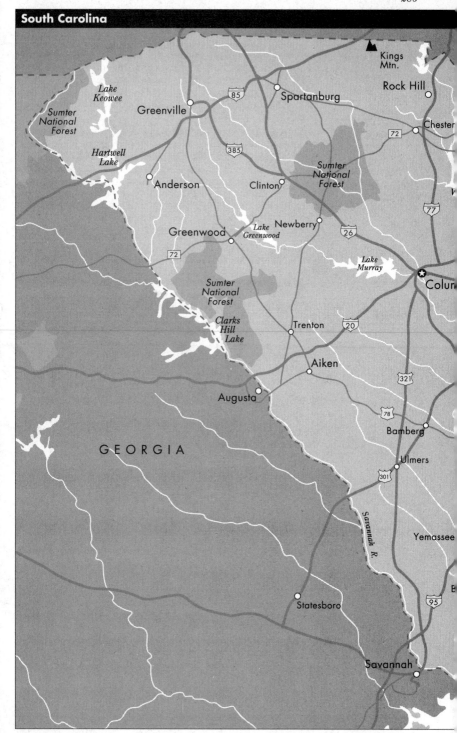

South Carolina

Kings
Mtn.

Rock Hill

Lake
Keowee

85

Spartanburg

Sumter
National
Forest

Greenville

72

Chester

385

Hartwell
Lake

77

Sumter
National
Forest

Anderson

Clinton

Newberry

26

Greenwood

Lake
Greenwood

72

Lake
Murray

Colum

Sumter
National
Forest

Clarks
Hill
Lake

Trenton

20

Aiken

321

Augusta

78

Bamberg

GEORGIA

Ulmers

301

Savannah R.

Yemassee

95

B

Statesboro

Savannah

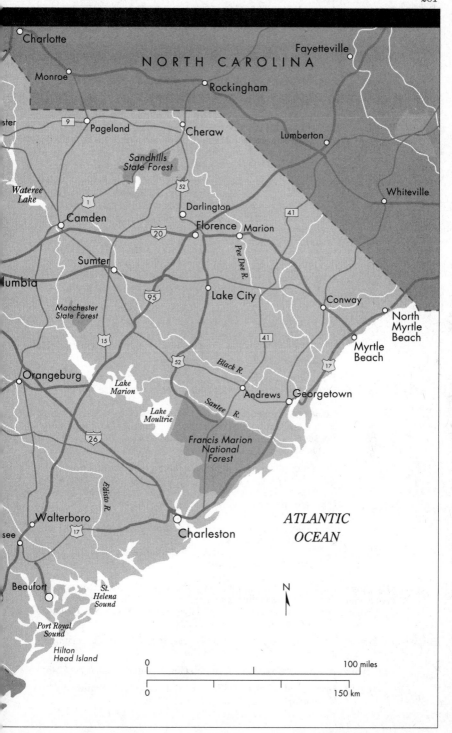

Charleston

At first glimpse, Charleston resembles an 18th-century etching come to life. Its low-profile skyline is punctuated with the spires and steeples of 181 churches, representing 25 denominations that have sought out Charleston as a haven (it was known for having the most liberal provisions for religious freedom of the 13 original colonies). Parts of the city appear stopped in time. Block after block of old downtown structures have been preserved and restored for both residential and commercial use. After three centuries of epidemics, earthquakes, fires, and hurricanes, Charleston has prevailed, and it is today one of the South's best-preserved cities.

Along the Battery, on the point of a narrow peninsula bounded by the Ashley and Cooper rivers, handsome mansions surrounded by gardens face the harbor. Called the "Charleston style," this distinctive look is reminiscent of the West Indies, and for good reason. Before coming to the Carolinas in the late 17th century, many early British colonists had first settled on Barbados and other Caribbean islands. In that warm and humid climate they had built homes with high ceilings and rooms opening onto broad piazzas at each level to catch welcome sea breezes. In Charleston, the settlers adapted these designs for other practical reasons. One new twist—building narrow two- to four-story houses (called single houses) at right angles to the street—emerged partly because of the British Crown's policy of taxing buildings according to frontage length. To save money (as well as to catch the prevailing winds), shrewd Charlestonians faced their houses to the side.

Each year, from mid-March to mid-April, the city opens its homes to visitors. In addition to tours of private homes, gardens, and churches, the Festival of Houses celebrates Charleston's heritage with symphony galas in stately drawing rooms, plantation oyster roasts, candlelight tours, and more. For more information, write to the Historic Charleston Foundation (51 Meeting St., Charleston 29401, tel. 803/722–3405).

But Charleston is more than a carefully polished and preserved relic of the past. It is a city with a vibrant cultural life, which finds its greatest expression in the renowned Spoleto Festival USA and its companion festival, Piccolo Spoleto, when hundreds of local and international artists, musicians, and other performers fill the city streets and buildings with sound and spectacle (*see* The Arts).

Arriving and Departing

By Plane **Charleston International Airport, in North Charleston, opened
Airports and new terminal facilities in 1985. It's on I–26, 12 miles west of
Airlines downtown Charleston, and is served by **American, Bankair, Delta, Eastern, United,** and **USAir.**

Between the Airport **Taxis** average $13, plus tip. By **car,** take I–26S to its terminus,
and Center City at U.S. 17, near the heart of the city.

By Train **Amtrak** (4565 Gaynor Ave., N. Charleston, tel. 800/872–7245).

By Bus **Greyhound** (89 Society St., tel. 803/722–1115), **Trailways** (100 Calhoun St., tel. 803/723–8649).

By Car I–26 traverses the state from northwest to southeast and terminates at Charleston. A favorite coastal route for north-south travelers is U.S. 17, which passes through Charleston.

By Boat Charleston harbor is along the Intracoastal Waterway.

Getting Around

By Taxi Fares within the city vary from company to company but average $2–$3 per trip. Companies include Everready Cab Co. (tel. 803/722–8383), Yellow Cab (tel. 803/577–6565), Safety Cab (tel. 803/722–4066), and Limo-Taxi (tel. 803/767–7111).

By Bus Regular bus service within the city is provided by **SCE&G** (South Carolina Electric and Gas Company) between 5:35 AM and 10 PM and to North Charleston until 1 AM. The cost is 50¢; at peak hours (9:30–3:30), senior citizens and disabled persons pay 25¢. Exact change is needed, and free transfers are available. SCE&G also operates the **DASH** (Downtown Area Shuttle) buses, new trolley-style vehicles that provide fast service on weekdays in the main downtown areas. The fares are the same. For schedule information, call 803/724–7368 (DASH) or 803/722–2226 (regular service).

Important Addresses and Numbers

Tourist Information **Visitor Information Center,** 85 Calhoun St., tel. 803/722–8338. Open weekdays 8:30–5:30, weekends 8:30–5.

Emergencies Dial 911 for emergency assistance.

Hospital The emergency rooms are open all night at **Charleston Memorial Hospital** (326 Calhoun St., tel. 803/577–0600) and **Roper Hospital** (316 Calhoun St., tel. 803/724–2000).

Dentist The **Dental Center** (86 Rutledge Ave., tel. 803/723–7242) provides dental care on short notice.

Guided Tours

Orientation Tours **Adventure Sightseeing** (tel. 803/762–0088), **Carolina Low-country Tours** (tel. 803/797–1045), and **Gateway Tours** (tel. 803/556–7059) offer van or motor-coach tours of the historic district. **Gray Line** (tel. 803/722–4444) offers similar motor-coach tours, plus seasonal tours to gardens and plantations.

Special-Interest Tours **Historically Speaking** (tel. 803/571–1787) offers a 100-minute van tour of the historic district with complimentary refreshments. **Livin' in the Past** (tel. 803/871–0791 or 723–0933) offers historically oriented van and minibus tours of the city and the plantations.

Carriage Tours **Charleston Carriage Co.** (tel. 803/577–0042) offers 40- to 50-minute horse-drawn-carriage tours through the historic district. **Old South Carriage Co.** (tel. 803/723–9712) has similar tours, but conducted by guides in Confederate uniforms. **Old Towne Carriage Co.** (tel. 803/722–1315) has carriage tours as well as semiprivate surrey tours. **Palmetto Carriage Tours** (tel. 803/723–8145) offers one-hour horse- and mule-drawn-carriage tours of the historic district.

Cassette Tours **Charles Towne Tours** (tel. 803/883–3320) and **Charleston Carriage Co.** (tel. 803/577–0042) rent self-paced cassette tours of the historic district.

Personal Guides   Contact **Associated Guides of Historic Charleston** (tel. 803/724–6419); **Charleston Guide Service** (tel. 803/747–3111); **Charleston Hospitality Tours** (tel. 803/722–6858), whose walking, car, and bus tours may include dinner and/or cocktails in antebellum homes; **Parker Limousine Service** (tel. 803/723–7601), which offers chauffeur-driven luxury limousine tours; or **Tours of Historic Charleston** (tel. 803/722–0026).

Walking Tours   Guided tours are given by **Charleston Carriage Co.** (tel. 803/577–0042), **Charleston Strolls** (tel. 803/766–2080), **Charleston Tea Party Walking Tour** (tel. 803/577–5896; includes tea in a private garden), and **Civil War Walking Tour** (tel. 803/722–7033).

Boat Tours   **Charles Towne Princess Gray Line Water Tours** (tel. 803/722–1112) and **Charleston Harbor Tour** (tel. 803/722–1691) offer nonstop harbor tours. **Fort Sumter Tours** (tel. 803/722–1691) includes a stop at Fort Sumter in its harbor tour. It also offers Starlight Dinner Cruises aboard a luxury yacht.

Exploring Charleston

Numbers in the margin correspond with points of interest on the Charleston map.

If you have just a day to spend in Charleston, you might begin with a carriage tour for the tidbits of history and humor that the driver-guides provide as they take you through the main streets of the historic district. This is the best way to decide where to go on your own. Next, browse through the shops of the Old Market area, where most of the carriage tours begin and end. After that, walk south along East Bay Street, past Rainbow Row (a row of pastel-painted houses near Tradd Street), or along any side streets on your way to your choice of the area's four house museums. Spend the rest of the day wandering the cool, palmetto-shaded streets, peeking into private gardens and churches of every stripe, discovering all the little surprises that reveal themselves only to those who seek them out.

If you have more time (and you really should), you can expand your itinerary by adding more sights within the same area; by adding a shopping excursion at the Shops at Charleston Place or along King Street; by including the Marion Square area, which has an excellent art museum and a house museum; or by adding excursions to magnificent plantations and gardens west of the Ashley River or to major historic sites east of the Cooper. There are also boat excursions and some very nice beaches for days when you just want to relax.

For a good overview of the city before you begin touring, drop by the Visitor Information Center to view *The Charleston Adventure,* a 30-minute film. *Admission: $3 adults; $1.50 children 6–12, under 6 free. Shown daily 9–5 on the half-hour.*

For another perspective, see *Dear Charleston: The Motion Picture.* This audacious 42-minute film depicts the city's unique history and personality through the voices of its residents, and through scenes from D. W. Griffith's *Birth of a Nation. Shown at two locations: Historic Preservation Society Visitor Center, 142 King St., tel. 803/723–4381; and Old Exchange and Provost Dungeon, 122 E. Bay St., tel. 803/792–5020. Admission: $3 adults; $1.50 children 7–12, under 7 free. Shown daily at both locations at 10, 11, noon, 2, 3, and 4.*

Marion Square
to the Battery

1
2

Starting at the **Visitor Information Center,** where there's free parking (for two hours; 50¢ per hour thereafter), head down Calhoun Street to Marion Square. Facing the square is the **Old Citadel Building,** built in 1822 to house state troops and arms. Here began the famed South Carolina Military College—The Citadel—now located on the banks of the Ashley River.

3

At 350 Meeting Street is one of Charleston's fine house museums, and a National Historic Landmark, the **Joseph Manigault Mansion.** An outstanding example of Adam-style architecture, it was designed by Charleston architect Gabriel Manigault in 1803 and is noted for its carved-wood mantels and elaborate plasterwork. Furnishings are British, French, and Charleston antiques, including rare tricolor Wedgwood pieces. *Tel. 803/723–2926. Admission: $3 adults; $1.50 children 3–12, under 3 free. Open Mon.–Sat. 10–5, Sun. 1–5.*

4

Across John Street, housed in a $6-million contemporary complex, is the oldest city museum in the United States. The **Charleston Museum,** founded in 1773, is one of the Southeast's major museums and is especially strong on South Carolina decorative arts. The 500,000 items in the collection—in addition to Charleston silver, fashions, toys, snuff boxes, etc.—include objects relating to natural history, archaeology, and ornithology. *360 Meeting St., tel. 803/722–2996. Admission: $3 adults; $1.50 children 3–12, under 3 free. Open Mon.–Sat. 9–5, Sun. 1–5. Three historic homes—the Joseph Manigault House, the Aiken-Rhett Mansion, and the Heyward-Washington House—are part of the museum, and a combination ticket can be bought for either all three and the museum ($9 adults) or any two ($5) or three ($7) houses at any of the four locations.*

5

Walk up Meeting Street to Wragg Street and take a right to reach the 1817 **Aiken-Rhett Mansion.** Furnished in a variety of 19th-century styles, with a heavy, ornate look overall, the house is still undergoing restoration and is especially interesting for that reason. *48 Elizabeth St. tel. 803/723–1159. Admission: $3 adults; $1.50 children 3–12, under 3 free. Open daily 10–5.*

6

If you've left your car at the visitor center, return now to retrieve it. From here you can either take an excursion to see the lovely **College of Charleston** (founded in 1770 as the nation's first municipal college, with a graceful main building constructed in 1828 after a design by famed Philadelphia architect William Strickland) and/or make a shopping tour of King Street, or you can proceed directly to the market area.

7

When you're ready for the market area, head for one of the many centrally located parking garages. Now is the time for a carriage tour, many of which leave from here (*see* Guided Tours). Our tour picks up again at **Congregation Beth Elohim** (90 Hassell St.), considered one of the nation's finest examples of Greek Revival architecture. It was constructed in 1840 to replace an earlier temple—the birthplace of American Reform Judaism in 1824—that was destroyed by fire. Visitors are welcome weekdays 10 AM–noon.

8

Follow Meeting Street south to Market Street, and at the intersection on the left you'll see **Market Hall.** Built in 1841 and modeled after the Temple of Nike in Athens, the hall is a National Historic Landmark. Here you'll find the **Confederate Museum,**

Aiken-Rhett
Mansion, **5**

American Military
Museum, **21**

Calhoun Mansion, **25**

Charleston Museum, **4**

Circular
Congregational
Church, **13**

City Hall, **19**

College of
Charleston, **6**

Congregation Beth
Elohim, **7**

Dock St. Theatre, **17**

Edmonston-Alston
House, **26**

Exchange
Bldg./Provost
Dungeon, **22**

French Huguenot
Church, **18**

Gibbes Art Gallery, **10**

Heyward-Washington
House, **23**

Joseph Manigault
Mansion, **3**

Market Hall, **8**

Nathaniel Russell
House, **24**

Old Citadel Bldg., **2**

Old City Market, **9**

Old Powder
Magazine, **14**

St. John's, **12**

St. Michael's, **20**

St. Philip's, **16**

Thomas Elfe
Workshop, **15**

Unitarian Church, **11**

Visitor Info., **1**

White Point
Gardens, **27**

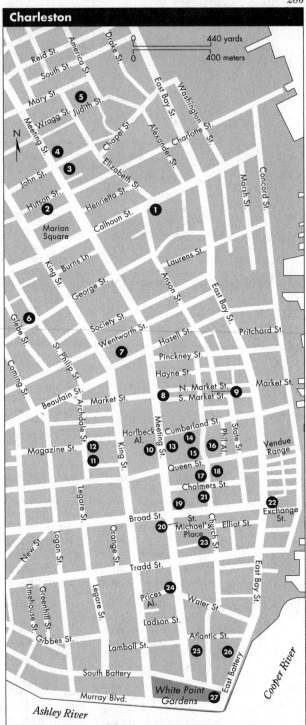

Charleston

where the Daughters of the Confederacy preserve and display flags, uniforms, swords, and other memorabilia. *188 Meeting St., tel. 803/723–1541. Museum admission: $1 adults; 25¢ children 6–12, under 6 free. Hours vary.*

Between Market Hall and East Bay Street is a series of low sheds that once housed produce and fish markets. Called ❾ **Old City Market,** the area now features restaurants and shops. There are still vegetable and fruit vendors here, too, along with local "basket ladies" busy weaving and selling distinctive sweet-grass, pine-straw, and palmetto-leaf baskets—a craft inherited from their West African ancestors—which are fast becoming collectors' items.

Time Out   This is a great area for some serious time out. Pick up batches of Charleston's famed benné (sesame) seed wafers at **Olde Colony Bakery** in the open-air market. Choose from 13 gourmet food stands in **The Gourmetisserie** in the Market Square shopping complex across South Market Street. Or indulge the urge to munch on oysters on the half-shell, steamed mussels, and clams at **A.W. Shucks** in nearby State Street Market.

Across the street is the **Omni Hotel at Charleston Place** (130 Market St.). You might wander over to peer at the lobby or have cocktails or tea in the intimate Lobby Lounge. The city's only world-class hotel is flanked by a four-story complex of upscale boutiques and specialty shops (*see* Shopping).

❿ Heading south on Meeting Street, we come to the **Gibbes Art Gallery.** Its collection of American art includes notable 18th- and 19th-century portraits of Carolinians and an outstanding group of more than 300 miniature portraits. Don't miss the miniature rooms—intricately detailed with fabrics and furnishings and nicely displayed in shadow boxes inset in dark-paneled walls—or the Tiffany-style stained-glass dome in the rotunda's 30-foot ceiling. *135 Meeting St., tel. 803/722–2706. Admission: $2 adults, $1 senior citizens and college students, 50¢ children under 18. Open Tues.–Sat. 10–5, Sun. and Mon. 1–5.*

For a little detour, head south on Meeting Street to Queen ⓫ Street, then west to Archdale. At no. 8 is the **Unitarian Church,** built in 1774. The building was remodeled in the mid-19th century after plans inspired by the Chapel of Henry VII in Westminster Abbey, including the addition of an unusual Gothic fan-tracery ceiling. *No regular visiting hours. Call 803/723–4617 10–noon weekdays in winter, Mon. and Fri. only in summer, to see whether someone can unlock the church.*

At the corner of Clifford and Archdale streets is the Greek ⓬ Revival–style **St. John's Lutheran Church,** built in 1817. Notice the fine craftsmanship in the delicate wrought-iron gates and fence. Organ aficionados may be interested in the 1823 Thomas Hall organ case. The church is open weekdays 9–1. Back at ⓭ Meeting Street, across from the Gibbes is the unusual **Circular Congregational Church.** Legend has it that its corners were rounded off so the devil would have no place to hide. The inside of this Romanesque-style church is simple but pretty, with a beamed, vaulted ceiling. It is open weekdays 9–1.

On Cumberland Street, one of Charleston's few remaining ⓮ cobblestoned thoroughfares, is the **Old Powder Magazine,** built

in 1713, used as a powder storehouse during the Revolutionary
War, and now a museum with costumes, furniture, armor, and
other artifacts from 18th-century Charleston. *79 Cumberland
St., tel. 803/722–3767. Admission: $1 adults, 50¢ students.
Open weekdays 9:30–4.*

⑮ It's a few steps down Church Street to the **Thomas Elfe Workshop,** the home and workplace of one of the city's famed early
furniture makers. Inside this restored miniature "single
house," original and replica Elfe furniture is on display. *54
Queen St., tel. 803/722–2130. Admission: $3. Tours weekdays
10–4:30, Sat. 10–noon. Closed Sun., holidays.*

⑯ At 146 Church Street is graceful **St. Philip's Episcopal Church.**
The late Georgian–style structure, the second on the site, was
completed in 1838. In its serene graveyard are buried some legendary native sons, including statesman John C. Calhoun and
DuBose Heyward, the author of *Porgy.*

⑰ The **Dock Street Theatre,** across Queen Street, was built on the
site of one of the nation's first playhouses. It combines the reconstructed early Georgian playhouse and the preserved Old
Planter's Hotel (ca. 1809). *135 Church St., tel. 803/723–5648.
Open weekdays noon–6 for tours ($1).*

⑱ At 110 Church Street is the Gothic-style **French Huguenot
Church,** the only U.S. church still adhering to the original Huguenot liturgy. A French-liturgy service is held each spring.
*Tel. 803/722–4385. Donations accepted. Open to visitors week-
days 10–12:30 and 2–4. Closed weekends, holidays, Jan.*

The intersection of Meeting and Broad streets is known as the
Four Corners of Law, because structures here represent federal, state, city, and religious jurisdiction. The County Court
House and the U.S. Post Office and Federal Court occupy two
corners.

⑲ The Council Chamber of the graceful 1801 **City Hall,** on the
northeast corner, has interesting historical displays as well as
fine portraits, including John Trumbull's famed 1791 portrait
of George Washington and Samuel F. B. Morse's likeness of
James Monroe. *Admission free. Open weekdays 9–5. Closed
holidays.*

⑳ On the last corner is **St. Michael's Episcopal Church,** modeled
after London's St. Martin's-in-the-Field. Completed in 1761,
this is Charleston's oldest surviving church. Climb the 186-foot
steeple for a panoramic view. *Open Mon., Tues., Thurs., Fri.
9–4:30; Wed. 9–3:30; Sat. 9–noon.*

From the Four Corners, head down Broad Street toward the
㉑ Cooper River. The **American Military Museum** displays hundreds of uniforms and artifacts from all branches of service,
dating from the Revolutionary War. *115 Church St., tel. 803/
723–9620. Admission: $2 adults, $1 children under 12, military in uniform no charge. Open Mon.–Sat. 10–6, Sun. 1–6.*

㉒ At the corner of East Bay Street stands the **Exchange
Building/Provost Dungeon.** The building itself was originally a
customs house. The dungeon was used by the British to confine
prisoners during the Revolutionary War; today, a tableau of
lifelike wax figures recalls this era. *East Bay and Broad Sts.,
tel. 803/792–5020. Admission: $2.50 adults, $2 senior citizens,
$1 children, Open Mon.–Sat. 9:30–5. Closed major holidays.*

Returning to Church Street and continuing south, you'll come
23 to the **Heyward-Washington House.** Built in 1772 by rice king
Daniel Heyward, it was the residence of President George
Washington during his 1791 visit. The mansion is notable for
fine period furnishings by such local craftsmen as Thomas Elfe
and includes Charleston's only restored 18th-century kitchen
open to visitors. *87 Church St., tel. 803/722–0354. Admission:
$3 adults; $1.50 children 3–12, under 3 free. Open Mon.–Sat.
10–5, Sun. 1–5.*

24 At 51 Meeting Street is the **Nathaniel Russell House,** headquarters of the Historic Charleston Foundation. Built in 1808, it is
one of the nation's finest examples of Adam architecture. The
interior is notable for its ornate detailing, its lavish period furnishings, and a "flying" circular staircase that spirals three
stories with no apparent support. *Tel. 803/723–1623. Admission: $3.50, children under 6 free. Open Mon.–Sat. 10–5, Sun.
2–5. A combination ticket with the Edmonston-Alston House
can be purchased at either location for $5.*

Continuing south, you'll come into an area where somewhat
25 more lavish mansions reflect a later era. The **Calhoun Mansion,**
at 16 Meeting Street, is opulent by Charleston standards, an
interesting reflection of Victorian taste. Built in 1876, it's notable for ornate plasterwork, fine wood moldings, and a 75-foot
domed ceiling. *Tel. 803/722–8205 or 577–9863. Admission: $5
adults; $4.50 senior citizens over 62; $3 children 6–13, under 6
free. Open daily 10–4, other times by appointment.*

26 The **Edmonston-Alston House,** at 21 East Battery, is an imposing 1828 Greek Revival structure with a commanding view of
Charleston harbor. It is tastefully furnished with antiques,
portraits, Piranesi prints, silver, and fine china. *Tel. 803/722–
7171. Admission: $3.50, children under 6 free. Open Mon.–
Sat. 10–5, Sun. 2–5.*

27 After all this serious sightseeing, relax in **White Point Gardens,**
on Battery Point, facing the harbor. It's a tranquil spot, shaded
by palmettos and graceful live oaks.

East of the Across the Cooper River Bridges, via U.S. 17, is the town of
Cooper River **Mt. Pleasant.** Here, along Shem Creek, where the area's fishing fleet brings in fresh daily catches, seafood restaurants
attract visitors and locals alike. Mt. Pleasant is home to **Patriots Point,** the world's largest naval and maritime museum.
Berthed here are famed aircraft carrier *Yorktown,* nuclear
merchant ship *Savannah,* vintage World War II submarine
Clamagore, and destroyer *Laffey.* Missiles, airplanes, and
weapons are also displayed. Tours are offered in all vessels, and
the film *The Fighting Lady* is shown regularly aboard the *Yorktown. Tel. 803/884–2727 or 800/327–5723. Admission: $7
adults; $6.50 senior citizens and military in uniform; $3.50
children 6–11, under 6 free. Open daily 9–6 Apr.–Oct., 9–5 rest
of year.*

From the docks here, Fort Sumter Tours' boats leave for 2¼-
hour cruises that include an hour-long stop at **Fort Sumter National Monument.** (The company also has boats leaving from
the Municipal Marina, on Charleston's west side.) This is the
only way to get there, as the fort is on a man-made island in the
harbor. *Tel. 803/722–1691. Cost: $7.50 adults; $3.75 children
6–12, under 6 free. Tours depart daily at 9, 10:15, noon, 1:30,*

2:30, 4 Easter weekend and June 15–Labor Day; call for schedules rest of year.

It was at Fort Sumter that the first shot of the Civil War was fired, when Confederate forces at Fort Johnson (now defunct) across the way opened fire on April 12, 1861. After a 34-hour bombardment, Union forces surrendered and Confederate troops occupied Sumter, which became a symbol of Southern resistance. The Confederacy managed to hold the fort—despite almost continual bombardment—for nearly four years, and when it was finally evacuated, Fort Sumter was a heap of rubble. Today National Park Service rangers conduct free guided tours of the restored structure, which includes a museum (also free) with historical displays and dioramas.

Continuing north out of Mt. Pleasant along U.S. 17, you'll find more "basket ladies" at roadside stands. If you have the heart to bargain, you *may* be able to purchase the baskets at somewhat lower costs than in Charleston.

SC 703 will take you to Sullivan's Island and **Fort Moultrie,** completed in 1809 and the third fort on this site. Here Colonel William Moultrie's South Carolinians repelled a British assault in one of the first Patriot victories of the Revolutionary War. The interior has been restored. A film and slide show tell the history of the fort. *W. Middle St., Sullivan's Island, tel. 803/883–3123. Admission free. Open daily 9–6 summer, 9–5 winter. Closed Christmas.*

Back on U.S. 17, about eight miles out of Charleston, is the 1681 **Boone Hall Plantation,** approached via one of the South's most majestic avenues of live oaks. The primary attraction is the grounds, with formal azalea and camellia gardens, as well as the original slave quarters—the only "slave street" still intact in the Southeast—and cotton-gin house. Visitors may also tour the first floor of the classic columned mansion, which was built in 1935 incorporating woodwork and flooring from the original house. *Tel. 803/884–4371. Admission: $4.50 adults; $1 children 6–12, under 6 free. Open Mon.–Sat. 8:30–6:30, Sun. 1–5 Apr.–Labor Day; Mon.–Sat. 9–5, Sun. 1–4 rest of year. Closed holidays.*

West of the Ashley River Vestiges of the Old South—and Charleston's beginnings—beckon as you cross the Ashley River Bridge. Take SC 171 north to reach **Charles Towne Landing State Park,** commemorating the site of the original Charleston settlement, begun in 1670. There's a reconstructed village and fortifications, English park gardens with bicycle trails and walkways, and a replica 17th-century vessel moored in the creek. In the animal park roam species native to the region for three centuries. A pavilion includes exhibits and a film about the region. Bicycle and kayak rentals and cassette and tram tours are available. *1500 Old Towne Rd., tel. 803/556–4450. Admission: $4 adults; $2 children 6–14, under 6 free; $2 senior citizens. Open daily 9–6 June–Aug.; 9–5 rest of year.*

Nine miles west of Charleston via the Ashley River Road (SC 61) is **Drayton Hall,** built between 1738 and 1742. A National Historic Landmark, it is considered the nation's finest example of Georgian Palladian architecture. The mansion is the only plantation house on the Ashley River to have survived the Civil War intact and serves as an invaluable lesson in history as well as architecture. It has been left unfurnished to highlight the original plaster moldings, opulent hand-carved woodwork, and other ornamental details. *Tel. 803/766–0188. Admission: $6 adults, $3 students, children under 6 free. Guided tours daily 10–4 Mar.–Oct. 10–3 rest of year. Closed major holidays.*

A mile or so farther on SC 61 is **Magnolia Plantation and Gardens.** The 50-acre informal gardens, begun in 1686, boast one of the continent's largest collections of azaleas and camellias and were proclaimed the "most beautiful garden in the world" by John Galsworthy. Nature lovers may canoe through the 125-acre Waterfowl Refuge, explore the 30-acre swamp garden along boardwalks and bridges, or walk or bicycle over 500 acres of wildlife trails. Tours of the manor house, built during the Reconstruction period, depict plantation life. Several nights weekly the gardens are open for strolls along lighted paths. There is also a petting zoo and a mini-horse ranch. *Tel. 803/571–1266. Admission: $7 adults; $6.50 senior citizens; $5 teens; $3 children 4–12, under 4 free. House tours $3 extra. Mar. 15–May 15, all prices $1 additional. Open daily 8–5.*

Middleton Place, four miles farther north on SC 61, has the nation's oldest landscaped gardens, dating from 1741. Design highlights of the magnificent gardens—ablaze with camellias, magnolias, azaleas, roses, and flowers of all seasons—are the floral *allées,* terraced lawns, and ornamental lakes. Much of the mansion was destroyed during the Civil War, but the south wing has been restored and houses impressive collections of silver, furniture, paintings, and historic documents. The stableyard is a living outdoor museum: here craftsfolk, using authentic tools and equipment, demonstrate spinning, blacksmithing, and other domestic skills from the plantation era. Farm animals, peacocks, and other creatures roam free. Rides in a vintage horse-drawn wagon are offered. *Tel. 803/556–6020. Gardens and stableyard open daily 9–5. Admission: $7 adults; $3.50 children 4–12, under 4 free. Prices slightly higher mid-Mar.–mid-June. House tours Tues.–Sun. 10–4:30, Mon. 1:30–4:30; $4 extra.*

The picturesque town of **Summerville,** about 25 miles northwest of Charleston via I–26 (Exit 199), is a pleasant place for a drive or stroll. Built by wealthy planters as an escape from hot-weather malaria, it's a treasure trove of mid-19th-century and Victorian buildings—many of which are listed in the National Register of Historic Places—with colorful gardens of camellias, azaleas, and wisteria. Streets often curve around tall pines, since a local ordinance prohibits cutting them down. This is a good place for a bit of antiquing in attractive shops.

Last but not least, about 24 miles north of Charleston via U.S. 52 is **Cypress Gardens,** a swamp garden created from what was once the freshwater reserve of a vast rice plantation. Explore the inky waters by boat, or walk along paths lined with moss-draped cypress trees, azaleas, camellias, daffodils, wisteria, and dogwood. Peak season is late March into April. *Tel. 803/553–0515. Admission (not including boat ride) Feb. 15–Apr. 30: $5 adults; $4 senior citizens; $2 children 6–16, under 6 free. Rest of year, $1 less and boat ride included in admission cost. Open daily 9–5.*

Charleston for Free

The Citadel Corps of Cadets Dress Parade. Visitors are welcome at the military college's parade at Summerall Field every Friday at 3:45 PM during the school year.

The Citadel Memorial Military Museum. Military documents and relics relating to the Civil War, the college, and its graduates are on display at this on-campus museum. *Tel. 803/792–6846. Open weekdays 2–5, Sat. 9–5, Sun. 10–5.*

Hampton Park Concerts in the Park. These concerts, held often on Sunday afternoons, are free. *For information, call the visitors bureau, tel. 803/723–7641 or 800/845–7108.*

Monday Night Recital Series. The College of Charleston (tel. 803/792–8228) presents guests and faculty artists in free musical performances during the school year.

What to See and Do with Children

American Military Museum (*see* Marion Square to the Battery in Exploring Charleston).

Boat Ride to Fort Sumter (*see* East of the Cooper River in Exploring Charleston).

Charles Towne Landing Animal Forest (*see* West of the Ashley River in Exploring Charleston). Birds, alligators, bison, pumas, bears, wolves, and many other animals roam in natural environments. Children's Days are held during the last two weeks of December.

Charleston Museum (*see* Marion Square to the Battery). The Discover Me Room, designed just for children, has computers and other hands-on exhibits.

Herbie's Antique Car Museum. Nearly 100 vehicles are on display. *2140 Van Buren Rd., N. Charleston, tel. 803/747–7207. Admission: $4, children under 12 free. Open daily 11–8.*

Magnolia Plantation and Gardens (*see* West of the Ashley River). The petting zoo and mini-horse ranch appeal to the young at heart of all ages.

Middleton Place (*see* West of the Ashley River). At this plantation, youngsters can ride in a horse-drawn wagon, pet farm animals, and watch craftsfolk demonstrate their skills.

Palmetto Islands County Park. This family-oriented nature park has a Big Toy playground, a two-acre pond, a canoe trail, an observation tower, and marsh boardwalks. Bicycles, pedal boats, and canoes can be rented in season. *On U.S. 17N, ½ mi past Snee Farm, turn left onto Long Point Rd., tel. 803/884–0832. Admission: $1. Open daily 10–6 Apr. and Sept., 10–7 May–Aug., 10–5 Oct.–Mar. Closed major holidays.*

Shelling. Kiawah Island has excellent shelling. If you're not staying at the private resort, you can shell at **Beachwalker Park,** the public beach at the west end of the island. *Tel. 803/762–2172. Parking fee: $2. Open daily 9:30–6:30 June–Aug.; weekends only Apr., May, Sept., Oct.*

Off the Beaten Track

Angel Oak. Reportedly the oldest living thing east of the Rockies, this 1,500-year-old giant has a 25½-foot circumference and a 151-foot limb spread. *From SC 700 turn left onto Bohicket*

Rd.; after about 1 mi, turn right at sign and follow dirt road, tel. 803/559–3496. Nominal fee. Visitors welcome daily 10–6.

Francis Marion National Forest. About 40 miles north of Charleston via U.S. 52, this site comprises 250,000 acres of swamps, vast oaks and pines, and little lakes thought to have been formed by meteors—a good place for picnicking, camping, boating, and swimming. (tel. 803/336–3248 or 887–3311). At the park's **Rembert Dennis Wildlife Center** (off U.S. 52 in Bonneau, tel. 803/825–3387), deer, wild turkey, and striped bass are reared and studied.

St. James Church. At Goose Creek, about 19 miles north of Charleston, is this remarkably well preserved church, built between 1708 and 1719. Not in use since 1808, it retains the original box pews, slave gallery, and pulpit. The British royal arms are still visible above the chancel. The sexton's house is nearby, and he will open the church on request. *U.S. 52N to U.S. 78; at junction, turn right at stoplight and bridge and drive to top of hill. Donation.*

Shopping

Most downtown Charleston shops and department stores are open from 9 or 10 AM to 5 PM. The malls are open 10–9 and on Sunday, 1–6. The sales tax is 5%. Generally, banks are open Monday through Thursday 8:30–5 and Friday from 8:30 to 6.

Shopping Districts. One of the most interesting shopping experiences awaiting visitors to Charleston is the colorful produce market in the two-block **Old City Market** at East Bay and Market streets. Adjacent to it is the **open-air flea market,** with crafts, antiques, and memorabilia. Here (and at stands along U.S. 17 north of Charleston, near Mt. Pleasant) women weave and sell baskets of grass (*see* Marion Square to the Battery in Exploring Charleston). A portion of the Old City Market where cotton was once auctioned, now called **The Market,** has been converted into a complex of specialty shops and restaurants. Other such complexes in the area are **Rainbow Market** (in two interconnected 150-year-old buildings), **Market Square,** and **State Street Market.** Also, some of Charleston's oldest and finest shops are on the main downtown thoroughfare, **King Street.**

Antiques   Charleston is one of the South's major cities for antiques shopping. King Street is the center. **Coles & Company** (84 Wentworth St., tel. 803/723–2142, and 185 King St., tel. 803/722–3388) is a direct importer of 18th- and 19th-century English antiques. **Livingston Antiques,** dealers in 18th- and 19th-century English and Continental furniture, clocks, and bric-a-brac, has two locations: a large one west of the Ashley (2137 Savannah Hwy., tel. 803/556–6162) and a smaller one in the historic district (163 King St., tel. 803/723–9697). **Vendue House Antiques** (9 Queen St., tel. 803/577–5462) sells 18th- and 19th-century English antiques and distinctive objets d'art.

Art Galleries   The **Birds I View Gallery** (119-A Church St., tel. 803/723–1276 or 795–9661) sells bird paintings and prints by Anne Worsham Richardson. The **Elizabeth O'Neill Verner Studio & Museum** (79 Church St., tel. 803/722–4246) is located in a 17th-century house where the late artist, one of Charleston's most distinguished, had her studio. The studio is now open to the public, as is a gallery of her pastels and etchings. Prints of her work are on sale at adjacent **Tradd Street Press** (38 Tradd St., tel. 803/722–4246). The **Virginia Fouché Bolton Art Gallery** (127 Meeting St., tel. 803/577–9351) has original paintings and limited-edition lithographs of Charleston scenes.

Gift Shops **Charleston Collections** (142 E. Bay St., tel. 803/722–7267, and Bohicket Marina Village, between Kiawah and Seabrook resorts, tel. 803/768–9101) has Charleston charms, prints, and candies, T-shirts, and more. **Charleston Ornaments** (188 Meeting St., The Market, tel. 803/723–6945) carries Christmas ornaments, plus cotton-boll and other novelty items.

One of a Kind Over two dozen upscale boutiques are clustered in a luxurious complex adjoining the Omni Hotel called **The Shops at Charleston Place** (130 Market St., tel. 803/722–4900). Included are branches of Jaeger, Laura Ashley, Gucci, Banana Republic, Polo/Ralph Lauren, Brookstone, Godiva, and Crabtree & Evelyn. Also here is Charleston's and London's own Ben Silver, premier purveyor of blazer buttons, with over 800 designs struck from hand-engraved dies, including college, monogram, British regimental, and specialty motifs. (Ben Silver also sells British neckties, embroidered polo shirts, and blazers.)

Period Reproductions **Historic Charleston Reproductions** (105 Broad St., tel. 803/723–8292) has superb reproductions of Charleston furniture and accessories, all authorized by the Historic Charleston Foundation. Royalties from sales contribute to restoration projects. At the **Thomas Elfe Workshop** (54 Queen St., tel. 803/722–2130), you'll find excellent 18th-century reproductions and objets d'art, Charleston rice beds, handmade mirrors, and Charleston pieces in silverplate, pewter, or porcelain. At the **Old Charleston Joggling Board Co.** (tel. 803/723–4331), these Low Country oddities can be purchased.

Participant Sports

Beaches South Carolina's climate allows swimming from April through October. There are public beaches at **Beachwater Park,** on Kiawah Island; **Folly Beach County Park** and **Folly Beach,** on Folly Island; **Isle of Palms;** and **Sullivan's Island.** Resorts with extensive private beaches are **Fairfield Ocean Ridge,** on Edisto Island; **Kiawah Island Resort; Seabrook Island;** and **Wild Dunes Resort,** on the Isle of Palms. This is definitely not a "swingles" area; all public and private beaches are family oriented.

Bicycling The **historic district** is level and compact, ideal for bicycling, and many city parks have biking trails. **Palmetto Islands County Park** also has trails. Bikes can be rented at **The Bicycle Shop** (tel. 803/722–8168), which offers a self-guided tour of the district; and at the **Charleston Carriage Co.** (tel. 803/577–0042), which also rents tandem bikes. **Pedal Carriage Co.** (tel. 803/722–3880) rents a sort of pedal "surrey with the fringe on top" for two riders (plus two children) and offers a 40-minute self-guided tour of the historic district; it also rents one-speed balloon-tire bikes.

Boardsailing Instructions are provided by **Sailsports** in Mt. Pleasant (tel. 803/884–1508) and **Time Out Sailing** at the Charleston marina (tel. 803/577–5979).

Fishing Fresh- and saltwater fishing is excellent along 90 miles of coastline. Surf fishing is permitted on many beaches, including

Palmetto Islands County Park's. Charter fishing boats offering partial- or full-day sails to individuals include the **J. J.** at Charleston marina (tel. 803/766–9816) and **Blue Water Sportfishing Charter** (tel. 803/554–5280. **Bohicket Yacht Charters** on Johns Island (tel. 803/768–1280) arranges charters for groups of four to six for full- or half-day sportfishing, shark fishing, flat-bottom-boat marsh fishing, shrimping, crabbing, shelling, and nature-observing expeditions.

Golf Public courses include **Charleston Municipal** (tel. 803/795–6517), **Patriots Point** (tel. 803/881–0042), **Plantation Pines** (9 holes; tel. 803/599–2009), and **Shadowmoss** (tel. 803/556–8251). **Kiawah Island** (tel. 803/768–2121) and **Wild Dunes** (tel. 803/886–6000) offer golf to nonguests on a space-available basis.

Jogging Jogging paths wind through **Palmetto Islands County Park,** and **Hampton Park** has a fitness trail.

Miniature Golf There are also three 18-hole **Putt-Putt Golf Courses** (tel. 803/797–7874) in the area and 36 holes of miniature golf at **Classic Golf** (tel. 803/881–9614).

Sailing Boats can be rented and yachts chartered from **Bohicket Yacht Charters** on Johns Island (tel. 803/768–1280).

Tennis Courts are open to the public at **Farmfield Tennis Courts** (tel. 803/724–7402), **Shadowmoss** (tel. 803/556–8251), **Kiawah Island** (tel. 803/768–2121), and **Wild Dunes** (tel. 803/886–6000).

Spectator Sports

Baseball The **Charleston Rainbows,** the San Diego Padres' minor-league team, play at College Park Stadium (701 Rutledge Ave., tel. 803/723–7241). For other sporting events, see the "Database" column in the sports section of the daily *News and Courier.*

Dining

by Eileen Robinson Smith

Formerly a travel editor for Ziff-Davis Publishing in New York and more recently the editor of Charleston Magazine, Ms. Smith, still Charleston-based, is a freelance food and travel writer.

Known for its Low Country specialties—she-crab soup, sautéed shrimp and grits, and variations on pecan pie—Charleston is also a hotbed of new American cuisine. Its chefs are busy creating marriages of the classical and the contemporary, of down-home cooking and haute cuisine. With the strong national interest in both seafood and Southern cooking, Charleston was chosen as the host city for the American Seafood Challenge. For the last three years, chefs from more than 30 states have competed in what has been called the "toughest hot food competition in the country." Locally, chefs and restauranteurs took advantage of the learning experience the Challenge provided.

82 Queen has not only just opened 102 North Market as a steakhouse. Robert Dickson, chef/opera singer, has moved his famous supper club to larger quarters at Planters Inn, 122 North Market. In his former location in the Rainbow Market is an elegant new restaurant, Chouinards.

Near St. Philip's Episcopal Church, at 158 Church Street, once the address of Le Madeleine, Pierre, the first maître'd at the Omni's Shaftesbury Room, has opened his own restaurant, calling it the obvious, Pierre's. For the college crowd, which can't get enough of the buffalo wings and pitchers of Killian's South African dark beer, there's now Humps at 14 Market Street.

Across the East Cooper Bridge, in the trendy suburb of Mount Pleasant, the Village Cafe, opened by chef Scott Roark whose talent kept Supper At Seven so well–booked, is a culinary oasis. Directly across the street, A.W. Shucks new mega-restaurant fronting Shem Creek (Mt. Pleasant's waterfront restaurant row) is a total renovation of the old Crab Net. Out on Folly Beach, the Sugar Reef Cafe, once just a luncheonette up from the surf shop, now has a chef, Terry Gouallard, and on week–ends, it is a feat to secure a table.

Things change and this year no business in Charleston is so exciting to watch as the hospitality industry.

The most highly recommended restaurants in each price category are indicated by a star ★.

Category	Cost*
Expensive	over $30
Moderate	$20–$30
Inexpensive	under $20

per person without tax (5% in South Carolina), service, or drinks

The following credit-card abbreviations are used: AE, American Express; CB, Carte Blanche; DC, Diners Club; MC, MasterCard; V, Visa.

Expensive
Low Country/
Continental
★

The Shaftesbury Room. Under the direction of master chef Joel Gourio de Bourgonnier (previously with Wild Dunes), an updated Charleston cuisine with an emphasis on seafood is featured. In addition to the regular menu is a moderately priced table d'hôte with entrees such as petite filet mignon with bordelaise and quail stuffed with cornbread and shellfish served with a peach sauce. Still formal, with its hardwood paneling and Venetian-glass chandeliers, the place has lightened up, thanks in part to the jazz combo, but the cuisine continues to be world-class. Still offered is the ever-so-special smoked-meat cart from which diners choose such appetizers as Norwegian salmon, chicken with apricot sauce, and tenderloin with horseradish cream. *130 Market St., tel. 803/722–4900. Jackets suggested. Reservations preferred. Dinner only. AE, CB, MC, V.*

Moderate
American
★

82 Queen. This popular restaurant, part of a complex of pink stucco buildings dating to the mid-1800s, is the unofficial headquarters for many of the city's annual events; during Spoleto, musicians perform in the courtyard garden. At the outdoor raw bar, tourists can meet and mingle with the locals. Low Country favorites like crab cakes are served with basil tartar sauce. The traditional commingles with innovations like scallops simmered in leek sauce over spinach fettuccine, garnished with toasted pine nuts. Ask about the homemade relishes, particularly the passion fruit/kiwi chutney. For dessert, the strawberry mocha mousse is exceptional. *82 Queen St., tel. 803/723–7591. Dress: informal. Reservations preferred for dinner. AE, MC, V.*

Low Country

The Moultrie Tavern. This reconverted brick warehouse, dating from 1833, is filled with artifacts and artwork from the Civil War era. Chef/owner Robert Bohrn, who greets guests in a

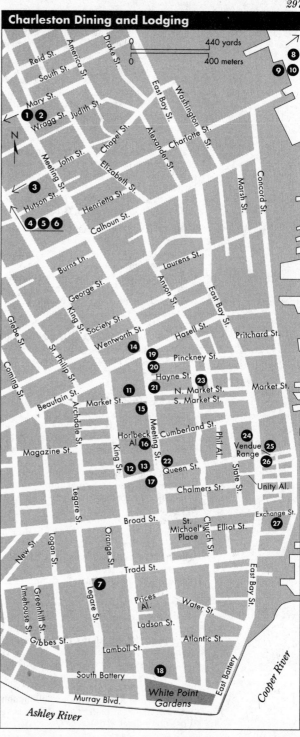

Dining
Athens, **1**
Barbadoes Room, **17**
Calif. Dreaming, **2**
Carolina's, **27**
82 Queen, **12**
Henry's, **23**
Moultrie Tavern, **25**
Queen St. Seafood Inn, **22**
Rusty Anchor, **8**
Shaftesbury Room, **11**
Shem Creek Bar & Grill, **9**

Lodging
Battery Carriage House, **18**
Best Western King Charles, **14**
Days Inn Hist. Dist., **16**
Econo Lodge, **4**
Elliott House Inn, **13**
Hampton Inn Airport, **5**
Heart of Charleston, **20**
Holiday Inn, Mt. Pleasant, **10**
Indigo Inn, **19**
Lodge Alley Inn, **24**
Meeting St. Inn, **15**
Mills House, **17**
Motel 6, **6**
Omni Hotel, **11**
Planters Inn, **21**
Sheraton Charleston, **3**
Sword Gate Inn, **7**
Vendue Inn, **26**

Charleston Dining and Lodging

Confederate uniform, is a historian and unearths his own relics. The fife-and-drum music plays continuously and the food and spirits are authentically 1860s. Try an early Southern specialty: baked oyster and sausage pie with puff pastry. *18 Vendue Range, tel. 803/723–1862. Dress: informal. Dinner reservations recommended. AE, MC, V. Closed Sat. lunch and Sun.*

Carolina's. European chic with its black lacquer, white, and peach decor, Carolina's is the brainchild of German restaurateurs Franz Meier and Chris Weihs. Many come here for the "appeteasers" and the late-night (until 1 **AM**) offerings, which include everything from baby back smoked ribs to pasta with crawfish and tasso (spiced ham) in cream sauce. Dinner entrees are selections from the grill: Carolina quail with goat cheese, sundried tomatoes and basil; salmon with cilantro, ginger, and lime butter; and lamb loin with jalapeño chutney. *10 Exchange St., tel. 803/724–3800. Dress: informal. Reservations suggested. AE, MC, V. Dinner only. Closed Sun.*

New American **Henry's.** Henry Hesselmer opened a grocery store here with a
★ second-story bordello and gambling room in 1928. Total renovation has restored the decor to a "late Prohibition" style; the Art Deco black-and-white-tile floors have been saved. Red-hot action has returned upstairs—though this time around with live jazz. Original items served at Henry's over the last 30 years have been re-created, for example, shrimp wando—shrimp, oysters, blue crab, and lobster in a veloute sauce served over fried grits. The new chef, Karl Schwerzler, formerly with Baker's Cafe, is incorporating his own creations, such as linguine Matriciana with bacon, peppers, onions, peppers, tomatoes, and parmesan cheese. *54 Market St., tel. 803/723–4363 or 723–4084. Dress: informal. Dinner reservations suggested. AE, MC, V.*

Seafood **Barbadoes Room.** This large, airy plant- and light-filled space has a sophisticated island look and a view out to a cheery courtyard garden. Entrees include such Charleston traditions as Middleton Shrimp—large shrimp sautéed in white wine with garlic and Dijon mustard and blended with heavy cream. A new treatment of Caesar salad, called South Caroline salad is prepared tableside, with spinach and romaine, toasted local pecans, and bleu cheese crumbles tossed with a Caesar-style dressing. There's an elegant and extensive Southern-style breakfast menu and a popular Sunday brunch. *115 Meeting St., tel. 803/577–2400. Jacket and tie suggested at dinner. Reservations required for Sun. and holiday brunch, suggested for dinner in season. AE, CB, DC, MC, V.*

Queen Street Seafood Inn. Surrounded by a white picket fence, it was converted from a two–story residence, c. 1880. Classical music is played and there is dining in the courtyard, weather permitting. The rooms are intimate, with period furnishings and decor—Victorian black and pink upstairs, lighter and softer downstairs. Especially recommended is a puff-pastry concoction called Bouche à la Reine; the filling varies from day to day—perhaps scallops and mushrooms in a cream sauce. For dinner try the duckling with loquart (sweeter cousin to the kumquat), sauce. The new chef, Hank Yaden, masterfully combines spices for such specials as sea trout broiled with lemon butter, and finishes with a dusting of lavender flowers. The peach crisp is a dense, moist, cinnamony delight, served hot with vanilla ice cream. The kitchen is very accommodating to those on restricted diets. *68 Queen St., tel. 803/723–7700. Jack-*

et and tie optional. Reservations recommended. AE, CB, DC, MC, V.

★ **Rusty Anchor.** Executive chef Terence McKelvey has a refreshing outlook on local American cuisine, which shows in his grilled fish served in a simple island style—for instance, the shrimp-and-scallops brochette in a garlic-and-lemon-butter sauce—and his Sullivan Island sauté: clams, oysters, shrimp, scallops, and dolphin in a sauce similar to a Mediterranean bouillabaise. All preparation is done in view of the diners, either in the open display kitchen or at the raw bar. Closed Sun. and Mon. *2213 Middle St. and Station 22½, Sullivan's Island, tel. 803/883–9131. Dress: informal. Reservations suggested, particularly for large parties and on weekend nights. AE, MC, V.*

Inexpensive **California Dreaming.** The floor-to-ceiling windows of this
American heavy-volume restaurant, in an impressive stone fort on the Ashley River, look out at night on the lights of the harbor. The crowds come for the great view, low prices, and bountiful platters of food, such as Texas smoked ribs, barbecued chicken, prime rib, and catch of the day. To make the wait bearable, take to the bar for a frothy frozen margarita. *1 Ashley Pointe Dr. (5 min from downtown), tel. 803/766–1644. Dress: informal. No reservations. AE, MC, V.*

Greek **Athens.** Located just six minutes from downtown, a sojourn here is like a Greek holiday. The *bouzouki* music is straight from the *Plaka* in Athens. George Koutsogiannaks, one of three owners, is the vocalist on tape. The *kalamari lemonato* (baby squid in lemon) is like that served in the *tavernas* on the isle of Hydra. Traditional dishes moussaka and pasticcio are mainstays, but in keeping with current health trends, the freshest of seafood appears on the special board and a vegetarian plate with eggplant, pita, feta cheese, stuffed grape leaves, and *spanakopita* (spinach pie) has been added. The homemade Greek pizza with 12 different spices is Charleston's best. *325 Folly Rd., Cross Creek Shopping Center, James Island, tel. 803/795–0957. AE, MC, V. Closed Sun. lunch.*

Seafood **Shem Creek Bar & Grill.** This pleasant dockside spot is perennially popular for its oyster bar and light fare (until 10 Mon.–Wed., until 1 AM Thurs.–Sun.). There's also a wide variety of seafood entrees, including a steam pot—lobsters, clams, oysters, and sausages with melted lemon butter or hot cocktail sauce—big enough for two. *508 Mill St., Mt. Pleasant, tel. 803/884–8102. Dress: informal. No reservations. AE, MC, V.*

Lodging

Hotels and inns on the peninsula are generally more expensive. Also, rates tend to increase during the Spring Festival of Houses (mid-March to mid-April) and the Spoleto Festival USA (late May to early June); at those times, reservations are essential. During Visitors' Appreciation Days, from mid-November to mid-February, discounts of up to 50% may apply. For a Courtesy Discount Card, write to the **Charleston Trident Convention and Visitors Bureau** (Box 975, Charleston 29402, tel. 803/723–7641 or 800/845–7108).

Three organizations offer rooms in homes, cottages, and carriage houses: **Charleston East Bed and Breakfast League** (1031 Tall Pine Rd., Mt. Pleasant 29464, tel. 803/884–8208), **Charles-**

ton **Society Bed & Breakfast** (84 Murray Blvd., Charleston 29401, tel. 803/723–4948), and **Historic Charleston Bed and Breakfast** (43 Legare St., Charleston 29402, tel. 803/722–6606). Those interested in renting condominiums or houses on the beach on the Isle of Palms—some with private pools and tennis courts—might contact **Island Realty** (Box 157, Isle of Palms 29451, tel. 803/886–8144 or 800/845–2546).

The most highly recommended properties in each price category are indicated by a star ★. For a map pinpointing locations, *see* Dining.

Hotel/Motel Category	Cost*
Very Expensive	over $100
Expensive	$75–$100
Moderate	$50–$75
Inexpensive	under $50

*double room; add 7% for taxes

The following credit-card abbreviations are used: AE, American Express; CB, Carte Blanche; DC, Diners Club; MC, MasterCard; V, Visa.

Hotels and Motels
Very Expensive
★ **Mills House Hotel.** Antique furnishings and period decor give great charm to this luxurious Holiday Inn property, a reconstruction of a historic hostelry on its original site in the historic district. There's a lounge with live entertainment, and excellent dining in the Barbadoes Room (*see* Dining). *115 Meeting St., 29401, tel. 803/577–2400 or 800/465–4329. 215 rooms. Facilities: pool. AE, CB, DC, MC, V.*

★ **Omni Hotel at Charleston Place.** The city's newest luxury hotel, this graceful, low-rise structure in the historic district is flanked by upscale boutiques and specialty shops (*see* Shopping). The lobby features a magnificent hand-blown Venetian glass chandelier, an Italian marble floor, and antiques from Sotheby's. Rooms are furnished with period reproductions. *130 Market St., 29401, tel. 803/722–4900 or 800/228–2121. 443 units, including 46 suites. Facilities: fitness center with heated pool, sauna, whirlpool, Nautilus; concierge floor; restaurants; lounges with entertainment. AE, CB, DC, MC, V.*

Expensive **Best Western King Charles Inn.** This inn in the historic district has spacious rooms furnished with period reproductions. *237 Meeting St., 29401, tel. 803/723–7451 or 800/528–1234. 91 rooms. Facilities: pool, dining room, lounge. AE, CB, DC, MC, V.*

Moderate–Expensive **Sheraton Charleston Hotel.** Some rooms and suites in this 13-story hotel outside the historic district overlook the Ashley River. Spacious rooms and suites are highlighted with Queen Anne furnishings, and there's concierge service. Live entertainment and dancing contribute to the lounge's local popularity. *170 Lockwood Dr., 29403, tel. 803/723–3000 or 800/325–3535. 337 rooms. Facilities: 4 lighted tennis courts, pool, jogging track, coffee shop, dining room. AE, CB, DC, MC, V.*

Moderate **Days Inn Historic District.** This inn is well located and attrac-
★ tively furnished. *155 Meeting St., 29401, tel. 803/722–8411 or*

800/325–2525. 124 units. Facilities: pool, dining room. AE, DC, MC, V.

Heart of Charleston Motor Inn. This long-established motor hotel draws loyal repeat visitors for its convenient courtyard parking and location across from the Charleston Convention Center. *200 Meeting St., Box 460, 29402, tel. 803/723–3451 or 800/845–2504. 118 rooms. Facilities: pool, coffee shop, lounge, beauty shop. AE, CB, DC, MC, V.*

Holiday Inn Charleston/Mt. Pleasant. Just over the Cooper River Bridge, a 10-minute drive from the downtown historic district, is this new full-service hotel. Everything has been graciously done: brass lamps, crystal chandeliers, Queen Anne-style furniture. Two suites have Jacuzzis. "High-tech suites" offer PC cable hookups, large working areas, glossy ultramodern furniture, and refrigerators. *250 U.S. 17 Bypass, Mt. Pleasant 29464, tel. 803/884–6000 or 800/465–4329. 158 rooms. Facilities: outdoor pool, sauna, exercise room, cable TV/ movies, meeting facilities and ballroom, concierge floor, laundry, restaurant, raw bar, lounge with DJ.*

Inexpensive **Econo-Travel Motor Hotel.** This budget-chain unit is eight miles from downtown. Contemporary-style rooms are spacious and well maintained. *4725 Arco Ln., N. Charleston 29405, tel. 803/ 747–3672 or 800/446–6900. 48 rooms. Facilities: cable TV/free movies. Senior citizen, military/government discounts. AE, CB, DC, MC, V.*

Hampton Inn Charleston Airport. This economy arm of Holiday Inns offers lower rates with full service amenities. Rooms are decorated in contemporary style. *4701 Arco Ln., N. Charleston 29418, tel. 803/554–7154 or 800/426–7866. 125 rooms. Facilities: pool, cable TV/free movies, suite for small meetings. AE, CB, DC, MC, V.*

Motel 6. This well-maintained motor inn, part of a budget chain, is 10 miles from the downtown historic district. The decor is cheerful, colorful, and contemporary. *2551 Ashley Phosphate Rd., N. Charleston, 29418, tel. 803/572–6590. 126 rooms. Facilities: pool, cable TV/movies. DC, MC, V.*

Inns and Guest Houses The charms of historic Charleston can be enhanced by a stay at one of its many inns, most housed in restored structures. Some are reminiscent of European inns; one is tastefully contemporary, tucked away on the grounds of a famous garden estate. For all, double-room rates range from $85 to $145 in peak season. For complete listings, consult the "Charleston Area Visitors Guide," published by the Charleston Trident Convention & Visitors Bureau (Box 975, 17 Lockwood Blvd., Charleston 29402, tel. 803/723–7641 or 800/845–7108).

Historic District **Battery Carriage House.** This small luxury guest house—one of Charleston's first inns—has handsomely furnished rooms with period furniture and kitchenettes. *20 S. Battery St., 29401, tel. 803/723–9881 or 800/845–7638. 10 rooms. Facilities: pool. AE, MC, V.*

★ **Indigo Inn.** All the rooms here focus on the picturesque interior courtyard and are furnished with 18th-century antiques and reproductions. The trademark "hunt breakfast" consists of homemade breads, ham biscuits, fruit, and coffee. There are six slightly more expensive suites—one with a Jacuzzi—in the nearby **Jasmine House,** a pre–Civil War Greek Revival structure. These have high ceilings, fireplaces, and Oriental rugs. *1*

Maiden Ln., 29401, tel. 803/577–5900 or 800/845–7639. 40 rooms. AE, MC, V.

Lodge Alley Inn. All of the various accommodations here are luxuriously appointed in traditional Charleston fashion with Oriental carpets and period reproduction furnishings. Room refrigerators are stocked with complimentary wine. The French Quarter Restaurant features a grand rotisserie. Adjacent is a lounge with an ornate bar. *195 E. Bay St., 29401, tel. 803/722–1611 or 800/845–1004. 34 rooms, 37 suites with kitchens, 1 2-bedroom penthouse. AE, MC, V.*

Meeting Street Inn. The rooms in this handsome 1870 structure are furnished in period. Each has a reproduction four-poster rice bed, and all open onto a piazza. Guests mingle in the courtyard garden for complimentary afternoon champagne and for evening cocktails and chamber music. *173 Meeting St., 29401, tel. 803/723–1882 or 800/845–7638. 54 rooms. Facilities: whirlpool, boardroom suite for meetings. AE, MC, V.*

★ **Planters Inn.** Rooms and suites here are beautifully appointed with opulent fabrics and furnishings, including mahogany four-poster beds and marble baths. There's a concierge and 24-hour room service. *112 N. Market St., 29401, tel. 803/722–2345 or 800/845–7082. 46 rooms and suites. AE, CB, DC, MC, V.*

Sword Gate Inn. Rooms in this, Charleston's oldest inn, are all furnished in antiques, including a large plantation bed or two. The four downstairs rooms have private entrances off the courtyard. A traditional Charleston breakfast is highlighted by host Walter Barton's cheese grits, and complimentary wine and cheese are served afternoons in the expansive ballroom. *111 Tradd St., 29401, tel. 803/723–8518. 6 rooms. AE, MC, V.*

★ **Vendue Inn.** Near the waterfront, this European-style inn in a renovated 1828 warehouse offers antiques-furnished public areas and guest rooms, with canopied four-poster beds and Oriental rugs. The adjacent **Vendue West,** in a restored 1800 house, has deluxe suites with fireplaces, wet bars, Jacuzzis, and marble baths. Complimentary wine and cheese are served afternoons in the courtyard, accompanied by chamber music. Concierge service is offered, and there is an elegant restaurant, Morton's. *19 Vendue Range, 29401, tel. 803/723–9980 or 800/845–7900. 30 rooms and suites. AE, MC, V.*

West of the Ashley
★ **Middleton Inn and Conference Center.** This contemporary-style lodge with sumptuously furnished rooms is located on the grounds of Middleton Place Plantation. Floor-to-ceiling windows are hung with wooden shutters, and working fireplaces are serviced by tools forged by the estate's blacksmith. There is a cafe. *Ashley River Rd. (U.S. 61), Middleton Place, 29407, tel. 803/556–0500. 55 rooms. Facilities: pool, tennis courts. AE, MC, V.*

Resort Islands The semitropical islands dotting the South Carolina coast near Charleston are home to some of the nation's finest resorts. A wide variety of packages makes them more affordable than you would imagine. Peak-season rates (during spring and summer vacations) range from $100 to $250 per day, double occupancy. Costs often drop considerably off-season.

Kiawah Island Resort. Choose from 150 inn rooms, 48 suites, and 500 completely equipped one- to four-bedroom villas in two luxurious resort villages on 10,000 wooded acres. There are 10 miles of fine broad beaches, two championship golf courses, two complete tennis centers, jeep and water safaris, land sailing, canoeing, surfcasting, fishing, and children's programs.

There's also a general store and shops. Dining options are many and varied: Low Country specialties in the Jasmine Porch and Veranda, Indigo House; Continental cuisine in the Charleston Gallery; lagoonside dining at the Park Cafe; casual dining in the Sand Wedge, Sundancers, Jonah's. *On Kiawah Island, 21 mi from Charleston (take U.S. 17S to Main Rd., take left and follow signs), Box 12910, Charleston 29412, tel. 803/768–2121 or 800/354–2924. AE, DC, MC, V.*

Seabrook Island Resort. There are 360 completely equipped one- to three-bedroom villas, cottages, and beach houses. Beach Club and Island Club, open to all guests, are centers for dining and leisure activities. Amenities include championship golf, tennis and equestrian centers, bicycling, water sports, pools, children's programs. *On Seabrook Island, 23 mi from Charleston (take U.S. 17S to SC 171S to SC 700, then follow signs), Box 32099, Charleston 29417, tel. 803/768–1000 or 800/ 845–5531. AE, CB, DC, MC, V.*

★ **Wild Dunes.** This lavish, 1,500-acre resort has 350 villa accommodations, each with a fully equipped kitchen and washer and dryer. There are two widely acclaimed championship golf courses, a racquet club, a yacht harbor on the Intracoastal Waterway, bicycling, nature trails, surfcasting, water sports, and children's programs. Guests enjoy beef specialties at The Club House and fresh seafoods at The Island House, where all dishes are created by a French master chef. There's a lounge with live entertainment. *On the Isle of Palms, 12 mi northeast of Charleston (take U.S. 17 to SC 703), Box 1410, Charleston 29402, tel. 803/886–6000 or 800/845–8880. AE, CB, DC, MC, V.*

The Arts

Pick up the comprehensive Schedule of Events at the Visitors Information Center (85 Calhoun St.) or at area hotels, inns, and restaurants. For an advance copy, contact **Charleston Trident Convention and Visitors Bureau** (Box 975, Charleston 29402, tel. 803/723–7641 or 800/845–7108). Also see "Tips for Tourists" each Saturday in *The News & Courier/The Evening Post.* And the weekend ARTSline (tel. 803/723–2787) gives information on arts events for the week.

Arts Festivals **Spoleto Festival USA.** Founded by renowned maestro Gian Carlo Menotti in 1977, Spoleto has become one of the world's greatest celebrations of the arts. For two weeks, from late May to early June, opera, dance, theater, symphonic and chamber music performances, jazz, and the visual arts are showcased in concert halls, theaters, parks, churches, streets, and gardens throughout the city. For information: Spoleto Festival USA (Box 704, Charleston, SC 29402, tel. 803/722–2764).

Piccolo Spoleto Festival. The spirited companion festival of Spoleto Festival USA showcases the best in local and regional talent from every artistic discipline. There are about 700 events—from jazz performances to puppet shows—held at 60 sites in 17 days, from mid-May through early June, and most performances are free. For a program, available May 1 each year, contact the Office of Cultural Affairs, Piccolo Spoleto Festival (133 Church St., Charleston 29401, tel. 803/724–7305).

Moja Arts Festival. Theater, dance, and music performances, art shows, films, lectures, and tours celebrating the rich heritage of the African continent are held at sites throughout the historic district the first two weeks in October. For information: The Office of Cultural Affairs (133 Church St., Charleston 29401, tel. 803/724–7305).

Concerts   The College of Charleston has a **Monday Night Recital Series** (*see* Charleston for Free). The **Charleston Symphony Orchestra** (tel. 803/723–7528) presents its Classics Concerts Series at Gaillard Municipal Auditorium (77 Calhoun St., tel. 803/577–4500). Its Brass Quintet plays at the Charleston Museum Auditorium (360 Meeting St., tel. 803/722–2996) and the Garden Theatre (371 King St., tel. 803/722–6230). Its Woodwind Quintet also performs at the Charleston Museum Auditorium. Guest artists at **Sarah Johnson & Friends** (tel. 803/577–0536)—a chamber music series held fall through spring at the Dock Street Theatre (135 Church St., tel. 803/723–5648)—have included Paula Robison and Eliot Fisk.

Dance   The **Charleston Ballet Theatre** (tel. 803/723–7334) and the **Charleston Civic Ballet** (tel. 803/722–8779 or 577–4502) perform at Gaillard Municipal Auditorium. The **Robert Ivey Ballet Company** (tel. 803/556–1343), a student group at the College of Charleston, gives a fall and spring program of jazz, classical, and modern dance at the Simons Center for the Arts.

Theater   The **Footlight Players,** the **East Cooper Theater,** and the **Young Charleston Theatre Co.** stage performances at the Dock Street Theatre. The East Cooper Theatre also stages some performances at the Garden Theatre. Performances by the College of Charleston's drama department and guest theatrical groups are presented during the school year at the **Simons Center for the Arts** (tel. 803/792–8228).

Nightlife

Beach Bar   **Windjammer** (tel. 803/886–8596), on the Isle of Palms, is an oceanfront spot featuring live rock music.

Dance Clubs   In the market area, there's **Fannigans** (tel. 803/722–6916), where a DJ spins Top-40 hits, and the best of beach music. The "shag", South Carolina's state dance, popularized in the early '60s, is alive and well here. **Juke Box** (tel. 803/723–3431), with a DJ, '50s and '60s music, and a '50s look (waitresses wear cheerleader outfits); and **Myskyns** (tel. 803/577–5595), with live rock, reggae, R&B, or other bands most nights and an 8-by-10 video screen.

Hotel Bars   The **Best Friend Lounge** (tel. 803/577–2400), in the Mills House Hotel, has a guitarist playing easy-listening tunes Monday–Saturday nights. **Water Colors** (tel. 803/722–4900), in the Omni Hotel at Charleston Place, has dancing Monday–Saturday nights, with a DJ, Top-40 hits, and videos.

Restaurant Lounges   **A.W. Shucks** (tel. 803/723–1151) is a popular spot for relaxed evenings set to taped easy-listening. **Cafe 99** (tel. 803/577–4499) has laid-back '60s and '70s music indoors and out by vocalists and guitarists. **East Bay Trading Co.** (tel. 803/722–0722) has a small dance floor in its lively bar and a DJ playing Top 40s Friday and Saturday nights.

Dinner Cruise   For an evening of dining and dancing afloat on the luxury yacht *Spirit of Charleston,* call 803/722–2628. *The Southern Star,* a reconverted paddlewheeler, also has dinner cruises and sails from the Ripley Light Marina near California Dreaming. Call

Bill Miller, 803/722–6182. *The Pride* operates from the same dock and is an 84-foot gaff-topsail schooner available for daily harbor excursions and cruises to Savannah, Georgia. Phone Capt. Bob, 803/795–1180.

Myrtle Beach and the Grand Strand

The Grand Strand, a resort area along the South Carolina coast, is one of the Eastern Seaboard's megafamily-vacation centers, and the state's top tourist area. The main attraction, of course, is the broad, beckoning beach—55 miles of it, stretching from the North Carolina border south to Georgetown, with Myrtle Beach at the hub. But the Strand has something for everyone: 48 championship golf courses, designed by such legends as Arnold Palmer, Robert Trent Jones, and Tom and George Fazio; excellent seafood restaurants; giant shopping malls and factory outlets; amusement parks, water slides, and arcades; a dozen shipwrecks for divers to explore; fine fishing; nine private campgrounds, most on the beach; plus paddlewheeler cruises, antique-car and wax museums, the world's largest sculpture garden, a version of the Grand Ole Opry, an antique pipe organ and merry-go-round, a minor-league baseball team, and a museum dedicated entirely to rice.

Getting Around

By Plane The Myrtle Beach Jetport is served by **American, American's American Eagle** affiliate; **Atlantis, Eastern's** affiliate; **Delta** and its **Atlantic Southeast** Airlines affiliate; and **USAir.**

By Car Located midway between New York and Miami, the Grand Strand can be reached from all directions via Interstates 20, 26, 40, 77, 85, and 95, which connect with U.S. 17, the major north–south coastal route through the Strand.

By Train **Amtrak** service for the Grand Strand is available through a terminal in Florence. Buses connect with Amtrak there for the 70-mile drive to Myrtle Beach.

By Bus Public transportation is provided by **Coastal Rapid Transit Authority** (tel. 803/248–7277). It operates daily between 6 AM and 1:15 AM. The fare is 75¢, exact change required.

By Taxi Service is provided by **Coastal Cab Service** in Myrtle Beach (tel. 803/448–4047).

Guided Tours

Palmetto Tour & Travel in Myrtle Beach (tel. 803/626–2660) and **Leisure Time Unlimited** in Myrtle Beach (Gray Line) (tel. 803/448–9483) offer tour packages, guide service, and charter service. At the **Georgetown County Chamber of Commerce and Information Center** (U.S. 17, tel. 803/546–8436), you can pick up free driving- and walking-tour maps or rent cassette walking tours. Also from here (Mar.–Oct.), you can take three different tours of historic areas: by tram, by 1840 horse-drawn carriage, or by boat.

Important Addresses and Numbers

Tourist Information
Georgetown County Chamber of Commerce and Information Center (U.S. 17, Georgetown 29442, tel. 803/546–8436). **Myrtle Beach Area Chamber of Commerce** (Box 2115, 1301 N. Kings Hwy., Myrtle Beach 29578, tel. 803/626–7444 or for literature only 800/356–3016).

Emergencies Dial 911 for emergency assistance.

Hospital The emergency room is open 24 hours a day at the **HCA Grand Strand General Hospital** (off U.S. 17 at 809 82nd Ave. Pkwy., Myrtle Beach, tel. 803/449–4411).

Dentist For emergency service, call **Sexton's Dental Clinic** (901 Medical Plaza, 82nd Ave. Pkwy., Myrtle Beach, tel. 803/449–0431).

Exploring the Grand Strand

Myrtle Beach—whose population of 26,000 increases to about 350,000 in summer—is the center of activity in the Grand Strand. It is here that you find the amusement parks and other children's activities that make the area so popular for family vacations, as well as most of the nightlife that keeps parents and teenagers happy after beach hours. North of Myrtle Beach, in the North Strand, there is Little River, with a thriving fishing and charter boat industry, and the several communities—each with its own small-town flavor—that make up North Myrtle Beach. In the South Strand, Surfside Beach and Garden City are family retreats of year-round and summer homes and condominiums. Farther south are Murrells Inlet, once a pirate's haven and now a popular fishing port, and Pawleys Island, one of the East Coast's oldest resorts. Historic Georgetown, the state's third-oldest city, forms the Strand's southern tip.

Our tour begins in **Myrtle Beach.** At the **Myrtle Beach Pavilion and Amusement Park,** you'll find activities for all ages and interests: thrill and kiddie rides, including the Carolinas' largest flume, plus video games, a teen nightclub, specialty shops, antique cars, and sidewalk cafes. *Ninth Ave. N and Ocean Blvd., tel. 803/448–6456. Fees for individual attractions; family discount book available. Open daily 1 PM–midnight late May–Sept., weekends rest of year.*

Nearby, at the **Guinness Hall of World Records,** fantastic human and natural phenomena spring to life through videotapes, replicas, and other displays. *911 N. Ocean Blvd., tel. 803/448–4611. Admission: $3.95 adults; $2.95 children 7–12, under 7 free. Open daily 10 AM–midnight mid-Mar.–early Oct. Closed rest of year.*

More of the unusual awaits at **Ripleys Believe It or Not Museum.** Among the more than 750 exhibits is an eight-foot, 11-inch wax replica of the world's tallest man. *901 N. Ocean Blvd., tel. 803/448–2331. Admission: $4.95 adults; $2.95 children 6–12, under 6 free. Open daily 10 AM–10 PM First week Mar.–mid-Oct. Closed rest of year.*

Drama, sound, and animation highlight religious, historical, and entertainment sections in the **Myrtle Beach National Wax Museum.** *1000 N. Ocean Blvd., tel. 803/448–9921. Admission:*

$4.50 adults; $2 children 6–12, under 6 free. Open daily 9 AM–9 PM Feb.–mid-Oct. Closed rest of year.

When your family's appetite for more raucous amusements has been sated, it's time to head out of town. Going south on Kings Highway, you'll come to **Murrells Inlet,** a picturesque little fishing village that boasts some of the most popular seafood restaurants on the Grand Strand. It's also a great place for chartering a fishing boat or joining a half- or full-day group excursion.

Three miles south, on the grounds of a Colonial rice plantation, is the largest outdoor collection of American sculpture, with works by such American artists as Frederic Remington and Daniel Chester French. **Brookgreen Gardens** was begun in 1931 by railroad magnate/philanthropist Archer Huntington and his wife, Anna, herself a sculptor. Today, more than 400 works are set amid beautifully landscaped grounds, with avenues of live oaks, reflecting pools, and over 2,000 plant species. Also on the 9,000-acre site is a wildlife park, an aviary, a cypress swamp, nature trails, and an education center. It's a lovely, soothing place for a picnic. *18 mi south of Myrtle Beach off U.S. 17, tel. 803/237–4218. Admission: $4 adults; $1 children 6–12, under 6 free. Tape tours, $1 extra. Open daily 9:30–4:45 except Christmas.*

Across the highway is **Huntington Beach State Park,** the 2,500-acre former estate of the Huntingtons. The park's focal point is the Moorish-style "castle" Atalaya, once the Huntingtons' home, now open to visitors in season. In addition to the splendid beach, there is surf fishing, nature trails, an interpretive center, a salt-marsh boardwalk, picnic areas, a playground, concessions, and a campground. *Tel. 803/237–4440. Admission free; parking fee in peak months; incidentals fees. Open daily during daylight hours.*

Farther south is one of the first summer resorts on the Atlantic coast, **Pawleys Island.** Prior to the Civil War, wealthy planters and their families summered here to avoid malaria and other fevers that infested the swampy coastal region. Four miles long and a half-mile wide, it's made up mostly of weathered old summer cottages nestled in groves of oleander and oak trees. The famed Pawleys Island hammocks have been handmade here since 1880. In several shops, you can watch them being fashioned of rope and cord by local craftsfolk (*see* Shopping).

Bellefield Nature Center, south on U.S. 17, is at the entrance of Hobcaw Barony, the vast estate of the late Bernard M. Baruch. Here he consulted with such guests as President Franklin D. Roosevelt and Prime Minister Winston Churchill. The nature center, operated by the Belle W. Baruch Foundation, is used for teaching and research in forestry and marine biology. *Tel. 803/546–4623. Admission free. Open weekdays 10–5, Sat. 1–5.*

Georgetown, on the shores of Winyah Bay, was founded in 1729 by a Baptist minister and soon became the center of America's Colonial rice empire. A rich plantation culture took root here and developed on a scale comparable to Charleston's. Today, oceangoing vessels reach Georgetown's busy port through a deepwater channel, and the town's prosperity is based on industry (such as its paper mill and an iron foundry) and tourism.

In the heart of town, the graceful market-meeting building, topped by an 1842 town clock and tower, has been converted into the **Rice Museum,** which traces the history of rice cultivation through maps, tools, and dioramas. *Front and Screven Sts., tel. 803/546-7423. Admission: $2 adults, $1 military, students free. Open weekdays 9:30-4:30, Sat. 10-4:30 (until 1 PM Oct.-Mar.), Sun. 2-4:30 PM. Closed major holidays.*

Nearby, **Prince George Winyah Episcopal Church,** named after King George II, still serves the congregation established in 1721. It was built in 1737 with bricks brought over from Mother England. *Broad and Highmarket Sts., tel. 803/546-4358. Donation suggested. Visitors welcome weekdays 9-4.*

Overlooking the Sampit River from a high bluff is the **Harold Kaminski House** (ca. 1760). It's especially notable for its collections of regional antiques and furnishings, and for its Chippendale and Duncan Phyfe furniture, Royal Doulton vases, and silver. *1003 Front St., tel. 803/546-7706. Admission: $4 adults; $3 senior citizens; $2 children 12-16, under 12 free. Open weekdays 10-5, tours hourly. Closed holidays, 2 weeks at Christmas.*

Twelve miles south of Georgetown, **Hopsewee Plantation,** surrounded by moss-draped live oaks, magnolias, and tree-size camellias, overlooks the North Santee River. The mansion is notable for its fine Georgian staircase and hand-carved Adam candlelight moldings. *U.S. 17, tel. 803/546-7891. Admission: $3 adults; $1 children 6-18, under 6 free. Open Tues.-Fri. 10-5 Feb.-Oct., other times by appointment. Grounds only, including nature trail, $1 per car.*

Hampton Plantation State Park, at the edge of the Francis Marion National Forest (*see* off the Beaten Track in Charleston section), preserves the home of Archibald Rutledge, poet laureate of South Carolina for 39 years until his death in 1973. The 18th-century plantation house is an excellent example of a Low Country mansion. The exterior has been restored; cutaway sections in the finely crafted interior show the changes made through the centuries. The grounds are landscaped, and picnic areas are available. *Off U.S. 17, tel. 803/546-9361. Admission: $1 adults; 50¢ children 6-18, under 6 free. Grounds free; open Thurs.-Mon. 9-6. House open Sat. 10-3, Sun. noon-3.*

What to See and Do with Children

Brookgreen Gardens (*see* Exploring the Grand Strand).

Huntington Beach State Park (*see* Exploring).

Myrtle Beach Grand Prix. Auto-mania heaven, it offers Formula 1 race cars, go-carts, bumper boats, mini-go-carts, kiddie cars, and mini-bumper boats for adults and children age 3 and up. *Two locations: U.S. 17 Bus., Myrtle Beach, across from Air Force base, tel. 803/238-2421; and Windy Hill, U.S. 17N, N. Myrtle Beach, tel. 803/272-6010. Rides priced individually, average ride $3.50. Open daily 10 AM-11 PM Mar. 10-Oct. 31.*

Myrtle Beach Pavilion and Amusement Park (*see* Exploring).

Myrtle Waves Water Park. There's splashy family fun for all ages in 17 rides and activities. *U.S. 17 Bypass and 10th Ave. N, Myrtle Beach, tel. 803/448-1026. Cost: $10.92, $8.27 after 3 PM,*

$5.25 after 5 PM Tues.–Thurs., children under 3 free. Open daily 9:30–6 (Tues.–Thurs. until 8) Memorial Day weekend–Labor Day, weekends only rest of May, after Labor Day–Sept. 30. Closed rest of year.

Shopping

Malls **Myrtle Square Mall** (2502 N. Kings Hwy., Myrtle Beach, tel. 803/448–2513) is an upscale complex with 71 stores and restaurants, and a new 250-seat Food Court. **Briarcliffe Mall** (10177 N. Kings Hwy., Myrtle Beach, tel. 803/249–2819) has 100 specialty shops, JC Penney, and K-mart. Both malls, the area's largest, are open Monday–Saturday 10–9:30 (until 9 in winter), Sunday 1–6.

Discount and Off-Price Outlets Off-price shopping outlets abound in the Grand Strand. **Waccamaw Pottery and Outlet Park** (U.S. 501 at the Waterway, Myrtle Beach, tel. 803/236–1100) is one of the nation's largest. In several buildings, over three miles of shelves are stocked with china, glassware, wicker, brass and pewter, and countless other items. Outlet Park has about 50 factory outlets with clothing, furniture, books, jewelry, and more. Open Monday through Saturday 9–10. The **Hathaway Factory Outlet** (tel. 803/236–4200), across from Waccamaw, offers menswear by Christian Dior, Ralph Lauren, and Jack Nicklaus and women's wear by White Stag and Geoffrey Beene, among others. Open daily 9–6 (until 8 Mon.–Sat. in summer).

Specialty Shops The **Hammock Shops at Pawleys Island** is a handsome complex of 17 boutiques and gift shops built with old brick brought from England as ballast. In one shop, summer visitors can see rope hammocks being made. Other wares include jewelry, toys, antiques, and designer fashions. The shops are open daily 10–5 in winter; Monday–Saturday 9:30–9, Sunday 12:30–6 in summer.

Beaches

All the Grand Strand beaches are family oriented, and almost all are public. The widest expanses are in North Myrtle Beach, where the sand stretches for up to an eighth of a mile from the dunes to the water at low tide. Those who wish to combine their sunning with nightlife and amusement-park activities can enjoy it all at Myrtle Beach. Vacationers seeking a quieter day head for the South Strand communities of Surfside Beach and Garden City, or historic Pawleys Island. All along the Strand, you can enjoy shell hunting, fishing, swimming, sunbathing, sailing, surfing, jogging, or just strolling.

Participant Sports

Fishing Because offshore waters along the Grand Strand are warmed by the Gulf Stream, fishing is usually good from early spring through December. Anglers can walk out over the Atlantic from 10 piers and jetties to try for amberjack, sea trout, and king mackerel. Surfcasters may snare bluefish, whiting, flounder, pompano, and channel bass. In the South Strand, salt marshes, inlets, and tidal creeks yield flounder, blues, croakers, spots, shrimp, clams, oysters, and blue-claw crabs. Some conveniently located marinas that offer both half- and full-day fishing and sightseeing trips are **Capt. Dick's** (U.S. 17 Bus.,

Murrells Inlet, tel. 803/651–3676), **Flying Fisherman** (U.S. 17 Bus., Murrells Inlet, tel. 803/651–5700), and **Hurrican Fleet, Vereen's Marina** (U.S. 17 at 11th Ave. N, N. Myrtle Beach, tel. 803/249–3571).

The annual **Grand Strand Fishing Rodeo** (Apr.–Oct.) features a "fish of the month" contest, with prizes for the largest catch of a designated species. The October **Arthur Smith King Mackerel Tournament** offers more than $350,000 in prizes and attracts nearly 900 boats and 5,000 anglers.

Golf The Grand Strand—known as the World's Golf Capital—has 48 public courses. Many are championship layouts by top designers. All share meticulously manicured greens, lush fairways, and challenging hazards. Spring and fall are the busiest seasons because of warm temperatures and off-season rates. An organization called **Golf Holiday** (tel. 803/448–5942), whose members include hotels, motels, condominiums, and golf courses along the Grand Strand, offers many package plans throughout the year.

Popular courses include: in Myrtle Beach, **Arcadian Shores Golf Club** (tel. 803/449–5217) and **Dunes Golf and Beach Club** (tel. 803/449–5914); in North Myrtle Beach, **Gator Hole** (tel. 803/249–3543), **Oyster Bay Golf Links** (tel. 803/272–6399), and **Robbers Roost Golf Club** (tel. 803/249–1471); and at Little River, **Marsh Harbor Golf Links** (tel. 803/249–3449).

Scuba Diving In summer, a large variety of warm-water tropical fish find their way to the area from the Gulf Stream. Off the coast of Little River, rock and coral ledges teem with coral, sea fans, sponges, reef fish, anemones, urchins, arrow crabs, and stone crabs. Several outlying shipwrecks are home to schools of spadefish, amberjack, grouper, and barracuda. Instruction and equipment rentals are available from **Myrtle Beach Scuba Center** (U.S. 501W, Myrtle Beach, tel. 803/448–2832).

Tennis There are over 150 courts throughout the Grand Strand. Facilities include hotel and resort courts, as well as free municipal courts in Myrtle Beach, North Myrtle Beach, and Surfside Beach. Among tennis clubs offering court time, rental equipment, and instruction are **Myrtle Beach Racquet Club** (tel. 803/449–4031), **Myrtle Beach Tennis and Swim Club** (tel. 803/449–4486), and Surfside Beach's **Grand Strand Tennis Club** (tel. 803/650–3330).

Water Sports Surfboards, Hobie Cats, Jet Skis, Windsurfers, and sailboats are available for rent at **Downwind Sails** (Ocean Blvd. at 29th Ave. S, Myrtle Beach, tel. 803/448–7245).

Spectator Sports

Baseball Between early April and late August, the **Myrtle Beach Blue Jays,** farm club for the Toronto Blue Jays, play about 70 home games at the 3,500-seat Coastal Carolina Stadium (tel. 803/347–3161), off U.S. 501 less than 10 miles from downtown Myrtle Beach.

Dining

A wealth of seafood, fresh from inlets, rivers, and ocean, graces the tables of coastal South Carolina. Enjoy it in lavish portions, garnished with hush puppies, cole slaw, and fresh vegetables, in many family-style restaurants. Or sample Continental or classic American preparations at elegant resorts and upscale restaurants. The most highly recommended restaurants in each price category are indicated by a star ★.

Category	Cost*
Very Expensive	over $25
Expensive	$15–$25
Moderate	$7–$15
Inexpensive	under $7

per person without tax (5% in South Carolina), service, or drinks

The following credit-card abbreviations are used: AE, American Express; CB, Carte Blanche; DC, Diners Club; MC, MasterCard; and V, Visa.

Georgetown **Rice Paddy.** This cozy restaurant is apt to be crowded at lunch,
Seafood when local business folk flock in for homemade vegetable soup,
★ garden-fresh salads, and sandwiches. Dinner is more relaxed, and the menu showcases broiled fresh seafood. Crabmeat casserole is a tasty specialty. So is veal scaloppine. *408 Duke St., tel. 803/546–2021. Dress: informal. Reservations not required. AE, MC, V. Closed Sun. Moderate.*

Murrells Inlet **Planter's Back Porch.** Sip cool drinks in the spring house of a
Seafood turn-of-the-century farmhouse, then have dinner in a garden
★ setting reminiscent of a 19th-century Southern plantation. Black wrought-iron chandeliers are suspended from high white ceiling beams, and hanging baskets of greenery decorate white latticework archways separating the fireplace-centered main dining room and the airy, glass-enclosed porch. You can't go wrong with baked whole flounder, panned lump crabmeat, or the hearty Inlet Dinner showcasing several fresh daily catches. *U.S. 17 and Wachesaw Rd., tel. 803/651–5263 or 651–5544. Dress: informal. Reservations not required. AE, MC, V. Closed Dec.–mid-Feb. Moderate.*

Myrtle Beach **Slug's Choice.** A Carolinas tradition, this immensely popular
Mixed Menu restaurant has a lounge overlooking the Intracoastal Waterway. It does serve fresh local seafood and some veal dishes, but the house specialties are prime rib, and steaks flame-grilled to order. There's a hefty salad bar. The restaurant is under the same management as nearby Slug's Rib, specializing in prime rib. *Slug's Choice: 10131 N. Kings Hwy., tel. 803/272–7781. Jacket and tie suggested. Reservations accepted. May close one month in winter—best to call. AE, CB, DC, MC, V. Moderate–Expensive. Slug's Rib: 9713 N. Kings Hwy., tel. 803/449–6419. Dress: informal. No reservations. AE, CB, DC, MC, V. Moderate–Expensive.*

Seafood **Rice Planter's Restaurant.** Dine on fresh seafood, quail, or
★ steaks grilled to order in a homey setting enhanced by Low Country antiques, rice-plantation tools and artifacts, and candlelight. Shrimp Creole is a house specialty; among the appetizers, don't miss the crab fingers! Bread and pecan pie are home-baked. *6707 N. Kings Hwy., tel. 803/449–3456 or 449–*

3457. Dress: informal. Reservations not required. AE, MC, V. Closed Dec. 25 and 26. Moderate.

Sea Captain's House. At this picturesque restaurant with a nautical decor, the best seats are in the windowed porch room, with its sweeping ocean views. The fireplace in the wood-paneled inside dining room casts a warm glow on cool off-season evenings. Menu highlights include she-crab soup, Low Country crab casserole, and avocado-seafood salad. Breads and desserts are home-baked. *3002 N. Ocean Blvd., tel. 803/448-8082. Also on U.S. 17 Bus., Murrells Inlet, tel. 803/651-2416. Both: Dress: informal. Reservations not required. AE, MC, V. Closed mid-Dec.–mid-Feb. Moderate.*

Southern Suppers. Here's hearty family dining in a cozy farmhouse filled with country primitive art; handmade quilts line the walls. The menu features an all-you-can-eat seafood buffet. You can also order down-home Southern specialties like fried chicken, country-fried steak, and country ham with red-eye gravy and grits. *U.S. 17S, midway between Myrtle Beach and Surfside Beach, tel. 803/238-4557. Dress: informal. Reservations not required. No liquor. MC, V. Closed Oct.–Feb. Moderate.*

Pawleys Island
American Regional
★

Pawleys Island Inn Restaurant and Bar. There are four dining rooms in this 18-year-old antebellum-style inn. It's especially pleasant to dine on the glass-enclosed porch; request this seating when you make reservations. Specialties include snapper sautéed in lemon butter, then baked; broiled lump-crab cakes; and shrimp Provençale with fresh spinach pasta. There's a children's menu, and all breads and desserts are baked on the premises. Under the same ownership is the adjacent Pawleys Island Inn Bakery, which seats 12 and serves sandwiches, salads, picnic boxes, and freshly baked breads. *U.S. 17, in the Hammock Shops at Pawleys Island, tel. 803/237-9033. Dress: informal. Reservations suggested. AE, DC, MC, V. Closed Sun., major holidays. Expensive.*

Lodging

Among other lodgings options, condominiums are popular on the Grand Strand, combining spaciousness and modern amenities and appealing especially to families. You can choose among cottages, villas, and hotel-style high-rise units. Maid service is frequently available. For the free directories *Grand Hotel and Motel Accommodations* and *Grand Condominium and Cottage Accommodations*, write the Myrtle Beach Area Chamber of Commerce (Box 2115, Myrtle Beach 29578, tel. 803/626-7444 or 800/356-3016).

Attractive package plans are available between Labor Day and spring break. Also, see Golf section in Participant Sports regarding golf packages. The most highly recommended properties in each price category are indicated by a star ★.

Category	Cost*
Very Expensive	over $100
Expensive	$65–$100

Moderate	$45–$65
Inexpensive	under $45

double room; add 7% for taxes

The following credit-card abbreviations are used: AE, American Express; CB, Carte Blanche; DC, Diners Club; MC, MasterCard; and V, Visa.

Georgetown
Inexpensive–
Moderate

Best Western Carolinian. This conveniently located in-town motor inn has spacious rooms with reproduction period furnishings. *706 Church St., 29440, tel. 803/546–5191 or 800/528–1234. 90 rooms. Facilities: pool, cable TV/movies, restaurant, lounge. AE, CB, DC, MC, V.*

Myrtle Beach
Very Expensive
★

Myrtle Beach Hilton and Golf Club. This luxurious high-rise oceanfront property—part of the Arcadian Shores Golf Club—is highlighted by a dramatic 14-story atrium. Spacious, airy rooms, all with sea views, are decorated in chic plum, mauve, gray, and rose tones and accented by ultracontemporary lamps and accessories. Two newly redecorated executive floors offer two-phone rooms and other amenities. *701 Hilton Rd., Arcadian Shores, 29577, tel. 803/449–5000 or 800/445–8667. 392 rooms. Facilities: 600-foot private beach, oceanfront pool, tennis, golf, restaurant, lounges, entertainment, shops, social program. AE, CB, DC, MC, V.*

Radisson Resort Hotel. The Grand Strand's newest luxury property, this 20-story glass-sheathed tower is part of the Kingston Plantation complex of shops, restaurants, hotels, and condominiums set amid 145 acres of oceanside woodlands. Guest rooms are highlighted by bleached-wood furnishings and attractive artworks. The balconied one-bedroom suites have kitchenettes. *9800 Lake Dr., 29577, tel. 803/449–0006 or 800/228–9822. 255 suites. Facilities: 2 restaurants and lounge; privileges at sports/fitness complex offering racquetball, tennis, squash, aerobics, exercise equipment, sauna, pools, whirlpool. AE, CB, DC, MC, V.*

Sheraton Myrtle Beach Martinique. (Formerly Sheraton Myrtle Beach Inn.) The oceanfront rooms in this luxury hotel have been recently remodeled and all have queen-size beds. There's also a grand new lobby. *7100 N. Ocean Blvd., 29578, tel. 803/449–4441 or 800/325–3535. 147 rooms, 86 efficiencies. Facilities: dining and dancing in glass-enclosed rooftop restaurant, live entertainment in bar, laundry, heated pool, wading pool, racquet club privileges, children's activity director. New conference and amenities center has full spa facilities. AE, CB, DC, MC, V.*

Best Western/The Landmark. The rooms in this high-rise oceanfront resort hotel are tastefully decorated in a modern style. Some have balconies and refrigerators. *1501 S. Ocean Blvd., 29577, tel. 803/448–9441 or 800/528–1234. 326 rooms. Facilities: pool, children's activity program, game room, dining rooms, lounges, nightclub, live nightly entertainment (see Nightlife). AE, CB, DC, MC, V.*

The Breakers Resort Hotel. The rooms in this oceanfront resort are airy and spacious, with contemporary decor. Many have balconies and refrigerators. *2006 N. Ocean Blvd., Box 485, 29578–0485, tel. 803/626–5000 or 800/845–0688. 391 rooms. Facilities: restaurant, 3 oceanfront pools, indoor and outdoor whirlpools, saunas, exercise room, restaurant, lounge, laundry, children's programs. AE, CB, DC, MC, V.*

Expensive **Holiday Inn Downtown.** This in-town oceanfront inn is right at the heart of the action. The spacious rooms have been newly redecorated in cool sea tones. After beach basking, you can prolong the mood in the inn's spacious, plant-bedecked indoor recreation center. *415 S. Ocean Blvd., 29577, tel. 803/448–4481 or 800/845–0313. 306 rooms. Facilities: oceanfront pool with bar, pool parties, heated indoor pool, snack bar, sauna, whirlpool, game room, restaurant, 2 lounges (1 with live entertainment). AE, CB, DC, MC, V.*

Driftwood-on-the-Oceanfront. Under the same ownership for over 50 years, this facility is popular with families. Some rooms are oceanfront; all have recently been redecorated in sea, sky, or earth tones. *1600 N. Ocean Blvd., Box 275, 29578, tel. 803/448–1544 or 800/448–1544. 90 rooms. Facilities: room refrigerators, 2 pools, laundry. AE, CB, DC, MC, V.*

Moderate– **Comfort Inn.** This new inn, 400 yards from the ocean, is clean,
Expensive well furnished, and well maintained. *2801 S. Kings Hwy., 29577, tel. 803/626–4444 or 800/228–5150. 153 rooms. Facilities: 8 Jacuzzi suites, 6 kitchen suites, outdoor pool, health club with whirlpool and sauna, cable TV, restaurant, par-3 golf course adjacent. AE, CB, DC, MC, V.*

Moderate **Cherry Tree Inn.** This rambling, low-rise oceanfront inn is in a quiet North Strand section and caters to families. It is furnished Scandinavian-style. *5400 N. Ocean Blvd., 29577, tel. 803/449–6425 or 800/845–2036. 35 rooms. Facilities: kitchens, cable TV, Jacuzzi, laundry, video games, heated pool (enclosed in winter). AE, MC, V.*

North Myrtle **Economy Inn.** This hotel, part of a chain, is across from the air-
Beach port and near Waccamaw Pottery. *3301 U.S. 17S, 29582, tel.*
Inexpensive *803/272–6196 or 800/446–6900. 40 rooms. Facilities: pool, cribs, cable TV. AE, CB, DC, MC, V.*

Pawleys Island **Quality Inn Seagull.** This is a very well maintained inn on a golf
Moderate course (excellent golf packages are available). The rooms are spacious, bright, and airy. *U.S. 17S, Box 153, 29585, tel. 803/237–4261 or 800/228–5151. 95 rooms. Facilities: pool, dining room, lounge with entertainment, in-room movies. AE, CB, DC, MC, V.*

The Arts

Theater productions, concerts, art exhibits, and other cultural events are regularly offered at the **Myrtle Beach Convention Center** (21st Ave. N, Myrtle Beach, tel. 803/448–7166) and during the school year at **Coastal Carolina College's** Wheelright Auditorium (U.S. 501, west of Conway, tel. 803/347–6206).

Nightlife

Clubs offer varying fare, including beach music, the Grand Strand's unique sound, which conjures up memories of the 1950s. During summer, sophisticated live entertainment is featured nightly at some clubs and resorts. Some hotels and resorts also have piano bars or lounges featuring easy-listening music.

In Myrtle Beach: **Sandals,** at the Sands Ocean Club (tel. 803/449–6461) is an intimate lounge with live entertainment. **Coquina Club,** at the Best Western Landmark Inn (tel. 803/448–

9441), features beach-music bands. **Studebaker's** (tel. 803/626–3855) is one of the area's hot night spots, with live beach music. At The Breakers Hotel, **Top of the Green Lounge and Sidewalk Cafe** (tel. 803/626–5000) is a popular spot, with nightly dancing and entertainment.

In North Myrtle Beach, the lounge at **Holiday Inn on the Ocean** (tel. 803/272–6153) showcases live bands.

In Murrells Inlet, **Drunken Jack's** (tel. 803/651–2044) is a popular restaurant with a lounge overlooking the docks and fishing fleets.

Carolina Opry offers music, comedy, and a variety show to combine the flavor of the Grand Ole Opry with a dash of Broadway. Entertainment for the whole family. *301 U.S. 17S, Surfside Beach, tel. 803/238–8888. Tickets $8–$10. Show at 8 PM, days vary with season. Closed Dec. 20–early Feb.*

Hilton Head and Beyond

Anchoring the southern tip of South Carolina's coastline is 42-square-mile Hilton Head Island, named after English sea captain William Hilton, who claimed it for England in 1663. It was settled by planters in the 1700s and flourished until the Civil War. Thereafter, the economy declined and the island languished until Charles E. Fraser, a visionary South Carolina attorney, began developing the Sea Pines resort in 1956. Other developments followed, and today Hilton Head's casual pace, broad beaches, wide-ranging activities, and genteel good life make it one of the East Coast's most popular vacation getaways.

Beaufort is a gracious antebellum town with a compact historic district preserving lavish 18th- and 19th-century homes. Southward lies Fripp Island, a self-contained resort with controlled access. And midway between Beaufort and Charleston is Edisto ("ED-is-toh") Island, settled in 1690 and once a notable center for cultivation of silky Sea Island cotton. Some of its elaborate mansions have been restored; others brood in disrepair. About the only contemporary touches on the island are a few cottages in a popular state park and modern villas in Fairfield Ocean Ridge Resort.

Getting Around

By Plane **Hilton Head Island Airport** is served by Atlantis, an Eastern affiliate, with nonstop flights to and from Atlanta and Charlotte. Most travelers use the **Savannah International Airport,** about an hour from Hilton Head via transfer bus or limousine, which is served by American, Continental, and United.

By Car The island is 40 miles east of I–95 (Exit 28 off I–95S, Exit 5 off I–95N).

By Taxi **Yellow Rose Cab** (tel. 803/681–6666) provides service in Hilton Head. Cabs here do not have meters; there is a flat rate of $6, plus a preset fare according to zone. For more than two passengers, an additional charge of $2 per person is levied.

Guided Tours

Low Country Adventures (tel. 803/681–8212) and **Regal Limousine of Hilton Head** (tel. 803/785–5466) offer tours as well as transportation from Savannah and Hilton Head Island airports. **Hilton Head Helicopters** (tel. 803/681–9120) offers sightseeing flights as well as shuttle service from Savannah's airport. Hilton Head's **Adventure Cruises** (tel. 803/785–4558) offers dinner, sightseeing, and murder-mystery cruises. Self-guided walking or driving tours are available through the **Beaufort County Chamber of Commerce** (tel. 803/524–3163).

Important Addresses and Numbers

Tourist Information
: **Beaufort County Chamber of Commerce,** Box 910, 1006 Bay St., Beaufort, 29901–0910, tel. 803/524–3163. Open weekdays 9–4:30, Saturday 10–3. **Hilton Head Island Chamber of Commerce,** Drawer 5647, Hilton Head Island, 29938, tel. 803/785–3673. Open weekdays 8:30–5:30, Saturday (June–Sept.) 10–4.

Emergencies
: Dial 911 for emergency assistance.

Doctor
: For nonlife-threatening emergencies, no appointment is necessary at **Family Medical Center** (South Island Square, U.S. 278, tel. 803/842–2900); open daily 8–8.

Exploring Hilton Head and Beyond

Lined by towering pines, wind-sculpted live oaks, and palmetto trees, Hilton Head's 12 miles of beaches are a major attraction of this semitropical barrier island. And its oak and pine woodlands, meandering lagoons, and temperate ocean climate provide an incomparable environment for golfing, tennis, water sports, beachcombing, and sea splashing.

Choice stretches of the island are occupied by various resorts, or "plantations," among them Sea Pines, Shipyard, Palmetto Dunes, Port Royal, and Hilton Head. In these, accommodations range from rental vacation villas and lavish private homes to luxury hotels. The resorts are also private residential communities, although many have restaurants, marinas, shopping areas, and/or recreational facilities that are open to the public. All are secured, and visitors cannot tour the residential areas unless arrangements are made at the visitor or security office near the main gate of each plantation.

In the south of the island, at the **Newhall Audubon Preserve,** you'll find unusual native plant life identified and tagged in a pristine 50-acre site. There are trails, a self-guided tour, and plant walks seasonally. *Palmetto Bay Rd., tel. 803/671–2008. Admission free. Open daily during daylight hours.*

Also in the south, and part of the Sea Pines resort, is the **Sea Pines Forest Preserve,** a 605-acre public wilderness tract. There are seven miles of walking trails, a well-stocked fishing pond, a waterfowl pond, and a 3,400-year-old Indian shell ring. Both guided and self-guided tours are available. *Tel. 803/671–7170. $3 per-car fee for nonguests. Open daily 7 AM–9:30 PM. Closed during the Heritage Golf Classic in April.*

The **Whooping Crane Conservancy,** on Hilton Head Plantation in the north, is home to rare semitropical birds, reptiles, and mammals. There are self-guided tours on a boardwalk and trail through the 137-acre black-gum swamp. (The boardwalk, leading through the rookery, is closed during breeding season, Feb.–July.) From September to March, there are Saturday-morning bird walks. *Tel. 803/681–5291. Admission free. Open daily during daylight hours.*

While on Hilton Head Plantation, you might stop to note the earthwork fortifications that mark the site of **Fort Mitchell**, built in 1812 on a bluff overlooking Skull Creek as part of a large system across the island's northern end.

Beach walks are conducted daily in season by the Environmental Museum of Hilton Head for a nominal fee (tel. 803/842–9197; the museum itself is years away from opening).

Off the island, there's the **Waddell Mariculture Research and Development Center,** three miles west. Here methods of raising seafood commercially are studied, and visitors are invited to tour its 24 ponds and the research building to see work in progress. *Sawmill Creek Rd., near U.S. 278–SC 46 intersection, tel. 803/681–8800. Admission free. Tours weekdays at 10 AM and by appointment.*

North of here is the waterfront city of **Beaufort.** Established in 1710, Beaufort achieved immense prosperity toward the close of the 18th century when Sea Island cotton was introduced as a money crop. Many of the lavish houses that the wealthy landowners and merchants built—with wide balconies, high ceilings, and luxurious appointments—today remain, a legacy of an elegant and gracious era.

Across the street from the Beaufort County Chamber of Commerce (where you can pick up maps, tours, and literature) is the handsome **George Elliott House,** which served as a Union hospital during the Civil War. It was built in 1840 in Greek Revival style, with leaded-glass fanlights, pine floors, and rococo ceilings. The furnishings include some fine early Victorian pieces. *1001 Bay St., tel. 803/524–8450. Admission: $3 adults, $2 children. Open weekdays 11–3, Sun. 1–3.*

Nearby, the **John Mark Verdier House,** an Adam-style structure built around 1790 and headquarters for Union forces during the war, has been restored and furnished as it would have been between 1790 and the visit of Lafayette in 1825. Guided tours are available. *801 Bay St., tel. 803/524–6334. Admission: $3 adults, $2 children under 15. Open Tues.–Sat. 11–3 Feb.–mid-Dec. Closed rest of year and Thanksgiving.*

Built in 1795 and remodeled in 1852, the Gothic-style arsenal was home of the Beaufort Volunteer Artillery. It now houses the **Beaufort Museum,** with prehistoric relics, Indian pottery, Revolutionary and Civil War exhibits, and decorative arts. *713 Craven St., tel. 803/525–7471. Donations requested. Open weekdays 10 AM–noon, 2–5 PM; Sat. 10 AM–noon. Closed Sun., holidays.*

St. Helena's Episcopal Church, dating from 1724, was also touched by the Civil War: It was turned into a hospital and gravestones were brought inside to serve as operating tables. *501 Church St., tel. 803/524–3163. Donations appreciated. Visitors welcome weekdays 8:30–6.*

Part of the 304-acre Historic Beaufort District, **Old Point** includes many private antebellum homes not open to visitors. Some may be open during the annual Fall House Tour, a mid-October weekend, and the Spring Tour of Homes and Gardens, in April or May. The rest of the year, you'll have to content yourself with appreciating the fine exteriors.

Before setting out to explore outlying areas, pause in the **Henry C. Chambers Waterfront Park** to rest and survey the scene. Its seven landscaped acres along the Beaufort River, part of the Intracoastal Waterway, include a seawall promenade, a crafts market, gardens, and a marina. Some events of the popular mid-July Beaufort Water Festival occur here.

Eighteen miles east of Beaufort via U.S. 21 is **Hunting Island,** a secluded domain of ocean beaches, semitropical woodlands, and the photogenic 140-foot-high **Hunting Island Lighthouse,** built in 1859 and abandoned in 1933. If you want to make the effort to climb the spiral staircase—all 181 steps—you'll be rewarded with sweeping vistas of the island, ocean, and marshland. The 5,000-acre barrier island is a popular state park offering three miles of broad swimming beach, hiking, nature trails, and surf, inlet, and lagoon fishing. *Nominal admission per car in summer. For cabin reservations, write Hunting Island State Park, Rte. 1, Box 668, Frogmore 29920, tel. 803/838–2011.*

Heading north from Beaufort on U.S. 21 to Gardens Corner, taking Rte. 17N to Rte. 174, and following that road east to the ocean will bring you to **Edisto Island** (80 mi from Beaufort). Here, magnificent stands of age-old oaks festooned with Spanish moss border quiet streams and side roads. Wild turkeys roam freely in open grasslands. Trawlers dock at rickety piers in an antiquated fishing village that looks like a monochromatic etching in early morning mists. Most of the island's inhabitants are descendants of former slaves, and they preserve many aspects of their African heritage, such as painting doorways and windowsills bright blue to ward off evil spirits.

Edisto Beach State Park, one of the state's most popular, offers three miles of beach with excellent shelling. There are cabins by the marsh and campsites by the ocean. The cabins are basic but clean, and offer full housekeeping facilities. *For information and reservations, contact: Superintendent, Edisto Beach State Park, 8377 State Cabin Rd., Edisto Island 29438, tel. 803/869–2156 or 869–3396.*

What to See and Do with Children

On Hilton Head Island, each major hotel and resort offers some **summer youth activities** or a full-scale youth program. Every summer hundreds of visiting youngsters join island youth in the weekly camps offered by the Island Recreation Center. **Day camp** activities include tennis lessons, beach trips, arts and crafts, games, contests, and special events. **Sports camps** include basketball, boardsailing, golf, racquetball, sailing, soccer, tennis, and volleyball. *Contact: Hilton Head Island Recreation Association, Box 6121, Hilton Head Island, 29938, tel. 803/785–9016.*

Most hotels and resorts offer **baby-sitting** lists. During daylight hours, some **day-care services** welcome drop-ins on an hourly basis for youngsters six months to six years; check the yellow pages; or ask your hotel's concierge or front-desk staff.

Hunting Island State Park (*see* Exploring Hilton Head and Beyond) has playgrounds and is a fine family picnicking site.

Off the Beaten Track

From Hilton Head Island, you can visit remote **Daufuskie Island** by boat. It was the setting for Pat Conroy's novel *The Water Is Wide*, which was made into the movie *Conrack*. Most inhabitants, descendants of former slaves, live on small farms. Remnants of churches, homes, and schools scattered among the live oaks, pines, palmettos, and semitropical shrubs serve as reminders of antebellum times, when the island was well populated and prosperous. With its unspoiled natural environment, Daufuskie won't remain off the beaten track for very long. Two major developments are under way. Boats offering excursions to the island from various marinas in Hilton Head include *The Adventure* in Shelter Cove Harbor (tel. 803/681–8222) and *The Gypsy* in Harbour Town Marina (tel. 803/842–4155).

South of Beaufort is **Parris Island,** home of the U.S. Marine Corps Recruit Depot, where visitors are welcome to observe recruit training. Guided tours are available. Also on the base, the **War Memorial Building Museum** features a collection of vintage uniforms, photographs, special exhibits, and weapons. On the grounds is a replica of the Iwo Jima flag-raising monument. *Museum: Tel. 803/525–2951. Admission free. Open daily 10–4:30. Closed major holidays.*

Shopping

Malls Major Hilton Head Island shopping sites include **Pinelawn Mall** (U.S. 278 at Matthews Dr., tel. 803/681–8907 or 681–9807), with 33 shops and six restaurants; and **Coligny Plaza** (Coligny Circle, tel. 803/842–6050), with 60-plus shops, restaurants, food stands, a movie theater, and a supermarket.

Antiques **Christina's Antiques Et Cetera** (Hilton Head Plaza, tel. 803/686–2320) features Oriental and European antiques and New Guinea primitives. **Den of Antiquity** (20 mi north of Hilton Head on U.S. 170, tel. 803/842–6711), the area's largest antiques shop, carries a wide assortment of Low Country and nautical pieces. **Harbour Town Antiques** (at Harbour Town, Hilton Head, tel. 803/671–5777) has an impressive collection of American and English furniture, plus unusual pieces of Oriental and English porcelain.

Art Galleries In Hilton Head, the **Red Piano Art Gallery** (220 Cordillo Pkwy., tel. 803/785–2318) showcases works by island artists and craftsfolk. In Beaufort, the **Rhett Gallery** (809 Bay St., tel. 803/524–3339) sells Low Country art by Nancy Ricker Rhett, William Means Rhett, Stephen Elliott Webb, and James Moore Rhett.

Jewelry On Hilton Head, **The Bird's Nest** (Coligny Plaza, tel. 803/785–3737) sells locally made shell and sand-dollar jewelry. **The Goldsmith Shop** (3 Lagoon Rd., tel. 803/785–2538) features classic jewelry, island charms, custom designs, and repairs. **Touch of Turquoise** (The Market on Palmetto Bay Rd., tel. 803/842–3880) sells authentic Indian jewelry, sand-dollar pendants, and more. In Beaufort, **The Craftseller** (210 Scott St., tel. 803/525–6104) showcases jewelry and other items by Southern craftsfolk.

One of a Kind **The Christmas Shop** (Plantation Center near Palmetto Dunes entrance, tel. 803/785–6002) sells Christmas ornaments and trees, plus toys, dolls, and gifts for all seasons. The **Wicker Warehouse** (130 Matthews Dr., tel. 803/686–5511) has baskets, planters, rattan and wicker furniture, straw hats, and more.

Beaches

On Hilton Head Island, the ocean side features wide stretches of gently sloping white sand, extending for the island's entire 12-mile length. Many spots remain secluded and uncrowded. Although resort beaches are reserved for guests and residents, there are about 35 public beach entrances from Folly Field to South Forest Beach near Sea Pines. Two main parking areas are at Coligny Circle, near the Holiday Inn, and on Folly Field Road, off U.S. 278 near the Hilton Head Island Beach and Tennis Resort. Signs along U.S. 278 point the way to Bradley, Burkes, and Singleton beaches, where parking space is limited.

Hunting Island State Park has three miles of broad swimming beaches. **Edisto Beach State Park** on Edisto Island also has nearly three miles of public beach.

Participant Sports

Bicycling There are pathways in several areas of Hilton Head Island (many in the resorts), and pedaling is popular along the firmly packed beach. Bicycles can be rented at most hotels and resorts. One of the oldest rental shops here is **Harbour Town Bicycles** (Graves Plaza, Hwy. 278, tel. 803/785–3546; Sea Pines Plantation, tel. 803/671–7300; and Palmetto Dunes Resort, tel. 803/671–5386).

Fishing On Hilton Head, you can pick oysters, dig for clams, or cast for shrimp. Each year a billfishing tournament and two king mackerel tournaments attract anglers to the island.

Golf Many golf courses on Hilton Head Island are ranked among the world's top 100. Several resort courses are open for public play. Each April, Sea Pines's Harbour Town course is the site of the MCI Heritage Golf Classic, drawing top PGA stars.

Horseback Riding Many trails wind through woods and nature preserves. There are five fully equipped stables in the Hilton Head area: **Lawton Fields Stable** in Sea Pines (tel. 803/671–2586), **Moss Creek Plantation Equestrian Center** (tel. 803/785–4488), **Rose Hill Plantation Stables** (tel. 803/757–3082), **Sandy Creek Stables** near Spanish Wells (tel. 803/681–4610), and **Seabrook Farm Stables** in Hilton Head Plantation (tel. 803/681–5415).

Tennis There are more than 300 courts on Hilton Head. Three resorts —**Sea Pines** (tel. 803/785–3333), **Shipyard Plantation** (tel. 803/785–2313), and **Port Royal** (tel. 803/681–3322)—are rated among the top 50 tennis destinations in the United States. Racquet clubs that welcome guest play on clay, composition, hardsurface, synthetic, and even a few grass courts include **Port Royal Tennis Club** (tel. 803/681–3322), **Rod Laver Tennis** at Palmetto Dunes (tel. 803/785–1152), **Sea Pines Racquet Club** (tel. 803/671–2494), and **Van der Meer Tennis Center** (tel. 803/785–

8388 or 800/845–6138). Each April, top professional women's stars participate in the Family Circle Magazine Cup Tennis Tournament at Sea Pines Racquet Club.

Windsurfing Lessons and rentals are available from **Windsurfing Hilton Head** at Sea Pines Resort's South Beach Marina (tel. 803/671–2643) and at Shelter Cove Plaza (tel. 803/686–6996).

Spectator Sports

Polo There are matches every other Sunday during spring and fall at **Rose Hill Plantation** (tel. 803/842–2828).

Dining

All along this stretch of South Carolina coastline, fresh seafood is showcased on menus. But Hilton Head Island is a cosmopolitan community, with restaurants to suit every palate. The most highly recommended restaurants in each price category are indicated by a star ★.

Category	Cost*
Very Expensive	over $25
Expensive	$15–$25
Moderate	$7–$15
Inexpensive	under $7

per person without tax (5% in South Carolina), service, or drinks

The following credit-card abbreviations are used: AE, American Express; CB, Carte Blanche; DC, Diners Club; MC, MasterCard; V, Visa.

Beaufort **The Anchorage House.** The pre-Revolutionary ambience of this
Continental 1765 structure is enhanced by period furnishings, candlelight, and gleaming silver and crystal. Sherry-laced she-crab soup, crabmeat casserole, and other Low Country specialties share the menu with such Continental selections as veal piccata and steak *au poivre. 1103 Bay St., tel. 803/524–9392. Jackets suggested at dinner. Reservations suggested. AE, CB, DC, MC, V. Closed Sun., major holidays. Moderate–Expensive.*

Hilton Head Island **Harbourmaster's.** With sweeping views of the harbor, this
Continental spacious, multilevel dining room offers such dishes as chateaubriand and New Zealand rack of lamb laced with a brandy demiglaze. Service is deft. *In Shelter Cove Marina, off U.S. 278, across from Palmetto Dunes, tel. 803/785–3030. Jacket required at dinner. Reservations required. AE, CB, DC, MC, V. Closed Sun. and for about a month in winter. Very Expensive.*

★ **The Barony.** An intimate series of softly lighted seating areas with "upscale country French" decor range off the main dining room, which is centered with a display of drop-dead desserts, marzipan flowers, and exotic cheeses and breads, spotlighted by a crystal chandelier. There's glittering crystal and silver, and a quartet of tuxedoed waiters for every table. In addition to the regular Low Country and Continental entrees, elegant low-calorie menus are offered, such as chilled coconut-and-pineapple soup, asparagus salad with quail eggs, sorbet, poached fillet of Dover sole with seafood mousse, and macé-doine of fresh fruits with raspberry sauce. *The Westin Resort, Hilton Head Island (formerly Hotel Inter-Continental). 135 S. Port Royal Dr., tel. 803/681–4000. Jacket and tie required. Reservations suggested. AE, CB, DC, MC, V. Closed Mon. Expensive–Very Expensive.*

Fulvio's. A rather elegant, formal atmosphere, reinforced by deft service, prevails in this popular dining room. The menu emphasizes Italian specialties, such as a hearty and luscious *cioppino di frutti di mare*—a tomato-based stew of shellfish and vegetables. *New Orleans Rd. and U.S. 278, in Shipyard Center, tel. 803/681–6001. AE, CB, DC, MC, V. Closed Sun., holidays, first 2 wks in Jan. Dinner only. Expensive.*

Low Country **Old Fort Pub.** Tucked away in a quiet site overlooking Skull Creek, this rustic restaurant specializes in such dishes as oyster pie, oysters wrapped in Smithfield ham, Savannah chicken-fried steak with onion gravy, and hoppin' john. *In Hilton Head Plantation, tel. 803/681–2386. Dress: informal. No reservations. AE, CB, DC, MC, V. No lunch Sun. Moderate.*

Seafood **Hemingway's.** This oceanfront restaurant serves pompano *en papillote*, trout amandine with herbed lemon-butter sauce, fresh grilled seafoods, and steaks, in a relaxed, Key West–type atmosphere. *Hyatt Regency Hilton Head, in Palmetto Dunes Resort, tel. 803/785–1234. Dress: informal. Reservations suggested. AE, CB, DC, MC, V. Moderate.*

Hudson's Seafood House on the Docks. This huge, airy, family-owned restaurant has its own fishing fleet; catches are rushed straight from the boats to the kitchens. The dining room always seems full, but service is quick and friendly and diners never feel rushed. There's a separate oyster bar, as well as an adjacent family-style restaurant, The Landing. *1 Hudson Rd., on the docks, tel. 803/681–2772. The Landing; 803/681–3363. Dress: informal. No reservations. AE, MC, V. Moderate.*

Lodging

Hilton Head Island is home to some of the nation's finest and most luxurious resort developments. **Sea Pines,** the oldest and best-known, occupies 4,500 choice, thickly wooded acres. Its three championship golf courses include renowned Harbour Town Links, designed by Pete Dye and Jack Nicklaus and one of the top 20 U.S. courses. There's a fine beach, two racquet clubs, riding stables, two shopping plazas, and a 500-acre forest preserve. Accommodations are in luxurious homes and villas fronting the ocean or the golf courses.

Sea Pines's emphasis on preserving the integrity of the island's ecology has set the tone for resorts that have followed. Among them, differences are subtle. In **Shipyard Plantation,** Marriott's Hilton Head Resort caters to groups from 50 to 1,500; its luxuriant garden setting, water sports, and fitness center make it a favorite with family vacationers as well. This plantation also has a wide array of villa condominiums, most overlooking an excellent golf facility with three championship nines. There's a racquet club and a small beach club.

Palmetto Dunes Resort includes the Hyatt Regency Hilton Head, the island's largest resort hotel. It has a concierge floor and extensive meeting space and services, making it especially appealing to groups. A good array of vacation packages attracts families as well. With kitchenettes and all-oceanfront rooms, the Mariner's Inn–A Clarion Hotel (also in Palmetto Dunes) is a great favorite with families and honeymooners. Palmetto Dunes is home of the renowned Rod Laver Tennis Center and has a good stretch of beach and three championship golf courses. In addition to its hotels, there are several luxury rental villa complexes overlooking the ocean.

At **Port Royal Plantation** is the new, super-luxurious Westin Resort, Hilton Head Island (formerly Hotel Inter-Continental Hilton Head Resort). With vast meeting spaces and an emphasis on upscale amenities, it caters to the upscale business traveler and middle-aged to older affluent vacationers. Not that families aren't warmly welcomed, but the atmosphere is a bit more formal than elsewhere on the island. Port Royal has three championship golf courses, which have hosted PGA events, and its racquet club offers play on clay, hard, and grass courts. There are also a few rental homes and a limited selection of villas.

Hilton Head Plantation, a private residential community, is on the northern, "quiet side" of the island. It has no rentals, but two of its golf courses are available for public play.

Not all lodgings are located within the resorts. The high-rise Holiday Inn, for example, occupies a choice patch of beach and is very popular with families and smaller groups. It's easily accessible from the main business area.

Hilton Head Central Reservations (Box 5312, Hilton Head Island, 29938, tel. 800/845–7018) is a good source of detailed information about various island resorts and properties. It represents almost every hotel, motel, and condominium-rental agency on the island.

Rates can drop appreciably in the off-season (on Hilton Head Island, Nov.–Mar.), and package plans are available year-round. The most highly recommended properties in each price category are indicated by a star ★.

Category	Cost*
Very Expensive	over $135
Expensive	$95–$135
Moderate	$50–$95
Inexpensive	under $50

double room; add 7% for taxes

The following credit-card abbreviations are used: AE, American Express; CB, Carte Blanche; DC, Diners Club; MC, MasterCard; V, Visa.

Beaufort
Inexpensive

Best Western Sea Island Motel. At this well-maintained resort inn in the downtown historic district, rooms feature period decor. *1015 Bay St., Box 532, 29902, tel. 803/524–4121 or 800/528–1234. 43 rooms. Facilities: pool, cable TV, restaurant, lounge. AE, CB, DC, MC, V.*

Holiday Inn of Beaufort. This motor inn is conveniently located for visitors to Parris Island or the Marine Corps Air Station.

U.S. 21 and Lovejoy St., Box 1008, 29902, tel. 803/524–2144 or 800/465–4329. 152 rooms. Facilities: heated pool, tennis, cable TV/movies, restaurant, lounge with live entertainment. AE, CB, DC, MC, V.

Edisto Island
Moderate–
Expensive

Fairfield Ocean Ridge Resort. This is a good choice for vacationers seeking to combine all the resort amenities with a get-away-from-it-all setting. There are accommodations in well-furnished two- and three-bedroom villa units tastefully decorated in contemporary style. *1 King Cotton Rd., Box 27, 29438, tel. 803/869–2561. 110 units. Facilities: pool, wading pool, beach, marina, fishing, tennis, golf, miniature golf, social and recreational programs, children's activities, nature trails, playground, restaurant, lounge, AE, CB, DC, MC, V.*

Fripp Island
Moderate–
Expensive

Fripp Island Resort. The resort encompasses the entire island, and access is limited to guests only. The two- and three-bedroom villas are contemporary in decor. *19 mi south of Beaufort via U.S. 21, 1 Tarpon Blvd., 29920, tel. 803/838–2441 or 800/845–4100. 133 units. Facilities: pools, tennis courts, championship golf course, full-service marina with rental boats, bicycle and jogging trails, laundry, children's program, 3 restaurants. AE, MC, V.*

Hilton Head Island
Very Expensive

Hyatt Regency Hilton Head. At this newly renovated oceanside hotel, the rooms have been lavishly redecorated. Some have balconies. *U.S. 278, in Palmetto Dunes Resort, Box 6167, 29938, tel. 803/785–1234 or 800/228–9000, 800/268–7530 Canada. 505 rooms. Facilities: pools, health club, sailboats, concierge floor, extensive convention facilities, cable TV/movies, coffee shop, dining rooms, lounges, entertainment, dancing. Guests have privileges at 3 18-hole championship golf courses and 25 hard, grass, and clay tennis courts at Palmetto Dunes, plus its 3 mi of private beach. AE, CB, DC, MC, V.*

★ **The Westin Resort, Hilton Head Island** (formerly Hotel Inter-Continental Hilton Head). Among the island's newest luxury properties, this horseshoe-shaped hotel sprawls in a lushly landscaped oceanside setting. The expansive guest rooms, most with ocean view, are furnished in a pleasing mix of period reproduction and contemporary furnishings. All have comfortable seating areas and desks. Public areas display museum-quality Oriental porcelains, screens, paintings, and furnishings. *At Port Royal Resort, 135 S. Port Royal Dr., 29928, tel. 803/681–4000 or 800/228–3000. 416 rooms. Facilities: pool and ocean swimming, water sports, health club, restaurants (see the Barony in Dining), lounge with live entertainment, pianist in elegant lobby lounge. AE, CB, DC, MC, V.*

Expensive–
Very Expensive

Mariner's Inn–A Clarion Hotel. There's a Caribbean-island feel to this five-story resort hotel set in an enclave. The grounds are beautifully landscaped. All oceanside, the rooms are spacious and colorfully decorated in a modern style. *In Palmetto Dunes Resort, 21 Ocean Ln., Box 6165, 29938, tel. 803/842–8000 or 800/845–8001. 324 rooms. Facilities: pool, health club, sauna, whirlpool, volleyball, canoeing, fishing, biking, sailing, restaurant, full resort privileges of Palmetto Dunes. AE, CB, DC, MC, V.*

Marriott's Hilton Head Resort. This oceanside hotel has spacious rooms with informally elegant tropical decor and ocean, garden, or forest views. The lobby is highlighted by a dramatic five-story atrium. Pathways wind amid lagoons and gardens to a wide, sandy private beach. *130 Shipyard Dr., Shipyard*

Plantation, 29928, tel. 803/842–2400 or 800/228–9290. 338 rooms and suites. Facilities: pool, exercise rooms, sauna, rental catamarans, restaurants, privileges at nearby golf and tennis clubs. AE, CB, DC, MC, V.

Expensive **Holiday Inn Oceanfront Resort.** This handsome high-rise motor hotel is located on a broad, quiet stretch of beach. The rooms are spacious and well furnished in a contemporary style. *S. Forest Beach Dr., Box 5728, 29928, tel. 803/785–5126 or 800/465–4329. 200 rooms. Facilities: outdoor pool, poolside bar, restaurant, lounge with entertainment, beauty salon, boat, children's programs, golf, tennis, marina privileges. AE, CB, DC, MC, V.*

Inexpensive– **Red Roof Inn.** This two-story inn at the center of the island is
Moderate especially popular with families. It's a short drive to the public beaches. *5 Regency Pkwy. (U.S. 278), 29928, tel. 803/686–6808 or 800/848–7878. 112 units. Facilities: cable TV/movies. AE, DC, MC, V.*

The Arts

Community Playhouse (Arrow Rd., tel. 803/785–4878) presents up to 10 musicals or dramatic productions each year and offers a theater program for youths. During the warmer months, there are free outdoor concerts at **Harbour Town** and **Shelter Cove.** Concerts, plays, films, art shows, theater—along with sporting events, food fairs, and minitournaments—make up Hilton Head Island's **SpringFest,** which runs for the entire month of March. For information, contact SpringFest (Box 5278-D, Hilton Head Island, SC 29938, tel. 803/842–3378).

Nightlife

Dancing At the **Battery** (tel. 803/681–4000), in The Westin Resort, Hilton Head Island, at Port Royal Resort, there's entertainment every night except Monday and dancing nightly to a five-piece band. At **Club Indigo** (tel. 803/785–1234), a large cabaret downstairs at the Hyatt Regency Hilton Head, there is dancing and two shows nightly Monday through Saturday. At the **Mockingbird Lounge** (tel. 803/842–2400), in the Marriott's Hilton Head Resort, Shipyard Plantation, there's a dance band at night Monday through Saturday. **Scarlett's** (tel. 803/842–8500), a sophisticated oceanfront night spot at Mariner's Inn, Palmetto Dunes, features smooth jazz nightly. At **W.G. Shucker's** (tel. 803/785–8050), a lively spot on Palmetto Bay Road, there's dancing nightly on the island's largest dance floor. **White Parrott** (tel. 803/785–5126), a locally popular lounge in the Holiday Inn Oceanfront Resort, has nightly entertainment.

Easy Listening **Cafe Europa** (tel. 803/671–3399), at the Lighthouse in Harbourtown, has nightly piano entertainment. **The Gazebo** (tel. 803/681–4000), The Westin Resort, Hilton Head Island's opulent lobby lounge overlooking tropical grounds and the ocean, offers classical entertainment at the grand piano afternoons and early evenings every night but Saturday. **Hemingway's Lounge** (tel. 803/785–1234), adjoining Hemingway's at the Palmetto Dunes Resort, has live entertainment in a casually elegant setting. **The Marsh Tacky** (tel. 803/681–4000), an oceanfront lounge at The Westin Resort, Hilton Head Island at Port Royal, has informal entertainment every night but Sunday. **Playful Pelican** (tel. 803/681–4000), the pool bar at the same location, has a live calypso band Tuesday through Sunday from 1 to 4 PM.

Elsewhere in the State

The State Capital **Columbia.** Centrally located in South Carolina, Columbia was founded in 1786 as the capital city. The Italian Renaissance style State Capitol dates from 1855, and contains rich appointments of marble, mahogany, art works, and a replica of Houdon's statue of George Washington. *Intersection of Main and Gervais Sts., tel 803/734–2430. Admission free. Guided tours every half hour. Open weekdays 9–noon and 1–4.*

The South Carolina State Museum, Columbia. Located in a large refurbished textile mill, the museum interprets in multifaceted exhibits South Carolina's history, archaeology, fine arts, and scientific and technological accomplishments. *301 Gervais St., tel. 803/737–4921. Admission: $3 adults; $2 senior citizens; $1.25 children, 6–17. Open Mon.–Sat. 10–5, Sun. 1–5, closed Christmas.*

Riverbanks Zoological Park, Columbia. Showcase for over 800 birds and animals, some endangered, in natural habitats, the Zoological Park is among the nation's best. It also offers a cage-free aviary, reptile house, aquarium, and breeding facilities for rare and fragile species. *Junction of I–26 and Greyston Blvd., tel. 803/779–8717. Admission: $3.25 adults, $1.25 children 6–12. Open daily 9–5, summer weekends until 6, closed Dec. 25.*

The Greenville County Museum of Art, Greenville. Housed in an innovative modern structure, the museum displays the largest public collection of Andrew Wyeth paintings in the nation. Also exhibited are works by Paul Jenkins, Jamie Wyeth, Jasper Johns, and noted Southern artists along with North American sculpture and Colonial-era art. Special events include films, lectures, seminars, and changing exhibits emphasizing contemporary art. *420 College St., tel. 803/271–7520. Admission free. Open Tues.–Sat. 10–5, Sun. 1–5, closed major holidays (open Easter).*

Kings Mountain National Military Park. The famous "turning point" Revolutionary War battle on October 7, 1780 was fought on this site. A contingent of colonial Tories commanded by Major Patrick Ferguson, the only British participant in the engagement, was soundly defeated by rag-tag patriot forces from the Southern Appalachians. Visitor Center exhibits, dioramas, and an orientation film describe the action. A paved 1½-mile self-guided trail leads through the battlefield. *20 mi NE of Gaffney off I–85 via marked side road which is entered in North Carolina then leads back into South Carolina, tel. 803/936–7921. Admission free. Open Memorial Day–Labor Day, daily 9–6; rest of year 9--5; closed Christmas and New Year's Day.*

8 Tennessee

Introduction

by Patricia and Edgar Cheatham

Mountains and music—these two gifts Tennessee was given in abundance and shares generously with millions of guests each year.

In Memphis, in the southwest corner of the state, on the shores of the Mississippi River, the blues were born. Beale Street produced or nurtured some of the finest talents of the genre, from W. C. Handy, who became known as the Father of the Blues, to Elvis Presley, the King of Rock and Roll. Today, with live music in Handy Park and in numerous nightclubs, Beale Street is once again alive with the sounds that made it a legend.

Nashville, of course, is Nashville—the country music capital of the world. Here, at the center of the state, there's country on every corner. In addition to stars' homes, recording studios, and country-related museums and other attractions, there's the Grand Ole Opry, the long-running radio-show extravaganza that has launched many a singer's and picker's career and is now part of a theme park built around live country music shows. Even the biggest fan will come away satisfied.

As for mountains, they don't come any more beautiful than the Great Smokies, part of the Appalachian chain, in East Tennessee (and shared by North Carolina). Covered with a dense carpet of wildflowers in spring and ablaze with foliage in autumn, the Smokies—named for the mysterious mantle of blue haze that so often blankets them—are a joy to hike, meander, or drive through. Spend some time in the little mountain towns and villages to sample homegrown bluegrass music and traditional cooking and crafts (like the making of fine wood dulcimers), along with the natural warmth of the people.

Memphis

Memphis was founded in 1819, but since long before that, the great river on whose shores it was built has exerted a powerful influence on the area. An Indian river culture that existed here from the 11th through the 15th century is documented in archaeological excavations, reconstructions, and exhibits at the Chucalissa Indian Village. The river itself is celebrated with a museum dedicated to its history—part of a unique entertainment-oriented park occupying an island in the river.

The other significant influence on the city has been the music that has flowed through it. W. C. Handy moved from Alabama to Memphis in 1902–3, drawn by the long-thriving music scene, and it was here that he produced most of the songs that made him famous. The recent history of legendary Beale Street reflects that of all modern Memphis. Economic decline in the mid-20th century brought the city to its knees, and the unrest following the assassination in 1968 of Dr. Martin Luther King, Jr., at the Lorraine Motel, just south of Beale, dealt a near-fatal blow. (The motel, at 406 Mulberry Street, is now closed but is scheduled to open in 1991 as the National Civil Rights Center.) Today, thanks to a proud group of local boosters whose efforts to save their city and their heritage can be seen at every turn, Memphis has been brought back to life and Beale Street bursts with clubs and restaurants, as it did in its heyday.

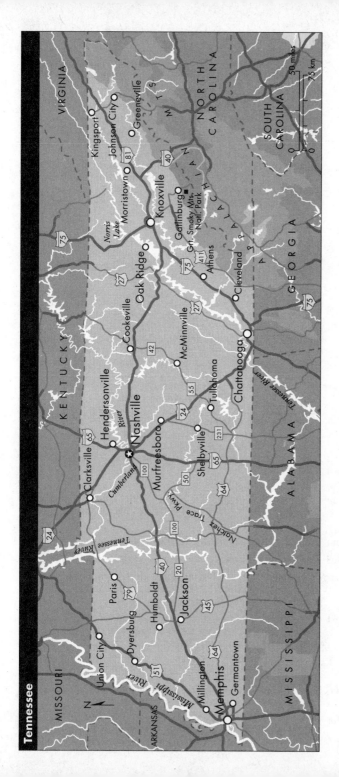

Tennessee

One young boy influenced by the blues, who went on to become the King of Rock and Roll, is remembered at Graceland, the estate where he lived, died, and lies buried. The great crowds that flock to the mansion are testament to the enduring legacy of Elvis's music.

For true blues fans, a good time to visit is during Blues Music Week in November, when the art form is celebrated with musical performances and other activities throughout the city. The week culminates in the National Blues Music Awards Show, which is attended by luminaries of the music world. For information on a three-day vacation package that includes admission to the awards show as well as to the jam afterward, contact the Blues Foundation (352 Beale St., 38103, tel. 800/334–5177). Most weekends throughout the year, there's plenty of blues to be heard on the front porch of the Handy home or in Handy Park (*see* Exploring Memphis).

Many people plan their visit to coincide with the month-long Memphis in May International Festival, at a time when the summer's heat and humidity have not yet begun to set in. Each year the cuisine, crafts, and other cultural offerings of a different country are saluted over four consecutive weekends. The first of these weekends sees the clubs and sidewalks of Beale Street playing host to a rollicking, blues-based Music Festival, and the second finds hordes of the hungry flocking to the river for the World Championship Barbecue Cooking Contest. A sports weekend featuring races on land and water follows, succeeded by the grand finale of Sunset Symphony, during which the Memphis Symphony plays on the banks of the Mississippi, and a soloist's powerful rendition of "Old Man River" brings the festival to an end and the crowd to its feet.

Arriving and Departing

By Plane
Airports and Airlines
Memphis International Airport is 9½ miles south of downtown. It is served by **American, Delta, Northwest, TWA, United,** and **USAir.**

Between the Airport and Center City
There is **taxi** and **limousine** service to downtown hotels. Taxi fare is about $10, limo fare $5.50. Both are operated by Yellow Cab (tel. 901/577–7777 taxi, 901/477–7700 limousine). By **car**, take I–240 to downtown.

By Train **Amtrak** (545 S. Main St., tel. 901/526–0052).

By Bus **Greyhound/Trailways** (203 Union Ave., tel. 901/523–7676).

By Car From Memphis, I–55 leads north to St. Louis and south to Jackson, Mississippi; I–40, east to Nashville and Knoxville. I–240 loops around the city.

By Boat The paddlewheel steamers *Delta Queen* and *Mississippi Queen* (tel. 800/543–1949) stop at Memphis on excursions between New Orleans, St. Louis, Cincinnati, and St. Paul.

Getting Around

By Taxi The fare is $1.75 for the first mile, 90¢ for each additional mile. There are stands at the airport and bus station.

By Bus Memphis Area Transit Authority (tel. 901/274–6282) buses cover the city and immediate suburbs. Weekdays, there is service from 4:30 AM to 11:15 PM; Saturday, 5 AM–8 PM; Sunday, 9 AM

–6:15 PM. The base fare is 85¢ (95¢ on express routes), $1 after 7 PM. Transfers cost 10¢. Exact change is required. There is short-hop service on designated buses between Front, Third, and Exchange streets from 9 AM to 3 PM and between downtown and the Medical Center complex from 7 AM to 6 PM (cost: 25¢).

Important Addresses and Numbers

Tourist Information
Visitors Information Center, 207 Beale St., 38103, tel. 901/526–4880. Open Monday–Saturday 9–5. Memphis Convention and Visitors Bureau, Morgan-Keegan Tower, 50 N. Front St., Suite 450, 38103, tel. 901/576–8181. Open weekdays 8:30–5.

Emergencies
Dial 911 for **police** and **ambulance** in an emergency.

Hospital
Near-downtown hospitals with 24-hour emergency service include **Baptist Memorial Hospital** (889 Madison Ave., tel. 901/522–5252) and **Methodist Hospitals of Memphis** (1265 Union Ave., tel. 901/726–7000).

Guided Tours

Orientation Tours
Both **Cottonland Tours** (tel. 901/774–5248) and **Gray Line** (tel. 901/942–4662) offer three-hour motor-coach tours that include downtown highlights as well as Graceland.

Special-Interest Tours
Cottonland Tours has gardens-and-galleries, Graceland, "Old Man River," shopping, nightlife, and Southland Greyhound Park excursions. **Gray Line** offers Elvis Memorial, nightlife, and Mud Island tours. **Memphis Unique Tours** (tel. 901/365–9267 or 800/235–1984) has three-day, two-night tours of Graceland or Mud Island River Park. **Blues City Tours** (tel. 901/522–9229) offers tours of Memphis and attractions, including Graceland, Mud Island, Beale Street; riverboat rides; and nightly tours which include dinner and a show. **Heritage Tours** (tel. 901/527–3427) explores the area's rich black cultural heritage.

Walking Tours
At the **Memphis Convention and Visitors Bureau** (*see* Important Addresses and Numbers), pick up a free downtown tour map.

Carriage Tours
Bluff City Buggy Co. (tel. 901/726–5000) and **Carriage Tours of Memphis** (tel. 901/527–7542) have horse-drawn carriage rides through the downtown area.

Boat Tours
Memphis Queen Cruise Line (tel. 901/527–5694) offers 1½-hour sightseeing cruises March through December and sailings to and from Mud Island mid-April through mid-October.

Exploring Memphis

Numbers in the margin correspond with points of interest on the Memphis and Downtown Memphis maps.

Downtown
① A good place to start is the **Visitors Information Center** on Beale Street (*see* Important Addresses and Numbers), where you can pick up free maps, brochures, and other literature about Memphis. There's free parking in lots behind the center.

② At Main Street and Beale is the magnificent 1928 **Orpheum Theatre,** a former vaudeville palace and movie theater, refurbished as a center for the performing arts. Step inside to admire its crystal chandeliers, gilt decorations, and ornate tap-

A. Schwab's, **3**

Chucalissa Indian Village, **16**

Dixon Gallery, **14**

Fuller State Park, **17**

Graceland, **15**

Handy Home, **6**

Handy Park, **4**

Magevney House, **8**

Mallory-Neeley House, **9**

Memphis Brooks Museum of Art, **12**

Mud Island, **7**

Old Daisy Theatre, **5**

Ornamental Metal Museum, **18**

Orpheum Theatre, **2**

Pink Palace Museum, **13**

Visitors Info., **1**

Woodruff-Fontaine House, **10**

Zoo & Aquarium, **11**

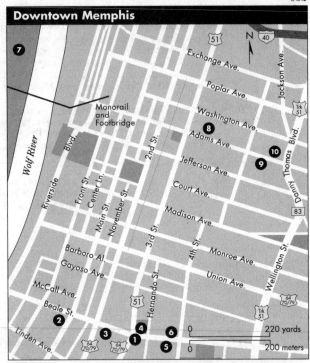

Downtown Memphis

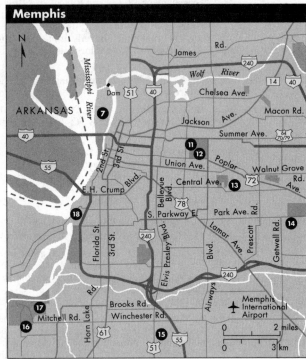

Memphis

estries. Proceeding east, you'll pass a bronze statue of Elvis. At 163 Beale Street you can step into the past at the highly eccentric, **③** 114-year-old **A. Schwab's** dry-goods store, where Elvis used to buy some of his glitzy threads and where you can pick up a **④** voodoo potion (*see* Shopping). In **Handy Park,** between Second and Third streets, pause to admire the statue of W. C. Handy clutching his famed trumpet.

⑤ At 329 Beale is the renovated **Old Daisy Theatre,** which today, as when it was built in 1918, runs silent short films (shown continuously 10–5 daily, free, tel. 901/525–1631). From here, you can take a tram tour with guides who will fill you in on Beale Street's musical past (*see* Guided Tours). Diagonally **⑥** across the street, at 352 Beale, is the **W. C. Handy Memphis Home and Museum.** (Call for an appointment 9–6 daily, tel. 901/527–2583; donation.) In this house (moved from its original location elsewhere in Memphis), where Handy wrote some of his most famous music, he is remembered through photographs, sheet music, and other memorabilia.

If you're traveling by car, you might want to retrieve it before setting out on the next part of the tour, or you can continue walking. Parking on Front Street between Poplar and Adams puts you in a good position to explore two very different areas: the Victorian Village Historic District and Mud Island.

Whether you get there by monorail, pedestrian walkway, or **⑦** boat (*see* Guided Tours), you must see **Mud Island,** a 52-acre, $63 million park that explores Memphis's intimate relationship with the river. There, at the **Mississippi River Museum,** 18 galleries bring the history of the Mississippi to life with exhibits ranging from scale-model boats to life-size, animated river characters (Mark Twain spins his tales anew here) to the Theater of River Disasters. But the most extraordinary exhibit is outside: **River Walk,** a five-block-long scale model of the Mississippi that replicates its every twist, turn, and sandbar from Cairo, Illinois, to New Orleans. Other features include shops, river-view restaurants serving regional foods, and a 5,064-seat amphitheater that hosts name entertainment. Mud Island's newest addition, the famed World War II B-17 bomber *Memphis Belle,* is housed in an open pavilion topped by a gleaming white dome. *The footbridge and monorail are at 125 Front St., tel. 901/576–7241. Pay-one-price ticket includes admission, round trip monorail, daily tours, films, and museum: $4 adults; $2.50 children 4–11, senior citizens over 59, and disabled; children under 4 free. Open daily 10 AM–10 PM Apr.–Thanksgiving; call for hours rest of year.*

To leave the 20th century behind, return to Front Street and walk east on Adams Street through the **Victorian Village Historic District,** comprising some 25 blocks on Adams between Front and Manassas. Here, 18 houses ranging from neoclassical to Gothic Revival have been restored to their appearance in the days when cotton was king. Most are privately owned, but the three that follow are open to the public.

⑧ The charming little white clapboard **Magevney House,** built in the 1830s, is Memphis's oldest dwelling and the former home of a pioneer schoolteacher. It's furnished with some of his original possessions. Magevney was a strong Catholic—the city's first Catholic church service was held in this house, and he later built the church next door. *198 Adams Ave., tel. 901/526–4464. Admission free. Open Tues.–Sat. 10–4.*

❾ The **Mallory-Neely House** is a 25-room Italianate Victorian home that contains original family furnishings. Note the hand-carved cornices and frescoed ceilings on the first floor, and the double front doors' stained-glass panels. *652 Adams Ave., tel. 901/523–1484. Admission: $4 adults, $3 students and senior citizens. Open Tues.–Sat. 10–4, Sun. 1–4.*

❿ The **Woodruff-Fontaine House** is an exquisite three-story French Victorian mansion. The grand drawing room is graced with the original parquet floors and large mirrors. Antique furnishings include Aubusson carpets, marble mantels, and a Venetian crystal chandelier. From the tower, gaze out at Memphis's skyline, then browse through the formal garden with its 100-year-old gingerbread playhouse and chapel. *680 Adams Ave., tel. 901/526–1469. Admission: $4 adults, $3 senior citizens and military, $1.75 children 6–18, children under school age free. Open Mon.–Sat. 10–4, Sun. 1–4.*

Fanning Out Two miles east of the Victorian district is **Overton Park,** where
⓫ the city's zoo and art museum are found. The **Memphis Zoological Gardens and Aquarium** is one of the South's most notable zoos. Here you can view more than 400 species on 36 wooded acres. There's a 10,000-gallon aquarium, a large reptile facility, and a natural African veldt setting for larger creatures. For the youngsters, there's an animal-contact area, a mini-locomotive, and carnival rides. *Tel. 901/726–4775. Admission: $3 adults, $1.50 senior citizens and children 2–11; free for all Mon. after 3:30 PM. Aquarium 25¢ extra for adults, 10¢ for children. Open daily 9–5 Apr.–Sept., 9–4:30 rest of year. Closed major holidays.*

⓬ The collections of the **Memphis Brooks Museum of Art,** also in the park, span eight centuries, including a notable collection of Italian Renaissance works, plus English portraiture, Impressionist and American modernist paintings, decorative arts, prints, photographs, and one of the nation's largest displays of Doughty bird figurines. *Tel. 901/722–3500. Donation. Open Tues.–Sat. 10–5, Sun. 1–5. Closed major holidays.*

⓭ Southeast of the park is the **Memphis Pink Palace Museum and Planetarium,** adjacent to the rambling 1920s pink marble mansion built by Clarence Saunders, whose Piggly Wiggly self-service stores were predecessors of today's supermarkets. Exhibits are eclectic, including natural and cultural history displays, a hand-carved miniature three-ring circus, and displays of African game. *3050 Central Ave., tel. 901/454–5600. Admission (museum/planetarium): $3/$2.50 adults; $2/$1.75 senior citizens and children 5–18, under 5 free. Open Tues.–Sat. 9:30–5 June–Labor Day, 9:30–4 rest of year; Sun. 1–5.*

⓮ A very different personal statement is made by the **Dixon Gallery and Gardens,** with 17 acres of formal and informal gardens and woodlands—a welcoming bucolic enclave near the heart of the city. The estate and its superb art collections were given to the community by the late Margaret and Hugo Dixon, philanthropists and cultural leaders. Included in the intimate museum are French and American Impressionist paintings,

British portraiture and landscapes, and the Stout collection of 18th-century German porcelain. The gardens display regional flowering plants and statuary. *4339 Park Ave., tel. 901/761–5250. Admission: $2 adults, $1 senior citizens and students; free for all on Tues. Open Tues.–Sat. 10–5, Sun. 1–5. Closed major holidays.*

Twelve miles southeast of downtown is perhaps the most visited Memphis attraction: **Graceland,** a poignant reminder of the many facets of fame. The tour of the Colonial-style mansion once owned by Elvis Presley reveals the spoils of stardom— from his gold-covered piano to his glittering show costumes— and a circuit of the grounds (shuttle service is available) leads inevitably to the tomb where he is buried. Separate tours are available of his touring bus and his jet, the *Lisa Marie,* named for his daughter. *3717 Elvis Presley Blvd. (I–55S to exit for Jackson, Miss., then exit for Elvis Presley Blvd.), tel. 901/332–3322 or 800/238–2000. Home tour admission: $7.50 adults, $4.75 children 4–12, under 4 free. Lisa Marie admission: $3.95 adults, $2.75 children 4–12, under 4 free. "Elvis Up Close" museum admission: $1.75. Touring bus admission: $1. Combination tickets are available. Parking: $1. Reservations suggested in summer. Open Wed.–Mon. 9–5 Nov.–Feb.; daily 9–5 Mar., Apr., Sept., Oct.; daily 8–5 May; daily 8–6 June–Aug. Closed major holidays.*

At the peaceful, thought-provoking **Chucalissa Indian Village,** about 10 miles southwest of downtown, you'll catch glimpses of a simple river culture that existed from AD 1000 to 1500. The four-acre reconstruction is operated by Memphis State University, and on-site archaeological excavations are often conducted during the summer. In the **C. H. Nash Museum,** you'll see prehistoric tools, pottery, and weapons and a free 15-minute slide presentation describing Chucalissa life and culture. Outside, skilled Choctaw craftsfolk fashion jewelry, weapons, and pottery. An annual August powwow is a highlight. The adjacent **T. O. Fuller State Park** (tel. 901/543–7581) offers camping, golf, and swimming. *1987 Indian Village Dr., tel. 901/785–3160. Admission: $1.25 adults; 50¢ children 6–11 and senior citizens; children under 6 free. Open Tues.–Sat. 9–5, Sun. 1–5. Closed major holidays.*

On the way back to downtown Memphis (via U.S. 61, following the green Tour Memphis signs) is the **National Ornamental Metal Museum,** the nation's only museum preserving the art and the craft of metalworking—from wrought iron to gold. There's also a working blacksmith shop and special exhibitions and demonstrations. *374 W. California St., tel. 901/774–6380. Admission: $1.50 adults; $1 senior citizens; 75¢ children 5–18, under 5 free; free to all on Wed. Open Tues.–Sat. 10–5, Sun. noon–5.*

The Hinterland From Memphis, you can branch out in various directions to explore quieter, historic byways that seem light-years removed from the busy river city. Driving northward along U.S. 51 through the fertile Mississippi River bottomlands brings you into the heart of King Cotton's domain. About 48 miles along the way, you'll come to **Henning,** a friendly little town remarkably untouched by its world acclaim. This is the boyhood home of Alex Haley, Pulitzer Prize–winning author of *Roots.* At the **Alex Haley State Historic Site and Museum,** you can visit the comfortable bungalow to see family portraits, mementos, and furnishings. *Haley St., tel. 901/738–2240. Admission: $2.50 adults, $1 children under 16. Open Tues.–Sat. 9–5, Sun. 10–5.*

Reelfoot Lake—about 55 miles farther on (via U.S. 51N and TN 21W), in Tennessee's northwest corner—gains a weird and mysterious beauty from a romantic scattering of cypress trees and charred stumps. The 13,000-acre lake was formed when earthquakes caused the Mississippi River to flood into the sinking land where a luxuriant forest once stood. The lake is a major sanctuary for American bald eagles from late November through mid-March. At **Reelfoot Lake State Resort Park** (tel. 901/253–7756), the Tennessee Department of Conservation conducts eagle-spotting tours.

From Memphis, you can also follow I-40 85 miles northeast to **Jackson,** a railroad hub that was home to Johnathan Luther (Casey) Jones. Immortalized in the "Ballad of Casey Jones," the famed engineer became a hero by staying aboard his locomotive in a vain attempt to stop his engine from plowing into another train. In Casey Jones Village (at U.S. 45 Bypass), the **Casey Jones Home and Museum** (tel. 901/668–2222) contains a diverse assortment of railroad memorabilia. On the grounds is a replica of Old No. 382, Casey's steam engine. The **Carl Perkins Music Museum** (tel. 901/668–0064), also in the village, has personal memorabilia of the "Blue Suede Shoes" man, along with items contributed by Elvis, the Beatles, and Johnny Cash. *Joint admission: $3 adults; $2 children 6–12, under 6 free. Both open Mon.–Sat. 9–5, Sun. 1–5, daily 8–8, June–Sept. Closed major holidays.*

One hundred miles east of Memphis via U.S. 64, then 10 miles south on TN 22, is **Shiloh National Military Park,** site of one of the Civil War's grimmest and most decisive battles. At the visitor center, you'll see a film explaining the battle's strategy, along with a display of Civil War relics. A self-guided auto tour leads past markers explaining monuments and battle sites. Almost 4,000 soldiers, many unidentified, are buried here in the national cemetery. *Tel. 901/689–5275. Visitor center open daily 8–6 May–Sept., 8–5 rest of year. Closed Christmas. Admission: $1 adults, children under 12 and senior citizens free.*

Nearby (TN 22S to TN 57E) is **Pickwick Landing Dam** (tel. 901/689–3135), one of the TVA's showcase hydroelectric projects. From the top of the dam, which rises high above the Tennessee River to create Pickwick Lake, there are sweeping views. You're welcome to visit the power plant during daylight hours. **Pickwick Landing State Resort Park** (tel. 901/689–3129) offers a resort inn, a restaurant, playgrounds, swimming beaches, picnic areas, and a par 72, 18-hole golf course.

Memphis for Free

Beale Street Substation Police Museum. Come in and browse through 148 years of Memphis police history, including confiscated weapons, photographs dating to the 1800s, and an old-style jail cell. *159 Beale St., tel. 901/528–2370. Open 24 hrs.*

Crystal Shrine Grotto. At this dramatic cavern of natural rock, quartz crystals, and other semiprecious stones, relief sculptures carved by artist Dionicio Rodriguez in the late 1930s depict scenes from the life of Jesus. *Memorial Park Cemetery, 5668 Poplar Ave., tel. 901/767–8930. Open daily 8:30–4:30.*

Laurel Hill Vineyard. A surprising find in the heart of town, this small winery offers tours that include a slide presentation and a wine tasting. *1370 Madison Ave., tel. 901/725–9128. Tours weekdays 10–12:30, 1:30–5.*

Memphis Botanic Gardens–Goldsmith Civic Garden Center. The outdoor gardens range over 87 acres and include Japanese, rose, iris, herb, wildflower, perennial, and cactus gardens, and azalea and dogwood trails. The Garden Center showcases tropical plants and hosts horticultural shows. *750 Cherry Rd., tel. 901/685–1566. Botanic Gardens open daily 8 AM–sunset. Garden Center open weekdays 9–4:30 year-round; weekends and holidays 1–4:30 Nov.–Feb., 1–5 rest of year.*

Stroh Brewery. You can take a guided tour of the ultramodern brewery and sample the finished product in the *Stroh Belle*, a replica of a Mississippi River sternwheeler. *5151 E. Raines Rd., tel. 901/797–2200. Tours weekdays 10:30–3:30.*

What to See and Do with Children

Adventure River. This new 25-acre water park has a giant wave pool, water slides, raft and inner-tube rides, a man-made river, a kiddie pool, and more. *6880 Whitten Bend Cove, tel. 901/382-WAVE. Open 10–8, weekends only in May, daily Memorial Day–Labor Day. Admission: $10.50 ages 10–61, $9.50 ages 4–9 (both $6.95 after 4 PM), under 4 and over 61 free.*

Chucalissa Indian Village (*see* Fanning Out).

Libertyland. At this family amusement park, there are 24 rides, ranging from thrillers to leisurely paddleboat excursions and rides for tots. Don't miss the 1909 hand-crafted carousel, one of the nation's oldest. There are also three live music shows. *940 Early Maxwell Blvd., tel. 901/274–1776. Admission: $6 adults and children over 4, $2 senior citizens over 55, children under 4 free. Thrill-ride ticket $5 extra. Open Sat. 10–8, Sun. noon–8 mid-Apr.–mid-June; Tues.–Sat. 10–8, Sun. noon–8 mid-June–late-Aug., weekend schedule resumes late Aug.–Sept. Closed rest of year.*

Meeman-Shelby Forest State Park. Get back to nature at this 12,500-acre park bordering the Mississippi, with boat rides, hikes, tours, arts and crafts, campfires, and games. *16 mi north of Memphis, off U.S. 51, tel. 901/876–5215. Admission free; some usage fees. Open daily 7 AM–10 PM.*

Memphis Zoological Gardens and Aquarium (*see* Fanning Out).

Mud Island (*see* Downtown). Younger children will especially like Huck's Backyard, a one-acre river-theme playground.

Off the Beaten Track

Agricenter International. This 1,000-acre complex showcases agricultural technology. Visit the hydroponics center, crop areas, aquaculture farm, forest and nature preserve, orchards, and vineyards. There's also a farmer's market and farm shows. *7777 Walnut Grove Rd., tel. 901/757–7777. Admission free. Open weekdays 8:30–5. Closed major holidays.*

Lichterman Nature Center. Within the city limits is a 65-acre wildlife sanctuary preserving forest, field, pond, and marsh habitats. Walk the banks of a 12-acre lake or follow animal tracks by a woodland stream; visit a greenhouse where native wildflowers are propagated or tour a hospital for wild animals. Youngsters can explore a discovery room with nature games or watch honey being made in observation hives. *5992 Quince Rd., tel. 901/767-7322. Open Tues.-Sat. 9:30-5, Sun. 1-5. Admission: $2.50 adults; $1.75 senior citizens, students, children 4 and over; children under 4 free.*

Shopping

Stores are generally open Monday-Saturday 10-6, Sunday 1-5 (in shopping malls, Mon.-Sat. 10-9, Sun. 1-6). Generally banks are open weekdays 8:30-4. First Tennessee Bank is open until 6:30 PM on Fridays.

Shopping Districts Over a dozen shopping centers and malls are scattered about the city. The **Mid-America Mall,** on Main Street between Beale and Poplar, is one of the nation's longest pedestrian malls. Here you'll find major department stores, boutiques, and restaurants amid trees, fountains, and sculptures. **Overton Square** (24 S. Cooper St., tel. 901/274-0671)—a three-block midtown shopping, restaurant, and entertainment complex in artfully restored vintage buildings and newer structures—features upscale boutiques and specialty shops.

Specialty Stores **The Woman's Exchange** (88 Racine St., Memphis, tel. 901/327-
Children's Clothes 5681) specializes in children's wear and handcrafted items. There's a Christmas shop in November and December.

Crafts and **The Checkerberry Shoppe** (2247 Germantown Rd. S, German-
Collectibles town, tel. 901/754-3601) has quilted wall hangings, country dolls, salt-glazed stoneware, handmade baskets, stained glass, miniatures, and antique reproductions. **Tanasi Crafts** (35 Charleston St., Moscow, tel. 901/527-5421) manufactures and sells Tennessee pewter and other crafts.

Elvis Memorabilia Six shops at **Graceland** (3717 Elvis Presley Blvd., tel. 901/332-3322 or 800/238-2000) sell every Elvis-related item imaginable, from cookie jars and T-shirts with his face plastered over them to Elvis records and tapes to collectible vintage items.

Off-Price Outlet **Factory Outlet Mall** (3536 Canada Rd., Exit 20 off I-40, Lakeland, tel. 901/386-3180) includes 50 stores with apparel, household goods, furniture, recreational items, and more.

One of a Kind **A. Schwab's** (163 Beale St., tel. 901/523-9782) is an old-fashioned dry-goods store whose motto is "If you can't find it at A. Schwab's, you're better off without it!" Elvis shopped here, and you can, too—for top hats, spats, tambourines, bow ties, dresses to size 60, and men's trousers to size 74. And everybody gets a free souvenir.

Participant Sports

Boating and You'll find boat rentals at **Meeman-Shelby Forest State Park** (16
Fishing mi north of Memphis off U.S. 51, tel. 901/876-5215), **Pickwick Landing State Resort Park** (in Shiloh, 15 mi south of Savannah off TN 128, tel. 901/689-3135), and **Reelfoot State Resort Park** (5 mi east of Tiptonville on TN 21, tel. 901/253-7756). You can fish year-round for bass, crappie, trout, bream, and catfish.

Golf The Memphis Park Commission (tel. 901/454-5740) operates eight public courses, the most central of which are **Overton**

Park (9 holes; tel. 901/725–9905) and **Galloway** (18 holes; tel. 901/685–7805).

Hiking There are trails at **Meeman-Shelby Forest State Park** (tel. 901/876–5215), **Shelby Farms Plough Recreation Area** (tel. 901/382–4250), **Lichterman Nature Center** (tel. 901/767–7322), and **T. O. Fuller State Park** (tel. 901/529–7581).

Horseback Riding **Shelby Farms Plough Recreation Area** (tel. 901/572–4278) offers hayrides as well as horses for riding.

Ice Skating The **Ice Capades Chalet,** in the Mall of Memphis (tel. 901/362–8877), is the area's only skating facility.

Jogging There are trails at **Shelby Farms Plough Recreation Area** (tel. 901/382–4250), which also has paddleboats, fishing, picnic areas, and nature walks.

Tennis The Memphis Park Commission (tel. 901/454–5755) operates several facilities that offer lessons, tournaments, and league play. The most centrally located is **Rogers** (tel. 901/523–0094), and **Ridgeway** (tel. 901/767–2889) has indoor courts.

Water Sports **Water-skiing** is available at the parks listed under Boating and Fishing.

Spectator Sports

Auto Racing The new 600-acre **Memphis International Motorsports Park** hosts weekly dirt-track and drag racing. *5500 Taylor Forge Rd., Millington, tel. 901/358–7223. Open Mar.–Nov.*

Baseball You can cheer for the **Memphis Chicks,** a class AA team of the Kansas City Royals and member of the Southern League, at Chicks Stadium (tel. 901/272–1687).

Dog Racing Greyhound racing draws hordes of Memphians and visitors into Arkansas, which allows pari-mutuel betting. **Southland Greyhound Park** is a posh facility, with closed-circuit viewing and a restaurant. *1550 N. Ingram Blvd. (via I–40 or I–55 from downtown Memphis), W. Memphis, AR, tel. 501/735–3670. Open early Apr.–early Nov. Under 18 not admitted.*

Football Each December a top Southern collegiate event—the **Liberty Bowl Football Classic**—is held at the Liberty Memorial Stadium (tel. 901/278–4747), which hosts the Memphis State University Tigers and other football teams.

Soccer The **Memphis Storm**—a professional soccer team—play home games during the November–March season at the Mid-South Coliseum (Mid-South Fairgrounds, tel. 901/767–4000).

Dining

by Tom Martin Not so long ago, Memphis offered little more than various neighborhood restaurants featuring "home cooking," several Chinese chop-suey houses, a handful of Italian spaghetti-and-lasagna spots, and numerous establishments serving pork barbecue. Even the city's few higher-priced restaurants served only the ordinary.

Tom Martin has reviewed restaurants for *Memphis* magazine since 1982. He also contributed the Memphis chapter to *Mariani's Coast-to-Coast Dining Guide.*

Happily, the dining choices have not only greatly expanded but dramatically improved in quality during the last 15 years. In addition to a number of restaurants serving imaginative American cuisine, Memphis now boasts many competent and attractive international dining rooms. Happily, too, hotel dining in Memphis, which used to mean tired menus and lifeless cooking, has been revitalized, and today the city's most inspired dishes are often served in its finer hotels.

Memphis's top culinary attraction, however, remains barbecue, and a visit to one of the 70-odd barbecue restaurants is recommended for anyone wanting to savor local color as well as tasty ribs. True fanciers may want to schedule their visit around the International Pork Barbecue Cooking Contest, which is held during the annual Memphis in May International Festival and draws 300 teams from around the world (as well as 250,000 spectators) for its three-day run on the banks of the Mississippi.

The most highly recommended restaurants in each price category are indicated by a star ★.

Category	Cost*
Very Expensive	over $50
Expensive	$40–$50
Moderate	$20–$40
Inexpensive	under $20

per person without tax (7.75% in Tennessee), service, or drinks

The following credit-card abbreviations are used: AE, American Express; CB, Carte Blanche; DC, Diners Club; MC, MasterCard; V, Visa.

Very Expensive
Continental

Justine's. Fresh roses from the restaurant's gardens adorn each table, and soothing piano music flows through the six dining rooms of this restored mansion, built in 1843. In operation over 30 years, Justine's is a gracious reminder of the style of the Old South. The New Orleans–influenced menu is hardly innovative, but it is reliable, especially the fresh and well-prepared seafood. Excellent specialties are crabs Justine, a crabmeat casserole with buttery sauce; broiled pompano with chives, parsley, and lemon; and beef tenderloin with artichoke hearts and béarnaise sauce. *919 Coward Pl., tel. 901/527–3815. Jacket and tie recommended. Reservations advised, especially on weekends. AE, DC, MC, V. Closed Sun.*

New American
★

Chervil's. The three-section room's soft lighting and pastel colors contribute to an intimate ambience, as do the guitarist's light jazz and classical selections. In this setting are served such delights as lobster ravioli with saffron, salad of warmed duck breast on a nest of radicchio, broiled tournedos of yellowfin tuna with fresh tomato chutney, and veal *forestière* with chanterelle mushrooms. *Holiday Inn Crowne Plaza, 250 N. Main St., tel. 901/527–7333. Jacket and tie recommended. Reservations accepted. AE, DC, MC, V. Closed Sun. and Mon.*

Nouvelle French
★

Chez Philippe. The decor—high ceilings, *faux* marble columns, huge murals depicting a masked ball—is wonderfully lavish,

Dining

Captain Bilbo's River Restaurant, **1**

Charlie Vergos' Rendezvous, **2**

Chervil's, **4**

Chez Philippe, **3**

Dux, **3**

The East India Company, Ltd., **21**

Genghis Khan's, **20**

Hemmings, **24**

John Wills' Barbecue Pit, **17**

Justine's, **7**

La Tourelle, **15**

Leonard's, **8**

Molly's La Casita, **12**, **19**

Palm Court, The, **13**

Wang's Mandarin House, **23**

Lodging

Days Inn Memphis Airport, **10**

Econo Lodge Airport, **18**

French Quarter Inn, The, **14**

Hampton Inn Airport, **11**

Holiday Inn Crowne Plaza, **4**

Howard Johnson's Motor Lodge, **9**

La Quinta Motor Inn-Medical Center, **6**

Lowenstein-Long House, **5**

Memphis Airport Hilton, **16**

Omni Memphis, **22**

Peabody, The, **3**

Downtown Memphis Dining and Lodging

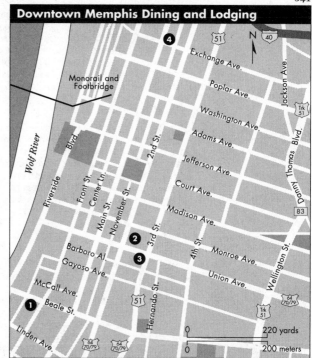

Memphis Dining and Lodging

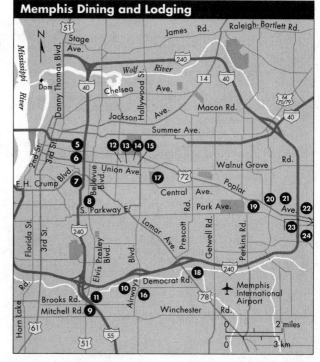

and lilting harp music adds a finishing touch of elegance. The service, by waiters in white tie, is impeccable. Most important, the cuisine—Memphis's most innovative and sophisticated—lives up to its regal setting. Specialties include cold mousse of salmon and scallops served with lobster aspic, fillet of sturgeon poached in pink rose vinegar, and medallions of veal and tuna marinated in paprika vinegar. *The Peabody Hotel, 149 Union Ave., tel. 901/529–4188. Jacket and tie recommended. Reservations advised. AE, DC, MC, V. Closed Sun.*

Expensive
French

La Tourelle. The quiet setting is reminiscent of a small country restaurant in France, with fine lace curtains and wood floors. Four-course prix fixe meals are served nightly, or you can order à la carte. Among the better appetizers are poached ravioli with a goat-cheese filling, and shrimp- and crab-filled pastries. Recommended entrees include red snapper with lobster cream sauce and pork loin braised with bourbon and prunes. *Overton Sq., 2146 Monroe, tel. 901/726–5771. Jacket and tie recommended. Reservations accepted. MC, V. Closed Mon.*

Indian

The East India Company, Ltd. This is Memphis's best Indian restaurant by far. The atmosphere is very elegant, and though the selection isn't vast, a good representation of Indian dishes is offered, including papadams, aloo samosa, and bajji as appetizers; tandoor chicken, masala lamb, and orange roughy in coriander sauce for entrees; and Indian breads such as nan, chapathis, and puri. *712 West Brookhaven Circle, tel. 901/685–8723. Dress: informal. Reservations accepted. AE, DC, MC, V. Closed Sun. Mon. lunch only.*

New American
★

Dux. Stylishly done up in black, white, and maroon, this pleasing hotel restaurant serves such popular specialties as seared tuna with black sesame seeds and ginger-scallion sauce, corn-and-red-pepper polenta with coriander and tomato relish, baked squab in phyllo pastry, and, for dessert, white chocolate charlotte with raspberry *coulis*. The restaurant's entrance is decorated with beautiful glass and ceramic ducks in honor of the real ones you'll see in the hotel's famous lobby. *The Peabody Hotel, 149 Union Ave., tel. 901/529–4199. Dress: informal. Reservations accepted. AE, DC, MC, V.*

Hemmings. An impressive new entry to Memphis dining, this restaurant is set in the distinctive Saddle Creek shopping development of suburban Germantown. The decor is in crisp shades of pale blue and ivory, with high ceilings and huge windows. The menu, inspired by the cooking of California and the American southwest, changes every few weeks. Typical of the creative choices are venison cutlets over grilled corn cakes with tomato salsa, pit-roasted breast of duck with bok choy and papaya chili sauce, and roasted quail with andouille sausage on a bed of grilled corn relish. *Saddle Creek shopping center, 7615 West Farmington Rd., Germantown, tel. 901/757–8323. Jacket and tie recommended. Reservations advised. AE, DC, MC, V.*

Northern Italian

The Palm Court. The restaurant is housed in what was once an ice-skating rink, but you'd never know it now: the space is filled with huge potted palms, and yards of gathered fabric form canopies around a central atrium. The menu features such distinctive regional dishes as *gnochetti* in cream, snails *Milanese* over angel-hair pasta, and lobster *fra diavolo* with red-pepper sauce. Desserts include zabaglione served over fresh strawberries. *210–1 Overton Sq. Ln., tel. 901/725–6797. Dress: informal. Reservations advised, especially on weekends. AE, DC, MC, V. Closed Mon.*

Moderate **Genghis Khan's.** This stylish restaurant is decorated in muted
Chinese greens, with subtle Chinese drawings adorning the walls. The food—an impressive selection of Hunan, Szechuan, and Mandarin specialties—is similarly refined. Among the better-than-average offerings are Hunan fish, beef with sesame, tangerine shrimp, and twice-cooked pork with Chinese vegetables. There's also a weekday luncheon buffet. *Clark Tower, 5100 Poplar Ave., tel. 901/763–0272. Dress: informal. Reservations accepted. AE, DC, MC, V.*

★ **Wang's Mandarin House.** This is a fast-paced local favorite, especially among those who favor highly spiced Szechuan and Mandarin fare. Only the decor here is subdued, with dark orange wallpaper, brown linens, and glass and natural-wood partitions that divide the room. Excellent first courses include cold noodles with sesame sauce and crisp spring rolls with chili sauce. Entrees include Mandarin Flower Basket, a woven rice-flower basket filled with shrimp and vegetables; and General Tsao's Chicken, large chunks lightly fried and served in a sweet brown sauce. The bar features live piano music. *1183 Park Place Mall, tel. 901/767–0354. Dress: informal. Reservations accepted. AE, MC, V.*

Seafood **Captain Bilbo's River Restaurant.** This riverfront establishment is one of Memphis's busiest restaurants, and though it seats over 300, the waiting list often exceeds one hour. Fortunately, you can listen to live music in the comfortable bar while you wait. The dishes served are simple but consistently well-prepared. Among the better offerings are shrimp in a brown butter sauce, flounder stuffed with shrimp and crabmeat, and fried oysters and shrimp. *263 Wagner Pl., tel. 901/526–1966. Dress: informal. No reservations. AE, MC, V.*

Inexpensive **Charlie Vergos' Rendezvous.** Charlie Vergos has become some-
Barbecue thing of a Memphis ambassador of barbecued ribs: Not
★ only does his downtown basement restaurant hosts thousands of tourists each year, but he also ships his ribs by air express all over the country. The decor here is museumlike: the walls are filled with memorabilia and bric-a-brac, from old newspaper cartoons to Essolene gas signs. But what packs in the crowds is the delicious pork loin plate and the barbecued pork ribs. *52 S. Second St., tel. 901/523–2746. Dress: informal. No reservations. AE, MC, V. Closed Sun. and Mon.*

★ **John Wills' Barbecue Pit.** John Wills parlayed his two victories in the International Pork Barbecue Cooking Contest into this successful restaurant, open since 1983. Attractive, with green tables, natural-wood booths, and cute photos of pigs adorning the walls, the busy establishment offers a wide selection of well-prepared barbecued meats, including beef and pork ribs, pork shoulder, beef brisket, and sausage. The barbecued beans are nicely spiced, and the coleslaw has a tart mustard seasoning. *2450 Central Ave., tel. 901/274–8000. Dress: informal. No reservations. AE, MC, V.*

Leonard's. This landmark has been around since 1932, and you'll still find excellent barbecue beneath its smiling neon pig. The waitresses who tend the small booths and plain tables are friendly and fast. The ribs are meaty and lean. The pork shoulder is chopped in large chunks and served with a mild sauce (hotter sauce from shaker bottles on each table can be added). The onion rings are legendary: huge, sweet slices, crisply fried. An excellent lemon icebox pie makes a fitting end to this visit to America's culinary past. *1140 S. Bellevue Blvd., tel. 901/948–1581. Dress: informal. No reservations. MC, V.*

Mexican **Molly's La Casita.** Molly Gonzales's roots in Mexican cooking,
★ Memphis-style, go back to the Lone Star restaurant, which her father started here in 1934. The Lone Star's not around anymore, but there are two La Casitas now open in Memphis, and both upbeat operations serve reliable Mexican food (though the Park Avenue outlet has the more attractive dining room). Some of the best entrees are the *chiles rellenos*—two *posia* peppers blackened and stuffed with cheese or meat, coated in a light egg batter and fried. Also good is the *pollo con mole* (chicken in the traditional unsweetened chocolate sauce), shrimp *fajitas*, and *arroz con pollo* (chicken with rice). *2006 Madison Ave., tel. 901/726–1873; 4972 Park Ave., tel. 901/685–1616. Dress: informal. No reservations. AE, MC, V.*

Lodging

Memphis hotels are especially busy during the spring, when the Memphis in May International Festival and April's Cotton Carnival are in progress, and in mid-August, when pilgrims observe Elvis Presley's death. Be sure to reserve well in advance during those times. To find out about B&Bs in Memphis, contact the **Bed & Breakfast in Memphis Reservation Service** (Box 41621, Memphis, 38174, tel. 901/726–5920).

The most highly recommended properties in each price category are indicated by a star ★. For maps pinpointing locations, *see* Dining.

Category	Cost*
Very Expensive	over $115
Expensive	$70–$115
Moderate	$50–$70
Inexpensive	under $50

*double room; add 11.75% for taxes

The following credit-card abbreviations are used: AE, American Express; CB, Carte Blanche; DC, Diners Club; MC, MasterCard; V, Visa.

Very Expensive **Omni Memphis.** This luxury property, a 27-story circular glass tower, is in the flourishing eastern suburbs near I–240. From your glass-walled aerie, you'll have sweeping vistas of the sprawling metropolis and its outskirts. *939 Ridge Lake Blvd., 38119, tel. 901/761–1234 or 800/228–9000. 380 rooms. Facilities: cable TV/movies, pool, health club, coffee shop, restaurant, lounge with live entertainment; arrangements for golf, spa, tennis privileges. AE, CB, DC, MC, V.*

★ **The Peabody.** After languishing in disrepair for two decades, and finally closing, this 12-story landmark downtown hostelry was impeccably restored and reopened in 1981. Guest rooms

were enlarged, refurbished, and redecorated with period reproduction furnishings. The lobby preserves its original
stained-glass skylights and ornate travertine marble fountain
—home to the hotel's famed resident ducks, who come down
each morning from their penthouse apartment and parade
across a red carpet to the stirring sounds of Sousa's "King Cotton March." Each afternoon, the ceremony is repeated as they
return to their rooftop "Duck Palace." *149 Union Ave., 38103,
tel. 901/529–4000 or 800/732–2639. 454 rooms. Facilities: indoor pool, health club, 4 dining rooms including Chez Philippe
and Dux (see Dining), lounge with live entertainment, lobby
bar serving cocktails and afternoon tea. AE, CB, DC, MC, V.*

Expensive **The French Quarter Inn.** With its mellow rose-brick exterior
★ and classic architectural lines, this pleasant New Overton
Square hostelry is reminiscent of an older, New Orleans–style
inn. All the one-bedroom suites have living rooms and whirlpool tubs, and some are balconied. *2144 Madison Ave., 38104,
tel. 901/728–4000. 106 suites. Facilities: cable TV/movies,
health club, pool. AE, CB, DC, MC, V.*

Holiday Inn Crowne Plaza. Memphis was the birthplace of Holiday Inns, and this is the flagship of the area's seven-inn fleet.
Adjacent to the downtown Convention Center, this sleek high-
rise hotel (18 floors) offers a concierge floor and sizable meeting
facilities, plus ample work space and lighting in the spacious
guest rooms and suites. The lobby lounge, a tasteful,
greenery-filled retreat, is a pleasant spot to relax and listen to
music from the grand piano. *250 N. Main St., 38103, tel. 901/
527–7300 or 800/465–4329. 400 rooms. Facilities: cable TV/
movies, indoor pool, health club, whirlpool, sauna, 2 restaurants, lobby lounge. AE, CB, DC, MC, V.*

Memphis Airport Hilton. Guest rooms are ranged around a five-
story, skylit, greenery-bedecked atrium lobby. Relax in the
well-equipped fitness centers or in a whirlpool-bath suite (with
kitchenette). The hotel has attractively priced packages for
weekend visitors. *2240 Democrat Rd., 38132, tel. 901/332–1130
or 800/445–8667. 380 rooms. Facilities: cable TV/movies, indoor pool, heated outdoor pool, 2 lighted tennis courts, 2-mi
jogging track, separate fitness centers for men and women, restaurant, lobby bar with wide-screen TV and piano, nightclub
lounge, video checkout. AE, CB, DC, MC, V.*

Moderate **Howard Johnson's Motor Lodge.** In the Executive section of this
★ two-story inn, rooms are extra-large, with a mini-living room,
spacious work table, good lighting, and comfortable over-
stuffed chairs. All rooms have private patios. The grounds are
expansive and well landscaped, in a resortlike setting. *3280
Elvis Presley Blvd., 38116, tel. 901/345–1425 or 800/654–2000.
128 rooms. Facilities: cable TV/movies, outdoor pool, wading
pool, playground, restaurant. AE, CB, DC, MC, V.*

Lowenstein-Long House. If you're on a budget but still want a
special lodging experience, this may be for you—especially if
you're into Victoriana. This castlelike mansion on an acre of
lawn was built at the turn of the century by department-store
magnate Abraham Lowenstein and is listed on the National
Historic Register. All the rooms are spacious, with high ceilings and large private baths. Some have four-poster beds and
fireplaces; none have TVs. *217 N. Waldran Blvd., 38105, tel.
901/527–7174. 8 rooms. Facilities: kitchen and laundry facilities. No credit cards.*

Inexpensive– **Days Inn Memphis Airport.** Accommodations at this completely
Moderate renovated three-story motor inn are light, sunny, well-maintained, and spacious. This is an especially good buy for the
economy-minded business traveler and visitor to nearby
Graceland. *1533 E. Brooks Rd., 38116, tel. 901/345–2470 or
800/325–2525. 242 rooms. Facilities: cable TV, meeting rooms,
dining room, lounge with dancing and wide-screen TV, oversize pool. AE, CB, DC, MC, V.*

Inexpensive **Econo Lodge Airport.** This well-kept two-story motor inn is
conveniently located near the airport and Graceland. King-size
beds and suites are available. *3456 Lamar Ave., 38118, tel. 901/
365–7335 or 800/446–6900. 100 rooms. Facilities: cable TV,
pool, meeting rooms. AE, CB, DC, MC, V.*

★ **Hampton Inn Airport.** This is a member of the economy-priced
system that's "cousin" to Holiday Inns. The building is a pleasing contemporary design. Spacious, well-lighted rooms have
Scandinavian-style teakwood furnishings. A hospitality suite
has comfortable chairs, tables, and an audiovisual unit. *2979
Millbranch Rd., 38116, tel. 901/396–2200 or 800/426–7866. 128
rooms. Facilities: cable TV/movies, pool. AE, CB, DC, MC, V.*
La Quinta Motor Inn–Medical Center. This two-story inn near
the medical center and midtown attractions offers spacious,
well-maintained rooms. King Plus rooms have a full-length mirror, a large working area, and an oversize bed. *42 S. Camilla
St., 38104, tel. 901/526–1050 or 800/531–5900. 130 rooms. Facilities: cable TV, outdoor pool. AE, CB, DC, MC, V.*

The Arts

For a complete listing of weekly events, check the Playbook section in the Friday *Memphis Commercial Appeal*, or see *Key
Magazine*, distributed at hotels, motels, restaurants, and
lounges. The Visitor Information Center will also provide an
up-to-date rundown of events.

Concerts During the warmer months, there are free concerts at noon
Monday, Wednesday, and Friday at the **Court Square Gazebo** in
the Mid-America Mall (tel. 901/526–6840). Big-name enter-
tainers and musical groups appear at the **Mud Island
Amphitheatre** (tel. 901/576–7241). Among the offerings at the
Orpheum Theatre (tel. 901/525–3000) are classical concerts.

Dance The Orpheum Theatre is also the scene of performances by two
dance companies: **Memphis Concert Ballet,** featuring professional dancers and celebrity guest artists; and **Tennessee Ballet
Company of Memphis,** with local performers.

Opera **Opera Memphis** performs October through February at the Orpheum Theatre (tel. 901/678–3021 for tickets).

Theater **Playhouse on the Square** (tel. 901/726–4656, Sept.–July) features the city's only repertory company. The **Orpheum Theatre**
(tel. 901/525–3000), an impeccably restored former vaudeville
palace, is the site of Broadway shows and other productions.
Center Stage, at the Jewish Community Center (901/761–0810),
and the **Circuit Playhouse** (tel. 901/726–5521, Sept.–June) offer
a wide variety of performances.

At **Memphis Children's Theatre** (tel. 901/452–3968), performances are directed, designed, and acted entirely by children.
Community theaters include **Theatre Memphis** (tel. 901/682–
8323), acclaimed as one of the best in the States, and **German-**

town **Community Theatre** (tel. 901/754–2680), in a restored schoolhouse. Memphis State's **University Theatre** (tel. 901/454–3975) and Rhodes College's **McCoy Theatre** (tel. 901/726–3839, Oct.–May) present dramatic and musical productions starring students, faculty, and guest performers.

Nightlife

Blues   **Blues Alley.** Listen to live blues and jazz while munching on Memphis barbecued ribs. *598 Marshall Ave., tel. 901/525–0193. Open nightly 5 PM–2 AM.*

Captain Bilbo's River Restaurant. This spot overlooking the Mississippi offers floor shows, live entertainment, and dancing nightly in the bar. *263 Wagner Pl., tel. 901/526–1966. Open Sun.–Thurs. 5–10:30, to 11 Fri.–Sat.*

Lou's Place. Live blues comes with barbecued ribs or catfish. *94 S. Front St., tel. 901/528–1970. Bands Wed.–Sat. 5 PM–2 AM.*

New Daisy Theatre. At this 600-seat concert hall, where B.B. King got his start, blues, jazz, and (predominantly) rock concerts are held. *330 Beale St., tel. 901/525–8979.*

Rum Boogie Cafe. There's live blues and dancing nightly. *182 Beale St., tel. 901/528–0150. Open Mon.–Thurs. 11:30 AM–1 AM, Fri. 11:30 AM–2 AM, Sat. noon–2 AM, Sun. noon–midnight.*

Nightclubs   **Alfred's on Beale.** One of the city's hottest dance clubs also serves food. Rock bands perform every Friday and Saturday night, and a DJ spins popular dance tunes during the week. *197 Beale St., tel. 901/525–3711. Open daily 11 AM–3 AM.*

Bad Bob's Vapors. This airport-area supper club that holds 1,000 people features dancing to two live country and rock 'n' roll bands daily. *1743 E. Brooks Rd., tel. 901/345–1761. Open daily 3 PM–3 AM.*

Club Royale. Nightly live entertainment (blues, oldies, pop) and a Sunday night singers' contest are featured. *349 Beale St., tel. 901/527–5404. Open Mon.–Sat. 5 PM–3 AM, Sun. 5 PM–1:30 AM.*

Proud Mary's. Described as an "old-style river bar," this club features live rock in a relaxed, slightly rustic atmosphere. *326 Beale St., tel. 901/525–8979. Open daily 4 PM–3 AM.*

Sir Lafs-A-Lot Comedy Club. There are professional live comedy acts, specialty dinners, and reservations are recommended. *535 S. Highland St., tel. 901/324–5653. Shows Wed., Thurs., Sun. 8:30 PM; Fri.–Sat. 8:30 PM, 10:45PM.*

Hotel Lounges   **Dad's Place.** Dance to Top 40, country, rock, and big band sounds nightly. *Ramada Inn SW Airport, 1471 E. Brooks Rd., tel. 901/332–3500. Open daily 4:30 PM–1 AM.*

Escape Hatch. This video/jukebox lounge offers country, pop, rock, and R&B at 50¢ a play. *Admiral Benbow Inn, 1220 Union Ave., tel. 901/725–0630. Open Mon.–Sat. 3–10 PM.*

Lobby Lounge. Enjoy cocktails or late-night pastries in a sumptuous hotel lobby. *The Peabody Hotel, 149 Union Ave., tel. 901/529–4000. Open weekdays 10:30 AM–12:30 AM, weekends until 1 AM.*

Tanasie's Supper Club. A nightclub singer performs Elvis, country, and light rock. *Ramada Inn SE Airport, 3896 Lamar Ave., tel. 901/365-6100. Shows Tues.–Fri. at 9 and 11 PM.*

Zeiggy's. At this video lounge, there's dancing and complimentary hors d'oeuvres nightly. *Holiday Inn–Memphis E, 5795 Poplar Ave., tel. 901/682-7881. Open Tues.–Sat. noon–2 AM, Sun. and Mon. noon–midnight.*

Overton Square Spots **Paulette's.** Come here for easy-listening piano music. *2110 Madison Ave., tel. 901/726-5128. Open Mon.–Thurs. 11 AM–11 PM, Fri. and Sat. 11 AM–midnight, Sun. 11 AM–9 PM.*

Studebaker's. A DJ spins discs from the fifties to the eighties. *2125 Madison Ave., tel. 901/274-1144. Open Mon.–Fri. 4 PM–3 AM, Sat. and Sun. 6 PM–3 AM.*

Nashville

Heralded as the Country Music Capital and birthplace of the "Nashville Sound," Tennessee's fast-growing capital city is also a leading center of higher education, appropriately known as the Athens of the South. Both labels fit. Far from developing a case of civic schizophrenia at such contrasting roles, Nashville has prospered from them both, becoming one of the middle South's liveliest and most vibrant cities in the process.

Much of Nashville's role as a cultural leader, enhanced by the presence of the new performing arts center, derives from the many colleges, universities, and technical and trade schools located here. Several, including Vanderbilt University, have national or international reputations, and many have private art galleries. As ancient Athens was the "School of Hellas," so Nashville fills this role in the contemporary South.

As every fan knows, it was Nashville's "Grand Ole Opry" radio program, which began as station WSM's "Barn Dance" in 1925, that launched the amazing country music boom. The Opry performs in a sleek $15 million Opry House now, but it's still as gleeful and down-home informal as it was when it held forth in the old Ryman Auditorium. Joining the Opry in Nashville are dozens of country music attractions—some large, some small, many begun by or memorials to individual stars.

You'll also enjoy forays into the surrounding Tennessee Heartland, a pocket of gently rolling Cumberland Mountain foothills and bluegrass meadows. It's one of the state's richest farming areas.

Arriving and Departing

By Plane Airports and Airlines Nashville Metropolitan Airport, approximately eight miles from downtown, is served by **American, American Eagle, Delta, Eastern, Northwest, Pan American, Southwest, United,** and **USAir.**

Between the Airport and Center City Airport **limousine service** (tel. 615/367-2305) to downtown is $8 for the first person and $4 for each additional person; the return-trip rate is $7. To reach downtown by **car,** take I–40W.

By Train Amtrak does not serve the Nashville area.

By Bus The **Greyhound/Trailways** terminal is at 8th Ave. S and McGavock St., tel. 615/256-6141.

By Car From Nashville, I–65 leads north into Kentucky and south into Alabama, and I–24 leads northwest into Kentucky and Illinois and southeast into Georgia. I–40 traverses the state east–west, connecting Knoxville with Nashville and Memphis.

By Boat The **Delta Queen Steamboat Co.** (tel. 504/586–0631) offers four-night paddlewheeler cruises between St. Louis and Nashville, with stops along the way.

Getting Around

By Bus **Metropolitan Transit Authority (MTA)** buses (tel. 615/242–4433) serve the entire county. Service on most routes begins at 4–5 AM and continues until 11:15 PM. The regular adult base fare is 75¢ (exact change required). For disabled persons, a van is available for downtown transport (tel. 615/351–RIDE).

By Trolley **Nashville Trolley Co.** (tel. 615/242–4433) also offers rides in the downtown area. The fare is 25¢ (exact change).

By Taxi The fare is a basic $1.50, plus 10¢ for each quarter-mile. It's best to phone for service: **Checker Cab** (tel. 615/254–5031), **Nashville Cab** (tel. 615/242–7070), **Yellow Cab** (tel. 615/256–0101).

Important Addresses and Numbers

Tourist Information **Nashville Area Chamber of Commerce,** 161 4th Ave. N, tel. 615/259–3900. Open weekdays 8–4:30. **Visitor Information Center,** I–65 and James Robertson Pkwy., Exit 85, tel. 615/242–5606. Open daily 8–5 (until 8 PM Memorial Day–Labor Day).

Emergencies Dial 911 for **police** and **ambulance** in an emergency.

Hospital The emergency room is open all night at centrally located **Baptist Hospital** (2000 Church St., tel. 615/329–5555) and **Vanderbilt University Medical Center** (1211 22nd Ave. S, tel. 615/322–7311).

Dentist For emergency service, contact any of three **American Dental Center** facilities: on Woodland St., tel. 615/256–2321; on Old Harding Pike, tel. 615/662–0035; or on Bransford Ave., tel. 615/292–3301.

24-Hour Pharmacy **Farmer's Market Pharmacy** (715 Jefferson St., tel. 615/242–5501).

Guided Tours

Orientation Tours Several companies offer tours that may include drives past stars' homes and visits to the Grand Ole Opry, Music Row, and historic structures. Among them are **American Sightseeing** (tel. 615/256–1200 or 800/826–6456), **Gray Line** (tel. 615/244–7330 or 800/251–1864), **Grand Ole Opry Tours** (tel. 615/889–9450), and **Nashville Tours** (tel. 615/889–4646).

Special-Interest Tours **Country & Western Round-Up Tours** (tel. 615/883–5555) offers a daily Twitty City/Johnny Cash Special motorcoach tour, which drives past homes of stars and visits Twitty City/Music Village USA and the House of Cash. **Johnny Walker Tours** (tel. 615/834–8585 or 800/722–1524) has an evening Music Village Nightlife Tour, which includes a Southern-style barbecue buffet dinner and top-name country entertainment in Music Village Theater. **Stardust Tours** (tel. 615/244–2335) offers a daily Music

Village Sunset Tour, which includes the Music Village Theater entertainment and buffet dinner. **Nissan** (tel. 615/459–1400) offers free tours of its vast, supermodern Smyrna auto plant on Tuesday and Thursday. Call for an appointment; only children in fifth grade or older are allowed on tours.

Walking Tours   At the Nashville Area Chamber of Commerce or the Visitor Information Center (*see* Important Addresses and Numbers), pick up a self-guided tour of downtown.

Excursion Boat   **Belle Carol Riverboat Co.** (tel. 615/244–3430 or 800/342–2355)
Tours   offers Cumberland River sightseeing, luncheon, and dinner cruises from the Nashville Old Steamboat Dock. From its dock, **Opryland USA** (tel. 615/889–6611) offers daytime cruises with Opryland-style entertainment and evening dinner cruises aboard its four-deck *General Jackson* showboat.

Exploring Nashville

Numbers in the margin correspond with points of interest on the Nashville and Downtown Nashville maps.

Nashville sprawls. In getting around, it helps to remember that the river horizontally bisects the central city. Numbered avenues, running north–south, are west of and parallel to the river; numbered streets are east of the river and parallel to it.

Downtown   Although considerably smaller, the Cumberland River has been as important to Nashville as the Mississippi has been to Memphis. That this is still true can be seen by any visitor to **❶** **Riverfront Park** at First Avenue and Broadway, a welcoming green enclave on the west bank of the Cumberland, with an expansive view of the busy barge traffic on the river. The park serves as a popular venue for summer concerts and picnics, as well as a docking spot for riverboat excursions (*see* Guided **❷** Tours). North on First Avenue is **Fort Nashborough.** High on the limestone bluffs overlooking the river that brought them to this place, the first settlers built a crude log fort in 1779 as protection and shelter. Today it has been painstakingly re-created to serve as a monument to their courage, and in five log cabins costumed interpreters evoke the indomitable spirit of the American age of settlement. *Tel. 615/255–8192. Donation. Open Tues.–Sat. 9–4. Closed major holidays.*

By the early 19th century, logs had given way to brick and marble. Downtown was thriving, and today it thrives anew, thanks to an extensive preservation program. From Fort Nashborough, turn left onto Church Street and you'll be in the **❸** heart of the **Historic Second Avenue Business District,** where 19th-century buildings have been handsomely restored to house offices, restaurants, boutiques, and residences.

Continue west on Church Street, which between Fourth and Eighth avenues is cobblestoned and tree-lined, retaining a picturesque quality reminiscent of a European town. At the **❹** corner of Fifth is the **Downtown Presbyterian Church,** an Egyptian Revival tabernacle (c. 1851) designed by noted Philadelphia architect William Strickland.

Strolling north on Fifth Avenue, you'll come to one of the city's finest contemporary structures: the James K. Polk Office **❺** Building, home to the impressive **Tennessee State Museum.** Here over 6,000 artifacts are displayed in settings that explore

Barbara Mandrell Country, **12**

Belmont Mansion, **23**

Belle Meade Mansion, **21**

Boxcar Willie's/Cars of the Stars, **17**

Car Collector's Hall of Fame, **14**

Cheekwood, **22**

Country Music Hall of Fame, **10**

Country Music Wax Museum, **15**

Downtown Presbyterian Church, **4**

Fort Nashborough, **2**

Hank Williams Jr. Museum, **13**

Hermitage, The, **25**

Hist. 2nd Ave. Bus. Dist., **3**

House of Cash, **26**

Jim Reeves Museum, **19**

Music Valley Wax Museum, **18**

Opryland USA, **16**

Parthenon, **20**

Performing Arts Center, **6**

Riverfront Park, **1**

Ryman Auditorium, **9**

State Capitol, **7**

Studio B, **11**

Tenn. State Museum, **5**

Traveller's Rest, **24**

Twitty City/Music Village USA, **27**

War Memorial Bldg., **8**

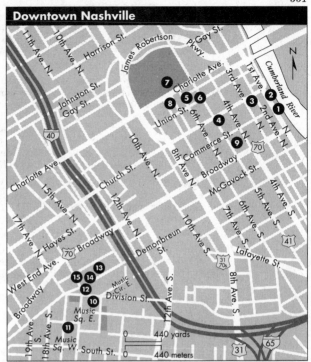

Downtown Nashville

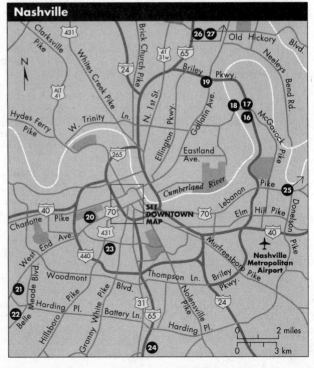

Nashville

life in Tennessee. Included are a log cabin, an exhibition of Indian life, and a demonstration of bygone printing techniques. ❻ (Also part of the complex is the **Tennessee Performing Arts Center.**) *505 Deaderick St., tel. 615/741–2692. Admission free. Open Mon.–Sat. 10–5, Sun. 1–5.*

❼ Walking west along Charlotte Avenue, you'll come to the Greek Revival **State Capitol,** also designed by Strickland, who was so impressed with his creation that he requested—and received —entombment behind one of the building's walls. On the grounds—guarded by statues of such Tennessee heros as Andrew Jackson—are buried the 11th U.S. president, James K. Polk, and his wife. *Tel. 615/741–0830 (Education Dept.). Open for free tours daily, 9–4. Closed major holidays.*

❽ On the corner of Seventh and Union is the **War Memorial Building,** built to honor the state's World War I dead and now housing a collection of military memorabilia. *Tel. 615/741–5383. Admission free. Open Mon.–Sat. 10–4, Sun. 1–4. Closed major holidays.*

Music Row The leap from state capital to music capital is not as great as it may seem. If you're walking, you might head down Fifth Avenue to pass recently renovated **Ryman Auditorium,** home of the ❾ Grand Ole Opry from 1943 to 1974 and now open for tours—a shrine for die-hard Opry fans. *116 Opry Pl. (Fifth Ave. N, between Broadway and Commerce Sts.), tel. 615/254–1445. Admission: $1.50 adults; 75¢ children 6–12, under 6 free. Open daily 8:30–4:30.*

By car, take the Demonbreun exit off I–40 to Music Row, the heart of Nashville's recording industry and a center for country ❿ music attractions. The ample free parking next to the **Country Music Hall of Fame and Museum** is convenient to all the country attractions clustered nearby and is another reason to begin your Music Row tour at Nashville's premier country music museum. Costumes, instruments, film, photos, insights: the Hall of Fame has it all (including Elvis Presley's "solid gold" Cadillac). A ticket for the Hall of Fame includes admission to the ⓫ legendary RCA **Studio B** a few blocks away. Elvis, Dolly Parton, and countless others once recorded here; now the studio is a hands-on exhibit area showing how records are produced. *4 Music Sq. E, tel. 615/256–1639. Admission: $6 adults; $1.75 children 6–11, under 6 free. Open daily 8–8 June–Aug., 9–5 rest of year.*

Those inspired by their visit to Studio B might stop by the **Recording Studios of America** (1510 Division St., tel. 615/254–1282) to record, at nominal cost, a demo tape of their own. ⓬ The studio is part of **Barbara Mandrell Country,** an intimate look at the career and family life of that superstar (including a replica of her bedroom). *Tel. 615/242–7800. Admission: $6.03 adults, $2.09 children. under 5 free. Open daily 9–5 Jan.–Mar., Sept.–Dec.; 8–8 June–Aug.*

The car seems to be as much a country music icon as the guitar, a fact underlined by two museums on Demonbreun Street. At ⓭ the **Hank Williams Jr. Museum,** family memorabilia includes Hank Sr.'s '52 Cadillac and Hank Jr.'s pickup truck. *1524 Demonbreun St., tel. 615/242–8313. Admission: $4 adults, children under 16 free with an adult. Open daily 8 AM–9 PM Oct.–Feb., 8–3 Oct.–Feb.*

⑭ A few doors away, the **George Jones Car Collectors' Hall of Fame** displays another of Elvis's Cadillacs (alongside one of George's), Webb Pierce's startling "silver dollar car," and 50 other flashy vehicles with country provenances. *1534 Demonbreun St., tel. 615/255–6804. Admission: $4 adults; $2.50 children 6–11, under 6 free. Open daily 9–5 Sept.–May, 8–8 June–Aug.*

⑮ In the same block, you'll find the guitars: At the **Country Music Wax Museum and Mall** are over 60 figures of country stars, complete with original stage costumes, and musical instruments. *118 16th Ave. S, tel. 615/256–2490. Admission: $3.75 adults, $1.75 children 6–12, under 6 free.* In same building is Waylon Jenning's private collection of 6 automobiles, including the General Lee used in the TV series, The Dukes of Hazzard. *Admission: $3 adults, $1.75 children. Open daily 9–8 June–Aug., 9–5 Sept.–May.*

Opryland ⑯ Country music lovers may continue their pilgrimage at **Opryland USA,** an attraction-filled show park just 15 minutes from downtown via Briley Parkway. The complex was created in part because the enormously popular Grand Ole Opry—65 years old and still going strong—had outgrown its old stomping grounds, the Ryman. Each weekend, top stars perform at the nation's oldest continuous radio show, in the world's largest broadcast studio (it seats 4,424). There are special matinees in summer. *To avoid disappointment, purchase tickets in advance. Request a ticket-order form from Grand Ole Opry, 2804 Opryland Dr., 37214, tel. 615/889–3060. Admission: Aug., 9–5 Sept.–May, reserved seats $12 evenings, $10 matinees; upper balcony $10.50 evenings, $8.50 matinees.*

The show park also offers more than a dozen live shows ranging from bluegrass bands to huge stage productions, and there are 22 thrilling rides, including brand-new Chaos, a $7-million indoor thriller combining a roller-coaster ride and spectacular audio-visual effects. The **Roy Acuff Musical Collection and Museum** (tel. 615/889–6700) contains memorabilia, including many guns and fiddles, of the "king of country music." Relocated to the same building in 1989 was **Minnie Pearl's Museum,** providing a nostalgic tour of her life. *Admission to the museums in Opryland Plaza is free; hours vary widely, so it's best to inquire locally.* The *General Jackson,* Opryland's new showboat, offers several cruises daily with a musical revue while you dine (tel. 615/889–6611). There's also dining at food stands or full-service restaurants, and shopping for trinkets or treasures. *Tel. 615/889–6700. Admission: $18.95 one day; $4 each day, 2nd and 3rd consecutive days; $54.70 3-day passport, including Grand Ole Opry matinee, daytime cruise, performance in Acuff Theatre (adjacent to Opry). Children under 3 free. Open weekends only late Mar.–May, Sept., Oct.; daily late May–Labor Day. Closed Nov.–late Mar. Hours vary widely but are generally 9–6 weekdays, 9–9 weekends except 9–9 daily in summer; call to be sure.*

⑰ Just north of Opryland USA, is **Boxcar Willie's Railroad Museum,** with displays depicting the life and travels of this Opry performer and "world's most famous hobo." In the same building is the inevitable **Cars of the Stars,** where classic cars share center stage with those of such country notables as Randy Travis, Dolly Parton, and Roy Acuff (about 45 cars in all). *2611*

*McGavock Pike, tel. 615/885–7400. Admission (Willie's/Cars/
both): $2/$3.50/$4.50 adults; $1.50/$3/$4 senior citizens; $1/
$1.50/$2 children 6–12, under 6 free. Both open daily 8 AM–9 PM
Memorial Day–Labor Day, 9–5 rest of year.*

⑱ Next door is **Music Valley Wax Museum of the Stars,** with life-
size wax figures of more country stars, and outside is the **Sidewalk of the Stars,** Nashville's version of Graumann's Chinese,
with the footprints, handprints, and signatures of over 200
country music performers. (Fame is also written in cement at
the Fountain Square shopping complex's lakeside **Star Walk,**
where 50 Grammy winners' pawprints are displayed on pedes-
tals at hip level so you can compare yours with theirs without
bending, while reading the stars' personally engraved
messages—*see* Shopping.) *2515 McGavock Pike, tel. 615/883–
3612. Admission: $3.50 adults, $3 senior citizens, $1.50 chil-
dren. Open daily 8 AM–9 PM. Memorial Day weekend–Labor
Day, 9–5 rest of year.*

Fans of Gentleman Jim Reeves will not want to miss the col-
⑲ lection of memorabilia at the **Jim Reeves Museum,** in an attractive 1794 house. This place continues the tradition of up close
and personal à la Barbara Mandrell: Jim's bedroom furniture is
on display, too. *1023 Joyce Lane (off Briley), tel. 615/226–2062.
Admission: $4 adults; $2 children 6–12, under 6 free. Open
daily 9–5.*

Farther Afield Apart from the many educational and cultural institutions that
lend credence to Nashville's Athens of the South sobriquet are
the gracious estates that form a necklace of emerald green
around the city. To get into the spirit, begin your tour at
⑳ Centennial Park's **Parthenon,** an exact copy of the Athenian
original right down to the Elgin Marbles. Newly renovated, including the addition of a huge statue of Athena, the Parthenon
houses an art gallery with changing exhibits. *Tel. 615/259–
6358. Admission: $2.50 adults, $1.25 senior citizens and children 6–17, under 6 free. Open Tues.–Sat. 9–4:30 (until 8 on
Thurs.), Sun. 1–4:30.*

㉑ **Belle Meade Mansion** is a stunning Greek Revival house, the
centerpiece of a 5,300-acre estate that was one of the nation's
first and finest thoroughbred breeding farms. It was also the
site of the famous Iroquois, the oldest amateur steeplechase in
America, which is still run each May but in nearby Percy Warner Park. A Victorian carriage museum continues the equine
theme. *110 Leake Ave., (from Centennial Park, head west on
West End Ave. and follow the signs for Belle Meade—not to be
confused with Belle Meade Blvd.), tel. 615/356–0501. Admission: $4 adults, $2.50 children 6–13, under 6 free. Open Mon.–
Sat. 9–5, Sun. 1–5.*

㉒ The Georgian-style mansion at nearby **Cheekwood** (take Harding Rd. east, turn right on to Belle Meade Blvd., and look for a
sign) is now a fine arts center, and the surrounding 55-acre
Tennessee Botanical Gardens showcases herbs, roses, irises,
daffodils, and area wildflowers. Greenhouses, streams, and
pools make this a delightful spot for a picnic. *Forrest Park Dr.,
tel. 615/352–5310. Admission: $3.50 adults; $2 senior citizens
and college students with ID, 50¢ children 6–17, under 6 free.
Open Mon.–Sat. 9–5, Sun. 1–5.*

㉓ **Belmont Mansion,** now on the campus of Belmont College, was
the home of Adelicia Acklen, Nashville's answer to Scarlett

O'Hara, who married "once for money, once for love, and once for the hell of it." This outstanding Italianate villa of the 1850s is a Victorian gem right down to its cast-iron gazebos. *Take Belle Meade Blvd. north from Cheekwood. Turn right on to West End Ave., then right on to Blakemore, which becomes Wedgewood. Turn right on to Magnolia Blvd., first left, then follow signs. Corner of Acklen Ave. and Belmont Blvd., tel. 615/269–9537. Admission: $3 adults, $1 children 6–12, under 6 free. Open Tues.–Sat. 10–4, also Mon., Jun–Aug. Closed major holidays.*

From here, take I–65 south to the first of two Harding Place exits to **Travellers' Rest,** the early 19th-century clapboard home of pioneer landowner John Overton. Following the fortunes of Overton, the law partner, mentor, campaign manager, and lifelong friend of Andrew Jackson, whose own home is nearby, the house metamorphosed from a 1799 four-room cottage to a 12-room mansion with Federal and Greek Revival additions. *636 Farrell Pkwy., tel. 615/832–2962. Admission: $3 adults, $1 children 6–16, under 5 free. Open Mon.–Sat. 9–5, Sun. 1–5.*

Forming the eastern end of this semicircle of homes is **The Hermitage,** 12 miles east of Nashville (I–40E to Old Hickory Blvd. exit), where the life and times of Tennessee's beloved Old Hickory are reflected with great care. Andrew Jackson built this mansion on 600 acres for his wife, Rachel, and both are entombed here. The **Andrew Jackson Center,** a 28,000-sq.-ft. museum, visitor, and education center, opened in 1989, contains many Jackson artifacts never before exhibited. A 16-minute film, "Old Hickory," is shown in its auditorium; the structure also includes Rachel's Garden Cafe and a museum store. Tours take you through the mansion, furnished with many original pieces. Across the road stands **Tulip Grove,** built by Mrs. Jackson's nephew, and **The Hermitage Church,** fondly known as "Rachel's Church." *4580 Rachel's Lane, Hermitage, tel. 615/889–2941. Admission (includes Tulip Grove and church): $7 adults; $6.50 senior citizens, $3.50 children 6–13, under 6 free. Open daily 9–5. Closed major holidays.*

In Hendersonville, 20 miles northeast of downtown Nashville (eight miles from The Hermitage), there are yet more shrines to country music notables. The **House of Cash** displays possessions and memorabilia of the "Man in Black," a legend in his own time, including some superb Frederic Remington bronzes. *700 Johnny Cash Pkwy., tel. 615/824–5110. Admission: $5 adults; $4 senior citizens; $1 children 6–12, under 6 free. Open Mon.–Sat. 9–5 early Mar.–early Nov.*

Twitty City/Music Village USA is not only the home of superstar Conway Twitty but also a 15-acre entertainment complex with live shows, shops, restaurants, and museums highlighting the life and times of such entertainers as Bill Monroe, Ferlin Husky, and Marty Robbins. *Music Village Blvd., Hendersonville, tel. 615/822–6650 or 800/345–9338. Admission: $8.50 adults; $4.25 children 7–12, under 7 free. Open daily 9–5.*

Nashville for Free

TV Tapings. Several shows produced at Opryland USA and other Nashville sites—including *Hee Haw* (June and October only) and TNN cable programs—are open to visitors, and most are free. *Call TNN Viewer Services at 615/883–7000 for schedules and to make reservations.*

Museum of Tobacco Art and History. The wide-ranging collections include antique pipes, tobacco jars, cigar-store figures, and snuff boxes. *800 Harrison St., tel. 615/242–9218. Open Tues.–Sat. 10–4.*

Entertainment in the Parks. The Metro Nashville Parks Department (tel. 615/259–6399) presents free summer concerts and outdoor arts shows in some of the area's 70 public parks.

What to See and Do with Children

Children's Discovery House. This is a youngster's dream, with bubble blowers on the front lawn, colored chalk by the sidewalks, dress-up clothes, a play store and play hospital, a nature collection, and more. *503 N. Maple St., Murfreesboro, tel. 615/890–2300. Open Tues.–Sat. 10–5, Sun. 1–5 (closes 1 hr earlier in summer). Admission: $3 adults; $2 children 2 and over, under 2 free.*

Cumberland Museum and Science Center. Children are invited to look, touch, smell, climb, listen, and explore. The planetarium has star and laser shows. *800 Ridley Blvd., Nashville, tel. 615/259–6099. Admission: $3 adults, $2 children 3–12 and senior citizens. Open Tues.–Sat. 9:30–5, Sun. 12:30–5.*

Fort Nashborough (*see* Downtown in Exploring Nashville).

Opryland USA (*see* Opryland in Exploring Nashville). The petting zoo especially delights the younger ones.

Picnicking. Get away for a day outdoors, picnicking, horseback riding, hiking, and walking through the nature preserves at 14,200-acre **J. Percy Priest Lake** (11 mi east of Nashville off I–40, tel. 615/889–1975) or 22,500-acre **Old Hickory Reservoir** (15 mi northeast of Nashville via U.S. 31E, tel. 615/822–4846).

Tennessee State Museum (*see* Downtown in Exploring Nashville). The walk-through and Civil War exhibits especially appeal to children.

Wave Country. This water park near Opryland has a large wave pool and a three-flume water slide. *Two Rivers Pkwy., off Briley Pkwy., tel. 615/885–1052. Admission: $4 adults; $3 children 5–12, under 4 free. Open daily 10–8 Memorial Day–Labor Day.*

Off the Beaten Track

Lynchburg is home to the **Jack Daniels Distillery,** where you can observe every step of the sour-mash-whiskey-making art. *¼ mi northeast of Nashville on TN 55, tel. 615/759–4221. Guided tours daily 8–4. Closed major holidays.*

During July and August, you can tour studios of some of the state's most talented craftsfolk at the **Joe L. Evins Appalachian Center for Crafts.** The sales gallery has crafts from throughout the Appalachian Mountains. *70 mi east of Nashville in Smithville (exit Rte. 273 off I–40, go 6 mi south on 56), tel. 615/597–6801. Open daily 9–5.*

At the **Loretta Lynn Ranch,** in Hurricane Mills, the singer's personal museum is housed in an old restored gristmill. Narrated hayride tours of the 3,500-acre ranch are offered during the summer; you can also tour her stately antebellum home. *I-40W to TN 13N, tel. 615/296-7700. Admission: $3 adults; $1 children 6-12, under 6 free. Open daily 8-5 Apr. 15-Oct. 31.*

Miss Mary Bobo's Boarding House is a Tennessee institution. Diners flock to the big two-story 1867 white frame house with a white picket fence to feast family-style at tables groaning with fried chicken, roast beef, fried catfish, stuffed vegetables and sliced tomatoes fresh from the gardens out back, corn on the cob, homemade biscuits, cornbread, pecan pie, lemon icebox pie, fruit cobblers, and strawberry shortcake. *½ block from the Public Square, Lynchburg, tel. 615/759-7394. Dress: informal. Reservations required, at least a week in advance in summer. One meal served each day, promptly at 1 PM, Mon.-Sat. Closed major holidays. Fixed price is $9 adults, $4 children under 12, including tax (no tipping permitted). MC, V.*

The most ambitious fraternity collection pales before the 25,000 assembled beer cans at the **Museum of Beverage Containers and Advertising.** Thousands of soda cans, bottles, and ephemera add to the celebration of all things fizzy. *Ridgecrest Dr., Goodlettsville, tel. 615/859-5236. Admission: $2 adults; $1 children under 12. Open Mon.-Sat. 9-5, Sun. 1-5.*

Old Stone Fort State Park, in Manchester (U.S. 41, tel. 615/728-0751), contains a walled structure believed to have been built at least 2,000 years ago. The scenic 600-acre site, on bluffs overlooking Duck River, is laced with waterfalls and has a visitor center, a nine-hole golf course, and campsites.

Alfred Stieglitz rewarded Fisk University's progressive arts program with a bequest from his collection of 20th-century paintings and his own superb photographs. These are now on display in the **Van Vechten Art Gallery** on the campus. Stieglitz's wife, Georgia O'Keeffe, helped install the collection, highlighted by her own paintings. The gallery also features African sculpture. *Fisk University at 17th Ave. N, tel. 615/329-8543. Admission: $2.50 adults, children free. Open Tues.-Fri. 10-5, weekends 1-5.*

Shopping

Major downtown stores are generally open Monday-Saturday 10-5. The shopping malls are open Monday-Saturday 10 to 9 or 9:30 and Sunday 1-6. Banks are generally open weekdays 8:30-3:30 (until 5 or 6 on Fri.).

Shopping Districts **Church Street** is the major downtown shopping area; there you'll find department stores, smaller chain stores, and numerous boutiques. **Fountain Square** (2244 Metro Center Blvd., tel. 615/256-7467) is a complex of 35 shops, a food court, pushcart vendors in season, and Star Walk (*see* Opryland)—all ranged round a 48-acre lake. There is free live entertainment nightly, from classical music to mime to dance.

Specialty Stores **Murfreesboro,** about 15 miles outside Nashville, calls itself the
Antiques Antique Center of the South. Pick up a free antiques shopping guide at Cannonsburgh Pioneer Village, a living museum of 19th-century life in the South (tel. 615/890-0355). In Nashville, browse for distinctive 18th- and 19th-century English antiques and art objects at **Madison Antique Mall** (404 Gallatin Rd. S, tel. 615/865-4677), **Nashville Antique Mall** (657 Wedgewood

Ave., tel. 615/256–1465), and **Smorgasbord Antique Mall** (4144-B Lebanon Rd., tel. 615/883–5789).

Arts and Crafts You'll find works of major regional artists at **Ambiance Art Gallery** (2137 Bandywood Dr., tel. 615/385–3161) and **Cumberland Gallery** (4107 Hillsboro Circle, tel. 615/297–0296). For pottery and ceramics, seek out **Forrest Valley Galleries,** a working studio (2218 Eighth Ave. S, tel. 615/298–2787).

Country and Western Wear Stores geared to the latest look in country clothing include **Alamo of Nashville** (324 Broadway, tel. 615/244–3803), **Boot Country** (2412 Music Valley Dr., tel. 615/883–2661), **Loretta Lynn's Western Stores** (120 16th Ave. S, tel. 615/256–2814; 435 Donelson Pike, tel. 615/889–5582), **Nashville Cowboy** (118 16th Ave. S, tel. 615/242–9497; 1516 Demonbreun St., tel. 615/242–9497), and **The Tennessee Saddlery** (Wilson Pike, Brentwood, tel. 615/373–9585).

Records and Tapes Fans can find good selections of records and tapes at **Conway's Twitty Bird Record Shop** (1530 Demonbreun St., tel. 615/242–2466), **Ernest Tubb Record Shops** (2414 Music Valley Dr., tel. 615/889–2474; 417 Broadway, tel. 615/255–7503; 1516 Demonbreun St., tel. 615/244–2845), and **The Great Escape** (1925 Broadway, tel. 615/327–0646; 139 Gallatin Rd. N, Madison, tel. 615/865–8052).

Farmer's Market Every day from late spring through early autumn, farmers and gardeners set up stands in a downtown area bounded by Seventh and Eighth avenues North and Jefferson Street.

Flea Market From treasures to just plain "junque"—you'll find it at the **Nashville Flea Market** at the Tennessee State Fairgrounds. Usually, at least 450 traders, craftsfolk, and dealers will be plying their wares the fourth weekend of every month (except Sept. and Dec.). *Tel. 615/383–7636. Admission free. Open Sat. 9–6, Sun. noon–6.*

Participant Sports

Boating and Fishing You'll find boat rentals at **J. Percy Priest Lake** (11 mi east of Nashville, off I–40, tel. 615/883–2351) and **Old Hickory Reservoir** (15 mi northeast of Nashville via U.S. 31E, tel. 615/824–7766).

Golf Among courses open to the public year-round are **Harpeth Hills** (tel. 615/373–8202), **Hermitage Golf Course** (tel. 615/847–4001), and **Rhodes Golf Course** (9 holes; tel. 615/242–2336). Hermitage is the site each April of the LPGA Sara Lee Classic.

Horseback Riding You can jog or canter on gentle steeds at **Riverwood Recreation Plantation and Riding Academy** (tel. 615/262–1794).

Ice Skating From September through April, there's indoor skating at **Ice Centennial** (tel. 615/320–1369), in Centennial Park.

Jogging Favorite sites include **Centennial Park,** the **Vanderbilt University running track, J. Percy Priest Lake,** and **Percy Warner Park.** The 1,700-plus-member running club Nashville Striders (tel. 615/254–0631) can recommend choice spots and will provide information on the many summer races.

Mini-Golf Enjoy this uniquely American family sport at **Grand Old Golf** (tel. 615/871–4701), across the street from the Opryland Hotel.

Tennis Several municipal tennis facilities offer good play. **Centennial Park Tennis Center** (tel. 615/327–9831) has grass and clay outdoor courts plus indoor courts.

Spectator Sports

Baseball You can root for the AAA **Nashville Sounds,** an affiliate of the Detroit Tigers, from April through August at Herschel Greer Stadium (tel. 615/242–4371).

Horse Show For 10 days from late August to early September, Shelbyville hums as visitors, horses, and riders come from all over the land for the **Tennessee Walking Horse National Celebration,** the world's greatest walking horse show. *Information: Box 1010, Shelbyville 37160, tel. 615/684–5915.*

Stock Car Racing Top drivers compete at the **Nashville Motor Speedway** (tel. 615/726–1818) from April through October.

Dining

by Beverly Garrison

Beverly Garrison is the food editor of The Tennessean.

The most highly recommended restaurants in each price category are indicated by a star ★.

Category	Cost*
Expensive	over $30
Moderate	$12–$20
Inexpensive	under $12

**per person without tax (7.75% in Tennessee), service, or drinks*

The following credit-card abbreviations are used: AE, American Express; CB, Carte Blanche; DC, Diners Club; MC, MasterCard; V, Visa.

Expensive
American

Cascades, Opryland Hotel. The newest of many restaurants at the Opryland complex, this tropical Eden—with huge granite rocks, rushing waterfalls, and over 8,000 live plants—gives diners the feeling of being transported to the South Pacific. Executive Chef Richard Gerst has placed emphasis on dietary concerns as well as good taste, providing a number of low-salt, low-fat, low-cholesterol dishes. Menu items include sautéed swordfish with fresh basil beurre blanc and veal scaloppine in a lemon-butter sauce. *2800 Opryland Dr., tel. 615/889–1000. No reservations. Dress: informal. AE, CB, DC, MC, V.*

★ **Chef Sigi's.** Culinary Olympic Gold Medal winner Siegfried Eisenberger believes in American cuisine and showcases it on a menu that changes every four weeks. Selections may include iced melon yogurt soup, Maryland crab cakes with remoulade sauce, or beef tips in creamy peppercorn sauce. The spacious and inviting interior is elegant but not intimidating. *3212 West End Ave., tel. 615/269–9999. Dress: informal. Reservations recommended. AE, DC, MC, V. No lunch Sat.; Sun., brunch only.*

The Merchants. A $3.2 million renovation of a historic property in downtown Nashville, this former hotel provides three levels of dining and an appealing outdoor patio. Specialties include

Dining

Arthur's, **15**

Cakewalk
Restaurant, **13**

Cascades, Opryland
Hotel, **20**

Chef Sigi's, **12**

F. Scott's, **16**

Julian's, **14**

Loveless Cafe, **9**

Mario's, **2**

Maude's Courtyard, **3**

Merchants, The, **7**

Mère Bulles, **8**

106 Club, **11**

Sperry's, **10**

Lodging

Best Western at
Opryland, **18**

Comfort Inn
Hermitage, **24**

Courtyard by
Marriott-Airport, **23**

Hampton Inn
Vanderbilt, **1**

Holiday Inn-Briley
Parkway, **22**

Hotel Watauga
House, **5**

Hyatt Regency
Nashville, **4**

La Quinta Motor
Inn, **17**

Opryland Hotel, **20**

Park Suite Nashville
Hotel, **21**

Ramada Inn Across
from Opryland, **19**

Stouffer Nashville
Hotel, **6**

Downtown Nashville Dining and Lodging

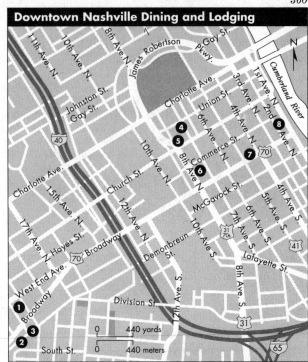

Nashville Dining and Lodging

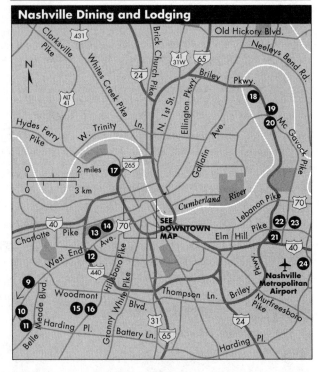

deep-fried alligator bits, the freshest seafoods, and meats grilled over native hardwoods. The menu changes to lighter fare in summer and all rolls, pastas, and pastries are made fresh daily. Save room for the Key lime pie. *401 Broadway, tel. 615/254–1892. Dress: informal. Reservations recommended. AE, CB, DC, MC, V.*

Classic French   **Julian's Restaurant Francais.** If you can't travel to the City of
★   Light, dine at Julian's instead, for here, in the intimate rooms of a turn-of-the-century town house, Chef Sylvain Le Coguic serves some of the best French cuisine this side of Paris. His creations include sautéed veal sweetbreads in Sauternes sauce with fresh wild mushrooms, and grilled breast of duckling in tart cherry sauce. *2412 West End Ave., tel. 615/327–2412. Jacket and tie suggested. Reservations suggested. AE, DC, MC, V. Closed Sun.*

Continental   **Arthur's.** *Romantic* is the word for this serene and sophisti-
★   cated restaurant featuring gourmet international cuisine. Be sure to save room for dessert, especially the Crown Royal Cake, a fruit-and-nut cake created for HRH, The Princess Royal, when she visited Nashville for the Royal Chase. The decor is lush, with lace curtains, velveteen-upholstered chairs, white linen, and fine silver service. *The Mall at Green Hills, tel. 615/383–8841. Jacket required. Reservations suggested. AE, DC, MC, V. Dinner only weekends, also Sun. brunch.*

Mére Bulles, The Wine Bar and Restaurant. There's an aura of casual elegance in this locally popular restaurant with brass-trimmed mahogany bar and changing artworks decorating mellow, exposed brick walls. Guests can enjoy tapas and drinks in the cozy lounge, then move into one of three intimate dining areas with views of the river. There's live entertainment nightly, usually jazz or folk music. Specialties include veal saltimbocca stuffed with honey-cured ham and Swiss cheese, and topped with chef Chris's special sauces; pesto Mére Bulles—shrimp and scallops with walnut pesto sauce served on a bed of shell pasta. There are 50 wines by the glass and a stock of over 170 selections by the bottle. *152 2nd Ave. N, tel. 615/256–1946. Jacket and tie suggested. Reservations accepted. AE, DC, MC, V.*

Northern Italian   **Mario's Ristorante Italiano.** Owner Mario Ferrari is the genius
★   behind this Nashville institution. Country music stars, visiting celebrities, and local society come here to see and be seen. The atmosphere is elegant, with lots of brass and an impressive wine collection on view, yet it's never stuffy. Pastas created by Chef Sandro Bozzatto are memorable, the seafood and veal— such as the *saltimbocca,* veal medallions with mozzarella, prosciutto, mushrooms, and fresh sage—equally palate-pleasing. *2005 Broadway, tel. 615/327–3232. Jacket required. Reservations required, 2–3 days ahead on weekends. AE, CB, DC, MC, V. Closed Sun.*

Moderate   **F. Scott's.** At this elegant cafe and wine bar, Nashville artist
American   Paul Harmon's bright avant-garde paintings stand out on the steel-gray-and-mauve walls. Chef Anita Hartel's creations include pasta with chicken and artichokes in a cream sauce, and braised lamb with mint sauce. F. Scott's has one of the largest wine lists in Nashville, with many fine wines available by the glass. *2220 Bandywood Dr., tel. 615/269–5861. Dress: informal. Reservations accepted. AE, MC, V.*

Sperry's. At first glance, Sperry's reminds the uninitiated of an old English pub, but that's where the resemblance ends. Sperry's has a country-club atmosphere, complete with a comfortable paneled bar where diners are pampered while they wait for a table. Steaks done to perfection—including blackened beef, cooked in a skillet with butter and Cajun spices—are the specialty of the house. Seafood items have become a close second, with Alaskan King Crab legs worthy of raves. *5109 Harding Rd., tel. 615/353–0809. Dress: informal. No reservations. AE, CB, DC, MC, V.*

Continental **Maude's Courtyard.** "Meet me at Maude's" is more than an advertising slogan—it's a way of life in Nashville. Owner Morton Howell III encourages his chefs to add personal flair to every dish. Some examples: lobster pasta with artichoke hearts, superb seafood gumbo—a true Louisiana recipe, scampi and scallops brochette, and veal florentine. A covered courtyard with a fountain and several fireplaces throughout the restaurant allow guests to choose their own ambience. Sundays, there's live jazz by the Bourbon Street Trio. *1911 Broadway, tel. 615/320–0543. Dress: informal. Reservations recommended. AE, CB, DC, MC, V. No lunch Sat.; Sun., brunch only.*

106 Club. A white baby grand and a bar of shiny black enamel and glass brick set the atmosphere in this intimate, Art Deco dining room in suburban Belle Meade. The cuisine is a mix of California nouvelle—such as veal medallions with litchi nuts, strawberries, and pistachios sautéed in a light sauce made from nuts and berries—and international favorites. The pasta primavera is one of the best in town. In the evening, the outdoor patio is a good place to relax with one of 106's rich desserts and listen to old and new melodies on the baby grand. *106 Harding Pl. tel. 615/356–1300. Jacket and tie suggested. Reservations suggested. AE, DC, MC, V.*

Inexpensive **Cakewalk Restaurant.** The first things to catch your eye at this *Mixed Menu* cozy bistro are the intriguing paintings by local artists on the turquoise walls. The eclectic cuisine is equally imaginative, blending the best of nouvelle California, a bit of Southwestern, and a dash of Cajun/Creole, with some down-home American specialties thrown in for fun. Desserts are to die for, especially the Kahlua cake, a four-layer chocolate cake laced with liqueur. *3001 West End Ave., tel. 615/320–7778. Dress: informal. Reservations recommended for dinner. DC, MC, V.*

Southern **Loveless Cafe.** An experience in true down-home Southern
★ cooking. Don't come for the decor—which is also down-home, including red-and-white-checked tablecloths—but, rather, for the feather-light homemade biscuits and preserves, country ham and red-eye gravy, and fried chicken. *8400 Hwy. 100, tel. 615/646–9700. Dress: informal. Reservations suggested, especially on weekends. No credit cards. Closed Mon.*

Lodging

Nashville offers a very impressive selection of hotel, motel, and all-suite accommodations in all price categories and levels of luxury. Although some establishments increase rates slightly during the peak summer travel season, most maintain the same rates year-round. Some downtown luxury hotels offer special weekend rates to attract guests to otherwise vacant rooms.

For information on B&Bs in the area, contact **Bed & Breakfast of Middle Tennessee,** (Box 40804, Nashville, 37204, tel. 615/297–0883). **Bed & Breakfast Host Homes of Tennessee** (Box 110227, Nashville, TN 37222, tel. 615/331–5244) has listings for homes here and throughout the state.

The most highly recommended properties in each price category are indicated by a star ★. For maps pinpointing locations, *see* Dining.

Category	Cost*
Very Expensive	over $100
Expensive	$75–$100
Moderate	$50–$75
Inexpensive	under $50

*double room; add 11.75% for taxes

The following credit-card abbreviations are used: AE, American Express; CB, Carte Blanche; DC, Diners Club; MC, MasterCard; V, Visa.

Very Expensive **Hyatt Regency Nashville.** Downtown near the State Capitol, this 28-story tower has Hyatt's signature vast, skylighted atrium lobby awash with greenery, along with the glassed-in elevators that still seem to fascinate all but the most blasé occupants. Rooms are extra spacious and contemporary in decor. The hotel is topped by Nashville's only revolving rooftop restaurant. *623 Union St., 37219, tel. 615/259–1234 or 800/228–9000. 478 rooms, including 32 suites. Facilities: cable TV/movies, restaurant, coffee shop, cocktail lounge, nightly dancing, live entertainment, recreational privileges at Y. AE, CB, DC, MC, V.*

★ **Opryland Hotel.** Adjacent to Opryland, this massive hostelry has recently almost doubled in size. Even if you don't stay here, come out to take a look—it's an attraction in its own right. The two-acre glass-walled Conservatory is a lush enclave of tropical vegetation, streams, waterfalls, statuary, and fountains. Just added is the Cascades, another skylighted interior space with streams, waterfalls, and a half-acre lake. The hotel claims to have more meeting space than any other in the nation. The culinary staff is directed by a member of the U.S. Culinary Olympics Team. *2800 Opryland Dr., 37214, tel. 615/889–1000. 1,891 rooms, including 92 suites. Facilities: 3 restaurants, coffee shop, 5 lounges with live entertainment, heated pool, wading pool, lighted tennis (fee). AE, CB, DC, MC, V.*

★ **Park Suite Nashville Hotel.** Near the airport and Opryland is this hotel of all suites, ranged around a nine-story parklike atrium lobby with live plants, meandering watercourses, and tropical birds. Suites are comfortably furnished in tasteful contemporary style; each has a wet bar, a refrigerator, and two color televisions. *10 Century Blvd., 37214, tel. 615/871–0033 or 800/432–7272. 296 suites. Facilities: cable TV/ movies, indoor pool, whirlpool, sauna, exercise room, free full buffet* *breakfast, dining room, lounge, live entertainment. AE, DC, MC, V.*

Stouffer Nashville Hotel. This luxurious new ultracontemporary high-rise hotel adjoins Nashville Convention Center and is also connected to the new Church Street Centre Mall with fine shops, restaurants, and entertainment. Spacious rooms are highlighted by period reproduction furnishings. Executive Club concierge floors offer extra privacy and personal services. *611 Commerce St., 37203, tel. 615/255–8400 or 800/ 468–3571. 673 units. Facilities: spa, indoor pool, whirlpool, sundeck, sauna, exercise facilities, cable TV, restaurant, coffee shop, cocktail lounge, 24– hr. room service, complimentary coffee and newspaper wake-up, garage, airport transportation. AE, CB, DC, MC, V.*

Hotel Watauga House. This downtown, vintage 1902 structure has been restored to its original Victorian grandeur. The suites, all with kitchenettes, are decorated in period. *222 Polk Ave., 37203, tel. 615/252–2500. 24 suites. Facilities: color TV, hot tub, sauna, party rooms.*

Expensive **Holiday Inn–Briley Parkway.** To while away your time between flights or Opryland visits, there's the trademark Holidome Indoor Recreation Center, with pool, sauna, whirlpool, game room, table tennis, pool tables, and putting green. Business travelers will appreciate the conference center and spacious, well-lighted guest rooms. *2200 Elm Hill Pike at Briley Pkwy., 37210, tel. 615/883–9770 or 800/465–4329. 394 rooms, including 4 suites. Facilities: cable TV, restaurant, lounge with live entertainment, coin laundry. AE, CB, DC, MC, V.*

Ramada Inn Across from Opryland. This contemporary-style, well-maintained new low-rise motor inn has the closest location to the theme park other than the Opryland Hotel. *2401 Music Valley Dr., 37214, tel. 615/889–0800 or 800/272–6232. 308 rooms, including 7 suites. Facilities: cable TV/movies, rental refrigerators, heated indoor pool, sauna, whirlpool, dining room, lounge, live entertainment. AE, CB, DC, MC, V.*

Moderate **Comfort Inn Hermitage.** Near the Hermitage, this inn offers first-rate accommodations, some with water beds or whirlpool baths. *5768 Old Hickory Blvd., 37076, tel. 615/889–5060 or 800/ 228–5150. 107 rooms, including 7 suites. Facilities: pool, cable TV/movies. AE, CB, DC, MC, V.*

★ **Courtyard by Marriott–Airport.** This handsome new low-rise motor inn with a sunny, gardenlike courtyard offers some amenities you'd expect in higher-priced hotels: spacious rooms, king-size beds, oversize work desks, and hot-water dispensers for in-room coffee. *2508 Elm Hill Pike, 37214, tel. 615/883– 9500 or 800/321–2211. 145 rooms, including 12 suites. Facilities: cable TV/movies, restaurant, lounge, heated indoor pool, sauna, whirlpool, exercise room. AE, CB, DC, MC, V.*

Inexpensive– Moderate **Best Western at Opryland.** Conveniently located near Opryland and other attractions, this chain unit offers rooms that are comfortable and bright. *2600 Music Valley Dr., 37214, tel. 615/889– 8235 or 800/528–1234. 212 rooms. Facilities: cable TV/movies, pool, restaurant, coffee shop, lounge with live entertainment, band and dancing nightly in season. AE, CB, DC, MC, V.*

Inexpensive **Hampton Inn Vanderbilt.** Near the Vanderbilt University cam-
★ pus, this inn is new, clean, and contemporary. The rooms are colorful and spacious. A multipurpose hospitality suite has a conference table, chairs, and an audiovisual unit for meeting

and business groups. *1919 West End Ave., 37203, tel. 615/329–1144 or 800/426–7866. 163 rooms. Facilities: cable TV/free movies, pool. AE, CB, DC, MC, V.*

La Quinta Motor Inn. The rooms here are especially spacious and well lighted, with a large working area and oversize bed. King Plus rooms have a full-length mirror and an ottoman. *2001 Metrocenter Blvd., 37227-0001. (1 mi north of downtown), tel. 615/259–2130 or 800/531–5900. 121 rooms. Facilities: cable TV, pool, 24-hr restaurant adjacent. AE, CB, DC, MC, V.*

The Arts

For a complete listing of weekly events, consult the Visitor Information Center or the local newspapers. For information on concerts and special events, call WSM Radio's entertainment line (tel. 615/889–9595) or TV Channel 5's hot line (Thurs.; tel. 615/248–5200). Ticketmaster (tel. 615/741–2787) has information on events at various Nashville venues.

Concerts Country music takes center stage at the 4,424-seat **Grand Ole Opry Auditorium** (tel. 615/889–3060). The Nashville Symphony Orchestra's classical and pops series and concerts by out-of-town groups are staged at **Andrew Jackson Hall** (tel. 615/741–7975), part of the Tennessee Performing Arts Center (TPAC). Chamber concerts take place at TPAC's **James K. Polk Theater** (tel. 615/741–7975). Some rock and country events are held at the **Nashville Municipal Auditorium** (tel. 615/259–6461). The **Starwood Amphitheatre** (tel. 615/793–5800) is the site of rock, pop, country, and jazz concerts, musicals, and special events; it's also the summer home of the Nashville Symphony. Vanderbilt University stages music, dance, and drama productions (many free) at its **Blair School of Music** (tel. 615/322–7651).

Festivals **Summer Lights.** The first weekend each June, more than half a million visitors attend Nashville's unique music and arts festival, showcasing top names and newcomers in pop, rock, jazz, country, classical, and reggae on five outdoor stages downtown. The work of 50 Tennessee visual artists are exhibited in warehouses and storefronts along First and Second avenues. Local cuisine is available from street vendors or sidewalk cafes, and clowns and other street entertainers fill the Family Arts Arcade. Most events are free. *Contact: Metro Nashville Arts Commission, 111 Fourth Ave. S, 37201, tel. 615/259–6374.*

International Country Music Fan Fair. For six days following Summer Lights, this celebration is staged at the Tennessee State Fairgrounds, Vanderbilt University's Dudley Field, and Opryland USA. There are more than 35 hours of musical events, autograph sessions with country music stars, and the Grand Masters Fiddling championship. *Contact: Fan Fair, 2804 Opryland Dr., 37214, tel. 615/889–6700.*

Theater **James K. Polk Theater** hosts touring Broadway shows and local theatrical performances. For theater-in-the-round, there's the **Andrew Johnson Theater.** The **Academy Theatre** (tel. 615/254–9103) hosts children's theater performances. **Chaffin's Barn** in Hendersonville (tel. 615/822–1800) offers dinner theater year-round, and a live country show is staged here daily Memorial Day–Labor Day.

Nightlife

Revues **Ernest Tubb Midnight Jamboree.** Here's a live radio show with performances by new talent as well as Opry stars, usually including Ernest himself. *2414 Music Valley Dr., tel. 615/889–2474. Show Sat. midnight–1 AM (arrive by 11:30 PM).*

Grand Ole Opry. If you can attend only one event, make it this one (*see* Opryland in Exploring).

Nightclubs **Boots Randolph's.** One of the city's landmark night spots, this sophisticated supper club features Boots—"Mr. Yakkety Sax"—at 9:30 (and 11:30 PM, if there's a crowd) in the showroom, and Jimmy Travis at 7:30 (and 10 PM) in the lounge. *209 Printers Alley (between Third and Fourth Aves.), tel. 615/256–5500. Open Mon.–Sat. 9–11 PM (or later).*

Heartthrob Cafe & Philadelphia Bandstand. Enjoy a buffet while rocking to fifties and sixties hits during early evening. Later, dance to contemporary hits on a two-tiered dance floor. *2200 Metro Center Blvd. (Fountain Square), tel. 615/259–3502. Bandstand open Mon.–Thurs. 5 PM–2 AM, Fri. 4 PM–3 AM, Sat. 7 PM–3 AM, Sun. 7 PM–2 AM.*

McGavocks Place II Nightclub. Here's dancing to live bands or recorded music with a DJ and music videos in a turn-of-the-century atmosphere. *Sheraton Music City Hotel, 777 McGavock Pike, tel. 615/885–2200. Open Mon.–Sat. 4 PM–2 AM, Sun. 6 PM–1 AM.*

Monroe's Bluegrass Country. This dinner club features top-name country and bluegrass entertainers, with plenty of room for dancing. The legendary Bill Monroe appears frequently. *2620 Music Valley Dr., tel. 615/885–0777. Open nightly 4 PM–2:30 AM. Reservations suggested.*

Stock Yard Bull Pen Lounge. Upstairs is a popular steak-and-seafood restaurant and lounge with live entertainment. Downstairs, the Bull Pen features dancin', pickin', and singin' as many of Nashville's big names show up for performances—both scheduled and unscheduled. *901 Second Ave. N and Stock Yard Blvd., tel. 615/255–6464. Open Mon.–Thurs. 7:30 PM–1 AM, Fri. and Sat. 7:30 PM–2 AM.*

Hotel Lounges **Alberts.** A DJ spins records, and there's a video screen and dance floor. *Marriott Hotel, I–40 at Briley Pkwy., tel. 615/889–9300. Open Mon.–Sat. 4 PM–1 AM.*

Aviator's. Laser lights accent dancing to contemporary and past hits. Complimentary hors d'oeuvres served weeknights 5–8 PM. *Park Suite Hotel, 10 Century Blvd., tel. 615/871–0033. Open Mon.–Sat. 4 PM–1 AM.*

Cascades Lounge. Country-jazz harpist Lloyd Lindroth entertains (6:30–11 Tues.–Sat.) amid the tropical splendor of Opryland Hotel's indoor garden, which features the "Dancing Waters," an intricate fountain electronically synchronized to accompany the harpist's evening performances. *2800 Opryland Dr., tel. 615/889–1000. Open Mon.–Sat. 11 AM–1 AM, Sun. 1–11 PM.*

Jack Daniel's Saloon. There's live entertainment nightly in this lounge adorned with memorabilia from the famed Lynchburg distillery. *Opryland Hotel, 2800 Opryland Dr., tel. 615/889–1000. Open Mon.–Sat. 11 AM–2 AM, Sun. noon–2 AM.*

Reflections Lounge. Live entertainment Friday and Saturday nights features top-name acts from throughout the country. *The Doubletree Inn, 2 Commerce Pl., tel. 615/244–8200. Open*

Mon.–Thurs. 4 PM–midnight, Fri.–Sat. 4 PM–1 AM. Reservations required.

Sessions. Enjoy Top-40 hits in a high-tech lounge with video screens. There's live entertainment on Friday and Saturday nights. *Hyatt Regency Nashville Hotel, 623 Union St., tel. 615/259–1234. Open Mon.–Sat. 4 PM–2 AM.*

East Tennessee

East Tennessee combines wholesome and savory vacation ingredients much as a skilled mountain cook creates a sumptuous down-home feast, with bounty from forests, fields, flowing streams, and the family farm. From the misty heights of the Great Smoky Mountains to the Holston, French Broad, Nolichucky, and Tennessee rivers, it offers a cornucopia of scenic grandeur and recreational offerings.

The highest and most rugged elevations are in the Great Smoky Mountains National Park, a cool and scenic retreat for those seeking relief from the heat of summer. The gateway city to the park is Gatlinburg, not too long ago a remote little place with a few hotels and some mountain crafts shops. Now hordes of visitors are attracted here for outdoor recreation. Neighboring Pigeon Forge—site of Dolly Parton's theme park, Dollywood, and numerous other tourist attractions—has become a favorite with family vacationers.

Mountain folkways often persist in smaller communities, but the major towns and cities—like Knoxville and Chattanooga— are up-to-date and quite diverse. Wherever you travel in East Tennessee, the glory of mountains and meadows, forests and farms, rivers and lakes, inspires you to pause, linger awhile, and refresh the spirit.

Getting Around

By Plane Knoxville Airport is served by **American Eagle, Delta** and its affiliate **Comair, Eastern Metro Express, Northwest, Trans World Express, United, United Express,** and **USAir.**

By Car I–75 runs north–south from Kentucky through Knoxville, then to Chattanooga, where it enters Georgia. I–81 enters East Tennessee from Virginia at Bristol and continues southwest until it ends at the junction with I–40 northeast of Knoxville. I–40 enters from North Carolina, traces a northwesterly course to Knoxville, then heads west. U.S. 11 joins Chattanooga with Knoxville.

By Train There is no Amtrak service in East Tennessee.

By Bus There are **Greyhound/Trailways** stations at Chattanooga (tel. 615/267–6531) and Knoxville (tel. 615/522–5141).

Guided Tours

In Knoxville, **Roger Q Tours** (tel. 615/584–6186) offers local and area guided sightseeing. In Pigeon Forge, **Mountain Tours and Pigeon River Bus Line** (tel. 615/453–0864) offers guided tours to Cades Cove, Cherokee (NC), Roaring Fork Motor Nature Trail, and out-of-the-way places in the Great Smoky Mountains. **Smoky Mountain Guide Service** (tel. 615/436–4919) in Gatlinburg has native guides for tours in the Smokies. Self-guided-tour maps and brochures are available at many local visitor information centers.

Important Addresses and Numbers

Tourist Information
Chattanooga Area Convention and Visitors Bureau (1001 Market St., Chattanooga 37402, tel. 615/756–8687). Knoxville Convention and Visitors Bureau (500 Henley St., Box 15012, Knoxville 37901, tel. 615/523–2316). Smoky Mountain Visitors Bureau (1004 Tuckaleechee Pike, Maryville 37801, tel. 615/984–6200). Upper East Tennessee Tourism Council (Box 375, Jonesborough 37659, tel. 615/753–5961).

Emergencies
Dial 911 for **police** and **ambulance** in an emergency.

Exploring East Tennessee

Numbers in the margin correspond with points of interest on the East Tennessee map.

The tour outlined on the following pages requires about three to five days for leisurely enjoyment. It takes you through cities and towns clustered in comfortable valleys, sprawled on upland plateaus, tucked away in hidden reaches of high mountains. Here and there you'll encounter poverty-ridden hardscrabble places, but many communities boast respectable economies and some have achieved enviable prosperity. Expect the unexpected from East Tennessee.

Knoxville
❶
We begin (and end) in **Knoxville**. In 1786, Patriot General James White and a few pioneer settlers built a fort here beside the Tennessee River. A few years later, territorial Governor William Blount selected White's fort as capital of the newly formed Territory of the United States South of the River Ohio and renamed the settlement after his long-time friend, Secretary of War Henry Knox. It flourished from the very beginning, and became the first state capital when Tennessee was admitted to the Union in 1796.

In the 20th century, Knoxville has been synonymous with energy: the headquarters of the TVA, with its vast complex of hydroelectric dams and impounded recreational lakes, is here, and during World War II, atomic energy was secretly developed at nearby Oak Ridge. Today the University of Tennessee adds its own energy—intellectual and cultural—to this dynamic city.

Enough of Knoxville's history has been preserved to interest rather than overwhelm visitors. At the **Governor William Blount Mansion,** a modest white frame structure dating from 1792, the governor and his associates planned the admission of Tennessee as the 16th state in the Union. The home is furnished with original and period antiques, along with memorabilia of Blount's checkered career. A visitor center in the adjacent **Craighead-Jackson House,** built in 1818, presents an introductory slide program, museum exhibits, and a glass collection. *200 W. Hill Ave., tel. 615/525–2375. Admission: $2.50 adults; $2 senior citizens; $1.50 children 6–12, under 6 free. Open Tues.–Sat. 9:30–5, Sun. 2–5 Apr.–Oct.; Tues.–Sat. 9:30–4:30 rest of year. Closed major holidays and Christmas week.*

Other eras of Knoxville's history can be savored at **James White's Fort** (tel. 615/525–6514), a series of seven log cabins

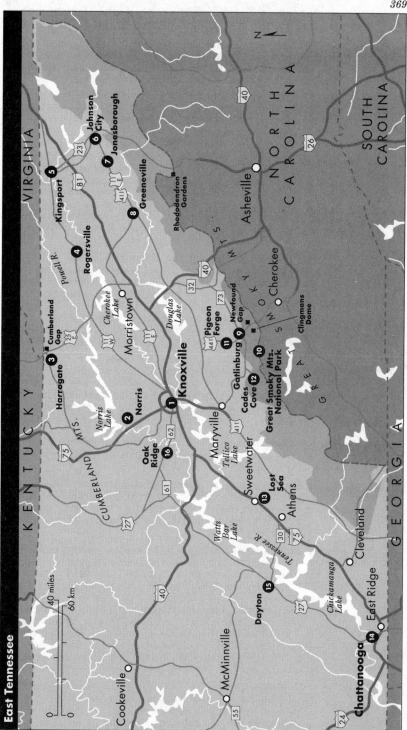

East Tennessee

with authentic furnishings and pioneer artifacts; the **John Sevier Historical Site** (tel. 615/573–5508), where Tennessee's first governor built his summer home, Marble Springs; and the **Armstrong-Lockett House** (tel. 615/637–3163), an eloquent farm mansion dating from 1834, now a showcase of American and British furniture, silver, and ornate appointments, along with terraces and fountains in Italianate gardens.

The **McClung Museum** (tel. 615/974–2144; free), on the University of Tennessee campus, has diverse collections of anthropology, natural history, geology, science, and fine arts. The **Knoxville Museum of Art** is at present located in the Candy Factory on the World's Fair grounds until construction of its 53,000-square-foot, $7-million new home is completed (scheduled for summer 1989). Major exhibitions include works by local artists, changing displays on loan, and nine miniature rooms with scale furnishings. *1010 Laurel Ave., tel. 615/525–6101. Admission: $2 adults, $1 students and senior citizens, children under 12 free, free to all Sun. Open Tues.–Sat. 10–5, Sun. noon–5. Closed between exhibits (call to be sure).*

The **Students' Museum and Akima Planetarium** contain displays of pioneer tools and clothes, mounted animals, and fresh- and saltwater aquariums. Youngsters especially like the hands-on and audiovisual exhibits. *516 Beaman St., in Chilhowee Park, tel. 615/637–1121. Admission: $1.75 adults; $1.25 senior citizens over 65 and children 6–16, 40¢ 2–5, under 2 free. Museum open weekdays 9–5, Sat. 1–5, Sun. 2–5. Planetarium shows Sat. and Sun. 2:30 PM. Closed major holidays.*

Plan on a full day at the **Knoxville Zoological Park,** famous for breeding large cat species and African elephants. The 1,100 animals include a rare red panda, wild creatures native to the African plains, polar bears, seals, and penguins. There are rides on a miniature steam train or an elephant, as well as a petting zoo. *In Chilhowee Park on Rutledge Pike S, 4½ mi east of I–40 Exit 392, tel. 615/637–5331. Admission: $4.50 adults; $2.75 children 3–12 and senior citizens; children under 3 free. Open daily 9:30–6 Apr.–Sept., 10–4:30 rest of year. Closed Christmas.*

For relaxed enjoyment and views of an especially scenic portion of the Tennessee River, step aboard the **Robert E. Lee** (tel. 615/522–4630 or 800/522–0630). One-hour sightseeing excursions as well as brunch and dinner cruises are offered April–December.

To the North and East ❷ From Knoxville, scenic U.S. 441 leads northwest to **Norris,** a distance of about 20 miles. This delightful planned town was built in 1948 as a workers' community during construction of the **Norris Dam,** TVA's first. The dam, which spans the Clinch River and impounds a 72-mile-long lake, has a visitor lobby and two overlooks. Some of the best views, though, are from **Norris Dam State Park** on Rte. 1 (tel. 615/426–7461). Here also is the **Lenoir Museum,** where Indian, pioneer, Civil War, and regional historical artifacts are displayed. A restored country store and an 18th-century gristmill (where you can purchase stone-ground cornmeal) are on the grounds.

The prime attraction at Norris is the **Museum of Appalachia,** where about 35 log structures—among them a molasses mill powered by mules—have been restored in a mountain-village setting. Period furnishings and implements are found in the buildings, and there are pioneer craft demonstrations and a working farm. Locals sometimes bring their musical instruments for an old-time hoedown. *On TN 61, 1 mi east of I–75 Exit 122, tel. 615/494–7680. Admission: $4 adults; $3 senior citizens; $2 children 6–15, under 6 free. Open daily 8 AM–dusk Apr.–Oct., 9–5 rest of year.*

3 A 50-mile drive northeast of Norris along I–75, U.S. 25W, and TN 63 leads to **Harrogate,** by the Virginia border. Here, at **Lincoln Memorial University,** founded in 1896, the Great Emancipator's principles and philosophies prevail. **Lincoln Memorial Museum** contains the world's third-largest collection of Lincolniana. One of the most poignant exhibits is the ebony-and-silver cane he carried to Ford's Theatre. *On campus, off U.S. 25E, tel. 615/869–3611, ext. 235. Admission: $3 adults; $2 senior citizens; $1 children 6–12, under 6 free. Open weekdays 9–4, Sat. 11–4, Sun. 1–4. Closed major holidays.*

4 From Harrogate, drive about 50 miles along U.S. 25E and 11W to **Rogersville,** a little hideaway East Tennessee town. Savor its undisturbed atmosphere, pleasant homes, churches, and ancient trees. Then linger a while.

5 A 28-mile drive along U.S. 11W through rolling hills, meadows, and woodlands brings you to thriving **Kingsport,** founded in 1761. At **Exchange Place,** a restored pioneer homestead, craftspeople demonstrate their skills in commodious log houses. Their handmade quilts, baskets, wood carvings, ceramics, and stuffed dolls are sold in nearby shops. *4812 Orebank Rd., tel. 615/288–6071 or 288–6613. Admission free. Open Sat. and Sun. 2–4:30, Mon. 10–1 May–Oct. Closed rest of week and year.*

The **Netherland Inn,** built in 1818, was for 150 years a stop on the Great Stage Road. Now restored as a museum, it features period furnishings and accessories, a flatboat, a garden, and a log cabin with displays for children. *2140 Netherland Inn Rd., tel. 615/247–3211. Admission: $2 adults, 75¢ students, children under 6 free. Open Fri.–Sun. 2–4:30 Apr.–Oct., by appointment other times.*

Bays Mountain Park on Rte. 4 (tel. 615/229–9447) is a remarkable sanctuary for native plants and animals. Here you'll find an interpretive center, self-guided nature trails, natural history programs, a small zoo, a planetarium, and (in season) float trips by barge on a large lake.

Heading South A 21-mile drive southeast along U.S. 23 brings you to **Johnson City,** an important center for agriculture, manufacturing, and education—it is home to Washington College, the oldest institution of higher education in the state, and East Tennessee State University, with more than 9,000 students.

6 At **Tipton-Haynes Historical Farm,** the 19-century main house, granary, horse barn, law office, and mountain still have been authentically restored. *4 mi south of U.S. 23 Exit 31 via University Pkwy. and S. Roan St., tel. 615/926–3631. Admission: $2 adults, $1.50 senior citizens, $1 students with adults. Open weekdays 10–4, weekends 2–5 Apr.–Oct.*

Rocky Mount, a two-story log mansion completed in 1772, was Governor William Blount's territorial capitol from 1790 until he moved to Knoxville two years later. Faithful restoration and careful selection of authentic furnishings testify to a simple yet eloquent pioneer lifestyle. There's also a cookhouse, slave quarters, a blacksmith shop, and a flax house. Exhibits and demonstrations focus upon the role of women in frontier times. Guided tours are available. *4 mi northeast on U.S. 11E, tel. 615/538-7396. Admission: $4 adults, $2.50 students, children under 6 free. Open Mon.–Sat. 10–5, Sun. 2–6 Mar.–Dec.; weekdays 10–5 rest of year. Closed Thanksgiving, Dec. 21– Jan. 5.*

About eight miles south via U.S. 11E/321, you'll drive into a veritable time warp: **Jonesborough,** the state's oldest town. Visitors admire a trio of antebellum churches, lovely vintage houses, brick and wooden fretwork shops, and the period Court House. Of the many special events held here, the most famous is October's National Storytelling Festival, when professional and amateur storytellers from all around the United States and abroad flock here for a weekend to enchant hordes of curious visitors. At the **Visitor Center and History Museum** (just off U.S. 11E on Boone St., tel. 615/753–5961), a slide show and exhibits describe the town's history.

After a 25-mile drive southwest along U.S. 11E/321, you'll come to the pleasant town of **Greeneville,** founded in 1783. Young Andrew Johnson settled here in 1826 after an arduous trek over the mountains from North Carolina, opened a tailor shop, and married. **Andrew Johnson National Historic Site** preserves his primitive tailor shop, the homestead where he lived from 1851 until his death in 1875, and his hilltop gravesite, marked by an elaborate monument. Displays in the visitor center include notes he made at his impeachment trial. *Depot and College Sts., tel. 615/638–3551. Admission to Homestead: $1 adults, children under 17 and senior citizens with Golden Age Passports free. Open daily 9–5. Closed Christmas.*

Sixty-one miles south via U.S. 321/411 is **Gatlinburg,** Tennessee's premier mountain resort town. Set in the narrow valley of the Little Pigeon River (actually a turbulent mountain stream), it has something for everyone. Family attractions include the **American Historical Wax Museum** (tel. 615/436–4462), the **Gatlinburg Sky Lift** (tel. 615/ 436–4307) to the top of Crockett Mountain, the **Guinness World Record Museum** (tel. 615/436–9100), and the **Ober Gatlinburg Tramway** (tel. 615/ 436–5423) to a mountaintop shopping mall.

Christus Gardens, in a quiet setting overlooking the river, exhibits life-size dioramas of Christ's ministry with background sacred music. Sculptures, a courtyard garden, biblical-era coins, and other artifacts may also be seen here. *4055 River Rd., tel. 615/436–5155. Admission: $4.50 adults; $1.50 children 7–11, under 7 free. Open daily 8 AM–9 PM Apr.–Oct., 9–5 rest of year.*

At the **Great Smoky Mountains National Park,** shared by North Carolina and Tennessee, the southern Appalachians reach their ultimate grandeur as 16 peaks soar more than 6,000 feet. From Gatlinburg, the northern gateway to the park, drive south along the scenic Newfound Gap Road (U.S. 441) to the Sugarlands Visitor Center at park headquarters. Here are informative films, exhibits, maps, and brochures about the park. Driving along on the Newfound Gap Road, stop often at scenic overlooks, perhaps taking time to explore one or more of the nature trails that lead off from many of them. The road ascends to **Newfound Gap** on the Tennessee–North Carolina border, a haunting viewpoint. From here, a seven-mile spur road leads to **Clingmans Dome**—at 6,643 feet, the highest point in Tennessee—where you can walk up a spiral pathway to the top of an observation tower for panoramic views of the Smokies. Spring and summer displays of wildflowers, dazzling rhododendron, and mountain laurel invite explorers to experience this most visited of national parks. But autumn is the favorite season for the spectacular foliage. *Tel. 615/436–5615. Open daily 8–7:30 Mar.–Oct., 8–4:30 rest of year. Closed Christmas Day.*

From Gatlinburg, follow the crowds half a dozen miles or so along U.S. 321/441 and you come to **Pigeon Forge,** with tourism amenities straddling the main thoroughfare for several miles. Popular visitor attractions (many seasonal) have burgeoned here, among them **Magic World** and **Ogle's Water Park** (*see* What to See and Do with Children), **Carbo's Police Museum** (tel. 615/453–1358), and the **Waltzing Waters** (water, light, and music show with popular Broadway tunes; tel. 615/428–5600).

A new dinner theater, **Dixie Stampede** (tel. 615/453–4400), offers a hearty chicken and ribs dinner mid-March–Thanksgiving weekend in a 1000-seat arena; it's accompanied by a colorful, all-new western-themed musical show and rodeo.

The 1830s-era **Old Mill** (tel. 615/453–4628) beside the Little Pigeon River still grinds corn, wheat, and rye on water-powered stone wheels. Here you can purchase flour, meal, grits, and buckwheat. Across the road is **Pigeon Forge Pottery** (*see* Shopping).

Dollywood, Dolly Parton's popular theme park, brings to life the folklore, fun, food, and music of the Great Smokies. In a re-created 1880 mountain village, scores of talented and friendly craftspeople demonstrate their artistry. Museum exhibits trace Parton's rise to stardom. The many amusement rides include a thrilling river raft trip, and "Thunder Express," a twisting, turning coaster ride through a dense backwoods setting. Live music shows are performed on the park's seven stages. Throughout the season, some of the nation's best known entertainers lead a line-up of over 200 performances in "Showcase of Stars." Occasionally Dolly shows up for a surprise appearance. The season ends with the gala National Crafts Festival in an old-fashioned harvest setting from late September to early November. When hunger strikes, try Aunt Fanny's Dixie Fixin's Restaurant for down-home mountain cookery. *700 Dollywood Ln., tel. 615/428–9400. Admission: $16.40 adults, $13.70 senior citizens, $11.50 children 4–11, under 3 free. Open last weekend Apr.–first weekend Nov., daily 9–6; extended hours mid-June–Labor Day weekend, most weekends; closed Thurs. May, Sept., Oct. Phone ahead to verify hours.*

To the West and Home From Pigeon Forge, drive west on U.S. 321, a lovely scenic route, for about 20 miles to the junction of TN 73, which becomes Laurel Creek Road, leading to **Cades Cove** in the Great Smoky Mountains National Park. Here an isolated mountain valley, farmhouses, barns, churches, and an old gristmill still in operation can be seen and visited via a loop road. From spring through autumn, special park ranger programs and demonstrations describe the pioneer agriculture, crafts, and folkways in the Cove. The Visitor Center (tel. 615/448–6967) has exhibits and provides information and literature. At the old gristmill you can take a tour and purchase stone-ground corn-meal. (Both open daily mid-Apr.–Oct.)

Drive southwest for 54 miles along U.S. 321, U.S. 441, and TN 68 for a visit to the **Lost Sea,** outside Sweetwater, where you can explore a 4½-acre underground lake by glass-bottom boat. *Tel. 615/337–6616. Admission: $6 adults; $3 children 6–12, under 6 free. Open daily 9 AM–dusk. Closed Christmas Day.*

Continue on TN 68 until you reach I–75, then take it south for 70 miles to **Chattanooga,** a city of Civil War battlefields, museums of all kinds (art, antiques, history, even knives), the world's steepest incline railway, and a famous choo-choo. **Point Park** (tel. 615/821–7786), a unit of the Chickamauga and Chattanooga National Military Park, commemorates a Union victory at the bloody Battle of Lookout Mountain. Views of the city and of the Tennessee River are stunning. The *Southern Belle* sternwheel steamboat (tel. 615/266–4488) offers sight-seeing excursions and brunch, dinner, and moonlight cruises on the scenic river from April to October.

Chattanooga Choo-Choo and Terminal Station commemorate the first major public passenger train service between the North and the South, which began in 1880. An engine and car of the original train are displayed, and you can ride an antique trolley, dine in a choice of restaurants (including one—the Station House—that is a dinner theater), browse through old-style shops, wander among floral displays, and see a fine exhibit of model railroads. The splendid Terminal Building, dating from 1905, is a gem. In its former main lobby, a magnificent, ornate dome rises 85 feet above an area now part of the Transcontinental restaurant. *1400 Market St., tel. 615/266–5000. Trolley rides: 50¢ adults, 25¢ children under 13. Model railroad exhibit: $1 adults; 50¢ children 6–12, under 6 free. Terminal open daily 11–10. Model railroad exhibit openMon.–Sat. 10–10, Sun. noon–5. Closed Christmas Day.*

The **Lookout Mountain Incline Railway** is the world's steepest, reaching a gradient of 72.7 percent. The ride is truly sensational: it feels like the cars are moving straight up and down the mountainside. A one-way trip lasts 20 minutes. *Station at base, 3917 St. Elmo Ave.; at the top, 827 E. Brow Rd.; tel. 615/821–4224. Round-trip fare: $4.50 adults, $2.75 children. Operates daily 8:30 AM–8:20 PM Memorial Day–Labor Day; daily 9–5:40 rest of year.*

A 36-mile drive north along U.S. 27 will bring you to **Dayton,** where the famous Scopes "Monkey Trial" was held in 1925. At the **Rhea County Courthouse,** the room where the trial took place has been preserved. There is also a small museum with displays about the trial. *301 New Market St., tel. 615/775–0187. Admission free. Open Mon., Tues., Thurs., Fri. 8–4; Wed., Sat. 8–noon. Closed major holidays.*

Sixty-two miles north along U.S. 27, I–40E, and TN 58 is **Oak Ridge,** the famous "atomic city," established secretly during World War II. Some of the original installations here include the **Oak Ridge National Laboratory,** still involved in programs of nuclear fission and magnetic fusion energy; the **Graphite Reactor,** 10 miles southwest, now a National Historic

Landmark, with a display area open to the public; and the **K-25 Visitors Overlook** for views of the **Oak Ridge Gaseous Diffusion Plant,** where uranium is enriched for use in nuclear reactors.

The **American Museum of Science and Energy** focuses upon uses of nuclear, solar, and geothermal energy, mainly for peaceful purposes. Exhibits include hands-on experiments, demonstrations, and computer games. A slide show furnishes valuable background on Oak Ridge and the museum. *300 Tulane Ave., tel. 615/576–3200. Admission free. Open daily 9–6 June–Aug., 9–5 rest of year. Closed major holidays.*

A drive of 22 miles on TN 62E brings you back to Knoxville, where our tour of East Tennessee concludes.

What to See and Do with Children

American Museum of Science and Energy, Oak Ridge (*see* To the West and Home in Exploring).
Chattanooga Choo-Choo and Terminal Station (*see* To the West and Home in Exploring).
Dollywood, Pigeon Forge (*see* Heading South in Exploring).
Knoxville Zoological Park (*see* Knoxville in Exploring).
Lost Sea, Sweetwater (*see* To the West and Home in Exploring).
Magic World. This theme park centered on a magic show also offers rides and a haunted castle. *607 N. Parkway, Pigeon Forge, tel. 615/453–7941. Admission: $8.95, children under 3 free; season pass $15.95. Open Apr.–Oct. Hours vary widely.*
Ogle's Water Park. This is a family park with a giant wave pool, a kiddie play area, eight water slides, and miniature golf. *1115 N. Parkway, Pigeon Forge, tel. 615/453–8741. Admission: $9.95 adults; $8.95 children 4–11, under 4 free. Open daily 10–8 June and July, 11–6 Aug.; weekends only 11–6 May and first half Sept.*
Students' Museum and Akima Planetarium (*see* Knoxville in Exploring).

Off the Beaten Track

Rhododendron Gardens. Atop 6,285-foot Roan Mountain on the border of Tennessee and North Carolina is the world's largest natural display of the multihued flowering shrub. Quiet pathways wend among the 600 acres of plants, which generally reach peak bloom in mid-June. So numerous are the varieties of plants and wildlife that naturalists from throughout the world come to observe and study. At nearby **Roan Mountain State Park,** there's a museum, a picnic area, a campground, a swimming pool, rental cabins, and a restaurant. *U.S. 19E to TN 143, tel. 615/772–3303. Open year-round.*

Shopping

Crafts   The mountain towns of East Tennessee are known for Appalachian folk crafts, especially wood carvings, corn-husk dolls, pottery, dulcimers, and beautiful handmade quilts. These crafts can be found in shops throughout the state, but a good central location for all of them is the **Great Smoky Arts and Craft Community,** a collection of 50 shops and craftsmen's studios along eight miles of rambling country road. Begun in 1937, the community includes workers in leather, pottery, weaving, hand-spun pewter, stained glass, quiltmaking, handcarving, marquetry, and more. Everything sold here is made on the premises by the 64 members. Also here are two restaurants and the popular Wild Plum Tearoom. *Off U.S. 321, 3 mi east of Gatlinburg, tel. 615/436–3808. For more information on the community and the special crafts shows held at Thanksgiving and Easter, write Box 366, Gatlinburg 37738.*

Other area shops selling mountain crafts are **Pigeon Forge Pottery** (301 Middle Creek Rd., Pigeon Forge, tel. 615/453–3883), where internationally esteemed tableware, vases, and bird and animal figurines are handmade and sold; **Ogle & Son's Broom Shop** (Brookside Village on U.S. 321, Gatlinburg, tel. 615/436–5931); and **Arrowcraft Shop** (576 Parkway, Gatlinburg, tel. 615/436–4604), with regional and other crafts.

Iron Mountain Stoneware plant. Hidden away in the northeastern corner of Tennessee and entirely surrounded by the Cherokee National Forest is the tiny village of Laurel Bloomery, the only place where the high-fired stoneware is made. It is also available through numerous retail outlets in the Appalachian Mountains. *TN 91, about 8 mi north of jct with U.S. 421, tel. 615/727–8888. Open daily 8–5. Closed Christmas Day.*

Participant Sports

Fishing At Norris Lake, there's seasonal angling for striped bass, walleye, white bass, and muskie. There are boat launch ramps (but no rentals) at **Norris Dam State Resort Park** (tel. 615/426–7461) and on Chickamauga Lake, near Chattanooga, at **Booker T. Washington State Recreational Park** (tel. 615/894–4955).

Golf East Tennessee courses open to the public include **Brainerd Golf Course** in Chattanooga (tel. 615/894–7131), **Whittle Springs Municipal Golf Course** in Knoxville (tel. 615/525–1022), **Bent Creek Mountain Inn and Country Club** in Gatlinburg (tel. 615/436–9333), **South Hills Golf Club** in Oak Ridge (tel. 615/483–5747), and **Warrior's Path State Park Golf Course** in Kingsport (tel. 615/323–4990).

Hiking An unusually elevated and scenic portion of the **Appalachian Trail** runs along high ridges in the Great Smoky Mountains National Park. The Trail can be easily reached at Newfound Gap from U.S. 441 (Gatlinburg, tel. 615/436–5615).

Horseback Riding **McCarter's Riding Stables** (tel. 615/436–5354) in Gatlinburg arranges guided horseback riding in the Great Smoky Mountains National Park from April through October.

Ice Skating A rink is open year-round at **Ober Gatlinburg Ski Resort** (tel. 615/436–5423).

Rafting and Canoeing **Expeditions, Inc.** (tel. 615/743–3221 or 743–7111; Mar.–Oct.), based in Erwin, south of Johnson City, provides guided whitewater ventures. Ocoee's **Cripple Creek Expeditions** (tel. 615/338–8441; Apr.–Oct.) offers canoe rentals and guided raft trips. **Hiwassee Outfitters** in Reliance (tel. 615/338–8115; mid-Mar.–early Nov.) has canoes, rafts, tubes, and funyaks. **Pigeon River Outdoors** in Gatlinburg (tel. 615/436–5008; Apr.–Oct.) offers guided whitewater raft trips.

Skiing At **Ober Gatlinburg Ski Resort** (tel. 615/436–5423 or, Nov.–mid-Mar. only, 800/251–9202), the slopes of Mount Harrison—reached by double and quad chairlifts—provide dramatic winter skiing. Summer skiing on grass and other surfaces is also available for those who must.

Dining

Mountain cooks have long been noted for preparing fresh ingredients many different ways. Corn remains the old standby, used in the making of grits, luscious muffins, cornbread, and savory spoonbread. At historic water-powered gristmills you can stock up on flour and cornmeal ground between massive antique limestone wheels. The limestone residue blends with the flour and meal, adding nutrients and flavor.

Barbecued ribs, thick pork chops, and generous slices of country ham with red-eye gravy rank as all-time favorites. Freshwater fish, such as varieties of trout, walleye, crappie, muskie, and catfish, will also be found in varied and delicious preparations (but remember to save room for home-baked pies and cobblers). The most highly recommended restaurants in each price category are indicated by a star ★.

Category	Cost*
Very Expensive	over $25
Expensive	$15–$25
Moderate	$10–$15
Inexpensive	under $10

per person without tax (7.75% in Tennessee), service, or drinks

The following credit-card abbreviations are used: AE, American Express; CB, Carte Blanche; DC, Diners Club; MC, MasterCard; V, Visa.

Chattanooga
Very Expensive–Expensive
★

The Green Room. A formal Georgian elegance dominates the spacious, columned dining room. Favorites from the basically Continental menu are smoked Barbary duckling basted with honey, soy, and ginger and served with scallions and rice cakes; and plantation pecan chicken breast with field mushrooms and a roasted tomato. The Jack Daniel's bread pudding is flavored with the famous Tennessee sour-mash whiskey. The moderately priced Sunday buffet is popular. *The Radisson Read House–A Plaza Hotel, 827 Broad St., tel. 615/266–4121. Jacket and tie required. Reservations suggested during the week, required Sun. and holidays. AE, DC, MC, V. Closed Mon. No lunch Tues.–Sat., no dinner Sun.*

★ **River Landing.** A different catch from nearby lakes and streams is featured on the menu each night, in such preparations as flounder baked in parchment and served with mushrooms and a cream sauce. The dining room, embellished with polished wood paneling, has an air of comfortable formality. Views of the Tennessee River through spacious windows and from the outdoor dining terrace are dramatic. *600 River Rd., tel. 615/267–6430. Dress: informal. Reservations advised on Fri. and Sat. evenings. AE, MC, V.*

Moderate–Inexpensive

Chatt's. Though located in a Howard Johnson Hotel, this restaurant is privately owned and managed. The shrimp-and-steak combination—jumbo shrimp sautéed in garlic butter and served with a tender rib-eye steak—is a house specialty. Fried cornbread accompanies homemade vegetable, bean, onion, red potato, creamed broccoli, and cauliflower soups. Brass accents, paintings, live greenery, white napery, candlelight, and comfortable armchairs provide a low-key, elegant ambience. *100 W. 21st St., tel. 615/265–3151. Dress: informal. No reservations. AE, CB, DC, MC, V.*

Gatlinburg
Expensive–
Moderate
★

Burning Bush Restaurant. Antique-style furnishings and accessories evoke a Colonial atmosphere; the menu is Continental. Broiled Tennessee quail and beef Rossini—an eight-ounce fillet served on an English muffin with Madeira sauce—are house specialties. Bountiful breakfasts are also featured. *1151 Parkway, tel. 615/436–4669. Dress: informal. Reservations recommended. AE, CB, DC, MC, V.*

Smoky Mountain Trout House. Of the eight distinctive trout preparations to choose from at this cozy restaurant, an old favorite is trout Eisenhower: pan-fried, using corn-meal breading and bacon flavorings, and served with bacon-and-butter sauce and a side dish of mushrooms. Prime rib, country ham, and fried chicken are also available. *410 N. Parkway, tel. 615/436–5416. Dress: informal. No reservations. AE, CB, DC, MC, V. Closed Dec.–Mar.*

Inexpensive
★

Ogle's Buffet Restaurant. Indulge in bountiful feasting, either in the soft-green-and-beige dining room or on the patio, which extends over a turbulent mountain river. The buffet tables offer five choices of country-style meat, such as fried chicken, prime rib, country ham; five vegetables fresh from the farm; and 70 fixin's for your salad. Don't overlook the sourwood honey. *On the Parkway near traffic light No. 3, tel. 615/436–4157. Dress: informal. No reservations. MC, V. Closes at 4 PM Sun.*

Pancake Pantry. A house specialty is Austrian apple-walnut pancakes covered with apple cider compote, black walnuts, apple slices, sweet spices, powdered sugar, and whipped cream. Other selections include waffles, omelets, sandwiches, soups, and fresh salads. Century-old brick, polished-oak paneling, rustic copper accessories, and spacious windows create a delightful ambience. Box lunches are available for mountain picnics. *628 Parkway, tel. 615/436–4724. Dress: informal. No reservations. Open daily 7 AM–4 PM June–Aug., 7 AM–3 PM rest of year. Closed Thanksgiving, Christmas Day.*

Knoxville
Expensive–
Moderate
★

Regas Restaurant. This cozy Knoxville classic, with fireplaces and original art, has been around for 70 years. The specialty, prime rib, is carefully aged on the premises, baked very slowly all day, then sliced to order and served with creamy horseradish sauce. *318 Gay St., tel. 615/637–9805. Dress: informal. Reservations advised. AE, CB, MC, V. Closed Sun., major holidays. No lunch Fri. and Sat.*

Moderate–
Inexpensive

Hawkeye's Corner, Too. The setting may be serious—a refurbished antebellum mansion, full of the atmosphere of the Old South—but Hawkeye's is about fun. Try the sweet-potato chips (on the menu, they're called "I yam what I yam") or the "Nimwads Special"—an open-faced sandwich of beef, turkey, jack cheese, broccoli, and hollandaise on whole wheat. A special dish is chicken teriyaki. The main seating areas are the glass-walled greenhouse and the sun room. There are also seats upstairs and on the open-air patio. *9000 Kingston Pike, tel. 615/ 693–7098. Dress: informal. Reservations accepted. AE, CB, DC, MC, V. Closed major holidays.*

Inexpensive **Bob Evans Farm Restaurant.** At this country-style restaurant, part of a chain, piquantly seasoned fresh country sausages in many varieties and flavors are the specialty. For accompaniment, you can choose from side orders of eggs, pancakes, biscuits, and grits. Though breakfast specialties are always available, there's also a full lunch and dinner menu. *5604 Merchants Center Blvd., tel. 615/689–8555. Dress: informal. No reservations. Open weekdays 6 AM–10 PM, weekends 24 hrs. Closed major holidays.*

Pigeon Forge **Cole's Mill House Restaurant.** At this restaurant in a renovated
Expensive–Moderate 19th-century home, seafood is emphasized, but you'll also find a Jack Daniels–glazed rib-eye steak and prime rib. The Double Derby pie is a pecan, chocolate, and caramel concoction. *115 S. River Rd., tel. 615/428–2307. Dress: informal. No reservations. MC, V.*

Moderate **Green Valley Restaurant.** Here's a place for family-style dining on country ham, homemade biscuits, and gravy for breakfast, sautéed rainbow trout or lobster tail for dinner. The well-lit room has a cathedral ceiling with exposed beams and a two-story fireplace. *804 S. Parkway, tel. 615/453–3500. Dress: informal. No reservations. AE, MC, V. Closed Christmas.*

Inexpensive **Apple Tree Inn Restaurant.** A traditional East Tennessee menu
★ is offered here, including fried chicken and a special spoonbread: a regal soufflé of cornmeal, flour, eggs, buttermilk, and seasonings, served hot from the baking dish. Order family-style or individually. At the center of the spacious dining room is an apple tree, which grows through an opening in the ceiling. *Parkway and Frances Rd., tel. 615/453–4961. Dress: informal. No reservations. AE, MC, V. Closed Dec.–Feb.*

Lodging

Some restored historic hotels in larger cities offer lodging in settings reminiscent of earlier times. The major resort areas of Gatlinburg and Pigeon Forge have abundant choices. For reservations at hotels, motels, chalets, and condominiums throughout the area, contact **Smoky Mountain Accommodations Reservation Service** (Rte. 4, Box 538, Roaring Fork Rd., Gatlinburg 37738, tel. 615/436–9700 or 800/231–2230). For B&B reservations, contact **Bed & Breakfast Host Homes of Tennessee** (Box 110227, Nashville 37222, tel. 615/331–5244).

In the categories below, the high-season summer and autumn rates are given; these drop considerably at other times of the year. The most highly recommended properties in each price category are indicated by a star ★.

Category	Cost*
Very Expensive	over $100
Expensive	$75–$100
Moderate	$50–$75
Inexpensive	under $50

*double room; add 11.75% for taxes

The following credit-card abbreviations are used: AE, American Express; CB, Carte Blanche; DC, Diners Club; MC, MasterCard; V, Visa.

Chattanooga
Expensive–
Moderate
★

Chattanooga Choo-Choo. The hotel adjoins the showcase 1905 Southern Railway Terminal, with restaurants, lounges, shops, exhibits, gardens, and operating trolley. Guest rooms stress luxurious appointments, especially the restored Victorian-era parlor cars converted to overnight aeries. *1400 Market St., 37402, tel. 615/266–5000. 363 units, including suites and 48 parlor cars. Facilities: cable TV, indoor and outdoor pools, whirlpools, lighted tennis courts, 3 dining rooms, coffee shop, lounge with entertainment. AE, DC, MC, V.*

★ **Radisson Read House–A Plaza Hotel.** A traditional favorite in the Mid-South, the Georgian-style Read House dates from the 1920s and has been impeccably restored to its original grandeur. The lobby, listed on the National Register of Historic Places, is highlighted by a large archway, stately columns, and panels of polished walnut. Guest rooms in the main hotel continue the Georgian motif; rooms in the annex are more contemporary. *827 Broad St., 37402, tel. 615/266–4121 or 800/228–9822. 250 rooms, including suites and 10 2-bedroom units. Facilities: cable TV, pool, sauna, whirlpool, dining room, restaurant, coffee shop, lounge. AE, DC, MC, V.*

Moderate–
Inexpensive

Howard Johnson Hotel. This five-story hotel, recently renovated, has a warm, contemporary atmosphere with greenery and cheerful accessories in public areas. Guest rooms in various styles feature modern art, wicker and rattan furnishings, and spacious work areas. *100 W. 21st St., 37408, tel. 615/265–3151 or 800/654–2000. 103 rooms. Facilities: cable TV, pool, coin laundry, game room, Executive Club, dining room, cocktail lounge. AE, CB, DC, MC, V.*

Inexpensive

Econo Lodge East Ridge. Rooms are spacious, contemporary in style, clean, and well-maintained. *6650 Ringgold Rd., 37412, tel. 615/894–1860 or 800/446–6900. 122 rooms. Facilities: TV, pool, restaurant. AE, CB, DC, MC, V.*

Gatlinburg
Very Expensive
★

Buckhorn Inn. This inn in a remote woodland setting about six miles outside the city has welcomed guests—including seclusion-seeking diplomats, government officials, and celebrities—for more than 40 years. The views of Mt. LeConte and the Great Smokies are spectacular. Inside, the country-inn atmosphere is reinforced by wicker rockers, paintings by local artists, a huge stone fireplace, and French doors that open onto a large stone porch. Breakfast and dinner are included in the rates and are hearty and warming: home-baked breads, creamed soups, marinated beef tenderloin, fruit tortes. *Off U.S. 321, Box 323, 37738, tel. 615/436–4668. 7 rooms with mountain-style furnishings, no phones or TV; 4 cottages with cable TV, cooking equipment, fireplace, screened porch; all units have private baths. Facilities: spring-fed lake for fishing, off-trail hiking in nearby Great Smoky Mountains National Park. No credit cards.*

Expensive–
Moderate
★

Holiday Inn Resort Hotel. The hotel is near the Convention Center and the aerial tramway, which in winter whisks ski addicts to the snowy slopes at Ober Gatlinburg. The Holidome Indoor Recreation Center is attractive and cheerful, with lavish plantings, a pool, and a spacious atrium. *333 Airport Rd., 37738, tel. 615/436–9201 or 800/465–4329. 402 rooms and suites. Facilities: cable TV, 2 indoor pools, outdoor pool, whirlpool, 2 saunas, putting green, coin laundry, pizza parlor, din-*

ing room, coffee shop, cocktail lounge, nightclub, live enter-tainment in season, meeting areas. AE, DC, MC, V.

Park Vista Hotel. This large hotel on a mountain ledge has mod-ern, lavishly decorated public areas and large, eloquently appointed guest rooms, each with a balcony overlooking color-ful garden grounds, the town of Gatlinburg, the Little Pigeon River, and the mountains beyond. The white, semicircular con-temporary tower, though handsome, seems rather out of place here in the Great Smoky Mountains. *Airport Rd. at Cherokee Orchard Rd., Box 30, 37738, tel. 615/436–9211 or 800/421–7275. 315 rooms and suites. Facilities: cable TV, indoor pool, saunas, whirlpool, health spa, coin laundry, restaurant, din-ing room, cocktail lounges, nightclub, live entertainment, meeting rooms. AE, CB, DC, MC, V.*

Moderate **Best Western Twin Islands Motel.** In the center of Gatlinburg, beside the surging Little Pigeon River, this motel is notable for its low-key contemporary architectural style. All rooms have balconies overlooking the river. *U.S. 441, Box 648, 37738, tel. 615/436–5121 or 800/223–8256. 107 rooms and suites, 5 kitchen units; whirlpool or waterbed units, king rooms with hot tubs, some fireplaces available. Facilities: cable TV, heated pool, fishing on premises, playground, coin laundry, restaurant. AE, CB, DC, MC, V.*

Inexpensive **Rainbow Motel.** Here is a small, neat, well-maintained lodging, a pleasant choice for budget-minded vacationers. *U.S. 321 (3 blocks east of U.S. 441), Box 1397, 37738, tel. 615/436–5887 or 800/422–8922. 41 rooms, including 1 with whirlpool, 1 efficien-cy, 2 2-bedroom units. Facilities: cable TV, heated pool, refrigerators available. AE, DC, MC, V.*

Knoxville **Hyatt Regency Knoxville.** This is a handsome, contemporary
Expensive– adaptation of an ancient Aztec pyramid atop a hill overlook-
Moderate ing the city and mountainous hinterlands. The nine-story
★ atrium lobby blends modern furnishings and artworks in Meso-american motifs with abundant flora and colorful accessor-ies. *500 Hill Ave. SE, Box 88, 37901, tel. 615/637–1234 or 800/ 228–9000. 386 rooms, including luxury suites, 3 2-bedroom units. Facilities: cable TV, pool, playground, exercise room, cocktail lounge, coffee shop, rooftop dining room. AE, DC, MC, V.*

Inexpensive **La Quinta Motor Inn.** Rooms are spacious and well lighted,
★ with convenient working areas. *258 Peters Rd. N, 37923, tel. 615/690–9777 or 800/531–5900. 130 rooms, including King Plus. Facilities: cable TV, heated pool. AE, DC, MC, V.*

Pigeon Forge **Holiday Inn.** This inn is situated in the middle of the action. The
Expensive– vast Holidome Indoor Recreation Center features lush green-
Moderate ery and activities for the entire family. Especially pleasant rooms and extra services are available on the concierge floor. *413 N. Parkway, 37863, tel. 615/428–2700 or 800/465–4329. 208 rooms and suites. Facilities: cable TV, restaurant, indoor pool, sauna, whirlpool, health club, coin laundry, game room, specialty shops. AE, CB, DC, MC, V.*

Expensive– **Days Inn.** Centrally located near major attractions, this five-
Moderate story inn features some ultramodern rooms with water beds and fireplaces. *425 N. Parkway, 37863, tel. 615/453–0056 or 800/325–2525. 119 units, including suites, 27 rooms with whirlpools, 11 efficiencies. Facilities: cable TV. AE, DC, MC, V.*

Moderate **Best Western Plaza Inn.** Located within easy reach of shops, restaurants, and family attractions, the inn offers amenities for the entire family. Rooms are spacious and well furnished, and some have refrigerators; some overlook mountain scenery, others an indoor swimming pool. *501 S. Parkway, Box 926, 37863, tel. 615/453–5538 or 800/232–5656. 140 rooms, including suites with fireplaces and whirlpool baths, and 2 2-bedroom units; waterbeds available. Facilities: cable TV, indoor and outdoor pools, saunas, game rooms. AE, CB, DC, MC, V.*

Inexpensive **Bilmar Motor Inn.** This is a clean, basic motel for budget-minded vacationers. *411 S. Parkway, 37863, tel. 615/453–5593. 52 rooms, 2 with whirlpool. Facilities: cable TV/movies, pool, wading pool. AE, MC, V.*

The Arts

Theater **Sweet Fanny Adams Theatre and Music Hall** in Gatlinburg (tel. 615/436–4038) offers original musical comedies, Gay '90s revues, and old-fashioned sing-alongs. **Archies Playhouse** in Pigeon Forge (tel. 615/428–3218) features comedy and music by *Hee Haw* star Archie Campbell and his friends. The **Backstage Playhouse** in Chattanooga (tel. 615/629–1565) is a weekend dinner theater. The **Carousel Theatre,** at the University of Tennessee in Knoxville (tel. 615/974–5161), presents professional and student players at a theater-in-the-round.

Religious Plays **The Kingdom Story** in Pigeon Forge (tel. 615/428–4456 or 800/451–1881) depicts the life of Jesus Christ evenings on the first weekend of the month, May through October, except Wednesdays. **The Smoky Mountain Passion Play,** depicting the life of Christ, and **Damascus Road,** the story of the Apostle Paul, are staged on alternate evenings at an outdoor theater in Townsend (tel. 615/448–2244 or 984–4111).

Concerts, Opera, and Dance Events at the **Tivoli Theater** in Chattanooga (tel. 615/757–5050) include concerts and operas. The **Knoxville Opera Company** (tel. 615/523–8712) sponsors New York Metropolitan Opera competitions each year, along with two locally produced operatic performances. The **Knoxville Symphony Orchestra** (tel. 615/523–1178) presents seven concerts a year, often with esteemed guest artists. **Lamar House Bijou Theater** in Knoxville (tel. 615/522–0832) offers seasonal ballet, concerts, and plays.

Nightlife

Chattanooga There is live entertainment in **Peacocks Lounge** of the Holiday Inn Lookout Mountain (tel. 615/265–0551) and dancing to live music at the lounges of the **Ramada Inn** (tel. 615/622–8353) and the **Sheraton City Center Hotel** (tel. 615/756–5150).

Gatlinburg At Ober Gatlinburg's **Old Heidelberg Restaurant** (take the aerial tramway from downtown; tel. 615/436–9256), there's dancing to DJ-selected rock and roll. You can watch wide-screen TV, warm your aching feet, and sip a toddy at the **Still Room Lounge** (tel. 615/436–5703), in Filbert's Restaurant. **Sadie and Dora's** (tel. 615/436–9201) at the Holiday Inn Resort Hotel features live entertainment and dancing. The **Park Vista Hotel** (tel. 615/436–9211) has upbeat entertainment and a DJ in the high energy Matrix Lounge. Spirits' Lounge at the new **Edgewater Hotel** (tel. 615/436–4151), features live country and easy-listening.

Knoxville **Annie's** (tel. 615/637-4484) features live jazz in a courtyard, plus a light menu. **Manhattan's** (tel. 615/525-4463), a lively saloon and grill in the "Old City," has Big Band music, entertainment Tues.–Sat., with free hors d'oeuvres 5–7 PM. At **Funny Bone Comedy Night Club** (tel. 615/588-5155), eat and drink while watching comedians from TV. At **Lord Lindsey's** (tel. 615/522-2178), there's a DJ and dancing on weekends. **Mom 'n Dad's Buffet & Bar** (tel. 615/524-4681), near the University of Tennessee at the Best Western Campus Inn, offers hot hors d'oeuvres and weekend entertainment. At **Nirt 'n Girty's Lounge** (tel. 615/546-7110), in the Best Western Cherry Tree Inn, there's hot and cold hors d'oeuvres, backgammon, a DJ, and a lighted dance floor.

Oak Ridge The **Reactor Room Lounge** (tel. 615/483-4371) at the Holiday Inn reflects Atomic City right down to dance floor, with lights that pulsate to the beat of the DJ's offerings.

9 Virginia

Introduction

by Francis X.
Rocca

Francis X. Rocca
is a writer based in
Alexandria,
Virginia.

Virginia does not have something for everyone. It does not have
a major-league sports franchise, for one thing (though the
Washington Redskins enjoy a loyal following). No, Virginia is
not an essential trip—unless you wish to understand the
United States.

This state ranks second to none as the venue of seminal events
in American history. English-speaking North America began
at Jamestown. The breach with England was instigated largely
in Williamsburg and then confirmed at Yorktown. The tensions
latent within the young nation were bloodily released on the
soil of the Old Dominion: more than two-thirds of the War Between the States was fought here.

Virginia has been recovering ever since from the ravages of civil war. Finally flourishing, it draws prestige from an antebellum legacy undisturbed by too much progress. The skyscrapers of Richmond spring out of a 19th-century cityscape.
Towns in the Shenandoah Valley look so authentically old that
they routinely serve as movie sets. Many important battlefields
and historic houses have been restored and opened to the public.

The Commonwealth's prehistory is also well defended, in the
vast official wilderness of state and national parks and forests.
The natural beauty is abundant and diverse: beaches on one
side, mountains on the other. The amount of unspoiled land,
both unsettled and cultivated, is a wonder in a state so crowded
with Civilization—but not, fortunately, with people.

Shenandoah Valley and the Highlands

The Shenandoah Valley is best known for its rugged beauty and
rural charm, yet its cities and towns have much to offer in the
way of history and culture. Staunton preserves the birthplace
of Woodrow Wilson, the 28th president of the United States and
the latest of eight from Virginia. Bath County, where the salu-
tary mineral waters flow, has been a fashionable resort for two
centuries. Lexington is a town dense with historic sites —
including the birthplace of Sam Houston and the last home of
Stonewall Jackson—and is practically unchanged in its appearance since the 19th century. Roanoke is the only city in the
country to have a mountain within its limits; its nickname, the
"Star City of the South," derives from the large illuminated
star topping the mountain the name also reflects Roanoke's
pride in its long-standing role as the cultural and commercial
center of western Virginia.

The Highlands in the southwest have been neglected by travelers, for no good reason. The scenery is too beautiful to ignore,
and there is plenty of indoor and outdoor recreation—in this region are seven state parks, three national parks, and six national forests. The town of Abingdon has a well-preserved
collection of 18th- and 19th-century buildings, hosts two renowned regional festivals, and is the home of the state theater
of Virginia, the Barter Theatre.

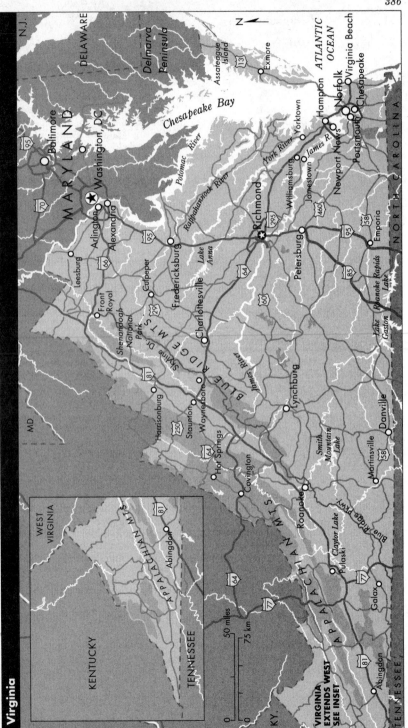

Virginia

N.J.

DELAWARE

MARYLAND

Delmarva Peninsula

Assateague Island

Exmore

113

ATLANTIC OCEAN

Baltimore

95

Washington, DC

70

Arlington

Alexandria

Chesapeake Bay

Potomac River

Hampton

Norfolk

Virginia Beach

Chesapeake

Portsmouth

Newport News

Yorktown

Williamsburg

Jamestown

460

York River

James R.

Leesburg

66

Front Royal

Culpeper

Fredericksburg

Rappahannock River

Lake Anna

Richmond

295

64

95

295

Petersburg

85

158

Emporia

NORTH CAROLINA

Shenandoah National Park

Skyline Dr.

29

Charlottesville

BLUE RIDGE MTS.

60

Lake Gaston

Roanoke Rapids

Lake

81

Harrisonburg

Staunton

250

Waynesboro

James River

Lynchburg

Danville

Hot Springs

64

Covington

Smith Mountain Lake

Martinsville

58

MD

Roanoke

Claytor Lake

Pulaski

Blue Ridge Pkwy.

Galax

WEST VIRGINIA

KENTUCKY

APPALACHIAN MTS.

Abingdon

81

77

TENNESSEE

VIRGINIA EXTENDS WEST SEE INSET

KY.

APPALACHIAN MTS.

Abingdon

81

TENNESSEE

50 miles

75 km

0

Getting Around

By Plane   Eight carriers, including **USAir,** serve Roanoke Municipal Airport. The Tri-City Regional Airport in Bristol, by the Tennessee state line, is served by **USAir/Allegheny,** and others.

By Car   I–81 and U.S. 11 run north–south the length of the Shenandoah Valley and continue on south into Tennessee. I–66 west from Washington, DC (90 miles to the east) passes through Front Royal to connect with 81 and 11 at the northern end of the Valley. I–64 connects them with Charlottesville, 30 miles to the east. Route 39 into Bath County connects with I–81 just north of Lexington. I–77 cuts off the southwest tip of the state, running north–south.

By Train   **Amtrak** has service three days a week to Staunton (One Middlebrook Ave.), en route between New York and Chicago. The same train stops at Clifton Forge (Ridgeway St.), for The Homestead resort.

By Bus   **Greyhound/Trailways:** Abingdon (465 W. Main St., tel. 703/628–6622), Lexington (631 Waddell St., tel. 703/463–2424), Roanoke (26 Salem Ave., tel. 703/342–6761), Staunton (100 S. New St., tel. 703/886–2424).

Guided Tours

The **Historic Staunton Foundation** (tel. 703/885–7676) offers free one-hour guided tours of the town every Saturday morning at 11, Memorial Day through October, departing from the Woodrow Wilson Birthplace (24 N. Coalter St.) A brochure is available for a self-guided tour.

For $6, the **Lexington Carriage Company** (tel. 703/463–9500) will take you around town in a horse-drawn carriage for 50 minutes, April–October. A walking-tour brochure is available at the Lexington Visitor Center (*see* Important Addresses and Numbers).

Important Addresses and Numbers

Tourist Information   **Bath County Chamber of Commerce,** Rte. 220, Box 57, Warm Springs 24484, tel. 703/839–5409. Open weekdays 8:30–4:30. For literature and maps 24 hours a day, stop by their gazebo at the intersection of Rtes. 39 and 220. **Front Royal/Warren County Chamber of Commerce,** 414 E. Main St., Front Royal 22630, tel. 703/635–3185. Open weekdays 9–5, Sat. 9–noon in summer. Closed Sun. **Lexington Visitor Center,** 102 E. Washington St., Lexington 24450, tel. 703/463–3777. Open daily 9–5. **Roanoke Valley Convention and Visitors Bureau,** 14 W Kirk Ave., Roanoke 24011, tel. 703/342–6025. Open weekdays 8:30–5. **Shenandoah Valley Tourist Information Center** (off I–81 at Exit 67), Box 1040, New Market 22844, tel. 703/740–3132. Open daily 9–5. **Historic Staunton Welcome Center,** 24 N. Coalter St., Staunton 24401, tel. 703/885–8097. Open daily 9–5, except Sun. in Jan. and Feb. **Washington County Chamber of Commerce,** 179 E. Main St., Abingdon 24210, tel. 703/628–8141. Open daily 9–5.

Emergencies   Dial 911 for emergency assistance.

Exploring Shenandoah Valley and the Highlands

Numbers in the margin correspond with points of interest on the Shenandoah Valley and the Highlands map.

1 It must be admitted that the justifiable fame of the **Skyline Drive** has its drawbacks. The holiday and weekend crowds in high season—spring or fall—can slow traffic (already held to a maximum speed of 35 mph) to a crawl and put enormous strain on the few lodges, campsites, and eating places along the way. But for those seeking easily accessible wilderness and stunning views, there are few routes that can compete with this one.

Starting at **Front Royal,** the Drive—easily reached from Interstates 64, 66, and 81—winds 105.4 scenic miles south over **2** the mountains of the **Shenandoah National Park** and affords spectacular vistas of the Shenandoah Valley to the west and the rolling country of the Piedmont to the east. The hundreds of miles of hiking trails (including a section of the Appalachian Trail), the canoeing on the Shenandoah River, and the trout fishing in the rushing streams provide many incentives for the action-minded, and the rangers supervise a variety of activities (outlined in the *Shenandoah Overlook*, a free newspaper you can pick up as you enter the park).

It's better to choose another route in the winter; most facilities are closed from November through April, and parts of the Drive itself can be closed due to treacherous conditions. So come during the fine weather, but bring a sweater—temperatures can be brisk. *For information, contact the Park Superintendent, Box 348, Rte. 4, Luray 22835, tel. 703/999–2229. Admission to the park and the Drive: $5 per car.*

You'll also want that sweater for one not-to-be-missed detour: **3** **Luray Caverns,** the largest in the state and only nine miles west of the Drive. For millions of years the water has seeped through the limestone and clay to create a variety of suggestive rock and mineral formations. The world's only "Stalacpipe Organ" is composed of stalactites hanging from the ceiling (stalag*mites* rise from the floor), which are tuned to concert pitch and tapped by rubber-tipped plungers under the organist's control. A one-hour tour starts every 20 minutes. *West on Rte. 211 from Skyline Dr., tel. 703/743–6551. Admission: $9 adults, $8 senior citizens, $4 children. Open daily 9–7 June 15–Labor Day, 9–6 Mar. 15–June 15 and after Labor Day to Nov. 14, 9–4 rest of year.*

The trip south on Skyline Drive ends at **Waynesboro,** which is 28 miles west of "Mr. Jefferson's Country" on I-64 (*see* Charlottesville Area). Those whose thirst for the picturesque is not **4** yet sated might continue south on the 470-mile-long **Blue Ridge Parkway,** a direct continuation of the Drive. It extends through the George Washington National Forest to Great Smoky Mountains National Park in North Carolina and Tennessee. Although the Parkway is less pristine, the higher mountains offer even better views, including a 360-degree panorama at **5** the **Peaks of the Otter Recreation Area,** near Roanoke. Like the Drive, it has a variety of lodges, waysides, and self-guided nature walks and a section of the Appalachian Trail; unlike the Drive, admission to the Parkway and its attractions is free.

Shenandoah Valley and the Highlands

389

1 Skyline Drive
2 Shenandoah National Park
3 Luray Caverns
4 Lexington
5 Peaks of the Otter Recreation Area
6 Mabry Mill
7 Staunton
8 Bath County
9 Natural Bridge
10 Natural Bridge
11 Roanoke
12 Booker T. Washington Birthplace
13 Mount Rogers National Recreation Area
14 Abingdon

Front Royal
Culpeper
Harrisonburg
Waynesboro
Blue Ridge Parkway
Goshen Pass
Hot Springs
The Homestead
Charlottesville
Appomattox Court House
Lynchburg
Smith Mountain Lake
Danville
Claytor Lake
Pulaski
Galax
Bon Aire

BLUE RIDGE MTS
APPALACHIAN MTS
Jefferson National Forest
Jefferson National Forest

WEST VIRGINIA
KENTUCKY
TENNESSEE
NORTH CAROLINA
VIRGINIA

James River

Skyline Dr.
Blue Ridge Pkwy.

N

0   50 miles
0   75 km

❻ Perhaps the point of greatest interest—certainly the most famous—is **Mabry Mill,** just north of Meadows of Dan and the junction with U.S. 58 at mile marker 176. This gristmill and sawmill features exhibitions of blacksmithing and other trades. *For more information, contact the Parkway Superintendent, Blue Ridge Pkwy., 700 Northwestern Plaza, Asheville, NC 28801, tel. 704/259–0701 or 259–0702.*

❼ Those who are content to forgo the Parkway and who leave the Drive and the wilderness at Waynesboro will find two interesting attractions 11 miles to the west in **Staunton** (pronounced "Stan-ton"), a town with a distinguished past. It was once the seat of vast Augusta County—formed in 1738 and encompassing present-day West Virginia, Kentucky, Ohio, and Indiana—and was briefly the capital of Virginia (the general assembly fled here from the British in 1781). It seems a fitting birthplace for a president.

In the **Woodrow Wilson House,** the president was born in 1856. The house has been restored, with period antiques and some original pieces, to reflect its time as the residence of an antebellum Presbyterian minister (which is what Woodrow's father was). Wilson's presidential limousine, a 1919 Pierce-Arrow sedan, is on display in the garage. *24 N. Coalter St., next door to the Welcome Center (I–81 to I–64 at Exit 57), tel. 703/885–0897. Admission: $3.50 adults, $3 senior citizens, $1 children. Open 9–6 daily Memorial Day–Labor Day, 9–5 Mar.–Memorial Day and Labor Day–Dec., 9–5 Mon.–Sat. rest of the year. Closed Thanksgiving, Christmas, and New Year's.*

Just outside town is the new **Museum of American Frontier Culture,** an outdoor living museum that shows the beginnings of agrarian life in America. Four genuine 18th-century farmsteads—American, Scotch-Irish, German, and English—will be fully operating by the summer of 1990; the first two are ready now. The attention to authenticity and detail is painstaking. For instance, master craftsmen were brought in from Ulster to thatch the roofs on farm buildings that were transported here from County Tyrone. Livestock have been backbred and ancient seeds germinated in order to create an environment accurate in all respects. *230 Frontier Dr. off I–81 at Exit 57 to Rte. 250W, tel. 703/332–7850. Admission: $4 adults, $3.60 senior citizens, $2 children. Open daily 9–8 Memorial Day–Labor Day, 9–5 rest of year.*

❽ Traveling south again on I–81, a side trip well worth the two-hour detour is bucolic **Bath County.** Take the scenic route: the **Goshen Pass,** a three-mile stretch of Route 39 that follows the Maury River through the Allegheny Mountains and is lush with rhododendrons in May. There are no traffic lights in all of Bath County, as the locals proudly point out; there are only 10 year-round residents per square mile. But for more than 200 years this peaceful area has been an important resort. Originally, visitors came for the healing thermal springs. Those treatments are no longer much in fashion, yet the sulfur waters still flow at Warm Springs, Hot Springs, and Bolar Springs (ranging from 77 to 106 degrees F.), and many swear by them.

Outdoor enthusiasts will find in Bath County many diversions —public and private, on water and land. *Call or write to the Virginia Division of Parks and Recreation, 203 Governor St., 306, Richmond 23219, tel. 804/786–2132.*

Of the various resorts in the area, **The Homestead** in Hot Springs has evolved into an attraction in its own right. Every imaginable luxury, diversion, and convenience is here for the guests, who at any one time number as many as 1,000. The golf course was laid out in 1892 and is one of the oldest in continuous use in the States. The first skiing in the South began here in 1959. Tennis, horseback riding, fishing, lawn bowling, skeet shooting, and archery are also available. Staying here is like taking a cruise on a mountain instead of a ship (*see* Lodging).

❾ Returning to I–81, travel 12 miles south to **Lexington,** where two deeply traditional Virginia colleges sit side-by-side, each with a memorial to a soldier who was also a man of peace.

Washington and Lee University is the sixth-oldest college in the United States, founded in 1749 as Augusta Academy. In gratitude for a donation from George Washington, it was renamed Washington College. After Robert E. Lee served as its president following the Civil War, it received its present name. The **Lee Memorial Chapel and Museum** on campus contains Washington's christening dress and many relics of the Lee family. Edward Valentine's statue of the recumbent general, behind the altar, is especially moving: the pose is natural and the expression gentle, in contrast to most monumental art, the martial in particular. Here you can appreciate the reverence Lee has inspired. *Tel. 703/463–8768. Admission free. Open Mon.–Sat. 9–5 Apr.–Oct., 9–4 rest of year; Sun. 2–5. Closed New Year's, Thanksgiving, and the following day, Dec. 24–26 and 31.*

Directly adjacent is the imposing, Gothic-style **Virginia Military Institute,** founded in 1839. Here the **George C. Marshall Museum** preserves the memory of a man who came to this West Point of the South because he could not get into the one in the North. He later served as chief of staff in World War II and eventually, most famously, as the secretary of state who conceived the plan to revive Western Europe after the war. Exhibits trace his brilliant career, which began as aide-de-camp to Black Jack Pershing in World War I. Marshall's Nobel Peace Prize is on display; so is the Oscar won by his aide Frank McCarthy, who produced the 1970 Best Picture, *Patton*. An electronic, narrated map tells the story of World War II in 45 minutes. *Tel. 703/463–7103. Admission free. Open Mon.–Sat. 9–5, Sun. 2–5. Mar.–Oct., Mon.–Sat. 9–4, Sun. 2–4 rest of year. Closed Thanksgiving, Christmas, and New Year's.*

The **V.M.I. Museum** is in the basement of the Institute's Jackson Memorial Hall. Stonewall Jackson's stuffed and mounted horse, Little Sorrel, is on display, as is the general's raincoat, pierced by the bullet that killed him at Chancellorsville. *Tel. 703/463–6232. Admission free. Open Mon.–Sat. 9–5, Sun. 2–5. Closed Thanksgiving and Christmas Eve through New Year's.*

Jackson's private life is on display just a few blocks away at the **Stonewall Jackson House.** He was devoted to physical fitness and the Presbyterian faith, careful with money, musically inclined, and fond of gardening. There is nothing remote about the modest professor you meet here, in the only house he ever owned. It is furnished with period pieces and a few of the general's belongings. He lived here only two years, while he taught physics and military science to the cadets at the Institute, until the War Between the States put his tactical genius to bloody use. *8 E. Washington St., tel. 703/463–2552. Admission: $3.50 adults, $2 children. Open Mon.–Sat. 9–5, Sun. 1–5 Sept.– May; Mon.–Sat. 9–6, Sun. 1–6 June–Aug.*

⑩ About 15 miles south of Lexington is the **Natural Bridge,** an impressive arch 215 feet high and 90 feet long that has been gradually carved out of the limestone by the Cedar Creek below. The arch really *is* a bridge, supporting a segment of U.S. 11. The Monocan Indians worshiped it as "The Bridge of God." George Washington surveyed it for Lord Fairfax, and evidently carved his own initials into the rock. Thomas Jefferson bought it and some surrounding acreage because he admired it as a wonder of the world. The constant background music is distracting and the sound-and-light show after dark is overkill, but the bridge itself is worth the price of admission. *I–81 to Exit 49 or 50, tel. in VA 800/533–1410 or 800/336–5727. Admission: $5 adults, $4 senior citizens, $2.50 children. Open daily 7 AM–dusk.*

Next door, the exhibits at **Natural Bridge Wax Museum** are less interesting than its factory tour: a look at the state-of-the-art process by which the realistic biblical and historical figures are assembled. You should not go out of your way, but it is right at the entrance to the bridge. *Tel. 703/291–2426. Admission: $4 adults, $2 children. Open daily 9–9 May–Aug., 10–6 Sept., Nov., Mar., and Apr.; Wed.–Sun. 10–4 Dec.–Feb.*

⑪ Fifty-four miles south of Lexington is **Roanoke.** At the heart of this quiet and cheerful city, a hub for the railroad and the arts, is Market Square. A restored warehouse here, called **Center in the Square,** contains three museums and a theater. The **Science Museum of Western Virginia** (tel. 703/343–7876) has displays on Virginia's natural history and computer games that entertain and inform on such topics as energy resources. Many of the exhibits are interactive and therefore especially appealing to youngsters. Shows are held in the planetarium on a varying schedule; call 703/343–STAR. The **Roanoke Valley Historical Society** (tel. 703/342–5770; admission free) displays a curious collection of regionalia, including prehistoric relics of the local Indians, from whose name for "shell wampum" the name Roanoke is derived. The **Roanoke Museum of Fine Arts** (tel. 703/342 –5760; admission free) does not have a big-name collection; the emphasis is regional. The best thing about it is that local artists flock here to work in the studios on the top floor. The **Mill Mountain Theater** presents musicals and Shakespearean and contemporary drama (*see* The Arts). *General information for Center in the Square, tel. 703/342–5700. All museums open Tues.–Sat. 10–5, Sun. 1–5; Science and art museums also open until 8 on Fri.*

Just a pleasant stroll away is the **Virginia Museum of Transportation,** devoted almost exclusively to trains. This is not surprising, since Roanoke got its start as a railroad town and is the headquarters of Norfolk and Western (formerly Norfolk Southern) Railway Co. The dozens of original train cars and engines, many built in town, include a massive "Nickel Plate" locomotive. The collections of the museum are unique, and its unabashed display of civic pride is peculiar to Roanoke. This museum captures the whole spirit of a town. *303 Norfolk Ave., tel. 703/342–5670. Admission: $3 adults, $2.50 senior citizens, $2 teens, $1.75 children. Open Mon.–Sat. 10–5, Sun. 12–5.*

⑫ Twenty miles southeast of Roanoke is **Booker T. Washington's Birthplace,** a restored plantation that is now a national monument. Born in slavery, this remarkable educator went on to advise presidents McKinley, Roosevelt, and Taft, and take tea with Queen Victoria. More important, he started Tuskegee Institute in Alabama and inspired generations of black Americans. *Rte. 116S to Burnt Chimney, then 6 mi 122N. Tel. 703/721–2094. Admission $1 adults, senior citizens and children free, family rate $3. Open daily 8:30–5. Closed Thanksgiving, Christmas, and New Year's.*

Back in Roanoke, you're ready for the long drive out through the rugged Highlands to Abingdon, about 135 miles to the southwest. The main route is I–81, but the longer, more scenic choice would be the Blue Ridge Parkway to I–77 to I–81. (This section of the Parkway includes the previously mentioned Mabry Mill.) Breaks along the route, or destinations in themselves, are the campgrounds, picnic areas, and lakes of the **Jefferson National Forest,** comprising 700,000 acres in patches widely scattered over this section of western Virginia and providing a habitat for bobcat, black bear, and bald eagle. The

⑬ focal point of this patchwork of parks is the **Mount Rogers National Recreation Area,** east of Abingdon, which contains the highest mountain in Virginia (5,729 feet), as well as an extensive network of trails for riding (for guided tours on horseback, *see* Participant Sports—and hiking—the Appalachian Trail crosses the border into Tennessee here. Hunting and fishing are permitted in season. *For information, contact the Forest Supervisor, 210 Franklin Rd. SW, Roanoke 24001, tel. 703/982–6270. For information on Mount Rogers only: Rte. 1, Box 303, Marion 24354, tel. 703/783–5196.*

⑭ **Abingdon** is a cultural crossroads in the wilderness, a town of 5,000 residents that draws tens of thousands of visitors annually with its fine resident theater company and exuberant local celebrations. The most popular attraction by far is the Virginia Highlands Festival in the first two weeks of August, which draws 150,000 people with its wide-ranging musical performances (everything from bluegrass to opera), exhibitions of mountain crafts, and over 100 antiques dealers. This is followed by the Burley Tobacco Festival, where country-music stars perform and prize farm animals are on proud display. *Call the Washington County Chamber of Commerce for information, including dates, which vary widely: tel. 703/628–8141.*

Throughout the summer, the prestigious **Barter Theatre** (*see* The Arts) draws an appreciative crowd. Hume Cronyn, Patricia Neal, Ernest Borgnine, and Gregory Peck are among the actors who began their careers here. The theater was organized by Robert Porterfield in 1932 to give work to penniless thespians and entertainment to cash-poor local farmers, who were welcome to barter for tickets with their surplus crops. They still accept barter, by the way.

What to See and Do with Children

Barter Theatre in Abingdon stages performances especially for kids during their regular season (*see* The Arts).
Lime Kiln Arts Theater (tel. 703/463–3074) in Lexington (*see* The Arts) stages afternoon shows for kids on the lawn of a natu-

ral amphitheater nicknamed the Baby Bowl, though it will accommodate not only toddlers but also restless older tykes.
Science Museum of Western Virginia (*see* Exploring Shenandoah Valley and the Highlands).

Off the Beaten Track

The locals in Roanoke will steer you toward more respectable and more expensive establishments, but not because they are ashamed of the **Texas Tavern** (114 Church Ave., tel. 703/342–4825); they just want to keep it to themselves. A sign says We Serve a Thousand, Ten at a Time, and indeed there are but ten stools. It is often packed, especially late at night, but wait your turn or else answer to one of the tough guys behind the counter. Chili is the specialty.

Participant Sports

Canoeing Canoe rentals are available through **Front Royal Canoe** (Rte. 340, near Front Royal, tel. 703/635–5440), **Downriver Canoe Company** (Rte. 613, near Front Royal, tel. 703/635–5526), and **Shenandoah River Outfitters** (Rte. 684, near Luray, tel. 703/743–4159).

Fishing To take advantage of the trout that abound in Shenandoah National Park—in some 50 streams—obtain a five-day Virginia fishing license, which is available in season (early April through mid-October) at concession along Skyline Drive.

Golf **Caverns Country Club Resort** (Rte. 211 in Luray, tel. 703/743–6551) has a par-72 18-hole course along the river. **Greene Hills Golf Club** (Rte. 33 in Stanardsville, tel. 804/985–7328) has an 18-hole course open to the public. **The Homestead** in Hot Springs (tel. 703/839–5500) has three.

Hiking There are 500 miles of trails through the **Shenandoah National Park.** The more popular trails are described in the guidebook available at the visitor centers.

Horseback Riding Guided tours of Mount Rogers National Recreation Area are offered by **Fairwood Stables** in Troutdale (tel. 703/677–3301).

Skiing **The Homestead** in Hot Springs (tel. 703/839–5500 or 800/336–5771) offers night skiing. **Massanutten Village Ski Resort** (off Rte. 33 in McGaheysville, tel. 703/289–9441) offers equipment rental and snowmaking.

Tennis **The Homestead** in Hot Springs (tel. 703/839–5500 or 800/336–5771) maintains 19 courts, including one all-weather. **Caverns Country Club Resort** (Rte. 211 in Luray, tel. 703/743–6551) has four courts. Many hotels throughout the region provide courts or have them nearby.

Spectator Sports

Thirty minutes northwest of Front Royal, in West Virginia, is the **Charles Town Race Track** (tel. 304/725–7001), where thoroughbred racing goes on year-round, every day except Tuesday and Thursday.

The new **Virginia Horse Center** in Lexington (tel. 703/463–2194) stages competitions—including showjumping, hunter trials, and multibreed shows—several days each week from mid-March through mid-November. Construction on a 4,000-seat indoor arena began in mid-1989.

In June and August, **jousting tournaments** are held at the Natural Chimneys area in Mt. Solon, south of Harrisonburg. The day's entertainment also includes a parade and crafts exhibitions. Admission: $2 adults, $1 children.

Dining

The most highly recommended restaurants in each price category are indicated by a star ★ .

Category	Cost*
Very Expensive	over $30
Expensive	$20–$30
Moderate	$10–$20
Inexpensive	under $10

*per person without tax (4.5% in Virginia), service, or drinks

The following credit-card abbreviations are used: AE, American Express; CB, Carte Blanche; DC, Diners Club; MC, MasterCard; V, Visa.

Abingdon **The Tavern.** This cozy, comfortable restaurant was a field hos-
American pital during the Civil War. Built in 1779, it is the oldest building in town. It has two small dining rooms, a cocktail lounge, and a dart room, all with fireplaces, stone walls, and brick floors. In warm weather, you can dine outdoors on a balcony overlooking historic Court House Hill, or on a brick patio surrounded by trees and flowers. The menu features excellent beef Wellington and rainbow trout from local waters, stuffed with crabmeat and shrimp and cooked in a white wine sauce. For dessert, try the homemade apple crisp. *222 E. Main St., tel. 703/628–1118. Dress: informal. Reservations not needed. AE, MC, V. Moderate.*

Lexington **The Palms.** Once a Victorian ice-cream parlor, this is now a full-
American service restaurant with indoor/outdoor dining. The tin ceiling is part of the original building, which dates to 1890. Wood booths line the walls of the plant-filled room. Food is prepared and presented with great care. Specialties include broccoli-cheese soup, charbroiled meats, and teriyaki chicken. There is a champagne brunch on weekends. *101 W. Nelson St., tel. 703/463–7911. Dress: informal. Reservations not needed. AE, MC, V. Inexpensive.*

Newbern **Valley Pike Inn.** This family-owned restaurant midway be-
Country tween Roanoke and Abingdon features fried chicken, country
★ baked ham, roast beef, homemade buttermilk biscuits, and old-fashioned fruit cobblers, all family-style. Wood walls and floor planks give the feeling of eating in a comfortable farmhouse. The inn was built in 1830 at an old stagecoach stop. *I–81 Exit 32, tel. 703/674–1810. Dress: informal. Reservations advised for groups of 5 or more. MC, V. Closed Mon.–Wed. Dinner only. No liquor. Inexpensive.*

Roanoke **Billy's Ritz.** A fun spot, comfortable and casual, with especially
American good soups and salads. *102 Salem Ave., tel. 703/342–3937.*

Dress: informal. Reservations not needed. AE, MC, V. Moderate.

French and Continental

★

The Library. This quiet, elegant restaurant decorated with shelves of books specializes in seafood dishes. *3117 Franklin Rd. SW (Picadilly Square shopping center), tel. 703/985–0811. Jacket required. Reservations advised. AE, CB, DC, MC, V. Closed Sun. Very Expensive.*

Staunton Country

Rowe's Family Restaurant. This homey restaurant, with a bright and comfortable dining room filled with booths, has been operated by the same family since 1947. Homemade baked goods are outstanding. Specialties include Virginia ham, steak, and chicken. *I–81 Exit 57, tel. 703/886–1833. Dress: informal. Reservations not needed. MC, V. Inexpensive.*

Warm Springs French and Regional

★

Waterwheel Restaurant. Part of a complex of five restored buildings, this restaurant is in a gristmill that dates back to 1700. A walk-in wine cellar, set among the gears of the original waterwheel, has 80 varieties of wines. The dining area is decorated with Currier and Ives and Audubon prints. Try the salmon steak, broiled and stuffed with smoked salmon, or the Chicken Fantasio, breast of chicken stuffed with wild rice, sausage, apple, and pecans. Desserts feature such old Virginia recipes as Apple Brown Betty, a deep-dish apple pie baked in bourbon. *Grist Mill Sq., tel. 703/839–2231. Dress: informal. Reservations advised. MC, V. No lunch Tues.–Thurs., Nov.–Apr. Closed Sun. and Mon. Expensive.*

Lodging

To see about staying in a private home or old, reconverted inn, contact the **Shenandoah Valley Bed & Breakfast Reservations Service** (Box 305, Broadway, VA 22815, tel. 703/896–9702). The most highly recommended properties in each price category are indicated by a star ★ .

Category	Cost*
Very Expensive	over $120
Expensive	$90–$120
Moderate	$50–$90
Inexpensive	under $50

double room, highest rate in peak season; add 4.5% for taxes

The following credit-card abbreviations are used: AE, American Express; CB, Carte Blanche; DC, Diners Club; MC, MasterCard; V, Visa.

Abingdon Very Expensive

★

Martha Washington Inn. Built in 1832 as a private house, turned into a college dormitory in 1860 and then into a field hospital during the Civil War, this spot across from the Barter Theatre has been an inn since 1935. Rooms are furnished with antiques, and some suites have fireplaces. *150 W. Main St., 24210, tel. 703/628–3161. 61 rooms with private bath, including 11 suites, some with whirlpool. Facilities: restaurant, lounge. AE, CB, DC, MC, V.*

Inexpensive **Alpine Motel.** At this remarkably clean motel, with the basic amenities, each room has a beautiful view of Virginia's two highest mountain peaks. *882 E. Main St. (I–81 Exit 9), 24210, tel. 703/628–3178. 19 rooms. Facilities: cable TV. AE, MC, V.*

Blue Ridge Parkway
Expensive
★
Doe Run Lodge. This resort at Groundhog Mountain, with beautiful vistas, is near the golf course, skiing, and hunting. *Mile Post 189, Rte. 2, Box 338, Hillsville 24343, tel. 703/398–2212. 38 condominium apartments with 2 or more bedrooms, including 7 villas. Facilities: tennis courts, outdoor pool, stocked fishing pond, restaurant open June–Oct. MC, V.*

Inexpensive
Rocky Knob Cabins. Rustic cabins with kitchens. No private baths. *Mile Post 174, Box 5, Meadows of Dan 24120, tel. 703/593–3503. DC, MC, V. Closed Labor Day–Memorial Day.*

Hot Springs
Very Expensive
★
The Homestead. Founded in 1891, this is the oldest resort in the United States and one of the most luxurious. It spreads out over 15,000 acres and includes a spa with natural mineral springs, three 18-hole golf courses, 19 tennis courts, 100 miles of riding trails, four ski slopes, four miles of streams stocked with rainbow trout, skeet shooting. All rooms are decorated in Victorian style; many have marble tubs and TV in the bathrooms. *U.S. 220, 24445, tel. 703/839–5500. 600 rooms. Facilities: 10 restaurants, one with orchestra and dancing; indoor/outdoor pools; complete health spa. AE, MC, V.*

Inexpensive
Roseloe Motel. A modest and very clean place with some kitchenettes. *Rte. 2, Box 590, 24445, tel. 703/839–5373. 14 rooms. MC, V.*

Lexington
Moderate–Expensive
Historic Country Inns. *Alexander-Withrow House,* built 1789; *McCampbell Inn,* 1809; and *Maple Hall,* 1850. All three inns are operated by the same family and decorated in period antiques, but with modern amenities. The first two, on the National Register, are across the street from each other in the historic district. The third, a former plantation house on 56 acres, is six miles north. *Main office: 11 N. Main St., 24450, tel. 703/463–2044. Facilities: TV, phone, bath in each room. Maple Hall has 3 mi of hiking trails, half-acre pond stocked with rainbow trout, outdoor pool, tennis courts, and restaurant. MC, V.*

Natural Bridge
Inexpensive–Moderate
Natural Bridge Hotel, Inn & Lodge. Within walking distance of the spectacular rock arch (though a shuttle service is offered), all three properties offer a beautiful setting and recreational facilities for the entire family. The hotel and inn have long porches with rocking chairs for enjoying views of the Blue Ridge Mountains; there's Colonial Virginia decor throughout. *U.S. 11 & Rte. 130, off I-91, Exits 49 or 50; Box 57, 24578, tel. 703/291–2121 or 800/336–5727; in VA 800/533–1410. Hotel: 90 rooms, including 2 honeymoon suites. Inn: 30 rooms. Lodge: 60 rooms. Facilities: restaurant, lounge, cafeteria, snack bar, outdoor pool, 2 tennis courts, walking trails. AE, DC, MC, V.*

Radford
Moderate
Best Western. Rooms are decorated in Colonial Virginia style, and most have views of the Valley and the Blue Ridge Mountains. *1501 Tyler Ave. (Rte. 177, Exit 35 off I–81), Box 1008, 24141, tel. 703/639–3000 or 800/528–1234. 104 rooms. Facilities: room hairdryer and phone, restaurant, lounge, indoor pool, whirlpool, sauna, gym. AE, DC, MC, V.*

Roanoke
Expensive
★
Hotel Roanoke. This Tudor-style hotel was built more than 100 years ago by the Norfolk and Southern Railroad. Although it's in the downtown area, it resembles a large, very elegant country inn. The equally elegant dining room was recently renovated. *19 N. Jefferson St., 24026, tel. 703/343–6992. 383*

rooms. *Facilities: excellent restaurant, indoor/outdoor pool.
AE, DC, MC, V.*

Moderate **Holiday Inn–Civic Center.** Convenient downtown location. *501
Orange Ave. (I–581 and Williamson Rd.), 24012. 153 rooms.
Facilities: restaurant and lounge, exercise room, outdoor pool.
AE, DC, MC, V.*

Smith Mountain   **Bernard's Landing.** This lakeside resort 45 minutes southeast
Lake   of Roanoke offers one- to three-bedroom kitchen-equipped ac-
Expensive   commodations, as well as a wealth of sporting opportunities.
*Rte. 166 off 122, Rte. 3, Box 462, Monita 24121, tel. 800/368–
3142. 62 units. Facilities: boating, sailing, fishing, swimming
(beach and pool), tennis, racquetball, sauna, Jacuzzi, weight
room, playground, restaurant. AE, MC, V.*

Staunton   **Belle Grae Inn.** At this restored Victorian mansion, built in
Moderate   1870, many rooms are furnished with rocking chairs and canopied or brass beds. Free breakfast and afternoon tea are
served. *515 W. Frederick St., 24401, tel. 703/886–5151. 12
rooms. Adults only. Facilities: bistro, with live music Wed.–
Sat., candlelight dinner in inn, light fare in garden restaurant.
AE, CB, DC, MC, V.*

★   **Frederick House.** Three restored town houses dating to 1810
make up this inn in the center of the historic district. All the
rooms are decorated with antiques. Adjacent is a pub and restaurant. *No smoking on the premises. 18 E. Frederick St.,
24401, tel. 703/885–4220. 11 rooms; each with bath, cable TV,
phones. AE, DC, MC, V.*

Warm Springs   **The Inn at Gristmill Square.** In two of five restored buildings,
Moderate–   on the same site as the Waterwheel Restaurant (*see* Dining),
Expensive   the rooms are individually decorated in Colonial Virginia style.
In addition to the inn and the restaurant, the complex has a
blacksmith's shop and a hardware store. *Rte. 645, Box 359,
24484, tel. 703/839–2231. 14 rooms, including 2 suites and 2 2-
bedroom apartments with kitchens. Facilities: restaurant,
pub, 3 tennis courts, outdoor pool, sauna. MC, V.*

The Arts

Dance   The regular company of the **Roanoke Ballet Theatre** (tel. 703/
345–6099) is joined by guest artists from around the world for
performances in spring and fall at theaters around town.

Music   **Garth Newel Music Center** in Hot Springs (tel. 703/839–5018)
runs a summer weekend chamber-music festival. Plan to picnic
on the grounds, and make reservations. There is also a special
program at Thanksgiving.

The **Roanoke Valley Chamber Music Society** (tel. 703/774–2899)
hosts distinguished visiting performers from October to May in
the Olin Theater on the campus of Roanoke College.

Theater   The **Lime Kiln Arts Theater** in Lexington (tel. 703/463–3074) is
just that: the ruins of a lime kiln—an outdoor rock-walled pit.
Here folk and classical concerts are given, in addition to performances of dramatic works both well-known and home-grown,
all summer long. The **Mill Mountain Theater** in Roanoke's Center on the Square (Market Sq., tel. 703/342–5740) is a regional
theater noted for producing the work of emerging playwrights.
The season at Abingdon's **Barter Theatre** (Main St., tel. 703/
628–2281) is April to October, with experimental productions

from June through August. Call in advance to barter for tickets, or pay the conventional way.

Nightlife

In Roanoke, **Billy's Ritz** (102 Salem Ave., tel. 703/342–3937) has pop music and a young professional crowd. At **The Homestead** in Hot Springs (U.S. 220, tel. 703/839–5500), there's ballroom dancing to live music nightly. In Abingdon, the **Act II Lounge** (150 W. Main St., tel. 703/628–3161) has dancing and entertainment nightly. The lounge is in the basement of the Martha Washington Inn and across from the Barter Theatre.

Charlottesville Area

Charlottesville is at the heart of "Mr. Jefferson's Country," as the locals proudly call it. The influence of the Sage of Monticello is inescapable anywhere in the Commonwealth (and far beyond its borders), but around here, in Albemarle County and in Orange County to the north, it is downright palpable. Also here are sites associated with other giants among his contemporaries and with crucial events in American history.

Since Jefferson founded the University of Virginia in 1819, this area has been a cultural center. The countryside has been discovered by an array of celebrities, including Jessica Lange and Sissy Spacek, who have settled here in recent years. A growing community of writers and artists is making this affluent area the "Santa Fe of the East Coast": a colony of the intellectual and the fashionable in a historic and natural setting.

Getting Around

By Plane Charlottesville-Albemarle Airport is served by **USAir** and **Henson.**

By Car Charlottesville is where U.S. 29 (north–south) meets I–64, which connects with Interstates 95 and 81.

By Train **Amtrak** trains originating in New York stop at Charlottesville's Union Station (810 W. Main St.) on the way to Chicago and to New Orleans three times a week and daily, respectively.

By Bus **Greyhound/Trailways** (310 W. Main St., tel. 804/295–5131).

Important Addresses and Numbers

Tourist Information **Thomas Jefferson Visitors Bureau and Center** (Rte. 20S, Box 161, Charlottesville, 22902, tel. 804/977–1783).

Emergencies Dial 911 for emergency assistance.

Hospitals Emergency rooms at **Martha Jefferson Hospital** (459 Locust Ave., tel. 804/293–0193) and **University of Virginia Hospital** (Jefferson Park Ave., tel. 804/924–2231) are open 24 hours.

Minor Emergencies **Prompt Care** (210 Hydraulic Rd., tel. 804/296–2273).

Exploring the Charlottesville Area

Start at the **Thomas Jefferson Visitors Center,** where you can get oriented. The people here are glad to answer your questions about attractions and accommodations in the area and the whole state. A free extensive permanent exhibition, "Thomas Jefferson at Monticello," provides background on the house and its legendary occupant. On display are artifacts recovered during recent archaeological excavations. Do not miss it, before or after Monticello; it will make the experience at least twice as rich, since there is so much that is not explained on the tour. *Rte. 20S from Charlottesville (Monticello exit off I–64), tel. 804/977–1783. Open weekdays 9–5 (until 5:30 Mar.–Oct.) Closed Thanksgiving, Christmas, and New Year's.*

Monticello is the most famous of Jefferson's homes, and his lasting monument to himself—an ingenious masterpiece created over more than 40 years. Not typical of any style, it is characteristic of Jefferson, who made a statement with every detail: the staircases are narrow and hidden because he considered them unsightly and wasteful of space, and contrary to plantation tradition, his outbuildings are in the back, not on the east side, where his guests arrived. In these respects, as in its very essence, Monticello was a subversive structure, a classical repudiation of the prevalent English Georgian style as well as of the colonial mentality behind it.

As if to reflect this revolutionary aspect, a concave mirror in the entrance hall presents you with your own image upside down. Throughout the house are Jefferson's inventions, including a seven-day clock and a "polygraph," a two-pen contraption with which he could make a copy of his correspondence as he wrote it. The Thomas Jefferson Center for Historic Plants features interpretive gardens, exhibits, and a sales area. The tour guides are happy to answer questions, but they have to move you through quickly since there is always another group waiting. It is impossible to see everything in one visit. *On Rte. 53 (off Rte. 20), 2 mi southeast of Charlottesville, tel. 804/295–8181 or 295–2657. Admission: $7 adults, $6 senior citizens, $2 children and military. Open daily 9–4:30 Nov.–Feb., 8–5 rest of year. Closed Christmas.*

Like its grand neighbor, modest **Ash Lawn** is marked by the personality of its owner. This is not the simple farmhouse built for James Monroe: he lived in the small L-shaped single story at the rear. A subsequent owner added the more prominent two-story section. Yet the furnishings are mostly original, and it is not hard to imagine him here at his beloved retreat. The small rooms are crowded with presents from notable contemporaries and souvenirs from his time as envoy to France. Such coziness befits the fifth president, the first from the middle class. Today Ash Lawn is a working plantation. Spectacular peacocks roam the grounds. *On Rte. 795 (off Rte. 53), 2 mi past Monticello, tel. 804/293-9539. Admission: $6 adults, $5.50 senior citizens, $2 children. Open daily 9–6 Mar.–Oct., 10–5 rest of year. Closed Thanksgiving, Christmas, and New Year's.*

Because of its proximity to Monticello and Ash Lawn, **The Historic Michie Tavern** also has become a popular attraction. Most of the complex was constructed in 1784 at Earlysville, 17 miles away, and moved here piece by piece in 1927. Costumed hostesses lead you into a series of rooms, where you hear recorded interpretations of the interiors. A visit here is not as entertaining or educational as the tour of the Rising Sun Tavern in Fredericksburg (*see* Exploring Northern Virginia): the narration is less informative, and the conditions are too tidy. The restaurant serves mediocre "Colonial" fare (fried chicken) for lunch. The old gristmill has a gift shop. *On Rte. 53 near Monticello, tel. 804/977-1234. Admission: $4.50 adults; $4 senior citizens, students, and the military; $2 children under 12. Open daily 9–5. Closed Christmas and New Year's.*

There's not really a whole lot to see in Charlottesville itself, though the visitor center on Route 20 (*see* Important Addresses and Numbers) does have a walking-tour map of the downtown historic district. The center also has a complete list of crafts and antiques shops, of which the city has a nice supply. The main shopping area is the Downtown Mall, spread along six blocks of Main Street. Fountains, outdoor restaurants, and restored buildings line the street, which has been bricked over and restricted to pedestrians. Among the area's unique shops are **Lewis Glaser Quill Pens** (107 W. Main St., tel. 804/293–8531), which sells feather pens and pewter inkwells, and **Paula Lewis** (4th and Jefferson Sts., in Historic Court Square, 2 blocks north of Main St., tel. 804/295–6244), which specializes in handmade quilts from across the country.

At the west end of town is the **University of Virginia,** one of the most distinguished institutions of higher education in the nation. It was founded and designed by Thomas Jefferson, who called himself its "father" in his own epitaph. Experts polled during the U.S. Bicentennial named his campus "the proudest achievement of American architecture in the past 200 years." You will be struck by the innovative beauty of the "academical village": it is subtle—almost delicate—and totally practical. Students vie for rooms among the original pavilions that flank the Lawn, a graduated expanse that flows down from the Rotunda, a half-scale replica of the Pantheon in Rome. Behind the pavilions are gardens and landscaping laced with serpentine walls. To arrange a free one-hour tour, call 804/924–3239.

Time Out Have lunch with UVA students at one of their haunts: **Martha's Café** (11 Elliewood Ave., tel. 804/971–7530). Try the enchiladas or a vegetarian entree. In warm weather, ask for a table on the patio, where the plantings are lush and appealing.

About an hour north of Charlottesville is another presidential residence, recently opened to the public. Originally the home of James Madison, **Montpelier** in its present condition has more to do with its 20th-century owners, the du Pont family, who enlarged and redecorated it. This dual legacy poses a dilemma in the restoration, since the house only vaguely resembles itself in Madison's day. Markings on walls, floors, and ceilings show the locations of underlying door and window frames, etc., as a preliminary step to future restoration work. The process of restoration is slow, to the credit of the painstaking preservationists of the National Trust. In the meantime, it takes your imagination and your guide's eloquent narration to appreciate the history of this mostly empty house.

The house can be seen only on a 1½- to 2-hour guided tour, which begins with a slide show on the history of the house, then takes you on a shuttle-bus tour of the farm and paddock area, followed by a tour of the mansion and another slide show, free time to wander the delightful grounds and gardens, and a shuttle-bus tour of the cemetery where James, Dolley, and other Madisons are buried. *On Rte. 20, outside the town of Orange, tel. 703/672–2728 or 672–2206. Admission: $5 adults; $4* *senior citizens; $1 children 6–12, under 6 free. Open daily 10–4. Closed major holidays.*

Less than two hours south of Charlottesville is an American shrine. The village of **Appomattox Court House** has been restored to its appearance on April 9, 1865, when Lee surrendered the Army of Northern Virginia to Grant. There are 27 structures, including the McLean House, in whose parlor the articles of surrender were signed. The self-guided tour is well mapped out and introduced by exhibits and slide shows in the reconstructed courthouse. First-person interpreters cast as soldiers and villagers answer questions in summer. *U.S. 29S to U.S. 460E to Rte. 24, tel. 804/352–8782. Admission: $1 adults, senior citizens and children free. Open daily 9–5, Mar. –Dec. Closed major holidays.*

What to See and Do with Children

At Charlottesville's **Virginia Discovery Museum,** kids can step inside a giant kaleidoscope or basketball star Ralph Sampson's actual uniform. Plays and musical performances are given, in addition to the permanent hands-on exhibits that are supposed to develop both the imagination and such everyday skills as tying shoes. *400 Ackley Lane, tel. 804/293–5528. Admission: $3 adults, $2 senior citizens and children. Open Tues.–Sat. 10– 4:30, Sun. 1:30–4:30. Closed Mon.*

Participant Sports

Golf **McIntire Park Golf Course** (tel. 804/977–4111) and **Pen Park Golf Course** (tel. 804/977–0615) offer nine holes each.

Tennis **The Boar's Head Inn** (*see* Lodgings) offers tennis to nonguests as well as guests. There are **public courts** at the intersection of 250 Bypass and McIntire Road and in Pen Park at Park Street and Rio Road (tel. 804/977–0615).

Spectator Sports

The **University of Virginia** is nationally or regionally ranked in several varsity sports. In season, you can watch the Cavaliers play first-rate ACC basketball in University Hall. There's also football at Scott Stadium, plus baseball, soccer, lacrosse, and more. Check *The Cavalier Daily* for listings.

Dining

All of the restaurants listed are in Charlottesville unless otherwise noted.

The most highly recommended restaurants in each price category are indicated by a star ★.

Category	Cost*
Very Expensive	over $30
Expensive	$20–$30

Moderate	$10–$20
Inexpensive	under $10

*per person without tax (4.5% in Virginia), service, or drinks

The following credit-card abbreviations are used: AE, American Express; CB, Carte Blanche; DC, Diners Club; MC, MasterCard; V, Visa.

Very Expensive
French
★
C&O Restaurant. A boarded-up storefront hung with an illuminated Pepsi sign conceals one of the best restaurants in town. Downstairs is a lively bistro serving pâtés, cheeses, and light meals. The stark white formal dining room upstairs features excellent regional French cuisine. Recommended are the coquilles St. Jacques—steamed scallops served in a sauce made of grapefruit juice, cream, and Dijon mustard—and, for an appetizer, the *terrine de campagne*, a pâté of veal, venison, and pork. The wine list includes 300 varieties. *515 E. Water St., tel. 804/971–7044. Upstairs, tie and jacket required; downstairs, informal. Reservations advised. Seatings at 6:30 and 9:30 for dining room. MC, V. Closed Sun.*

The Galerie. Set amid woods and cornfields seven miles from town is an elegant restaurant reminiscent of a French country inn. Specialties include Norwegian salmon with raspberry and lime sauce; duckling braised in port wine and shallot sauce; and rich desserts like *vacherin glacé*—layers of grilled meringue and French vanilla ice cream topped with unsweetened whipped cream and chestnut sauce. The wine list includes 190 varieties. *Rte. 250W, tel. 804/823–5883. Tie and jacket required. Reservations advised. MC, V. Closed Mon. and Tues.*

Expensive
American
Old Mill Room. In a onetime gristmill (built in 1834), prints and posters of the mill, a fireplace, and wrought-iron chandeliers set the mood as waiters and waitresses in Colonial dress serve such offerings as prime rib and veal Oscar—veal topped with crabmeat, asparagus spears, and béarnaise sauce. Light meals are served in the Tavern downstairs. *In the Boar's Head Inn, U.S. 250W (3 mi from town), tel. 804/296–2181. Dress: informal. Reservations advised. AE, CB, DC, MC, V.*

International
★
Eastern Standard. Here's another restaurant with a formal dining room upstairs and a bistro downstairs. Dining room specialties include rainbow trout stuffed with shiitake mushrooms, wild rice, and fontina cheese; oysters cooked in a champagne and caviar sauce; and loin of lamb with mint pesto. Curries and stirfried Asian dishes are also offered. The bistro is crowded and lively, with taped music, primarily jazz and rock. It serves pastas and light meals. *West End, Downtown Mall, tel. 804/295–8668. Dress: informal. Reservations advised for dining room. AE, MC, V. Dinner only. Upstairs closed Sun.*

Moderate
American
The Hardware Store. Deli sandwiches, burgers, salads, seafood, and ice cream from the soda fountain are the specialties in this former Victorian hardware shop. The store was built in 1890, and some of the original wood paneling and brick walls remain. There's outdoor dining in the warm months. *316 E. Main St., tel. 804/977–1518. Dress: informal. Reservations not needed. MC, V. Closed Sun. No dinner Mon.*

Pizza
Crozet Pizza. Twelve miles west of Charlottesville, you'll find some of Virginia's best pizza. There are 18 different toppings to

choose from, including snow peas and asparagus spears. On weekends take-out must be ordered hours in advance. *Rte. 240, Crozet, tel. 804/823–2132. Dress: informal. Reservations not needed. No credit cards. Closed Sun. and Mon. Moderate.*

Lodging

A B&B service for the area is **Guesthouse Bed & Breakfast, Inc.** (Box 5737, Charlottesville 22905, tel. 804/979–7264 or 979–8327). The most highly recommended properties in each price category are indicated by a star ★.

Category	Cost*
Very Expensive	over $120
Expensive	$90–$120
Moderate	$50–$90
Inexpensive	under $50

*double room, highest rate in peak season; add 4.5% for taxes

The following credit-card abbreviations are used: AE, American Express; CB, Carte Blanche; DC, Diners Club; MC, MasterCard; V, Visa.

Downtown Charlottesville
Very Expensive

Omni Charlottesville. A recent addition to the luxury chain, this attractive hotel looms over the Downtown Mall. The decor is a mixture of modern and Colonial. *235 W. Main St., 22901, tel. 804/971–5500. 209 rooms. Facilities: multilevel restaurant, bilevel lounge with live entertainment, atrium lobby lounge, indoor/outdoor pools, fitness center with saunas, whirlpool, exercise room. AE, CB, DC, MC, V.*

200 South Street Inn. Two historic houses, one of them a former brothel, have been combined and restored to create this old-fashioned inn in the historic district. Furnishings throughout are English and Belgian antiques. Many rooms have private sitting rooms, fireplaces, and whirlpools. *200 South St., 22901, tel. 804/979–0200. 20 rooms, all with private bath and canopy beds. AE, MC, V.*

Near the University
Expensive

University Hilton. An elegant hotel a mile from town. *2350 Seminole Trail (U.S. 29, 3 mi north of jct. Rte. 250 Bypass), 22901, tel. 804/973–2121. 252 rooms. Facilities: indoor/outdoor pools, 2 tennis courts, jogging trails, 2 restaurants, lounge. AE, DC, MC, V.*

Moderate

Best Western–Cavalier Inn. Next to the university and an easy drive to Monticello. *105 Emmet St., Box 5647, 22905, tel. 804/296–8111 or 800/528–1234. 118 rooms. Facilities: outdoor pool, restaurant and lounge, cable TV. AE, DC, MC, V.*

★ **English Inn.** This inn is a motel treatment of the bed-and-breakfast theme on a large but comfortable scale. Breakfast is a full country buffet, served in a 150-year-old, transplanted Tudor-style dining room with fireplace. There's an attractive three-story atrium lobby with cascading plants. Suites feature king-size beds and reproduction antiques; the other rooms have modern furnishings. *2000 Morton Dr. (jct. U.S. 29 and Rte. 250 Bypass), 22901, tel. 804/971–9900. 88 rooms, including 21 king suites with sitting room and wet bar. Facilities: large indoor* *pool, sauna, exercise equipment, restaurant lounge, cable TV. AE, CB, DC, MC, V.*

Inexpensive **Econo Lodge.** Basic chain lodgings next to the university. *400 Emmet St., 22903, tel. 804/296–2104. 60 rooms. Facilities: outdoor pool. AE, DC, MC, V.*

Farther Afield **Boar's Head Inn.** At this luxurious, quiet resort on two small
Expensive lakes, rooms and suites are simple but elegant, furnished mostly with antiques. Some suites have fireplaces, some are efficiencies, and some rooms have king- or queen-size beds. *U.S. 250 (3 mi from town), Box 5307, Charlottesville 22905, tel. 804/296–2181. 175 rooms, 11 suites. Facilities: 5 restaurants (see Dining); complete health club, with 3 pools, squash and racquetball courts, tennis; biking; fishing; hot-air balloon rides. AE, CB, DC, MC, V.*

★ **Mayhurst.** This old Victorian building is a cozy and comfortable B&B about a half-hour northeast of Monticello, surrounded by 36 acres of woods and hiking trails. It was built in 1859 by the grandnephew of James Madison. All the rooms are decorated with early Victorian antiques. Afternoon tea is served. *Box 707 (U.S. 15), Orange 22960, tel. 703/672–5597. 6 rooms with private bath, and a guesthouse. Facilities: pond for fishing and swimming. MC, V.*

The Arts

Dance, music, and theater events of every kind take place all year at the **University of Virginia.** Check *The Cavalier Daily* for details. The **McGuffey Art Center** (201 2nd St., NW, tel. 804/295–7933), housed in a converted school building, contains the studios of painters and sculptors, and is also the scene of musical and theatrical performances.

Nightlife

Folk **Miller's** (109 W. Main St. Downtown Mall, tel. 804/971–8511) is a large and comfortable bar that also hosts jazz musicians.

Jazz At the nightclub downstairs in the **C&O** (515 E. Water St., tel. 804/971–7044), they play not just jazz but often rock, R&B, bluegrass, and even reggae.

Rock The **Mine Shaft** (1107 W. Main St., tel. 804/977–6656) has a dance floor and a lineup of regional bands.

Singles Postgraduate students are strongly represented at the bar at **Eastern Standard** (Downtown Mall, tel. 804/295–8668).

Northern Virginia

Much of this region has been subsumed into the official and residential life of Washington, DC, and has prospered as a result. The affluent and cosmopolitan Northern Virginians are somewhat estranged from the rest of the Commonwealth, yet they are proud of their distinction as Virginians. As their economy grows, they are protecting the historic treasures they hold in trust for the rest of the nation.

Old Town Alexandria remains apparently unsuburbanized; its hundreds of 18th- and 19th-century buildings are collectively listed in the National Register of Historic Places. Fairfax and

Arlington counties are thriving as satellites of Washington (Tyson's Corner in Fairfax County now has more commercial office space than Miami, Florida) and contain some of America's most precious acreage: Mount Vernon and Arlington Cemetery, respectively. Fredericksburg, only an hour from the nation's capital, seems much farther away: a quiet, well-preserved Southern town, with a 40-block National Historic District. But Fredericksburg was once the bloody scene of conflict, as was Manassas (Bull Run), 26 miles from Washington—site of some of the most savage battles of the Civil War. The gracious lifestyle of the old South survives in Loudoun County, less than an hour from Washington, where fox hunting and steeplechasing fill leisure hours.

Getting Around

By Plane **Washington National Airport** in Arlington is served by all major U.S. airlines. **Washington Dulles International Airport** in Loudoun County has departures for most destinations in this country and the world.

By Car I–95 runs north–south along the eastern side of the region. I–66 runs east–west, perpendicular to I–95, cutting off the top third of the region.

By Train There are **Amtrak** stations in Alexandria (110 Callahan Dr.) and Fredericksburg (Caroline St. and Lafayette Blvd.)

By Bus **Greyhound/Trailways:** Fairfax (4103 Rust St., tel. 703/273–7770), Fredericksburg (1400 Jefferson Davis Hwy., tel. 703/373–2103), Springfield (6583 Backlick Rd., tel. 703/451–5800).

Guided Tours

Guided walking tours of Alexandria from April through November 30 begin at the Ramsay House Visitor's Center (221 King St., tel. 703/838–4200). You can take a guided bus tour of Fredericksburg, for one or two hours, departing from the Visitor's Center (706 Caroline St., tel. 703/373–1776 or 800/678–4748).

Important Addresses and Numbers

Tourist Information **Alexandria Tourist Council,** at the Ramsay House Visitor's Center, 221 King St., Alexandria 22314, tel. 703/549–0205. Open daily 9–5. **Arlington Visitor's Center,** 735 S. 18th St., Arlington 22202, tel. 703/521–0772. Open daily 9–5. **Fairfax County Tourism and Convention Bureau,** 8300 Boone Blvd., Suite 450, Vienna 22180, tel. 703/790–0600. Open daily 9–5. **Fredericksburg Visitor's Center,** 706 Caroline St., Fredericksburg 22401, tel. 703/373–1776. Open daily 8:45–7 mid-June through Labor Day; 9–5 rest of year. All closed major holidays.

Emergencies Dial 911 for emergency assistance.

Minor Emergencies In Fredericksburg, the **Medic 1 Clinic** is at 3429 Jefferson Davis Highway (tel. 703/371–1664).

Exploring Northern Virginia

Numbers in the margin correspond with points of interest on the Northern Virginia map.

First in war, first in peace, and first on our tour is George **①** Washington, whose **Mount Vernon,** 16 miles south of the city that bears his name, is today the most visited house museum in the United States. About 30% of the furnishings are original; the rest are carefully selected and authenticated antiques.

Washington considered himself, first and foremost, a farmer. His farmhouse was a formal one, certainly, but none of the embellishments disguised the noble practicality of its purpose. In the ornate dining room, guests ate at simple trestle tables assembled from boards and sawhorses. More of a sage than an intellectual, he read mostly for practical reference; his enormous library of 900 volumes (now mostly dispersed) was composed largely of presents from the authors. The outbuildings are precisely restored, including the kitchen and stable, and a bit farther on are the graves of George and Martha Washington, laid to rest in the land they loved so well. *From DC, take any Virginia-side bridge to the George Washington Memorial Pkwy. (which becomes Mt. Vernon Memorial Hwy. to the south) and follow signs, tel. 703/780–2000. Admission: $5 adults, $4 senior citizens, $2 children under 12. Open daily 9–5 Mar.–Oct., 9–4 rest of year.*

Near Mount Vernon—on land given by Washington to his nephew Lawrence Lewis and step-daughter, Nelly Custis, as a **②** wedding gift—is **Woodlawn.** Designed by the architect of the Capitol, William Thornton, to resemble Lewis's boyhood home, Kenmore, in Fredericksburg, it was begun in 1800, then furnished well but not lavishly, to accommodate and entertain a family of many children. Today, the formal gardens are well maintained and include a large collection of rare old-fashioned roses. *14 mi south of DC on U.S. 1, and 3 mi from Mount Vernon on the George Washington Memorial Pkwy., tel. 703/557–7880. Admission: $4 adults, $3 senior citizens and students. Open daily 9:30–4:30. Closed Thanksgiving, Christmas, and New Year's.*

Also on the grounds of Woodlawn is the **Pope-Leighey House,** **③** designed by Frank Lloyd Wright and built in 1940. It has no Washington-family connection; it is here because when highway construction augured its destruction on its original site nearby, the National Trust stepped in and moved it to Woodlawn, where it makes a nice contrast to the Federal mansion. The longer you look around and the more that is explained, the more of its peculiar beauty is revealed. It is not to every taste, but it *is* an architectural education. *Tel. 703/557–7880. Admission: $4 adults, $3 senior citizens and students. Open daily 9:30–4:30 Mar.–Dec., weekends only Jan. and Feb. Combined ticket to Woodlawn and Pope-Leighey House: $7 adults, $5.50 senior citizens and students.*

Unlike Mount Vernon, **Gunston Hall,** 15 miles away in Lorton, **④** is rarely crowded with visitors. This was the home of a lesser-known George: George Mason, father of the Bill of Rights. He was one of the framers of the Constitution, then refused to sign it because it did not prohibit slavery, adequately restrain the powers of the federal government, or include a bill of rights. The interior, with its carved woodwork in styles from Chinese to Gothic, has been meticulously restored, with paints made from the original recipes and with carefully carved replacements for the intricate mahogany medallions in the moldings. The grounds—with formal gardens featuring large boxwood

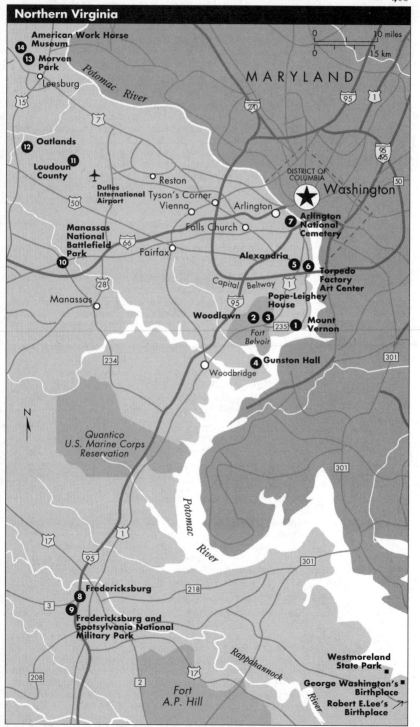

hedges—may look familiar, since the last scene in the 1987 movie *Broadcast News* was filmed here, by the gazebo. *U.S. 1S to VA 242S, tel. 703/550-9220. Admission: $3 adults, $2.50 senior citizens, $1 children. Open daily 9:30-5. Closed Christmas.*

5 Nine miles north of Mount Vernon is **Alexandria,** where the Mount Vernon Memorial Highway becomes the George Washington Memorial Parkway. Established in 1749, this city once dwarfed Georgetown, which is just across the Potomac. That was before the Revolution. Today Alexandria proudly maintains an identity separate from that of the federal capital. The historic area is Old Town; its main arteries are Washington Street (the parkway as it passes through town) and King Street, which divide the town east–west and north–south, respectively. The shopping (art, antiques, and specialty) is of high quality, as are the sights. Most points of interest are on the east (Potomac) side of Washington Street. Visit them on foot if you are prepared to walk for 20 blocks or so. Parking is usually scarce, but the Tourist Council (*see* Important Addresses and Numbers) will give you a 72-hour parking permit for the two-hour metered zones, along with a walking tour map and other information.

Among the town's attractions is the **boyhood home of Robert E. Lee,** where he lived off and on for 13 years. The 1795 Georgian town house is furnished in antiques that reflect life in the 1820s. *607 Oronoco St., tel. 703/548-8454. Admission: $2 adults, $1.50 senior citizens, $1 children. Open Mon.–Sat. 10-4, Sun. noon-4. Closed Thanksgiving and Dec. 15–Feb. 1.*

Across the street is the **Lee-Fendall House,** built in 1785 by an in-law and lived in by Lees until 1903. The interior reflects styles from a variety of periods and includes Lee-family furnishings. Labor leader John L. Lewis lived here from 1937 until 1969. *614 Oronoco St., tel. 703/548-1789. Admission: $2 adults, $1 children. Open Tues.–Sat. 10-3:45, Sun. noon-3:45. Closed holidays.*

Christ Church looks much the same as it did when George Washington worshiped here. His pew and that of Robert E. Lee, who was confirmed in the church, are marked by silver commemorative plates. The churchyard contains the graves of several Confederate dead, among others. *Washington and Columbus Sts. at Cameron St., tel. 703/549-1450. Admission free. Open Mon.–Sat. 9-5, Sun. noon-4:30. Closed (except for services) major holidays.*

Time Out   Take a break for a pint of Guinness or Harp and perhaps a ploughman's lunch (pickles and cheese) at **Murphy's Grand Irish Pub** (713 King St., tel. 703/548-1717). At night this brickwalled pub and restaurant, on two floors of an 18th-century building, resounds with an Irish sing-along.

Gadsby's Tavern Museum comprises two buildings: the tavern and the hotel. The former was built in 1770, 22 years before the latter. General Washington reviewed his troops for the last time from the steps of this building. Lafayette was entertained here during his 1824 visit. The rooms in the tavern have been convincingly restored to their appearance in the 1790s. *134 N. Royal St., tel. 703/838-4242. Admission: $2 adults, $1 children. Open Tues.–Sat. 10-5, Sun. 1-5. Closed major holidays.*

Modern Alexandria is represented by the extremely popular
❻ **Torpedo Factory Art Center.** About 170 artists and craftsmen
have their studios (with wares for sale) within this renovated
waterfront building where torpedo parts were manufactured
during the two world wars. The center also houses exhibits of
the city's archaeology program (one of the nation's largest and
oldest) and laboratories, where you can observe work in progress. *105 N. Union St., tel. 703/838–4565. Admission free.
Center: open daily 10–5 except major holidays. Archaeology
Section: open Tues.–Sat. 10–5; lab open Fri.–Sat. 11–5.*

From Alexandria, proceed northward on the Parkway and take
in the skyline of Washington, DC across the river. This is the
single best, most comprehensive panorama of the famous buildings and monuments in the nation's capital. At Memorial
Bridge, cross over into Washington and turn back around. It is
worth leaving Virginia for just a moment in order to make this
❼ most impressive approach to **Arlington National Cemetery.** Directly behind you, on the Washington side, is the Lincoln
Memorial; ahead, high atop a hill, is Robert E. Lee's Arlington
House, and a little below it is the eternal flame that marks the
grave of John F. Kennedy. All are in line with the bridge. The
symbolism of this arrangement is stunning.

In the cemetery are thousands of veterans buried beneath simple white headstones. The many famous Americans interred
here include President Taft, Oliver Wendell Holmes, George C.
Marshall, Joe Louis, and John and Robert Kennedy. In and
around the Tomb of the Unknown Soldier are the graves of men
killed in both world wars, Korea, and Vietnam. It is guarded
constantly by members of the Old Guard: 1st Battalion (Reinforced), 3d Infantry. A changing-of-the-guard ceremony takes
place every half-hour from 8 to 5. Apr.–Sept., hourly the rest of
the year. *Tel. 703/545–6700. Admission free. Open daily 8–5
Nov.–Mar., 8–7 rest of year.*

Within the cemetery is **Arlington House,** where Robert E. Lee
lived for 30 years, until his job obliged him to leave the proximity of the Union capital. The Union confiscated the estate during
the Civil War, when Arlington began to function as a cemetery.
The massive house is of Greek Revival design, reminiscent of a
temple, and is furnished in antiques and reproductions. The
view of Washington from the portico is as gorgeous as the sight
of the house from the bridge. *Tel. 703/557–0613. Admission
free. Open daily 9:30–4:30 Oct.–Mar., 9:30–6 rest of year.
Closed Christmas and New Year's.*

A narrated bus tour of Arlington National Cemetery, with
stops at Arlington House, the Tomb of the Unknown Soldier,
and the Kennedy graves, is given by Tourmobile (tel. 202/554–
7950). Tours leave from the visitor center on the site starting at
8:30 AM. Cost: $2.50 adults, $1.25 children.

❽ Fifty miles south of Washington on I–95 is **Fredericksburg,**
which rivals Alexandria and Mount Vernon for Washington-
family associations. The first president lived at nearby Ferry
Farm (across the Rappahannock River) between the ages of six
and 16 and later bought a house for his mother here, near his
sister and brother.

Washington's only sister, Betty, married her cousin Fielding
Lewis in 1750, and they built **Kenmore** a few years later. The
plain exterior belies the lavish interior; these have been called

some of the most beautiful rooms in America. The plaster moldings in the ceilings are outstanding and even more ornate than Mount Vernon's. Of equal elegance are the furnishings, including a large standing clock that belonged to Betty's mother, Mary. In the reconstructed kitchen next door you can enjoy tea and Mary Washington's gingerbread after the tour. *1201 Washington Ave., tel. 703/373-3381. Admission: $4 adults, $2 children. Open daily 9–5 Mar.–Nov., 10–4 rest of year. Closed Christmas Eve and Day, and New Year's Eve and Day.*

In 1760, George Washington's brother Charles built as his home what became the **Rising Sun Tavern,** a watering hole for such pre-Revolutionary patriots as the Lee brothers, Patrick Henry, Washington, and Jefferson. A "wench" in period costume leads the tour without stepping out of character. From her perspective you watch the activity—day and night, upstairs and down—at this busy institution. In the tap room, you are served spiced tea. *1306 Caroline St., tel. 703/371-1494. Admission: $2 adults, 50¢ children. Open daily 9–5 Mar.–Nov., 10–4 rest of year. Closed Thanksgivng, Christmas Eve and Day, and New Year's Eve and Day.*

On Charles Street is the modest white **Home of Mary Washington.** George purchased it for her in 1772, and she spent the last 17 years of her life here, tending the charming garden where her boxwood still flourishes and where many a bride and groom now come to exchange their vows. *1200 Charles St., tel. 703/373-1569. Admission: $2 adults, 50¢ children. Open daily 9–5 Mar.–Nov., 10–4 rest of year. Closed Thanksgiving, Christmas Eve and Day, and New Year's Eve and Day.*

Dr. Mercer might have been more careful than most other Colonial physicians, yet his methods will make you cringe. At his **Apothecary Shop,** a costumed hostess will explicitly describe amputations and cataract operations. You will also hear about therapeutic bleeding and see the gruesome devices used in Colonial dentistry. This is an informative if slightly nauseating look at life two centuries ago. *Caroline and Amelia Sts., tel. 703/371-3486. Admission: $2 adults, 50¢ students. Open daily 9–5 Mar.–Nov., 10–4 rest of year. Closed Thanksgiving, Christmas Eve and Day, and New Year's Eve and Day.*

The **James Monroe Museum and Memorial Library** is the tiny one-story building where the man who was to be the fifth president of the United States practiced law from 1787 to 1789. In this building are many of Monroe's possessions, collected and preserved by his family until this century, including the desk on which Monroe signed the doctrine named for him. *908 Charles St., tel. 703/373-8426. Admission: $2.50 adults, 50¢ children. Open daily 9–5. Closed Thanksgiving, Christmas Eve and Day, and New Year's Eve and Day.*

Time Out   Stop for a gourmet sandwich or some quiche at the **Made in Virginia Store Deli** (807 Caroline St., tel. 703/371-2030). Do not skip the rich desserts.

Four nearby Civil War battlefields—Fredericksburg, Chancellorsville, the Wilderness, and Spotsylvania Courthouse—
➒ constitute the **Fredericksburg and Spotsylvania National Military Park.** All are within 17 miles of Fredericksburg. At the in-town visitor's center for the park, there's a slide show about the battles and look at two floors of exhibits. On the fields, signs

and exhibits point out moments in the battles. *1013 Lafayette Blvd. (U.S. 1), tel. 703/373–4461. Admission free. Open 8:30–6:30 June 15–Labor Day, weekdays, 9–5 and weekends 9–6 rest of year. Closed Christmas and New Year's.*

Heading west from Washington instead of south brings you to another major Civil War battlefield: **Manassas National Battlefield Park.** The self-guided tour begins at the visitor center, which offers exhibits and audiovisual presentations that greatly enhance the visit. Here the Confederacy won two important victories—and Stonewall Jackson won his famous nickname. It's a 26-mile drive: take I–66 west to Route 234 (don't be fooled by the earlier Manassas exit for Route 28); the visitor center is half a mile north on the right. *Tel. 703/754–7107. Admission: $1 adults, children under 12 and senior citizens free. The visitor center is open daily 8:30–6 in summer, 8:30–5 rest of year; the park is open until dusk.*

After Manassas, return to I–66, following it west to U.S. 15, the road to horse country. The major towns here, in **Loudoun County,** are Leesburg and Middleburg, where residents claim the living is some of the best in Virginia and prove it with their gracious homes, fox hunts, and steeplechases. Touring the well-tended countryside is a pleasure; its history is detailed in exhibits at the **Loudoun County Museum and Visitors Center** in Leesburg (16 W. Loudoun St., tel. 703/777–0519). This is the place to pick up information on scenic drives and area attractions. Of the latter, three in particular capture the horsey atmosphere of this fine green county.

Oatlands, six miles south of Leesburg on U.S. 15, is a former 5,000-acre plantation built by a great-grandson of the famous King Carter. In 1827, a stately portico was added to the original 1803 manor house. The house has been beautifully restored, and the manicured fields that remain host a variety of public and private equestrian events from spring to fall—including April's popular Loudoun Hunt Point-to-Point, a steeplechase that brings out the whole community for picnics on blankets and tailgates, and Draft Horse and Mule Day in late summer, when competing teams flex their muscles in pulling contests and craftspeople spread out their wares for an all-day fair. *Tel. 703/777–3174. Admission: $5 adults, $4 students and senior citizens; children under 12 free weekdays. Other charges apply for special events. Open Mon.–Sat. 10–5, Sun. 1–5. Closed from just before Christmas until mid-Mar.*

A mile north of Leesburg is **Morven Park,** a mansion open to the public, as well as a stronghold of horsedom: The **Westmoreland Davis Equestrian Institute** (a private riding school), the **Winmill Carriage Museum** (boasting over 100 horse-drawn vehicles), and the **Museum of Hounds and Hunting** make their home on this 1,200-acre estate. The price of admission includes entrance to 16 rooms in the mansion and the two museums. *Rte. 7 north from Leesburg, then follow signs, tel. 703/777–2414. Admission: $4 adults, $3.75 children, $2 senior citizens. Open Tues.–Sat. 10–5, Sun. 1–5 Memorial Day–Labor Day. Closed mid-Oct.–first week in May, weekends only at other times (call ahead).*

This may be Thoroughbred country, but the workhorse gets his day in the sun at Paeonian Springs's **American Work Horse Museum,** where two enormous live Clydesdales greet visitors.

Here, the exhibits point out this unsung hero's contributions to the growth of our nation. *Rte. 7 west from Leesburg to Rte. 662, tel. 703/338–6290. Admission free. Open Wed. 9–5 Apr.–Oct., other times by appointment.*

What to See and Do with Children

The **Pet Farm Park** in Vienna, Fairfax County, is inhabited by ostriches, giant tortoises, baboons, zebras, and other exotica, plus domestic farm animals. The whole family can take a hayride, and there are pony and elephant rides for the children. *Adjacent to Lake Fairfax, on Hunter Mill Rd., at the intersection of Leesburg Pike (Rte. 7) and Rte. 606, tel. 703/759–3636 or 759–3637. Admission: $4.95 adults; $3.95 senior citizens and children, under 2 free. Open daily 10–5 May 15–Labor Day; weekdays 10–3, weekends 10–5 rest of year.*

At **Wolf Trap Farm Park,** also in Vienna (Rte. 7, I–495 Exit 10W), performances for children—including mime, puppets, animal shows, music, drama, and storytelling—are held throughout the year. The first Saturday of each month from October through May, there are two shows a day in The Barns ($4; tel. 703/255–1939). From mid-July through August, daily performances take place at the outdoor Theater in the Woods (admission free; tel. 703/255–1823). On Labor Day weekend, a three-day International Children's Festival brings together performers from the States and abroad (admission per day: $6 adults, $4 children; tel. 703/255–1939).

Off the Beaten Track

On display at Alexandria's 333-foot-high **George Washington Masonic National Memorial** is furniture and regalia that Washington used while Charter Master of the local Masonic Lodge. Exhibits that demystify the legendary international organization, explaining its traditions, aims, and activities—unless there is something they are not telling us. Every 45 minutes until 4 PM, an elevator tour takes you to the top for a singular view of the town and Washington nearby. *A 20-min walk from the river, or ride the DASH bus west on King St. to Shooter's Hill (60¢ exact change, includes transfer for return trip). Admission free. Open daily 9:15–3:45. Closed Thanksgiving, Christmas, and New Year's.*

Participant Sports

Bicycling The **Mount Vernon Bicycle Trail** (tel. 703/285–2598) is 17 miles of asphalt along the shore of the Potomac and through Alexandria. Bicycles are available for rental by the hour or day at the six-mile **Burke Lake Park Bicycle Trail** (tel. 703/323–6600) in Fairfax County. For a free map of Arlington County's Bikeway System, call 703/528–2941. The **Fredericksburg Visitor's Center** (tel. 703/373–1776) has mapped out rides of three, nine, and 20 miles that take in the historical and natural beauty of the town.

Golf **Algonkian Park** in Leesburg (tel. 703/450–4655), **Burke Lake Park** in Fairfax (tel. 703/323–6600), and **Shannon Green Resort** in Fredericksburg (tel. 703/786–8385) have 18-hole courses.

Ice Skating Indoor rinks include **Fairfax Ice Arena** (tel. 703/323–1131) and **Mount Vernon Recreation Center** (tel. 703/768–3223).

Tennis There are dozens of public courts all over the Virginia suburbs of Washington; many are lighted and some are accessible to the disabled. For a directory, call 703/941–5000.

Spectator Sports

Check the sports pages of the *Washington Post* or the *Fairfax Journal* for events at George Mason University, which run the gamut of intercollegiate athletics. The Fredericksburg *Freelance Star* lists events at Mary Washington College.

Dining

The most highly recommended restaurants in each price category are indicated by a star ★.

Category	Cost*
Very Expensive	over $30
Expensive	$20–$30
Moderate	$10–$20
Inexpensive	under $10

per person without tax (4.5% in Virginia), service, or drinks

The following credit-card abbreviations are used: AE, American Express; CB, Carte Blanche; DC, Diners Club; MC, MasterCard; V, Visa.

Alexandria
Early American

Old Gadsby's Tavern. Located in Old Town, this tavern will take you back 200 years with its decor, cuisine, and unique entertainment. While you dine, John Douglas Hall, in the costume and character of an 18th-century gentleman, performs on the lute and chats about the latest news and gossip of Colonial Virginia. The tavern, built in 1792, was a favorite of George Washington's, and he is remembered today on the menu, with George Washington's Favorite Duck: cornbread-stuffed roast duck with fruit-and-madeira sauce. Other special offerings are Colonial Game Pye, of lamb, pork, and rabbit; Sally Lunn bread; and rich English trifle. Upstairs is a museum showing authentic table settings and the section of the tavern that was once a hotel. *138 N. Royal St., tel. 703/548–1288. Dress: informal. Reservations advised. AE, MC, V. Moderate.*

Greek
★

Taverna Cretekou. Whitewashed stucco walls and brightly colored macramé tapestries bring the Mediterranean to the center of Old Town. In the warm months, you can dine in the canopied garden. The Lamb Exohikon—lamb baked in a pastry shell—and the swordfish kabob are especially good. All wines served are Greek. *818 King St., tel. 703/548–8688. Dress: informal. Reservations advised. AE, CB, DC, MC, V. Closed Mon. Moderate.*

Arlington
New American

Windows. This award-winning restaurant is appropriately named, for it offers diners a spectacular view of the Potomac and the Washington monuments across the river. The menu changes daily, with everything fresh and in season. The chef specializes in exotic versions of familiar dishes. Try roasted loin of Texas jackrabbit, served with baby corn and squash in truffle butter; or grilled menemsha, a swordfish steak with fuji sprouts, served on a bed of crisp fried spinach with spicy black-bean sauce. *1000 Wilson Blvd., tel. 703/527–4430. Tie and jacket required. Reservations advised. AE, DC, MC, V. Closed Sun. No lunch Sat. Very Expensive.*

Vietnamese   **Cafe Dalat.** Photos and silkscreens of Vietnamese scenery decorate this restaurant, which caters to the area's large Vietnamese population. Try the Fairy Combination, crispy noodles with chicken, scallops, shrimp, and mixed vegetables; beef wrapped in grape leaves; or any fish dish. Portions are generous. *3143 Wilson Blvd., tel. 703/276–0935. Dress: informal. Reservations not needed. No credit cards. Inexpensive.*

Fredericksburg   **Chimneys Tavern.** Built in 1772 and reportedly haunted by the
American   ghosts of several past residents (including President Chester A. Arthur's wife), this handsome old house is now a restaurant serving regional specialties. Try the rack of lamb with tarragon, or veal Virginia—veal topped with Smithfield ham and backfin crabmeat. There's an extensive wine list. *623 Caroline St., tel. 703/371–9229. Dress: informal. Reservations advised. AE, CB, DC, MC, V. Closed Mon. Moderate.*

P.K.'s. This is a conventional and comfortable surf-and-turf restaurant with a 19th-century atmosphere. *2051 Plank Rd. (Rte. 3), tel. 703/371–3344. Dress: informal. Reservations not needed. AE, CB, DC, MC, V. Moderate.*

Great Falls   **L'Auberge Chez François.** At this spot about 35 minutes north-
Country French   west of Arlington, Alsatian cuisine is served in a country-inn
★   atmosphere. The building, of white stucco and dark exposed beams, is set on six acres, with a garden that can be seen from the dining room. Inside, two fireplaces, flowered tablecloths, and stained glass set the mood for such specialties as salmon soufflé—fillet of salmon topped with a mousse of scallops and salmon and a white-wine or lobster sauce. *332 Springvale Rd. (Rte. 674), tel. 703/759–3800. Jacket required. Reserve 2 weeks ahead. AE, MC, V. Closed Mon. Dinner only (from 2 PM on Sun.). Very Expensive.*

Tyson's Corner   **Clyde's.** This is a superior branch of the popular Georgetown
American   pub. Its four dining rooms offer a choice of styles—such as the Palm Terrace, with high ceilings and lots of greenery—but all are basically Art Deco; one room is formal. The menu is long and eclectic; it always includes fresh fish of the season, in such preparations as trout Parmesan. The wine list is equally long. Quality is high, and service is attentive. *8332 Leesburg Pike, tel. 703/734–1901. Dress: informal (except jacket in formal room). Reservations suggested. AE, CB, DC, MC, V. Expensive.*

Lodging

The most highly recommended properties in each price category are indicated by a star ★.

Category	Cost*
Very Expensive	over $120
Expensive	$90–$120

Moderate	$50–$90
Inexpensive	under $50

*double room, highest rate in peak season; add 4.5% for taxes

The following credit-card abbreviations are used: AE, American Express; CB, Carte Blanche; DC, Diners Club; MC, MasterCard; V, Visa.

Alexandria
Very Expensive
★

Morrison House. This small, luxurious hotel in Old Town is decorated in Federal style throughout, complete with four-poster beds. Afternoon tea is served as it must have been 200 years ago. *116 S. Alfred St., 22314, tel. 703/838–8000. 45 rooms, including 3 suites. Facilities: 24-hr butler and room service, French restaurant. AE, CB, DC, MC, V.*

Holiday Inn–Old Town. This luxury hotel in 1988 completed a $4-million refurbishment. The rooms are decorated in Federal style, with such high-tech touches as "executive phones" with computer-modem capabilities. Bathrooms have marble tubs and floors. *480 King St., 22314, tel. 703/549–6080 or 800/HOLIDAY. 227 rooms. Facilities: indoor pool and sauna, restaurant, disco. AE, DC, MC, V.*

Arlington
Very Expensive

Marriott Crystal Gateway. This modern, elegant hotel caters to the business traveler and the tourist who wants to be pampered. Its two towers rise 17 stories above the highway. Inside, there's black marble, blond wood, Oriental touches, and lots of greenery. Rooms are modern. *1700 Jefferson Davis Hwy. 22202, tel. 703/920–3230 or 800/228–9290. 702 rooms, including 110 suites. Facilities: indoor/outdoor pools; health spa with whirlpool, sauna, and exercise rooms; 4 restaurants and lounges; nightclub. AE, CB, DC, MC, V.*

Expensive

Holiday Inn–National Airport. A basic high-rise Holiday Inn off the highway, with modern, cheerful decor and a convenient location a mile from the airport. *1489 Jefferson Davis Hwy., 22202, tel. 703/521–1600 or 800/HOLIDAY. 306 rooms, including 11 suites. Facilities: outdoor pool, restaurant bar; adjacent to racquetball club. AE, CB, DC, MC, V.*

Fredericksburg
Moderate

Best Western–Johnny Appleseed. This family-oriented two-story motel is five minutes from the battlefields. Rooms are motel basic; queen-size beds are available. *543 Warrenton Rd. (U.S. 17 at Jct. I–95), 22405, tel. 703/373–0000 or 800/528–1234. 90 units, including 1 suite and 4 efficiencies. Facilities: outdoor pool, playground, nature trail, volleyball, restaurant, free HBO. AE, CB, DC, MC, V.*

Moderate

Hampton Inn. A cheerful and comfortable new motel on the interstate, near the historic district. *2310 Plank Rd., 22401, tel. 703/371–0330 or 800/HAMPTON. 166 rooms, including king suites with whirlpools. Facilities: outdoor pool. AE, CB, DC, MC, V.*

Tyson's Corner
Expensive

Ramada Hotel. This luxury hotel and convention center has spent $21 million on renovation and additions recently. It is a high-rise property on the highway, about 10 miles west of Arlington. *7801 Leesburg Pike (Rte. 7 and I–495), 22043, tel. 703/893–1340. 404 units, including meeting room and king suites. Facilities: indoor pool, sauna, whirlpool, exercise room, restaurant, nightclub. AE, CB, DC, MC, V.*

The Arts

The **Fairfax County Council of the Arts** (tel. 703/642–0862) is a clearinghouse for information on performances and exhibitions all over Northern Virginia.

The **Wolf Trap Farm Park for the Performing Arts,** in Vienna, operates out of a grand outdoor pavilion in the warmer months, and the rest of the year in the Barns (18th-century farm buildings transported from upstate New York). The best performers appear here, in programs that span the whole range of musical entertainment except extreme rock, plus dance. It is one of the major performing-arts venues for the entire area around Washington. (*see also* What to See and Do with Children). *I–495 Exit 10W, tel. 703/255–1860. The Barns: tel. 703/938–2404.*

The **Harris Theater** at George Mason University (tel. 703/425–3900) is the scene of acclaimed student drama. The **Lazy Susan Dinner Theater** (tel. 703/550–7384) has a varied program all year long.

Nightlife

Bluegrass　In Arlington, **Whitey's** (tel. 703/525–9825) is a crowded, noisy, and irresistible dive with a loyal following of diverse ages and backgrounds.

Irish and Folk　**Murphy's Grand Irish Pub** in Alexandria (tel. 703/548–1717) has a fire blazing in winter and boisterous entertainment all year.

Jazz　Upstairs at Alexandria's **Two Nineteen** (tel. 703/549–1141) there's jazz, or hang out in the sports bar in the basement.

Singles　**Clyde's** in Tyson's Corner (tel. 703/734–1901) is famous all over the DC area as a mecca for unattached professionals.

Richmond

At the fall line of the James River, 71 miles southeast of Charlottesville, is the capital of the Commonwealth: Richmond. Discovered in 1607, it replaced Williamsburg as the capital in 1779 and became the capital of the Confederate States in 1861.

Richmond's historical significance alone makes it an important place to visit; moreover, it is a metropolis surprisingly lively and sophisticated for its size (the population is under a quarter of a million—second in Virginia to bustling Norfolk's, which approaches 300,000). Following years of urban decay, this pinnacle of the Old South is prospering anew. Long a center for shipping and banking, it has fostered high-technology and the heavier industries in order to flourish. The results can be seen in the array of distinctive neighborhoods, each with its own pleasures to offer the visitor.

Monument Avenue is a wide thoroughfare lined with stately houses, divided by a verdant median, and punctuated by statues of Civil War heroes. Two of the major streets retain their traditional identifications: Main with banks and Grace with shops. Shockoe Slip is several blocks of warehouses converted into a fashionable shopping-and-entertainment zone on Cary Street, between 12th and 15th streets. The Fan District—so called because its streets fan out to the west from Laurel Street

—is bordered by Monument Avenue on the north, Main Street on the south, and The Boulevard on the west. This treasury of restored turn-of-the-century town houses has been the "hip" neighborhood for at least a decade. It should, in time, be succeeded as such by venerable Church Hill to the east (the area around St. John's Church, at 25th and Broad Sts.), which is still more fashionable than safe after dark.

Arriving and Departing

By Plane   Richmond International Airport, newly expanded at a cost $34 million, is served by 12 airlines, including **USAir,** the major regional carrier. A taxi ride downtown from the airport is $16–$18.

By Train   **Amtrak** trains headed north toward New York and south toward Florida or Newport News pass through here daily. The station is at 7519 Staples Mill Road.

By Bus   **Greyhound/Trailways** (2910 N. Boulevard, tel. 804/254–5910).

By Car   Richmond is at the intersection of Interstates 95 and 64, which run north–south and east–west, respectively. U.S. 1 also runs north–south by the city.

Getting Around

For bus and trolley route, schedule, and fare information 24 hours a day, call 804/358–GRTC.

By Bus   Public buses run from 5 AM to 12:30 AM daily. Fares are 75¢–$1.25, exact change.

By Trolley   Trolley service is available within downtown Richmond between 11 AM and 11:50 PM. The fare is 25¢, exact change.

By Taxi   Taxis are metered and charge $1.50 per mile, $1 for each extra passenger.

Important Addresses and Numbers

Tourist Information   The **Virginia Division of Tourism** maintains an office in the Old Bell Tower on the grounds of the Capitol (9th St., tel. 804/786–4484). The **Metro Richmond Visitor's Center** is at 1700 Robin Hood Road (Exit 14 off Interstates 95 and 64, tel. 804/358–5511).

Emergencies   Dial 911 for emergency assistance.

Minor Emergencies   There are 24 walk-in medical-care centers in and around town; check the Yellow Pages for those nearest you.

Dentist   **Walls & Collado, D.D.S., P.C.,** 6710 Midlothian Tpk. (tel. 804/745–6696) offers walk-in service and has a doctor on call in case of emergency.

24-Hour Pharmacy   **People's Drug Store,** 2730 W. Broad St. (tel. 804/359–2497).

Guided Tours

Orientation Tour   On weekends, the **Cultural Link Trolley,** leaving from the Science Museum, makes a continuous 55-minute loop, stopping at 34 cultural and historic landmarks. You can pace yourself, getting on and off when and where you like. *Tel. 804/358–GRTC.*

Cost: per day: $5 adults, $2.50 children, under 5 free. Runs Sat. 10–5, Sun. 12:30–4.

Guided Tours **Historic Richmond Foundation** (tel. 804/780–0107) gives various bus and walking tours. **Winning Tours** (804/358–6666).

Boat Tours **Heritage Cruise Line** (tel. 804/222–5700) offers lunch and dinner voyages on the James on a three-deck, air-conditioned paddle wheeler replica from April through October. **Historic Richmond Foundation.** (tel. 804/780–0107) offers specialized scenic-tour and dining cruises.

Exploring Richmond

Numbers in the margin correspond with points of interest on the Richmond map.

Start downtown at the **Court End** district, the heart of old Richmond, which includes seven national historic landmarks, three museums, and 11 other buildings on the National Register of Historic Places—all within eight blocks. At any one of the museums you will receive a self-guided walking tour with the purchase of a discount block ticket ($5 adults, $4.50 senior citizens, $2 children), good for all admission fees.

1 The first museum, the **John Marshall House,** was built in 1790 by the Chief Justice of the Supreme Court, who was also secretary of state and ambassador to France. It is now fully restored and furnished with a convincing mix of period pieces and heirlooms. *9th and Marshall Sts., tel. 804/648–7998. Admission: $5 adults, $4.50 senior citizens, $2 children. Open Tues.–Sat. 10–5, Sun. 1–5. Closed major holidays.*

2 The **Valentine Museum,** in the former home of sculptor Edward Valentine, is devoted to the life and history of Richmond. Exhibits include early American clothing and toys. The building will remain open throughout its current extensive restoration, which is fascinating to observe in progress. *1015 E. Clay St., tel. 804/649–0711. Admission: $3.50 adults, $3 senior citizens, $2.75 students, $1.50 children. Open Mon.–Sat. 10–5, Sun. 1–5, Memorial Day–Labor Day; Mon.–Thurs. 10–7, Fri.–Sun. 10–5, rest of year.*

3 The **Museum and White House of the Confederacy** are better seen in that order. The former offers elaborate permanent exhibitions on the Civil War era. The "world's largest collection of Confederate memorabilia" features such relics as the sword General Lee wore for the surrender at Appomattox. At the White House, next door, preservationists have painstakingly re-created the interior as it was during the Civil War, when Jefferson Davis lived here. *1201 E. Clay St., tel. 804/649–1861. Admission to both sites (1 site): $5 ($3) adults; $4.50 ($2.50) senior citizens; $2 ($1.25) children 7–12, under 7 free. Open Mon.–Sat. 10–5, Sun. 1–5. Closed holidays.*

4 The **Virginia State Capitol** was designed by Thomas Jefferson in 1785. Inside is a wealth of sculpture, including busts of each of the eight presidents Virginia has given the nation; also the famous life-size, and lifelike, statue of George Washington by Houdon. In the old Hall of the House of Delegates, Robert E. Lee accepted the command of the Confederate forces in Virginia. Also on the grounds is the Old Bell Tower, where you can get travel information about the whole state. *Capitol Sq., tel. 804/*

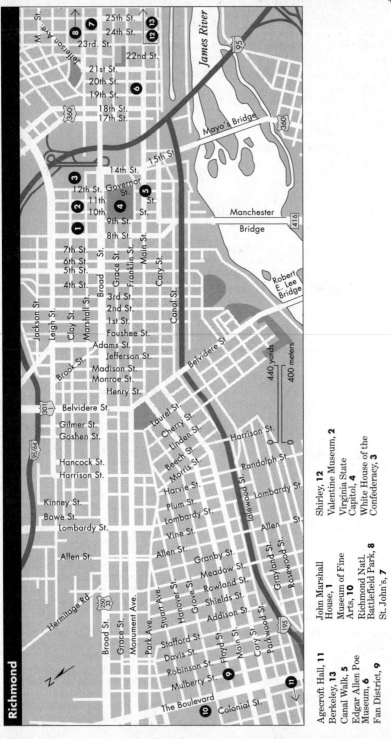

Richmond

James River

James River

25th St.
24th St.
23rd St.
22nd St.
21st St.
20th St.
19th St.
18th St.
17th St.

Jefferson Ave. W.

Jefferson Ave. W.

Mayo's Bridge

15th St.
14th St.
12th St.
11th St.
10th St.
9th St.
8th St.

Governor St.

Manchester Bridge

Broad St.
Grace St.
Franklin St.
Main St.
Cary St.

Canal St.

7th St.
6th St.
5th St.
4th St.
3rd St.
2nd St.
1st St.

Robert E. Lee Bridge

Jackson St.
Leigh St.
Clay St.
Marshall St.

Foushee St.
Adams St.
Jefferson St.
Madison St.
Monroe St.
Henry St.

Brook St.

Belvidere St.

Belvidere St.

Belvidere St.
Gilmer St.
Goshen St.

Laurel St.
Cherry St.
Linden St.
Beech St.
Morris St.

Harrison St.

Hancock St.
Harrison St.

Randolph St.

Kinney St.
Bowe St.
Lombardy St.

Harvie St.
Plum St.
Lombardy St.
Vine St.

Lombardy St.

440 yards
400 meters

Idlewood St.

Allen St.

Allen St.

Allen St.

Granby St.
Meadow St.
Rowland St.
Shields St.
Addison St.

Grayland St.
Rosewood St.

Hermitage Rd.

Broad St.
Grace St.
Monument Ave.

Park Ave.
Stuart Ave.
Hanover St.
Grove St.

Stafford St.
Davis St.
Robinson St.
Mulberry St.

Floyd St.
Main St.
Cary St.
Parkwood St.

Colonial St.

The Boulevard

N

Agecroft Hall, **11**
Berkeley, **13**
Canal Walk, **5**
Edgar Allen Poe
Museum, **6**
Fan District, **9**

John Marshall
House, **1**
Museum of Fine
Arts, **10**
Richmond Natl.
Battlefield Park, **8**
St. John's, **7**

Shirley, **12**
Valentine Museum, **2**
Virginia State
Capitol, **4**
White House of the
Confederacy, **3**

*786–4344. Admission free. Open daily 9–5 Apr.–Nov.; Mon.–
Sat. 9–5, Sun. 1–5 rest of year. Closed Thanksgiving, Christmas, and New Year's.*

❺ The **Canal Walk** starts south of the Capitol at 12th and Main and
follows the locks of the James River–Kanawha Canal, designed
by George Washington. At 12th and Byrd, under the archway,
watch a free slide show (daily 9–5) about the history of the canal. Follow the river to **Brown's Island,** across from the ruins of
an iron foundry. The island, terminus of the scenic walk, boasts
a heliport and some unique sculptures, and hosts concerts in
season.

Leaving downtown Richmond, follow Main Street east to the
❻ Church Hill Historic District and the **Edgar Allan Poe Museum,**
inside the Old Stone House. Poe never lived in the house, built
in 1737, that his disciples have turned into a shrine, with some
of his possessions on display. The Raven Room is hung with il-
lustrations inspired by his most famous poem. *1914 E. Main
St., tel. 804/648–5523. Admission: $3 adults, $2 senior citizens,
$1 students. Open Tues.–Sat. 10–4, Sun. and Mon. 1:30–4.
Closed Christmas.*

❼ Three blocks north is Broad Street, leading east to **St. John's
Episcopal Church.** For security reasons, the rebellious Second
Virginia Convention met here, instead of at Williamsburg, and
on March 23, 1775, Patrick Henry delivered at this church the
speech in which he insisted: "Give me liberty or give me death!"
*25th and Broad Sts., tel. 804/648–5015. Admission: $2 adults,
$1.50 senior citizens, 50¢ children. Open Mon.–Sat. 10–3:30,
Sun. 1–3:30. Closed Christmas Eve and Day, and New Year's
Eve and Day.*

At the eastern end of Broad Street is the visitor center for the
❽ **Richmond National Battlefield Park,** the launching point for
tours of the Richmond and other Civil War battlefields in the
surrounding countryside. Here you can watch a movie about
the city during the war and a slide show about the battlefields,
then pick up a map to use on your self-guided tour. *3215 E.
Broad St., tel. 804/226–1981. Admission free. Open daily 9–5.
Closed Christmas and New Year's.*

Returning west on Broad Street, turn south on Boulevard,
❾ ❿ where you will find the **Fan District** and the **Virginia Museum of
Fine Arts.** The museum's most startling exhibits have to be
Duane Hanson's true-to-life wax figures: with their contemporary, unglamorous attire, and provocative poses they fool
visitors all the time. But the paintings by Goya, Renoir, Monet,
and van Gogh are quite real, and so are the African masks, Roman statuary, Oriental icons, and five Fabergé eggs.
*Boulevard and Kensington St., tel. 804/367–0844. $2 donation
suggested. Open Tues.–Sat. 11–5 (Thurs. until 10), Sun. 1–5.
Closed July 4, Thanksgiving, Christmas, and New Year's.*

Just west of the Fan District, in the Windsor Farms neighbor-
⓫ hood, is **Agecroft Hall,** built in the 15th century in Lancashire
and transported here in 1925. Set amid gardens, it contains an
extensive assortment of Tudor and early Stuart furniture and
art plus a few priceless anomalies, such as a Ming vase. *4305
Sulgrave Rd., tel. 804/353–4241. Admission: $2 adults, $1.50
senior citizens, $1 students. Open Tues.–Sat. 10–4, Sun. 2–5.
Closed major holidays.*

Take VA 5 east toward Williamsburg to see two historic plantation houses less than half an hour from Richmond. The most
⑫ impressive fact about **Shirley** is that the same family, the
Carters, have lived here for 10 generations. Their claim to the
land goes back to 1660, when it was settled by a relative, Edward Hill. The house was built in 1723; Robert E. Lee's mother
was born here. Your first view of the elegant Georgian manor is
a dramatic one: the house stands at the end of an allée lined by
towering Lombardy poplars. Inside, the impressive hall staircase rises for three stories without any visible support. *VA 5E
to Rte. 608, tel. 804/829–5121. Admission: $6 adults, $5 senior
citizens, $4 students under 22, $3 children under 13. Open daily 9–5. Closed Christmas.*

⑬ Continue east a bit on VA 5 for **Berkeley.** It is said that the first
Thanksgiving was celebrated not in Massachusetts but here, on
December 4, 1619. The plantation was later the home of U.S.
president William Henry Harrison. The Georgian brick house,
built in 1726, is furnished with period antiques, not original
pieces. The gardens are in excellent condition, particularly the
boxwood hedges. There is a restaurant on the premises, with
seating indoors and out. *VA 5E, then follow signs, tel. 804/795–
2453. Admission: $6.50 adults, $4 children, $5.85 senior citi-
zens. Open daily 8–5. Closed Christmas.*

What to See and Do with Children

The **King's Dominion** entertainment complex is strictly for children, but parents may revert to childhood under its influence.
The more than 100 rides include simulated white-water rafting
and a stand-up roller coaster. There is also a monorail ride
through a game preserve and shows by trained dolphins and
cartoon characters. *22 mi north on I–95, Doswell exit, tel. 804/
876–5000. Admission: $16.95 adults and children, $12.45 senior citizens, under 2 free. Parking: $2. Open daily 9:30–8 (until
10 July–Aug.). Closed Oct.–Mar.*

Shopping

In general, banks are open weekdays 9–3, Saturdays 9–noon.
Shops open at 10 AM Monday–Saturday, noon on Sunday. Malls
stay open until 9 PM Monday–Saturday, 6 PM Sunday; downtown
stores close at 5:30.

6th Street Marketplace, as you might guess, is between 5th and
7th—also between Grace and Leigh. Here you'll find more than
100 specialty shops, chain stores, and eateries. Next door are
Thalhimers and **Miller & Rhoads,** the best-known department
stores in Virginia.

Shockoe Slip (E. Cary St., between 12th and 15th Sts.), in the
cobblestoned tobacco warehouse district of the 18th and 19th
centuries, has boutiques and branches of such upscale stores as
Beecroft & Bull and **The Toymaker of Williamsburg.**

At the **Farmers Market** (17th and Main Sts.) fresh produce is
sold directly by the farmers. Nearby are boutiques, art galleries, and antiques shops, many in converted warehouses and
factories.

Participant Sports

Within Richmond and the three suburban counties, there are open to the public—for free or at a nominal charge—405 tennis courts, 45 swimming pools, 20 golf courses, and seven miles of fitness trails. The following are just a few of the facilities available; the Visitor's Center and Division of Tourism have complete listings.

Golf **The Crossings,** 20 minutes north of downtown in Glen Allen (tel. 804/266–2254), has an 18-hole course open to the public.

Jogging There is a **running track** in the park around the Randolph pool (on Idlewood St.) and a **fitness track** in Byrd Park (off The Boulevard).

Rafting From April through October, the **Richmond Raft Co.** (tel. 804/222–7238) offers guided white-water rafting through the heart of the city on the James River (Class 3 and 4 rapids), float trips upriver, and overnight camping/rafting trips.

Swimming Among the city-run outdoor pools—open only in summer—are the **Randolph pool** (on Idlewood Ave.), which has a little park with a running track and tennis and basketball courts, and the **Bell Meade pool** (off Jefferson Davis Hwy.); call the City Dept. of Recreation and Parks for more information, 804/780–5930. The **YWCA** (6 N. 5th St., tel. 804/643–6761) has an indoor pool that is open to members of any YWCA and guests of Richmond hotels.

Tennis **Byrd Park** (off The Boulevard) has lighted courts.

Spectator Sports

The **Richmond Coliseum** (tel. 804/780–4956), which seats 12,000, hosts ice shows, basketball games, wrestling matches, and tennis tournaments.

Auto Racing Twice a year, in September and February, races are held at the **Richmond Fairgrounds Raceway** (I–64, Exit Laburnum Ave. tel. 804/329–6796).

Baseball The Richmond Braves, a Triple-A farm team for Atlanta, play at **The Diamond** (tel. 804/359–4444), a new 12,500-seat stadium.

Basketball Randolph-Macon College, University of Richmond, Virginia Commonwealth University, and Virginia Union University are listed in the *Times-Dispatch* and the *News Leader*.

Dining

The most highly recommended restaurants in each price category are indicated by a star ★.

Category	Cost*
Very Expensive	over $30
Expensive	$20–$30
Moderate	$10–$20
Inexpensive	under $10

per person without tax (4.5% in Virginia), service, or drinks

The following credit-card abbreviations are used: AE, American Express; CB, Carte Blanche; DC, Diners Club; MC, MasterCard; V, Visa.

Very Expensive | **La Petite France.** The atmosphere is formal, with emerald green walls and tuxedoed waiters. The traditional food and service set the standard for Richmond's best. Specialties include Dover sole amandine and chateaubriand. *2912 Maywill St., tel. 804/353–8729. Jacket and tie required. Reservations advised. AE, CB, DC, MC, V. Closed Sun. and Mon.*
Classic French |

Expensive | **The Aviary.** This is a sleek and modern restaurant, decorated with colorful papier-mâché parrots and serving such fare as New York strip steak with tomato-basil hollandaise sauce. *901 E. Cary St., tel. 804/225–8219. Dress: informal. Reservations advised. AE, MC, V. No lunch Sat. Closed Sun.*
International
★ |

Nouvelle Cuisine | **Patrick Henry's.** Two 1858 houses were restored and joined to make this restaurant and inn (upstairs there are three suites with kitchenettes and fireplaces). The dining room is Colonial in atmosphere, with antiques and fireplaces; there's also an English-style pub in the basement and a garden cafe. Especially popular dishes are the crisp roasted duck with crushed-plum sauce, and the "crabcakes"—here, crabmeat and spices in a puff pastry. *2300 E. Broad St., tel. 804/644–1322. Dress: informal. Reservations advised. AE, DC, MC, V. Closed Mon.*

Moderate | **Bird in Hand.** This Shockoe Bottom–area spot is frequented by local artists, whose works grace the walls. The upstairs room, for formal dining, features such specialties as tenderloin stuffed with prosciutto and mushrooms, rolled in black peppercorns, and topped with béarnaise sauce. Downstairs, Mexican food, salads, and sandwiches are served. *1718–20 E. Main St., tel. 804/788–1100. Dress: informal. Reservations advised. AE, MC, V. Closed Mon. dinner, Sat. lunch, and Sun.*
American |

Inexpensive | **Joe's Inn.** Spaghetti—especially spaghetti à la Greek, with feta and provolone cheese baked on top—is the specialty, but try the sandwiches, too. The regulars, who predominate at this local hangout in the Fan District, make outsiders feel right at home. *205 N. Shields Ave., tel. 804/355–2282. Dress: informal. Reservations not needed. AE, MC, V.*
American |

Lodging

The most highly recommended properties in each price category are indicated by a star ★ For a map pinpointing locations, *see* Dining.

Category	Cost*
Very Expensive	over $120
Expensive	$90–$120
Moderate	$50–$90
Inexpensive	under $50

**double room, highest rate in peak season; add 4.5% for taxes*

The following credit-card abbreviations are used: AE, American Express; CB, Carte Blanche; DC, Diners Club; MC, MasterCard; V, Visa.

Richmond Dining and Lodging

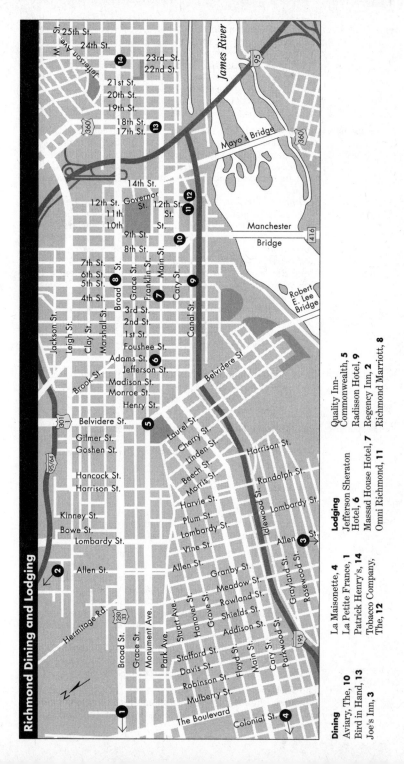

Dining
Aviary, The, **10**
Bird in Hand, **13**
Joe's Inn, **3**

La Maisonette, **4**
La Petite France, **1**
Patrick Henry's, **14**
Tobacco Company,
The, **12**

Lodging
Jefferson Sheraton
Hotel, **6**
Massad House Hotel, **7**
Omni Richmond, **11**

Quality Inn-
Commonwealth, **5**
Radisson Hotel, **9**
Regency Inn, **2**
Richmond Marriott, **8**

Very Expensive
★

Jefferson Sheraton Hotel. A winding, 26-step staircase reputedly used as a model for the one in the movie *Gone With the Wind* graces the lobby of this famous old downtown hotel. Built in 1895, it is a National Historic Landmark recently restored to its former glory by Sheraton. Guests are given passes to the YMCA spa across the street. *Franklin and Adams Sts., 23220, tel. 804/788–8000 or 800/343–6320. 273 rooms, including 26 suites. Facilities: 3 restaurants, lounges. AE, CB, DC, MC, V.*

Expensive

Radisson Hotel. This luxurious hotel in the center of the business district offers rooms with views of the Richmond skyline or the James River. *555 E. Canal St., 23219, tel. 804/788–0900 or 800/333–3333. 300 rooms. Facilities: indoor pool, health club with Jacuzzi and saunas, 2 restaurants, 2 lounges, nightclub. AE, DC, MC, V.*

Richmond Marriott. The lobby of this luxury hotel near the 6th Street Marketplace has a marble floor and crystal chandeliers; rooms are furnished in a contemporary style. Concierge service is offered. *500 E. Broad St., 23219, tel. 804/643–3400 or 800/228 –9290. 400 rooms. Facilities: 3 restaurants, nightclub, indoor pool, exercise room, tanning parlor. AE, DC, MC, V.*

Omni Richmond. This luxury hotel in the James Center Complex, next door to Shockoe Slip, opened in 1987. Rooms are furnished in contemporary style, and the lobby is homey despite the Italian marble. *100 S. 12th St., 23219, tel. 804/344– 7000 or 800/THE–OMNI. 375 rooms. Facilities: indoor/outdoor pool; sun deck; health club with racquetball, squash courts, indoor track, Nautilus, whirlpool, saunas; 3 restaurants; bar. AE, CB, DC, MC, V.*

Moderate

Quality Inn–Commonwealth. This brick high rise is located in the heart of downtown. *515 W. Franklin St., 23220, tel. 804/ 643–2831. 175 rooms and suites. Facilities: outdoor pool, restaurant, bar, beauty parlor. AE, CB, DC, MC, V.*

Inexpensive

Massad House Hotel. This attractive hotel, set in the heart of the downtown area, resembles an old-fashioned English inn. *11 N. 4th St., 23219, tel. 804/648–2893. 64 rooms. Facilities: restaurant. MC, V.*

The Arts

The campus of Virginia Commonwealth University is usually teeming with artistic activity. Events here and throughout the city are listed in the *Times-Dispatch* and the *News-Leader*.

Theater

Barksdale Theatre, in historic Hanover Tavern (tel. 804/ 537–5333), was the first dinner theater in the country, founded in 1953. Performances are given Wednesday through Saturday. Touring companies are often featured at the **Carpenter Center** (tel. 804/782–3900), a restored 1928 motion-picture palace. A unique Moorish-style auditorium called **The Mosque** (tel. 804/ 780–4213), at Main and Laurel streets, is worth a peek even when the stage is dark. The **Swift Mill Creek Playhouse** (tel. 804/748–4411) is a dinner theater set in a 17th-century gristmill. The Virginia Museum of Fine Arts maintains an equity theater, **Theatre Virginia** (tel. 804/367–0831).

Music

The **Richmond Symphony** (tel. 804/788–1212), more than 30 years old, often features internationally known guest performers. Members of the orchestra perform as **The Sinfonia** for concerts of chamber music; and with popular guest artists, the versatile orchestra plays as **The Richmond Pops.**

Dance There are two professional ballet companies in town: the **Richmond Ballet** (tel. 804/359–0906) and the more experimental **Concert Ballet of Virginia** (tel. 804/780–1279).

Nightlife

Comedy The **Richmond Comedy Club** (1218 E. Cary St., tel. 804/745–3166) is modeled on successful establishments in New York and Los Angeles.

Dancing An imaginative selection of pop hits is performed live at **New Horizon Cafe** (1203 W. Broad St., tel. 804/353–4743).

Folk At **The Jade Elephant** (909 W. Grace St., tel. 804/353–9674) you can enjoy cheap, well-made drinks while you listen to performers who usually appear solo.

Jazz **Bogart's** (203 N. Lombardy St., tel. 804/353–9280) is a cozy club.

Rock **The Flood Zone** (18th and Main Sts., tel. 804/644–0935) is a converted recording studio where you can listen and dance to live music, or listen and watch from the balcony.

Tidewater and the Eastern Shore

The Historic Triangle comprises Williamsburg, Jamestown, and Yorktown, sites that figure crucially in the preindependent history of the United States. Williamsburg, once the capital of a colony that extended into present-day Minnesota, is now most famous for its Historic Area, restored to 18th-century perfection. Jamestown is where the English first settled successfully in North America; it is no longer an inhabited town. Yorktown, the site of the last major battle of the War of Independence, remains a living—albeit minuscule—community. The towns are linked by the scenic, 23-mile-long Colonial Parkway.

The enormous port of Hampton Roads—located where the Chesapeake Bay and the James River converge, and comprising Hampton, Newport News, and Norfolk—has been crucial in the discovery and settlement of this nation, the struggle for its independence, and the conflict that nearly dissolved its union. Past violence and hardship are a dramatic background for the busy and prosperous present day.

On the peninsula, Hampton hosts a famous weekend jazz festival in June and the even bigger "Bay Days" extravaganza, including fireworks and boat races, for three days in September. Norfolk is the U.S. headquarters for the North Atlantic Treaty Organization (NATO), which is honored in the annual Azalea Festival during the third week of April, when a queen from the year's honored member nation is chosen amid parades, air shows, dances, and exhibitions. The celebration resumes on the first full weekend in June during Harborfest, when the tall ships and more than one million guests come to town.

Virginia Beach is one of the most popular East Coast resorts. It is not a quiet seaside retreat but an entertainment mecca more likely to be enjoyed by the young. For those who crave natural beauty, largely undisturbed, the nearby Eastern Shore is an exquisite reward.

Getting Around

By Plane Patrick Henry International in Newport News and Norfolk International is served by **USAir/Allegheny.**

By Car I–64 runs northwest to intersect with I–95 at Richmond and southeast to the peninsula. U.S. 58 and VA 44 connect I–64 to Virginia Beach. U.S. 13 runs north from Virginia Beach over the Chesapeake Bay Bridge-Tunnel to the Eastern Shore.

By Train **Amtrak** trains stop at Williamsburg (468 N. Boundary St.) on their way from New York, Washington, and Richmond to Newport News. There is daily Amtrak service to Newport News (9304 Warwick Blvd.) from Boston and points in between.

By Bus **Greyhound/Trailways:** Hampton (22 S. Armistead Ave., tel. 804/722–9861), Newport News (9702 Jefferson Ave., tel. 804/599–3900), Norfolk (701 Monticello Ave., tel. 804/627–5641), Virginia Beach (2402B Pacific Ave., tel. 804/422–2998), Williamsburg (468 N. Boundary St., tel. 804/229–8750).

Guided Tours

Orientation Tours **Colonial Williamsburg** offers two-hour guided walking tours of the Historic Area every day. The **Norfolk Tour** (tel. 804/441–5266) is a free self-guided driving or walking tour of the city's most popular attractions; at each you can pick up a leaflet with directions to the others, which are marked with blue-and-gold signs. From April through October the **Norfolk Trolley** (tel. 804/623–3222) takes you on a guided tour of the historic downtown area, letting you on and off as you please. Tickets are sold at the TRT kiosk outside the Waterside. Cost: $1.50 adults; 75¢ children, senior citizens, and the disabled.

Boat Tours The **Elizabeth River Ferry** from the Waterside in Norfolk to Portsmouth is faster and more fun than the tunnel, and it operates every day all year long. Cost: 50¢ adults; 25¢ children, senior citizens, and the disabled. The *Carrie B* (tel. 804/393–4735), a reproduction Mississippi riverboat, cruises Hampton Roads to give you a look at the naval shipyard, as well as the site of the Civil War battle between the *Monitor* and the *Merrimac*. **Wharton's Wharf** (tel. 804/245–1533) in Newport News offers a comprehensive cruise of the harbor, and some special voyages on the James and the Intracoastal Waterway. On the Eastern Shore, you can take a guided tour of the Assateague Channel on a cruise boat or a Wildlife Safari boat ride through the Chincoteague National Wildlife Refuge from **Island Cruises** (tel. 804/336–5511).

Special Tours **Colonial Williamsburg** offers a variety of tours, including "According to the Ladies," which provides a female perspective on 18th-century America, and "The Other Half," which focuses on the experience of black residents.

Important Addresses and Numbers

Tourist Information **Chincoteague Chamber of Commerce** (Box 258, Chincoteague 23336, tel. 804/336–6161), **Eastern Virginia Chamber of Com-**

merce (Box 147, Accomac 23301, tel. 804/787–2460), **Hampton Tourist Information Center** (710 Settlers Landing Rd., Hampton 23669, tel. 804/727–6108), **Norfolk Convention and Visitors Bureau** (236 E. Plume St., Norfolk 23510, tel. 804/441–5266), **Virginia Peninsula Tourism and Conference Bureau** (8 San Jose Dr., Suite 3B, Newport News 23606, tel. 804/873–0092), **Virginia Beach Visitors Center** (19th St. and Pacific Ave., Virginia Beach 23451, tel. 804/425–7511), **Williamsburg Area Tourism and Conference Bureau** (Drawer GB, 201 Penniman Rd., Williamsburg 23187, tel. 804/ 253–0192).

Emergencies   Dial 911 for emergency assistance.

Minor Emergencies   **First Med. of Williamsburg** (tel. 804/229–4141) and **Community Emergency Care Center** (tel. 804/253–6005) in Williamsburg. **Sentara Medical Care Centers** in Hampton (tel. 804/723–1313), Newport News (tel. 804/599–6117 and 838–4288), Norfolk (tel. 804/583–0404), and Virginia Beach (tel. 804/671–1674).

Exploring Tidewater and the Eastern Shore

Numbers in the margin correspond with points of interest on the Tidewater and the Eastern shore map.

❶ Begin at **Colonial Williamsburg,** which is a marvel. The Historic Area comprises 173 acres of restored buildings populated by costumed interpreters and craftspeople. In the various shops you can observe coopers, milliners, wigmakers, and other tradesmen at their tasks, and their wares are for sale nearby. The taverns serve period-style food and beverages.

Begin at the visitor center, where you buy your tickets. Here you can watch an introductory movie, starring Jack Lord (of "Hawaii Five-O" fame) as an apocryphal patriot in the early 1770s. *I–64 Exit 56, tel. 804/229–1000. Admission: The Patriot's Pass ($25 adults, $12.50 children) is good for a year and admits the bearer to every Colonial Williamsburg–run site, including Bassett Hall and Carter's Grove Plantation. A range of less expensive tickets is available for those who haven't the time or inclination to see every site. Tickets are also sold at the courthouse in the Historic Area. In winter, some of the sites close down on a rotating basis; Carter's Grove closes in Jan. and Feb.; otherwise, every attraction except DeWitt Wallace (whose hours change frequently) is open daily. For a Vacation Planner, write Colonial Williamsburg, Box C, Williamsburg, VA 23187 (or call 800/HISTORY).*

A good three or four days can be spent in Colonial Williamsburg alone—there's so much to see and do. Be sure to allow enough time, because this place is too good to rush through. You have to tour the Historic Area on foot, but in case you get tired, shuttle buses follow a route along the perimeter of the area and will take you to and from the visitor center. There are some 25 attractions on and off broad, mile-long Duke of Gloucester Street, which serves as the spine of the whole area; you should start at its east end, which is closest to the visitor center and includes the building that made the town so important.

At the east end of Duke of Gloucester is the **Capitol,** where you can take an informative tour that explains the earliest stages in the development of American democracy from its English parliamentary roots. Here the pre-Revolutionary House of Burgesses, made up of the rising gentry, challenged the bigger

Tidewater and Eastern Shore

MARYLAND

Assateague Island 12

Chincoteague Island 13

Temperanceville

Crisfield

Cedar Island
Great Fox
Island

Bloxom

14 NASA's Wallops
Visitor Center

Modest Town

Nelsonia

Smith
Island

E A S T E R N

Potomac
River

Watts
Island

Chesapeake Bay

Tangier
Island

Onancock

Tasley

Cedar Island

S H O R E

Pungoteague

Wachapreague

Parramore
Island

Quincy

Exmore

Rappahannock River

13

Hog
Island
Bay

Hog Island

V I R G I N I A

Cobb Island
Bay

Cobb Island

17

Oyster
Bay

Wreck Island

Mobjack
Bay

South
Bay

Cape
Charles

York River

Yorktown
Battlefield

Cape Charles
Lighthouse

Colonial
Williamsburg

6 7 Yorktown

Busch Gardens

Fisherman's
Island

1 3

238

Poquoson

2

5 4

Carter's Grove
Plantation

Chesapeake Bay
Bridge-Tunnel

Jamestown
Island

Cape Henry
Memorial

64

Jamestown
Settlement

8 Hampton

Virginia
Beach

James River

Newport
News

60

11

9

Hampton
Roads

13 44 64

0   10 miles

10 Norfolk

0   15 km

Portsmouth

Chesapeake

17

T I D E W A T E R

264

landowners who sat on the royally appointed Council, an almost medieval institution. It was the House that eventually arrived at the resolutions that amounted to rebellion. In the courtroom you will hear the harsh Georgian sentences meted out: for instance, petty theft was a capital crime. Note this official building's ornate interior, characteristic of aristocratic Virginia—a marked contrast to the plain town meeting halls in New England, where other Founding Fathers were governing themselves.

The **Governor's Palace,** at the center of Duke of Gloucester Street, was completed in 1720 for Alexander Spotswood, and after the Revolution it housed the Commonwealth's first two governors, Patrick Henry and Thomas Jefferson. It burned in 1781; a 20th-century reconstruction stands on the original foundation. Nothing inside is original, but the antiques are matched to an extraordinary inventory of 16,000 items. The lavish decorations include 800 guns and swords arrayed on the walls and ceilings of several rooms.

Anchoring the west end of the street is the **Wren Building,** part of the campus of the College of William and Mary, the second-oldest college in the United States (founded in 1693). This building, erected in 1695, was based on the work of Sir Christopher Wren, the London architect for whom it was named—and who never made it to the Colonies. The professors' Common Room suggests Oxford and Cambridge, which were models for this institution. Jefferson studied and later taught law here—to James Monroe, among others.

Sharing the limelight with the handsome public buildings, restored homes, tidy reconstructed shops, and costumed interpreters are three very personal legacies from some modern-day benefactors of this historic town. The Public Hospital serves as Colonial disguise for the relatively new **DeWitt Wallace Decorative Arts Gallery** on Francis Street, where furniture, textiles, prints, metals, and ceramics from England and America are on display. The collection includes a famous full-length portrait of Washington by Charles Willson Peale. The **Abby Aldrich Rockefeller Folk Art Center,** a mile away on South England Street (a good time to take the shuttle bus), is a showcase for American "decorative usefulwares," such as toys, furniture, weathervanes, and quilts, along with folk paintings and sculptures. This is a populist complement to the exquisite DeWitt Wallace. Eclectic and precious furnishings make **Bassett Hall** a most personal house museum. Mr. and Mrs. John D. Rockefeller, Jr., who bankrolled the restoration of Colonial Williamsburg, beginning in the 1920s, lived in this two-story 18th-century house among Chinese, American, and English antiques. The 19th-century Turkish prayer rugs are outstanding specimens.

About six miles east of Williamsburg on U.S. 60 is the palatial **②** **Carter's Grove Plantation.** The house, built in 1750, is more luxurious than others of the period, since it was built as a showcase by Carter Burwell, whose grandfather King Carter had made his fortune elsewhere among the family's vast holdings. Though atypical, it is perfectly authentic and the epitome of Williamsburg in all its educational glamour. *Tel. 804/229-1000. Admission included in Patriots Pass; separately, $6.50. Open daily 9–5. Closed Jan., Feb., first 2 weeks in Dec.*

❸ For sheer contrast, you might stop at **Busch Gardens,** three miles east of Williamsburg on U.S. 60. This 360-acre, razzle-dazzle family entertainment park features water and other rides, shows, and eight European hamlets (*see* What to See and Do with Children).

❹ Nine miles west of Williamsburg on the Colonial Parkway is **Jamestown Island,** the site, in 1607, of the first permanent English settlement in North America. All that is left of the city is its foundations and the ruins of a 1639 tower—now part of the Memorial Church, built on the site of the original. The island is ringed by a five-mile nature drive. There are guided tours daily during the summer and on weekends in the spring. *Tel. 804/229–1733. Cost: $5 per car, $2 per pedestrian or cyclist. Open daily 9–6:30 June–Labor Day, 9–dark rest of year. Closed Christmas.*

As you leave the island (which is linked by a small isthmus to the rest of Virginia), stop at **Glass House Point,** at the park entrance, to observe a demonstration of glass-blowing, an unsuccessful business venture of the early colonists.

❺ Adjacent to Jamestown Island is **Jamestown Settlement,** a living-history museum formerly known as Jamestown Festival Park. A version of the early fort has been built, and within it "colonists" cook, make armor, and tell of a hard life under thatched roofs and between walls of wattle and daub. In the Indian Village, enter a wigwam and watch a costumed interpreter make tools and pottery. Stroll to the pier and inspect reproductions of the boats in which the settlers arrived. *Between Rte. 31 and Colonial Pkwy., tel. 804/229–1607. Admission: $5 adults, $2.50 children. Open daily 9–7 June 15–Aug. 15, 9–5 rest of year. Closed Christmas and New Year's.*

❻ Fourteen miles east of Williamsburg on the Parkway is **Yorktown Battlefield.** In the visitor center here is a museum with George Washington's original field tent, pitched and furnished as it was during the fighting. You can see the battlefield by self-guided auto tour, stopping at the signs. For $2 the gift shop will rent you a cassette player with a taped tour to hear as you drive around. *Tel. 804/898–3400. Admission free. Visitor center open daily 8:30–5:30, with extended hours in the spring, summer, and fall. Closed Christmas.*

On the western edge of the battlefield is the **Yorktown Victory Center,** where you will find a Continental Army encampment, with tents and a covered wagon. Costumed soldier-interpreters will try to enlist you and then answer your questions. Indoor sight-and-sound presentations are arranged along a street of a generalized 18th-century town. *Exit Colonial Pkwy. at VA 238, tel. 804/887–1776. Admission: $5 adults, $2.50 children. Open daily 9–7 June 15–Aug. 15, 9–5 rest of year. Closed major holidays.*

❼ Follow Route 238 into **Yorktown,** whose Main Street is a picturesque array of preserved 18th-century buildings, many still in use. **Moore House,** where the terms of surrender were negotiated, and **Nelson House,** the residence of a Virginia governor and signer of the Declaration of Independence, are open for tours in summer. On adjacent Church Street is **Grace Church,** built in 1697 and still an active Episcopal congregation.

Thirty miles south of Williamsburg on I–64, near the tip of the Virginia peninsula, is **Hampton,** the oldest existing continuous English-speaking settlement in the United States. Little from the earliest days survives because of repeated shellings and conflagrations over the years. Hampton's **Fort Monroe,** dating to 1834, is the only active-duty fort in the nation that is enclosed by a moat. A federal stronghold in Confederate territory, it was attacked by the *Merrimac* and defended by the *Monitor* in their famous battle near here. After the war, Confederate President Jefferson Davis was imprisoned for two years in a casemate (a chamber for the artillery within a fort's wall), which is now the **Casemate Museum.** Exhibits tell of the fort's history. (A resort hotel on the grounds, the Chamberlin, has seen better days, but its roof gardens offer a fine view of the area.) *Rte. 258 (Mercury Blvd.), tel. 804/727–3391. Admission free. Open daily 10:30–5.*

It is not well known that the U.S. space program began in Hampton, the first headquarters of NASA. The history of the future is on display at the **Langley Research Center,** where astronauts trained for Project Mercury and Apollo missions. The visitor center has exhibitions on both aeronautics and space exploration, with artifacts from the moon landings, including a lunar rock. *Follow signs off I–64, tel. 804/865–2855. Admission free. Open Mon.–Sat. 8:30–4:30, Sun. noon–4:30. Closed Easter, Thanksgiving, Christmas, and New Year's.*

Adjacent to Hampton is **Newport News** and the **Mariner's Museum,** whose exhibits cover the history of seafaring in all its aspects. Some of the hand-carved models are so tiny you must look at them through magnifying glasses; all are completely accurate. Full-size vessels are on display in surprising numbers, among them a sailing yacht, a speedboat, an Indian bark canoe, a gondola, and even a Japanese submarine. A boat is usually under construction in one gallery. $3 million has been spent for renovation. *I–64, Exit 62A, tel. 804/595–0368. Admission: $3 adults, $2.50 senior citizens, $1.50 children. Open Mon.–Sat. 9–5, Sun. noon–5. Closed Christmas.*

The third town in the triumvirate that makes up the port of Hampton Roads, and the only one not on the peninsula, is **Norfolk.** It is reached by way of the Hampton Roads Bridge-Tunnel. There is plenty to see in this old navy town, but it is rather spread out, so you will have to drive.

Gardens-by-the-Sea (Norfolk Botanical Gardens), 175 acres close by the airport, is well known for abundant azaleas and camellias. From March into September, boats and trackless trains carry visitors along seasonal routes to different plants and flowers, including 4,000 roses and even a palm tree. *Azalea Garden Rd., off Norview Ave. (Airport exit off I–64), tel. 804/441–5385. Admission: $2. Boat and train tours: $2. Open daily 8:30–dusk.*

The **Hermitage Foundation Museum** is a 16th-century English Tudor–style house reproduced by Gilded Age textile tycoons. Inside is this country's largest private collection of Oriental art, including a 1,400-year-old marble Buddha from China, plus art from the Middle East, India, Europe, and America. You may picnic outside on the 12 acres along the Lafayette River. *7637 North Shore Rd., tel. 804/423–2052. Admission: $3 adults, $1 children under 18, military free. Open Mon.–Sat.*

10–5, Sun. 1–5. Closed Thanksgiving, Christmas, and New Year's.

By any standards, the **Chrysler Museum** qualifies as a major American art museum; works by such artists as Gainsborough and Roy Lichtenstein suggest the collection's variety and stature. Still, the comfortable exhibition spaces make this an inviting, rather than intimidating, experience. *Olney Rd. and Virginia Beach Blvd., tel. 804/622–ARTS. Admission free. Open Tues.–Sat. 10–4, Sun. 1–5. Closed July 4, Thanksgiving, Christmas, and New Year's. Closed Mon.*

The **Douglas MacArthur Memorial** is the burial place of the controversial war hero. Rooms adjoining the mausoleum house mementos of his career. Next door his staff car is on display and a 24-minute biography is screened continuously. *Bank St. and City Hall Ave., tel. 804/441–2965. Admission free. Open Mon.– Sat. 10–5, Sun. 11–5. Closed Thanksgiving, Christmas, and New Year's.*

The **Moses Myers House,** built in 1792, is exceptional not just for its elegance; Norfolk's first Jewish resident lived here. The original furnishings include family portraits by Gilbert Stuart and Thomas Sully. *323 E. Freemason St., tel. 804/622–1211. Admission: $2 adults, $1 students, military free. Jan.–Mar.: open Tues.–Sat. noon–5. Rest of year: open Tues.–Sat. 10–5, Sun. noon–5. Closed July 4, Thanksgiving, Christmas, and New Year's.*

The **Waterside,** at 333 Waterside Drive, is a shopping center billed as "Tidewater's festival marketplace." It is decorated in a nautical motif, appropriate to its location on the harbor. This is a comfortable place to eat and shop, and its TRT kiosk is the launching point for several tours (*see* Guided Tours).

Time Out **Doumar's** (20th St. and Monticello Ave., tel. 804/627–4163) is a drive-in restaurant founded in 1934 by the inventor of the ice cream cone. Veteran waitresses carry to your car the specialties of the house: barbecue, natural limeade, and ice cream in fresh waffle cones made according to the original recipe.

The **Naval Base** is an impressive sight. This is the home of more than 125 ships of the Atlantic and Mediterranean fleets, including the USS *Theodore Roosevelt,* a nuclear-powered carrier with a crew of 6,300—the second-largest warship in the world. In the winter, call the Naval Base Tour Office to schedule a sailor-guide to ride for free in your car. Tour buses operate April through October, departing from the TRT kiosk at the Waterside and from the Naval Base Tour Office. *Hampton Blvd., tel. 804/623–3222 or 444–7955. Admission: $4 adults; $2 children, senior citizens, and the disabled.*

① **Virginia Beach** is 18 miles east of Norfolk, on the Atlantic Ocean. Here you will find the exquisite little **Adam Thoroughgood House,** built in 1636 and betraying its medieval English influences with every brick. The farmhouse's 17th-century garden is equally charming. *1636 Parish Rd., tel. 804/ 460–0007. Admission: $2 adults, $1 children. Open Tues.–Sat. 10–4:30, Sun. noon–5, Apr.–Dec.; Tues.–Sat. noon–5 rest of year. Closed Thanksgiving, Christmas, and New Year's.*

The sea is the subject at the **Virginia Marine Science Museum.** This massive facility, with more than 200 exhibits, became the most visited museum in the state in its first year of operation. You can predict the weather with computers, travel to the bottom of the sea in a simulated submarine, watch fish up close in tanks that re-create different underwater environments, and go birdwatching out back in the salt marsh, on a deck equipped with long-range scopes. *General Booth Blvd., ¼ mi south of the Rudee Bridge, tel. 804/425–FISH. Admission: $3.50 adults, $2.75 senior citizens and $2 children. Open daily 9–5, Fri.– Sat. until 9, June 15–Sept. 15.*

Take U.S. 13 north from Virginia Beach over the 17.5 miles of an engineering marvel: the **Chesapeake Bay Bridge-Tunnel.** This is a rare experience: you're surrounded by the sea while never leaving the comfort of your car. There is an observation pier and restaurant at the midpoint. On the other side is the Eastern Shore, where the wildlife, sea, and sun are abundant and humans, even in fashionable Chincoteague, are not.

Continue north on U.S. 13 for 63 miles to VA 175 to find the most unspoiled spot on the Eastern Shore: unpopulated **Assateague Island,** a 37-mile-long wildlife refuge and recreational area that extends into Maryland. The beaches and trails for hiking and biking are extensive and uncrowded. In addition to the exquisite scenery, as many as 300 species of birds can be seen here, including migrant geese and swans. The most famous residents are the wild ponies, supposedly descended from Spanish workhorses who survived a shipwreck off these shores. *Admission: $3 per car and $1 per pedestrian or cyclist. Wildlife drive closed to cars before 3 PM. The visitor center (tel. 804/336– 6577) is open daily 9–4.*

Chincoteague, smaller and closer to shore, has a hardy, self-reliant population. On the last Thursday of July the ponies from Assateague are driven across the channel to Chincoteague, where they are placed at auction; those unsold swim back home. The rest of the year is less exciting, but the proximity to fine beaches and natural beauty make the whole summer here a pleasant and relaxing vacation time. The **Oyster Museum** tells the history of the area. *Main St., tel. 804/336–6117. Admission: $1 adults, 25¢ children. Open daily 11–4:45 June–Aug., weekends 11–4:45 Mar.–May and Sept.–Nov. Closed Dec.– Feb.* Both the museum and the Oyster Festival on Columbus Day weekend (a food fair with oysters in every form from stew to fritters) celebrate a great local industry. *Tickets to the festival are limited to 2,000 and must be purchased well in advance from the Chamber of Commerce, tel. 804/336–6161.*

NASA's Wallops Visitor Center is near Chincoteague on Wallops Island, at the site of early rocket launchings. Satellites are sent up from here occasionally, but what goes on mostly is atmospheric research. There is a collection of spacecraft, plus exhibits and videos about the space program. *Tel. 804/824– 2298. Admission: free. Open July–Aug., daily 10–4; Thurs.– Mon. 10–4 rest of year. Closed major non-summer holidays.*

What to See and Do with Children

In addition to guided walking tours especially for children (age four and older), **Colonial Williamsburg** often organizes special "Programs for Young People." Inquire at the courthouse.

Busch Gardens—a theme park based on "The Old Country," with environments evoking England, France, Italy, and Germany—is a mecca for the little ones, though not their exclusive preserve. There are rides, including a suspended roller coaster and water rafting; music and dancing; and plenty of food and drink (including Anheuser-Busch beer, for grownups). *3 mi east of Colonial Williamsburg on U.S. 60, tel. 804/253–3350. All-day tickets are $18.95, with different rates for longer and shorter visits. Parking $2. Hours vary widely; call to confirm. Open weekends only in Apr., daily May–Labor Day, Fri.–Tues. Labor Day–Oct. Closed Nov.–Mar.*

Beaches

Along Water Street (Rte. 238) in **Yorktown** is a public beach for swimming and fishing. Right over the bridge across the York River, at **Gloucester Point,** is one that also has boat ramps. Beware of sea nettles (jellyfish) in July and August. The 14 miles of beach along the Chesapeake Bay in Norfolk are called **Ocean View Beaches.** The waters are, of course, much calmer than the ocean, and safer for children. There is good fishing here for sea trout and flounder. **Virginia Beach** has 28 miles of oceanfront. Nonetheless, it gets crowded during the summer. The lively boardwalk scene may be more of an attraction at that time of year. On the Eastern Shore, five miles of well-maintained beach, with bathhouses and picnic areas, are on the southern end of Assateague Island, at **Tom's Cove Hook.** Nearby, the ponies roam the 10 miles of **Wild Beach,** which is not supervised.

Participant Sports

Bicycling
: Colonial Williamsburg ticketholders can rent bicycles at the Lodge on South England Street; everyone else can try **Bikesmith** (tel. 804/229–9858). A 20-mile route is mapped out in the pamphlet "Biking through America's Historic Triangle," available at bike shops.

Canoeing
: **Wild River Outfitters** (tel. 804/497–4890) in Virginia Beach rents canoes and kayaks.

Fishing
: Charters are offered in season (Apr. or May through Oct.) by **Al Hartz Poquoson Charter Boats** (tel. 804/868–6821) and **Chesapeake Charter Service** (tel. 804/723–0998). For angling, try **Airfield Lake,** six miles east of Wakefield on Route 628. On Chincoteague Island, boat rentals, bait, and tackle are available through **Barnacle Bill's** (tel. 804/336–5188), **Captain Bob's** (tel. 804/336–6654), and **R&R Boats** (tel. 804/336–5465).

Golf
: **Colonial Williamsburg** (tel. 804/229–1000, ext. 3120) operates two courses, nine- and 18-hole. **Kingsmill Resort** (tel. 804/253–3906), near Busch Gardens, has two courses. **Hampton Golf and Tennis** (tel. 804/727–1195) has an 18-hole course. **Newport News Park** (tel. 804/886–2848) offers an 18-hole course. **Lake Wright** (tel. 804/461–2246) in Norfolk and **Cypress Point** (tel. 804/490–8822) in Virginia Beach have 18-hole courses.

Tennis
: In Williamsburg, **Colonial Williamsburg** (tel. 804/229–1000, ext. 3169) has six courts, **Kingsmill** (tel. 804/253–3945) has 10 clay and two hard courts open to the public, and there are public courts at **Kiwanis Park** on Longhill Road and at Quarterpath Park on Pocahontas Street. **Hampton Golf and Tennis** (tel. 804/

727–1194) offers seven courts, and there are 14 at **Owl Creek** (804/422–4716) in Virginia Beach.

Water Sports In Virginia Beach, **Chick's Beach Sailing Center** (tel. 804/481–3067) has Windsurfer rentals and lessons. They also rent Hobie Cats, Jet Skis, and Windsurfers; and **Lynnhaven Dive Center** (tel. 804/481–7949) and **Scuba Ventures** (tel. 804/481–3132) offer scuba lessons, gear, and trips.

Spectator Sports

The **College of William and Mary** in Williamsburg fields varsity or club teams in football, basketball, baseball, track, wrestling, field hockey, soccer, swimming, tennis, and gymnastics. Check the weekly listings in the *Virginia Gazette* for specifics.

Auto Racing **Langley Speedway** (tel. 804/865–1992) in Newport News features late-model stock cars, grand stock, All-American stock, and ministock. Races are run March through September.

Baseball The **Peninsula Pilots** play at the War Memorial Stadium in Hampton (tel. 804/244–2255) April through August. The **Tidewater Tides** play at Metropolitan Park in Norfolk (tel. 804/461–5600) April through September.

Golf Kingsmill in Williamsburg hosts the **Anheuser-Busch Classic** every July.

Tennis The **Wightman Cup** women's tennis tournament is held at Williamsburg in October.

Dining

The most highly recommended restaurants in each price category are indicated by a star ★.

Category	Cost*
Very Expensive	over $30
Expensive	$20–$30
Moderate	$10–$20
Inexpensive	under $10

per person without tax (4.5% in Virginia), service, or drinks

The following credit-card abbreviations are used: AE, American Express; CB, Carte Blanche; DC, Diners Club; MC, MasterCard; V, Visa.

Hampton
American
Fuller's. The slogan here is "Eat Dirt Cheap." Basic and satisfying fare—spaghetti, baked ham, barbecue, hamburgers—is served at this place, family-run since 1901. *Mallory and County, tel. 804/723–9754. Dress: informal. Reservations not needed. No credit cards. Inexpensive.*

Seafood
★
Victor's. The rich soups set the standard for a superior meal. Specialties are veal scalloppine sauté, with Riesling sauce and chanterelle mushrooms, and venison with Zinfandel sauce and mushrooms. There's a long wine list and a wide choice of desserts. The place has a contemporary look, with a mauve and green interior. During the week, a piano player and a classical guitarist entertain. Service is enthusiastic and polite. *700 Set-*

tlers Landing Rd., in the Radisson Hotel, tel. 804/727–9700. Dress: informal. Reservations advised. AE, DC, MC, V. Expensive.

Norfolk **Kelley's.** This sports bar offers the best cheeseburgers in town,
American as well as delicious homemade soups. There's musical entertainment on Sunday nights. *1408 Colly Ave., tel. 804/623–3216. Dress: informal. Reservations not needed. AE, MC, V. Inexpensive.*

Italian **Il Porto.** Plenteous portions of pasta, seafood, and veal are served in a dining room with a river view, and on the terrace in the warm months. The bar is bright and commodious, and there's a piano player to entertain most nights. *The Waterside, tel. 804/627–4400. Dress: informal. Reservations advised. AE, MC. Moderate.*

Seafood **The Ship's Cabin.** The steaks are as good as the fish—the filet-
★ mignon-and-crabcake combination is perfect if you're really hungry—and there's a variety of fresh breads, including blueberry bread that's almost a dessert in itself. *4110 E. Ocean Ave., tel. 804/480–2526. Dress: informal. Reservations advised. AE, CB, DC, MC, V. Expensive.*

Virginia Beach **The Lighthouse.** There may be no better place in town for fresh
Seafood seafood, especially shrimp and lobster. The six dining rooms all overlook the ocean or the inlet. *1st St. and Atlantic Ave., tel. 804/428–7974. Dress: informal. Reservations advised. AE, DC, MC, V. Expensive.*

Williamsburg **The Regency Room.** This restaurant in the Williamsburg Inn is
Continental the place to dine if you're looking for an elegant atmosphere,
★ attentive service, and excellent cuisine. Crystal chandeliers, oriental silkscreen prints, and full silver service set the tone. Specialties include rack of lamb, carved at the table; lobster bisque; and rich ice cream desserts. *S. Francis St., tel. 804/229–1000. Tie and jacket required for dinner and Sun. brunch; informal for breakfast and lunch. Reservations advised. AE, MC, V. Very Expensive.*

Country French **Le Clos des Marchands.** This is a cozy place with a country-inn atmosphere in the heart of the historic district. The chunky soup of scallops, flounder, and other fish in a garlic-mayonnaise sauce is an uncommon treat, as is the Delmonico steak with peppercorn sauce. *433 Prince George St., tel. 804/220–3636. Dress: informal. Reservations advised. MC, V. Moderate.*

International **The Trellis.** Although it's in an old Colonial building, the hard-
★ wood floors, ceramic tiles, and green plants evoke the feeling of being in a country inn in the Napa Valley. There are five small, cozy dining rooms, one overlooking historic Duke of Gloucester Street. The wine vault has 8,000 bottles, most from California vineyards, a few from Virginia. Try the grilled swordfish served with crispy fried leeks and sautéed onions, and Death by Chocolate dessert, seven layers of chocolate topped with cream sauce. *Merchant Sq., tel. 804/229–8610. Dress: informal. Reservations advised. AE, MC, V. Expensive.*

Yorktown **Nick's Seafood Pavilion.** This riverside eatery has a wide selec-
Seafood tion of fresh seafood—including seafood shish kebab (lobster, shrimp, scallops, tomatoes, peppers, mushrooms, and onion, served with pilaf and topped with brown butter) and a buttery lobster pilaf—along with Chinese dishes and a fine baklava.

Water St., tel. 804/887–5269. Dress: informal. Reservations advised. AE, CB, DC, MC, V. Moderate.

Lodging

Cottages on Chincoteague Island are available for rental through **Vacation Cottages** (Rte. 1, Box 547, East Side Dr., Chincoteague 23336, tel. 804/336–3720). The most highly recommended properties in each price category are indicated by a star ★.

Category	Cost*
Very Expensive	over $120
Expensive	$90–$120
Moderate	$50–$90
Inexpensive	under $50

*double room, highest rate in peak season; add 4.5% for taxes

The following credit-card abbreviations are used: AE, American Express; CB, Carte Blanche; DC, Diners Club; MC, MasterCard; V, Visa.

Hampton
Moderate

Holiday Inn Hampton. Halfway between Colonial Williamsburg and Virginia Beach is this complex of buildings set on 13 beautifully landscaped acres. A recent addition is a four-story atrium with plants and fountains. *1815 W. Mercury Blvd., 23666, tel. 804/838–0200 or 800/HOLIDAY. 325 rooms. Facilities: indoor/outdoor pools, whirlpool, sauna, fitness course, exercise and game rooms, restaurant, lounge. AE, DC, MC, V.*

Norfolk
Expensive
★

Hilton–Airport. Don't let the gray cement exterior scare you away. Inside, this 2½-year-old highway-side Hilton is very pleasant. The six-story hotel has a concierge floor, an atrium, some king-size beds and free shuttle service to the airport. *1500 N. Military Hwy., 23502, tel. 804/466–8000. 250 rooms, including 4 suites. Facilities: outdoor pool, tennis, health club, 2 restaurants, 2 lounges with live jazz weekends, coffee shop. AE, DC, MC, V.*

Moderate

Holiday Inn–Waterside. Some rooms in this 12-story downtown inn have king-size beds and recliners. *700 Monticello Ave., Norfolk, 23501, tel. 804/627–5555. 347 rooms. Facilities: outdoor pool, restaurant, nightclub. AE, CB, DC, MC, V.*

Inexpensive

YMCA of Tidewater. An amazing bargain. This is a co-ed Y, with daily maid service, private baths. *312 W. Bute St., 23510, tel. 804/622–6328. 68 single rooms, 4 family rooms, 4 doubles. Facilities: health club, with indoor pool, indoor track, racquetball court, Nautilus. MC, V.*

Virginia Beach
Very Expensive

Cavalier Hotels. This resort complex combines the original Cavalier hotel—a 1920s six-story building on a hill, with traditional decor—and a modern, oceanfront high rise across the street. *Atlantic Ave. and 42nd St., 23451, tel. 804/425–8555 or 800/446–8199. 408 rooms. Facilities: private beach, indoor/outdoor pools, tennis and platform tennis, children's wading pool, playground, children's activities, baby-sitting service, 4 restaurants, 2 lounges with nightly entertainment in season. AE, CB, DC, MC, V.*

Moderate **Idlewhyle Motel.** This motel right on the beach usually caters to families, who can choose either efficiencies or guest rooms. *Atlantic Ave. and 27th St., 23451, tel. 804/428–9341. 23 rooms, 23 efficiencies. Facilities: coffee shop, indoor pool, sundeck. AE, MC, V.*

Williamsburg
Very Expensive
★

The Williamsburg Inn. Adjacent to the Historic Area, and owned and operated by Colonial Williamsburg, the inn is the grand hotel of Williamsburg. Built in 1932, it is decorated in luxurious English Regency style throughout. The surrounding Colonial houses, also part of the inn, are decorated in Federalist style but with modern kitchens and baths. The Tazewell Club—a $5-million facility with full fitness offerings as well as conference rooms and executive suites—is available to guests of any of the Colonial Williamsburg operated properties. *136 E. Francis St. 23185, tel. 804/229–1000 or 800/HISTORY. 232 rooms, 150 in inn, 82 in Colonial houses. Facilities: outdoor pool, golf, tennis, health club, restaurant, lounge, tavern. AE, MC, V.*

Expensive **The Motor House.** This newly renovated motel—another official Colonial Williamsburg hostelry—is on the grounds of the visitor center. Rooms are in separate buildings set in a pine grove. All inn facilities are open to motel guests. *Information Center Dr., 23187, tel. 804/229–1000 or 800/HISTORY. 219 rooms. Facilities: 2 pools, miniature golf, putting green, tennis, playground, cafeteria, restaurant. AE, MC, V.*

Moderate **Heritage Inn.** This is a charming and comfortable inn one mile from the Historic Area. The three-story building is about 25 years old and decorated inside and out in Colonial style. *1324 Richmond Rd., 23185, tel. 804/229–6220 or 800/782–3800. 54 rooms. Facilities: outdoor pool with patio, restaurant. AE, CB, DC, MC, V.*

Inexpensive **Bassett Motel.** Three blocks from the Historic Area, this single-story brick property is quiet, well run, and family oriented. *800 York St. (U.S. 60), Williamsburg, 23185, tel. 804/229–5175. 18 rooms. MC, V.*

The Arts

Music A variety of popular song and dance shows (country, gospel, opera, German folk) are held in several theaters at **Busch Gardens,** and the 5,000-seat Royal Palace Theater there features famous pop stars of every kind. The 10,000-seat W&M Hall at the **College of William and Mary** is also the scene of concerts by well-known artists on tour. The **Virginia Opera,** at Norfolk Center Theater (tel. 804/623–1223), is widely acclaimed for its regular company, and international stars have performed as guests. The season (Oct.–Mar.) often features world and American premieres. Concerts of all kinds are held year-round at the **Scope Center** (tel. 804/441–2161) in Norfolk.

Theater Student drama at the **College of William and Mary** (tel. 804/253–4272) goes on during the school year. In Norfolk, the **Virginia Stage Company** (tel. 804/627–1234) performs at Wells Theatre, Broadway shows on tour appear at **Chrysler Hall** (tel. 804/441–2161), and the **Tidewater Dinner Theater** (tel. 804/461–2933) performs Thursday through Sunday.

Nightlife

Rock **The Veranda** at the Fort Magruder Inn near Williamsburg (tel. 804/220–2250) has a bar with some music and a transient crowd. **The Coach House** in Norfolk (tel. 804/489–7454) is a showcase for oldies and rockabilly. **The Inn Place** (tel. 804/599–4488) is the most popular spot for rock in Newport News.

Jazz A multigenerational crowd forms at **The Judge's Chambers** in Norfolk (tel. 804/625–1016). **Artifacts** is a piano bar in the lobby of the Norfolk Airport Hilton (tel. 804/466–8000).

Dance At the **Orient Express,** in the Norfolk Airport Hilton (tel. 804/466–8000), the latest dance tunes are performed live. **After Dark** in Hampton (tel. 804/838–7078) hosts every kind of live music. Each weekend, Portsmouth's **The Max** (tel. 804/397–1866) features dancing to Top-40 tunes and hits from the fifties on a stainless-steel dance floor in a glass-enclosed atrium.

Index

Abby Aldrich Rockefeller Folk Art Center, 431
Abingdon, VA, 385, 392, 395, 396, 399
Acadiana area, LA, 159–160
the arts, 171
beaches, 165
children, 167
emergencies, 160
guided tours, 159–160
lodging, 163, 168–171
map of, 161
nightlife, 171–172
restaurants, 164, 166, 168–171
sightseeing, 160–167
sports, 168
transportation, 159
Acadiana Park Nature Station, 164
Acadian Village, 164
Adam Thoroughgood House, 434
Adventure River (water park), 337
Afro-American Cultural Center, 235
Agecroft Hall, 421
Agricenter International, 337
Agriculture and Forestry Museum, 200
Aiken, SC, 279
Aiken-Rhett Mansion, 285
Airliewood (historic house), 214
Alabama, 20–67 See also Birmingham; Mobile and Gulf Coast; Montgomery
map of, 21
Alabama Department of Archives, 38
Alabama Shakespeare Festival, 37
Alabama Space and Rocket Center, 63
Alabama Sports Hall of Fame Museum, 23
Alexandria, VA,

409–410, 414, 416, 417
Alex Haley State Historic Site, 335
Alliance Theatre, 80
Alonzo Herndon Home, 82
American Historical Wax Museum, 372
American Military Museum, 288
American Museum of Science, 375
American Work Horse Museum, 412
Anderson's Cottage, 186
Andrew Johnson National Historic Site, 372
Andrew Low House, 103
Apothecary Shop, 411
Appomattox Court House, VA, 402
Aquarium of the Americas, 137
Arlington, VA, 414–415, 416, 417
Arlington (mansion), 25
Arlington House, 410
Arlington National Cemetery, 410
Armand Broussard House, 163
Armstrong-Lockett House, 370
Arts, the. See under cities and areas
A. Schwab's (shop), 333
Asheville, NC, 266–271
Ash Lawn (Monroe estate), 400
Assateague Island, VA, 435
Atlanta, GA, 69–95
the arts, 80, 93–94
children, 82–83
climate, 5
emergencies, 73
free attractions, 82
guided tours, 73

lodging, 79, 91–93
maps of, 70–71, 86
nightlife, 94–95
restaurants, 85–91
shopping, 83–84
sightseeing, 73–83
sports, 85
transportation, 69, 72–73
Atlanta-Fulton County Public Library, 79
Atlanta Historical Society, 81
Atlanta Symphony Orchestra, 80, 94
Audubon Park and Zoo, 140
Audubon State Commemorative Area, 176
Ave Maria Grotto, 63
Avery Island (salt dome), 163
Azalea Trail Festival, 54

Baby-sitting, 16
Balfour House, 223
Banner Elk, NC, 277
Barbara Mandrell Country, 352
Barnard Observatory, 216
Barter Theatre, 398
Bassett Hall, 431
Bath County, VA, 390–391
Baton Rouge-Plantation Country, LA, 172
the arts, 181
children, 178
emergencies, 173
guided tours, 173
lodging, 181–182
map of, 175
nightlife, 181
restaurants, 179–180
sightseeing, 173–178
sports, 178
transportation, 172–173
Bayou Teche country, 162

Bay St. Louis, MS, 191
Bays Mountain Park, 371
Beaches. See under cities and areas
Beachwalker Park, 292
Beale Street Substation Police Museum, 336
Beaufort, SC. See Hilton Head-Beaufort
Beaufort Museum, 317
Beauregard-Keyes House, 137
Beauvoir (mansion), 188
Beaver Creek, MS, 199
Beaver Creek, NC, 273
Bellefield Nature Center, 307
Belle Meade Mansion, 354
Bellingrath Gardens and Home, 52, 54
Belmont Mansion, 354–355
Belzoni, MS, 224
Berkeley (plantation), 422
Bethabara Park, 256
Biloxi, MS, 187–189, 191–193
Biltmore Estate, 267
Bird City (sanctuary), 163
Birmingham, AL, 20–36
the arts, 35–36
children, 27
climate, 4
emergencies, 21
free attractions, 27
guided tours, 23
lodging, 33–35
maps of, 24, 31
nightlife, 36
restaurants, 23, 25, 26, 27, 30–32, 33
shopping, 28

sightseeing, *23–28*
sports, *29*
transportation, *22*
Birmingham
Museum of Art, *23*
Birmingham Turf
Club, *27*
Birmingham Zoo, *26*
Black Heritage Trail
(Savannah), *92, 99*
Black history tours,
3
Blowing Rock, NC,
272, 276
Blue Ridge Mountain
Frescoes, *273*
Blue Ridge Parkway,
272–273, 388
Bluff Hall, *64*
Booker T.
Washington's
Birthplace, *393*
Boone, NC, *273,
277*
Boone Hall
Plantation, *290*
Botanical and
Japanese Gardens,
26–27
Botanical Garden,
81
Boxcar Willie's
Railroad Museum,
353
Boyhood Home of
Robert E. Lee, *409*
Boyle, MS, *225*
Breaux Bridge, LA,
164, 169, 172
Bridgeport, AL, *65*
British travelers, *3–4*
Brookgreen Garden,
307
Brown's Island, VA,
421
Burnside, LA, *180*
Busch Gardens
(amusement park),
432, 436
Bynum Mounds
(prehistoric site),
199

Cades Cove, TN, *373*
Calhoun Mansion,
289
Cape Hatteras
National Seashore,
263
Capital City Club, *79*

Capitol Building
(MS), *206*
Carbo's Police
Museum, *373*
Carencro, LA, *169*
Carl Perkins Music
Museum, *336*
Carowinds
(amusement park),
235
Car rentals, *14*
Cars of the Stars
(exhibit), *353*
Carter's Grove
Plantation, *431*
Casemate Museum,
433
Casey Jones Home,
336
The Castle (historic
house), *80*
Cathedral Garden, *138*
Cathedral of St. John
the Baptist, *103*
Cathedral of St. John
the Evangelist, *164*
Cathedral of St.
Peter the Apostle,
202
Cedar Grove (historic
house), *223*
Cedarhurst (historic
house), *214*
Center for the Study
of Southern Culture,
215
Chapel Hill, NC. *See*
Raleigh-Durham-
Chapel Hill
Charleston, SC, *279,
282–305*
the arts, *303–304*
beaches, *294*
children, *292*
climate, *5*
emergencies, *283*
free attractions, *292*
guided tours, *283–284*
lodging, *299–303*
map of, *286*
nightlife, *304–305*
restaurants, *295–299*
shopping, *293–294*
sightseeing, *284–293*
sports, *294–295*
transportation,
282–283
Charles Towne
Landing State Park,
290

Charlotte, NC,
229–246
children, *228–229*
emergencies, *232*
guided tours, *232*
lodging, *243–245*
map of, *234*
nightlife, *245–246*
restaurants, *239–243*
shopping, *237–238*
sightseeing, *232–237*
sports, *238–239*
transportation,
231–232
Charlottesville area,
VA, *399–405*
the arts, *405*
children, *402*
emergencies, *399*
lodging, *404–405*
nightlife, *405*
restaurants, *401,
402–404*
sightseeing, *399–402*
sports, *402*
transportation, *399*
Chattanooga, TN,
*367, 374, 377–378,
380–382*
Chattanooga
Choo-Choo and
Terminal, *374*
Cheekwood
(mansion), *354*
Chesapeake Bay
Bridge-Tunnel, *435*
Childersburg, AL, *63*
Children, traveling
with, *14–16. See
also under cities and
areas*
Children's Discovery
House, *356*
Chincoteague Island,
VA, *428, 436*
Chitimacha Indian
Reservation, *162*
C. H. Nash Museum,
335
Christ Church, *409*
Christ Episcopal
Church, *123*
Christus Gardens, *372*
Chrysler Museum,
434
Chucalissa Indian
Village, *335*
Church of St.
Charles Borromeo,
166

Church of St.
Lawrence, *267*
Circular
Congregational
Church, *287*
The Citadel (military
college), *285, 292*
The Citadel
Memorial Military
Museum, *292*
Clamagore
(submarine), *289*
Clarksdale, MS, *220,
225*
Cleveland, MS, *220*
CNN Center, *80*
College Hill
Presbyterian
Church, *216*
Colonial
Williamsburg, *428,
429, 431, 435, 439*
Columbia, SC, *279*
Columbus, MS, *194,
207*
Condo rentals, *14*
Confederate
Museum, *285, 287*
Congregation Beth
Elohim, *285*
Connemara
(Sandburg estate),
268
Corinth, MS, *195, 196*
Country Music Hall
of Fame and
Museum, *352*
Country Music Wax
Museum and Mall,
353
Cox-Deasy House, *52*
Craighead-Jackson
House, *368*
Crawfish Festival,
164
Creole Nature Trail,
165
Cretien Point
Plantation, *166–167*
Crystal Shrine
Grotto, *336*
Cullman, AL, *63*
Cumberland Island
National Seashore,
117, 119
Cumberland Museum
and Science Center,
356
Cypress Gardens, *291*
Cypress Swamp, *199*

Daufuskie Island, SC, *319*

Davidson, NC, *237*

Davis Planetarium, *201*

Dayton, TN, *374*

Decatur, AL, *66*

Deer Island, *187*

Delta area, MS, *219–223*
children, *224*
emergencies, *220*
lodging, *224–227*
map of, *221*
nightlife, *227*
restaurants, *224–227*
shopping, *224*
sightseeing, *220–224*
sports, *224*
transportation, *219*

Delta Blues Museum, *220*

Demopolis, AL, *63*

Design Works Bookstore, *104*

Desoto Lake, *219*

DeSoto State Park, *63*

Destrehan Plantation, *178*

DeWitt Wallace Decorative Arts Gallery, *431*

Dexter Avenue King Memorial Church, *38*

Disabled travelers, *16*

Discovery Place Museum (Birmingham), *27*

Discovery Place Museum (Charlotte), *233*

Disharoon House, *204*

Dixon Gallery, *334*

Dock Street Theatre, *288*

Doll House (shop), *189*

Dollywood (theme park), *373*

Douglas MacArthur Memorial, *434*

Downtown Presbyterian Church, *350*

Drayton Hall (mansion), *290–291*

Duck, NC, *265–266*

Dungeness (Carnegie estate), *119*

Dunleith (mansion), *205–206*

Durham, NC. *See* Raleigh-Durham-Chapel Hill

East Tennessee, *328, 367–383*
the arts, *382*
children, *375*
emergencies, *367*
guided tours, *367–368*
lodging, *379–382*
map of, *369*
nightlife, *382–383*
restaurants, *377–379*
shopping, *375–376*
sightseeing, *368–375*
sports, *376–377*
transportation, *367*

Ebenezer Baptist Church, *74*

Edgar Allan Poe Museum, *421*

Edisto Beach State Park, *318*

Edisto Island, SC, *315, 318, 324*

Edmonston-Alston House, *289*

1850 House, *136*

Elizabeth II State Historic Site, *262*

Elvis Presley Birthplace, *198, 206*

Elvis Presley Lake, Campground, Chapel and Park, *198*

Emerald Mound (Indian mound), *204*

Emerald Village (gold mine), *274*

Emmet Park, *102*

Energy Explorium (museum), *235*

Englesing House, *204*

Ethel Wright Mohamed Stitchery Museum, *224*

Eudora Welty Library, *202*

Eufaula, AL, *66*

Eunice, LA, *166*

Evangeline Country, *163*

Exchange Building-Provost Dungeon, *282*

Exchange Place (homestead), *288*

Executive Mansion (NC), *248*

Falconer House, *41*

False River, *177*

Faulkner and Yoknapatawpha Conference, *218*

Fernbank Science Center, *82*

Festivals and seasonal events, *6–12*

First Presbyterian Church (Charlotte), *233*

First Presbyterian Church (Port Gibson), *204*

First Skyscraper, *138*

First Union Tower, *233*

First White House of the Confederacy, *40*

Fisk University, *357*

Five Points South (outdoor museum), *25*

Flat Rock, NC, *268*

Florence, AL, *20*

Fontaine House, *334*

Forsyth Park, *99, 105*

Fort Frederica National Monument, *123*

Fort Condé, *52*

Fort Jackson, *106*

Fort Massachusetts, *188*

Fort Mitchell, *317*

Fort Monroe, *433*

Fort Morgan, *55*

Fort Moultrie, *290*

Fort Nashborough, *350*

Fort Payne, AL, *63*

Fort Pulaski, *105*

Fort Raleigh, *262*

Fort Sumter National Monument, *289*

Fourth Ward Park, *233*

Fox Theatre, *80*

Francis Marion National Forest, *293*

Franklin, LA, *162*

Franklin, NC, *269*

Fredericksburg, VA, *410–411, 415, 416*

Fredericksburg National Military Park, *411*

Freedom Park, *236*

French Camp, MS, *199*

French Huguenot Church, *288*

Fripp Island, SC, *315, 324*

Frisco Native American Museum, *262*

Fulton County Stadium, *75*

Funtime USA (amusement park), *189*

Furnace Master Inn, *28*

Gadsby's Tavern Museum, *409*

Gage House, *204*

Gainswood (mansion), *64*

Gallier House, *137*

Galloway House, *202*

Gardens-by-the-Sea, *433*

Garner Green House, *203*

Gatlinburg, TN, *367, 372, 375, 378, 380–381, 382*

General Richard Montgomery (riverboat), *41*

George C. Marshall Museum, *391*

George Elliott House, *317*

George Jones Car Collectors' Hall of Fame, *353*

Georgetown, SC, *307–308, 311, 313*

George Washington Carver Museum, *67*

George Washington Masonic National Memorial, *413*

Georgia. *See also* Atlanta; Savannah festivals, *6–12*

Golden Isles, *117–126*
maps of, *70–71*
Okefenokee Wildlife
Refuge, *124–126*
Georgia Governor's
Mansion, *81*
Georgia State
Capitol, *75*
Georgia Trust for
Historic
Preservation, *81*
Gibbes Art Gallery,
287
Glass House Point,
432
Glendale Springs,
NC, *273*
Golden Isles area,
GA, *117–126*
map of, *118*
Goldsmith Civic
Garden Center, *337*
Goodlettsville, TN,
357
Goose Creek, SC, *293*
Goshen Pass, *390*
Governor Shorter
Mansion, *41*
Governor William
Blount Mansion, *368*
Grace Church, *432*
Graceland (Presley
estate), *330, 335*
Grand Chenier, LA,
165
Grand Coteau, LA,
166
Grandfather
Mountain, *274*
Grand Gulf Military
Monument, *204*
Grand Ole Opry, *349,
353*
Grand Strand-Myrtle
Beach area, SC, *279,
305–315*
the arts, *314*
beaches, *309*
children, *308–309*
emergencies, *306*
guided tours, *305*
lodging, *312–314*
nightlife, *314–315*
restaurants, *310–312*
shopping, *309*
sightseeing, *306–309*
sports, *310*
transportation, *305*
Grand Village of the
Natchez Indians, *206*

Great Falls, VA,
415
Great River Road
State Park, *222*
Great Savannah
Exposition, *99*
Great Smoky Arts
and Craft
Community, *375*
Great Smoky
Mountains National
Park, *372*
Greenbrook Flowers
(historic home),
203
Greeneville, TN,
372
Green-Meldrim
House, *104*
Greenville, MS, *219,
222, 225*
Guinness World
Records Museums
Gatlinburg, *372*
Myrtle Beach, *306*
Gulf Islands National
Seashore, *187*
Gulf Marine State
Park, *187*
Gulfport, MS, *188,
192–193*
Gulf Shores, AL,
50–51, 55, 56–57
Gulf State Park, *55*
Gunston Hall, *407*

Hampton, VA, *427,
433, 437, 438, 440*
Hampton Plantation
State Park, *308*
Handy Park, *333*
Hank Williams, Jr.
Museum, *352*
Hank Williams
Memorial, *42*
Harold Kaminski
House, *308*
Harrogate, TN, *371*
Haskins Williams
House, *25*
Heaven on Earth
Amusement Park,
167
Hendersonville, TN,
355
Henning, TN, *335*
Henry C. Chambers
Waterfront Park,
318
Herbie's Antique Car

Museum, *292*
Hermann-Grima
House, *139*
The Hermitage
(Jackson estate), *355*
Hermitage
Foundation
Museum, *433*
Heyward-Washington
House, *289*
Hezekiah Alexander
Homesite, *235*
Highlands United
Methodist Church,
25
High Museum of Art,
79
Hillsborough, NC,
249
Hilton Head-
Beaufort area, SC,
279, 315–326
the arts, *325*
beaches, *320*
children, *318–319*
emergencies, *316*
guided tours, *316*
lodging, *322–325*
nightlife, *325–326*
restaurants, *321–322*
shopping, *319–320*
sightseeing, *316–319*
sports, *320–321*
transportation,
315–316
Historic Albemarle,
259–260
Historic Michie
Tavern, *400*
Historic New Orleans
Collection, *138*
Hobcaw Barony
(estate), *307*
Holly Springs, MS,
213–218
Home exchanges, *15*
Home of Mary
Washington, *411*
The Homestead
(resort), *391*
Hopsewee Plantation,
308
"Horn in the West"
(outdoor drama), *273*
Hotels. *See* lodging
*under cities and
areas*
Hot Springs, VA, *390,
397*
Houma, LA, *160*

Houmas House, *177*
House of Cash, *355*
House of Mayors, *41*
Hunting Island, SC,
318
Huntington Beach
State Park, *307*
Huntsville, AL, *63*

Imperial Calcasieu
Museum, *165*
Impressions Gallery,
201
Indianola, MS, *224*
Iron Mountain
Stoneware plant,
376
Isaiah Davenport
House, *102*
Isles of Palms, SC,
303
Ivy Green (Keller
home), *65*

Jacinto, MS, *196*
Jack Daniels
Distillery, *356*
Jackson, MS
children, *206*
climate, *5*
lodging, *208–210*
nightlife, *212*
restaurants, *203, 208*
shopping, *207–208*
sightseeing, *199–205*
sports, *208–210*
transportation, *194*
Jackson, TN, *336*
James K. Polk
Memorial, *236*
James Monroe
Museum and
Memorial Library,
411
Jamestown Island,
VA, *432*
James White's Fort,
368
Jarnagin Company,
207
Jasmine Hill
Gardens, *42*
Jeff Busby State
Park, *199*
Jefferson Island (salt
dome), *165*
Jefferson National
Forest, *393*
Jekyll Island, GA,
119, 120–121

Jim Bowie Museum, *166*

Jim Reeves Museum, *354*

Jockey's Ridge State Park, *262*

Joe L. Evins Center for Crafts, *356*

John Mark Verdier House, *317*

John Marshall House, *419*

John Sevier Historical Site, *370*

Johnson City, TN, *371*

Jonesborough, TN, *372*

Joseph Manigault Mansion, *285*

J. P. Coleman State Park, *196*

Julian Price Park, *273*

Juliette Gordon Low House, *103*

Jungle Garden, *163*

Kate Freeman Clark Art Gallery, *214*

Kenmore (mansion), *410–411*

Kiawah Island, SC, *292*, *303*

Kill Devil Hills, NC, *260*, *264*, *266*

King's Dominion (amusement park), *422*

Kingsport, TN, *371*

King-Tisdell Cottage (museum), *105*

Kitty Hawk, NC, *260*

Knoxville, TN, *367*, *370*, *378–379*, *381*

Knoxville Museum of Art, *370*

Knoxville Zoo, *370*

LaBranche House, *138*

Lafayette, LA, *160*, *164*, *169*, *171*

Lafayette County Courthouse, *215*

Lafayette Natural History Museum, *164*

Laffey (ship), *289*

Lafitte's Blacksmith Shop, *138*

Lake Charles, LA, *159*, *165*, *167*, *170*

Langley Research Center, *433*

Latta Plantation Park, *235*

Laura S. Walker State Park, *125*

Laurel Bloomery, TN, *376*

Laurel Hill Vineyard, *337*

Lee-Fendall House, *409*

Lee Memorial Chapel and Museum, *391*

Leesburg, VA, *412*

Legion Field, *27*

Lenoir Museum, *370*

Le Petit Théâtre du Vieux Carré, *142*

Lexington, VA, *385*, *391*, *395*, *397*

Libertyland (amusement park), *337*

Lichterman Nature Center, *337*

Liddell-McNinch House, *233*

Lime Kiln Arts Theater, *393*

Lincoln Memorial University and Museum, *371*

Linville, NC, *274*, *277*

Linville Caverns, *274*

Little River Canyon, *65*

Little St. Simons Island, GA, *124*

Live Oak Gardens, *165*

Lodging. *See under cities and areas*

Longfellow-Evangeline State Commemorative Area, *164*

Longue Vue House, *141*

Longwood (octagonal house), *206*

Lookout Mountain Incline Railway, *374*

Lookout Mountain Trail, *65*

Loretta Lynn Ranch, *356*

"The Lost Colony" (drama), *262*

Lost Sea (underground lake), *374*

Loudoun County Museum, *412*

Louis Armstrong Park, *139*

Louisiana, *128–181* *also* Acadiana area; Baton Rouge; New Orleans festivals, *6–12* map of, *130–131*

Louisiana Arts & Science Center, *174*

Louisiana Governor's Mansion, *176*

Louisiana State Museum, *136*

Louisiana State University, *176*

Lucas Tavern, *40*

Luray Caverns, *388*

Lurleen Burns Wallace Memorial Museum, *40*

Lynchburg, TN, *356*

Mabry Mill, *390*

McCartys of Merigold (shop), *222*

McClung Museum, *370*

McElreath Hall (museum), *81*

Madame John's Legacy (historic house), *138*

Madewood (mansion), *177*

Magevney House, *333*

Magic World (theme park), *373*

Magnolia Hall, *205*

Magnolia Mound Plantation, *176*

Magnolia Plantation and Gardens, *291*

Malbis Greek Orthodox Church, *55*

Mallory-Neely House, *334*

Manassas National Battlefield, *412*

Manship House, *203*

Manteo, NC, *260*, *264–265*

Marine Education Center, *187*

Marine Life (aquarium), *189*

Mariner's Museum, *433*

Market Hall, *285*

Martha Vick House, *223*

Martin Luther King, Jr. Historic District, *74*

Massie Heritage Center, *96*, *105*

Meeman-Shelby Forest State Park, *337*

Memphis, TN, *328* the arts, *346–347* Beale Street, *328*, *336* children, *337* emergencies, *331* free attractions, *336–337* guided tours, *331* lodging, *344–346* map of, *332* nightlife, *347* restaurants, *339–344* shopping, *338* sightseeing, *331–336* sports, *338–339* transportation, *330–331*

Memphis Botanic Garden, *337*

Memphis Brooks Museum of Art, *334*

Memphis in May Festival, *330*

Memphis Pink Palace Museum, *334*

Memphis Zoo, *334*

Merieult House, *138*

Merigold, MS, *220*, *225–226*

Middleburg, VA, *412*

Middleton Place (gardens), *291*

Mill Mountain Theater, *392*

Millsaps-Buie House, *203*

Minnie Pearl's Museum, *353*

Mintmere Plantation, *163*

Mississippi, *183–227* *also* Delta area; Mississippi Gulf

Coast; Natchez
Trace
festivals, *6–12*, *183*
Holly Springs and
Oxford, *213–219*
map of, *184*
Mississippi Arts
Center, *201*
Mississippi
Governor's Mansion,
201
Mississippi Gulf
Coast, *185*
beaches, *189*
children, *189*
emergencies, *186*
guided tours, *186*
lodging, *190–193*
nightlife, *193*
restaurants, *188*,
190–193
shopping, *189*
sightseeing, *186–189*
sports, *189*
transportation,
185–186
Mississippi Museum
of Art, *201*
Mississippi River
Museum, *333*
Miss Mary Bobo's
Boarding House, *357*
Mobile-Gulf Coast
area, AL, *50–62*
the arts, *62*
beaches, *55*
children, *56*
emergencies, *52*
guided tours, *51*
lodging, *60–62*
map of, *53*
nightlife, *62*
restaurants, *58–60*
shopping, *56–57*
sightseeing, *52–56*
sports, *57–58*
transportation, *51*
Moja Arts Festival,
303–304
Montgomery, AL,
36–50
the arts, *50*
children, *42*
emergencies, *38*
free attractions, *42*
guided tours, *38*
lodging, *48–50*
maps of, *39*, *45*
nightlife, *50*
restaurants, *44–48*

shopping, *42–43*
sightseeing, *38*
sports, *43*
transportation, *37*
Montgomery Zoo, *42*
Monticello (Jefferson
estate), *400*
Montpelier (Madison
estate), *401*
Montrose (mansion),
214
Moore House, *432*
Morgan City, LA, *162*
Morris House, *202*
Morven Park, *412*
Moses H. Cone Park,
273
Moses Myers House,
434
Mound State
Monument, *65*
Moundville, AL, *65*
Mount Holly (historic
house), *222*
Mount Pleasant, SC,
289
Mount Rogers
National Recreation
Area, *393*
Mount Vernon
(Washington estate),
407
Mud Island (park),
333
Murfreesboro, TN,
356
Murrells Inlet, SC,
307, *311*
Musée Conti Wax
Museum, *139*
Museum of the
Confederacy, *419*
Museum of American
Frontier Culture,
390
Museum of
Appalachia, *370–371*
Museum of Beverage
Containers, *357*
Museum of Coastal
History, *122*
Museum of Southern
Decorative Arts, *256*
Museum of Hounds
and Hunting, *412*
Museum of Tobacco
Art and History, *356*
Music Valley Wax
Museum of the
Stars, *354*

Myrtle Beach, SC.
See Grand Strand-
Myrtle Beach area
Myrtle Beach Grand
Prix, *308*
Myrtle Beach
National Wax
Museum, *306*
Myrtle Beach
Pavilion–Amusement
Park, *306*
The Myrtles (haunted
house), *177*
Myrtle Waves Water
Park, *308*

Nags Head, NC, *263*,
264
Napoleonville, LA,
180
Nashville, TN, *348*
the arts, *358–359*
children, *349–350*
climate, *5*
emergencies, *349*
free attractions, *349*
guided tours, *349–350*
lodging, *354*, *356–358*
map of, *351*
nightlife, *359–360*
restaurants, *353–356*
shopping, *351–352*
sightseeing, *350–355*
sports, *352*
transportation,
348–349
Natchez, MS, *194*,
205–206, *210–211*
Natchez Trace area,
MS, *194*
children, *206–207*
emergencies, *195*
guided tours, *195*
lodging, *208–212*
map of, *197*
nightlife, *212*
restaurants, *208–212*
shopping, *207*
sightseeing, *196–206*
sports, *208*
transportation, *194*
Natchez Trace
Parkway, *194*
Nathaniel Russell
House, *289*
National Military
Park (Vicksburg),
223
National Ornamental
Metal Museum, *335*

Natural Bridge, *392*,
397
Natural Bridge Wax
Museum, *392*
Nature Museum, *236*
Nature Science
Center of
Winston-Salem, *256*
Naval Aviation
Museum, *56*
Naval Base (Norfolk),
434
Nelson House, *432*
Neptune Park, *122*
Netherlands Inn
(museum), *371*
Newbern, VA, *395*
New Georgia
Railroad, *78*
Newhall Audubon
Preserve, *316*
New Iberia, LA, *160*,
162–163, *168*
New Orleans, LA, *128*
the arts, *156–157*
children, *142*
climate, *5*
directions in, *128*, *129*
emergencies, *132*
free attractions, *141*
French Quarter, *128*,
133, *137*, *153–154*,
155
guided tours, *132–133*
lodging, *151–156*
maps of, *134–135*,
148–149
nightlife, *157–159*
restaurants, *139*,
144–151
shopping, *142–143*
sightseeing, *133–142*
sports, *143–144*
transportation, *129*,
132
New Orleans
Museum of Art
(NOMA), *141*
New Orleans
Pharmacy Museum,
139
Newport News, VA,
427, *428*, *429*, *433*,
437
Nightlife. *See under
cities and areas*
Noccalula Falls, *65*
Norfolk, VA, *427*,
428, *429*, *433*, *438*,
440

Norris, TN, *370*

Norris Dam State Park, *370*

North Beach, *165*

North Carolina, *229–277 See also* Charlotte; Outer Banks area; Raleigh-Durham-Chapel Hill

Asheville, *266–271*

High Country, *271–277*

map of, *230*

North Carolina Museum of History, *248*

North Carolina Museum of Life and Science, *249*

North Carolina Museum of Natural Sciences, *248*

North Carolina Transportation Museum, *236*

Northeast Mississippi Museum, *196*

Northern Virginia, *405*

the arts, *417*

children, *413*

emergencies, *406*

guided tours, *406*

lodging, *415–416*

map of, *408*

nightlife, *417*

restaurants, *409, 411, 414–415*

sightseeing, *406–413*

sports, *413–414*

transportation, *406*

Nottoway (plantation), *177*

Oak Alley (historic house), *177*

Oakleigh (mansion-Holly Springs), *214*

Oakleigh (mansion-Mobile), *52*

Oakley Plantation House, *176*

Oak Ridge, TN, *375, 383*

The Oaks (historic house), *196*

Oak View (historic building), *203*

Oatlands (plantation), *412*

Ober Gatlinburg Tramway, *372*

Ocean Springs, MS, *186, 193*

Ocracoke Island, NC, *263, 266*

Ogle's Water Park, *373*

Okefenokee Wildlife Refuge, *117, 124–126*

Old Arsenal Museum, *174*

Old Capitol Building (Mississippi), *200*

Old Citadel Building, *285*

Old Confederate Post Office, *41*

Old Country Store, *204*

Old Daisy Theatre, *333*

Older travelers, *16–17*

Old Mill, *373*

Old Pack Library, *267*

Old Powder Magazine (museum), *287–288*

Old Salem Village, *255*

Old Settlers Cemetery, *233*

Old State Capitol (Louisiana), *174*

Old Stone Fort State Park, *357*

Old Ursuline Convent, *137*

Old U.S. Mint, *137*

Omni sports arena, *80*

Opelousas, LA, *166, 171*

Opryland USA (show park), *353*

Orange County Historical Museum, *249*

Ordeman-Shaw House, *40*

Oregon Inlet Bridge, *262*

Orpheum Theatre, *331*

Our Lady of

Guadelupe Church, *139–140*

Outer Banks area, NC, *259–266*

beaches, *263*

lodging, *265–266*

map of, *261*

restaurants, *264–265*

sightseeing, *260–263*

sports, *263–264*

Overcarsh House, *233*

Overton Park, *334*

Owens-Thomas House, *102*

Oxford, MS, *213–219*

Oyster Museum, *435*

Package deals, *3*

Palmetto Islands County Park, *292*

Parris Island, SC, *319*

The Parthenon, *354*

Pass Christian, MS, *189*

Passports, *3*

Patriots Point, *289*

Patterson's Mill Country Store, *249*

Pawleys Island, SC, *307, 309, 312, 314*

Pea Island National Wildlife Refuge, *262*

Peaks of the Otter Recreation Area, *388*

Pensacola, FL, *56*

Pentagon Barracks, (museum), *174*

Pet Farm Park, *413*

Photographic film, *13*

Pickwick Hotel, *26*

Pickwick Landing State Resort Park, *336*

Piedmont Park, *81*

Pigeon Forge, TN, *367, 373, 376, 379, 381–382*

Pike Pioneer Museum, *66*

Pitot House, *141*

Plains, LA, *178*

Plane travel, *4, 15–16*

Pleasure Island, AL, *54, 55*

Point Mallard Park, *66*

Pope-Leighey House, *407*

Port Gibson, MS, *204, 206*

Port Hudson State Area, *176*

Portsmouth, VA, *441*

Preservation Hall (jazz club), *138*

Prince George Winyah Episcopal Church, *308*

Pullen Park, *249*

Radford, VA, *397*

Raleigh-Durham-Chapel Hill, NC, *246*

children, *249*

climate, *5*

emergencies, *247*

guided tours, *247*

lodging, *252–254*

nightlife, *254*

restaurants, *248, 251–252*

shopping, *249–250*

sightseeing, *247–249*

sports, *250–251*

transportation, *246–247*

Red Mountain Museum, *26*

Reed Gold Mine, *236*

Reelfoot Lake, *336*

Rembert Dennis Wildlife Center, *293*

Restaurants. *See under cities and areas*

Reynolds House, *256*

Rhea County Courthouse, *374*

Rhododendron Gardens, *375*

Rice Museum, *308*

Richmond, VA, *417*

the arts, *426–427*

children, *422*

emergencies, *418*

guided tours, *418–419*

lodging, *424–426*

map of, *420*

nightlife, *427*

restaurants, *423–424*

shopping, *422*

sightseeing, *419–422*

sports, *423*

transportation, *418*

Richmond National Battlefield Park, *421*

Ridgeland Crafts Center, *199*
Ripley's Believe It or Not Museums
Myrtle Beach, *306*
New Orleans, *142*
Riverfront Park, *350*
Riverside Cemetery, *268*
River Walk, *333*
Roan Mountain State Park, *375*
Roanoke, VA, *385*, *392*, *393*, *395–396*, *397–398*
Roanoke Island, NC, *262*
Roanoke Museum of Fine Arts, *392*
Roanoke Valley Historical Society, *392*
Rockefeller Wildlife Refuge, *165*
Rocky Mount (mansion), *371–372*
Rocky Springs, MS, *203*
Rodney, MS, *204*
Rogersville, TN, *371*
Rosalie (mansion), *205*
Rosedale, MS, *222*
Rosedown Plantation and Gardens, *176*
Rowan Oak (Faulkner home), *216*
Roy Acuff Museum, *353*
Royal Peacock Night Club, *75*
Ruffner Mountain Nature Center, *27*
Russell Cave National Monument, *66*
Rust College, *214*

Sabine Wildlife Refuge, *165*
St. Andrew's Episcopal Cathedral, *201*
St. Francisville, LA, *177*
St. Helena's Episcopal Church, *317*
St. James Church, *293*

St. John's Episcopal Church (Montgomery), *40*
St. John's Episcopal Church (Mount Holly), *222*
St. John's Episcopal Church (Richmond), *421*
St. John's Lutheran Church, *287*
St. John Oak, *164*
St. Joseph's Catholic Church, *204*
St. Louis Cathedral, *136*, *140*
St. Martin de Tours (church), *163*
St. Martinville, LA, *163*, *171*
St. Michael's Episcopal Church, *288*
St. Peter's Cemetery, *216*
St. Peter's Roman Catholic Church, *41*
St. Philip's Episcopal Church, *288*
St. Simons Island, GA, *124*
Salter's Island, GA, *106*
Sam Houston Jones State Park, *165*
Samuel Clemens Riverboat, *174*
San Francisco (historic house), *178*
Savannah, GA, *96–117*
children, *107*
emergencies, *98*
free attractions, *106–107*
guided tours, *98–99*
lodging, *113–116*
maps of, *100–105*, *111*
nightlife, *116–117*
restaurants, *109–113*
shopping, *108*
sightseeing, *99*, *107–108*
sports, *109*
transportation, *97*
Savannah (ship), *289*
Savannah Science Museum, *107*
Scarbrough House, *100*

Schiele Museum of Natural History, *236*
Science Museum (Charlotte), *233*
Scopes "Monkey Trial" site, *374*
Seabrook Island, SC, *303*
Sea Island, GA, *121*
Sea Pines Forest Preserve, *316*
Sea Pines resort, *316*, *322*
Selma, AL, *66*
Sequoyah Caverns, *66*
Shadows-on-the-Teche (plantation), *162–163*
Shearwater Pottery and Showroom, *186*
Shenandoah National Park, *388*
Shenandoah Valley-Highlands area, VA, *385*
the arts, *398–399*
children, *393–394*
emergencies, *387*
guided tours, *387*
lodging, *396–398*
map of, *389*
nightlife, *399*
restaurants, *395–396*
sightseeing, *388–393*
sports, *394–395*
tourist info, *387*
transportation, *387*
Shiloh National Military Park, *336*
Ship Island, MS, *181*
Ships of the Sea Museum, *101*
Shirley (plantation), *422*
Shopping. *See under cities and areas*
Shorter Mansion, *66*
Sidewalk of the Stars, *354*
Siege of Savannah, site of, *99*
Six Flags over Georgia, (theme park), *82*
16th Street Baptist Church, *23*
Skidaway Island Marine Science Complex, *107*
Skyline Drive, *388*

Sliding Rock (water slide), *268*
Sloss Furnace (ironworks), *23*, *25*
Smith Mountain Lake, VA, *398*
Smith Park, *202*
South Carolina, *279–326 See also* Charleston; Grand Strand-Myrtle Beach area; Hilton Head-Beaufort area
map of, *280–281*
Southdown Plantation, *153*, *162*
Southeastern Center for Contemporary Art, *256*
Southern Belle (steamboat), *374*
Southern Living (magazine), *28*
Southern Museum of Flight, *28*
Southern University, *176*
Southside Baptist Church, *26*
Spirit of Vicksburg (riverboat), *223*
Spoleto Festival USA, *282*, *303*
Sports. *See under cities and areas*
Springfield (plantation), *204*
State Capitol (AL), *38*
State Capitol (NC), *248*
State Capitol (TN), *352*
State Capitol Building (LA), *173*
State Historical Museum (MS), *200*
State Legislative Building (NC), *248*
Staunton, VA, *390*, *396*, *398*
Stephen C. Foster State Park, *126*
Stone Mountain Park and Village, *78*, *83*
Stonewall Jackson Museum, *391*
Streetcar Named Desire, *137*

Students' Museum and Planetarium, 370

Sturdivant Hall, 66–67

Sullivan's Island, SC, 290

Sulphur, LA, 165

Summerville, SC, 291

Summer Waves (water park), 120

Superdome (stadium), 132

Surfside Beach, SC, 315

Suwanee Canal, 125

Swan House, 81

Swinging Bridge, 274

Tanglewood Park, 256

Tannehill Historical State Park, 28

Taylor, MS, 217

Teague House, 41

Telfair Mansion, 103

Temple Mickve Israel, 104

Temple Sibyl, 27

Tennessee, 322. See also East Tennessee; Memphis; Nashville map of, 329

Tennessee Botanical Gardens, 354

Tennessee Performing Arts Center, 352

Tennessee State Museum, 350

Texas Tavern, 394

Tezcuco (historic house), 177

Theatre for the Performing Arts, 139

Thomas Elfe Workshop, 288

Thomas Jefferson Visitors Center, 399–400

Thomas Wolfe Memorial, 267

Tidewater-Eastern Shore area, VA, 427–441

the arts, 441

beaches, 436–437

children, 435–436

emergencies, 429

guided tours, 428

lodging, 439–441

map of, 430

nightlife, 441

restaurants, 438–439

sightseeing, 429–436

sports, 437–438

transportation, 428

Timing the visit, 4–6

Tipton-Haynes Historical Farm, 371

Tishomingo State Park, 196

T. O. Fuller State Park, 335

Torpedo Factory Art Center, 410

Tour groups, 2–3

Townsend, TN, 382

Troy, AL, 66

Tullie Smith Plantation, 81

Tupelo, MS, 194, 195, 198, 208, 211–212

Tupelo Museum, 198

Turn-of-the-Century House, 162

Tuscumbia, AL, 65

Tuskegee, AL, 67

Tweetsie Railroad (theme park), 273

Twitty City/Music Village USA, 355

Tybee Island, GA, 106, 108

Tyson's Corner, VA, 415, 417

Underground Atlanta complex, 75

Unitarian Church (Charleston), 287

University of Mississippi, 215

U.S. Courthouse (Jackson), 201

USS *Alabama*, 55

USS *Cairo*, 223

Valentine Museum, 419

Valle Crucis, NC, 274

Valley Head, AL, 66

Van Vechten Art Gallery, 357

Vicksburg, MS, 220, 222–223, 226–227

Vienna, VA, 413, 416

Virden-Patton House, 202

Virginia, 385–441 also Northern Virginia; Richmond; Shenandoah Valley-Highlands; Tidewater-Eastern Shore Charlottesville area, 399–405 map of, 386

Virginia Beach, VA, 429, 430, 437, 439, 440

Virginia Discovery Museum, 402

Virginia Living Museum, 436

Virginia Marine Science Museum, 434–435

Virginia Museum of Fine Arts, 414

Virginia Museum of Transportation, 385

Virginia State Capitol, 421

Virginia Zoo, 436

Visas, 3

Voodoo Museum, 138

Waddell Mariculture Research Center, 317

W. A. Gayle Planetarium, 42

Wallops Visitor Center (NASA), 435

War Memorial Building Museum, 319

Warm Springs, VA, 396

Washington, MS, 204

Washington Artillery Park, 136

Water Circus, 373

Water Country USA (water park), 436

Waterville USA (water park), 56

Wave Country (water park), 356

Waveland, MS, 189

Waverley Mansion, 207

Waynesboro, VA, 388

W. C. Handy Home, 333

Weaverville Milling Company, 268

Wesley Monumental Church, 104

Westmoreland Davis Equestrian Institute, 412

White Castle, LA, 181

White Point Gardens, 289

Whooping Crane Conservancy, 318

Williamsburg, VA, 429, 430, 440–441

Williamsburg Pottery Factory, 437

Williams Gallery, 138

Windsor (mansion), 204

Winery Rushing, 222

Wing Haven Gardens and Bird Sanctuary, 236

Winmill Carriage Museum, 412

Winston-Salem, NC, 255–258

Wisner Children's Village, 140

Wolf Trap Farm Park, 413, 417

Woodlawn (mansion), 407

Woodrow Wilson House, 390

Woodruff Park, 78

World Congress Center, 79

Wright Brothers National Memorial, 260

Wynton M. Blount Cultural Park, 37

Yellow Fever House, 214

Yorktown, VA, 432, 436, 439

Yorktown Battlefield, 432

Yorktown (ship), 289

Zebulon B. Vance Birthplace, 267

Zoo Atlanta, 83

Personal Itinerary

Departure *Date*

Time

Transportation

Arrival *Date*   *Time*

Departure *Date*   *Time*

Transportation

Accommodations

Arrival *Date*   *Time*

Departure *Date*   *Time*

Transportation

Accommodations

Arrival *Date*   *Time*

Departure *Date*   *Time*

Transportation

Accommodations

Personal Itinerary

Arrival *Date*   *Time*

Departure *Date*   *Time*

Transportation

Accommodations

Arrival *Date*   *Time*

Departure *Date*   *Time*

Transportation

Accommodations

Arrival *Date*   *Time*

Departure *Date*   *Time*

Transportation

Accommodations

Arrival *Date*   *Time*

Departure *Date*   *Time*

Transportation

Accommodations

Addresses

Name	*Name*
Address	*Address*
Telephone	*Telephone*
Name	*Name*
Address	*Address*
Telephone	*Telephone*
Name	*Name*
Address	*Address*
Telephone	*Telephone*
Name	*Name*
Address	*Address*
Telephone	*Telephone*
Name	*Name*
Address	*Address*
Telephone	*Telephone*
Name	*Name*
Address	*Address*
Telephone	*Telephone*
Name	*Name*
Address	*Address*
Telephone	*Telephone*
Name	*Name*
Address	*Address*
Telephone	*Telephone*

Fodor's Travel Guides

U.S. Guides

Alaska
Arizona
Atlantic City & the
  New Jersey Shore
Boston
California
Cape Cod
Carolinas & the
  Georgia Coast
The Chesapeake Region
Chicago
Colorado
Dallas & Fort
  Worth

Disney World & the
  Orlando Area
Florida
Hawaii
Houston &
  Galveston
Las Vegas
Los Angeles, Orange
  County, Palm Springs
Maui
Miami, Fort Lauderdale,
  Palm Beach
Michigan, Wisconsin,
  Minnesota

New England
New Mexico
New Orleans
New Orleans (Pocket
  Guide)
New York City
New York City (Pocket
  Guide)
New York State
Pacific North Coast
Philadelphia
The Rockies
San Diego
San Francisco

San Francisco (Pocket
  Guide)
The South
Texas
USA
Virgin Islands
Virginia
Waikiki
Washington, DC
Williamsburg

Foreign Guides

Acapulco
Amsterdam
Australia, New Zealand,
  The South Pacific
Austria
Bahamas
Bahamas (Pocket
  Guide)
Baja & the Pacific
  Coast Resorts
Barbados
Beijing, Guangzhou &
  Shanghai
Belgium &
  Luxembourg
Bermuda
Brazil
Britain (Great Travel
  Values)
Budget Europe
Canada
Canada (Great Travel
  Values)
Canada's Atlantic
  Provinces
Cancun, Cozumel,
  Yucatan Peninsula

Caribbean
Caribbean (Great
  Travel Values)
Central America
Eastern Europe
Egypt
Europe
Europe's Great
  Cities
Florence & Venice
France
France (Great Travel
  Values)
Germany
Germany (Great Travel
  Values)
Great Britain
Greece
The Himalayan
  Countries
Holland
Hong Kong
Hungary
India, including Nepal
Ireland
Israel
Italy

Italy (Great Travel
  Values)
Jamaica
Japan
Japan (Great Travel
  Values)
Jordan & the
  Holy Land
Kenya, Tanzania,
  the Seychelles
Korea
Lisbon
Loire Valley
London
London (Great
  Travel Values)
London (Pocket Guide)
Madrid & Barcelona
Mexico
Mexico City
Montreal &
  Quebec City
Munich
New Zealand
North Africa
Paris
Paris (Pocket Guide)

People's Republic of
  China
Portugal
Rio de Janeiro
The Riviera (Fun on)
Rome
Saint Martin &
  Sint Maarten
Scandinavia
Scandinavian Cities
Scotland
Singapore
South America
South Pacific
Southeast Asia
Soviet Union
Spain
Spain (Great Travel
  Values)
Sweden
Switzerland
Sydney
Tokyo
Toronto
Turkey
Vienna
Yugoslavia

Special-Interest Guides

Health & Fitness
  Vacations
Royalty Watching

Selected Hotels of
  Europe

Selected Resorts and
  Hotels of the U.S.
Shopping in Europe

Skiing in North America
Sunday in New York

9331